Digital Rights Management for E-Commerce Systems

Dimitrios Tsolis
University of Patras, Greece

Lambros Drossos
TEI of Messolonghi, Greece

Spyros Sioutas
Ionian University, Greece

Theodore Papatheodorou
University of Patras, Greece

INFORMATION SCIENCE REFERENCE

Hershey · New York

Director of Editorial Content:	Kristin Klinger
Director of Production:	Jennifer Neidig
Managing Editor:	Jamie Snavely
Assistant Managing Editor:	Carole Coulson
Typesetter:	Carole Coulson
Cover Design:	Lisa Tosheff
Printed at:	Yurchak Printing Inc.

Published in the United States of America by
Information Science Reference (an imprint of IGI Global)
701 E. Chocolate Avenue, Suite 200
Hershey PA 17033
Tel: 717-533-8845
Fax: 717-533-8661
E-mail: cust@igi-global.com
Web site: http://www.igi-global.com

and in the United Kingdom by
Information Science Reference (an imprint of IGI Global)
3 Henrietta Street
Covent Garden
London WC2E 8LU
Tel: 44 20 7240 0856
Fax: 44 20 7379 0609
Web site: http://www.eurospanbookstore.com

Library of Congress Cataloging-in-Publication Data

Digital rights management for e-commerce systems / Lambros Drossos ... [et al.].

    p. cm.

Includes bibliographical references and index.

Summary: "This book highlights innovative technologies used for the design and implementation of advanced e-commerce systems facilitating digital rights management and protection"--Provided by publisher.

ISBN 978-1-60566-118-6 (hardcover) -- ISBN 978-1-60566-119-3 (ebook)

1. Electronic commerce--Technological innovations. 2. Copyright and electronic data processing. 3. Data protection. 4. Computer security. I. Drossos, Lambros, 1961- II. Title: Digital rights management for ecommerce.

HF5548.32.D54 2009

005.8--dc22

                    2008022547

British Cataloguing in Publication Data
A Cataloguing in Publication record for this book is available from the British Library.

All work contributed to this book set is original material. The views expressed in this book are those of the authors, but not necessarily of the publisher.

List of Reviewers

Cappellini Vito
University of Florence, Italy

Golfinopoulos Christos
Athens University of Law, Greece

Likothanasis Spiridon
University of Patras, Greece

Makris Christos
University of Patras, Greece

Nikolopoulos Spiros
SilkTech O.E., Greece

Ronchi Alfredo
Politecnico di Milano, Italy

Skodras Athanasios
Hellenic Open University, Greece

Stilios Georgios
TEI of Ionian Islands, Greece

Tsolis Dimitrios
University of Patras, Greece

Table of Contents

Section I
Overview

The specific section is providing an overview of the terms, methodologies, architectural issues and technological perspectives of digital rights management in e-commerce systems.

Section II
Protecting Digital Rights in E-Commerce Systems

In this section, an in-depth analysis of technological means for copyright protection of multimedia files is presented. Specifically, the most advanced watermarking algorithms and applications for multimedia are analyzed and evaluated.

Section III
Distributing, Managing, and Transacting Digital Rights in E-Commerce Systems

This section deals with the issues of distribution, management, and exploitation of copyrighted material and its digital rights through e-commerce systems. The issues are very important as they set the landscape and its restrictions regarding the transaction of digital rights via networks, Web services, and the Internet.

Section IV
Strategies and Case Studies

This section is presenting strategies and case studies of the use of digital rights management in organizations and sectors like cultural heritage.

Section V
Legislative Issues

The legal issues are being analyzed, aiming at pointing out the most crucial legislative parameters that affect digital rights management and the distribution of copyrighted material online through e-commerce systems.

Detailed Table of Contents

Section I
Overview

The specific section is providing an overview of the terms, methodologies, architectural issues and technological perspectives of digital rights management in e-commerce systems.

Chapter I

       Alfredo M. Ronchi, Politecnico di Milano, Italy

This chapter provides an overview on Intellectual Property Rights and related subjects including some approaches to IPR protection management and privacy.

Chapter II

       Ioannis Kostopoulos, University of Patras, Greece
       Penny Markelou, University of Patras, Greece
       Ioannis Panaretou, University of Patras, Greece
       Athanasios Tsakalidis, University of Patras, Greece

This chapter highlights the need for using copyright protection tools in our digital transactions. The legal framework and current activities of organizations as WIPO (World Intellectual Property Rights Organization) is also provided in this chapter, along with the existing DRM technologies and the future research directions in this field.

   Evanthia Tsilichristou, University of Patras, Greece
   Spiridon Likothanasis, University of Patras, Greece

The basic principle of watermarking is the addition of the watermark signal to the host data that copyright protection should apply. The addition is taking place in a way that the watermark signal is discreet and secure among the rest signals. Its retrieval, either partial or complete from the rest of signals, must also be possible only by using a secret key. This chapter analyzes the digital video watermarking. First its applications, requirements, and the most important trends will be presented, then some of the most significant techniques of the specific process will be described.

Section III
Distributing, Managing, and Transacting Digital Rights in E-Commerce Systems

This section deals with the issues of distribution, management, and exploitation of copyrighted material and its digital rights through e-commerce systems. The issues are very important as they set the landscape and its restrictions regarding the transaction of digital rights via networks, Web services, and the Internet.

   Nikos Nikolaidis, Aristotle University of Thessaloniki, Greece
   Ioannis Pitas, Aristotle University of Thessaloniki, Greece

Intellectual property rights protection and management of multimedia data is necessary for the deployment of e-commerce systems involving transactions on such data. Recently, replica detection or fingerprinting has emerged as a promising approach for the rights management of multimedia data. In this chapter, a review of two replica detection techniques is presented. The first technique utilizes color-based descriptors, an R-tree indexing structure and Linear Discriminant Analysis (LDA), to achieve image replica detection. The second technique is a video fingerprinting method that utilizes information about the appearances of individuals in videos along with an efficient search and matching strategy.

   Shiguo Lian, France Telecom R&D, Beijing, China

This chapter investigates the digital fingerprinting technology that is used to trace illegal distributors in multimedia content distribution. The background and basic knowledge of digital fingerprinting-based multimedia distribution is reviewed. Then, some existing fingerprinting algorithms are introduced and compared. Additionally, the methods to embed the fingerprint securely are overviewed and analyzed. As an example, the secure audio distribution scheme is presented, and its performances are evaluated. Finally, some open issues and the future trends in digital fingerprinting are proposed.

Chapter IX

Tom S. Chan, Southern New Hampshire University, USA
Shahriar Movafaghi, Southern New Hampshire University, USA
J. Stephanie Collins, Southern New Hampshire University, USA

Any business that wishes to control access to and use of its intellectual property is a potential user of Digital Rights Management (DRM) technologies. Traditional DRM has a passive, one-way downstream consumption of content from producer to consumer focusing primarily on concerns of digital rights enforcement. This model does not translate well to the education environment where openness, informal decision making, sharing of ideas and decentralization are valued. Collaboration and multiple authorships are common in the educational environment, as is the repurposing and modification of digital content used for teaching and learning. A DRM system for educational content distribution must be substantially more sophisticated and flexible than what is currently available, to gain support in the educational community.

Chapter X

Dimitrios P. Meidanis, SilkTech S.A., Greece
Spiros N. Nikolopoulos, SilkTech S.A., Greece
Emmanouil G. Karatzas, SilkTech S.A., Greece
Athanasia V. Kazantzi, SilkTech S.A., Greece

This chapter investigates intellectual property rights clearance of as part of e-commerce. Rights clearance is viewed as another online transaction that introduces certain technological and organizational challenges. An overview of the current intellectual property rights legislation is used to describe the setting in which business models and digital rights management systems are called to perform safe and fair electronic trade of goods. The chapter focuses on the technological aspects of the arising issues and investigates the potentials of using advanced information technology solutions for facilitating online rights clearance. A case study that presents a functioning online rights clearance and protection system is used to validate the applicability of the proposed approaches.

Section IV
Strategies and Case Studies

This section is presenting strategies and case studies of the use of digital rights management in organizations and sectors like cultural heritage.

Chapter XI

Dimitra Pappa, National Centre for Scientific Research "Demokritos", Greece
Lefteris G. Gortzis, Telemedicine Unit Department of Medical Physics, University of Patras,
Greece

When designing a DRM system, an integrated view over a number of parameters is required to understand their interdependencies. The external business environment, as determined by market conditions and related decisions of regulatory and normative authorities, can play a significant role. For example, DRM measures have to comply with intellectual property laws that provide a framework for protecting different forms of subject matter (i.e., copyright, patent, trademark, industrial design rights, trade secret, etc.). In this chapter we discuss and investigate a holistic framework for the development of value added DRM solutions using as basis Leavitt's diamond. In his effort to analyze organizational change, Leavitt (1965) proposed the classification of organizations as a four-dimensional diamond, in which Task, Technology, People, and Structure are interrelated and mutually adjusting.

The issue addressed in this chapter is the design implementation and evaluation of a watermarking application, especially focused on the protection of Cultural Heritage. The application described here is focusing on protecting digital surrogates of high-quality photographs of artifacts, monuments and sites, and on countering copyright infringement of online digital images. This is achieved by the integration of an innovative watermarking method to a specialized and usable user—interface. The system is specifically applied to "Ulysses" the Official Cultural Portal of the Hellenic Ministry of Culture (HMC).

Digital Rights Management (DRM) describes a set of functionalities which control access to, and the use of, copyright material. In particular, they focus on the acquisition of revenue from copyright material, and the prevention of its re-use and misuse in the online environment. This document describes a DRM system in the cultural heritage sector. The value of the DRMS to the content repositories and also to the end users is described.

Section V
Legislative Issues

The legal issues are being analyzed, aiming at pointing out the most crucial legislative parameters that affect digital rights management and the distribution of copyrighted material online through e-commerce systems.

The purpose of this chapter is to provide a brief overview of the legal framework available at EU level that applies to DRM information and Technological Protection Measures. For this reason, the relevant legal instruments are identified and briefly described. At the same time, an effort has been made to identify the most important points of concern that arise from the interpretation and application of the law. The review concludes by reference to the ongoing discussion over DRM designs in an effort to best combine the requirements of the law into technological solutions and vice-versa.

DRM systems have been implemented in the past few years by the Content Industry as the panacea against all copyright (and Intellectual Property Rights in general) infringements over the Internet. The chapter shall attempt to assess the validity of this statement, identifying its strengths and record up to modern times, and highlighting its shortcomings in an increasingly complex e-commerce (Web 2.0) environment.

Foreword

Due to the large spread of the Internet, e-commerce systems are getting more and more important as a new and effective method to distribute, transact, and exploit digital multimedia content. Interactive applications and graphic user interfaces, digital image, sound and video databases, e-payment systems, and e-licensing mechanisms are only a minor element of the existing and arising possibilities.

At the same time, intellectual property rights (IPR) protection and management of multimedia content has gradually become a critical issue.

- Advances in technology have improved the ability to reproduce, distribute, manage, and publish information. Reproduction costs are significantly lower for both legitimate IPR holders, (content owners) and those infringing intellectual property legislation. However, digital copies are perfect replicas. Computer networks have changed the economics of distribution; networks enable the worldwide distribution of multimedia content on a rapid and low cost basis. As a consequence, it is easier and less expensive, both for the legitimate rights holder to distribute their work, and for an individual to create and distribute unauthorized copies. Finally, the World Wide Web has fundamentally altered the publication channels, allowing everyone to become a publisher with global reach. This causes severe scepticism to the Digital Content Industry's organizations, which are consequently reluctant to distribute digital content through e-commerce systems, unless certain technically secure protection mechanisms are being implemented.
- The production and sharing of information in electronic form has been integrated into modern life, directly affecting intellectual property legislation. Today, common everyday activities such as file downloading or forwarding information retrieved from the Web may sometimes violate intellectual property laws. Other activities such as making copies of information for private use may require difficult interpretation of fair use provisions of the law to simply justify their legality. As a consequence, individuals in their daily lives have the capability and the opportunity to access and copy vast amounts of digital information, yet lack a clear picture of what is acceptable or legal. On the other hand, the necessary amendments of legislation in several cases do not fully cope with the problem, resulting in certain legislative weaknesses.
- A fundamental problem is that institutions of the Digital Content Industry want to make information widely available for educational or commercial reasons, but the legal environment renders this difficult. Where the rights-holders are known, this can be negotiated, but the costs of clearing the rights for digital images obtained by an individual for non-commercial purposes can be prohibitively expensive. The rights can be categorised as *legal, transactional,* or *implicit.* Legal are those rights that are got automatically (e.g., inherent copyright) or by some legal procedure (e.g., by applying for a patent). Transactional rights are those that are got or given up by buying or sell-

ing them (e.g., buying a book or selling a manuscript). Finally, implicit rights are defined by the medium that carries the information.

Digital rights management (DRM) refers to controlling and managing rights to digital intellectual property. The need for control and management has increased now that digital network technologies have taken away the implicit control that content owners get with legacy media. DRM systems combine a handful of technological solutions such as watermarking, data encryption, information systems, databases, e-commerce applications, so as to deal with the issue of the protection and management of copyrighted digital content.

The aim of this book is to investigate the field of DRM systems by giving an understanding of many relative publications appeared in the past 10 to 15 years, an overview of previously obtained, but also new results, and acquainting readers of active interest with the main approaches in this fascinatingly interesting and complicated direction. It intends "to open the door" for various specialists of different areas to this new and stimulating field of research activity. Design, implementation, and application through e-commerce systems and recommendations, key points, case studies, disputes, and limitations of these technological solutions, are thoroughly discussed in this book.

Each chapter of the book describes a part of this challenging area. The book is structured in five sections that deal with subjects ranging from purely low-level technical subjects to legislative and high-level systemic and procedural details. Of course the task of the authors is very hard, since each of these chapters could be an entire book by its own; to give important and comprehensive information that covers each subject in a satisfactory way.

Section I of the book provides an overview of the terms, methodologies, architectural issues, and technological perspectives of DRM in e-commerce systems. In Section II, an in-depth analysis of technological means for copyright protection of multimedia files is given. Section III deals with the issues of distribution, management, and exploitation of copyrighted material and its digital rights through e-commerce systems. The strategies and case studies of the use of DRM in organizations and sectors like cultural heritage are presented in Section IV. Finally, in Section V, the legal issues and the most crucial legislative parameters affecting DRM and the online distribution of copyrighted material through e-commerce systems are analyzed.

Professor A. N. Skodras
Hellenic Open University, Greece

Athanasios Skodras received the BSc degree in physics from Aristotle University of Thessaloniki, Greece, in 1980, the Diploma degree in computer engineering & informatics, in 1985 and the PhD degree in electronics, in 1986 from the University of Patras, Greece. Since 1986 he has been holding teaching and research positions at the Departments of Physics and Computer Engineering & Informatics of the University of Patras, and the Computer Technology Institute, Patras, Greece. Currently he is professor of Computer Science, School of Sciences and Technology, Hellenic Open University. During the academic years 1988-89 and 1996-97 he was a visiting researcher at the Department of Electrical and Electronic Engineering, Imperial College, London, UK. His current research interests include image and video coding, digital watermarking, fast transform algorithms, real-time digital signal processing and multimedia applications. He has authored or co-authored over 60 technical papers, 4 books, and holds 2 international patents. Dr. Skodras serves as an associate editor for the IEEE Transactions on Circuits and Systems II: Analog & Digital Signal Processing, as an associate editor for Pattern Recognition, and as a reviewer for numerous journals and conferences. He also serves as the chair of the IEEE CAS & SSC chapters in Greece, and as the technical coordinator of the WG6 on image and video coding of the Hellenic Organization for Standardization. He was appointed as the technical program chair for the 13th IEEE Int. Conference on Digital Signal Processing (DSP-97), and as the general Co-Chair for the 14th IEEE Int. Conference on Digital Signal Processing (DSP 2002). He is the co-recepient of the first place Chester Sall Award for the best paper in the 2000 IEEE TRANSACTIONS ON CONSUMER ELECTRONICS. Dr. Skodras is a Chartered Engineer, Senior Member of the IEEE, and member of the IEE, EURASIP and the Technical Chamber of Greece.

Preface

Borrowing a book from a library is now a typical, simple and costless procedure. A whole universe of knowledge is available to anybody, which establishes a basis for lifetime education for all of society. The act of borrowing a book seems easy, but it is based on a complicated mechanism involving laws, publication policies and many financial and technological parameters. This mechanism might be in balance and in everyday use, but this balance can be affected by the rapid digitization of the information provided (the books). The problem can be proven in a simple way: a book can be borrowed by one or two people at the same time within the same library. An electronic book can be borrowed by anyone with a telephone line, a computer and an Internet connection. From the Internet user's point of view, this news is positive; the library owns a book which is never exclusively borrowed and is always available for countless readers. In fact, this library is open twenty-four hours a day, seven days a week. On the other hand, this news is very stressful for publishers and writers. How many copies will be sold or published while digital networks allow worldwide access to digital information? How many books, movies, pieces of music and other, copyrighted information can be created, published and sold on the Internet while, to enable worldwide access for readers, listeners and viewers, one digital copy is enough? These initial thoughts and problems should not lead to aggressive and dangerous actions, which restrict or disallow access to cultural, scientific, educational and entertainment resources. This is the worst news for the Internet user and e-inclusion to Information Society is threatened.

The aforementioned simple (as it seems) problem describes exactly the modern digital dilemma that Randall D. (2001) predicted. The World Wide Web is a powerful vehicle for publishing and distributing information and is the world's largest infrastructure for making digital copies of this information. It is a technology with which free and efficient access to information could grow at an unbelievable pace but, at the same time, it could prove to be a force that deepens the discrimination line between those who have access to it and those who do not.

According to the House of Representatives (1998), Information Society technologies are changing the most common methods of providing access to digital content. The information available in digital form increases on a daily basis; the Internet is connecting worldwide digital content; and the World Wide Web is providing an efficient platform consisting of access services, which act as a gateway to scientific and cultural resources, music, movies and video archives. The technologies which provide access to digital content also provoke important problems concerning the protection and management of intellectual property rights (IPR) for this digital content. This happens mainly because technology supports efficient access to and enables the copying of copyrighted information. As a result, many legislative rules and laws for IPR, which refer to physical objects, are almost invalid for digital objects. The specific problem becomes even more intense as broadband Internet is applied worldwide and any Internet user has fast data transfer rates at his or her disposal. Other examples which prove the size of the problem include the free distribution of copyrighted music and movies through the Internet and the online sale of copyrighted digital art and cultural images without permission.

Digital rights management for e-commerce systems is a proposed solution for IPR protection and management. These systems combine a handful of technological solutions such as watermarking, data encryption, information systems, databases, and e-commerce applications so as to deal with the issue of the protection and management of copyrighted digital content.

The term digital rights management (DRM) was coined by some combination of vendors, their marketers, and industry analysts in the late 1990s, as Katzenbeisser and Petitcolas (2000) mention. Thus, defining DRM has become difficult and a better question to ask is "What has DRM become?" When content (information) is created, the control of a set of rights to that content is inherited by the owner, allowing browsing, editing, printing, executing, copying, etc. Traditionally, those rights have accrued from three sources:

- **Legal:** Rights that someone gets either automatically under law (such as inherent copyright) or by some legal procedure (such as applying for a patent).
- **Transactional:** Rights that someone gets or gives up by buying or selling them, such as buying a book or selling a manuscript to a publisher.
- **Implicit:** Rights defined by the medium that the information is in.

The most important aspect of DRM is that the first two sources of rights have not changed much with the advent of technologies such as the Internet, cell phones and MP3 files. Various parties have called for a complete replacement of the intellectual property (IP) law, but this has not happened and is not going to. Legislators have responded to new technologies by creating Directives and Acts.

Transactions have not changed that much, either, regardless of the fact that they can be performed over the Internet through e-commerce systems. The same laws apply, the same money is used, and the same goods can be purchased. What has really changed is the implicit nature of rights when applied to traditional media. The Internet has made these implicit rights explicit. This engenders problems and opportunities for content providers as well as consumers.

Understanding the implicit rights of traditional media types, the next example is considered. If a book is purchased, the buyer has rights to the content in the book. Some are legal (it is a breach of copyright law to make copies of the book and sell them) and other transactional (someone pays money for the right to read the book, to lend it, or to give it away). Most rights, however, derive from what is easy and what is difficult to do with the technology of a printed book.

Digital rights management refers to controlling and managing rights to digital intellectual property. The need for control and management has increased now that digital network technologies have taken away the implicit control that content owners get with legacy media.

It is the aim of this book to present the state of the art technologies for digital rights management systems, which are designed, implemented and applied through e-commerce systems and to discuss recommendations, key points, disputes and limitations of these technological solutions.

The main objective of the book is to concentrate on new innovative technologies used for the design and implementation of advanced e-commerce systems, which facilitate digital rights management and protection for the transacted content. Specifically, the focus will be on technologies such as data encryption and watermarking (Wayner, 2002), peer to peer networks, very large databases, digital image, sound and video libraries, multimedia content based services, electronic licensing, digital certificates, rights expression languages, metadata standards, etc., which are used within the e-commerce systems. In addition, special focus will be given to implemented e-commerce systems, whose aim is to support organizations active in the sectors of entertainment, content industry, music, cinema and culture and to protect, manage, exploit and disseminate multimedia content and its intellectual property rights.

THE CHALLENGES

E-commerce systems are becoming more and more important as a new and effective method to distribute, transact and exploit digital multimedia content. Interactive applications and GUIs, digital image, sound and video databases, e-payment systems, and e-licensing mechanisms are a few of the many opportunities created through the evolution of e-commerce.

In this framework, intellectual property rights (IPR) protection and management of multimedia content is gradually becoming a critical issue, primarily because reproduction costs are much lower for both legitimate IPR holders (content owners) and those infringing intellectual property legislation. Further, digital copies are perfect replicas and computer networks have changed the economics of distribution. Networks enable the distribution of multimedia content worldwide and do so cheaply and quickly. As the US Computer Science and Telecommunications Board (1999) has described, it is easier and less expensive both for the rights holder to distribute a work and for an individual to make and distribute unauthorized copies. Finally, the World Wide Web has fundamentally altered the publication of information, allowing everyone to be a publisher with worldwide reach.

In addition, the production and sharing of information in electronic form has been integrated into everyday life, directly affecting intellectual property legislation. Today, casual everyday activities such as downloading files and forwarding information found on the Web can, at times, violate intellectual property laws. Other activities, such as making copies of information for private use, may require difficult interpretation of fair use provisions of the law to simply justify their legality. Consequently, individuals have the capability and the opportunity to access and copy vast amounts of digital information, yet lack a clear picture of what is acceptable or legal. On the other hand, the necessary amendments of legislation in several cases does not fully address with the problem, resulting in certain legislative weaknesses.

A fundamental problem is that institutions of the Digital Content Industry want to make information widely available for educational or commercial reasons, but the legal environment makes this difficult. Where the rights-holders are known, this can be negotiated, but the costs of clearing the rights for digital images taken by an individual for non-commercial purposes can be prohibitively expensive.

The consequences of the aforementioned parameters are obvious and digital content is being used, copied, distributed and published without the necessary license. In many cases, commercial exploitation is also taking place without the necessary legal provisions and permissions by the copyright owners. An Internet user with an average ADSL connection at home who utilizes peer to peer networks for exchanging data has the ability to transfer more than 25Gbytes of digital content per day. This content may include music, movies, television series, documentaries, books, photographs and images of all kind. In addition, copyrighted content of the world's cultural heritage is being distributed and sold through the Internet. More than 4.000 illegal copies of the Picasso's "Guernica" are published on the Internet and more than 1,000 digital images of the Athens Parthenon are being sold through digital image stores without permission by the copyright owner. The music and movie industries are facing economic losses, and this directly affects the jobs of thousands of people. In addition, the phenomenon of unauthorized use of digital content on the Internet causes skepticism within Digital Content Industry organizations, who are not willing to distribute digital content through e-commerce systems, unless certain technical protection means are being applied.

SEARCHING FOR A SOLUTION

Universities, research institutes, laboratories and corporations who are active in dealing with the issue of protection and management of IPR of digital content aim mainly at providing a safe environment for content distribution and publication (Cox, Miller & Bloom, 2002). The US Government, the European Union, Canada, Japan, Russia and all the countries with a developed content industry have recognized the need for finding effective solutions for this important issue. The intensive activity is proved by the establishment of many governmental bodies and committees, which are dealing with the issue and its legal, financial and social aspects and, in parallel, by many funded research projects, which aim at developing technologies for copyright protection and management.

These projects concentrate on new innovative technologies used for the design and implementation of advanced e-commerce systems, which facilitate digital rights management and protection for the transacted content. Specifically, the focus is on technologies such as:

- Methodologies and techniques of content digitization
- Geographically dispersed and interoperable databases
- Peer to peer networks
- Metadata for digital rights management
- Digital image, video and audio processing
- Telecommunications and signal processing
- Digital watermarking of multimedia content
- Unique identification systems for digital objects
- Internet technologies
- E-commerce systems
- Electronic licensing mechanisms and applications
- New and innovative file formats
- Streaming applications for audio and video
- Rights expression computer languages

The use of the aforementioned technologies provides solutions, applications and information systems, which aim at digital rights protection and management. This book provides an in-depth analysis of all the above technological solutions and their combination and use in integrated e-commerce systems.

ORGANIZATION OF THE BOOK

The book is organized into five semantic sections and includes fifteen chapters. A brief description of each section and chapter follows:

Section I, "*Overview*," the specific section provides an overview of the terms, methodologies, architectural issues and technological perspectives of digital rights management in e-commerce systems.

Chapter I, "*Intellectual Property Rights*" this chapter provides an overview of Intellectual Property Rights and related subjects, including some approaches to IPR protection management and privacy.

Chapter II, "*Digital Rights Management: A New Trend or a Necessity?*" in this chapter, the need for using copyright protection tools in our digital transactions is highlighted. The legal framework and the current activities of organizations as World Intellectual Property Rights Organization (WIPO) is also provided in this chapter, along with the existing DRM technologies and the future research directions in this field.

Section II, *"Protecting Digital Rights in E-Commerce Systems"* In this section, an in-depth analysis of technological means for copyright protection of multimedia files is presented. Specifically, the most advanced watermarking algorithms and applications for multimedia are analyzed and evaluated.

Chapter III, *"Image Watermarking"* digital watermarking is an appropriate solution for copyright protection of digital rights. This technology allows a secret message to be hidden in an image file, without the detection of the user. The watermark is not apparent to the user, and does not in any way affect the use of the original file. The watermarking information is predominantly used to identify the creator of a digital image file. This chapter presents the basic terms and definitions as well as the most advanced watermarking methodologies.

Chapter IV, *"Watermarking Techniques for DRM Applications"* This chapter presents a mathematical formulation to define a digital watermarking model, and lists and discusses general requirements with more emphasis given to aspects of security, robustness and imperceptibility. After this general discussion, the two main classes of digital watermarking schemes, namely the spread-spectrum watermarking and the side-informed watermarking are explained by highlighting their main advantages and drawbacks. This analysis is completed by providing a detailed description of a practical implementation of a digital image watermarking scheme, designed in the past years by the authors. Next, the use of watermarking systems in the framework of a DRM is analyzed. Finally, future trends are discussed and the conclusions are drawn.

Chapter V, *"Watermarking and Authentication in JPEG 2000"* This chapter introduces JPEG2000 as an application field for image authentication and the new technology of digital image watermarking. The new compression format has a lot of unexplored characteristics that both the watermarking and the authentication communities should carefully take into account. Thus, a brief introduction to the standard is given at the beginning, discussing its structure, features, novelties and capabilities. Following that introduction, watermarking techniques are presented, at first into the wavelet domain (the DWT is part of the JPEG2000 core) and then right into the JPEG2000 pipeline.

Chapter VI, *"Securing and Protecting the Copyright of Digital Video Through Watermarking Technologies"* The basic principle of watermarking is the addition of the watermark signal to the host data that copyright protection should apply. The addition is taking place in a way that the watermark signal is discrete and secure among the rest signals. Its retrieval, either partial or complete, from the rest of signals must be possible only by using a secret key. In this chapter, digital video watermarking is analyzed. Its applications, requirements and the most important trends are presented and some of the most significant techniques of the specific process are described.

Section III, *"Distributing, Managing, and Transacting Digital Rights in E-Commerce Systems"* This section deals with the issues of distribution, management and exploitation of copyrighted material and its digital rights through e-commerce systems. The issues are very important as they set the landscape and its restrictions regarding the transaction of digital rights via networks, web services and the Internet.

Chapter VII, *"Digital Rights Management of Images and Videos Using Robust Replica Detection Techniques"* Intellectual property rights protection and management of multimedia data is necessary for the deployment of e-commerce systems involving transactions on such data. Recently, replica detection or fingerprinting has emerged as a promising approach for the rights management of multimedia data. In this chapter, a review of two replica detection techniques is presented. The first technique utilizes color-based descriptors, an R-tree indexing structure and linear discriminant analysis (LDA) to achieve image replica detection. The second one is a video fingerprinting method that utilizes information about the appearance of individuals in videos along with an efficient search and matching strategy.

Chapter VIII, "*Digital Fingerprinting Based Multimedia Content Distribution*" In this chapter, the digital fingerprinting technology that is used to trace illegal distributors in multimedia content distribution is investigated. First, the background and basic knowledge of digital fingerprinting based multimedia distribution are reviewed. Then, some existing fingerprinting algorithms are introduced and compared. Additionally, the methods to embed the fingerprint securely are overviewed and analyzed. As an example, the secure audio distribution scheme is presented, and its performances are evaluated. Finally, some open issues and the future trends in digital fingerprinting are proposed.

Chapter IX, "*A Digital Rights Management System for Educational Content Distribution*" Any business that wishes to control access to and use of its intellectual property is a potential user of digital rights management (DRM) technologies. Traditional DRM has a passive one-way downstream consumption of content from producer to consumer and focuses primarily on concerns of digital rights enforcement. This model does not translate well to the education environment where openness, informal decision making, sharing of ideas and decentralization are valued. Collaboration and multiple authorships are common in the educational environment, as is the repurposing and modification of digital content used for teaching and learning. A DRM system for educational content distribution must be substantially more sophisticated and flexible than what is available right now to gain support in the educational community.

Chapter X, "*Digital Rights Management and E-Commerce Transactions: Online Rights Clearance*" This chapter investigates intellectual property rights clearance as part of e-commerce. Rights clearance is viewed as another on-line transaction that introduces certain technological and organizational challenges. An overview of the current intellectual property rights legislation is used to describe the setting which business models and digital rights management systems are utilized to perform safe and fair electronic trade of goods. The chapter focuses on the technological aspects of the arising issues and investigates the potentials of using advanced information technology solutions for facilitating on-line rights clearance. A case study that presents a functioning on-line rights clearance and protection system is used to validate the applicability of the proposed approaches.

Section IV, "*Strategies and Case Studies*" The section presents strategies and case studies of the use of digital rights management in organizations and sectors such as cultural heritage.

Chapter XI, "*Digital Rights Management in Organisations: A Critical Consideration with a Socio-Technical Approach*" When designing a DRM system, an integrated view of a number of parameters is required, so as to understand their interdependencies. The external business environment, as determined by market conditions and related decisions of regulatory and normative authorities, can play a significant role. For example, DRM measures have to comply with intellectual property laws that provide a framework for protecting different forms of subject matter (copyright, patent, trademark, industrial design rights, trade secret, etc.). This chapter discusses and investigates a holistic framework for the development of value added DRM solutions using Leavitt's diamond as a model. In his effort to analyse organisational change, Leavitt (1965) proposed the classification of organisations in four-dimensional diamond, in which Task, Technology, People, and Structure are interrelated and mutually adjusting.

Chapter XII, "*An Advanced Watermarking Application for the Copyright Protection and Management of Digital Images of Cultural Heritage Case Study: 'Ulysses'*" The issue addressed in this chapter is the design implementation and evaluation of a watermarking application, especially focused on the protection of cultural heritage. The application described here focuses on protecting digital surrogates of high quality photographs of artifacts, monuments and sites and on countering copyright infringement of on-line digital images. This is achieved by the integration of an innovative watermarking method to a specialized and usable user interface. The system is specifically applied to "Ulysses" the Official Cultural Portal of the Hellenic Ministry of Culture (HMC).

Chapter XIII, *"Digital Rights Management in the Cultural Heritage Arena: A Truth or a Myth?"* Digital rights management (DRM) describes a set of functionalities which control access to, and the use of, copyrighted material. In particular, they focus on the acquisition of revenue from copyright material, and the prevention of its re-use and misuse in the online environment. This document describes a DRM system in the cultural heritage sector. The value of the DRMS to the content repositories and also to the end users is described.

Section V, *"Legislative Issues"* In this section, legal issues are analyzed and the most crucial legislative parameters which affect digital rights management and the distribution of copyrighted material on-line through e-commerce systems are discussed.

Chapter XIV, *"Digital Rights Management: A European Law Perspective"* The purpose of this chapter is to provide a brief overview of the legal framework available at EU level that applies to DRM information and technological protection measures. For this reason, the relevant legal instruments are identified and briefly described, while at the same time an effort has been made to identify the most important points of concern that arise from the interpretation and application of the law. The review concludes by reference to the ongoing discussion over DRM designs in an effort to best combine the requirements of the law into technological solutions and vice-versa.

Chapter XV, *"Legal Issues for DRM: The Future"* DRM systems have been implemented in the past few years by the Content Industry as the panacea against all copyright (and intellectual property rights in general) infringements over the Internet. The chapter attempts to assess the validity of this statement, identifying its strengths and record until today and highlighting its shortcomings in an increasingly complex e-commerce (Web 2.0) environment.

REFERENCES

Cox, I. J., Miller, M. L., & Bloom, J. A. (2002). *Digital Watermarking.*. Morgan Kaufann Publishers.

Computer Science and Telecommunications Board, National Research Council. (1999). The Digital Dilemma: Intellectual Property in the Information Age (pp. 2-3). Washington: National Academy Press.

House of Representatives. (1998). *Digital Millennium Copyright Act.*

Katzenbeisser, S., & Petitcolas, F. A. P. (2000). *Information Hiding - techniques for steganography and digital watermarking* (pp. 95-172). Artech House, Computer Series.

Randall, D. (2001) *The Digital Dilemma*, Communications of the ACM pp. 80, Volume 44.

Wayner, P. (2002). *Disappearing Cryptography - Information Hiding: Steganography and Watermarking* (Second, pp. 291-318). Morgan Kaufmann.

Acknowledgment

The editors would like to acknowledge the help of all involved in the collation and review process of the book, without whose support the project could not have been satisfactorily completed.

Thanks go to all the authors who contributed to this book supporting in parallel the high quality and innovation of the produced result. Most of the authors of chapters included in this book also served as referees for chapters written by other authors. Thanks go to all those who provided constructive and comprehensive reviews.

Special thanks also go to the publishing team at IGI Global, whose contributions throughout the whole process from inception of the initial idea to final publication have been invaluable. In particular to Ross Miller, Julia Mosemann and Jessica Thompson, who continuously prodded via e-mail for keeping the project on schedule.

Dr. Dimitrios Tsolis, Prof. Lambros Drossos,
Ass. Prof. Spyzos Sioutas & Prof. Theodore Papatheodorou
Editors

Section I
Overview

The specific section is providing an overview of the terms, methodologies, architectural issues and technological perspectives of digital rights management in e-commerce systems.

Chapter I
Intellectual Property Rights

Alfredo M. Ronchi
Politecnico di Milano, Italy

ABSTRACT

"Creativity is one of the highest forms of human energy. It is a defining human trait that enables us to design and use tools, while giving us the ability to solve problems. In the modern world, creativity and its outcome–innovation–are credited as the greatest predictors for economic advancement, equal to, or surpassing, investments. Creativity can be a vehicle for empowerment and fulfilment or, if denied or abused, it can lead to frustration, apathy, alienation, and even violence. The role of creativity has been magnified by the explosive developments in Information and Communication Technologies. ICTs are the most powerful means to produce, preserve, and communicate the fruits of human creativity, including information, know-how, knowledge, and works of art." (ICT and Creativity: Towards a global cooperation for quality contents in the Information Society – The Vienna Conclusions 2005)

INTRODUCTION

Creativity is one most significant assets of the human kind. Creativity makes the difference between humans and other creatures, human creativity is probably powerful and pervasive.

Human may express creativity in different ways with different media so we enjoy musicians, composers, singers, painters, sculptors, actors, movie directors, architects, industrial designers, writers, engineers, ..., computer scientists and more. All of them are able to "add" something special to a simple mix of common ingredients: lines, notes, colours, words, instructions etc. The element they "add" it should be named "brain juice", it is due to their own intellect. In such a way creativity is the inner engine of innovation.

Of course creativity does not start usually from "tabula rasa (from scratch)" it takes into account and is influenced by the cultural background and previous experiences and "products". All this happens voluntarily or involuntarily. Painters create their own style, even the most "break through" one, starting from the "elaboration" of the existent ones. Composers are frequently influenced by other artists as well as architects and industrial designers.

Obviously speaking about innovation and inventions it is a common understanding that no one use to sit down and think: Now I will invent something that does not exist at all!

Sometimes the recipe includes part or a set of parts of already existent "objects".

From time to time it happens that the original aim of the invention or research is not exactly or at all the real one on the market. Trying to better the efficiency of water pumps it happens to invent steam engines, researching on "peer to peer" secure wireless communication meet a "bug" later on called "broadcasting", trying to help to solve the problem of deaf invent one of the most significant and pervasive "object" of the twentieth century: the transistor.

Major part of the times the "quid" due to creativity and innovation capacity is disclosed to the public as soon as the "creation" is available to the people. The "disclosure" of the artefact inspires other "authors" enabling them to go one step beyond or just to clone it. It happens every day in every field: music, painting, engineering, architecture, industrial design etc.

It is a common understanding that creative people (and companies) invest time and resources in order to make some progress. Productivity and return of investment in this field are not easy to estimate, we can simply refer to average figures. Of course there are differences amongst painters, musicians and scientists.

Here it come the dilemma: do we consider such achievements human kind advances and in some way patrimony of the humanity freely accessible and reusable by anyone or do we consider wiser to protect it as the result of "personal" investments and efforts? And more in detail: how intellectual property laws might embrace the apparently paradoxical goals of motivating individual creation and preserving the ultimate benefits of that creation for the common good.

This chapter provides an overview on Intellectual property rights and related subjects including some approaches to IPR protection management and privacy[1].

DIGITAL PLAYGROUND

Intellectual property includes copyrights, patents, trademarks and trade secrets. The present chapter will mainly focus on intellectual property rights with specific reference to the digital world.

As we already considered intellectual property is key issue in any field of activity. One of the usual reference points in attributing the paternity of an artefact is the ownership or "registration" of the "original". So we use to refer to the manuscript, the negative, the technical sketches etc. All this was in the world of "analogue". What happens in the digital domain?

Recently we faced the so called "digital revolution" that influenced a number of fields of activity with opportunities and threats.

The digital technology has meaningfully increased the expressive opportunities of creative people both offering new form of expression and drastically reducing the production costs of prototypes and products.

Significant examples are the music and video fields where the production costs have drastically come down allowing young talents to approach their own productions. In addition in the computer games field and even more in the Web publishing field the use of easy access[2] technologies has concurred to offer the possibility to express themselves even to talented people not particularly skilled in computer science.

In addition to all the above, digital technologies and in particular the Internet have completely overturned the concept of commercial and distribution goods.

Every product that can assume the digital format can be cloned to the infinite with costs tending to zero.

A copy of a digital object is always equal to itself, without loss of quality. This aspect has deep repercussions on the ontological side, digital objects represents a completely new class of objects. There is no more the concept of ownership of the original, in the digital world *access* means *ownership*.

Furthermore this aspect take us to having to reconsider some ontological aspects and an interesting comparison with what happened with the introduction of "print", when all the "content" that could be reduced to sequences of lines of text organized in pages could be reproduced to infinite with minimal costs in comparison to the previous model of the hand copy[3].

What happened later on is well known, the text format prevailed on other communication formats influencing the information transmission to take the linear format.

Today "digital objects" can easily be cloned and more, they can easily be transmitted instantaneously all over the world enabling new ways to access information. Access to information publishing has drastically lowered and anyone today can reach a public unforeseeable until some years ago, it is enough to post on a Web site, be a blogger or upload to YouTube[4].

In the last decades we faced two related processes, the increasing role of electronic devices in our everyday life and the "rush to digital formats".

Institutions, organisations and private companies launched a midterm programme converting their own archives in digital format.

Even people at home started a "personal data" conversion toward digital format: documents, music, movies, drawings and photos left their original format and medium reshaped in "bitstreams" on digital media.

All this on one side may be a worry; from the other side thinking to expression and creativity of the young people is surely a remarkable benefit.

In this way, on the network, a great melting pot, groups of interest and forums, services of content sharing and a lot more are born and die every day.

A new class of objects probably does not fit within the same guidelines defined for already known objects. The new class has deep influence on different aspects such as: ownership, access, use, validity, quality, privacy and more.

If the author looses the control on the "artefact" he is no more responsible for the quality and the validity of the "artefact". This was one of the basic problems in the implementation of computer aided design in architecture and engineering.

Traditional (analogue) media were segmented and had their own terminology and economics. While the content elements of digital multimedia do not bring up new legal problems, the combination and uses of them do. The term "multimedia" can not only apply to text, images and music on hard disk, CD-ROM, DVD, podcasting etc., but also to networked resources, video on demand and other interactive services including ecommerce.

Questions to be answered are:

- Is multimedia a collaborative work (where the authors' rights belong to the different creators and have to be transferred by contract to the producer) or a collective work (where, from the outset, the rights belong to the publisher)?
- If multimedia were to be legally considered as a databank, this would raise other sets of rights problems, under existing national legislation and proposed EU harmonization that is currently being discussed.
- Does the inclusion of a work in a multimedia resource constitute a new form of exploitation or is it the adaptation of a pre-existing work? Many existing contracts have provision for the assignment of unknown methods of exploitation but most do not include rights of adaptation. Ancillary rights in existing contracts do not cover new media subsequently introduced.

Digital forms also introduce many new complications in relation to aspects such as image manipulation, downloading to disc or hard copy printout, networking etc. Reproducing a copyright protected work in electronic form is considered a restricted act, but in many EU and non-EU countries the status under copyright law of temporary (transient) electronic storage of protected works (i.e. in RAM memory) during acts of loading, transmission or screen display has been debated for a long time. With the rapid rate of technology development it is going to be necessary to regularly update agreements.

Multimedia is ravenous for content and, realistically, we have to start valuing the price of the various elements of content on a new basis.

COPY RIGHT OR COPY LEFT?

Back to the general topic let us start from the two main approaches to creativity management. This takes us to two main different "chunk of thought": copy right and copy left. Traditionally, copyright and copy left have been regarded as concepts in antithesis: the first one concerned with the strict protection of authors' rights, the other ensuring free circulation of ideas encouraging further achievements.

If we consider copyright in its extreme form, it would mean that all works fulfilling the condition of copyright protection, regardless of by whom, when and where they were created, are "unavailable" to the public at large. Such a total "unavailability" to the public goes beyond the necessity to respect authors' rights and would also be socially harmful, the law provides for some exceptions. Public domain is one of these exceptions.

In the field of art and culture the copy left vision follows the Medicean[5] idea to let the mankind, without any restriction due to social status or worth, enjoy the beauty of art.

People interested in this subject developed different studies and approaches. While on the subject of copyright, protecting ingenuity, products and generally speaking "brain juice" ensuring financial support to authors in order to enable further developments of the products there is a vast and global legislation, with corresponding applicative complications, few studies have been made on copy left, the dark side of the moon; the commonly held idea is that it begins where copyright's boundaries cease, spreading over a no man's land of more or less illegal exploitation. As a natural evolution of this double vision more recently an innovative approach was developed, from all right reserved to some rights reserved the new approach in the field of intellectual right management: Creative Commons.

Let us start from Public Domain and Copy Left.

Public Domain[6] & Copy Left

The concept of public domain does not relate to precise definition. Sometimes when we refer to public content it is not clear if this means accessible to the public, property of the public or simply accessible for free[7].

Basically the concept of public domain covers "anything that is not protected by copyright and related rights, regardless of the reason for the lack of protection in a given case".

Of course this does not apply for the categories of objects that could not be potentially protected or does not share any similarity with the protection-covered categories. This means that images, music, lyrics, ... might be of public domain but neither air nor the sea or the sunset are usually, if not metaphorically, considered in the public domain. In order to be protected or fall under public domain intellectual creations must satisfy at least some of the criteria provided for in the laws.

An easy definition of public domain, even taking into account the number of objects involved, is "objects no more copyrighted or for some reason not copyrighted". Is we consider the concept in a narrower sense, public domain does not cover non-material creations[8], which are not, or cannot be, works.

Even if it is in the same sphere of concepts the so called "fair use" must not be mistaken for public domain. Fair use means that "the rights to which the creator or other parties are entitled are limited in such a way that, under specified conditions, other persons may use the protected work in the way that has been defined[9]". Nevertheless the artefact is protected by law even if there are some limitations; moral rights, if applicable[10], are always protected.

Trying to summarize the main groups of artefacts that can be said to fall within the public domain category[11]:

a.   Ones that for some reason are not and could not be protected,
b.   Ones that used to be protected but are not any more due to lapse/progress of time,
c.   And ones that have never been protected because they were created in a time when copyright did not exist yet in today's meaning, or when it did not protect a given category of works.

Unprotected Works[12]

If a work satisfies the general conditions of protection that copyright provides for, it can be excluded from protection only exceptionally and this is done under express provision of the law in force. Various kinds of public documents, such as texts of the law, court decisions, descriptions of patents, etc. can serve as typical examples. Public interest requires that everybody should have access to them and may use them for their own purpose, and that is why they have been excluded from protection.

Works that are No Longer Protected[13]

Although copyright shows considerable similarity to ownership law, it is different in that it is temporary. Law gives a monopoly right to the right holder to use the work for a period of time. Once the period is over, the work enters the public domain and everybody can use it, generally without restrictions. As it applies to all possible kinds of works, copyright is the most frequent and the most important case of public domain, and so the concept is sometimes used to refer to those works for which the duration of protection has ended.

Protection periods are determined by the provisions of a given country's law with major influence exerted on their substance by, respectively, international agreements binding the country or Community legislation binding the EU Member States. It must be remembered that, due to changes in regulations, a state's entry into various agreements at different times and the occasional cases of copyright renewal, establishing whether a given work already belongs or still does not belong to the public domain can become difficult.

Works that Have Never Been Protected[14]

Works for which copyright was never created because, at the time of their creation, no copyright was in force that would give such protective rights to the creators do not benefit from protection. This can be exemplified by literary and artistic works of old masters. In their case, however, even if their works were protected, protection would have terminated long ago.

Whether a work or creation is part of the public domain is determined by the legislation of the state in which the problem is considered. It must be borne in mind that the law in various states may vary considerably, in this respect, from one to another.

Once we have checked if the artefact we are interested in is public domain how can we manage? Is there any limitation in use or any constraint?

Artefacts in the public domain may, in principle, be freely used by anybody. Nevertheless, this does not mean that there are no constraints. More specifically we cannot forget, at least were explicitly protected, moral rights such as "paternity" or what we will define later on "integrity". In addition, before using the artefact, we must check if, by chance, there is any other "protection" such as trademarks or specific agreements.

As we mainly considered public domain as the area "no more copyrighted", let us consider now the area "not copyrighted" or by the will of the authors freely accessible by anybody. Copyleft, they say, is a zone of free creativity to which anyone can access, looking at his own personal advantage and/or the advantage of the community.

The copy left phenomenon in the digital sector has exploded on the Internet after decades of "physical" exchanges of data and code within "developer's communities" or "special interest groups".

The Internet has dramatically changed the information sector almost as it happened in the television sector thanks to the creation of commercial broadcasting televisions. The threshold to access a broad audience lowered from media tycoons to Webmasters and "Internauts".

The only media allowing access to broad audience before the Internet were: newspapers, radio and television. Thanks to the Internet similar audience should be reached simply posting information in a newsgroup or on a Web site.

In addition the Internet not only offers infinite opportunities for exchanging messages, finding and publishing information, but also gives free access to information which once was the pertinence of closed circles or specialised publications[15] and for which, at the moment at least, no one dreams of asking any kind of payment.

The software programmes themselves, in the formula of freeware, have multiplied to as the extent that very few indeed are totally inaccessible, without at least a demo or trial version[16]. New media and related modification in social behaviour are pushing changes in right management. The intensive use of digital music and movies is pushing "majors" to change their policies and market models.

Market models affected very much even access to the Network, once available only by payment of expensive subscriptions, suddenly become free. It was enough that one single telecom operator started the new policy as it already happened for Web browsers and an infinite number of plug-ins.

So it can be said that the Net, with its capillary opening up to communication, has revolutionised the balance, in the favour of copyleft with its totally innovative dynamics.

How then may we regard the new problematic arising from this situation, in which copyright is not cancelled but taken for granted, in which payment for access is abolished but the philosophy of profit-making according to market rules is retained?

The OCCAM-UNESCO Observatory[17] has been researching this phenomenon and here we wish to give a brief analysis, beginning with the principal junctures between which this is articulated: free access, freeware, shareware.

Free Access

This is widely diffused on the Internet, since the important providers have learned that rivals are jumping one step ahead on Web communication, i.e. to the portals.

The contingent phenomenon, linked to the opening-up of new markets in which it is necessary to acquire ever wider slices whatever be the cost, is becoming structural as much as the firm's worth or its stock market value grows proportionally to the services offered and acquired customer loyalty.

So even in the most rigorous marketing oriented attitude can be found a value which is in continual growth, transferred from traditional material goods to the actual immaterial and identified by the number of users acquired - little does it matter how briefly, the time of evaluation is exceedingly rapid. The key example of such behaviour is in the figures of "customers" of the Internet access providers or mobile telecom operators paying zero for the service but anyway considered a significant company asset.

The rule of *copyleft* has thus become the winning weapon in the new market; value has been shifted from the product covered in copyrights to the attention of the user, his habits in every possible detail, in order to pin down his changing moods and whims and single out adequate productive solutions.

Freeware

This concerns the free software programmes, they are basically in the public domain. Sometimes they are available in source code sometimes simply the executable one. Some software companies decided to freely distribute demo version of the product with limited functions for free, offering the improved or professional version by payment.

This obviously is far cheaper than a wide advertising campaign, which, based as it would be on immaterial goods, would be attempting to sell solutions which would be difficult for buyers to conceive.

The logic of profit has thus moved from the product itself to the practice of its application by the user. This is ever more evident and accelerated with e-trading, which, with its on-line stock market service transfers the added value from the software to the transactions wrought.

Shareware

This is basically very similar to the previous one but it involves limited time span for trials then users have to pay a fee in order to use the product. This may be as a balance of a full registration of the product enabling all the functionalities or simply the clearance of the patrimonial rights.

Copyright

"What is worth copying is probably worth protecting." The idea to protect intellectual property stands on two main pillars: protect investments and creativity plus assure moral rights to the author.

Ancient Greeks believed that verbal communication of relevant events it was enough, considering "not essential" all the rest; philosophers and authors such as Socrates and Homer committed to oral tradition their own art and thought. Later on some philosophers trying to protect their intellectual property rights decided to create a written version of their own ideas and keep that in safe places such as the *nàos*[18] of temples.

This section will give a rough idea of IPR management both from the European and American point of view. In order to ease the description let us call "author" the owner of the rights and "publisher" the one that needs to acquire the rights and "artefact" or "work of art" the subject of the rights

What do we put under the umbrella named Intellectual Property? Intellectual property (IP) includes intangible assets, such as brands, designs, logos, documents, photos, and also human capital or know-how.

Intellectual property means that certain "authors" enjoy exclusive rights to use intangible protected "artefacts". If, therefore, an artefact is protected for the benefit of a person, it means that, in principle, no other party can use it without the right holder's consent[19].

A typical case study concerns the use of a picture representing an artefact e.g. sculpture/painting. In order to clear all the potential rights we must take into account and negotiate intellectual property rights with the owner of the artefact, the author and last but not less important the author of the picture. Photography is from long time an intellectual product like drawings and paintings so it is protected by law.

What happens in the digital domain? Using "content" materials in interactive multimedia requires acknowledgement and/or negotiation of "new[20]" intellectual property rights. As digital information has no geographical borders, legislation and agreements must be developed in the international social and legal context. The differences in national copyright law are currently a barrier to the development and distribution of multimedia products.

This is even more relevant if the core business of the company is related to content production and distribution. As an example, let us take into account "memory institutions[21]" like museums. In most cases, museums want to distribute images and text related to their collections as part of their educational mission of making their collections physically and intellectually accessible. Nevertheless, they are concerned that, in order to maintain the aesthetic integrity of the original work of art they should exercise control over the dissemination and quality of this material. Licensing rights and reproduction fees are also an important economic asset to most museums. Every museum will have to develop policies and expertise in the implications of digital publishing (joint ventures, going it alone etc.), basically as they have done with print, slides, film and video.

The Nature of Copyright

Which Class of Artefacts are Protected?

Dealing with Public Domain we already tried to define the artefacts potentially protected by copyright, we know that copyright does not protect concepts, ideas, processes, functionalities, utilities, facts, etc. Basically we might consider as a primary list of artefacts: literary works, musical composition, sound recordings, dramatic works, pictorial & graphic works, photography & audiovisual works, architectural and sculptural works.

Who Owns the Rights?

First of all who is in charge for the acknowledgment and/or clearance of the rights? We use to speak about the "author" or any other subject having the right. Who are the authors/creators (copyright holders) of the digital form? This has become an even more complex question with the development of interactive multimedia now comprised of authors of text and image: writers, museums databases, artists and the estates of deceased artists, photographers; museums as owners or controllers of photographic records of works; "subsidiary rights holders" including music, film, video; software authors; compilers of a new resource. Copyright may also attach to the actual digital scanning of an image.

They should be some relatives, the owner... It may happen that more the one "subject" owns the rights. This is the case of the picture of an artefact or more frequently creative work due to a group of "creative people" has it happens for movies or music.

Which are the Rights?

The copyright owner has the right to maintain the integrity of the work and protect it from piracy: to control reproduction, adaptation, distribution, public performance and public display of a work and to control the creation of derivative works plus some "moral" rights in the "continental" view. Widespread lack of understanding of the subject leads to emphasis on copyright protection rather than sensible and necessary exploitation of copyright. There is no required registration of copyright, no registration system and no central clearinghouse for information as to who owns or who can clear rights in relation to a particular work or performance. This is sometimes a significant barrier to the "use" of some artefacts.

Copyright protects certain rights inherent in a creative work. Here we face two main approaches, the one usually called Anglo-Saxon and the one called Continental/Medicean. Basically they differ because of the set of concerned rights: patrimonial and/or moral.

The Anglo-Saxon approach focus on the economic aspects, it mainly considers the payment of fees to the copyright owner.

Patrimonial Rights:

- Copy / Reproduction
- Distribution
- Modification
- Adaptation
- Public Performance

- Public Display
- Digital Transmission

Moral Rights:

- Attribution / Paternity
- Integrity
  ○ Context
  ○ Mutilation

The first "right" is no doubt the right to be recognised as the author of the work: paternity. This right cannot be sold[22].

Speaking about "paternity" an interesting habit has its origins because of computer game copyright polices applied by Atari® in the developing phase of that market. The company in fact did not recognize personal rights to employs authors of the games; they decided to protect the intellectual property as a company asset.

In such a way the first Easter Egg was born. Easter Eggs are special characteristics or messages hidden inside the game.

Warren Robinett, the creator of Adventure®, plans a secret room that contained his name in luminous letters with the colours of the rainbow. In order to approach the room players must find a special grey pixel somewhere in the computer game and bring it back to the beginning of the game. In a decade the secret characteristics become the norm both in computer games and in the most common computer science applications.

Do you remember the duel between the "icons" of WinWord® and WordPerfect® fought "live" simply creating empty macro named SPIFF and clicking on the credits of WinWord® itself or the complete list of the team that has developed Windows 95® simply clicking of the Microsoft® credits?

Back to the list of rights, for sure the second right is the right to make copies or reproduce/use it. This right is the foundation of music, movie and software market at least.

The list of rights continues with distribution, modification, adaptation and related to those: public performance, public display, digital transmission.

Then we enter the sphere of rights close to the moral side. They are: the right of integrity and lastly the right to withdraw the artefact from the "market".

The right of integrity is then subdivided in two branches: "context" and "mutilations".

Where context means the use of the artefact in an appropriate/approved context (e.g. a soundtrack associated to a video clip promoting illegal behaviours). Mutilation is typically an excerpt or the artefact that does not transfer the author's message or even if the artefact is completely reproduced it loses the original meaning. A typical example is the fight between movie directors and broadcasters in the early stages of the commercial television in Europe. Promotional spots within the movies break the "integrity" of the artefact compromising the fruition of the artefact itself.

Modification and adaptation are often used in turning novels or plays on stage in movies or music in soundtracks. The right to adapt is needed even to turn movies in DVDs.

How Can they be Transferred?

Intellectual property rights may be transferred accordingly with different formats:

- Exclusive or non exclusive, exclusive may be partial (one specific use) or total (all the possible uses);
- Addressing a specific scope or for any scope present and future;
- One or more rights;
- Addressing a specific time frame or "forever";
- Addressing a specific media or for any media already existent and future.

Due to such a richness of formats it happens that the publisher may have already negotiated some rights but the one needed is not included in the set. This was a very common situation when Interactive Virtual Reality exploded and at the early beginning of the Internet. CD producers have already acquired the right to use the "content" for CD ROMs but they need to negotiate "new" rights in order to use them for interactive virtual reality applications or Web sites.

Case Study: Museums

Museum as Owner

To what extent does a museum own the works it shows? A museum has to consider the copyright and moral rights attached not only to the works held in the museum collections, but also to material of others that may be used in collection management systems and in other information systems or sources.

In general terms, the copyright and moral rights attaching to a work of art (including photographs) belong to the "author" or "creator" for the duration of his/her life or their lives and to his/her heirs for a period after their death[23].

Many "works of art" in museums collections will be out of authors'/artists' copyright and in the public domain. The museum (or other owner) may control physical access to the work but does not usually own intellectual property rights.

The copyright attaching to any photograph of the work of art likewise belongs to the photographer unless the photographer is an employee of the organization for which the photograph has been taken (e.g. the museum) or unless there is an agreement transferring copyright to the organization in question.

The control of access to the work of art may obviously represent a financial asset to the museum or other owner. It can also be seen as part of the museum's responsibility to preserve, authenticate and accurately represent material in their collections. This involves not only copyright but also moral rights: to protect the integrity of the images and the identification of the author/artist. It would be conducive to good working relationships for museums to take the initiative on the subject of rights agreements at the time of new acquisitions entering the collection or new photographic records being commissioned, possibly utilizing standard forms of rights agreement. This becomes even more critical when the museum may subsequently wish to disseminate images via a network, whether for collection management, research or public access.

Museum as User of Copyright Material

Most museums are both providers and users of copyright material. Copyright protection arises when a work is "fixed" in any tangible medium of expression. Therefore use of a work without identifying the copyright owner (or his/her agent) and obtaining a license from them may result in copyright infringement. As a general rule, it is safe to assume that any right not expressly granted is reserved by the copyright owner and that one does not have the right. All relevant rights should be expressly stated in a rights license. Multimedia and other applications of "new media technology" are not clearly covered in many traditional rights agreements.

THE LEGAL FRAMEWORK

Historically there have been two different European approaches to intellectual property rights. On the one hand are those countries for which the concept of author's rights put emphasis on protecting the moral rights of the creator: the right to claim authorship, to insist on the integrity of the work and to prevent false attribution of the work (e.g. in France and Italy, where these rights are not assignable and continue in perpetuity).

On the other hand are those countries who emphasized copyright law focussing on exploitation (e.g. Great Britain).

Copyright legislation in Great Britain and the USA now encompasses moral rights but implementation is still not universal and the extent of moral rights protection varies from country to country. Other legal issues may be taken into consideration such as privacy rights and publicity rights in the USA. More recently *The Digital Millennium Copyright Act (DMCA)* was issued in the USA. DMCA Criminalizes technologies instead of behaviour such as most reverse engineering of copyrighted material and some computer security R&D. With the DMCA it becomes illegal to speak about and publish results stating vulnerabilities in systems used to protect copyright and to circumvent "copyright management information" even if no illegal copying occurs. Nevertheless DMCA had some negative impacts on the development of the information society. Because it is illegal to disseminate information about weaknesses in security systems used for copyright protection the security of information infrastructure weakened, researchers in the field of computer security have to consult a lawyer before developing their activity?

One or both of the Berne Convention for the Protection of Literary and Artistic Works and the Universal Copyright Convention have been signed by most countries, world-wide (but not fully implemented in all aspects by all signatories) as has the Rome Convention for the Protection of Performers, Producers of Phonograms and Broadcasting. These conventions lay down only minimum terms of protection of the rights to which they refer, leaving the contracting States free to grant longer terms.

International Regulations

Berne Convention

- Provides the International Minima WTO TRIPs
- Incorporates the International Minima

- Incorporates Berne
- WTO Enforcement

The Global Dimension: WTO & TRIPS

As we already considered Intellectual Property has a global dimension for this reason we must consider how this fundamental aspect is taken into account in worldwide agreements. One of the most relevant global "agreements" is no doubt the World Trade Organisation (WTO). The WTO is operational since January 1, 1995 as a kind of follow up of the first General Agreement on Tariffs and Trade (GATT 1947-48) Agreement. The basic scope of GATT was initially no more than gradually remove trade barriers.

Due to the fact that intellectual property issues have been recognized as a crucial element of international trade one of the pillars of the WTO is TRIPS.

A global agreement is needed because the protection of intellectual property rights varied significantly between various states. In the perspective of global trade this is a major obstacle for obvious reasons, the main one, of course, being the territoriality of IP protection. As it will be recalled later on there is another relevant obstacle, in many countries they were highly inadequate or absent, leaving human creations of mind devoid of effective protection. The lack of intellectual property protection causes relevant drawbacks especially in developing countries were foreign investments and technology transfer is the main leverage for development.

TRIPS is an abbreviation for Agreement on Trade-Related Aspects of Intellectual Property Rights. It acknowledges the pre-existing regime and tries to build on it instead of replacing previous conventions[24]. It is currently one of the most important international agreements in the field of IP law. In consideration of the acronym and general framework intellectual property is handled from the business perspective. In addition TRIPS is a comprehensive regulation it covers copyright, patents, designs, trade secrets, integrated circuits and geographical indications, whereas international IP conventions usually only deal with a specific category of IP rights (e.g. copyright, industrial property, neighbouring rights, etc.).

Countries subscribing the TRIPS Agreement must introduce minimum standards of protection for WTO members, thus facilitating international trade.

TRIPS brought the minimum standard of protection under the Berne Convention. In the specific field of software: Art. 10.1 stipulates that computer programs are to be protected as literary works under the Berne Convention emphasizing the role of copyright as the basic instrument of software protection and, at the same time, required that the term of protection be the same as in the case of literary works; Art. 10.2 clarifies that databases and other compilations of data or other material, on the condition that they are intellectual creations, must be protected as such under copyright, even if they include data that, as such, are not protected under copyright.

Important provisions concerning related rights were placed in art. 14. For example, art. 14.5 expanded the 20-year term of protection required under the Rome Convention to 50 years.

All major world economies are WTO[25] members, including the USA, the EU and China, and the others, such as Russia, want to join. Actually EU is representing all member states within the WTO.

EUROPEAN REGULATION INITIATIVES

The law follows, often much later, technical development. Most of present copyright law does not adequately reflect current (and likely future) developments in digital publishing, especially in the actual broad sense. Some people now feel that copyright will not be able to cope with digital developments in IT and will eventually be replaced by contract law or by copyright-on-demand arrangements.

In 1993-94 the *CIAGP (Conseil International des Auteurs des Arts Graphiques et Plastiques et des Photographes)*, made up of artists rights societies in many countries, drew up draft proposals for agreements on digital imaging and interactive multimedia. These proposals were later on considered by its parent body *CISAC (Conféderation Internationale des Sociétés des Auteurs et Compositeurs)*, although they did not include recommended tariffs, they could and should provide a basis for an important step forward, providing the individual Societies can, between themselves, agree on the terms and basis of implementation. On September 1993 the German Publishers Association has produced a Guide to the Negotiation of License Agreements for the Utilization of Published Works in On-line Databases.

International conferences on Interactive Multimedia and World Wide Web technology increasingly feature sessions on the topic of Intellectual Property Rights and their implications but there is still no sign of a basis for international proposals for model agreements.

Outside Europe, there have been a number of initiatives by consortia of museums in the USA, setting out to establish and protect the position of museums. Similarly there are initiatives by consortia of Photographers in the USA.

On September 1993 the *Coalition for Networked Information*, Washington DC, produced an interesting research report on *Rights for Electronic Access and Delivery of Information (READI)* Project. This has been followed by the deliberations and a preliminary report in July 1994 of the USA *Working Group on Intellectual Property Rights of the National Information Infrastructure (NII) Task Force*, which highlight the problem that sources of valuable intellectual property are not being made available over the networks because of the absence of reasonable assurance that intellectual property rights will be respected.

The *Multimedia Subcommittee of the Copyright Council* of Japan's *Agency for Cultural Affairs* considered the establishment of a centralised organisation for copyright information in a preliminary report in 1993. In 1994, the *Multimedia Committee* of the Japan's *Institute of* Intellectual *Property* (MITI) proposed a *Digital Information Centre*, a collective administrative centre at which information on copyrighted works could be readily accessible and clearance approval efficiently obtained.

Again in Japan, Copymart is a contract-based model for the collective licensing of copyright, which would comprise two databases - the *"copyright market"* (CRM), where rights holders can file their copyright information including a brief description of works and sale or license agreements and the *"copy market"*, where copies of works are distributed to customers upon request and payment.

In the US, there was a proposal for a *Multimedia Clearinghouse*, with copyright owners participating on a voluntary basis.

Photo Library Agencies in the UK and the US started to work with CD/DVD and on-line networking, providing clients with images that are copyright cleared for the purposes declared on-line by the client followed by the payment of the appropriate fee by the client.

The *World Intellectual Property Organisation (WIPO)* studied the establishment of an international system of assigning, on request, identifying numbers to certain categories of literary and artistic works and to phonograms. These identifying numbers may also be used for the electronic (particularly digital) means applied to control the extent of use and, possibly, to identify the protected material used.

Exhibit 1.

Name	Authors	photographers	performers/recordings
Berne Convention	50 years after death	25 years from making	
Rome convention			20 years from performance/fixation
EU harmonization	70 yrs after death	70 years after death	50 years from performance
USA	50 yrs after death/75 yrs from publ.	-	75 years from publication
Japan	50 yrs after death	-	30 years from performance/fixation

*Scans, like **photos** of photos are not new works protected by IRC or neighbouring rights, if not precluded in contracts*

Within the *WIPO* organisation the *Electronic Frontier Foundation (EFF)* stressed that the dream of making all published works available to everyone in the world was today available through technology. The digital world and the Internet provided the promise of universal access to knowledge stored in the world's libraries.

The French *Agency for Protection of Programs (APP)* has developed such an international identification system for software at the request of *WIPO*.

Significant among specialist conferences was *Legal Aspects of Multimedia and GIS* organised in Lisbon, October 1994 by the *Legal Advisory Board (LAB), DGXIII of the European Commission*. This included the presentation of drafts of several wide-ranging and, in some respects, controversial papers commissioned by the Commission. Given that the clearing of intellectual property rights is complicated, time consuming and therefore costly, there is an urgent need for simple, understandable licensing and model contracts on the part of the providers to encourage and facilitate integrity on the part of the users.

The Commission of the European Communities addressed the problems of harmonization of copyright legislation within the European Union (EU) in a Green Paper in 1988 leading to legislation harmonizing the terms of protection of Copyright and certain related rights which has been approved by the European Parliament and implemented in July 1995. This represents a considerable step forward only applying to the legislation of EU member countries (although many EFTA EEA countries harmonize with the EU) anyway there are still many exceptions to the norm.

The 70 year EU harmonisation will mean that some artists whose work is already out of copyright will come back into copyright. The EU Directive does not apply to works of non-EU origin, from countries that offer a shorter period of protection (e.g. the USA, life plus 50 years after death of the artist), where the protection will be for the shorter period. Copyright Protection of computer programs was the first example of harmonisation in the field of copyright within the EC (1991), followed by Rental and Lending Right in 1992, and copyright related to satellite broadcasting and cable transmission in 1993. The EU has also published a draft Directive for harmonisation of the legal protection of Databases, but has, so far, done very little on moral rights.

The administration of rights in the music industry (as compared with the visual arts) is much more developed but highly complex. Attempts are currently being made to find workable solutions for music rights, in the new situations arising from the development of interactive multimedia, including encouraging moves towards one- stop copyright clearance. Linear media in the film and TV sectors are also highly complex and questions arise as to how interactive a use has to be before it becomes non-linear.

Copyrighting Software

This section provides a quick overview on the law of software copyright in the European Union, with particular reference to the Community Directive on the subject (Directive 91/250/EEC). This section does not cover the laws of countries outside the European Union.

Software copyright does not essentially differ from any other sort of copyright. Nevertheless there are some aspects of copyright law that are specific to software.

The EC Directive gives a programmer[26] a rich set of rights on his own creation: it is unlawful for anyone other than the owner of the rights to run the program, copy the program, modify the program or distribute the program, except with the permission of the rights owner.

Please note that under the term "copy" there are many different meanings ranging between the usual copies "disk to disk" up to reverse engineering, with the only exception of the backup copy, always allowed.

All this applies to the software itself not to the rich set of knowledge and ideas behind the program. This basically means that there is no restriction in being "inspired" by a product. Copyright mainly protects the format, the shape, the appearance of the product not the idea itself.

In order to protect the *idea*, the *concept* a patent is needed. It is a very well known problem, we can simply remind the case of VisiCalc©, the first spreadsheet, conceived by Dan Bricklin, young student at the Harvard Business School in 1978. The idea behind VisiCalc© was revolutionary at that time, nothing similar was known in the traditional set of tools. At that time the American office of Patents and Trademarks (PTO) did not issue any patent for software applications because they were not considered products or processes. So it was impossible to protect the revolutionary idea behind VisiCalc and in a glimpse many competitors developed their own spreadsheets: SuperCalc®, Context MBA®, MS Multiplan®, 123 Lotus®, Quattro®, MS Excel®, etc without the payment of any fee to Bricklin.

Copyrighting Standards[27]

A recent initiative launched in the USA is addressed to protect as an intellectual product the "standards". Controversies over intellectual property (IP) in standards have been common in the past decade. At that time IT and standards disputes have mainly been about patents, now a new wave of controversies is due to copyrights claimed by standard setting organisations (SSOs) as to standards produced by committees formed by or under their aegis, especially when governments mandate use of these standards. Actually such controversies are limited to healthcare and ecommerce sectors but should extend to other relevant sectors.

CASE STUDY: THE MALAYSIAN MULTIMEDIA SUPER CORRIDOR

We already explored the relevance of creativity in the field of development policies, the need to protect intellectual capital and the legal framework addressed to such a protection. Consequently it is worth to take into account a case study build almost from scratch in a very interesting environment.

The Multimedia Super Corridor[28] in Malaysia developed with the aim to act as a global reference centre for multimedia production, faced IPR and cyber law problems.

Conceptualized in 1996, the MSC Malaysia has since grown into a thriving dynamic ICT hub, hosting more than 900 multinationals, foreign-owned and home-grown Malaysian companies focused on multimedia and communications products, solutions, services, research and development.

Malaysia is a member of the World Intellectual Property Organization (WIPO), Paris Convention, Berne Convention and signatory to the Agreement on Trade Related Aspects of Intellectual Property Rights (TRIPS).

With the implementation of the Multimedia Super Corridor, the Government makes a commitment to MSC Malaysia-Status companies in one of the 10-Point Bill of Guarantees to provide a comprehensive regulatory framework of intellectual property protection and cyber laws to facilitate and assist the development of a truly ICT and multimedia environment.

Intellectual Property Protection

The *Trade Marks Act 1976* provides for a registration system for marks (e.g. logos, brands, signs) used in relation to goods and services. The registration of a mark in relation to specified goods or services is valid for ten (10) years from date of filing and is renewable indefinitely. The *Patents Act 1983* provides for a registration of patents and utility innovations (20 years) in Malaysia. The *Copyright Act 1987* confers the exclusive right to the owner of a copyright for a specific period. There is no system of registration for copyright in Malaysia; a work that is eligible is protected automatically. The *Industrial Designs Act 1996* implements a system for the registration (5 years) of an "industrial design" in Malaysia. The *Layout Designs of Integrated Circuits Act 2000* set out, inter alia, the criteria for the protection (10 years) of the layout design of integrated circuits and the extent of protection conferred upon the right holder. The *Geographical Indications Act 2000* specifies the process for registration of geographical indications, to prevent misuse of the names of places which identify both the geographical origins and the products. The *Optical Discs Act 2000* provides for the licensing and regulation of the manufacture of optical discs, such as VCD, DVD, CDs, etc in Malaysia.

Cyberlaws

The *Digital Signature Act 1997* is an enabling law that allows for the development of, amongst others, e-commerce by providing an avenue for secure on-line transactions through the use of digital signatures. The *Communications and Multimedia Act 1998* provides a regulatory framework to cater for the convergence of the telecommunications, broadcasting and computing industries, with the objective of, among others, making Malaysia a major global centre and hub for communications and multimedia information and content services. The Malaysian Communications and Multimedia Commission were appointed on the 1st November 1998 as the sole regulator of the new regulatory regime. The *Copyright (Amendment) Act 1997* provides to make unauthorised transmission of copyright works over the Internet an infringement of copyright.

The *Computer Crimes Act 1997* created several offences relating to the misuse of computers. Among others, it deals with unauthorized access to computer material, unauthorized access with intent to commit other offences and unauthorized modification of computer contents. The *Telemedicine Act 1997* is intended to provide a framework to enable licensed medical practitioners to practice medicine using audio, visual and data communications.

AN INNOVATIVE APPROACH: CREATIVE COMMONS

As already stated digital technology, and in particular the Internet, has completely overturned traditional ideas about distribution. Any work that can take a digital form can be infinitely reproduced and delivered directly on the desk or handheld appliances at minimal cost. In addition digital technology has enabled new form of expression and new class of authors. Digital music, video clips, animations, multimedia content are created and exchanged more easily reaching a huge audience almost instantaneously. Peer to peer technology enables on the fly exchange of content unleashing incredible opportunities to share personal content and activate added value chains of cooperation.

Intellectual property rights management and even the concept of IPR itself has to be revised in order to better fit and do not constrain creativity and innovation. Cooperative and social products of creativity are boosted by the Internet and represent a completely new way to develop products.

In order to match a similar scenario *Creative Commons*[29] organisation was established some years ago.

Creative Commons is a nonprofits organization that offers flexible copyright licenses for creative works providing a range of protections and freedoms for authors, artists, and educators. The ideal genesis of the concept is built upon the "all rights reserved" concept of traditional copyright to offer a voluntary "some rights reserved" approach.

Baseline Rights and Restrictions in all Licenses

All Creative Commons licenses have many important features in common. Every license will help the author:

- Retain your copyright
- Announce that other people's fair use, first sale, and free expression rights are not affected by the license

Every license requires licensees:

- To get your permission to do any of the things you choose to restrict—e.g., make a commercial use, create a derivative work
- To keep any copyright notice intact on all copies of your work
- To link to your license from copies of the work
- Not to alter the terms of the license
- not to use technology to restrict other licensees' lawful uses of the work

Every license allows licensees, provided they live up to your conditions:

- To copy the work
- To distribute it
- To display or perform it publicly
- To make digital public performances of it (e.g., Webcasting)
- To shift the work into another format as a verbatim copy

Every license:

- Applies worldwide
- Lasts for the duration of the work's copyright
- Is not revocable

Note that this list of features does not apply to the Public Domain Dedication, our Sampling Licenses, or Founder's Copyright.

Creative Commons Licenses

This paragraph describes each of the six main licenses listed starting with the most restrictive type author can choose and ending with the most accommodating type author can choose.

It's also helpful to know there are a set of baseline rights all six licenses offer to others and a list of things to think about before choosing a license.

Attribution Non-commercial No Derivatives (by-nc-nd)
It allows others to download your works and share them with others as long as they mention you and link back to you, but they can't change them in any way or use them commercially. (most restrictive)

Attribution Non-commercial Share Alike (by-nc-sa)
This license lets others remix, tweak, and build upon your work non-commercially, as long as they credit you and license their new creations under the identical terms.

Attribution Non-commercial (by-nc)
This license lets others remix, tweak, and build upon your work non-commercially, and although their new works must also acknowledge you and be non-commercial, they don't have to license their derivative works on the same terms.

Attribution No Derivatives (by-nd)
This license allows for redistribution, commercial and non-commercial, as long as it is passed along unchanged and in whole, with credit to you.

Attribution Share Alike (by-sa)
This license lets others remix, tweak, and build upon your work even for commercial reasons, as long as they credit you and license their new creations under the identical terms.

Attribution (by)
This license lets others distribute, remix, tweak, and build upon your work, even commercially, as long as they credit you for the original creation. (least restrictive)

Other licenses
Creative Commons organisation also offers a set of other licenses for more specialized applications.

Choosing a License

Offering your work under a Creative Commons license does not mean giving up author's copyright. It means offering some of your rights to any member of the public but only on certain conditions.

What conditions? All of CC licenses require that you give attribution in the manner specified by the author or licensor (attribution, non commercial, no derivative works, share alike)

Taking a License

How it works the license? When the author has made the choices, he will get the appropriate license expressed in three ways:

*   **Commons Deed.** A simple, plain-language summary of the license, complete with the relevant icons;
*   **Legal Code.** The fine print that you need to be sure the license will stand up in court;
*   **Digital Code.** A machine-readable translation of the license that helps search engines and other applications identify your work by its terms of use.

Once the author has done this he should include a Creative Commons "Some Rights Reserved" button on the site, near his work. This button will link back to the Commons Deed, so that the world can be notified of the license terms. If the author finds that his license is being violated, he may have grounds to sue under copyright infringement.

CREATIVITY, PRODUCTION AND MARKET

Besides the traditional advertising information packs which have always been produced in the audiovisual field by governments and corporations, the Web is being invaded by the free and subjective need of individuals to communicate and become active protagonists of communication, freed at last from media uni-directionality.

New forms of communication and expression are emerging such as: blogs, shared collections of photos and videos, shared surfing history or personal video broadcasting[30].

Thoughts, emotions, beliefs become messages and works, sometimes of exceeding value, having no links to market values because they spring from primary exigencies of the creative him/her self and community relationships.

While in the past century very few managed to get past the expensive threshold of production for a mass market, now we are entering a phase in which collective creativity begins to produce for markets which are finely divided and "sectorised".

We are thus passing from "elite creativity for a mass market" to "mass creativity for elite markets".

This new passage is determining a profound upset in the productive, distributive, communicational, educational and social set-ups, which is irreversible.

From being *"generalist"*, television becomes digital and thematic, broadcasting changes to narrow casting, interactivity breaks down the unidirectional message into myriad fragments adaptable to each single user, who thus becomes the subject of the market rather than the object.

The selective capacity of the individual to latch on to tastes, trends, emotions and desires is such that anything may be custom-made, from clothes to gadgets, education or entertainment, and may be automatically renewed as required and promptly delivered to home.

The Web world, which has such a disconcertingly immense galaxy of options, may be comfortably controlled by selection on the part of each live user, whether an individual or a community, absolutely instantaneously, through paying rental services with minimum but constant fees, simply like the mass fluxes which polarised the immense riches of the past.

New mass consumerism will therefore take the form of intelligent software, free and custom-made, which will remain with the customer in every phase of his life (and , very likely, post mortem as well) with all the solicitude of an old housekeeper, accustomed to anticipate future needs and whims, and able to regulate the purse-strings.

DIGITAL RIGHTS MANAGEMENT AND CLEARANCE

It is reasonable that in the era of digital communication the management of IPR should be delegated to digital procedures. The amount of content and services produced and delivered in digital format is so huge that there is no chance to apply any traditional approach.

Use of *DRM* is sometimes the only way to enable content or service exchanges or the creation of compound services *"assembling"* different contributions even on the fly.

From a functional perspective, *DRM* means many things to many people. For some it is simply about the technical process of securing content in a digital form. To others, it is the entire technical process of supporting the exchange of rights and content on networks like the Internet. For convenience, *DRM* is often separated into two functional areas:

- The identification and description of intellectual property, rights pertaining to works and to parties involved in their creation of administration (digital rights management)
- The (technical) enforcement of usage restrictions (digital management of rights)

DRM may therefore refer to the technologies and/or processes that are applied to digital content to describe and identify it and/or to define, apply and enforce usage rules in a secure manner.

It is also important to distinguish between *"access control"*, *"copy protection"* and *"the management of intellectual property rights"* highlighting their respective boundaries.

An *access control system* manages a user's access to content, usually achieved through some kind of password protection. However, once access to the content has been granted, no further protection is applied. Thus, once a user has access to the content, it is no longer possible to control what is done with that content. This type of protection is often employed on Websites where a simple access control mechanism suffices.

A *copy protection system* is designed to signal the extent of allowed copying and serial copying, if any, that is defined by the associated "usage information" with respect to any instance of delivered content, and to implement and enforce the signalled behaviour in consumer equipment. The notion of copy protection can be extended to control the movement of content within and outside the user domain, encompassing re-distribution over the Internet.

A fully enabled *intellectual property rights management system* covers the processing of all rights information for the electronic administration of rights, sometime including contractual and personal information, to enable end to end rights management throughout the value chain. By its nature, *DRM* may require access to commercially sensitive information (as opposed to copy information and usage signalling). The use of such a system will enable very granular control of content, enabling rights owners to apply sophisticated usage models.

This process of managing intellectual property rights inevitably involves the extensive use of *DRM* technologies. Such technologies can be embedded into many components, from those that reside on a single device, such as a *Personal Digital Assistant* ("PDA") to those to be found in commercial Internet Servers run by major companies and organizations.

Protection of Rights

How can we manage intellectual property rights in a global market? Both in consideration of the *non uniform legal framework* and taking into account that some regions of the world *do not protect intellectual property* by law? Third but not less important the *digital piracy* phenomenon.

Starting from the case of absence of legal basis in order to protect intellectual property we can simply outline how it will be difficult to develop a conventional market in such a framework, specific content and entire products should be cloned and sold without any local legal infringement. The case study of software applications offers a clear example.

Considering different legal frameworks and digital-piracy, mayor efforts are done in order to harmonize the international regulatory framework as it happens in the case of *Creative Commons* even on the side of traditional IPR protection there are a number of initiative such as *Creative Commons, BSA®* and *NetAssociate®*. Copyrighted products use to have an explicit licence agreement to be accepted or not before starting the application the first time.

In addition to the regulatory framework IPR should be actively protected thanks to some methods such as:

- Watermarking and digital watermarking
- Trusted systems
- Encryption
- Hard keys
- Soft keys
- .. more

Of course nowadays we may be interested in protecting not only *texts, audio tracks,* images and *movies* but even *three dimensional models,* for this reason major protection systems may cope with all data types.

An additional key aspect to be adequately taken into account is the availability or not of an unprotected preview of the content.

Watermarking and Digital Watermarking

Watermarking should be *classical* or *digital* (visible or invisible). The most effective ones must contain, duly encoded, major details of the copyright agreement such as:

- Information about the owner of rights
- Information about the customer
- Information about possible use
- Timeframe and validity
- ... and more

Visible *watermarking* is mainly used by image banks or photographer in order to protect their own images, no matter if the image is highly compromised by the mark.

Customers can access the watermarked copy merely in order to choose and post the order for the image.

Invisible watermarking is usually preferred because it is more suitable for visual material that has to be shown as is preventing unauthorised copies and redistribution.

There are two more characteristics of such method, on one side it must be *robust* on the other side it must be *easily identified and managed automatically* even from partial or modified copies of the original.

Robust means that even if we edit and modify the original image both using digital filters and lowering resolution even cutting subparts of the image the watermark will be readable.

The possibility to *manage automatically* the set of information associated with digital watermarking enables the automatic check of potential copyright infringements. This is one of the basic features in

Exhibit 2.

Name	Digital Watermarking
Invention:	First related publications date back to 1979. However, it was only in 1990 that it gained a large international interest.
Definition:	Imperceptible insertion of information into multimedia data.
Concept:	Insertion of information, such as a number or text, into the multimedia data through slight modification of the data.
Requirements:	Imperceptible. Robust or fragile, depending on application.
Applications:	Copyright protection, labelling, monitoring, tamper proofing, conditional access.
Commercial potential:	Unsure. Although many watermarking companies exist, few of them seem fully profitable for the moment..

order to make economically valuable the protection process. In addition *robust* methods enable copyright identification even from reproductions on different media (e.g. printed copies).

Of course automation is a basic keyword otherwise authors must collect books and magazines in addition to Web sites in order to identify potential infringements, and this will cost usually far more than the payment of rights.

This method is basically suitable for visual material with some limits in the field of motion pictures where the most diffused options are: visible "*watermarking*" adding logos or textual information on the movie, data encryption disabling frames display from unauthorised copies.

Trusted Systems

The concept was developed many years ago starting from the idea to establish a "*trust*" relation amongst different interconnected devices. They must share a kind of "*code of conduct*" enabling or disabling a set of basic actions such as "*load in memory*", "*save a copy*", "*print*", "*display*" and more.

Any kind of digital information processed via trusted systems will obey to the rules. A customised version of this approach was even included in some advanced releases of the *mpeg* format.

Encryption

This method is suitable for any kind of data, even for three dimensional data models. It was very useful on the occasion of the Internet technology development phase when bandwidth wasn't enough in order to transfer very large data sets so that encrypted data set were distributed on CD ROMs and on line decryption keys were sold on the Internet.

Hard Keys

The use of hard keys in order to protect digital content, mainly software, was one of the first methods broadly diffused in the past. Hardware locks are sometimes simply represented by a "*special*" floppy disk, sometimes embedded in the keyboard or linked to the CPU serial number, sometimes installed in a chip to be permanently connected to an I/O port[31].

One of the mayor drawbacks of the method was the frequent troubles caused to the registered customers due to malfunction of the key.

Soft Keys

Soft keys are still one of the most diffused methods in order to access digital resources such as applications, data and services. This method was considerably bettered thanks to the synergies with Internet connections. Simply consider on line registration of software products, on line activation of access credit (e.g. mobile phone prepaid cards)

... More

There are a number of slightly different technologies and methods addressed to IPR or data protection. Some of them mainly rely on software some need to be associated to hardware components; some more use a combination of hard and soft components.

Recent solutions take advantage from *"scratchable" pre paid cards* in order to access MP3 files on the Internet. Following this approach we are getting close to secure identification and digital signatures.

DIGITAL OBJECT IDENTIFIERS

This topic is in some way related with IPR. It addresses the following issue: how can we create a *"robust"* reference pointing to a digital object? We all know very well that any kind of reference or link to a digital object is a *"fragile"* information.

Digital objects appear somewhere, without any *"publishing protocol"* then they are duplicated, moved from one Web site to another one. How can we rely on digital references? How to find a solution?

Physical objects are in some way traced so we may know where they are. Paper based documents are usually safely stored in archives or libraries clearly identified within inventories. In addition books, magazines, etc are identified by information printed on the colophon and a special code: ISBN, ISSN etc. ISBN code is assigned on the basis of a global identification system using thirteen digits in order to identify any book printed on the planet.

Following this approach the idea to associate a *unique alphanumeric code* to each digital object was borne. Thanks to the European Commission eContent framework the idea was turned in reality releasing the *DOI System®[32]*.

The *DOI System®* allows *"content objects"* identification in the digital environment. *DOI® names* are assigned to any entity for use on digital networks.

They are used to provide current information, including where they (or information about them) can be actually found on the Internet. Information about a digital object may change over time, including where to find it, but its *DOI name* will not change.

A *Digital Object Identifier* is a unique name (not a location) for an *"entity"* populating the Internet. A DOI guarantees persistent and actionable identification of digital *"objects"*; furthermore it provides interoperable exchange of managed information on digital networks.

As already expressed above, unique identifiers are essential for the management of information in any digital environment. We may assign identifiers related to a specific context and time; let us consider potential benefits due to *"universal unique identifiers"*. Where *"universal"* means: unique identifiers which may be re-used in a different context and time without consulting the *"official"* content owner/publisher.

If we should like to reach this goal we must design and manage identifiers in order to enable such interoperability and their use in services outside the direct control of the issuing organisation. The concept of interoperability itself adds to the list the requirement of persistence to an identifier across time, once defined in relation with a digital object, the identifier is valid forever and will always refer to the same digital object.

Because of the independence of services from the issuing organisation they are by definition arbitrary, consequently interoperability implies the requirement of extensibility.

Thanks to extensibility there is always the opportunity to *"extend"* the description of the provided services to the new one.

Thanks to the design specification of the *DOI System* a *DOI name* can be a representation of any logical entity. *DOI* is a generic framework applicable to any digital object, providing a structured, extensible means of identification, description and resolution.

To ensure consistency the whole system is built on top of several existing standards which have been brought together and further developed. The entire system has been accepted as an ISO standards itself (ISO TC46/SC9).

ICT AND PRIVACY

In the relation between the sphere of private and ICT it will have to find, in a near future, a satisfactory equilibrium for all.

These technologies on one side apparently render the humans self-sufficient and may push them to become selfish, isolate themselves managing in a mediate way great part of the contacts and relations with the rest of the world and, from the other side, they produce and leave an incredible number of *"evidences"* and files documenting nearly moment by moment our existence.

The *"tracking"* of humans is nearly complete, the more technology he uses the more is *"visible"*. In the United States, by Law, the familiar GSM mobile phone system must enable user localization within a range of ten meters, third generation portable phones on board AGPS allows to localize with optimal approximation the position of the customer, car on board GPS/navigation systems as well.

Today we enjoy 2D or 3D positioning based on three up to nine or more *"visible"* satellites, the near future European positioning system service, named Galileo, will better the overall performance enabling additional location dependent services, actually in advanced beta testing phase.

The inner and external video-surveillance systems connected to computer vision based systems are able to identify a person, a vehicle and their behaviour both in 2D and in 3D.

ATM transactions and credit card usage indicate our movements and our taste or lifestyle. The content of our PC and our surfing on Internet is subject to spyware, fishing, hacking, leading to, in the optimistic vision, the creation of personal profiles in the world of e-commerce applications, but all this pertains to a different context...

To draw some conclusions it was already introduced to the public by its inventor, on the occasion of the *World Wide Web Conference 2004*, a *"total recall"* digital memory system in some way similar to the one used in Arnold Schwarzenegger's movie. This wearable system is based on a CCD mounted on thin glasses connected with a micro computer hosting some hundreds of gigabytes. The system takes a picture each second or fraction of time. *"If we lose something"*, tells the inventor, *"we simply have to press rewind"*.

Of course this looks more as a new gadget; anyway privacy issues are relevant even in the field of culture, because of our ideas, attitude, religion or general behaviour. Sometimes privacy not only relates to user profiles and tracking, there is risky information in cultural data banks too. The exact location of an artefact[33], the presence of a specific artefact in a temporary exhibition[34], even the inclusion of a stolen artefact in the police's catalogue of thefts[35] is to be considered risky information.

On the same stream there are concerns related to the generalised use of *RFID*. They give machines not merely an imperfect way of sight; they give them *"X-ray"* vision. Cyber pickpockets will play to *"who's got the Rolex"* or even simply *"who's got the iPod"*[36].

Privacy and Personal Data Management

Due to the increasing diffusion of on line applications and the need to process and file personal information such as name, address, telephone, email address and more... national authorities all over the world started to take into account potential infringements of privacy due to hackers. There were some relevant actions even at international level addressed to care about personal information amongst the others the crack of the customer's data set of a very well known underwear trade mark and the consequent publication of "very personal" information regarding "music and movie" stars.

Rules and obligations may differ from country to country from continent to continent but basically it is recognised and protected the relevance of personal information, it is mandatory to ask for an explicit approval every time we store such information in any format, it is mandatory as well to ask for an explicit approval every time we need to update them, communicate or transfer part of them to a different subject. In addition a responsible for personal information has to be nominated and referenced care of the organisation.

The management of personal information stored in PDAs and mobile phone does not differ so much.

FUTURE RESEARCH DIRECTIONS

This trend specifies how *copyright* and *copyleft* are twin faces of the same coin, complementary and equally necessary: it thus becomes evident that from the harmonic balance of these two exigencies a form of communication which is at the same time open, free and democratic may arise.

The development of *copyleft* is thus functional to the new economy and should be incremented in order to increase access to the new media and raise the educational level of the underprivileged classes, in the awareness that heavily unbalanced situations create social tension and war.

In this crucial moment of globalisation which we are living it is necessary, without ignoring the dramatic game of rival markets, to be able to identify the weak points that the market can induce, if we do not wish to confine behind besieged bulwarks the few present users and abandon in dangerous "infopoverty" the majority of the world population.

This is why the protection of *copyright*, if correctly applied, can valorise the creativity of all those having access to the new communication tools. This discriminating threshold can now be widened and allow general entrance very rapidly thanks to the use of *copyleft*.

Under such a circumstance, technology does not help because delivers everyday new generations of "digital objects" increasingly different from traditional ones. How can we manage the rights of a cooperative artefact created in on the Internet? How to manage the rights of future generation of digital artefacts enabled from technology? People sometimes are in trouble looking for the "author" of a specific artefact they found somewhere on the Internet. If it is a natural trend to become "prosumers[37]" do we think that the future of creativity will follow the "wiki's way of thought"? There are a number of studies trying to find out an innovative approach to intellectual property issues. IPR clearance has to be as transparent as possible to the users, in this way we will solve the problem. One of the approaches is to do not try to change the behaviour of users in its place to find a transparent mechanism ensuring both the same approach and the clearance of rights. One of the basic ideas is to apply a "flat rate" for the compensation of the rights. This rate is usually defined on the basis of statistics and if spread on a wide range of users is not really expensive. Some national legislation applied this "delta" at the "source" increasing the cost of storage media such as musical CD ROMs or DVDs, other approaches prefer to refer to Internet access providers and size the rate on the basis of the tracked content traffic.

Here comes a potential drawback of similar "statistics" based rates, they concern even the users non involved in copyrighted content fruition, they pay for something that they are not going to enjoy. More recent models and experiments in the most advanced field - eMusic are re-using the commercial television or "newspaper for free" approach: agreements with the Majors, rights cleared by the commercial sponsors and music download for free.

REFERENCES

Cohen, J. E. (2001). *DRM and privacy.* ACM, pp. 46-49. http://doi.acm.org/10.1145/641205.641230.

Davis, R. (2001). *The digital dilemma.* ACM, pp. 77-83. http://doi.acm.org/10.1145/359205.359234.

Erickson, J. S. (2001). *Fair use, DRM, and trusted computing.* ACM, pp. 34-39, http://doi.acm.org/10.1145/641205.641228.

Frank, S. (2005, September). RFID is x-ray vision. Communication *of the ACM, 48*(9).

Nic, G., Digital rights management, copyright, and napster. *ACM Communications.* www.acm.org/sigs/sigecom/exchanges/volume_2/2.2-Garnett.pdf.

Samuelson, P. (2001). Intellectual property for an information age: Introduction. ACM, pp. 66-68. http://doi.acm.org/10.1145/359205.359230.

Samuelson, P. (2001). Does information really have to be licensed.

ACM, pp. 15-20. http://doi.acm.org/10.1145/285070.285073

Samuelson, P. (2001). *DRM {and, or, vs.} the law.* ACM, pp. 41-45. http://doi.acm.org/10.1145/641205.641229.

Samuelson, P. (2006, June). Copyrighting standards: Should standards be eligible for copyright protection. *Communication of the ACM, 49*(6).

Willingmyre, G. T. Current topics in IPR protection in the context of global standard-Setting processes. http://www.wipo.int/sme/en/documents/ip_standards2.htm

Sai Ho, K. (2002, August). Digital rights management for the online music business. *ACM SIGecom Exchanges, 3(*3), 17-24.

Digital Object Identifier (DOI) numbers. See http://www.doi.org for more information.

Intellectual property related organisations (Web sites tested on Aug 2007)

IPR Helpdesk organization: http://www.ipr-helpdesk.org

World Intellectual Property Organisation (WIPO): www.wipo.int/

Electronic Frontier Foundation (EFF): www.eff.org

CIAGP (Conseil International des Auteurs des Arts Graphiques et Plastiques et des Photographes): cisac.org

CISAC (Conféderation Internationale des Sociétés d'Auteurs et Compositeurs): cisac.org

Agency for Protection of Programs (APP): app.legalis.net

Società Italiana Autori ed Editori – www.siae.it

Legal Advisory Board (LAB) of the European Commission: http://europa.eu.int/ISPO/legal/en/lab/lab-def.html

BSA – Business Software Alliance: www.bsa.org

NetAssociate / MacAfee: www.nai.com

ADDITIONAL READING

Berne Convention: http://www.wipo.int/treaties/en/ip/berne/trtdocs_wo001.html

The Digital Millennium Copyright Act (DMCA) Software Copyright: http://www.copyright.gov/legislation/dmca.pdf

TRIPS - Agreement on Trade-Related Aspects of Intellectual Property Rights: http://www.wto.org/english/tratop_e/trips_e/t_agm0_e.htm

The Community Directive on software copyright Directive 91/250/EEC: http://europa.eu.int/ISPO/legal/en/ipr/software/software.html

Creative Commons Web site http://creativecommons.org

Ronchi, A. M. *eCulture: Cultural content in the digital age.* Springer, ISBN: 978-3-540-75273-8

OASIS, Policy on Intellectual Property Rights: http://www.oasis-open.org/who/intellectualproperty.php

Intellectual Property aspects of World Wide Web authoring : www. http://www.ipr-helpdesk.org

ISO, "MPEG Strides Forward with ISO/IEC 14496-2" in ISO Bulletin May 2002. http://www.iso.ch/iso/en/commcentre/isobulletin/articles/2002/pdf/mpeg02-05.pdf

ANSI, Guidelines for Implementation of the ANSI Patent Policy: http://public.ansi.org/ansionline/Documents/Standards%20Activities/American%20National%20Standards/Procedures,%20Guides,%20and%20Forms/PATPOL.DOC

Microsoft's Standards Licensing Program: http://www.microsoft.com/mscorp/ip/standards/

IEEE, Understanding Patent Issues During IEEE Standards Development: http://standards.ieee.org/board/pat/guide.html

Caplan, P., Patents and Open Standards (2003): http://www.niso.org/press/whitepapers/Patents_Caplan.pdf

ENDNOTES

[1] This chapter offers an extended overview on IP management and privacy, a synthetic approach to IP and privacy is included in the book: Alfredo M. Ronchi, *eCulture: cultural content in the digital age,* Springer ISBN: 978-3-540-75273-8

[2] like as an example Macromedia Flash©

[3] Like observed by Prof. Francisco Antinucci – in such a context manuscripts produced by amanuensi are not to be considered like our books, they are more similar to a painting commissioned to an artist. Manuscripts were commissioned to amanuensi by people that was well informed about the content of the manuscript, the copy were usually personalised and refined ad personam.

[4] YouTube available at http://www.youtube.com/

[5] Medici family, Renaissance - Florence

[6] May you need further information please refer to European IPR Helpdesk organization: http://www.ipr-helpdesk.org

[7] The definition of public information is many times one of the controversial aspects in EC funded projects.

[8] E.g. concepts, ideas (in term of protection we have to refer, if applicable, to patents)

[9] We keep the definitions used by IPR Helpdesk organization.

[10] Some national legislations does not take into account moral rights.

[11-14] We keep the definitions used by IPR Helpdesk organization.

[15] Sometimes relevant information are still locked within private sections of Web sites secued by passwords.

[16] Shareware and free trial version

[17] www.occam.org – part of UNO GAID project

[18] *Nàos* – the most protected and private part of ancient temples.

[19] This is one of the main reason why public domain exist.

[20] As we will see later rights are usually cleared for a specific use under specific circumstances.

[21] Museums, archives, art galleries, etc.

[22] Paternity is a right but in some way is not acknowledged by companies.

[23] Taking into account different continents this time span is between 50 and 70 years

[24] Paris Convention for the Protection of Industrial Property of 1883 (Art. 1 par. 2 defines the scope of the Convention as including "patents, utility models, industrial designs, trademarks, service marks, trade names, indications of source or appellations of origin, and the repression of unfair competition") - Berne Convention for the Protection of Literary and Artistic Works of 1886 (Copyright).

[25] 148 WTO member states in 2007

26   Generally speaking, the programmer who writes the program owns the rights. If more than one programmer wrote the code, the Directive provides for co-ownership. If the programmer is employed the employer owns the rights, if there is not a different agreement. If specified within the contract the rights are freely assignable.

27   Pamela Samuelson, Copyrighting standards: should standards be eligible for copyright protection? – Communication of the ACM June 2006, vol 49, Number 6

28   This section provides a summary of the features of the MSC, further information available at MSC official Website: www.msc.my

29   http://creativecommons.org/ - this section is derived (with excerpts) and directly related to the Creative Commons information set and Web site.

30   E.g. photo archivehttp://www.thesimplegallery.com.nyud.net:8080/pictures.php. Slide show pro http://www.slideshowpro.net/product_sspdir.php - and social Web applications – e.g. delicious Web site

31   One of the most diffused devices in the world of PCs was the Autodesk parallel port hard key.

32   DOI® and DOI.ORG® are registered trademarks and the "doi>" logo is a trademark of the International DOI Foundation.

33   Christian art artefact hosted by churches or monasteries

34   Thieves may find a less known artefact in minor art galleries or exhibits.

35   In the past this was the evidence of authenticity both for thieves and receivers. The same may happen for the Unique ID.

36   Frank Stjano, RFID is x-ray vision, Communication of the ACM September 2005 volume 48 number .9

37   The new role of both producer and consumer.

Chapter II
Digital Rights Management:
A New Trend or a Necessity

Ioannis Kostopoulos
University of Patras, Greece

Penelope Markelou
University of Patras, Greece

Ioannis Panaretou
University of Patras, Greece

Athanasios Tsakalidis
University of Patras, Greece

ABSTRACT

This chapter highlights the need for using copyright protection tools in our digital transactions. The main tools of copyright protection, such as cryptography, data hiding, and watermarking, along with the security framework where these tools can be used is also presented. However, all these tools and methods can be used only inside a specific technological and legal framework. This gap between technology and traditional human activities is bridged by developing the Digital Rights Management systems which is presented as a necessary mechanism to provide integrated e-services over the Internet. The legal framework and the current activities of organizations as WIPO (World Intellectual Property Rights Organization) is also provided in this chapter with the existing DRM technologies and the future research directions in this field.

INTRODUCTION

The spreading of internet and web technologies during the last years has leaded the world to technological infrastructures where the information can be exchanged freely and rapidly. The content providers are investing to new ways of making profits and offering new services concerning their digital products. The internet and its evolution was the best vehicle for the content providers to offer their services world wide. However, in contradiction with the traditional ways of copying where each copy of the original work has reduced quality, the digital information can be copied perfectly and every copy will be identical with the original one (Lyon, 2001). Moreover, the services that have been used today over the internet are giving the opportunity to spread these copies in all over the world, without geographical limitations.

Although www has imposed a tremendous change in the way of thinking, reducing the actual value of information, the digital content is still valuable and it should be protected. The protection of intellectual rights of digital content is concerned to be one of the big problems (CSTB, 1999; Crawford, 1999) of the digital age. Digital Rights Management Systems (DRM) (Duhl & Kevorkian, 2001) in addition with security measures (Cohen, 2003; Ingemar et al., 2002; Wipro Technologies, 2001) is essential for the protection of digital property. DRM systems (Heng, 2001, Renato, 2001a, Renato, 2001b; DCITA, 2003; Schmidt et al., 2004) are already in use to prevent people abusing information that is copyright protected. Most of the current solutions provide external applications to ensure data protection management (Russ, 2001). The current trend though, is to provide embedded applications and not external. This can be done in three ways:

- Hardware-embedded DRM systems
- DRM tools attached on the operating system
- Development of DRM functionality controllers embedded to the operating system

A Digital Right Management mechanism is needed, so as to produce an integrated protection and management framework, able to diminish the possibilities of inappropriate usage and unauthorised copying. That's where Digital Right Management (DRM) systems are focused. Right's management is a necessity, because the term combines all those techniques and methodologies aiming to define and model actions, dealings and violations of intellectual rights.

COPYRIGHT PROTECTION TOOLS

In the beginning of the third millennium, the use of digital means has become an inseparable piece of everyday life. Digital photography, video, medical images, satellite images, sounds etc. are some indicative examples. In many cases digital objects are intended to be published, either on the internet or in widely used mediums. Organizations, museums, digital libraries, need to protect their Intellectual Property Rights (IPR) on this kind of media.

In the past, the scientific community along with commercial organizations has invested in order to find reliable methods to protect digital media. During the last decade digital watermarking, based on the idea of information hiding, originally introduced in the 5th century BC (Katzenbeisser & Petitcolas, 2002), gave a solution to the problem of designing such mechanisms to protect media.

This chapter is providing information about the currently used technologies in order to protect the digital content (Documents, images, videos, sound, graphics etc.) from unauthorized use, along with the technologies that detect the unauthorized use (Qiong et al., 2003; Lyon, 2001). These technologies are considering a variety of tools that related both with software and hardware. More specifically these tools focused on:

*   Security and integrity of operational systems.
*   Cryptography.
*   Data hiding and digital watermarking techniques.

Security and Integrity

In computer security, an *access control list (ACL)* is a list of permissions attached to an object (Microsoft, n.d; Wikipedia, n.d). The list specifies who is allowed to access the object and what operations are allowed to be performed on it. In an ACL-based security model, when a subject requests to perform an operation on an object, the system first checks the list for an applicable entry in order to decide whether or not to proceed with the operation.

Systems that use ACLs can be classified into two categories, discretionary and mandatory. A system is said to have discretionary access control if the creator or owner of an object can fully control access to the object, including, for example, altering the object's ACL to grant access to anyone else. A system is said to have mandatory access control (also known as "non-discretionary access control" in the security literature) if it enforces system-wide restrictions that override the permissions stated in the ACL.

Traditional ACL systems assign permissions to individual users, which can become cumbersome in a system with a large number of users. In a more recent approach called role-based access control, permissions are assigned to roles, and roles are assigned to users.

Microsoft Windows Rights Management Services (RMS) is information protection technology that works with RMS-enabled applications to help safeguard digital information from unauthorized use -both online and offline, inside and outside of the firewall (Microsoft, n.d). RMS enforces an organization's security strategy by protecting information through persistent usage policies, which remain with the information, no matter where it goes. Organizations can use RMS to help prevent sensitive information -such as financial reports, product specifications, customer data, and confidential e-mail messages -from intentionally or accidentally getting into the wrong hands.

Cryptography

The cryptographic algorithms and procedures are very old. In Ancient Greece and Rome they used techniques and cryptographic devices in order to encode and decode messages (Katzenbeisser & Petitcolas, 2002; Wikipedia, n.d.). From that period till today the field of cryptography has made significant improvement. Especially during the Second World War cryptography was the main instrument for secret communication between spies, military, diplomats etc. The development of computers made possible the construction of more complex cryptographic algorithms and more powerful mechanisms for secure communication.

Cryptography is usually linked with two processes, the encryption and decryption process. The encryption process is operated by using a key and a cryptographic algorithm and the original data (plaintext) converted to encrypted data (ciphertext). The key as a secret parameter can be used also during the decryption process (Symmetric cryptography) where from encrypted data derived the original data or a second key is used for that purpose (asymmetric cryptography), depending the application. In public-key cryptosystems, the public key may be freely distributed, while its paired private key must remain secret. The *public key* is typically used for encryption, while the *private* or *secret key* is used for decryption. In addition to encryption, public-key cryptography can be used to implement digital signature schemes. A digital signature is reminiscent of an ordinary signature; they both have the characteristic that they are easy for a user to produce, but difficult for anyone else to forge.

The cryptographic technologies can be used to control the copyrighted material and protect the Intellectual Rights of the copyright holders, in DRM systems. In the whole world there are several laws and directives today that prevent the unauthorized use of copyrighted material and set a legislation framework that should be respected from all users or providers of digital content

Data Hiding and Digital Watermarking Techniques

The digital watermarking technique is a standard tool today for copyright protection of multimedia objects. The different types of watermarks concerning their characteristics (robustness/fragility, capacity, quality of watermarked object, security etc.), their visibility (visible, imperceptible watermarks) and they have a direct impact on DRM systems design (Ingemar et al., 2002; Katzenbeisser & Petitcolas, 2002).

Digital watermarking of images exploits the fact that digital images contain redundant data that can be used to hide the information of the image owner. The latter information is called digital watermark. The redundancy of the image data is also exploited by image compression techniques in order to reduce the amount of data that represent an image.

The directions that have been followed in the design of a watermarking method are:

a.   Modification of cover data in the frequency domain (Cox et al., 1996; Gilani et al., 2002)
b.   Modification of the cover data in the spatial domain (Kutter et al., 1997; Armeni et al., 2000; Van Schyndel et al., 1994; Yeung & Mintzer, 1997)

Recent advances in watermarking technologies introduce algorithms working in both spatial and frequency domain (Yu et al., 2003; Shih & Wu, 2003).

Perceptible Watermarks

The perceptible/visible watermark is usually connected with the embedding process where a pattern or company logo is inserted in the image or video content in a visible way, without altering the content of the original image/video. The watermark intends to protect the original work so as every attempt to remove it or destroy it will be difficult and should result the watermarked work destruction. Therefore the visible watermark can be inserted in whole image/video or in a part of it depending on the owner needs.

Imperceptible Watermarks

The invisible or imperceptible watermarks are digital information that embedded in the original work (image/video/sound) in a way that the Human Visual or Hearing System cannot detect it. The detection of the watermark can be achieved algorithmically, by using a watermark detection system (software/hardware).

Depending the application there are several types of imperceptible watermarks:

a. Watermarks that destroyed when the attacker modifies the watermarked object. These watermarks used for content authentication.
b. Watermarks that remain intact after several modifications are used for copyright protection of a digital object.

DIGITAL RIGHTS MANAGEMENT

Unfortunately, there is not a commonly agreed definition for DRM. The term, according to the World Wide Web Consortium (DRM, 2000), covers the description, recognition, protection, control, commerce, monitoring and tracking of all the possible usage types concerning digital content - including the relationship management between the digital object's owners.

According to (Katzenbeisser & Petitcolas, 2002), DRM is a term that is used to describe a range of techniques which collect information for rights and right holders, so as to manage copyrighted material; and the conditions under which these materials will be distributed to the users.

DRM refers to the protection of the intellectual properties of digital content by controlling the actions of the authorized end user to the digital content. It gives the digital object's owner the ability to

Figure 1. DRM lifecycle

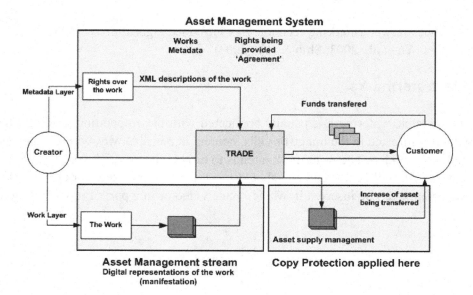

securely distribute valuable content such as books, photos, videos, magazines; at the same time helps the owner manage the content, avoiding unauthorized usage or copying.

Figure 1 represents DRM lifecycle.

DRM Systems: Overview

A DRM system is a chain of services and hardware technologies that controls the authenticated usage of digital content; it also manages any actions or results that the aforementioned usage causes throughout the lifecycle of the content.

A typical DRM system may comprise the following:

- File and content recognition systems
- Languages for attribute management
- Different file types.
- Techniques and methods of digital content distribution
- Metadata

It can be applied to any business or organization that deal with sensitive or confidential information and needs to protect valuable digital assets, controlling the distribution and usage of these assets. A DRM system is essential when the digital content:

- Must be accessible to certain groups of people and not available to others
- Should be used in a different way by different user types
- Is tracked and checked according to the flow of the process under which is being used

Previously, Digital Rights Management (DRM) focused on security and encryption as a means of solving the issue of unauthorized copying, which locks the content and limits its distribution to only those who pay. This was the first-generation of DRM, and it represented a substantial narrowing of the real and broader capabilities of DRM (Renato I., 2001a).

The second-generation of DRM covers the description, identification, trading, protection, monitoring and tracking of all forms of rights usages over both tangible and intangible assets including management of rights holders' relationships. Additionally, it is important to note that DRM is the "digital management of rights" and not the "management of digital rights". That is, DRM manages all rights, not only the rights applicable to permissions over digital content (Renato I., 2001a).

In designing and implementing DRM systems, there are two critical architectures to consider. The first is the functional architecture, which covers the high-level modules or components of the DRM system that together provide an end-to-end management of rights. The second critical architecture is the information architecture, which covers the modelling of the entities within a DRM system as well as their relationships. There are many other architectural layers that also need to be considered, such as the Conceptual, Module, Execution, and Code layers (Hofmeister et al., 2000).

Figure 2. Functional architecture

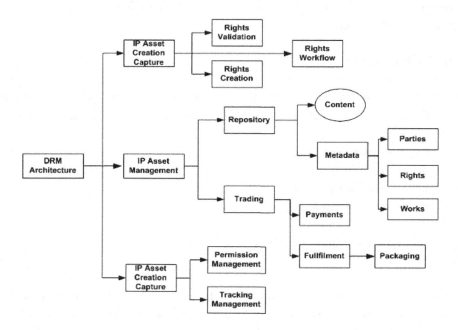

Figure 2. Functional architecture

Functional Architecture

The overall DRM framework suited to building digital rights-enabled systems can be modelled in three areas:

- **Intellectual Property (IP) asset creation and capture:** How to manage the creation of content so it can be easily traded. This includes asserting rights when content is first created (or reused and extended with appropriate rights to do so) by various content creators/providers
- **IP asset management:** How to manage and enable the trade of content. This includes accepting content from creators into an asset management system. The trading systems need to manage the descriptive metadata and rights metadata (e.g., parties, usages, payments, etc.)
- **IP asset usage:** How to manage the usage of content once it has been traded. This includes supporting constraints over traded content in specific desktop systems/software
- While the above models comprise the broad areas required for DRM, the models need to be complemented by the functional architecture that provides the framework for the modules to implement DRM functionality (Figure 2).

The functional architecture stipulates the roles and behaviour of a number of cooperating and interoperating modules under the three areas of Intellectual Property (IP): Asset Creation, Management, and Usage.

The IP Asset Creation and Capture module supports:

- **Rights validation:** To ensure that content being created from existing content includes the rights to do so
- **Rights creation:** To allow rights to be assigned to new content, such as specifying the rights owners and allowable usage permissions
- **Rights workflow:** To allow for content to be processed through a series of workflow steps for review and/or approval of rights (and content)

The IP Asset Management module supports:

- **Repository functions:** To enable the access/retrieval of content in potentially distributed databases and the access/retrieval of metadata. The metadata covers Parties, Rights and descriptions of the Works
- **Trading function:** To enable the assignment of licenses to parties who have traded agreements for rights over content, including payments from licensees to rights holders (e.g., royalty payments)

In some cases, the content may need to go through fulfillment operations to satisfy the license agreement. For example, the content may be encrypted/protected or packaged for a particular type of desktop usage environment.

The IP Asset Usage module supports:

- **Permissions management:** To enable the usage environment to honor the rights associated with the content. For example, if the user only has the right to view the document, then printing will not be allowed.
- **Tracking management:** To enable the monitoring of the usage of content where such tracking is part of the agreed to license conditions (e.g., the user has a license to play a video ten times). This module may also need to interoperate with the trading system to track usage or to record transactions if there is payment due for each usage

Together, these three modules provide the core functionality for DRM systems. These modules need to operate within other, existing e-business modules (such as shopping carts, consumer personalization, etc.) and digital asset management modules (such as version control, updates, etc.). Additionally, the modules would support interoperability, trust, standard formats, openness and other principles (Erickson, 2001).

Ideally, these modules would be engineered as components to enable systems to be built in a modular fashion. However, this implies a set of common and standard interfaces/protocols between the modules. As DRM matures, the industry will move towards such standardization.

The functional architecture is only part of the solution to the challenges of DRM. Rights Management can become complex remarkably quickly. As a result, DRM systems must support the most flexible information model possible to provide for these complex and layered relationships. The information architecture provides this (Renato I., 2001a).

Figure 3. Information architecture – Core Entities Model

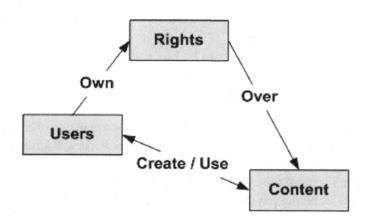

Information Architecture

The information architecture deals with how the entities are modelled in the overall DRM framework and their relationships. The main issues that require addressing in the development of a DRM Information model include:

- Modeling the entities
- Identifying and describing the entities
- Expressing the rights statements

Modelling the Entities

It is important to adopt a clear and extensible model for the DRM entities and their relationship with other entities. Existing work in this area includes the <indecs> project (INDECS, 2002). The basic principle of the <indecs> model is to clearly separate and identify the three core entities: Users, Content, and Rights as shown in Figure 3. Users can be any type of user, from a rights holder to an end-consumer. Content is any type of content at any level of aggregation. The Rights entity is an expression of the permissions, constraints, and obligations between the Users and the Content. The primary reason for this model is that it provides the greatest flexibility when assigning rights to any combination or layering of Users and Content. The Core Entities Model also does not constrain Content from being used in new and evolving business models.

This model implies that any metadata about the three entities needs to include a mechanism to relate the entities to each other.

Identifying and Describing the Entities

All entities need to be both identified and described. Identification should be accomplished via open and standard mechanisms for each entity in the model. Both the entities and the metadata records about the entities must be identifiable. Open standards such as Uniform Resource Identifiers (URI, n.d.) and Digital Object Identifiers (DOI, 2007) and the ISO International Standard Textual Work Code (ISO, n.d.) are typical schemes useful for Rights identification.

Content should be described using the most appropriate metadata standard for that genre (for example, the EDItEUR ONIX standard (EDItEUR ONIX, n.d.) for books and the IMS Learning Resource Meta-data Information Model (IMS, n.d.) for educational learning objects). It is also critical that such metadata standards do not themselves try to include metadata elements that attempt to address rights management information, as this will lead to confusion regarding where to describe such rights expressions. For example, the ONIX standard has elements for a number of rights holders (e.g., Authors and Publishers) and Territories for rights and single Price information (the latter poses a problem in setting multiple prices depending on what rights are traded). In such cases, following the <indecs> model should take precedence.

To describe Users, vCard (RFC, n.d.) is the most well-known metadata standard for describing people and (to some extent) organizations. An additional and important part of the Rights model is to articulate the role that the User has undertaken with respect to Content. A comprehensive list of roles can be found in the MARC Relators code list (MARC, n.d.).

Expressing Rights Statements

The Rights entity allows expressions to be made about the allowable permissions, constraints, obligations, and any other rights-related information about Users and Content. Hence, the Rights entity is critical because it represents the expressiveness of the language that will be used to inform the rights metadata.

Rights expressions can become complex quite quickly. Because of that, they are also modelled to understand the relationships within the rights expressions. This has been evidenced in the Open Digital Rights Language (ODRL, n.d.) and a paper by Gunter et al. (2001).

Rights expressions should consist of:

- **Permissions (i.e., usages):** What you are allowed to do
- **Constraints:** Restrictions on the permissions
- **Obligations:** What you have to do/provide/accept
- **Rights holders:** Who is entitled to what

LEGISLATIONS

This section presents the international conventions and agreements for the protection of intellectual properties starting with the very early attempts and its revisions, till the current legislation system and laws (Owens & Akalu, 2004).

Berne Convention

The *Berne Convention for the Protection of Literary and Artistic Works* (Berne Convention, 1979), usually known as the *Berne Convention*, is an international agreement about copyright, which was first adopted in Berne, Switzerland in 1886. The convention enriched and revised a lot of times since then: completed at Paris in 1896, revised at Berlin in 1908, completed at Berne in 1914, revised at Rome in 1928, at Brussels in 1948, at Stockholm in 1967 and at Paris in 1971, and was amended on September 28, 1979. It is worth to mention that United States refused initially to become a party to the Convention due to the major changes that required in its copyright law. Finally, they signed it on March 1989. Greece became a party to the Conversion with the law 100/1975 (FEK A' 162). Today, 163 countries are parties to the Berne Convention.

It was developed after a proposal of Victor Hugo and constitutes the first attempt for the copyright of works of authors. The Convention rests on three basic principles and contains a series of provisions determining the minimum protection to be granted, as well as special provisions available to developing countries which want to make use of them. It states that all works except photographic and cinematographic shall be copyrighted for at least 50 years after the author's death, but the parties are free to provide longer terms (Berne Convention, 1886).

WIPO

The *World Intellectual Property Organization (WIPO)* (WIPO, 2007) was created in 1967. Its stated purpose was *"to encourage creative activity, (and) to promote the protection of intellectual property throughout the world"*. The predecessor to WIPO was the BIRPI (Bureaux Internationaux Réunis pour la Protection de la Propriété Intellectuelle, French acronym for United International Bureau for the Protection of Intellectual Property), which had been set up in 1893 to administer the Berne Convention for the Protection of Literary and Artistic Works and the Paris Convention for the Protection of Industrial Property in 1883 [46]. The latter Convention applies to industrial property in the widest sense, including patents, marks, industrial designs, utility models (a kind of "small patent" provided for by the laws of some countries), trade names (designations under which an industrial or commercial activity is carried on), geographical indications (indications of source and appellations of origin) and the repression of unfair competition. 1967, BIRPI became WIPO, which, since 1974, is an organization within the United Nations in order to promote the protection of intellectual property throughout the world.

Currently, WIPO has 184 member states, administers 24 international treaties (16 on industrial property, 7 on copyright, plus the convention creating WIPO), is headquartered in Geneva, Switzerland, and carries out a rich and varied program of work, through its member States and secretariat that seeks to (WIPO Convention, 1967):

- Harmonize national intellectual property legislation and procedures
- Provide services for international applications for industrial property rights
- Exchange intellectual property information
- Provide legal and technical assistance to developing and other countries
- Facilitate the resolution of private intellectual property disputes
- Marshal information technology as a tool for storing, accessing, and using valuable intellectual property information

WIPO Copyright Treaty

The *WIPO Copyright Treaty (WCT)* (Paris Convention, 1883; WCT, 1996) is a special Agreement under the Berne Convention. Any Contracting Party (even if it is not bound by the Berne Convention) must comply with the substantive provisions of the 1971 (Paris) Act of the Berne Convention for the Protection of Literary and Artistic Works (1886). The Treaty mentions two subject matters to be protected by copyright: (a) computer programs, whatever may be the mode or form of their expression, and (b) compilations of data or other material ("databases"), in any form, which by reason of the selection or arrangement of their contents constitute intellectual creations. As to the rights of authors, the Treaty deals with three: (a) the right of distribution, (b) the right of rental, and (c) the right of communication to the public. Each of them is an exclusive right, subject to certain limitations and exceptions.

WPPT

WIPO Performances and Phonograms Treaty (WPPT) (WPPT, 1996) deals with intellectual property rights of two kinds of beneficiaries: (a) performers (actors, singers, musicians, etc.), and (b) producers of phonograms (the persons or legal entities who or which take the initiative and have the responsibility for the fixation of the sounds). The Treaty entered into force on May 20, 2002. The Director General of WIPO is the depositary of the Treaty.

TRIPS Agreement

The *Agreement on Trade Related Aspects of Intellectual Property Rights (TRIPS)* (TRIPS, 1994) is an international Agreement administered by the World Trade Organization (WTO) that sets down minimum standards for many forms of intellectual property regulation. It was negotiated at the end of the Uruguay Round of the General Agreement on Tariffs and Trade (GATT) in 1994.

The TRIPS Agreement contains requirements that nations' laws must meet for:

- Copyright rights, including the rights of performers, producers of sound recordings and broadcasting organizations
- Geographical indications, including appellations of origin
- Industrial designs
- Integrated circuit layout-designs
- Patents
- Monopolies for the developers of new plant varieties
- Trademarks
- Trade dress
- Undisclosed or confidential information

The TRIPS Agreement introduced intellectual property law into the international trading system for the first time, and remains the most comprehensive international agreement on intellectual property to date. States that were very unlikely to join the Berne Convention (e.g. Russia and China) have found the prospect of this membership a powerful enticement. Furthermore, unlike other treaties on intellectual property, TRIPS specifies enforcement procedures, remedies, and dispute resolution procedures. Greece legalizes the Agreement with the law 2290/1995.

DMCA

The *Digital Millennium Copyright Act (DMCA)* (DMCA, 1998) is a United States copyright law which implements two 1996 WIPO treaties. It criminalizes production and dissemination of technology, devices, or services that are used to circumvent measures that control access to copyrighted works and criminalizes the act of circumventing an access control, even when there is no infringement of copyright itself. It also heightens the penalties for copyright infringement on the Internet.

ESA

The Electronic Signatures Act (ESA) (Public Law No: 106-229) (ESA, 2001b) went into effect on October 2000 and gives electronic contracts the same weight as those executed on paper. The purpose of this Act is *"to establish the basic framework for electronic signatures in order to achieve the security and reliability of electronic documents and to promote their use, thereby expediting nationwide electronic connectivity and ultimately improving convenience in people's living standard"* (ESA, 2001a). The act has some specific exemptions or preemptions, notably the provision concerning student loans. Although the act enables documents to be signed electronically, the option to do so lies solely with the consumer. In other words, no portion of the act requires you to sign documents electronically, you retain the right to use "paper & ink" documents at your discretion. The act specifically avoids stipulating any "approved" form of electronic signature, instead leaving the method open to interpretation by the marketplace. Any number of methods is acceptable under the act. Methods include simply pressing an *I Accept* button, digital certificates, smart cards and biometrics.

TECHNOLOGICAL PROTOTYPES

DRM technology standards initiatives have to fulfill a number of challenges. Some standards are created to confront relatively narrow and specific problems while others are more broad and general. Furthermore, there are many organizations with an interest in the area, many of which are not standards bodies in the usual sense. In this section, we overview the prototypes, standards and metadata used in DRM systems.

DOI

Digital Object Identifier (DOI) (DOI, 2007) is an identification system for intellectual property in the digital environment. It has evolved as an effort of the Association of American Publishers (AAP) (AAP, 2007) in 1996. In 1998, International DOI Foundation (IDF) was created to advance development and promotion of DOI concept. Its goals are to provide a framework for managing intellectual content, link customers with publishers, facilitate electronic commerce, and enable automated copyright management not only for the publishing industry but for many others industries (for example, music).

Figure 4. DOI structure

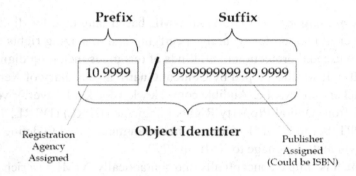

Figure 5. Examples of valid DOIs

10.0011 / 0999999991

10.0011 / 0999999991.1

10.0011 / 0999999991.01.0001

10.0011 / 0999999991.0.1.01

DOI names are assigned to any entity (documents, publications and other resources) for use on digital networks. These names are unique, persistent (i.e. they do not become invalid) and have high availability (i.e. they do not depend on a single Web server being up and running) for use over their lifetime (like bar codes), while standard Web URLs can change over time (Rosenblatt, 1997). Other information about the digital object may change over time, including where to find it, but its DOI name will not change. DOIs actually are in line with the Internet Engineering Task Force's preliminary specifications for Uniform Resource Names (URNs), a more general standard than URLs. This standard would facilitate interoperability between DRM and non-DRM systems such as content management and electronic commerce systems.

DOIs have a simple syntax, which is depicted in Figure 4. The general DOI structure has two components, a prefix and a suffix, separated by a forward slash (/). The combination of a prefix for the Registrant and unique suffix provided by the Registrant avoids any necessity for the centralized allocation of DOI numbers. The two components together form the DOI.

The prefix of all DOIs starts with "10", which distinguishes them from any other implementations. The next component of the prefix is a number (string) that corresponds to the publisher (or other intellectual property owner) that assigns the DOI.

The DOI suffix identifies the entity and may be any alphanumeric string chosen by the Registrant (e.g. sequential number, legacy identifier, etc.). It could be comprised of multiple nodes (Figure 5) that are separated by a dot (.). Node 1 is the whole work and legacy identifier node (highest structural level). In reflecting that, the full ISBN or other standard identifier should be used in the first node of the DOI suffix. Nodes 2 and following are the component nodes. The addition of a node creates a new DOI, which will need to be registered (AAP, 2000).

XrML

Extensible Rights Markup Language (XrML) is an XML-based language for digital rights management. It provides a universal method for securely specifying and managing rights and issuing conditions associated with the use and protection of all kinds of resources including digital content, as well as services (XrML, 2007). It was developed by Content Guard, a subsidiary of Xerox, and supported by Microsoft. Other backers are Adobe, Audible.com, Hewlett-Packard, OverDrive, Portal Software and Xerox. XrML stem from Digital Property Rights Language (DPRL) (DRRL, 1998) that was first introduced in 1996. DPRL became XrML when the meta-language (used to define the language) was changed from a Lisp-style meta-language to XML in 1999.

Contrary to DOI, which is simple conceptually and syntactically, XrML is a rich language of specifications. Its purpose is to expand the usefulness of digital content, resources, and web services to rights holders, technology developers, service providers and users by providing a flexible, extensible, and interoperable industry standard language that is platform, media, format and business independent. It supports an open architecture and can be integrated with both existing and new DRM systems (Heng, 2001).

The XrML data model consists of four entities: *principal, resource, right,* and *condition* and the relationship between them. These determine the full context of the rights that are specified. A principal encapsulates the identification of a party to whom rights are granted. A resource is the "object" to which a principal can be granted a right (e.g. e-book, audio file, video file, image, email service, B2B transaction service, or even a piece of information). A right is the "verb" that a principal can be granted to exercise against some resource under some condition. Finally, a condition specifies the terms, conditions, and obligations under which rights can be exercised (Wang et al., 2002).

Its latest release, XrML 2.0, expands the capabilities of a digital rights language to enable developers to establish the rights and conditions needed to access web services in addition to digital content. It also contains additional capabilities in the areas of extensibility, security, and life cycle management. Recent actions in several standards bodies, most notably MPEG, OeBF and OASIS, have positioned XrML to become the world wide industry standard for a digital rights language.

ICE

Information and Content Exchange (ICE) (Hunt, 2000) is an XML-based protocol used for electronic business-to-business (B2B) content management. It was originally developed in 1998 by industry content providers and software vendors. ICE specification provides businesses with a common language and an architecture to facilitate automated Web content syndication (information exchange, sharing and reuse between Web sites) for traditional publishing contexts and e-commerce uses and relationships.

By using XML, both syndicators and their subscribers (a syndicator produces content that is consumed by subscribers) have an agreed-upon language in which to communicate. The protocol defines the roles and responsibilities of syndicators and subscribers, specifies the format and method of content exchange, and provides support for management and control of syndication relationships. The system uses a client-server architecture.

The protocol covers four general types of operations (ICE, 1998): (a) subscription establishment and management, (b) data delivery, (c) event logs and (d) miscellaneous. A relationship starts with the subscription establishment. The subscriber obtains a catalog of possible subscriptions offers (including terms such as delivery policy, usage reporting, presentation constraints, etc.) from the syndicator and then subscribes to particular ones. The primary message exchanges center on data delivery. The protocol is able to manage special situations and conditions and to diagnose problems by event logs that automatically exchanged between subscribers and syndicators. Finally, a significant number of mechanisms for supporting miscellaneous operations (protocol parameters renegotiation, unsolicited ad-hoc notifications, queries, etc.) is supported.

With the latest release, ICE 2.0, robust content syndication is supported in a Web Services environment for the first time. It is defined as a W3C XML Schema, replaces the ICE 1.1 messaging structure with SOAP messaging protocol, and provides WSDL scripts to facilitate syndication as a Web service. ICE is considered as the best solution for those editors that want to build their own syndication architecture. It facilitates the building of flexible and reliable services and allows them to keep the profits of the transactions. ICE comprises an important protocol in DRM standardization field.

SDMI

Secure Digital Music Initiative (SDMI) was an initiative of music industry that formed in late 1998. Its purpose was to develop technology specifications to protect the playing, storing and distributing of digital music and consequently prevent music piracy. SDMI was a direct response to MP3 file format booming, which allowed digital music of good quality to be distributed via the Internet and forced the music industry to take new measures. In this way, consumers were provided with a convenient access to online music and new digital distributions systems to enable copyright protection.

In June, 1999, they defined a standard for manufacturing portable devices that can play both unprotected and protected music formats (SDMI, n.d.). The audio files contained a digital watermark, an inaudible message hidden in music to provide copyright information to devices like MP3 players and recorders.

In September 2000, SDMI announced a public challenge with an Open Letter to the Digital Community, invited interested parties to attempt to crack their proposed digital watermarking schemes. The protection scheme was cracked by a team at Princeton led by Professor Edward Felton (SDMI, 2001). So, any device implementing an algorithm based on the same reasoning would inevitably be cracked too.

The last press release from SDMI.org dated May 18, 2001. SDMI admitted that there was no concensus for adoption of any combination of the proposed technologies, although the digital watemark remains in widespread use.

XMCL

Extensible Media Commerce Language (XMCL), a rights specification language, was announced in June 2001 by RealNetworks Inc and is supported by 27 companies (e.g. Adobe, America Online, IBM, InterTrust Technologies, EMI, Sony Pictures Digital Entertainment and Sun). XMCL, as XrML and ICE, is an interchange format for the specification of content copyright information based on XML language. It describes usage rules that apply to multi-media content and is designed to communicate these rules in an implementation independent manner for interchange between business systems (e.g.

web store fronts, customer tracking and management) and trusted delivery and playback systems (e.g. DRM implementations responsible for enforcing the rules described in the language) (Ayars, 2002).

XMCL describes the minimum, self-complete set of business rules under which digital media is licensed for consumer use (XMCL, 2001). These business rules support multiple business models including rental, subscription, ownership, and video on demand/pay-per-view. When a business system authorizes a customer transaction for digital media, it generates a XMCL document that is then acted upon and enforced by a specific trusted system. The generated XMCL document is submitted to the trusted system through the APIs of the trusted system (e.g. HTTP POST, RPC call, API call).

ODRL

Open Digital Rights Language (ODRL) initiative aimed at developing and promoting an open standard for rights expressions. ODRL is intended to provide flexible and interoperable mechanisms to support transparent and innovative use of digital resources in publishing, distributing and consuming of electronic publications, digital images, audio and movies, learning objects, computer software and other creations in digital form (Renato, 2002). It is an open source language without license requirements.

ODRL is based on an extensible model for rights expressions which involves a number of core entities and their relationships. Three are the core entities of the model: *assets*, *rights* and *parties*. The first include any physical or digital content, should be uniquely identified, may consists of many subparts, may be in many different formats and may also be encrypted to enable secure distribution of content. The second entity includes *permissions* which can then contain *constraints*, *requirements*, and *conditions*. Finally, *parties* include end users and rights holders. With these three core entities, the model can then express or revoke *offers* (proposals from rights holders for specific rights over their assets) and *agreements* (when parties enter into contracts or deals with specific offers).

ODRL is more comprehensible in modeling the rights than XMCL. Its current version is 1.1, based on XML and provides a standardization mechanism that is independent from the content and the way of transport. It presents some resemblances with the XrML but also enough differences. ODRL has major application in media sector transactions and books publications and sales, while XrML is of general aim.

THE FUTURE OF DRM SYSTEMS

DRM technology faces several issues that have to be addressed. In the future, DRM enabled business models will grow dramatically. DRM technology will certainly improve over time and enhance new features, supporting business models that are endorsed by content providers.

The adoption of a DRM system is not easy; they are costly, complex and not fully secure. The success of Digital Right Management systems will be based in a number of other factors, including the balance between protection of intellectual rights and privacy.

A balanced, successful DRM system must be a combination of technological, business and legal concerns in a functional, open and acceptable framework.

Digital Right Management is inevitably one of the greatest challenges for content communities. But, what is it going to happen from now on?

First of all, the business models that need DRM will dramatically increase. Successful DRM business models will represent a gradual composition of traditional business models and models which are based on information technology and internet. The only concrete assumption is that different business models will succeed in different business areas.

DRM technology will be improving constantly. A major success factor is to be incorporated at the Computers' core technology and not provided as an additional software product. They are three possible ways that this can happen:

- **Build DRM into the PC's Hardware.** This is the most effective way to do it with respect to security.
- **Bundle the Software into the Operating System Distribution.** With this method, every PC that comes with an operating system may include a DRM controller that applies to all content types.
- **Build DRM Controller Functions Directly into the Operation System.** The system call to open files, as a built-in DRM controller, should determine whether the user has the rights to the file and then make the file available, possibly decrypting it in the process.

Another important factor that must be addressed is the open-standard issue. For instance, the Digital Object Identifier is vitally important. It is almost a no-barrier choice as a standard content identifier that also allows online reference. Yet DOI risks being pigeonholed as a standard that applies only to book and journal publishing.

DRM can be used as the vehicle, for content providers, to run and catch up with the easy spread of their proprietary information. This battle will certainly go on – but there is a great possibility to be able to control and manage a great amount of this information. There are several issues that have to be solved but yet DRM can lead the way.

FUTURE RESEARCH DIRECTIONS

DRM technology constantly faces new challenges. As the business models that need to incorporate digital right management mechanisms multiply, the research community must constantly address new ideas, models and variations of a typical DRM system. The goal must be the provision of different solutions to each and every alternative case (business model).

A core research direction is inevitably the adoption of concrete privacy models. "Privacy" and "Security" are often misused as common terms. Technologically, security is easier to be addressed. On the other hand, privacy often is not defined unambiguously. The variation in the way different people understand privacy is an open problem. Thus, a significant issue for researchers is to provide a unique definition of the privacy issues that can be modelled in a way, able to be addressed in such a technological platform.

As already mentioned in this chapter, among the success factors of a Digital Right Management information system is the balance between protection and usability. The latter, usability, should take into account both technical and functional requirements. As businesses grow in a new internet-oriented environment, technology is also reforming rapidly. New, open standards are continuously brought up and new interoperability needs occur. The need of a fully open and dynamically customisable standard is still a major problem. Researchers must foresee the future of technology in conjunction with the specifications of a Digital Right Management system and integrate technological solutions with new methods of intellectual property safeguarding.

Another vital issue that will be probably the key for the establishment of DRM technology is the level of interconnection between hardware and software modules and the integration methods to a DRM solution that the customer and the companies can trust. The previous generation of DRM solutions was deployed mainly in software and thus was vulnerable to attack. The early DRM solutions were fragmented and attempted to work by themselves being incompatible by design and not having trusted hardware to rely on. They were also designed as static closed devices. Thus, multilevel hardware and software modules must set to work together in a way that the users are able to easily understand (openness) and also the issue of trust as regards as intellectual property is guaranteed.

Finally, although no technical solution can be perfectly designed, the future of DRM systems finally embraces the concepts of system renewability and key revocation. These evolutionary concepts are very important to be addressed providing a very promising research field for the future.

REFERENCES

AAP (2000). *Association of American Publishers – AAP, numbering standards for E-Books*, Version 1.0. Retrieved February 1, 2008 from http://www.publishers.org/digital/numbering.pdf.

AAP (2007). Association of American Publishers – AAP. Retrieved February 1, 2008 from http://www.publishers.org.

Armeni, S., Christodoulakis, D., Kostopoulos, I., Stamatiou, Y., & Xenos, M. (2000, June). A transparent watermarking method for color images. *First IEEE Balcan Conference on Signal Processing, Communications, Circuits, and Systems*. Istanbul, Turkey.

Ayars, J. (2002). *XMCL – eXtensible media commerce language*. RealNetworks, Inc., W3C. Retrieved February 1, 2008 from http://www.w3.org/TR/xmcl.

Berne Convention (1886). *Summary of Berne Convention for the protection of literary and artistic works*. Retrieved February 1, 2008 from http://www.wipo.int/treaties/en/ip/berne/summary_berne.html.

Berne Convention (1979). *Berne Convention for the protection of literary and artistic works*. Retrieved February 1, 2008 from http://www.wipo.int/export/sites/www/treaties/en/ip/berne/pdf/trtdocs_wo001.pdf.

Cohen, J. (2003). DRM and Privacy. Communications of the ACM, 46(4), 46-49.

Cox, I., Kilian, J., Leighton, T., & Shamoon, T. (1996). A secure, robust watermark for multimedia. *First Workshop on Information Hiding*. Newton Institute, University of Cambridge.

Crawford, D. (1999). *Intellectual property in the age of universal access*. ACM Publications.

CSTB (1999). *The digital dilemma: Intellectual property in the information age*. Prepublication Copy, Computer Science and Telecommunications Board, US National Research Council: National Academy Press.

DCITA (2003). *A guide to digital rights management*. Department of Communications Information Technology and the Arts. Retrieved February 1, 2008 from http://www.dcita.gov.au/drm.

DMCA (1998). *Digital millennium copyright act*. Retrieved February 1, 2008 from http://www.gseis. ucla.edu/iclp/dmca1.htm.

DOI (2007). *Digital object identifier – DOI*. Retrieved February 1, 2008 from http://www.doi.org.

DRM (2000). *Digital rights management workshop*. Retrieved February 1, 2008 from http://www. w3.org/2000/12/drm-ws/.

DRRL (1998). *Digital property rights language – DPRL, manual and tutorial - XML edition, Version 2.00*. Retrieved February 1, 2008 from http://xml.coverpages.org/DPRLmanual-XML2.html.

Duhl, J., & Kevorkian, S. (2001). *Understanding DRM systems*. IDC White Paper.

EDItEUR ONIX (n.d.). *EDItEUR ONIX international standard*. Retrieved February 1, 2008 from http://www.editeur.org/onix.html.

Erickson, J. (2001). Information objects and rights management. *D-Lib Magazine, 7*(4). Retrieved February 1, 2008 from http://www.dlib.org/dlib/april01/erickson/04erickson.html.

ESA (2001a). *Electronic signature act*. Retrieved February 1, 2008 from http://unpan1.un.org/intradoc/groups/public/documents/APCITY/UNPAN025695.pdf.

ESA (2001b). *Electronic signatures act*. Retrieved February 1, 2008 from http://www.ecsi.net/help/help_esig.html.

Gilani, S., Kostopoulos, I., & Skodras, A. (2002, July 1-3). Adaptive color image watermarking. *14th IEEE International Conference on Digital Signal Processing*. Santorini, Greece.

Gunter, C., Weeks, S., & Wright, A. (2001). *Models and languages for digital rights*. InterTrust Star Lab Technical Report STAR-TR-01-04. Retrieved February 1, 2008 from http://www.star-lab.com/tr/star-tr-01-04.pdf.

Heng, G. (2001). Digital rights management (DRM) using XrML. *T-110.501 Seminar on Network Security*.

Hofmeister, C., Nord, R., & Soni, D. (2000). *Applied software architectures*. Addison-Wesley.

Hunt, B. (2000). *Information and content exchange (ICE) reference version*. Retrieved February 1, 2008 from http://www.infoloom.com/gcaconfs/WEB/paris2000/S21-04.HTM.

ICE (1998). *Information and content exchange protocol – ICE*. W3C. Retrieved February 1, 2008 from http://www.w3.org/TR/NOTE-ice.

IMS (n.d.). *IMS learning resource meta-data information model (Version 1.1)*. Retrieved February 1, 2008 from http://www.imsproject.org/metadata/mdinfov1p1.pdf.

INDECS (2002). *Interoperability of data in E-Commerce systems*. Retrieved February 1, 2008 from http://www.indecs.org.

Ingemar, C., Miller, M., & Bloom, J. (2002). *Digital watermarking.* Morgan Kaufmann Publishers.

ISO (n.d.). *ISO international standard textual work code.* Retrieved February 1, 2008 from http://www. nlc-bnc.ca/iso/tc46sc9/istc.htm.

Katzenbeisser, S., & Petitcolas, F. (2002). *Information hiding – Techniques for steganography and digital watermarking.* Atrech House Inc.

Kutter, M., Jordan, F., & Bossen, F. (1997). Digital signature of color images using amplitude modulation. *Proceedings of the SPIE, Storage and Retrieval for Image and Video Databases V,* 518-526.

Lyon, G. (2001). The Internet marketplace and digital rights management. *Report to the U.S. Department of Commerce,* USA.

MARC (n.d.). *MARC code list for relators.* Retrieved February 1, 2008 from http://lcweb.loc.gov/marc/relators/re0003r2.html.

Microsoft (n.d.). Retrieved February 1, 2008 from http://www.microsoft.com.

ODRL (n.d.). *Open digital rights language.* Retrieved February 1, 2008 from http://odrl.net/.

Owens, R., & Akalu, R. (2004). Legal policy and digital rights management. *Proceedings of the IEEE, 92*(6), 997-1003. Retrieved February 1, 2008 from http://ieeexplore.ieee.org/Xplore/login.jsp?url=/iel5/5/28864/01299173.pdf.

Paris Convention (1883). *Paris Convention for the Protection of Industrial Property.* Retrieved February 1, 2008 http://www.wipo.int/export/sites/www/treaties/en/ip/paris/pdf/trtdocs_wo020.pdf.

Qiong, L., Safavi-Naini, R., & Sheppard, N. (2003). Digital rights management for content distribution. *Australian Information Security Workshop (AISW2003).* Adelaide, Australia.

Renato, I. (2001a). Digital rights management (DRM) architectures. *D-Lib Magazine, 7*(6).

Renato, I. (2001b, January 22-23). Open digital rights management. *W3C Digital Rights Management Workshop.* Sophia Antipolis, France.

Renato, I. (2002). *Open digital rights language (ODRL), Version 1.1.* IPR Systems, W3C. Retrieved February 1, 2008 from http://www.w3.org/TR/odrl.

RFC (n.d.). *RFC 2426 vCard Profile.* Retrieved February 1, 2008 from http://www.ietf.org/rfc/rfc2426.txt.

Rosenblatt, R. (1997). Solving the dilemma of copyright protection online. *The Journal of Electronic Publishing (JEP), 3*(2). Retrieved February 1, 2008 from http://www.press.umich.edu/jep/03-02/doi.html.

Russ, A. (2001). *Digital rights management overview.* SANS Institute.

Schmidt, A., Tafreschi, O., & Wolf, R. (2004). Interoperability challenges for DRM systems. *Reviewed Papers about Virtual Goods.* Technische Universitat Ilmenau, Germany.

SDMI (2001). *Reading between the lines: Lessons from the SDMI challenge*. Princeton University. Retrieved February 1, 2008 from http://www.cs.princeton.edu/sip/sdmi.

SDMI (n.d.). *Secure digital music initiative – SDMI, protection through encryption*. Retrieved February 1, 2008 from http://www.benedict.com/Digital/Internet/SDMI.aspx.

Shih, F., & Wu, S. (2003). Combinational image watermarking in the spatial and frequency domains. *Elsevier, Pattern Recognition, 36*, 957-968.

TRIPS (1994). *Agreement on trade-related aspects of intellectual property rights*. Retrieved February 1, 2008 from http://www.wto.org/english/tratop_e/trips_e/t_agm0_e.htm.

URI (n.d.). *Uniform resource identifiers (URI): Generic syntax*. IETF RFC2396. Retrieved February 1, 2008 from http://www.ietf.org/rfc/rfc2396.txt.

Van Schyndel, R., Tirkel, A., & Osborne, C. (1994). A digital watermark. *Proceedings of IEEE International Conference on Image Processing (ICIP-94), 2*, 86-90.

Wang, X., Lao, G., DeMartini, T., Reddy, H., Nguyen, M., & Valenzuela, E. (2002). XrML – eXtensible rights markup language. *Proceedings of the ACM Workshop on XML Security*. New York: ACM Press. (pp. 71-79).

WCT (1996). *WIPO copyright treaty*. Retrieved February 1, 2008 from http://www.wipo.int/treaties/en/ip/wct/trtdocs_wo033.html.

Wikipedia (n.d.). *Wikipedia*. Retrieved February 1, 2008 from http://www.wikipedia.com.

WIPO (2007). *World intellectual property organization*. Retrieved February 1, 2008 from http://www.wipo.org.

WIPO Convention (1967). Convention establishing by the world intellectual property organization. *Preamble, Second Paragraph*. Retrieved February 1, 2008 http://www.wipo.int/treaties/en/convention/trtdocs_wo029.html.

Wipro Technologies (2001). *Digital watermarking: A technology overview*. White Paper.

WPPT (1996). *WIPO performances and phonograms treaty*. Retrieved February 1, 2008 http://www.wipo.int/treaties/en/ip/wppt/trtdocs_wo034.html.

XMCL (2001). *XMCL – eXtensible media commerce language*. Retrieved February 1, 2008 from http://www.xmcl.org/index.html.

XrML (2007). Extensible rights markup language – XrML. *2.0 Specification*. Retrieved February 1, 2008 from http://www.xrml.org.

Yeung, M., & Mintzer, F. (1997). An invisible watermarking technique for image verification. *Proceedings of ICIP '97*. Santa Barbara, CA.

Yu, G., Lu, C., & Liao, H. (2003). A message-based cocktail watermarking system. *Elsevier, Pattern Recognition, 36*, 969-975.

ADDITIONAL READING

Gantz, J., & Rochester, J. (2004). *Pirates of the digital millennium: How the intellectual property wars damage our personal freedoms, our jobs, and the world economy.* FT Prentice Hall.

Harte, L. (2006). *Introduction to digital rights management (DRM); Identifying, tracking, authorizing and restricting access to digital media.* Althos Publishing.

Rosenblatt, B., Trippe, B., & Mooney, S. (2001). *Digital rights management: Business and technology.* Wiley Publications.

Safavi-Naini, R., & Yung, M. (2005). *Digital rights management: Technologies, issues, challenges and systems.* Lecture Notes in Computer Science.

Tassel, J. (2006). *Digital rights management: Protecting and monetizing content.* Focal Press.

Zeng, W., Yu, H., & Lin, C. (2006). *Multimedia security technologies for digital rights management.* Academic Press.

Section II
Protecting Digital Rights in E–Commerce Systems

In this section, an in-depth analysis of technological means for copyright protection of multimedia files is presented. Specifically, the most advanced watermarking algorithms and applications for multimedia are analyzed and evaluated.

Chapter III
Image Watermarking

Nikos Tsirakis
University of Patras, Greece

ABSTRACT

This chapter describes image watermarking, the most common and widespread category of media files are images. The evolution of the Internet and the ease by which images can be duplicated and distributed has led to the need for effective copyright protection tools and techniques in order to provide a secure way to the producers and the owners of these media files. These techniques are described below with an introduction to information hiding. Various software products have been introduced with an aim to address these growing concerns; some categories are presented here. The fundamental technique which allows an individual to add hidden copyright notices or other verification messages to digital images is called digital image watermarking and constitutes the main part of the chapter. Finally authors provide future trends and directions of image watermarking.

INTRODUCTION

For the past few years, little focus has been given to copyright issues of digital media. However, as the World Wide Web becomes a dominant Internet tool, providing huge volumes of information, many copyright owners are concerned about protecting the copyright of their digital images. Digital watermarking is an appropriate solution that can assist to ensure their rights. This technology allows a secret message to be hidden in an image file, without the detection of the user. The watermark is not apparent to the user, and does not affect in any way the use of the original file. The watermarking information is predominantly used to identify the creator of a digital image file.

BACKGROUND

The growth of computer networks has helped any type of information to be transmitted and exchanged over the Internet. Due to the convenience of copy and reproduction of digital images, the copyright protection issue is nowadays more important in the Internet environment. Moreover there are many modern digital libraries that have replaced the conventional. All these facts in combination with the ease of duplication of digital information have led to the need for effective copyright techniques and tools for protecting digital image copyright. Image watermarking has come to prevent from the unauthorized use of the images commercially. Watermark as a technique is an invisible signature embedded inside an image to show authenticity or proof of ownership. This method discourages unauthorized copying and distribution of images especially over the Internet and ensures that a digital picture has not been altered.

HISTORY OF INFORMATION HIDING

In this section we are going to give some important landmarks about information hiding without intending to cover the whole history of it. Information hiding techniques belong to a wide category of techniques that try to embed a signal, called digital signature or copyright label or watermark in the initial data. These techniques combine many different scientific areas like cryptography, digital signal processing, communication theory, etc. Generally there are two basic methods of information hiding, cryptography and steganography which overlap in some cases because they share some techniques.

Cryptography is about protecting the content of a message with the use of disguise. The initial message is called the *plain text* and the disguised message is called the *cipher text*. The process of converting this plain text to a cipher text is called enciphering or in other words encryption. The opposite process is called deciphering or decryption. Encryption protects content during the transmission of the data from the sender to receiver. However, after receipt and subsequent decryption, the data is no longer protected and is clear. While cryptography is about protecting the content of messages, steganography is about concealing their very existence.

Figure 1. A classification of information hiding techniques (Based on Birgit Pfitzmann, 1996)

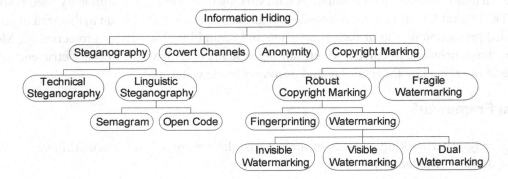

Steganography lies in devising astute and undetectable methods of concealing the message themselves. It comes from Greek roots (στεγανός, γραφείν), literally meaning «covered writing» (Clarendon Press, 1933), and is usually interpreted to mean hiding information in other information. Examples include sending a message to a spy by marking certain letters in a newspaper using invisible ink. Steganography hides messages in plain sight rather than encrypting the message. It is embedded in the data and does not require secret transmission. A whole other branch of steganography is linguistic steganography which consists of linguistic or language forms of hidden writing (David Kahn, 1996).

There has been a growing interest, by different research communities, in the fields of steganography, digital watermarking and fingerprinting. This led to some confusion in the terminology. For this reason in Figure 1 we present a classification of various information hiding techniques.

DIGITAL WATERMARKING

Digital watermarking technology is an emerging field in computer science, cryptography, signal processing and communications. A digital watermark is a signal which is permanently embedded into digital data like images, audio, etc. This signal can be detected or extracted by special programs in order to make assertions about the data. After this procedure the watermark is hidden in the host data in a way that it is inseparable from the data and it is resistant to many operations such as degrading the host file. Finally the work is still accessible but permanently marked. Digital watermarking is an enabling technology for several applications and strategies which can provide many advantages. More precisely digital watermarking can give the opportunity to the owner of a digital file to mark the data invisibly or visibly. There are many techniques and algorithms that provide this way to the owners. This mark can be used to serialize a piece of data as it is sold or used as a method to mark a valuable image file. Generally a watermark has to be robust enough to resist any attack and at the same time not to alter the value of the data that is being protected. The contents of an image file can be marked without visible loss of value or dependence on specific formats. The message is hidden in the image and stays below the human visible threshold for the image.

Both steganography and watermarking describe techniques that are used to imperceptibly convey information by embedding it into the cover-data. However, steganography typically relates to covert point-to-point communication between two parties. Thus, steganographic methods are usually not robust against modification of the data, or have only limited robustness and protect the embedded information against technical modifications that may occur during transmission and storage, like format conversion, compression, or digital-to-analog conversion. Since the digital watermarking field is still relatively young and has contributors from several disciplines with varying traditions, the terminology used is still quite diverse. The Digital Watermarking is intended by its developers as the solution to the need of providing value added protection on top of data encryption and scrambling for content protection (S. Mohanty, 1999). The basic principle of current watermarking systems is comparable to symmetric encryption as to the use of the same key for encoding and decoding of the watermark.

General Framework

In general, any watermarking consists of three parts, the watermark, a watermarking encoder and a respective decoder (Mohanty, 1999).

Watermark

Each digital file owner has a unique watermark or alternatively can use different watermarks in different files. The verification algorithm authenticates the object by determining both the owner and the integrity of the file.

Encoding Process

In the encoding process we denote an image by I, a signature by S and the watermarked image by I'. E is an encoder function, it takes an image I and a signature S, and it generates a new image which is called watermarked image I', i.e.

$$E(I, S) = I'$$

The signature S may be dependent on image I. In such cases, the encoding process described by the above equation still holds. Figure 2 illustrates the encoding process.

Decoding Process

In the decoding process a decoder function D takes an image J whose ownership is to be determined and recovers a signature S' from the image. In this process an additional image I can also be included which is often the original and un-watermarked version of J. This is due to the fact that some encoding schemes may make use of the original images, in the watermarking process, in order to provide extra robustness against intentional and unintentional corruption of pixels. Mathematically,

$$D(J, I) = S'$$

The extracted signature S' will then be compared with the owner signature sequence by a comparator function C_δ and a binary output decision will be generated. It is 1 if there is a match and 0 otherwise. C is the correlator, $x = C_\delta(S', S)$ and δ is certain threshold. Without loss of generality, a watermarking scheme can be treated as a three- tuple (E, D, C_δ). The following figures demonstrate the decoder and the comparator.

Figure 2. Watermark encoder (Based on Mohanty, 1999)

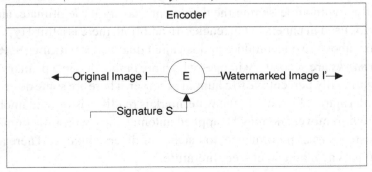

Figure 3. Watermark decoder (Based on Mohanty, 1999)

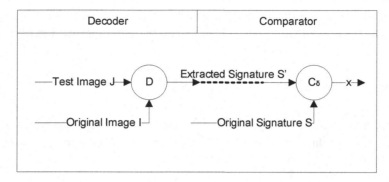

Figure 4. Watermark comparator (Based on Mohanty, 1999)

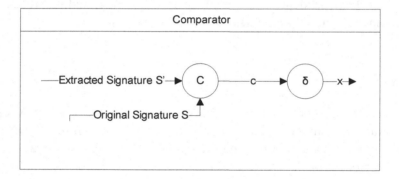

TYPES OF DIGITAL WATERMARKS

In digital watermarking the embedded data may be either visible or invisible (F. Mintzer, 1997). Visible and invisible watermarks both serve to deter theft but they do so in very different ways. Visibility is a term associated with the perception of the human eye. A watermarked image in which the watermark is imperceptible, or the watermarked image is visually identical to its original constitutes an invisible watermarking. Examples include images distributed over internet with watermarks embedded in them for copyright protection. Visible watermarks are especially useful for conveying an immediate claim of ownership. The main advantage is that they virtually eliminate the commercial value of the document to a would-be thief without lessening the document's utility for legitimate, authorized purposes. Examples include logos used in papers in currencies. In addition, there is a third type which is a result of the combination of the above two techniques and is called dual watermarking (S. P. Mohanty, 1999).

The *visible watermarks* are secondary images which are embedded in a primary image. In this case the watermark is intentionally perceptible to a human observer. There are some desired technical properties in this type of watermarks. First of all, the watermark is readily visible and unobtrusive. Moreover, the watermark is hard to remove, and may be applied automatically with little human intervention and labor, and with consistent visual prominence, to batches of diverse images. There are very few visible watermarking techniques available in current literature.

Invisible watermarks are watermarks where the embedded data are not perceptible, but may be extracted by a computer program. On the one hand, invisible image watermarks may change, or disappear, if a watermarked image is altered. It is generally desired that the watermarks are very sensitive to many sorts of image processing. These watermarks are called *fragile invisible watermarks* because it is desired that they can be altered or destroyed by most common image processing techniques. On the other hand, invisible image watermarks that persist even if someone tries to remove them are called robust image watermarks, since they are desired to survive intentional attacks.

Dual watermarks are a combination of visible and invisible watermarks. Initially, a visible watermark is being inserted in the original image and then an invisible watermark is added to the already visible watermarked image. More precisely as long as a visible watermark is there on the image, we can be sure about the ownership of this image. In any other case where the visible watermark is being tampered intentionally we can know the extent of tampering by the invisible watermark detection algorithm which is available. This technique works for both gray and color images.

IMAGE WATERMARKING APPLICATIONS

Digital watermarks are particularly attractive for signals constituting a continuous stream such as audio or video signals. For digitally transmitted signals, it must not be possible to detect the marking without an appropriately parameterized detector from either the encoded or the decoded signal and must be robust against digital-to-analog conversions. Generally there are many different applications for digital watermarking. Below are presented four main categories of these applications.

Copyright Protection

One of the traditional watermark applications is the protection of intellectual property through technical means, which is generally known as copyright protection. Generally, this application involves two distinct stages: (1) watermark embedding to indicate copyright and (2) watermark detection to identify the owner (Swanson, 1998). Embedding a watermark requires three functional components: (a) a watermark carrier, which is a list of data elements, selected from the un-watermarked signal, which are modified during the encoding, (b) a watermark generator, and (c) a carrier modifier, which generates noise signals to the selected carrier.

The watermark approach to this application area is particularly mentioned at numerous publications in the field (Cox, 1995; Koch, 1995) and many digital watermarking techniques have been developed to protect the copyright of different types of multimedia content such as images, video and audio signal. However, without regard to multimedia type, digital watermarking techniques can be divided into two main categories: visible and invisible. The idea behind the visible watermark is equivalent to stamping a watermark on paper, while, on the other hand, invisible watermarking is more complex. It is most often used to identify copyright data, like author, distributor, and so forth (Arnold, 2003).

Under another perspective, measures taken in order to protect the intellectual property can be grouped into two main categories, according to whom the protection is against. The first category includes protection techniques against other providers, while the second one encompasses protection against the illegal use by end users (Arnold, 2003). The main distinction between them lies in the fact that, whereas a content provider has to expose himself in order to profit from the image creations, the end users may distribute the altered material anonymously. Therefore, many image techniques that can be applied in the first case turn out to be ineffective for the second one. However, the technical requirements are more or less the same for both categories (Morimoto, 1999): the watermark has to remain invisible to the users, be independent of the data format, be detected without the original content and, finally, be uniquely identified by some kind of keys.

Image Authentication

The existence of more and more available tools for digital signal processing, which give the user the opportunity to make changes to either visual or audio content without leaving traces, leads to the undesired result of losing the credibility of digital data. This makes sense since occasional changes may alter the initial content, causing doubts about the true origin of the digital signal. For example, compression of an image I results in a new image I' which is still considered to be authentic. To overcome this critical problem, it is necessary to take measures in order to make it possible to verify the authenticity of an image recorded in digital form. Digital watermarking is a very promising solution to this problem (Barni, 2004).

A general authentication system has to fulfill the following requirements in order to be evaluated: sensitivity, robustness, security, portability, location of manipulated area and recovery capability. Generally, authentication of the host image may be accomplished either by (semi-) fragile or robust watermarking techniques (Barni, 2004). With fragile watermarking the hidden information is lost or altered as soon as the host image undergoes any modification (Walton, 1995; Yeung, 1998; Kundur, 1999). This is taken as evidence that data has been tampered with. In the special case of a semi-fragile watermarking, we have to assure that hidden information survives only a certain kind of allowed manipulations and therefore, a special scheme has to be applied. The use of robust watermarking for data authentication, on the other hand, relies on a different mechanism. A summary of the host image is computed and inserted within the image itself. Information about the data origin is embedded together with the summary. To prove data integrity, the information conveyed by the watermark is recovered and compared with the actual content of the sequence: their mismatch is taken as an evidence of data tampering.

Data Hiding

The process of embedding information into digital images without causing perceptual degradation is called data hiding. One of the most important problem we are dealing with is the creation of a data hiding scheme which will fulfill the following major requirements: 1) hiding the highest possible amount of information without affecting the visual quality of the host data, 2) being invisible, 3) being robust. The watermark must be invisible so that its presence does not affect the quality of the to-be-protected data. On the other hand, it must be resistant against the most common image manipulations.

In order to create the above scheme, it is important to understand the mechanisms underlying human vision (Cox, 1997; Tewfik, 1997; Wolfgang, 1999). Basically, a model describing the human visual perception is based on two main concepts: the contrast sensitivity function and the contrast masking model. The first concept is concerned with the sensitivity of the human eye to a sine grating stimulus, while the second concept considers the effect of one stimulus on the delectability of another.

Recently, this idea of embedding information into digital images has been progressively applied to other purposes as well, such as broadcast monitoring, image authentication, copyright protection, fingerprinting, copy prevention or control, metadata binding, and so on.

Over the last few years, a variety of digital watermarking and data hiding techniques have been proposed for such purposes. However, most of the methods developed today are for grayscale and color images (Swanson et al., 1998), where the gray level or color value of a selected group of pixels is changed by a small amount without causing visually noticeable artifacts. These techniques cannot be directly applied to binary document images where the pixels have either a 0 or a 1 value, since arbitrarily changing pixels on a binary image causes very noticeable artifacts. Therefore, different classes of embedding techniques have been developed. These techniques for binary document images can be classified according to one of the following embedding methods: text line, word, or character shifting, fixed partitioning of the image into blocks, boundary modifications, modification of character features, modification of run-length patterns, and modifications of half-tone images.

Covert Communication

Covert communication is a method of sending secret messages. Given the fact that the communication has to be encrypted, it is considered to be one of the earliest applications of watermarking. Historically, it traces back at least to the ancient Greeks, when the art of keeping a message secret was used for military applications (Barni, 2004). A covert communication scheme has been formulated by Simmons (Simmons, 1984) as "the prisoner's problem", in which we consider two prisoners in separate cells trying to pass messages back and forth. Their problem is that they rely on the prison warden to act as a messenger between them. To avoid any illegal communication, the warden inspects all the messages sent by the prisoners and punishes them every time he discovers that a message has malicious content, such as an escape plan. Therefore, the prisoners have to find a way to disguise the escape-plan messages by hiding them in innocuous messages.

In the case of image covert interchange, it is important to ensure that a secure covert "channel" for communication can always be established. It is also important to be able to calculate the capacity of this channel. The exploitation of a hidden communication channel for improved transmission is gaining more and more consensus. From the source coding point of view, it can help to design more powerful compression schemes where part of the information is transmitted by hiding it in the coded bit stream. From a channel coding perspective, it can be exploited to improve the resilience of the coded bit stream with respect to channel errors (self-correcting or self-healing images).

Although a great deal of research has been carried out aiming at designing robust watermarking techniques, very little attention has been paid to analyzing or evaluating the effectiveness of such techniques for steganographic applications. Instead, most of the work developed so far has focused on analyzing watermarking algorithms with respect to their robustness against various kinds of attacks attempting to remove or destroy the watermark.

IMAGE WATERMARKING ALGORITHMS

Image watermarking algorithms can be classified into fragile watermarking and robust watermarking (Petitcolas, 1999).

Fragile watermarks are destroyed as soon as the object is modified too much. This can be used to prove that an object has not been "doctored" and might be useful if digital images are used as evidence in court. The basic idea underlying these techniques is to insert a specific watermark, generally independent of the image data, so that any attempt to alter the content of an image will also alter the watermark itself.

Robust watermarks have the following property: it is infeasible to remove them or make them useless without destroying the object at the same time. This usually means that the mark should be embedded in the most perceptually significant components of the object. The aim of these methods is to discriminate between malicious manipulations, such as the addition or removal of a significant element of the image, and global operations preserving the semantic content of the image.

Most methods currently proposed for providing image authentication are based on a fragile watermark in opposition to robust watermark classically used for copyright protection. The latter form is the very challenging and attracts most research. Usually a digital image watermarking algorithm must be robust against a variety of possible attacks. Current watermarking techniques usually insert one bit of information in many pixels or alternatively transform coefficients and use classical detection schemes to recover the watermark information. These techniques are mostly referred to as spread-spectrum approaches, due to their similarity to spread-spectrum communication systems. Unlike the general digital communication system, where the channel characteristics is known or estimated, an image channel is hard to be defined because it can be transformed to many different domains, such as DCT domain, Wavelet-Transform domain, etc. Therefore an image channel has different capacity and probability of error, with respect to different representations. Especially for still image watermarking, watermark embedding is applied directly to the pixel values in the spatial domain or to transform coefficients in a transform domain such as the discrete cosine transform (DCT) or discrete wavelet transform (DWT) (Podilchuk, 2001).

For instance in (Chen, 1999) authors interpret the watermarking problem as a digital communication problem. In addition, they show the trade-off between the criteria concerning the performance of watermarking techniques and finally an adaptive coding-rate watermarking scheme based on spread spectrum communication technique is proposed. Lately in (Mohanty, 2006) authors present a VLSI architecture that can insert invisible or visible watermarks in images in the DCT domain. The proposed architecture exploits pipelining and parallelism extensively in order to achieve high performance.

Algorithm Attributes

The characteristics of a watermarking algorithm are normally tied to the application that was designed for. The following merely explain the words used in the context of watermarking.

- **Imperceptibility:** In watermarking we traditionally seek high fidelity, i.e. the watermarked work must look like the original.
- **Robustness:** It is more a property and not a requirement of watermarking. The watermark should be able to survive any reasonable processing inflicted on the carrier (carrier here refers to the content being watermarked).
- **Security:** The watermarked image should not reveal any clues of the presence of the watermark, with respect to un-authorized detection, or statistical undetectability or unsuspicious which is not the same as imperceptibility.

IMAGE ATTACKS

Image attacks are generally divided into 6 categories (Michiels, 2006). According to these attacks someone can destroy, or at least reveal significant limitations of several marking schemes.

- **Geometrical:** Flipping, cropping, rotation with possible additional cropping, uniform and non uniform scaling as for example with or without changing of aspect ratio, rolling as for example shifting of rows or columns, affine transformations, up and down-sampling, defo-process and general geometric transformations (Delannay, 2004)
- **Noising:** Are attacks that consist of the addition of noise like gaussian and multiplicative gaussian noising, poisson noising, laplacian noising, salt-and-pepper noising.
- **Denoising:** Are attacks that consist of the removal of noise like gaussian filtering, mean filtering, median filtering, midpoint filtering.
- **Format-compression:** Here belong all manipulations concerning the image format like JPEG compression and format changing.
- **Image Processing:** Are attacks with all common image processing transformations such as color quantization, black-and-white and grey-level transformation, gamma correction, histogram modification and finally sharpening (Stirmark, 2007).
- **Malicious:** Here are all the remaining attacks, intended to remove the watermark such as collusion attack, copy attack, rows or columns removal, Stir-Mark attacks, rows or columns removal, synchronization removal and template removal.

Although the above classification makes it possible to have a clear separation between the different classes of attacks, it is necessary to note that very often a malicious attacker applies not only a single attack at the moment, but rather a combination of two or more attacks.

FUTURE TRENDS OF IMAGE WATERMARKING

Image watermarking has progressed beyond an immature technology. Watermarking future is quite bright. Image watermarking as a content identifier for content metadata is on the rise and will be deployed by many content owners in the very near future. With the technology of the Internet, more sophisticated implementations of steganography are necessary. The process of image watermarking is needed to protect the huge amounts of content over the Internet. One of the most pressing issues is copyright protection.

Unfortunately, according to what the image watermarking attacks have shown, only little of the techniques that are employed nowadays are indestructible. Researchers and engineers still need to develop image watermarking techniques that are as reliable as their paper ancestors were and cost-effective enough so as to be widely implemented on a commercial basis. Only when these watermarks become robust enough to resist all attacks, will content providers to be willing to deliver real, high quality multimedia over public networks, such as the Internet.

CONCLUSION

Image watermarking technology is an emerging field in computer science, cryptography, signal processing and communications. The watermarking research is more exciting as it needs collective concepts from all the fields along with Human Psychovisual analysis, Multimedia and Computer Graphics. The watermark may be of visible or invisible type and each has got its own applications. The watermarking research progresses very fast and numerous researchers from various fields focus on developing some workable scheme.

FUTURE RESEARCH DIRECTIONS

The interest in watermarking technology is high, both for academia and industry and although many technical problems have been addressed, there are many more yet to be solved. Many of the techniques developed for watermarking are based on a solid understanding of communications and signal processing principles, but there are still many technical challenges to be solved such as monitoring and policing techniques for copyright infringement and ways to prevent distortions from particular applications in the future. In addition, there is a need for a more sophisticated watermark embedding and detection functions and improvement of the watermark invisibility via powerful techniques. Finally despite recent advances, watermarking security is still a largely unexplored field.

Many companies have already been active in digital watermarking research. Some of them have created new techniques for image protection and have included these techniques in their products. Security technology can be vulnerable, if it is not based on current research. However, if the technology is combined with proper legal enforcement, industry standards and respects of the privacy of individuals seeking to legitimately use intellectual property, image watermarking will encourage content creators to trust the Internet more as it has become a large repository of digital files. As a fact, it is expected that a great deal of effort must still be put into research before digital image watermarking can be widely accepted as legal evidence of ownership.

Generally there are many development challenges in image watermarking. Problems like lack of standardization, lack of a set of precise and realistic requirements for watermarking systems and lack of agreement on the definition of a common benchmark for method comparison lead to further developments and improvements in order to provide the end user with what he is expecting. In this chapter we meant to summarize the salient features and directions of watermarking research and the interested reader is encouraged to explore the references for more details.

REFERENCES

Arnold, M., &Schmucker, M., & Wolthusen, S. D. (2003). Techniques and applications of digital watermarking and content protection. Artech House.

Barni, M., & Bartolini, F. (2004). Watermarking systems engineering: Enabling digital assets security and other applications. *Signal Processing & Communication*. Marcel Dekker.

Chen, T. P.-C., Chen, Y.-S., & Hsu, W.-H. (1999, July). Adaptive-rate image watermarking based on spread spectrum communication technique. *3rd World Multiconference on Circuits, Systems, Communications and Computers (CSCC'99)*. Athens, Greece.

Clarendon Press. (1933). *The Oxford English dictionary: Being a corrected re-issue*. Oxford.

Cox, I. J., Kilian, J., Leighton, F. T., & Shamoon, T. (1995). Secure spread spectrum watermarking for multimedia. *Technical Report 95-10*. NEC Research Institute.

Cox, I., & Miller, M. L. (1997, February). A review of watermarking and the importance of perceptual modeling. *Proceedings of SPIE, 3016. Human Vision and Electronic Imaging II*, 92-99. Bellingham, WA.

Delannay, D. (2004, April). Digital watermarking algorithms robust against loss of synchronization. *PhD thesis*. Laboratoire de Telecommunications et Teledetection : Universite Catholique de Louvain.

Fabien A. P., Petitcolas, R. Anderson, J., .& Kuhn, M. G. (1999). iInformation hiding – A survey. *Proc. IEEE 87*, 1062-1078.

Kahn, D. (1996). The history of steganography. *Proceedings of the First International Workshop on Information Hiding*.

Koch, E., & Zhao, J. (1995, June). Towards robust and hidden image copyright labeling. In I. Pitas, (ed.), *Proceedings of 1995 IEEE Workshop on Nonlinear Signal and Image Processing*. Neos Marmaras, Greece, (pp. 452-455).

Kundur, D., & Hatzinakos, D. (1999, July). Digital watermarking for telltale tamper proofing and authentication. *Proceedings of the IEEE, 87*(7), 1167-1180.

Michiels B., & Benoit, M. (2006). Benchmarking image watermarking algorithms with open watermark. *14th European Signal Processing Conference - EUSIPCO06*, Florence, Italy.

Mintzer, F., Braudaway, G. W., & Yeung, M. M. (1992, October). Effective and ineffective digital watermarks. *Image Processing, 3*, 9-12.

Mohanty, S. (1999). *Digital watermarking: A tutorial review*.

Mohanty, S. P., Ramakrishnan, K. R., & Kanakanhalli, M. S. (1999). A dual watermarking technique for images. *In Proceedings of the 7th ACM International Multimedia Conference (ACMMM,) 2*, 49-51.

Mohanty, S. P., Ranganathan, N., & Balakrishnan, K. (2006, May). A dual voltage-frequency VLSI chip for image watermarking in DCT domain. *IEEE Transactions on Circuits and Systems II (TCAS-II), 53*(5), 394-398.

Morimoto, N. (1999). Digital watermarking technology with practical applications. *Information Science Special Issue on Multimedia Information Technology*, 1,2(4).

Pfitzmann, B. (1996). Information hiding terminology - Results of an informal. ISBN 3-540-61996-8. *Results of an informal plenary meeting and additional proposals*, pp. 347-350.

Podilchuk, C. I., & Delp, E. J. (2001, July). Digital watermarking: algorithms and applications. I*EEE Signal Processing Magazine, 18*(4), 33-46.

Simmons, G. J. (1984). The prisoners' problem and the subliminal channel. *In Proc. CRYPTO'83*, 51-67. Plenum Press.

Stirmark [online]. Available at http://www.petitcolas.net/fabien/watermarking/stirmark/.

Swanson, M., Kobayashi, M., & Tewfik, A. (1998, June). Multimedia data embedding and watermarking technologies. *IEEE Proceedings, 86*(6), 1064-1087.

Tewfik, A. H., & Swanson, M. (1997, July). Data hiding for multimedia personalization, interaction, and protection. *IEEE Signal Processing Magazine, 14*(4), 41-44.

Wolfgang, R. B., Podilchuk, C. I., & Delp, E. J. (1999, July). Perceptual watermarks for digital images and video. *Proceedings of IEEE, 87*(7), 1108-1126.

Yeung, M. M., & Mintzer, F. C. (1998, July). Invisible watermarking for image verification. *Journal of Electronic Imaging, 7*(3), 578-591.

ADDITIONAL READING

Certimark. Available at http://vision.unige.ch/certimark/.

Checkmark. Available at http://watermarking.unige.ch/checkmark/.

Openwatermark. Available at http://www.openwatermark.org/.

Optimark. Available at http://poseidon.csd.auth.gr/optimark/.

Stirmark audio. https://amsl-smb.cs.uni-magdeburg.de/smfa//main.php

Stirmark. Available at http://www.petitcolas.net/fabien/watermarking/stirmark/.

Watermark Evaluation Testbed. Available at http://www.datahiding.com/.

Juergen Seitz, Ed. Digital Watermarking for Digital Media. ISBN 1-59140-518-1 Idea Group, Inc. 2005.

Mauro Barni and Franco Bartolini. Watermarking Systems Engineering. ISBN: 0-8247-4806-9 Marcel Dekker, Inc. 2004.

Ingemar Cox, Jeffrey Bloom, and Matthew Miller. Digital Watermarking, Principles & Practice. Morgan Kaufmann, first edition, 2001.

Wei Lu, Hongtao Lu, Fu-Lai Chung. Feature based watermarking using watermark template match. ISSN:0096-3003 Applied Mathematics and Computation, Volume 177, Issue 1, June 2006.

Benoit Macq, Jana Dittmann, and Edward J. Delp. Benchmarking of image watermarking algorithms for digital rights management. Proceedings of the IEEE, 92(6):971–984, June 2004.

J. F. Delaigle, C. Devleeschouwer, B. Macq, and I. Langendijk. Human Visual System Features Enabling Watermarking. Proc. IEEE Int. Conf. Multimedia Expo, vol. 2, 2002, pp. 489—492.

J. Dittmann, P. Wholmacher, and K. Nahrstedt. Using cryptographic and watermarking algorithms. IEEE Multimedia, 8(Oct-Dec):54–65, 2001.

V. Solachidis, A. Tefas, N. Nikolaidis, S. Tsekeridou, A. Nikolaidis, and I. Pitas. A benchmarking protocol for watermarking methods. In IEEE Int. Conf. on Image Processing (ICIP'01), Thessaloniki, Greece, pages 1023–1026, 2001.

S. Voloshynovskiy, S. Peirera, V. Inquise, and T. Pun. Attack-modeling: towards a second generation watermarking benchmark. Signal Processing, 81:1177–1214, 2001.

S. P. Mohanty, K. R. Ramakrishnan, and M. S. Kanakanhalli, "A DCT Domain Visible Watermarking Technique for Images", in Proceedings of the IEEE International Conference on Multimedia and Expo (ICME) (Vol. 2), pp.1029-1032, 2000.

G.Voyatzis and I.Pitas, "Protecting Digital Image Copyrights: A Framework", *IEEE Computer Graphics & Applications*, Jan/Feb 1999, pp.18-24.

M.Ramkumar and A.N.Akansu, "Image Watermarks and Counterfeit Attacks: Some Problems and Solutions", Proc. of Content Security and Data Hiding in Digital Media, Newark, NJ, USA, May 14 1999.

Liehua Xie and Gonzalo R. Arce. Joint wavelet compression and authentication watermarking. In Proceedings of the IEEE International Conference on Image Processing, ICIP '98, Chicago, IL, USA, 1998.

J.J.K. O'Ruanaidh and T.Pun, "Rotation, Scale and Translation Invariant Spread Spectrum Digital Image Watermarking", *Signal Processing*, Vol.66, No.3, May 1998, pp.303-317.

Wenwu Zhu, Zixiang Xiong, and Ya-Qin Zhang. Multiresolution watermarking for images and video: a unified approach. In Proceedings of the IEEE International Conference on Image Processing, ICIP '98, Chicago, IL, USA, October 1998.

J.P.M.G. Linnartz, A.C.C. Kalker, G.F. Depovere and R. Beuker, "A reliability model for detection of electronic watermarks in digital images", Benelux Symposium on Communication Theory, Enschede, October 1997, pp. 202-209.

M.D.Swanson, et al., "Transparent Robust Image Watermarking", *Proc IEEE International Conf. on Image Processing, ICIP-96*, Vol.3, pp 211-214.

KEY TERMS

Copyright Protection: It is the attribute that a digital file can have where it gives the original producers various rights including the right to prevent others from making copies. It is one of the major institutional measures designed to secure producers' incentive to create useful products in these markets.

Digital Privacy: It is closely related to the freedoms of expression, association and assembly. In other words it is similar to the protection of the confidentiality of digital data.

Image Fingerprinting: It is a technique which embeds a digital signal in image files and may contain information on the end user. This can be used to trace the source of copyright infringement.

Image Authentication: It is the ability to ensure that a digital image has not been modified after capture. It provides the ability to detect if an image has been altered or if it is identical to the original captured or compressed image. This is done using computer software and/or hardware to generate a fingerprint of the image.

Invertibility Attack: It creates counterfeit watermarks in the same digital product to cause confusion therefore prevent rightful assertion of ownership.

Robust Watermarks: Watermarks where the embedded information should be reliably decodable after alterations of the marked data. Often the level of robustness is dictated by the application.

Still Image: Non-moving visual information such as graphs, drawings, pictures, or video frames not processed by the video CODEC portion of the VTU. This differs from freeze-frame images which are processed by the video CODEC portion of the VTU.

Chapter IV
Watermarking Techniques for DRM Applications

Alessandro Piva
University of Florence, Italy

Roberto Caldelli
University of Florence, Italy

Alessia De Rosa
University of Florence, Italy

Mauro Barni
Università di Siena, Italy

Vito Cappellini
University of Florence, Italy

ABSTRACT

The need to safeguard the property rights of multimedia content from unauthorized copying and the possibility to determine the true owners of the asset can be faced by resorting to efficient digital watermarking systems. This chapter presents a mathematical formulation to define a digital watermarking system and describes the general requirements to be satisfied, with more emphasis given to the aspects of security, robustness, and imperceptibility. After this general discussion, the two main classes of digital watermarking schemes, namely the spread-spectrum watermarking and the side-informed watermarking are explained by highlighting their main advantages and drawbacks. This analysis is completed by the description of a practical implementation of a digital image watermarking scheme. Finally, the use of watermarking systems in the framework of a DRM is deeply analyzed.

INTRODUCTION

Data hiding technology, introduced in the early 90's (Barni, 2004; Cox, 2001) allows to hide a signal or some information into a digital content (an audio file, a still image, a video sequence or a combination of the above), usually named host data. To embed the hidden information in the host data, data hiding techniques apply minor modifications to the host content in an imperceptible manner, where the modifications are related to the embedded information.

The hidden information can be retrieved afterwards from the modified content by detecting the presence of these modifications by means of computing operations.

In general, data hiding technologies allow to provide a communication channel multiplexed into original content (Kalker, 2001), through which it is possible to transmit some information, depending on the application at hand, from a sender to a receiver. In the first years, the research on data hiding was mainly devoted to offer a solution to the problem of copyright protection of digital content.

Copyright protection of multimedia data has been accomplished in the past by means of cryptography algorithms to provide control over data access and to make data unreadable to non-authorized users. However, encryption systems do not completely solve the problem, because once encryption is removed there is no more control on the dissemination of data; a possible solution is given by data hiding of multimedia works to allow their dissemination to be tracked. In this way the number of permitted copies is not limited, but the possibility exists to control the path the original work has been disseminated through.

In this class of application, data hiding was termed digital watermarking, and the hidden information, defined digital watermark, was some code conveying information related to the creator, the distributor, the customer, or licensing terms between them.

According to this design, in the realisation of really effective DRMSs watermarking technologies can undoubtedly play an important role. In fact the need to safeguard the property rights of the multimedia content from an unauthorised copying and the possibility to determine the true owners of the asset can be solved through the use of efficient digital watermarking systems.

The chapter is organized as follows. First of all, a mathematical formulation to define a digital watermarking model is given, and general requirements are listed and briefly discussed, with more emphasis given to the aspects of security, robustness and imperceptibility. After this general discussion, the two main classes of digital watermarking schemes, namely the spread-spectrum watermarking and the side-informed watermarking are explained, by highlighting their main advantages and drawbacks. This analysis is completed by the detailed description of a practical implementation of a digital image watermarking scheme, designed in the past years by the authors. Next, the use of watermarking systems in the framework of a DRM is analyzed. Finally, future trends are discussed and the conclusions are drawn.

MATHEMATICAL FORMULATION OF THE WATERMARKING PROBLEM

A digital watermarking system can be modelled as described in Figure 1 (Barni, 2004). The inputs of the system are a certain application dependent information, and the original host content, that could be an audio file, an image or a video sequence, here indicated as C. The to-be-hidden information is usually represented as a binary string $b = (b_1, b_2, ..., b_k)$, referred as the watermark code. The watermark embedder

Figure 1. The proposed model describing a digital watermarking system

hides the watermark code *b* into the host asset **C** to produce a watermarked content **Cw**, usually making use of a secret information *K* needed to tune some parameters of the embedding process and to allow the recovery of the watermark only to authorized users having access to that secret information.

The functionality's of the watermark embedding process can be further split into three main tasks: information coding; data embedding; watermark concealment, as indicated in Figure 2.

With *information coding*, the information message *b* is transformed into a watermark signal *w* = $(w_1, w_2, ..., w_n)$ which is more suitable for embedding in the content. As it happens in a digital communication system, the watermark code *b* may be used to modulate a much longer spread-spectrum sequence, or it may be transformed into a bipolar signal, or it may be mapped into the relative position of two or more pseudo-random signals in the case of position-encoded-watermarking. Eventually, *b* may be left as it is, thus leading to a scheme in which the watermark code is directly inserted within the host. In this case the watermark signal *w* coincides with the watermark code *b*.

Moreover, before coding, the watermark code may be channel-coded to increase robustness against possible attacks. As a matter of fact, it turns out that channel coding greatly improves the performance of any watermarking system.

In *data embedding*, given the host asset **C**, the watermark signal *w*, and, possibly, a key K, the watermarked content is generated by an embedding function. To embed the watermark code into the original content, watermarking techniques apply minor modifications to the host data in a perceptually invisible manner, where the modifications are related to the to-be-hidden data. In general, embedding is achieved by modifying a set of features $f = (f_1, f_2, ..., f_n)$ extracted by the host content, with the watermark signal *w*, according to a proper embedding rule that depends on the particular watermarking scheme, obtaining a set of watermarked features $f_w = (f_{w1}, f_{w2}, ..., f_{wn})$. The modified features are then reinserted into the content on behalf of the original ones, thus obtaining the watermarked content.

The main concern of the embedding part of any data hiding system is to make the hidden data imperceptible. This requirement is satisfied through the *watermark concealment* procedure, that can be achieved either implicitly, by properly choosing the set of host features to be modified and the embedding rule, or explicitly, by introducing a concealment step after watermark embedding; in this case, the original content **C** is usually required. To accomplish this task, the properties of the human senses must be carefully taken into account, since imperceptibility ultimately relies on the exploitation of the imperfections of such senses. Thereby, still image and video watermarking will rely on the characteristics of the Human Visual System (HVS), whereas audio watermarking will exploit the properties of the Human Auditory System (HAS).

Figure 2. The watermark embedding process can be divided into 3 steps

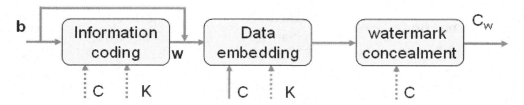

The second element of the model represented in Figure 1, the *watermark channel,* takes into account for all the processing operations and manipulations, both intentional and non-intentional, the watermarked content may undergo during its distribution and fruition, so that consequently the watermarked content can be modified into a new version $\mathbf{C'}_w$.

The third element of the model is the tool for the recovery of the hidden information from $\mathbf{C'}_w$: the extraction of the hidden data may follow two different approaches: the detector can look for the presence of a specific message given to it as input, thus only answering yes or no, or the system (now called decoder) reads the sequence of bits hidden into the watermarked content without knowing it in advance. These two approaches lead to a distinction between *readable* watermarking algorithms, embedding a message that can be read, and *detectable* watermarking algorithms, inserting a code that can only be detected. In the former case, the bits contained in the watermark can be read without knowing them in advance; in the latter case, one can only verify if a given code is present in the document, i.e. the watermark can only be revealed if its content is known in advance. Detectable watermarking is also known as 1-bit watermarking since, given a watermark, the output of the detector is just *yes* or *no*. Note that in readable watermarking, the decoding process always results in a decoded bit stream, however, if the asset is not marked, decoded bits are meaningless.

An additional distinction may be made between systems that need to know the original content $\mathbf{C}$ in order to retrieve the hidden information, and those that do not require it. In the latter case we say that the system is *blind*, whereas in the former case it is said to be *non-blind*.

Another distinction of the algorithms can be done on the basis of the key K used in the decoding/detection process. If the secret key for the detection/decoding process is the same used for embedding, we refer to *symmetric* watermarking schemes. These techniques present an intrinsic lack of security, since the knowledge of K is likely to give attackers information sensitive for the removal of the watermark from the watermarked content. In order to overcome the above problems, increasing attention has been given to the development of *asymmetric* methods (Furon, 2001). In such schemes two keys are present, a private key, K_s, used to embed the information within the host signal, and a public key, K_p, used to detect/decode the watermark (often K_p is just a subset of K_s). Knowing the public key, it should be neither possible to deduce the private key nor to remove the watermark (unlike in asymmetric cryptography, knowledge of K_s may be sufficient to derive K_p; additionally, the roles of the private key and the public key can not be exchanged). More details about the importance of asymmetric watermarking in security oriented applications may be found in (Barni, 2003).

REQUIREMENTS

Before a deeper analysis of watermarking algorithms, requirements watermarking techniques have to fulfil will be listed. Whereas the three most important ones, that is *security*, *robustness* and *imperceptibility* will be described in the next three subsections, in the sequel the others will be briefly discussed.

Depending on the application at hand, the watermarking algorithm should allow a predefined number of bits to be hidden (defined *payload* or watermark *capacity*). General rules do no exist here, however, system designers should keep well in mind that the number of bits which can be hidden into data is not unlimited, nay very often is fairly small.

Even in the absence of attacks or signal distortions, the probability of failing to detect the embedded watermark (false-negative error probability) and of detecting a watermark when, in fact, one does not exist (false- positive error probability), must be very small (*Trustworthy detection*). Usually, statistically-based algorithms have no problem in satisfying this requirement, however such an ability must be demonstrated if watermarking is to be legally credible.

It should be possible to embed a set of different watermarks in the same image, in such a way that each code can be detected by the authorised user (*Multiple embedding*). This feature is useful in fingerprinting applications, where the copyright property is transferred from the content owner to other customers. Moreover, we can not prevent someone from watermarking an already watermarked work.

Great attention should be given to watermark invertibility as well. Craver et al. in (Craver, 1998) stated that for a watermarking scheme to be successfully used to demonstrate rights ownership, non-invertibility of the watermark has to be granted. Furthermore, this is only a necessary condition to be satisfied, since, more generally, non-quasi-invertibility is needed. Without going into much details, we can say that a watermark is invertible if it is possible to generate a false watermark and a fake original document which is perceptually equal to the true one, such that by embedding the false watermark in it a document which is equal (*invertibility*) or perceptually equal (*quasi invertibility*) to the true marked one is obtained.

Security

At dawn of watermarking systems, performances were measured by proving them with respect to different issues such as payload, perceivability and robustness. In particular, this last one was felt as mandatory to grant algorithm resistance against a possible attacker who acted by means of various image processing tools such as filtering, color changing, compression, geometric transformations and so on. Anyway, not too much consideration has been paid to analyze problems related to system security, that is to determine if there was one or more weak links to permit an attacker to circumvent the whole system or to use it in illegal manner. In fact, with the term *attacks to security* has to be intended all those strategies that a hacker can put in practice, on the basis of what he knows and he does not, to fake the response of the watermarking algorithm. Only recently, it has been started to give relevance to this kind of problem and to reconsider most of the design approach from this new point of view. This is mainly due to the fact that when watermarking systems, apparently robust, have been tested in an actual insecure environment they have miserably failed. Open challenges like the one recently proposed in the BOWS (Break Our Watermarking System) contest (BOWS, 2006) has to be considered on this line.

Before starting the discussion it would be interesting to give a basic definition of what is intended with the term security talking about watermarking. In literature many celebrate phrases which deal with security exist. In particular we would like to cite one that is maybe the eldest and that focuses on a message to be kept in mind when debating on security, not only of watermarking systems. This is the *Kerchoffs* law (Kerchoffs, 1883) that establishes that *security cannot be based on algorithm secrecy but on one or more secret keys used by the algorithm itself.* After having reported this important paradigm, let us try to propose a general definition for security in watermarking framework among the various that can be found in literature and that will be adopted as reference: *security refers to the inability of unauthorised users to access the additional channel created with watermarking* (Kalker, 2001). The main difficulty when talking about security in watermarking is the lack of a defined general framework in which globally analyse all the elements involved in security aspects and, almost always, it is necessary to refer, time to time, to a specific application case; usually, in fact, it is the application at hand which determines ad-hoc requirements and levels of security. Sometimes, anyway, there are some important issues to be taken into account and that can constitute a sort of a "best practice" to follow when a watermarking algorithm is called to operate:

- What is available to the attacker to help his illegal action
- Which kind of attack procedure the attacker can put in practice
- What the attacker wishes to do

What is Available to the Attacker to Help his Illegal Action

The first issue regards the definition of what the hacker knows and/or owns to succeed in making a successful action. The greater the information the easier the attack to security: the effort to be done by the attacker in terms of resources (e.g. computational time, number of attempts, etc.) is reduced by any availability he has. First of all, it has to be considered if the attacker can benefit of the knowledge of the watermarking algorithm (public algorithm) to perform, for instance, a reverse engineering operation by selecting the watermarked features. He also could have at his disposal the decoding/detection system, and on the basis of which software/hardware devices he has access to, being helped in performing his action. In such a situation he could read the embedded code or on the contrary he could have access only to the detector, in this case he can realize if a watermark is present or not but not which information has been encoded. Similar considerations can be made for the eventuality that the attacker has the knowledge of one or more secret keys used by the algorithm during the watermark embedding and/or the watermark extraction phases. Another crucial issue to be analysed concerns the possibility that the hacker owns multiple watermarked copies so he can check more than one copy of the same watermarked asset or different documents watermarked with the same system and try, by means of a certain analysis (e.g. making a collusion attack (Doerr, 2003; Caldelli, 2004)), to understand something more on the watermarking algorithm he is cracking or make it fails.

Which Kind of Attack Procedure the Attacker can Put in Practice

Another issue to be considered basically concerns the manner the attacker performs his action, in fact in the "game" between him and the watermarking system designer, he can play *fairly* or *unfairly*. In the first case, the attacker only uses the means and the knowledge he has got and tries to carry out diverse kinds of attack that are feasible according to the application at hand and to the specific characteristics of that system; he can analyse the algorithm to understand if there exists one or more trojan horses to fool the system. Many are the attacks that have been proposed in literature depending on the application such as sensitivity attack, Holliman&Memon attack, collage attack, etc. In the second case, the hacker tries to illegally discover some secret information (e.g. secret keys, watermarking parameters), he does not possess, to use them to crack the system and does it in every possible way. It is obvious to comprehend that in a real application framework the hacker will be always an unfair player and this is the less favourable situation for the watermark designer.

What the Attacker Wishes to Do

The third issue to be evaluated concerns what the hacker could wish to achieve through his illegal action and how much sophisticated is the result he wants to obtain. It also depends on the kind of watermark, if it is robust or fragile, and partially if this watermark is adopted for an application such as authentication or copyright protection. A common malevolent activity performed could be to decode the hidden bits; in this case the attacker wishes to read the information encoded within the digital object to possibly re-encode it into a fake document. Other actions might be to destroy hidden bits (the attacker only wants to erase the message the watermark carries, obviously this action is simpler), to alter the hidden bits (the attacker tries to modify the hidden bits to insert a proper information for creating a fake document) or to make undetected modifications, in this circumstance the attacker is not interested in making the watermark unreadable or undetectable but he wants to perform some small modifications that are not revealed by the decoder, this is the specific case of digital asset integrity. Sometimes the pirate could want to leak some information to perform a successive unauthorized action against the watermarking system, for instance, trying to understand which are the secret keys.

After having introduced which are the basic rules to be attended to improve security of a watermarking system, it is also proper to point out that a substantial help could come from the integration of watermarking algorithms with cryptography tools, at the protocol level. As compared with watermarking, in fact, cryptography allows to establish the security level of a technique more formally, and many secure tools have been developed and largely used today. Starting from this, some interesting solutions have been recently proposed in the field of Zero-Knowledge Watermarking (ZKW) (Adelsbach, 2002). With the use of such techniques, it is possible to reduce the amount of sensible information that is exchanged among the untrustworthy players (e.g. during a transaction within a DRM system).

Robustness

One of the merits of watermarking technology is to embed directly the informative data in the content without resorting to an attached header, but, on the other side, this can lead to a loss of information each time the host data are undergone to any transformation or processing. *Watermark robustness* refers to the capability of the hidden message to survive possible host signal manipulations. It is important to point out what is intended with the term "host signal manipulations" to better differentiate the case of robustness by that of security, treated in the previous section. Usually manipulations are divided into two categories: *non-malicious* which do not explicitly aim at removing the watermark or at making it unreadable, and *malicious* manipulations, which precisely aims at damaging the hidden information (Barni, 2004).

Roughly speaking we could say that the first class deals with robustness of the watermark, that is the watermark algorithm must tolerate those attacks that can occur during the normal use of the asset.

Their nature and strength is strongly dependent on the application for which the watermarking system is devised; among these we have lossy compression, geometric and temporal manipulations, digital to analogue conversion, extraction of asset fragments (cropping), processing aimed at enhancing asset quality (e.g. noise reduction), etc.

Consequently, we can assess that the second class (malicious) refers to watermark security, that is the watermarking technique must be invulnerable with respect to an attack (e.g. collusion, sensitivity) whose main goal is just to remove or make the watermark unrecoverable. Sometimes, within this category of attacks, there is a further subdivision between *blind* (do not exploit any knowledge on the algorithm) and *informed* (exploit some knowledge on the algorithm). It is quite immediate to understand that the border between robustness and security is not well drawn, in fact it can happen that normal non-malicious transformations such as filtering can be adopted by themselves or together with other security attacks, for malevolent purposes.

Anyway, after this distinction, it is worth trying to propose a qualitative evaluation of the level of required robustness the hidden data must guarantee by referring to four general cases, usually considered in literature, in fact it would not be possible to establish a precise degree of robustness without fixing a specific application in which the watermarking algorithm is called to work. Let us see these four cases:

Secure watermarking: This case encompass copyright protection, ownership verification or other security-oriented applications and the watermark must survive both non-malicious and malicious manipulations. In secure watermarking, the loss of the hidden data should be achievable at the expense of a significant degradation of the quality of the host signal and consequently a depreciation of the digital asset. When considering malicious manipulations it has to be assumed that the attackers know the watermarking algorithm and thereby they can conceive ad-hoc watermark removal strategies. As to non-malicious manipulations, they include a huge variety of digital and analog processing tools, including lossy compression (e.g. JPEG/JPEG-2000), linear and non-linear filtering, cropping, editing, scaling, D/A and A/D conversion, analog duplication, noise addition, and many others that apply only to a particular type of media. Thus, in the image case, we must consider zooming and shrinking, rotation, contrast enhancement, histogram manipulations, row/column removal or exchange; in the case of video we must take into account frame removal, frame exchange, temporal filtering, temporal resampling; finally, robustness of an audio watermark may imply robustness against echo addition, multirate processing, reverb, wow-and-flutter, time and pitch scaling. It is, though, important to point out that even the most secure system does not need to be perfect, on the contrary, it is only needed that a high enough degree of security is reached. In other words, watermark breaking does not need to be impossible (which probably will never be the case), but only difficult enough.

Robust watermarking: In this case it is required that the watermark be resistant only against non-malicious manipulations. Of course, robust watermarking is less demanding than secure watermarking. Application fields of robust watermarking include all the situations in which it is unlikely that someone purposely manipulates the host data with the intention to remove the watermark. At the same time, the application scenario is such that the, so to say, normal use of data comprises several kinds of manipulations which must not damage the hidden data. Even in copyright protection applications, the adoption of robust watermarking instead than secure watermarking may be allowed due to the use of a copyright protection protocol in which all the involved actors are not interested in removing the watermark.

Semi-fragile watermarking: This is the case of applications in which robustness is not a basic requirement, mainly because the host signal is not intended to undergo any manipulations, but a very limited number of minor modifications such as moderate lossy compression, or quality enhancement. This is the case, for example, of data labelling for improved archival retrieval, in which the hidden data is only needed to retrieve the host data from an archive, and thereby it can be discarded once the data has been correctly accessed. It is likely, though, that data is archived in compressed format, and that the watermark is embedded prior to compression. In this case, the watermark needs to be robust against lossy coding. In general, a watermark is considered as semi-fragile if it survives only a limited, well-specified, set of manipulations leaving the quality of the host document virtually intact.

Fragile watermarking: A watermark is said to be fragile, if the information hidden within the host data is lost or irremediably altered as soon as any modification is applied to the host signal. Such a loss of information may be global, i.e. no part of the watermark can be recovered, or local, i.e. only part of the watermark is damaged. The main application of fragile watermarking is data authentication, where watermark loss or alteration is taken as an evidence that data has been tampered with, whereas the recovery of the information contained within the data is used to demonstrate data origin.

Furthermore, after this classification for the diverse degrees of robustness, we can generally say that robustness against signal distortion is better achieved if the watermark is placed in perceptually significant parts of the signal. This is particularly evident if we consider the case of lossy compression algorithms, which operate by discarding perceptually insignificant data not to affect the quality of the compressed image, audio or video. Consequently, watermarks hidden within perceptually insignificant data are likely not to survive compression. Achieving watermark robustness, and, to a major extent, watermark security, is one of the main challenges watermarking researchers are facing with, nevertheless its importance has sometimes been overestimated at the expense of other very important issues such as watermark capacity and protocol-level analysis.

Imperceptibility

As stated in the previous sections one of the main requirements a watermarking system must satisfy is the possibility of making the embedded watermark imperceptible to a human observer. Such a requirement has two main reasons: one concerning a quality point of view, i.e. the watermarked content should not be degraded by the watermark insertion, but on the contrary it should be perceptually identical to the original content; the other reason is from a security point of view, i.e. possible hackers should be prevented from locating if and where the hidden information has been embedded within the original data. Since in most of the cases the end users of the watermarked content are human observers or listeners (e.g. an exception occurs when watermarking is used for remote sensing multispectral images, for which invisibility should be granted with respect to classification tools), the importance of having a good knowledge of the characteristics of the *Human Visual System* (HVS) and *Human Auditory System* (HAS) appears with evidence. In fact, having a clear idea of the mechanisms underlying the perception of visual and auditory stimuli can help in fine tuning the watermark embedding phase for making the embedded signal imperceptible; in particular it is important to know how the user is able to perceive or not perceive certain stimuli. In the following we describe the main principles characterizing the HVS (firstly) and the HAS (secondly) (Barni, 2004).

Even if the *Human Visual System* is certainly one of the most complex biological devices far from being exactly described, each person has daily experience of the main phenomena which influence the ability of the HVS to perceive (or not to perceive) certain stimuli. By observing two copies of the same image, one being a disturbed version of the other, it is readily seen where the noise is more or less visible, thus letting to derive some very general rules:

• Disturbs are less visible in highly textured regions than in uniform areas
• Noise is more easily perceived around edges than in textured areas, but less easily than in flat regions
• The human eye is less sensitive to disturbs in dark and bright regions

In the last decades, several mathematical models have been developed to describe the above basic mechanisms. Basically, a model describing the human visual perception is based on two main concepts: the *contrast sensitivity function* and the *contrast masking model*. The first concept is concerned with the sensitivity of the human eye to a sine grating stimulus; as the sensitivity of the eye depends strongly on display background luminance and spatial frequency of the stimulus (as evidenced by the general rules reported above), these two parameters have to be taken into account in the mathematical description of human sensitivity. The second concept considers the effect of one stimulus on the detectability of another, where the stimuli can be coincident (*iso-frequency masking*), or non coincident (*non iso-frequency masking*) in frequency and orientation; specifically the masking effect indicates the visibility reduction of one image component due to the presence of other components. A mathematical model which considers all the recalled phenomena should result in an equation that provides the minimum level of contrast (i.e. the *Just Noticeable Contrast - JNC*) necessary to just detect a sine wave of a given frequency and orientation superimposed to another stimulus (the masking one) at a given frequency and orientation.

Regarding the *Human Audio System*, it is still possible to give a mathematical formula that indicates the minimum level sound (i.e. the *Sound Pressure Level - SPL*) necessary to a young listener with acute hearing to perceive, in a quiet environment, a pure tone stimulus at a given frequency. In addition it has to be taken into account the *masking effect*, that is the phenomenon by which a sound stimulus is not perceived by the HAS if it is near in frequency to another higher level stimulus. Such a masking effect depends on the characteristics of the two considered sound stimuli: specifically, if the stimulus is a pure tone or a narrow band stimulus (also called noise sound). It is convenient to distinguish three cases: 1) a noise sound masking a pure tone sound; 2) a pure tone sound masking a noise sound; 3) a noise sound masking a noise sound. The first case is the more effective one and the pure tone is easily masked by the noise sound (we suppose that the pure tone signal has frequency equal to the central frequency of the band of the noise sound): if the masking signal has a SPL around 5 *dB* higher than the SPL of the pure tone, it completely masks the pure tone. In the other two cases, the SPL of the masking signal must exceed the SPL of the stimulus to be masked more than 20 dB. Of course, when the frequencies of the two considered sound stimuli do not correspond, the detection threshold is reduced, proportionally to the distance between the frequencies.

After the analysis of the models of human perception, let us see how such concepts can be exploited for better hiding information into host content. Basically, we distinguish two different approaches for considering HVS/HAS characteristics during the data embedding process. The former approach considers the selection of appropriate features that are most suitable to be modified, without dramatically affecting perceptual content quality; in other words, the idea is to locate which features can better mask the embedded data. By following the second approach, the inserted data, embedded into the host content without a particular care for the selection of the most suitable features, are adapted to the local content for better reducing their perceptibility.

Let us first consider the concealment process through *feature selection*. In this case a set of features belonging to the host content has to be properly selected for the watermark embedding. But there is the binding requirement that, for a correct recovery of the watermark, the same set of features are identified for the detection/decoding phase, thus imposing an a-priori fixed choice. To be more explicit, let us make an example concerning the choice of the features in the *host content domain*. By taking into account that disturbs are less visible in highly textured regions than in uniform areas, one can choose to watermark those blocks of the content that have a large degree of texture: a simple function can measure the variance of the block and based on this value classifies it as suitable or not suitable for embedding. During the recovery phase, any processing applied to the watermarked content, could modify the classification produced by the same function, thus making the selection of the blocks really unpredictable.

The situation is different in the case of the *transformed domain* techniques. In general we have in fact seen that both the HVS and the HAS are less sensitive to disturb having high or very low frequencies; it is then common to partition the frequency range into two regions, one of which used for the embedding step. Since this partition is fixed, and not estimated time by time during the embedding phase, the problem outlined for the host content domain case does not raise now. In particular, the choice of the frequency range to be watermarked is a compromise between the imperceptibility and the robustness requirement, since the high frequencies will be the first to disappear due to many common attacks such as compression, low-pass filtering, etc..

Similar considerations are valid for the *hybrid techniques*. In particular the situation for block-based transforms is identical as for the transform domain case, high frequency coefficient are usually preferred for watermark embedding, in order to reduce watermark perceptibility. The same objective can be reached in the DWT (Discrete Wavelet Transform) case by performing embedding in the finest sub-bands.

We can conclude that perceptual data hiding through feature selection is not very easy to be performed. In particular, if it is desired that watermark recovery has to be achieved also after possible attacks, that can make the selected features no longer available or identifiable, the sole possibility is to select the features on a fixed basis. This choice, nevertheless, implies that the embedded data are not always inserted into the most suitable image features.

The other possibility for perceptual watermarking is to perform concealment through *signal adaptation*: in the following we briefly describe two possible approaches for adapting the watermark signal to the local host content.

In the first case we make use of *perceptual masks* giving a measure of the insensitivity to disturbs for each sample of the host content. Let us suppose to have a copy of the content C_w watermarked without taking care about perceptibility issues (e.g. uniformly) and the original host content C. If the perceptual mask M taking values in $[0,1]$ has the same dimensions of the content, we can obtained a perceptual watermarked content C'_w by mixing C and C_w through M:

$$C'_w = \bar{M} \otimes C + M \otimes C_w,$$

where $\otimes$ is the sample by sample product, and $\bar{M}$ is the masking function whose elements are the complement to 1 of the elements of M. Let us note that such an approach is valid apart from the domain where watermark embedding has been performed and the embedding rule. An example of a watermarking system based on signal adaptation through perceptual masks is given in the following when the scheme proposed by Piva et al. is described (Piva, 1999).

Following the second approach for concealment through *signal adaptation*, we make use of a criterion establishing the maximum amount of modification that can be sustained by the host data: this can be defined both in the host content domain (independently on the features used for embedding) or directly in the embedding features domain. It is defined an imperceptibility region around the host data: if watermark embedding brings the host data outside this region, hence the applied modifications will be perceptible, otherwise no. When the imperceptibility region is not defined in the same domain where embedding is performed, it is possible to use optimization techniques for tuning the strength of the watermark signal in the embedding domain in such a way to satisfy the imperceptibility constraint in the domain where this is defined. An example of this approach has been described by Pereira et al. (Pereira, 2001), where the perceptibility constraint is defined in the spatial domain, while the embedding is performed in the block DCT domain. In the case in which the imperceptibility constraint is given in the same domain where the embedding is performed, the simplest imperceptibility region is defined component wise, i.e. a maximum possible modification is given for each component of the host feature set. As an example, for an image watermarking scheme working in the hybrid block DCT domain, for each frequency coefficient of the block a perceptual threshold imposing a limit on the watermarked coefficients is fixed by referring to the default quantization matrices defined in the compression algorithm (e.g. JPEG). A more refined model defining the imperceptibility threshold for each frequency coefficient in the DCT blocks, has been proposed by Watson and takes into account the iso-frequency masking effect (Watson, 1993).

DATA EMBEDDING

The idea of watermark embedding can be expressed by referring to the communication theory. In fact, the information embedded within the digital content (the watermark) can be seen as the message that has to be transmitted over the channel (the host content). In order to provide an appropriate system which results resistant to natural interference or jamming and secure against unauthorized detection, in the second half of 90's, the Spread Spectrum (SS) techniques have been borrowed for communication literature and applied for proposing a new class of watermarking algorithms: the Spread Spectrum watermarking. In the late nineties, in the watermarking area a new idea, based on the work of Costa (Costa, 1983) was introduced, namely the side-informed watermarking, where the host content does not behave as disturbing noise, so that an improvement with respect to Spread Spectrum watermarking algorithms is achieved. In the following subsections the two paradigms are analyzed.

Spread-Spectrum Watermarking

Spread Spectrum techniques are methods by which energy generated at one or more discrete frequencies is deliberately spread or distributed in time or frequency domains. In particular, these techniques employ pseudorandom number sequences (noise signals) to determine and control the spreading pattern of the signal across the allotted bandwidth. The noise signal can be used to exactly reconstruct the original data at the receiving end, by multiplying it by the same pseudorandom sequence: this process, known

Figure 3. The watermark encoding and casting scheme for a Spread Spectrum watermarking system

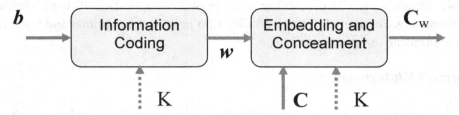

as "de-spreading", mathematically constitutes a correlation of the transmitted pseudorandom number sequence with the receiver's assumed sequence.

The application of SS techniques to digital watermarking is illustrated in Figure 3: the information sequence *b* (watermark code of length k) is spread spectrum modulated into a signal *w* (watermark signal of length $n \gg k$) before embedding such information within the host content **C**. Usually $w = (w_1, w_2, ..., w_n)$ is a pseudorandom noise and its components are random variables drawn from a given probability density function.

The embedding function could be a simple weighted addition:

$$f_{wi} = f_i + \gamma \, w_i,$$

or a multiplicative rule:

$$f_{wi} = f_i + \gamma \, w_i f_i$$
$$f_{wi} = f_i + \gamma \, w_i |f_i|$$

where f_i are the features $f = (f_1, f_2, ..., f_n)$ extracted by the host content, $f_w = (f_{w1}, f_{w2}, ..., f_{wn})$ are the watermarked features, and γ is a scaling factor controlling the watermark strength. The watermark energy can be locally adapted to the host content by exploiting its perceptual characteristics (the concealment step), as it has been described in the previous section concerning the imperceptibility requirement. The second equation referring to the multiplicative embedding lets the watermark to be dependent only on the magnitude of the host features rather than on their sign values.

Depending on the data recovery phase, i.e. if the system is detectable or readable, the information sequence *b* is spread spectrum modulated for producing the watermark signal *w*. In a detectable watermarking system, each message *b* is transformed into a pseudorandom sequence *w* (e.g. *b* can be the seed for the pseudorandom noise generation), whose presence is verified at the receiver side (e.g. through a correlation between *w* and the received features). In a readable watermarking system, a spread spectrum watermarking signal *w* is amplitude modulated by the antipodal version of the bit string *b* (i.e. $b_i = 0 \rightarrow -1$; $b_i = 1 \rightarrow +1$). In particular *w* is split into k random non-overlapping subsets and then each of the k bits modulates the samples of each different subset. At the receiver side the bit sequence *b* is recovered from the watermarked content. A secret key K can be used, if necessary, either in the encoding or casting step.

An example of an additive spread spectrum watermarking scheme has been developed by Kalker et al. (Kalker, 1999) for DVD protection. An important example of a multiplicative and detectable spread spectrum watermarking system is the work of Cox et al. (Cox, 1997), which has strongly influenced subsequent watermarking research. Another example of a multiplicative SS watermarking algorithm has been presented by Barni et al. (Barni, 2003b), who proposed an optimal and blind decoding and detection of multiplicative watermarks.

Side-Informed Watermarking

By referring to Figure 3, we can note that during the coding phase the knowledge of the original host content C, that must be treated as disturbing noise at the detector/decoder side, is not exploited. Additionally, also in the embedding step the knowledge of the host features is not taken into account and the watermark insertion is a mixing function of the watermark w and the feature set f: in such a case we refer to blind embedding. On the contrary, the host features are known by the encoder and can be exploited for increasing the reliability of the transmission. The watermark channel shown in Figure 4 refers to a communication system with side information at the transmitter: specifically, the information regarding the host content C can be both exploited in the embedding phase, thus referring to watermarking with *informed embedding*, and in the coding phase, thus referring to watermarking with *informed coding*.

The idea of informed coding is to achieve, from a given watermark code b, different watermark signals for different host contents; in other words, starting from a given message b, we select between several alternative code vectors (a set of watermark signals) by choosing the one that best fits the host feature set. Such an idea refers to the so called dirty-paper codes, based on the work of Costa (Costa, 1983) that studied the case of writing on a dirty piece of paper. Costa considered a particular channel with two noise sources that are additive, white and Gaussian; the first noise source represents the dirt on the paper where the message has to be written and Costa showed that if the transmitter uses the knowledge of the first AWGN noise source for producing the message to be transmitted over the channel affected by the second unknown AWGN noise source, hence the first noise source has no effect on the channel capacity. In the watermarking case the first noise source, i.e. the dirty paper, is the host content, whereas the to be transmitted message is the watermark signal; the second noise source represents distortions that may occur for normal processing or malicious tampering. Even if the channel studied by Costa is rather different from a true watermarking channel (the hypothesis of noise sources that are AWGN is not realistic), such a result implies that the design of a watermarking system can greatly benefit from the application of side information during the watermark coding phase.

Figure 4. The watermark encoding and casting scheme for a Side-Informed watermarking system: if the host content is exploited in the coding/embedding step we respectively refer to informed coding/informed embedding

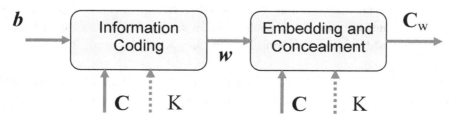

Figure 5. Informed embedding: example of the adaptation of watermark signal (w_1 and w_2 versus w) to the host contents (C_1 and C_2 respectively) following the informed embedding paradigm

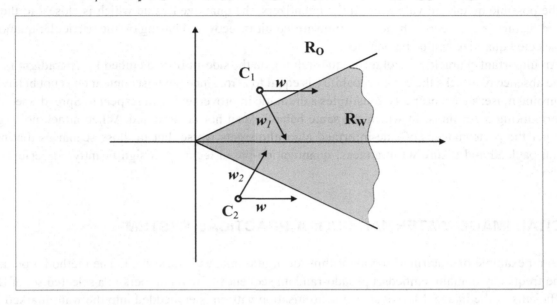

Regarding the informed embedding, a simplified example of exploiting the knowledge of **C** during the embedding procedure, is to adapt the watermark energy depending on the perceptual characteristics of the features $f = (f_1, f_2, \ldots, f_n)$ extracted by the host content, that is the watermark $w = (w_1, w_2, \ldots, w_n)$ is locally amplified or attenuated depending on f before it is mixed with the host feature set. More generally, following the informed embedding paradigm, the watermark is properly chosen based on the host content. For example, let us consider Figure 5: we can see the space of the host content as divided into two regions: the region of the original contents ($\mathbf{R_O}$) and the region of the watermarked contents ($\mathbf{R_W}$), also called the detection or decoding region (if a detectable or readable watermarking system is considered respectively): the watermark embedding procedure so consists in moving an original content toward the region $\mathbf{R_W}$ (in grey in Figure RR). If we adopt a simple additive embedding function, the watermarked content is achieved as the sum of the original content and the watermark. In the case of blind embedding, the same watermark is added to any given content (e.g. C_1 and C_2 in Figure 5), whereas in the case of informed embedding the most suitable watermark is chosen for each content (e.g. w_1 and w_2 in Figure 5 are selected in order to move the original content deeper inside the watermarked region, even if the energy of the watermark signals is constant).

If the informed coding is considered together with the informed embedding, for the same watermark message b a set of possible watermark signals is considered and consequently a set of detection/decoding sub-regions forms the region $\mathbf{R_W}$. In such a case, the informed coding lets the selection of the most suitable watermarked sub-region in which the particular original content has to be mapped; while the informed embedding lets deciding how to move the host content within the selected sub-region.

Examples of watermarking algorithms that simultaneously apply the informed coding and embedding belong to the class of Quantization Index Modulation (QIM) methods (Chen, 2001): here watermarking is achieved by quantizing the host features according to a set of predefined quantizers: the specific quantizer (within the set) is chosen basing on the message to be transmitted, and the specific quantized value to give to the host feature is selected to be closest to the feature itself. At the decoder side, among all the possible quantized values of all the quantizers, the quantized value which is closest to the received feature is considered; hence, the transmitted bit is recovered basing on the particular quantizer the selected quantized value belongs to.

An important characteristic of techniques relying on the side-informed embedding paradigm is that in the absence of attacks the error probability is equal to zero, since the host content does not behave as disturbing noise; such a property constitutes a dramatic improvement with respect to Spread Spectrum watermarking algorithms, in which the same behavior can not be assumed. When attack noise gets stronger the performances of side-informed algorithms gets worse, but in those scenarios that need a high payload and assure weak attacks, quantization-based techniques significantly outperform SS methods.

DIGITAL IMAGE WATERMARKING: A PRACTICAL SYSTEM

Here, an example of watermarking algorithm for digital images is described. The method, operating in the frequency domain, embeds a pseudo-random sequence of real numbers in a selected set of DFT coefficients of the image. Moreover, a synchronisation pattern is embedded into the watermarked image, to cope with geometrical attacks, like resizing and rotation. After embedding, the watermark is adapted to the image by exploiting the masking characteristics of the HVS, thus ensuring the watermark invisibility. An optimum blind decoder based on statistical decision theory allows a robust watermark detection (Piva, 1999; Barni, 2001).

Watermark Embedding

The watermark embedding process, sketched in Figure 6, can be decomposed in three steps, as described in the previous watermarking model.

Figure 6. The watermark embedding process of the described watermark algorithm

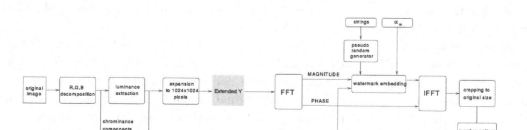

In *information coding*, a seed S, a sequence of four integers, is obtained by properly coding two strings, a character string, maximum 16 characters long, and a number string, maximum 8 digits long. This seed is used to generate a pseudo-random sequence of real number with period 2^{121}, and uniform distribution in the interval [0,1]. The sequence is then scaled and translated in [-1,1], in order to obtain a null mean.

In *data embedding*, from the original color image **C**, the luminance, where the watermark will be embedded, is extracted. The luminance in thus extended to a fixed size of 1024x1024 pixels. This step allows the system to be robust against cropping (Piva, 1998). Next, the FFT is applied to the extended luminance **Y**: two 1024x1024 matrices are obtained, representing the magnitude and the phase of the DFT coefficients. Watermark casting interests the magnitude only, so that robustness against image translations is automatically achieved. In order to build a blind system, which do not require the original image in detection, the position and the number of coefficients to be modified is fixed a priori. In particular, 66.384 elements belonging to the medium range of the spectrum are chosen, in order to achieve a compromise between robustness and invisibility. The watermark embedding rule is the following:

$$f_{wi} = f_i + \gamma\, w_i f_i$$

where f_{wi} represents the watermarked DFT magnitude coefficient, f_i the corresponding original, w_i is a sample of the watermark sequence, and γ is the watermark energy. The modified DFT matrix is inverted, and the image is cropped to the original size, obtaining a watermarked luminance **Y'**.

The system described so far is robust against translation and cropping, but it is weak against resizing or rotation. In fact, these attacks modify the DFT spectrum in such a way that we are no more able to find the watermarked coefficients. To cope with such attacks, we need to find the original size and position of the image, without the use of the original image. To do so, we add pixel by pixel a periodic reference pattern to the watermarked luminance:

$$f(x,y) = A rect\left(\frac{1}{T}x\right) rect\left(\frac{1}{T}y\right)$$

In the frequency domain, four peaks, with position depending on T, are correspondingly added to the spectrum of the watermarked luminance. The T value has to be chosen such that the frequency pulses are far from the DC component (so that the peaks can be distinguished from the image spectrum), and are not in the high frequency region (so that the peaks are not removed if low pass filtering is applied): a good compromise has been found by fixing T between 4 and 8 pixels.

When the watermarked and synchronised image is processed by means of a rotation or a resizing, a spectrum analysis will allow to reveal these peaks. Depending on their new position, the estimation of the geometric attack the image has undergone will be obtained, allowing to reverse the attacks.

The *watermark concealment* procedure applies a spatial visual masking process, based on a masking image **M** giving a measure of the insensitivity to noise of the original image pixel by pixel. The mask **M** is a grey level image having the same size of the original image, appearing brighter in the regions where the human eye is more sensitive to noise, and darker where the watermark can be embedded with an higher energy without a visual quality degradation. It is obtained by processing the original luminance according to many possible approaches (Bartolini, 1998). Thus, given the original luminance

Y, the watermarked luminance **Y'** and the mask **M**, another watermarked luminance $\mathbf{Y_M}$ is constructed by means of the masking process, realised in the spatial domain pixel by pixel:

$$\mathbf{Y_M} = \mathbf{MY} + (1 - \mathbf{M})\mathbf{Y}'$$

It is worth noting that where $\mathbf{M} = 0$ (that is in the darker regions of the mask), the watermark energy is higher and $\mathbf{Y_M} = \mathbf{Y}'$; whereas where $\mathbf{M} = 1$ (that is in the brighter regions), the watermark energy is null and $\mathbf{Y_M} = \mathbf{Y}$. Finally, to obtain the watermarked colour image, the watermarked luminance $\mathbf{Y_M}$ is combined to the original colour components, obtaining the watermarked RGB bands.

Watermark Detection

In watermark detection step, the system is asked to decide if a given mark, provided by the user, is present into an image or not (*detectable* technique), without resorting to the original image.

The decoder can decide the presence or the absence of a mark by comparing a decoding function against a predefined threshold. With regard to error detection probability, the decoder is optimum according to the Neyman-Pearson decision criterion: fixed a maximum value for the false alarm detection probability (in our case equal to 10^{-6}), the decoder minimises the missing watermark detection probability. In the following, the main steps of the detection process, shown in Figure 7, are described.

Given a watermarked color image, the luminance $\mathbf{Y_w}$, where the watermark will be looked for, is extracted and then extended by means of zero padding to the reference size of 1024x1024 pixels. To this image, the FFT is applied. This step is required for the synchronisation pattern detection. After synchronisation, a new expansion and a new FFT computation will be required, in order to carry out the watermark detection process.

The FFT of the watermarked luminance is analysed in order to extract the peaks corresponding to the synchronisation pattern. Their position will reveal if on the image a resizing or a rotation has been carried out, and, in this case, also the extent of these modifications. This is possible since a rotation or a resizing of the image corresponds to an equal rotation or resizing of its FFT magnitude.

Let us note with *PR* the reference pattern, that is the synchronisation signal introduced in watermark casting, and with *PS* the synchronisation pattern, that is the distorted synchronisation signal extracted in this step; the comparison between the two signals allows to find the transformation T_E linking the two patterns: $T_E \{PR\} = PS$

Figure 7. The watermark detection process of the described watermark algorithm

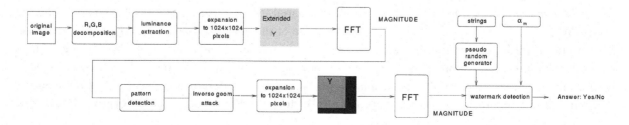

It is possible to demonstrate that a generic geometric transformation can be represented by means of an equivalent transformation, consisting of a rotation by an angle α, a resizing with scaling factors Δ_X (in the horizontal axis) and Δ_Y (in the vertical axis), and a new rotation by an angle β. Thus, T_E can be represented as the product of the matrices corresponding to each of the three simple geometric operations (Piva, 1999):

$$T_E = \begin{pmatrix} \cos \beta & -\operatorname{sen} \beta \\ \operatorname{sen} \beta & \cos \beta \end{pmatrix} \begin{pmatrix} \Delta_x^{-1} & 0 \\ 0 & \Delta_y^{-1} \end{pmatrix} \begin{pmatrix} \cos \alpha & -\operatorname{sen} \alpha \\ \operatorname{sen} \alpha & \cos \alpha \end{pmatrix}$$

Next step is given by the application of the inverse geometrical transformations to the watermarked luminance in order to obtain an image without geometrical attacks, where the watermark can be looked or.

The new watermarked luminance obtained after the synchronisation process is extended by means of zero padding, in order to obtain an image having a reference size of 1024x1024 pixels. To this image, the FFT is applied in order to carry out the watermark detection process.

The problem of watermark detection is the following: given a possibly watermarked image luminance Y_w, we want to know if a watermark w^* is present in Y_w or not. Since the position of the watermarked FFT coefficients is known, these coefficients can be selected obtaining a vector of elements. Thus, the input parameters are:

- The vector $f_w = (f_{w1}, f_{w2}, ..., f_{wn})$ of the watermarked FFT coefficient's amplitudes
- The watermark sequence $w^* = (w^*_1, w^*_2, ..., w^*_n)$ generated using as seed the two strings we are looking for
- The mean watermark energy used in watermark embedding, considered as a fixed parameter

An optimum criterion to verify if a given code is present in an image is derived based on statistical decision theory (Barni, 2001). Two hypotheses are defined: the image contains the watermark we are looking for (hypotheses H1) or the image does not contain this mark (hypotheses H0). Relying on Bayes theory of hypothesis testing, the optimum criterion to test H1 versus H0 is minimum Bayes risk; the test function results to be the likelihood ratio function L that has to be compared to a threshold λ:

- If $L > \lambda$, the system decides the watermark w^* is present
- If $L < \lambda$, the system decides the watermark w^* is absent

To choose a proper threshold λ, a constraint on the maximum false positive probability is fixed and the Neyman-Pearson criterion (Barni, 2001) is adopted to design the optimum decoder.

As a matter of fact, the function $L(y)$ depends on the knowledge of the probability density function of the watermarked features so that a procedure to estimate a posteriori the pdf of the DFT coefficients has been derived. By relying on the analysis carried out on a large set of images, it has been derived that the magnitude of a generic DFT coefficient follows a *Weibull* distribution. The estimation of the parameters of the Weibull distribution is done on the watermarked image, by means of the Maximum Likelihood criterion. At this aim, it is supposed that the DFT coefficients of the watermarked image belonging to small sub-regions of the spectrum are characterised by the same statistic parameters. The region of the DFT spectrum, where the watermark is embedded, is divided into 16 sub-regions: in each of the 16 groups of coefficients, the parameters characterising the Weibull function are estimated. See (Barni, 2001) for more details.

In summary, the detection process can be decomposed in the following steps:

- Generation of the watermark w^*
- Estimation of the Weibull parameters into the 16 regions composing the watermarked area of the spectrum
- Computation of $L(y)$ and λ
- Comparison between $L(y)$ and λ
- Decision

The decoder can detect the watermark presence also in highly degraded images. In particular, the system is robust to sequences of different attacks, such as rotation, resizing, and JPEG compression, or such as cropping, resizing and median filtering.

WATERMARKING BASED DRM

The problem of digital content piracy is one of the major problem to be solved in the world of ICT and technical instruments are to be provided to avoid that major content producers risk seeing their business being drastically reduced because of the ease by which digital contents can be copied and redistributed for instance in P2P infrastructures. This is the reason why digital rights management systems (DRMS) (Kundur, 2004) have been indicated, in the last years, like a possible answer to such a claim and much attention both from industry and from research has been dedicated to these systems.

Among the various technologies that can contribute to set up a reliable DRM system, digital watermarking has gathered much approval, basically thanks to its potentiality of persistently attaching some additional information to the content itself. Many potential applications such as ownership proofing, copy control, user tracking and so on, could be implemented by resorting to a DRMS based on data hiding techniques. DRM technology could benefit from digital watermarking in several ways, as it is evident by the variety of watermarking- based systems addressing DRM problems proposed in the literature.

Trying to give a general definition of what a DRM system is seems to be quite arduous, anyway a *DRMS can be considered as an ensemble of services, connected through a network environment, cooperating together, to allow the protection of the IPR of multimedia data, on the basis of terms and conditions agreed among the involved parties, and to control their delivery and usage.*

DRM can make possible for commercial publishers to distribute valuable content electronically, without destroying the copyright holder's revenue stream. DRM can also be used in other settings to enable safe distribution of digital content including, for example, document management within and between corporations, protected email, medical patient records handling, and government service access. At a minimum, a well-designed DRM system should provide:

- **Governance:** DRM is different from classical security and protection technologies. Conventional media distribution systems based on conditional access techniques protect media during transmission using a control model based on direct cryptographic key exchange. DRM systems, on the other hand, implement control, or governance, via the use of programming language methods executed in a secure environment.

- **Secure association of usage rules with information:** DRM systems securely associate rules with content. These rules determine usage of the content throughout its lifecycle. Rules can be attached to content, embedded within content (e.g., via watermarking), or rules can be delivered independently of content.

- **Persistent protection:** DRM systems are designed to protect and govern information on a persistent basis throughout the content's commercial lifecycle. Protection is frequently provided using cryptographic techniques. Encrypted content is protected even as it travels outside of protected distribution channels.

According to the previous classification and to better highlight the different composing parts, a complete technological scheme which incorporates all possible means for rights management and protection can be treated as composed by two separated functional units:

- **Digital Property Management (DPM):** That is a system concerned with the management of intellectual property related to the contents. As described in the following, DRMS should include a set of services and solutions:
  o Identification Systems;
  o Metadata for IPR management;
  o Rights management programming languages;
  o Data Format definitions;
  o Delivery methods and technologies.

- **Technical Protection Means (TPMs) or Digital Rights Enforcement (DRE):** That is a set of technologies to secure and protect multimedia contents from an unauthorized use, and to enforce usage policies so that the content is used only for the terms and the conditions agreed during purchase. TPMs can include:
  o Security and integrity of OS and computer networks
  o Encryption of transferred data
  o *Watermarking of multimedia content*
  o Tracking the use of the protected content

These TPMs are called to work together within a DRM infrastructure and their action is usually complementary. In fact, for example, once the DRM system has identified the intellectual property of a given data, and has set the rules for its usage, it is necessary to grant that such rules are enforced, through a so called *persistent* content protection, that is the content protection has to stay with the content itself along all its life, from delivery to the users enjoyment. A digital content can be transferred securely to an user through Internet by means of cryptographic algorithms. However, cryptography systems do not solve the problem of unauthorised copying. Once an authorised user decrypts the work, there is no more control on his/her possible illegal actions: for example, the recipient could save and copy the content in an unprotected format and redistribute the digital copy to many other users without reduction in quality. Therefore, the protection problem in DRM systems goes beyond simply granting the access to the content only to authorised users, but concerns also the support of restrictions of the content usage rights also after the digital asset is delivered to the end user. All these problems are faced by the Technical Protection Means.

It is important to note that the security model where TPMs have to work is different from the common cryptographic model where there are two trusted parties trying to exchange a message in a way that an attacker sitting in between is unable to recover the information. In this case, it is not possible to separate honest and dishonest users. A malicious user (cracker), once the protected content is delivered to his/her device, may try to break the security system with unlimited time and resource. Since Internet is an open distribution channel, the attacker can publish his breaking tool on Internet, so that anyone can download it and crack the protection scheme.

In the light of these considerations, it is easy to understand that techniques such as *digital watermarking* can be particularly appreciated due to fact that they provide the chance to attach a code to a multimedia document in such a way that the code is persistent with respect to the possible changes of format the document may undergo. The digital insertion of marks to individualize, trace, and control usage of a digital copy, even when it is transformed into analog signals, will be one of the pillars of future DRM systems. To fully exploit the potentiality of this peculiar characteristic, the concept of persistent association has been developed during the past few years. The basic idea is to associate a unique identifier (UI) to each multimedia creation. The UI is embedded inside the document itself by means of a watermarking primitive and is used for indexing a database where more detailed information (not only related to IPR) can be retrieved (see Figure 8).

The use of watermarking for tightly attaching a UI to a document has been widely proposed in diverse occasions such as the Content ID Forum Specification (cIDf, 2002), in the framework of the MPEG-21 standardization process (MPEG-21, 2002), and so on. Watermarking has been indicated as a basic tool to permit the implementation of several application scenarios mainly related to image/video distribution. On of these ones it is surely the digital cinema distribution in which the content exhibited in a theatre room is rescanned by a camera during the exhibition.. In this circumstance, watermarking allows to trace the room identification and time of a projection, In this kind of scenario, the retrieval of the parameters of an unauthorized copy can be helped by using the original version of the content.

Figure 8. The persistent association of an UI to each multimedia document, a player can request the licensing information from an IPR database and, as a consequence, apply the corresponding copyright policy to the document

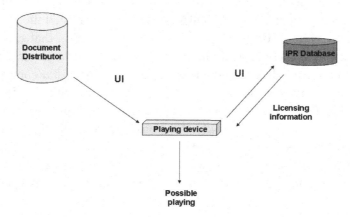

Another one it could be the broadcast scenario, in which a specific content is broadcasted to set-top decoders; watermarking has to allow to trace the content and to control the copy. Another possible application might be the publication over the Internet of digital images/videos.

Each scenario has specific requirements regarding the watermarking technology to be deployed. First of all, the watermark should be able to survive the types of transformations typically encountered in the life of a document, including conversions to and from the analogue domain (i.e., the watermark should be robust). It is also required that the association created by means of watermarking is secure (i.e., it should resist transformations deliberately performed for removing it). Authorized users should be able to remove or at least change the status of the watermark, but when this is done without authorization, it should be possible to obtain sufficient evidence of the former presence of a watermark to be used in forensic examinations. A DRM protocol based on the persistent identification of the multimedia document to be enjoyed should work by querying an IPR database with the UI extracted from the document and by analyzing the returned licensing rules (MPEG-21 has been also investigating the standardization of languages for the description of the rights associated with a multimedia document (MPEG-REL, 2003)) to decide if and how the document can be used. Such an approach allows a much higher flexibility than the simple protocols of ownership verification, copy control, or infringement tracking that we have seen above. The cost of this is a major complexity of the verification process that requires a trusted archive to be queried.

Finally, it is worth mentioning that the concept of persistent association, as approached by MPEG-21, can also have a wider scope: it is, in fact, foreseen that the persistent association could regard not only an UI but also transactions identifiers (thus implementing a generalized fingerprinting service), users, and temporal information (i.e., a time stamp).

Anyway, as we have previously seen, data hiding techniques can endure many types of attacks, and up to today no technique has exhibited enough resilience against all of them. These considerations urged researchers to find novel approaches to the problem of DRM, and there have been some proposals in which watermarking can still be helpful. The main assumption is that it is (at least today) almost impossible to design a secure watermarking technique, but it is really feasible to get a robust one. The main approach thus consists of trying to motivate users neither to attempt to remove the watermark nor to distribute the legally acquired and watermarked document for free. This could be obtained by assigning the function of enhancing the host data content to the watermark (Kalker, 1999): as an example, the watermark could give access to discounts on other documents or to update services to a more sophisticated version of the document or to other added-value services (trials on other products, bonus programs, etc.). In this way, the users would not be motivated to remove the watermark as this would deprive them of the associated advantages; they are not motivated to distribute the watermarked document as well since this would mean giving that advantages to others. Similarly, users would be not motivated to illegally acquire non-watermarked documents as this would not offer them the enhanced values associated with the watermark. This approach mainly requires that the watermark is resistant to the copy attack to avoid dishonest users transferring the advantages associated with a given document to another. Furthermore, the integration with effective cryptography protocols is required in order to avoid misuses. The use of a watermark associated with the added-value information, instead of the simpler format-header based approaches, is still motivated by the characteristic of persistence of the watermark. Indeed, this approach does not appear to be very effective: it would be really successful only if the added value services associated with the watermark were really of high value. On the contrary, what is of most interest for the widest part of the users is the document itself and not the possibly associated added values.

DRM in the Bricks Project: An Example

The European project BRICKS (Building Resources for Integrated Cultural Knowledge Services) (Bricks Project, 2007) has researched and implemented advanced open source software solutions for the sharing and the exploitation of digital cultural resources and can be an example of how transactions of digital items could be managed. The BRICKS Community is a worldwide federation of cultural heritage institutions, research organizations, technological providers, and other players in the field of digital libraries services. The BRICKS Cultural Heritage Network provides access to and fosters, through its architecture based on the B-Nodes, the European digital memory. In each B-Node a DRM module is implemented to deal with security issues. The role of the DRM module inside the BRICKS Security Architecture is basically that of defining and enforcing digital rights on content and services. The direct integration of a DRM component into the Security Architecture brings this functionality directly into the core of the BRICKS framework, ready to be leveraged by all the other services. In order to provide IPR protection, the following functionality is required.

Digital rights definition: The DRM Layer uses the MPEG 21 Rights Expression Language (REL) to define rights and conditions associated with the use and protection of digital content and services. The REL is defined as an XML based grammar. Its main functionality is to define rights, in term of which parties are allowed to use a resource, which rights they have and the terms and conditions that have to be fulfilled in order to be able to use those rights. MPEG-REL model provides the ability to map existing licenses such as Creative Commons, ROMEO, JORUM+, etc.

Digital rights enforcement: There is obviously no utility to define rights if they aren't enforced in any way. The DRM Layer cooperates with the Security Management Layer to block every user operation that can violate rights defined using the DRM tools.

Digital rights protection: Once outside the BRICKS environment, the digital content must still be protected and its usage be traced. This kind of protection is implemented into the DRM module as a Watermarking and Data Encryption Service, that provides among other means to embed a reference to the license acquired to obtain a content and the ability to check if a content (an image in particular) has been downloaded from the BRICKS environment.

FUTURE TRENDS

In the next future, DRM systems will probably continue to evolve in order to provide infrastructures for media distribution which can grant a higher level of interoperability and security, having to deal with heterogeneous consumer devices, media formats, communication protocols and security mechanisms. This effort, which also regards watermarking technologies, is mainly a technical effort and this is not enough to overcome the existing hurdles to achieve an interoperable and secure architecture for multimedia services. A standardization process could help, but, as well-known, standards are rarely applied on a world-wide basis.

It is worth pointing out that given the social nature of DRMS, technologists must take into account the involved sensitive legal aspects to be able to design broadly accepted technologies.

So it is clear that DRM is a field of growing activity in which innovation interacts with emerging business models, legal policy and social norms. Due to this is easy to understand that an integrated action which involves technical aspects, legal issues, business policies and standards could lead to a feasible solution or, at least, to widely accepted models.

Strictly speaking from the point of view of watermarking technologies, it can be seen that scientific community has been researching, in the last years, much more in the field of security; in fact the requirement that a watermarking algorithm has to operate in a hostile environment (e.g. a component of a DRM system) in which a possible hacker might try to crack the process has become the new frontier for watermarkers. Open contests such as BOWS (Break Our Watermarking System) (BOWS, 2006) and BOWS-2 (BOWS-2, 2007) that has been launched on the internet go in this direction. In each of these contests some images marked with an unknown watermarking algorithm have to be "unmarked" trying to maintain the better final perceptual quality; the participants could obviously use any approach they preferred to achieve the aim: exactly what happens when a DRM system, based on watermarking, is working in un-trusted scenario. Such a new trend in watermarking techniques design will probably better satisfy most of the needs that business models and media providers had in the past and surely still have nowadays, but that state-of-the-art solutions could not definitely match.

CONCLUSION

The conversion from analogue media to digital media has doubtless led to a large amount of benefits: in order to capitalize the digital content distribution and fruition, all the actors involved in such a digital chain must be assured in their own rights, e.g. the owner of a digital content wants to receive proceeds for selling it, whereas the buyer wants to make use, without restriction, of the content he bought. In the last years, Digital Rights Management Systems (DRMS) have been indicated as a possible solution for the promotion and the large diffusion of digital media distribution environments. A DRM system can be considered as an ensemble of services, connected through a network environment, co-operating together, to allow the protection of the IPR of multimedia data, on the basis of terms and conditions agreed among the involved parties, and to control their delivery and usage. Several technologies, usually complementary, are requested to work together for achieving a reliable DRM system; among them, digital watermarking has gathered much approval, basically thanks to its potentiality of persistently attaching some additional information to the content itself. DRM technology could benefit from digital watermarking in several ways, due to the different functionalities a watermarking system can realize such as ownership proofing, copy control, user tracking and so on, that can be exploited in a DRM chain.

By starting from such considerations, this chapter has been mainly devoted to the presentation and discussion of digital watermarking technology, letting the last part of the chapter to the analysis of DRMS based on watermarking techniques. Basing on the particular purpose the watermarking technology serves, different requirements must be satisfied: during the chapter the fundamental requirements have been discussed, with particular reference to security, robustness and imperceptibility issues. Furthermore, the two main approach for watermark embedding (namely the Spread-Spectrum and the Side-Informed) has been presented and analysed. An image watermarking system, previously proposed by the authors, has been also described, for giving an example of a practical implementation of a watermarking scheme.

Even if no watermarking system proposed so far can completely assure the high level of security and robustness potentially required in a DRM scenario, much interest is still focused on watermarking technology and its powerful application for developing useful DRM systems. To one side, the research for improving watermarking security in a DRM chain is in progress; on the other hand, novel approaches for using watermarking in a DRM system are proposed, taking into account the current watermark weaknesses.

FUTURE RESEARCH DIRECTIONS

It is possible to identify three possible research areas related to the use of watermarking in DRM applications that seem to be open to new research activity, namely distribution models, customer rights protection, and secure watermark detection.

In classical distribution models, the watermark embedding process is carried out by a trusted server before releasing the content to the user. However this approach is not scalable and in large scale distribution systems the server may become overloaded. In addition, since point-to-point communication channels are required, bandwidth requirements could become prohibitive. A proposed solution is to use client-side watermark embedding. Client-side watermark embedding systems transmit the same encrypted version of the original content to all the clients but a client-specific decryption key allows to decrypt the content and at the same time implicitly embed a watermark. When the client uses his key to decrypt the content, he obtains a uniquely watermarked version of the content. The security properties of the embedding scheme usually guarantees that obtaining either the watermark or the original content in the clear is of comparable hardness as removing the watermark from the personalized copy (Emmanuel, 2001; Crowcroft, 2000; Parviainen, 2001; Kundur, 2004; Lemma, 2006; Anderson, 1997; Adelsbach, 2006; Celik, 2007).

The customer's rights problem relates to the intrinsic problem of ambiguity when watermarks are embedded at the distribution server: a customer whose watermark has been found on unauthorized copies can claim that he has been framed by a malicious seller who inserted his identity as watermark in an arbitrary object. Buyer-seller protocols have been designed as a possible solution to this problem. Buyer-Seller Protocols rely on cryptographic primitives to perform watermark embedding ; the protocol assures that the seller does not have access to the watermarked copy carrying the identity of the buyer, hence he cannot distribute or sell these copies. In spite of this, the seller can identify the buyer from whom unauthorized copies originated, and prove it by using a proper dispute resolution protocol (Memon, 2001; Lei, 2004; Zhang, 2006; Kuribayashi, 2005; Ahmed, 2006).

In the watermark detection process, a system has to prove to a verifier that a watermark is present in certain content. Proving the presence of such a watermark is usually done by revealing the required detection information to the verifying party. All current applications assume that the verifier is a trusted party. However, this is not always true, for instance if the prover is a consumer device. A cheating verifier could exploit the knowledge acquired during watermark detection to break the security of the watermarking system. A possible solution is represented by Zero-knowledge watermark detection (ZKWD) schemes. In general, a zero-knowledge watermark detection algorithm is an interactive proof system where a prover tries to convince a verifier that a digital content is watermarked with a given watermark without disclosing it. In contrast to the standard watermark detector, in ZKWD the verifier is given only properly encoded (or encrypted) versions of security-critical watermark parameters. Depending on the particular protocol, the watermark code, the watermarked object, a watermark key or even the original unmarked object is only available in encrypted form to the verifier.

The prover runs the zero-knowledge watermark detector to demonstrate to the verifier that the encoded watermark is present in the object in question, without removing the encoding. A protocol run will not leak any information except for the unencoded inputs and the watermark presence detection result (Craver, 2001; Craver, 1999; Adelsbach, 2005; Adelsbach, 2001; Troncoso, 2007; Piva, 2006; Malkin,2006).

REFERENCES

Adelsbach, A., Katzenbeisser, S., & Sadeghi, A.-R. (2002). Crytpography meets watermarking: Detecting watermarks with minimal or zero knowledge disclosure. *In XI European Signal Processing Conference, EUSIPCO' 02, 1,* 446-449. Toulouse, France.

Barni, M., Bartolini, F., De Rosa, A., & Piva, A. (2001). A new decoder for the optimum recovery of non-additive watermarks. *IEEE Transactions on Image Processing, 10*(5), 755-766.

Barni, M., Bartolini, F., De Rosa, A., & Piva, A. (2003). Optimum decoding and detection of multiplicative watermarks. *IEEE Transactions on Signal Processing, 51*(4), 1118-1123.

Barni, M., Bartolini, F., & Furon, T. (2003). A general framework for robust watermarking security. *Signal Processing, 83*(10), 2069–2084.

Barni, M., & Bartolini, F. (2004). Watermarking systems engineering: Enabling digital assets security and other applications. Marcel Dekker (Ed).

Bartolini, F., Barni, M., Cappellini, V., & Piva, A. (1998). Mask building for perceptually hiding frequency embedded watermarks. *In 5th IEEE International Conference on Image Processing ICIP'98, 1,* 450-454. Chicago, Illinois, USA.

BOWS (2006). *Break our watermarking system.* From http://lci.det.unifi.it/BOWS.

BOWS-2 (2007). *Break our watermarking system,* 2nd Ed., From http://bows2.gipsa-lab.inpg.fr.

Bricks Project, (2007). From http://www.brickscommunity.org/

Caldelli, R., Piva, A., Barni, M., & Carboni, A. (2005). Effectiveness of ST-DM watermarking against intra-video collusion. *In 4th International Workshop on Digital Watermarking, IWDW 2005, LNCS, 3710,* 158-170. Siena, Italy.

Chen, B., & Wornell, G. (2001). Quantization index modulation: A class of provably good methods for digital watermarking and information embedding. *IEEE Transaction on Information Theory, 47,* 1423-1443.

Costa, M. (1983). Writing on dirty paper. *IEEE Transaction on Information Theory, 29,* 439-441.

Cox, I. J., Kilian, J., Leighton, T., & Shamoon, T. (1997). Secure spread spectrum watermarking for multimedia. *IEEE Transaction on Image Processing, 6,* 1673-1687.

Craver, S., Yeo, B., & Yeung, M. (1998). Technical trials and legal tribulations. *Communications of the ACM, 41*(7), 44-54.

Doerr, G., & Dugelay, J. L. (2003). New intra-video collusion attack using mosaicing. *In IEEE International Conference Multimedia Expo., 2,*505-508. Baltimora, USA.

Furon, T., Venturini, I., & Duhamel, P. (2001). An unified approach of asymmetric watermarking schemes. In E.J. Delp and P.W. Wong (Ed.), *Security and Watermarking of Multimedia Contents III, Proc. SPIE, 4314* , 269-279). San Jose, CA.

Kerckhoffs, A. (1883). La cryptographie militaire. *Journal des sciences militaires, 9,* 5-83.

Kalker, T., Depovere, G., Haitsma, J., & Maes, M. (1999). A video watermarking system for broadcast monitoring. In E.J. Delp and P.W. Wong (Ed.), *Security and Watermarking of Multimedia Contents, Proc. SPIE, 3657,* 103-112. San Jose, CA.

Kalker, T. (2001). Considerations on watermarking security. *In IEEE Multimedia Signal Processing, MMSP'01 Workshop,* 201-206. Cannes, France.

Kundur, D., Lin, C.-Y., Macq, B., & Yu, H. (2004). Special issue on enabling security technologies for digital rights management. *Proceedings of the IEEE, 92*(6), 879-882.

Piva, A., Barni, M., & Bartolini, F. (1998). Copyright protection of digital images by means of frequency domain watermarking. In Schmalz (Ed.), *Mathematics of Data/Image Coding, Compression, and Encryption, Proc. of SPIE, 3456,* 25-35. San Diego, California.

Piva, A., Barni, M., Bartolini, F., Cappellini, V., De Rosa, A., & Orlandi, M. (1999). Improving DFT watermarking robustness through optimum detection and synchronisation. In *GMD Report 85, Multimedia and Security Workshop at ACM Multimedia '99,* 65-69. Orlando, Florida.

MPEG REL, ISO/IEC FDIS 21000-5 (2003). *Information technology - Multimedia framework - Part 5: Rights expression language.*

N5229 (2002). Requirements for the persistent sssociation of identification and description of digital items, ISO/IEC *JTC1/SC29/WG11,* (MPEG-21—Requirements).

Pereira, S., Voloshynovsiy, S., & Pun, T. (2001). Optimal transform domain watermark embedding via linear programming. *Signal Processing, 81*(6), 1251-1260.

The Content ID Forum, (2002). *cIDf Specification v. 1.1.* Tokyo, Japan.

Watson, A.B. (1993). DCT quantization matrices visually optimized for individual images. *In Human Vision, Visual Processing and Digital Display IV, Proc. SPIE, 1913* 202-216. Bellingham, WA.

ADDITIONAL READING

Adelsbach, A. & Sadeghi, A.-R. (2001). Zero-knowledge watermark detection and proof of ownership. *In 4th International Workshop on Information Hiding, IH'01, Springer Lecture Notes in Computer Science, 2137,* 273-288. Pittsburgh, PA, USA.

Adelsbach, A., Rohe, M., & Sadeghi, A.-R. (2005). Non-interactive watermark detection for a correlation-based watermarking scheme. *In Communications and Multimedia Security, Springer Lecture Notes in Computer Science, 3677*, 129-139. Salzburg, Austria.

Adelsbach, A., Huber, U., & Sadeghi, A.-R. (2006). Fingercasting – Joint fingerprinting and decryption of broadcast messages. *In 11th Australasian Conference on Information Security and Privacy, Springer Lecture Notes in Computer Science, 4058*, 136-147. Melbourne, Australia.

Ahmed, F., Sattar, F., Siyal, M. Y., & Yu, D. (2006). A secure watermarking scheme for buyer-seller identification and copyright protection. *EURASIP Journal on Applied Signal Processing.*

Anderson, R. J., & Manifavas, C. (1997). Chameleon - A new kind of stream cipher. *In 4th International Workshop on Fast Software Encryption, FSE '97*, 107-113. London, UK: Springer-Verlag.

Celik, M., Lemma, A., Katzenbeisser, S., & van der Veen, M. (2007). Secure embedding of spread-spectrum watermarks using look-up tables. *In International Conference on Acoustics, Speech and Signal Processing, ICASSP'07, IEEE Press. 2*, 153-156. Honolulu, Hawaii, USA.

Craver, S. (1999). Zero knowledge watermark detection. *In 3rd International Workshop on Information Hiding, IH'99, Springer Lecture Notes in Computer Science, 1768*, 101-116. Dresden, Germany.

Craver, S., & Katzenbeisser, S. (2001). Security analysis of public-key watermarking schemes. *In M. S. Schmalz (Ed.) SPIE, Mathematics of Data/Image Coding, Compression and Encryption IV, with Applications, 4475*, 172-182. San Diego, CA.

Crowcroft, J., Perkins, C., & Brown, I. (2000). *A method and apparatus for generating multiple watermarked copies of an information signal.* WO Patent No. 00/56059.

Emmanuel, S., & Kankanhalli, M. (2001). Copyright protection for MPEG-2 compressed broadcast video. *In IEEE Int. Conf. on Multimedia and Expo, ICME 2001*, 206-209. Tokyo, Japan.

Kundur, D. (2004). Video fingerprinting and encryption principles for digital rights management. *Proceedings of the IEEE, 92*(6), 918-932.

Kuribayashi, M., & Tanaka, H. (2005). Fingerprinting protocol for images based on additive homomorphic property. *IEEE Transactions on Image Processing, 14*(12), 2129-2139.

Lei, C.-L., Yu, P.-L., Tsai, P.-L., & Chan, M.-H. (2004). An efficient and anonymous buyer-seller watermarking protocol. *IEEE Transactions on Image Processing, 13*(12), 1618-1626.

Lemma, A., Katzenbeisser, S., Celik, M., & van der Veen, M. (2006). Secure watermark embedding through partial encryption. *In International Workshop on Digital Watermarking (IWDW 2006), Springer Lecture Notes in Computer Science, 4283*, 433-445. Jeju Island, Korea.

Malkin, M., & Kalker, T. (2006). A cryptographic method for secure watermark detection. *In 8th International Workshop on Information Hiding, IH'06, Springer Lecture Notes in Computer Science, 4437*, 26-41. Old Town Alexandria, Virginia, USA.

Memon, N., & Wong, P. (2001). A buyer-seller watermarking protocol. *IEEE Transactions on Image Processing, 10*(4), 643-649.

Parviainen, R., & Parnes, P. (2001). Large scale distributed watermarking of multicast media through encryption. *In International Federation for Information Processing, Communications and Multimedia Security Joint working conference IFIP TC6/TC11, 192*, 149-158. Darmstadt, Germany.

Piva, A., Cappellini, V., Corazzi, D., De Rosa, A., Orlandi, C., & Barni, M. (2006). Zero-knowledge ST-DM watermarking. In P. W. Wong and E. J. Delp (Ed.), *Security, Steganography, and Watermarking of Multimedia Contents VIII, Proc. SPIE, 6072*, 291-301. San Jose, CA, USA.

Troncoso, J. R., & Perez-Gonzalez, F. (2007). Efficient non-interactive zero-knowledge watermark detector robust to sensitivity attacks. In P. W. Wong and E. J. Delp (Ed.), *Security, Steganography, and Watermarking of Multimedia Contents IX, Proc. SPIE, 6505*. San Jose, CA, USA.

Zhang, J., Kou, W., & Fan, K. (2006). Secure buyer-seller watermarking protocol. *IEE Proceedings on Information Security, 153*(1), 15-18.

Chapter V
Watermarking and Authentication in JPEG2000

V. E. Fotopoulos
Hellenic Open University, Greece

I. D. Kostopoulos
University of Patras, Greece

ABSTRACT

This chapter introduces JPEG 2000 as an application field for image authentication and the new technology of digital image watermarking. The new compression format has many unexplored characteristics that both the watermarking and the authentication communities should carefully take into account. Thus, a brief introduction to the standard is given at the beginning, discussing its structure, features, novelties, and capabilities. Following that introduction, watermarking techniques are presented, at first into the wavelet domain (the DWT is part of the JPEG2000 core), and then into the JPEG 2000 pipeline. The effects of the various standards' parameters in this process are carefully investigated. Then, authentication mechanisms of JPEG 2000 images are described and we peek into JPSEC, part-8 of JPEG 2000 that deals with issues of watermarking and authentication.

INTRODUCTION

Since the mid 1980s, ITU (International Telecommunications Union) and ISO (International Organization for Standardization) have joined efforts in order to establish a new standard for efficient compression of grayscale and still color images. The result of this process has been named "JPEG" (Joint Photographic Experts Group) and has been established as international standard IS 10918-1 in 1991. Very soon, the JPEG image format (jpg) has became the most commonly used format. New features were soon added. However, some of them required costly licensing, while some of the more than 40 available options, were mutually exclusive. Thus, only basic functionalities were adopted from most users. To correct the mistakes of the past, to take account of new trends (e.g. wavelets) and to adapt to the increased needs and requirements of modern multimedia and Internet applications, a new standard was required. Under these circumstances, almost a decade later, JPEG2000 emerged ("JPEG 2000", 2007). The new standard provided a unified coding system for different types of still images (bilevel, gray scale, color, multicomponent) with different characteristics (natural, medical, remote sensing etc.) allowing different imaging models (client/server, real time transmission, image library archival etc.). The system performs superior to older standards by achieving great compression ratios while retaining image quality at the same time. Part I of the standard (ISO/IEC 15444-1, 2007) can be used on a royalty and fee-free basis. All these lead to the conclusion that it is only a matter of time before JPEG2000 will become widely accepted.

Watermarking and authentication for digital images are also new technologies, descendants of the last decade. The main reason for their introduction was the fact that digital images are quite easy to duplicate, forge or misuse. One of the most important applications of watermarking is the protection of the images' copyright while authentication aims to the verification of the content, investigate if an image is tampered or not and if it is, to identify the locations that these alterations have occurred. Both technologies need in order to succeed, the inclusion of side-information into the original image. That is obviously the reason why lossy compression schemes often cause to them great problems. Part of the watermarking or authentication information may be discarded along with insignificant (presumed) parts of the original image's content, as a side effect in order to achieve better compression. Very few techniques have been proposed to cope with this problem and this is the motivation behind this chapter.

This chapter is organized in four parts. The first one, is a short presentation of the JPEG2000 structure, features, novelties introduced and capabilities. Following that introduction, the second part describes watermarking, at first into the wavelet domain (the DWT is part of the JPEG2000 core) and then right into the JPEG2000 pipeline. The effects of the various standard's parameters are also described in this part. In the third part the authentication mechanisms of JPEG 2000 images are described along with parameters that affect the watermarking process as image capacity and quality. The last part is the shortest and describes in brief JPSEC, part-8 of JPEG2000 that deals with such cases.

JPEG2000: AN OVERVIEW OF THE STANDARD

The new standard has come to serve a wide variety of applications like the Internet, mobile communications, medical imagery, remote sensing, color facsimile, printing and scanning, digital photography, e-commerce, digital libraries and many more. Of course, each of these areas imposes certain requirements that the new standard should fulfil in the best possible way. So the implementation of JPEG2000 provides the following:

- **Superior low bit-rate performance:** The new standard performs superior according to its predecessors for very low bit-rates. It is now possible to compress grayscale images with high detail, under 0.2 bpp. Of course Internet and mobile communications, as well as network applications greatly benefit from this feature.
- **Continuous-tone and bilevel compression:** Various kinds of images are supported by the new compression system. The algorithm is capable of compressing images of various dynamic ranges (eg. from 1 to 16 bpp for each color component). This turns beneficial for a variety of applications

like compound document compression, facsimile, graphics and images with binary and near to binary regions, alpha and transparency planes.

- **Lossless and lossy compression:** The new standard can provide both kinds of compression within the same codestream. There are applications like medical imaging, digital libraries and prepress imagery, in which image information loss can not be tolerated. In such cases the lossless part of the codestream is used while in the other cases (web browsing, network transmission over client/ server applications) the lossy part can be used instead. JPEG2000 also allows progressive lossy to lossless buildup.

- **Progressive transmission and decoding:** It is possible to transmit images progressively and decode at the receiver with increasing pixel accuracy or spatial resolution. This a valuable feature for web browsing and digital libraries.

- **Regions Of Interest:** In almost every image, there are regions that contain more important information content than others. In JPEG2000 one can define these regions of interest (ROI) and allocate more bits for their coding than for the rest of the image.

- **Open Architecture:** JPEG2000 allows optimization for different image types and applications.

- **Error resilience:** The new standard provides robustness to bit errors that may cause catastrophic decoding failures. That is essential, especially when images are transmitted over noisy channels (e.g. wireless networks).

- **Fixed-rates, fixed-sizes, limited workspace memory:** It is possible to specify the exact number of bits allocated for a group of consecutive pixels or for the whole codestream. Except for the profound advantage of this feature, it is also possible for devices of limited memory (like scanners and printers) to function with the new format.

Table 1. JPEG2000 standardisation process

Part	Description	CFP[a]	Current IS version[#]
1	JPEG 2000 Image Coding System: Core Coding System	Mar-97	ISO/IEC 15444-1:2004
2	JPEG 2000 Image Coding System: Extensions	Mar-97	ISO/IEC 15444-2:2004
3	Motion JPEG 2000	Dec-99	ISO/IEC 15444-3:2007
4	Conformance Testing	Dec-99	ISO/IEC 15444-4:2004
5	Reference Software	Dec-99	ISO/IEC 15444-5:2003
6	Compound Image File Format	Mar-97	ISO/IEC 15444-6:2003
7	Technical Report: Guideline of minimum support function of Part 1	Withdrawn	
8	JPSEC: Secure JPEG 2000	Mar-02	ISO/IEC 15444-8:2007
9	JPIP: Interactivity tools, APIs and protocols	Mar-02	ISO/IEC 15444-9:2005
10	JP3D:3-D and floating point data	Mar-02	FDIS[*] in March 2007
11	JPWL: Wireless	Jul-02	ISO/IEC 15444-11:2007
12	ISO Base Media File Format	Oct-02	ISO/IEC 15444-12:2005
13	An entry level JPEG 2000 encoder		FDIS[*] in April 2007

[a] *CFP: Call for Papers* [#] *IS: International Standard* [*] *FDIS: Final Draft for International Standard*

- **Security:** One of the last parts of the standard that have been approved is JPSEC (Part 8) which deals with security, authentication, data integrity and protection of copyright and intellectual property rights issues.

The standardisation procedure of JPEG2000 is given in the following table. Of the thirteen parts, ten are completed and published, one has been withdrawn and two are in the phase of final draft. Since all of the finished parts are copyrighted material of ISO and ITU-T, thus not freely distributable, interested readers can get the final committee draft (FCD) from the Committee Draft web page of the JPEG2000 website ("Welcome to JPEG", 2007).

JPEG2000 Compression Engine

In order to protect images that are going to be compressed by JPEG2000, one must be familiar with the standard's compression engine. This engine does not look any different from the original JPEG's. The image is subject to a discrete frequency transform, the transformed coefficients are quantized and then entropy encoded to form the compressed bitstream. At the receiver, the process is inverted: entropy decoding, inverse quantization and inverse transform. However there are radical differences in various stages of the process. Let's have a closer look into the system:

- The source image is decomposed into components.
- The image components are (optionally) decomposed into rectangular tiles. The tile-component is the basic unit of the original or reconstructed image.
- A wavelet transform is applied on each tile. The tile is decomposed into different resolution levels.
- The decomposition levels are made up of subbands of coefficients that describe the frequency characteristics of local areas of the tile components, rather than across the entire image component.
- The subbands of coefficients are quantized and collected into rectangular arrays of "code blocks."
- The bit planes of the coefficients in a code block (i.e. the bits of equal significance across the coefficients in a code block) are entropy coded.

Figure 1. JPEG2000 encoder

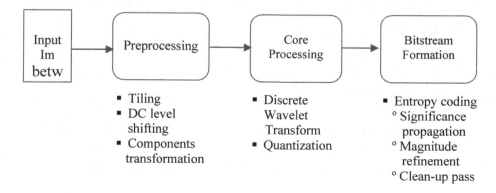

- The encoding can be done in such a way that certain regions of interest can be coded at a higher quality than the background
- Markers are added to the bit stream to allow for error resilience.
- The code stream has a main header at the beginning that describes the original image and the various decomposition and coding styles that are used to locate, extract, decode and reconstruct the image with the desired resolution, fidelity, region of interest or other characteristics.

A more detailed view is required, in order to identify the various parts in which a watermarking/authentication system could possibly interfere. For this reason, the coding process is decomposed in three parts (although there is some overlapping between them): preprocessing, core processing and bitstream formation (Figure 1).

Preprocessing

This part includes the *tiling process*, the *dc level shifting* and the *components transformation*. Tilling is the process of partitioning the original image into smaller, non-overlapping square blocks. Then, each of the blocks is independently coded. The tile, is the basic unit of the original/reconstructed image. By using small tiles, memory usage requirements are significantly decreased and it is also possible to decode selectively, certain parts of the original. The size of the tiles is user-selected and it is the same for all of them with the exception of tiles at the image boundary. Tiling may produce blocking effects, similar to the original JPEG if the tile size is too small and if this is combined with low bit rate coding.

Because of the filters involved in the core of JPEG2000, the input data should have a zero-centered dynamic range. For this reason, if the original pixel intensities are unsigned integers, dc level shifting is performed by subtracting a value of 2^{N-1} where N is the bit depth of the image component. The inversion should be performed at the decoder (adding the bias of 2^{N-1}). If the data are already signed, no shifting is performed.

Components transformation, generally improves the compression efficiency. Speaking of color images which are usually represented in the RGB color space, all three of these components are highly correlated. Thus a transformation to another space like YC_bC_r decorrelates the input data allowing for better compression. Two types of transformations are supported from the standard, the *reversible component transformation* (RCT) and the *irreversible component transformation* (ICT). The ICT can be used for lossy compression only and it is suitable for use with the 9/7 irreversible wavelet transform while RCT can be used for both lossy and lossless compression, combined with the 5/3 reversible wavelet transform. The formuli for the forward and inverse RCT and ICT are given in Table 2.

Core Processing

The core processing part consists of three different stages: the *discrete wavelet transform*, the *quantization* and the *entropy coding* processes. The discrete wavelet transform (DWT) has been the successor to the discrete cosine transform (DCT) that was used in the original JPEG. Each of the tiles that the image consists of, is analyzed via the DWT to different decomposition levels (Vetterli, 2001; Usevitch, 2001). Only power of 2 decompositions are allowed according to Part I of the standard (Figure 2). The 2D-DWT is separable, that means that for each input block, a filtering operation is carried out row by row and another one is carried out column by column. Order is not important. There can be two kinds

Table 2. Lossy and lossless transformation formuli

	ICT	RCT
Forward	$\begin{pmatrix} Y \\ C_b \\ C_r \end{pmatrix} = \begin{pmatrix} 0.299 & 0.587 & 0.114 \\ -0.16875 & -0.33126 & 0.5 \\ 0.5 & -0.41869 & -0.08131 \end{pmatrix} \cdot \begin{pmatrix} R \\ G \\ B \end{pmatrix}$	$\begin{pmatrix} Y \\ U \\ V \end{pmatrix} = \begin{pmatrix} \frac{R+2G+B}{4} \\ R-G \\ B-G \end{pmatrix}$
Inverse	$\begin{pmatrix} R \\ G \\ B \end{pmatrix} = \begin{pmatrix} 1.0 & 0 & 1.402 \\ 1.0 & -0.34413 & -0.71414 \\ 1.0 & 1.772 & 0 \end{pmatrix} \cdot \begin{pmatrix} Y \\ C_b \\ C_r \end{pmatrix}$	$\begin{pmatrix} G \\ R \\ B \end{pmatrix} = \begin{pmatrix} Y - \frac{U+V}{4} \\ U+G \\ V+G \end{pmatrix}$

of filters: lowpass and highpass. In that way, we have four subbands at each decomposition level, LL, LH, HL and HH. The first letter shows the kind of filter applied to rows and the second, the kind of filter applied to columns. Usually, the filters used are the Daubechies 9-tap/7-tap for the case of irreversible transform (Antonini, Barlaud, Mathieu, Daubechies, 1992) and the Le Gall 5-tap/3-tap for the reversible transform (Adams, Kossentini, 2000). There can be 0 to 32 levels of decomposition in JPEG2000 but usually, 4 to 8 are adequate.

There are two types of quantization: Uniform quantization with dead zone about the origin (used in Part I) and trellis coded quantization, TCQ (used in Part II). Quantization is a process that reduces the magnitude of the coefficients but also reduces the precision of their representation. Therefore this process is lossy, unless the quantization step is 1 and the coefficients are integers (e.g. those produced by the 5/3 reversible transform). A coefficient y in subband b is quantized with quantization step Δ_b via the following formula:

$$q = sign(y) \cdot \left[\frac{|y|}{\Delta_b} \right]$$

where q is the quantized value. It is possible for different subbands to have different quantization steps. All quantized values are signed integers even though the original values might be unsigned. All coefficients are expressed in sign-magnitude representation before coding.

Bitstream Formation

The entropy coder takes as input, non-overlapping rectangles called *code blocks*. The typical size of a code block is between 32x32 and 64x64 elements. Three spatially consistent rectangles taken from the same resolution level from each of the three subbands form a *precinct*.

Each code block is coded independently from the others and the code blocks of each subband are coding a bit plane, starting with the most significant bit plane to the least significant one (Taubman, 2000; Taubman et al., 2000).

The individual bit planes of the coefficients in a code block are coded within three coding passes. Each of the coding passes collects contextual information about the bit plane data. This contextual information is used by the arithmetic coder and its internal state to generate a compressed bit stream.

Each coefficient bit in the bit plane is coded in only one of the three coding passes, the *significance propagation*, the *magnitude refinement* and the *cleanup* pass. For each of these passes, contexts are created which are provided to the arithmetic coder (Taubman et al., 2000; Marcellin, Gormish, Bilgin & Boliek, 2000).

In significance propagation pass, a bit is coded if two conditions are satisfied. The location of this bit has to be not significant and at least one of the eight bits of its neighbourhood has to be significant. If a coefficient is significant then it takes the value of one for the creation of the context, otherwise it takes the value of zero. This pass includes the bits of the coefficients that are insignificant and the context is given to the arithmetic coder and the decoded coefficient bit is returned.

In the second pass (magnitude refinement) all bits that are significant are coded, except these bits that become significant after the first pass (significance propagation pass). The context that is used in this pass is related with the summation of the significance state of the horizontal, vertical and diagonal neighbourhoods of a bit.

The final pass (clean-up) is related with all these bits that have not been encoded during the previous two passes. This pass is not restrained to use the neighbor context but it also uses a run-length context.

Packets and Layers

Packets and layers are the fundamental structures of the code stream generation. The compressed bit streams for each code block in a precinct, create the body of a packet. The layers are consisted of sets of packets, by taking one packet from each precinct of each resolution level. Both packets and layers can be interpreted as quality increments for resolution levels or for the entire full resolution image correspondingly (Marcellin et al., 2000). The usage of layers by the decoder improves the image quality and the final bit stream is structured to be a layer sequence.

Once the whole image is processed and the data are compressed, a post-processing operation passes over all the compressed code blocks. Depending on the target bit rate or distortion this operation determines the truncation of the code block's bit stream (Taubman, 2000; Taubman & Zalkor, 1994).

Remarkable Features of the Standard

In parallel with the new compression standard's engine, extra features enhance it in order to fulfill the demands of the modern technological age. These features are *Region of Interest Coding, Scalability, Error Resilience, Visual Frequency Weighting* and *new file formats with IPR capabilities.*

Although all of the aforementioned features are very important, the application of watermarking in JPEG2000 compressed images is closely related with the IPR capabilities of the new format. These capabilities include the embedding of XML-formatted information into the image file in order to accompany the image data with metadata. These metadata are associated with the image vendor, the image properties the existence of IPR information in the image data etc. The new format (JP2) (Boliek, Houchin & Wu, 2000) gives the opportunity to embed extra metadata into the image, but this is not a substitute for the watermarking/authentication mechanisms used today. In the next section these mechanisms are well described and the already proposed methods are presented.

WATERMARKING AND JPEG2000

Watermarking against lossy compression has always been an interesting challenge. Many of the existing literature techniques are inefficient against the JPEG standard. But times are changing and now the time has come to face the next generation in image compression standards: JPEG2000. With the new standard, superior quality for the same compression ratio can be achieved or similar quality for higher compression ratio, you can take whichever view suits you best. Since it is easier now to retain quality by achieving smaller file sizes, this is quite desirable. Thus compression ratios of less than 0.5bpp will become common practice. The problem is that although these images will be visually pleasant, watermarking methods have to evolve in order to survive such high compression. Is the watermarking community ready to undertake that challenge?

Very few works directly relate watermarking with JPEG2000. In the majority of the literature, the new standard is considered as yet another attack. Others examine the effects that the various JPEG2000 coding parameters cause to the watermark's detection. There is also a third category that proposes incorporating watermarking into the JPEG2000 coding pipeline or using it as an important factor in the marking/retrieval process. These may be few but they are of great practical interest. Of course there are lots of papers that deal with watermarking in the wavelet domain. Since the heart of the new standard is the wavelet transform, these works may be seen as the pioneers of watermarking in the JPEG2000 domain. All of these categories will be discussed in the following sections.

Wavelet Domain Watermarking

DCT has always been a very popular transform among the image research community. Its computational simplicity combined with great energy compaction, attracted the interest of the JPEG committee which used it in the core of the JPEG standard, a compression scheme which dominated the field for more than a decade. During that time, the Wavelet transform for image applications has also become popular and corresponding interest was increasing rapidly. The use of the wavelet-based *Embedded Block Coding with Optimized Truncation* (EBCOT) in the JPEG2000 standard has established the wavelet transform as the most interesting transform for compression research. So it was highly expected that many watermarkers have used the DWT as an alternative to the DCT for their schemes. Wavelet based schemes are mainly classified according to the type of watermark (pseudorandom noise sequence, logo or other), the coefficients' selection strategy (approximation, details or mixed) and the detection method (blind, semi-blind, non-blind). Of course other classifications are possible based on the application target or other factors.

First wavelet based watermarking schemes appear around 1995 and for the embedding, the approximation image is selected. For a 3-level wavelet decomposition, this band of coefficients is actually a miniature of the original image (dimensions are 1/8 of the originals). In that way traditional spread spectrum and spatial techniques can be easily used since these methods do not exploit the special features that the wavelet decomposition provides. Examples of these works can be found in Liang, Xu, & Tran (2000), Ohnishi & Matsui (1998), Tzovaras, Karagiannis, & Strintzis (1998), Corvi & Nicchiotti (1997), Nicchiotti & Ottaviano (1998), Perreira, Voloshynovskiy & Pun (2000), Xie & Arce (1998).

Detail based methods as in Kim, Kwon & Park (1999), Kim & Moon (1999), Barni, Bartolini, Cappellini, Lippi & Piva (1999), Xia, Boncelet & Arce (1998), Kundur (1999), are a bit different. The coefficients distribution in the detail bands is different compared to the approximation. There are only a few coefficients large enough to carry the watermark and a careful selection strategy is required. To define a selection threshold, the level of decomposition, orientation and subband energy can be utilized. Since the number of appropriate coefficients in each band is small, usually contribution is gathered from all the detail bands in all decomposition levels. An advantage coming out of this practice is that if the watermark is found in one of them, there's no need to search the others, reducing the detection's computational cost. This characteristic makes such methods appealing for real time applications. There are also techniques that use all of the bands, approximation and details for additional robustness (Davoine, 2000).

Built-In Approaches

There's no better way to confront a situation, than being part of it. If someone wants to make code that is JPEG2000 robust, the best way is to put his/her mark inside the coding pipeline. In any other cases, the results will be suboptimal. The next logical question is "in which exact part of the encoder, should I intervene by putting my mark?". One option is to put the mark right after the DWT. In that case though, the scheme wouldn't make any difference to conventional wavelet based methods. Of course an interesting variation would be to insert the mark into the intermediate coefficients from the lifting stages as Seo et al. (2001). Using Daubechies 9-7 filter banks involves four lifting stages and a final scaling stage. In that case, authors propose to insert an extra lifting scheme between the second and third lifting stage (raising the number of lifting stages to five) in which only half of the coefficients are different from those of the previous stage (Figure 3). The whole alteration is based on a tuning parameter ω which selects the frequency characteristics of the desired coefficients. Actually the resulting coefficients correspond to the filtering of the input sequence with a high pass filter; the impulse response of this filter is tuned by the ω variable. If $\omega=0$, the transform is the same as the original DWT (the extra stage is redundant). Authors' experiments show that using values of ±0.1, ±0.2, for ω leads to improved robustness comparing to final stage DWT based methods, while the quality of the image and transparency of the mark are preserved. The scheme can be easily integrated into the JPEG2000 coding and consequently benefit real-time applications like watermarking for digital still cameras, video monitoring e.t.c. The ω parameter, except from selecting the coefficients' characteristics, can also be used as an auxiliary secret key.

One may argue that embedding directly into, or right after the DWT, would cause many problems. In the case of JPEG2000 coding, this can be true. Problems lie in the fact that the DWT is followed by quantization and bitstream truncation in order to achieve the bit rate constraint. Before the end of the coding process, the mark will be already weakened. As an alternative, Su & Kuo (2003) propose to bypass the quantization procedure and hide data in the coding stage. Their intention is to hide a large number of bits rather than doing it in a robust way, so their primary goal is to achieve high payloads. However, the bitstream optimization is quite a hard challenge for their goal. So their method works only for high bit rate with lazy mode coding. The coding stage (right after quantization) is a 2-tier structure. The first tier consists of three passes: significance propagation, magnitude refinement and cleanup. The authors take advantage of the fact that in lazy mode, during the magnitude refinement passes, except for the four most significant bit-planes, the rest of the passes are raw coded. Thus, a large number of bits can easily be changed at this place in order to conceal the secret information. The goal of high payload is achieved in that way (smaller images can easily be embedded into the cover image), there's no problem with the decoding process (since only raw data are altered, not arithmetic coded) while the information can be progressively retrieved during decoding. Progressive retrieval is possible because during the first of the raw coded passes, the last part of the info is hidden. That means that the first part is hidden at the last pass. Since decoding is exactly the reverse procedure, the parts of the hidden data are backwards retrieved thus achieving progressive extraction.

Although great discussion is done about where is it most appropriate to put the mark, before or after the quantization of the coefficients, there's also a third view; using the quantization to engrave the mark. Meerwald (2001) uses a method proposed by Chen & Wornell (2000) and further analyzed by Eggers & Girod (2000) called *Quantization Index Modulation*. In this technique, the watermark bit determines which quantizer should be used from a set of available quantizers. The watermark sequence is a binary sequence with a size of a few hundred bits. The author recognizes the problem that conventional techniques have with the number of suitable coefficients for embedding. To circumvent that, he uses coefficients from both the details and approximation subbands to support his scheme. The distribution of the mark's energy is adjusted so that more energy is placed in those coefficients that the human eye is less sensitive to their changes. JPEG and JPEG2000, blurring and sharpening are used for testing purposes and results are quite satisfactory.

Parameterization Effects

Usually, when watermarking methods are tested for lossy compression, the parameter involved is compression ratio. In JPEG2000, compression ratio is only one of the available options to the coder. Other also important parameters include the filter kernels used, regions of interest, levels of decomposition, tile size and many more. Such an advanced (and consequently complex) compression algorithm, is definitely multi-parametric and it is not wise to ignore all these parameters during the testing procedure. This was the motivation between Fotopoulos & Skodras work (2002) in which, the authors put all of the aforementioned parameters under the microscope. The image used is 'Lena' which undergoes a full block transform. Three different transforms are used (DCT, Hartley, Subband DCT). First of all, from

Figure 3. Adding an extra lifting stage for watermarking purposes (Seo et al., 2001)

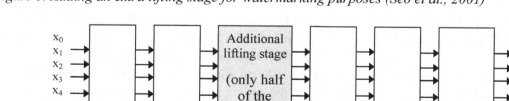

Figure 4 it seems that the detector's value falls almost linearly while compression increases. In Figure 5, the tile size effects are depicted. As tile size decreases, the detector's value also decreases. This can be reasoned because tilling with smaller block sizes leads to inefficient coding (supposing that the bit rate is constant – 0.5bpp in that case). It is obvious from the figure that tile sizes of 64 and 128 pixels, produce a fall of almost 15%-20% to the detectors value while a tile size of 512 makes almost no difference to the detection (almost same output with and without tiling).

In Figure 6 the target parameter is the kernel of the filters used. Three different kernels are tested, the well known Daubechies bi-orthogonal 9/7, a 2 (low-pass) x 10 (high-pass) filter and Brislawn-Treiber. It is evident that the selection of the kernel is crucial for the watermark's detection. Daubechies filter outperforms the others while the Brislawn-Treiber reduces the output to a range of 10%-20%. Thus, different filters perform differently and if a real time application is involved, for example a digital camera that saves in j2k file format with a fixed kernel in the encoder, the selection of the filter is of prime importance if watermarking is performed on the fly.

The region of interest (ROI) subject is also important. Two options are currently available, circular and rectangular regions. If full block-transform is employed, then reducing the size of the ROI reduces the detector's output accordingly. It is difficult in that case to retrieve the mark if the ROI is less than 20%-25% (supposing for a required fixed bit rate of 0.5bpp). If embedding is based in smaller blocks, then chances are better. The same stands for second generation watermarking schemes that are based on previous examination of the cover image. Of course in that case the content of the ROI is also important, not only its size.

Minguillón, Herrera-Joancomartí & Megías (2003) also evaluate JPEG2000 parameters but they start from a different perspective. Their watermarking scheme is non-oblivious in the sense that the original image is needed for the correct decoding of the mark. A JPEG2000 version of the original image is used to locate pixels that differ from the original after compression. Then, these positions are selected for embedding. The mark is a binary sequence, encoded with an error correction code (ECC), replicated as many times as needed to reach the number of candidate pixels. The resulting sequence is encrypted and a logical operation follows to produce the final version, prior to embedding. The final insertion of

Figure 4. Effect of compression ratio to the detector's output (x-Hartley, o-DCT, *-Subband DCT)

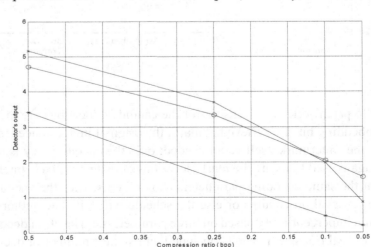

Figure 5. Effect of tile size to the detector's output (x-Hartley, o-DCT, *-Subband DCT)

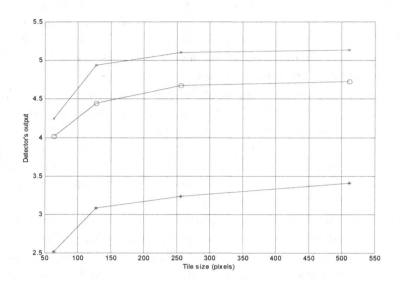

Figure 6. Effect of filter kernels to the detector's output (x-Hartley, o-DCT, *-Subband DCT)

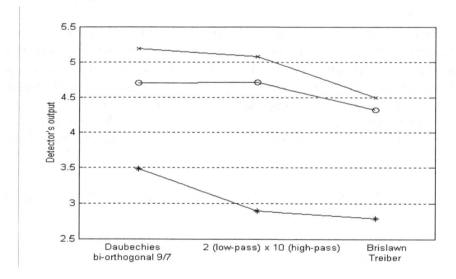

the mark is similar to patchwork; the intensities of the candidate locations are increased or decreased according to the embedding bit. To retrieve the mark, the original image is needed in order to find the mark's location but the watermark itself is not needed; only the encoding key is needed to decrypt it. JPEG2000 is once again used to locate the mark (locations of different pixels intensities).

It is obvious that the same encoding parameters should be used for the encoding during both the embedding and the retrieval procedures or else the scheme will fail. The authors are checking their scheme's capacity and imperceptibility based on three parameters: (a) levels of decomposition, (b) block size and (c) integer or real transform. They conclude that smallest number of decomposition achieves highest capacity while smallest block size achieves lowest. Real and integer transforms perform similarly in terms of capacity except for very high bit rates in which integer transforms is almost lossless meaning that only a small portion of the image's pixel is available for marking.

For robustness issues, the Stirmark benchmark is used. Attacks involve different kinds of filtering, JPEG compression, cropping, row/column removal and geometric attacks (rotation, cropping and scaling). From the 20 different experimental JPEG2000 encoding sets, the conclusion drawn is that each of the sets performs different. That means that encoding parameters should be seriously chosen in order to maximize robustness. Experimental results favor the set that consists of a real wavelet transform with 4 decomposition levels and a block size of 8.

JPEG2000 as an Attack

In this category of works, JPEG2000 is simply considered as yet another attack. No special care is taken during the algorithm's design which is simply tested against compression with various bit rates. One of the two publicly available versions of the encoder is usually used, JJ2000 or Jasper. Testing is always based on the bit rate parameter. The lowest the bit rate, the worst the detectors perform. It seems that 0.3-0.1 bpp is the range in which the watermarks start finding great difficulties to survive and under 0.1 bpp the majority of the methods easily fail (speaking of blind detection algorithms). By far, the most complete comparative study of various schemes for different bit rates can be found in Meerwald's webpage ("Robustness: JPEG 2000 compression", 2007)

AUTHENTICATION AND JPEG2000

An alternative application of watermarking technologies in JPEG2000 domain is image authentication. While one of the major directions of digital watermarking aims to protect the ownership of digital images, the safeguarding of the image content is essential. The research community has been activated during the last years to construct effective mechanisms following this direction (Eskicioglu, 2003). Since a lot of work has been done in order to design watermarking mechanisms for image authentication in earlier image formats, the new compression standard meets the research community in a moment that very few attempts have already approached this topic.

Standardization organizations have adopted the deployment of content authentication mechanisms that can be offered in companion with the digital images or by embedding them in the image data.

The image authentication field is stretched to cover the questions of whether a digital image is altered, whether the content of the image has been tampered, which particular regions, colors or image parts have been altered and finally if these changes can be recovered.

Classification of Image Authentication Techniques

Considering the nature of the watermark and the application that uses an image authentication technique, the image authentication techniques are classified in different categories. The first category of image authentication techniques aims at the integrity check of the image data. Authentication in terms of data integrity originates from cryptography. According to these techniques, if even one bit of the data that compose the image changes, the watermarked image is regarded as non authentic. In these methods, the watermark information is embedded in the original image in a way that it can easily be destroyed after any modification of the data. By this watermark property, in these methods the watermark is called *fragile*.

A second category includes the techniques that authenticate the image content. The main idea behind these techniques is that some modifications of the image data do not affect the image content. If for example a watermarked image has to be JPEG compressed (with high quality) then the data of the image will change but the image content will be identical. In these techniques the watermark information must be robust to actions that do not alter the image content and at the same fragile to actions that destroy the image content. The watermark in these techniques is called *semi-fragile* (Walton, 1995; Wu & Liu, 1998).

Some of the techniques that belong to the previously mentioned categories, can also localize the alterations of a watermarked image. This extra characteristic is related with the algorithmic design of those techniques and the nature of the watermark that is embedded in the original image (Bhattacharjee & Kutter, 1998; Kailasanathan, Safavi-Naini & Ogunbona, 2001).

Finally the self-embedding techniques have not been appeared yet in JPEG2000 authentication domain. In the past such techniques have been proposed in order to embed a highly compressed version of the original image into itself (Barni, Bartolini & Fridrich, 2000; Lin & Chang, 2000; Kostopoulos, Gilani, & Skodras, 2002). This operation is giving the opportunity next to the watermark detector to localize the alterations and to reconstruct the content of the image that has been destroyed (Figure 8).

Image authentication techniques can be combined with techniques that protect the copyright ownership in order to have a multipurpose watermarking scheme (Lu & Liao, 2001). Since these schemes have been applied in other image formats with excellent results, similar methods can be expected with application to the new compression standard.

Capacity Issues and Suitability of JPEG2000 for Image Authentication

It is necessary for all watermarking applications to contain redundant information in the host data that can be used in order to embed the watermark. This field has been studied well from researchers that work

Figure 7. The watermarked image and the altered image

Figure 8. The altered positions and the reconstructed image

in image compression and image watermarking field. The interest of researchers in image compression field is focused on the existence of redundant data that can be truncated in order to achieve the desirable compression ratio, while the interest of researchers in image watermarking field is focused on the existence of redundant data that can be used in order to embed the watermark information in host data.

It is obvious that in compressed image formats the amount of redundant information has been minimized during the compression procedure. Degrading the image quality by applying an image compression technique, the space for watermark embedding is becoming smaller and smaller.

The data of the image that can be used in order to embed a watermark are considered as a secret channel. The volume of these data can be theoretically estimated and in watermarking terminology, it is called *image capacity*. Depending on the image format, for images with the same dimensions and number of colors, image capacity varies. In general, in compressed image formats the image capacity is lower than non-compressed formats.

Very few attempts have been done to estimate the image capacity in JPEG2000 domain (Wong, Yeung & Au, 2003). These estimations are based on the *Human Visual System* (HVS) and more specifically to the *Just Noticeable Difference* (JND) of each Discrete Wavelet Transform coefficient. Authors have adopted the Watson's model (1997) to estimate the JND of transform coefficients.

The capacity estimation is achieved by making two basic assumptions. The first assumption is that input and output images are in JPEG2000 format with the same characteristics and the second assumption is that the image dimensions do not change during the watermarking process. The purpose of the method is to estimate the JND of each wavelet coefficient and by these estimations to measure the noise that can be added to the coefficients without affecting the image quality. Experimental results show that the estimated capacity depends on the compression bit rate. For compression of 1 bpp the capacity of a typical image (Lena 512x512) is estimated to 25 kbits, while for compression of 2 bpp the estimated capacity exceeds 150 kbits.

The capacity of the watermarking algorithm has also been estimated from Meerwald (2001), where for different window sizes and sub-block sizes the image capacity has been calculated and for images with dimensions 512x512, achieved capacities were 85, 194 and 383 bits, while respective PSNRs were 32.05, 31.45 and 32.09 dB.

Nature of the Watermark Information

Authentication techniques are divided in different categories depending on the volume and nature of the watermark. Therefore, there are watermarking systems that embed watermarks in order to decide about the image alterations, systems that embed watermarks in order to localize these alterations and finally systems that localize the alterations and reconstruct the image content that have been destroyed.

The watermark represents either a reference pattern that if destroyed the detector of the watermarking system responds that the watermarked image is altered, either a hash value of the image content or an approximation of the image content. Some methods (Zhishou et al., 2004; Grosbois, Gerbelot & Ebrahimi, 2001) are using cryptographic hash functions (SHA, MD2, MD4 etc.) in order to generate digests of the whole image or image code-blocks. The products of these functions are digital signatures with a fixed length (e.g. 160 bits). For extra security, the hash value can be encrypted before the embedding process. The encryption applied in order to avoid the hash value replacement after an attack, an action that disorients the watermark detector. The hash value encryption can be achieved by using a typical public-key cryptosystem (DES, RSA, etc.) (Schneier, 1995).

Since JPEG2000 is a more complicated image format, researchers have followed different approaches in order to authenticate the image content. Such an approach is presented from Peng, Deng, Wu & Shao (2003) where the authentication mechanism is used to authenticate the sub-images transcoded by a single original image codestream. These sub-images can have different qualities, resolutions, components and special regions.

As described in the beginning of the chapter, the packet generation process consists of five distinct steps. These steps are tile decomposition in tile-components, tile component transformation into resolution levels, resolution level partition into several precincts, precinct partition into several layers and finally packet formation from the bit stream corresponding to a given tile component, resolution level, precinct and layer.

The overall authentication process is based on a Merkle (1989) hash tree construction, using the source of a JPEG2000 codestream. The usage of this structure is giving the opportunity to the end user to authenticate any subset of the data values in combination with auxiliary information. Along with the Merkle hash tree a signature of the root value of the tree is computed.

The end user on a second step, requests the sub-image with its characteristics (resolution and quality) and the provider sends the corresponding packets. The provider sends also to the end user the signature of the root value accompanied with the auxiliary information that will be used in order to authenticate the sub-image.

Figure 9. Grosbois et al. embedding scheme

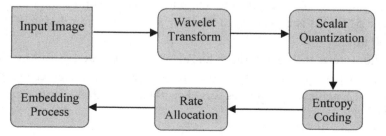

A different approach is followed by Meerwald (2001). He has designed a technique that is able to localize the image alterations by using a semi-fragile watermark. The watermark in this case is consisted of coefficients in the approximation image of the wavelet domain. In order to construct an algorithm that will be able to authenticate pixel blocks of size 8x8 the author has selected to apply the Wavelet Transform (three decomposition steps). This technique is differentiated from the others while it is able to localize particular areas (blocks) of the image that could be altered. At the same time the watermark is embedded with semi fragile way in the host data.

Authentication Information Embedding

One of the crucial considerations of the researchers when designing a watermarking scheme applied to compressed images is where exactly to perform the embedding process. In Grosbois et al., (2001) the authors embed the watermark information between the entropy coding and rate allocation procedures (Figure 9). They are exploiting an interesting feature of the bit stream construction where a termination marker exists. The arithmetic decoder stops reading from the bit stream after this termination marker, so the watermark information is embedded there without affecting the arithmetic decoding process. The disadvantage of this choice is the short volume of the data that can be hidden after the termination marker since this amount of data increases the code stream bit-rate.

In the previous approach a digital signature is used for authenticating the image codestreams. The embedding process has a weak point since it embeds extra information (authentication watermark) at the end of each code-block bit stream (Figure 10). In that way, the method is vulnerable to cut and paste attacks because of the fact that the authentication process is applied in code-blocks and not to the whole image codestream. However, this feature is giving the advantage to the method to localize the alterations of the image content.

Another interesting approach is followed by Meerwald (2001). In that work a technique called Quantization Index Modulation (QIM) is used where the information of the watermark is acted as an index to select a quantizer from a set of possible quantizers. The watermarking process is presented in Figure 11.

Figure 10. Modifying the code-blocks

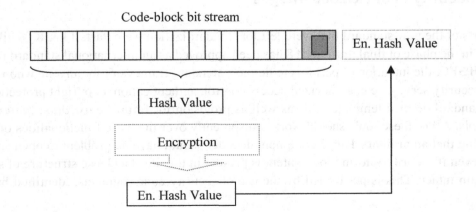

Figure 11. Meerwald's embedding process

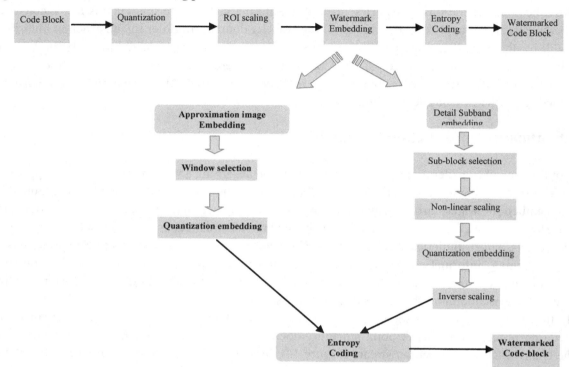

The technique serves both the needs of Ownership Protection and Tamper Detection (Authentication) Applications. The path with bold fonts corresponds to the authentication process and the path with normal fonts corresponds to the ownership protection process.

The Tamper Detection is achieved by using one wavelet coefficient to authenticate image blocks. In order to have a good spatial resolution for the tamper detection these coefficients are taken from the third decomposition step, giving the opportunity to the watermark detector to authenticate and localize changes in blocks of 8x8 pixels.

JPSEC : Security in JPEG2000 Images

The last parts of the new standard that were left for standardization were Parts 13 & 8. While the first is currently in the phase of final draft, part 8 has been approved as an international standard in May'07. Known as JPSEC, the intention of part 8 is to define a standard framework for anyone who would like to provide security services e.g. authorized access control, authentication, copyright protection. There are some standard defined template tools as well as provision for future *registration authority* (RA) provided tools. All of these tools should work transparently over the basic functionalities of the standard, meaning that an ordinary Part 1 compliant decoder should have no problem to open and show a j2k image, even if security information content is present in the file. The basic structure of such a file should remain intact. This is performed by the use of security code segments, identified by specific markers in the bitstream that are ignored by non-part 8 compliant decoders. The two different categories of security code segments are:

- **SEC:** Marked in the stream as 0xFF65, this code segment is found in the header of the JPEG2000 file. Information provided here, may apply to the whole image or specific parts of it. For these reason, in each tool's syntax, there is a *zone of influence* field (ZOI) that identifies the tool-affected parts.
- **INSEC:** Identified in the stream as 0xFF94, this code segment can be found anywhere in the codestream. This marker provides additional security comparing to SEC, as well as alternative implementation schemes.

The forms of the two code segments are given in Figure 12.

One must note here, that for the case of SEC segment, the tool syntax part, may involve the use of several different tools, not only one. Tools are the means by which the RAs provide the aforementioned security services through JPSEC. At the time that part 8 was in final draft form, ten different tools were presented in Annex B. These tools are:

- A flexible access control scheme for JPEG 2000 codestreams
- A unified authentication framework for JPEG 2000 images
- A simple packet-based encryption method for JPEG 2000 bitstreams
- Encryption tool for JPEG 2000 access control
- Key generation tool for JPEG 2000 access control
- Wavelet and bitstream domain scrambling for conditional access control
- Progressive access for JPEG 2000 codestream
- Scalable Authenticity of JPEG 2000 Code-streams
- JPEG 2000 data confidentiality and access control system based on data splitting and luring
- Secure scalable streaming and secure transcoding

Figure 12. Security code segments inside the JPEG2000 bitstream

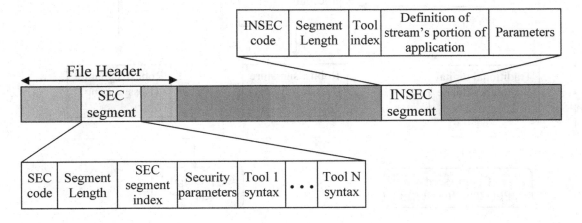

This list's tools are indicative. In the future many more, modern and advanced tools may become available. As can be observed, most tools address access control, encryption and authentication issues. Notably, there is not even one watermarking tool (at least at the time of writing of this chapter). This is due to patent restrictions. Most of the companies involved in watermarking, have patentized their methods and this is contrary to the openness of the new standard. However, if permission is given for a watermarking tool to be used license free, then there is no problem for the JPSEC framework to include it in the future.

It is not the intention of this chapter to analyse all of these tools. The main targets are watermarking and authentication. Since watermarking is currently absent in JPSEC, a brief discussion will be given on the authentication tools. In the work that led to the second tool of the list (Zhishou, Gang, Qibin, Xiao, Zhicheng, & Shi, 2004) an authentication framework is proposed against unauthorized modifications of digital images in JPEG2000 format. The aim of the authentication framework is to provide a flexible mechanism for different applications and user/provider requirements. The framework is suitable for all kinds of compressed and uncompressed images using the JPEG2000 encoder and it can be used to apply different watermarking techniques to them. A new parameter called Authentication bit Rate is introduced in order to achieve the desirable authentication robustness level. This parameter is also serving a variety of image authentication applications since it gathers all application's needs in a simple parameter. This mechanism is able to use the traditional digital signatures in case the required robustness of the watermark is to be fragile or robust signatures in case the required robustness of the watermark is to be semi fragile. In the next flowchart (Figure 13), this general framework is depicted.

In tool number eight (Peng, Deng, Wu & Shao, 2003) a proposal of guarantying the authenticity of the received image data by the end user without trustworthy servers and networks is formulated.

Figure 13. An Authentication framework for JPEG2000 images

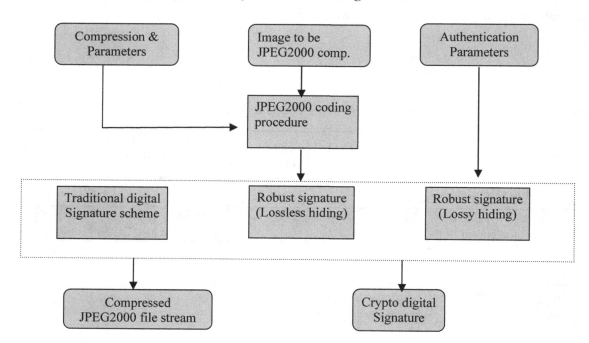

According to this proposal the authentication data on an image code stream and its verification by the end users are performed with three modules. The image provider generates an Integrity Check Value (ICV) of the image using a hash algorithm an then signs on the ICV to generate a digital signature of the image using a public key cryptosystem (e.g. RSA). When the end user requests a portion of the image, the provider sends to him the requested portion along with the Subsidiary Integrity Tokens (SIT) of the unsent portion of the image. Finally the end user verifies the authenticity of the received image portion by using the received digital signature and the SIT's.

CONCLUSION

In this chapter, a short overview of the new standard has been given. Through this, the possible places for watermarking have been identified. Methods proposed for each place in the coding pipeline (into the transform, after it, in the quantization stage, in the coding stage) have been presented. Each of these cases has specific advantages and disadvantages. Embedding at the transform coefficients is very compatible with older methods for which great expertise exist. On the other hand, quantization and coding may lead to significant loss of the watermark's energy. Quantization methods avoid quantization errors but haven't been thoroughly tested yet. None of the presented schemes has become part of the standardization procedure due to patent related issues. The effect of parameters selection for coding has also been discussed. Experiments with levels of decomposition, tile size, regions of interest, filter kernels, compression ratios, prove that the coding strategy is crucial for the survival of the watermark.

As far as authentication is concerned, the complexities of the standard along with the limited bibliography have restrained this activity. Proposed techniques are mostly based on the data integrity check in order to authenticate digital images by using cryptographic hash functions. However, more general frameworks have been proposed that include the application of different watermarking techniques for image authentication, in terms of content authentication. Most work on this field, is coming from the teams that contributed to the standard like Prof. Ebrahimi's team at EPFL, and Infocomm Research, Singapore.

FUTURE RESEARCH DIRECTIONS

It is obvious that watermarking in the JPEG2000 domain currently constitutes a promising research area. There are still many places in the coding pipeline in which the watermark can be embedded. There are various arguments about the place of embedding but coding stage embedding seems to be the most promising because no errors are introduced by the previous stages. A good idea could be that a non legitimate user, could decode the image with errors, or inferior quality while the rightful user will have the best quality possible. Quality control watermarking/data hiding is an open issue in JPEG2000 as it is for all lossy image compression formats.

Authentication of digital images in JPEG2000 format is a research field that also attracts the interest of the research community during the last years. Of all techniques, most interesting are the self-correcting ones, those that can partially or fully reverse the tampering. The practical value of such schemes is enormous.

Concluding this section, it seems that in the next years the field of watermarking and authentication of digital images in JPEG2000 format will attract more of the interest of the research community and new powerful protection mechanisms will be provided. The recent release of the JPSEC, will give researchers the opportunity to conform and include their tools in the JPEG2000 codestream. Currently, the number of available tools is very limited, so there's plenty of space for work in this area.

REFERENCES

Adams, M., & Kossentini, F. (2000). Reversible iInteger-tTo-iInteger wWavelet tTransforms for iImage cCompression: Performance eEvaluation and aAnalysis. *IEEE Transactions on Image Processing, 9*(6), 1010-1024.

Antonini, M., Barlaud, M., Mathieu, P., & Daubechies, I. (1992). Image coding using the wavelet tTransform. *IEEE Transactions on Image Processing, 1*(2), 205-220.

Barni, M., Bartolini F., & Fridrich, J. (2000, September). Digital watermarking for the authentication of the AVS Data. *Eusipco2000.* (Sep. 4-8, 2000, Tampere, Finland).

Barni, M., Bartolini, F., Cappellini, V., Lippi, A., & Piva, A. (1999). A DWT-based technique for spatio-frequency masking of digital signatures. *Proceedings of the 11th SPIE Annual Symposium, Electronic Imaging '99, Security and watermarking of multimedia contents*, P. W. Wong (ed.), *3657*, 31-39.(January 1999, San Jose, CA), P. W. Wong (Ed.), vol. 3657, 31-39.

Bhattacharjee S., & Kutter, M. (1998, October 4-7). Compression tolerant image authentication. *International Conference on Image Processing ICIP'98.* (October 4-7, 1998, Chicago, IL).

Boliek, M., Houchin J. S., & Wu, G. (2000, September). JPEG 2000 next generation image compression system features and syntax. *Proceedings of the Intl Conf. on Image Processing ICIP 2000 2*, 45-48. , (September 2000, Vancouver, Canada), vol. II, 45-48.

Chen, B., & Wornell, G. (2000). Preprocessed and postprocessed quantization index modulation methods for digital watermarking. *Proceedings of SPIE: Security and Watermarking of Multimedia Contents II, Electronic Imaging 2000*, (January 2000, . San Jose, CA).

Corvi, M., & Nicchiotti, G. (1997, June). Wavelet-based image watermarking for copyright protection. *Scandinavian Conference on Image Analysis SCIA '97.* , (June 1997, Lappeenranta, Finland).

Davoine, F. (2000). Comparison of two wavelet based image watermarking schemes. *Proceedings of the IEEE International Conference on Image Processing ICIP 2000*, (September 2000,. Vancouver, Canada).

Eggers, J., & Girod, B. (2000). Quantization watermarking. *Proceedings of SPIE: Security and Watermarking of Multimedia Contents II, Electronic Imaging 2000*, (January 2000,. San Jose, CA).

Eskicioglu, A. M. (2003). Protecting intellectual property in digital multimedia networks (Invited Paper). *IEEE Computer, Special Issue on Piracy and Privacy, 36*(7), 39-45.

Fotopoulos, V., & Skodras, A. N. (2002, July 1-3). JPEG2000 parameters against watermarking. *Proceedings of the 14th Int. Conf. on Digital Signal Processing DSP 2002* (July 1-3, 2002, Santorini, Greece), vol. *2*, 713-716. Santorini, Greece

Grosbois, R., Gerbelot, P., & Ebrahimi, T. (2001, July 29th-August 3rd). Authentication and access control in the JPEG 2000 compressed domain. *Proceedings of the SPIE 46th Annual Meeting, Applications of Digital Image Processing XXIV* (July 29th- August 3rd, 2001,. San Diego, CA).

ISO/IEC JTC1/SC29 15444-1. (2007). Information technology—JPEG 2000 image coding system: Core coding system.

"JPEG 2000". (2007). Retrieved August 07, 2007, from http://www.jpeg.org/jpeg2000.html

Kailasanathan, C., Safavi-Naini, R., & Ogunbona, P. (2001, June 3-6). Image authentication surviving acceptable modifications. *IEEE-EURASIP Workshop on Nonlinear Signal and Image Processing NSIP'01.1* (June 3-6, 2001).

Kim, J. R., & Moon, Y. S. (1999, October). A robust wavelet-based digital watermark using level-adaptive thresholding. *Proceedings of the 6th IEEE International Conference on Image Processing ICIP '99, (October 1999, Kobe, Japan), vol.II2*, 226-230. Kobe, Japan

Kim, Y.-S., Kwon, O.-H., & Park, R.-H. (1999). Wavelet- based watermarking method for digital images using the human visual system. *Electronic Letters 35*(6), 466-467.

Kostopoulos, I., Gilani, S. A. M., & Skodras, A. N. (2002, July 1-3). Color image authentication using a self-embedding technique. *Proceedings of the 14th Int. Conf. on Digital Signal Processing DSP 2002* (July 1-3, 2002, . Santorini, Greece).

Kundur, D. (1999, October). Improved digital watermarking through diversity and attack characterization. *Proceedings of the ACM Workshop on Multimedia Security '99*, 53-58, (October 1999,. Orlando, FL), 53-58.

Liang, J., Xu, P., & Tran, T. D. (2000, March). A robust DCT-based low frequency watermarking scheme. *34th Annual Conference on Information Sciences and Systems, 1*, TA5 1-6. (March 2000, Princeton, NJ), vol. *I*, TA5 1-6.

Lin, C.-Y., & Chang, S.-F. (2000, January). Semi-fragile watermarking for authenticating JPEG visual content. *Proceedings of the SPIE International Conference on Security and Watermarking of Multimedia Content II, 3971*, 140-151. (Jan 2000, San Jose, CA), vol. 3971, 140-151.

Lu, C. S., & Liao, H. Y. M. (2001). Multipurpose watermarking for image authentication and protection. *IEEE Transactions on Image Processing, 10*(10), 1579-1592.

Marcellin, M. W., Gormish, M., Bilgin, A., & Boliek, M. (2000, March). An overview of JPEG 2000. *Proceedings of IEEE Data Compression Conference*, 523-541(March 2000, . Snowbird, UT), 523-541.

Meerwald, P. (2001, May). Quantization watermarking in the JPEG 2000 coding pipeline. Communications and multimedia security issues of the new century., *IFIP TC6/TC11, Fifth Joint Working Conference on Communications and Multimedia Security, CMS'01*, 69-79. (May 2001, Darmstadt, Germany), 69-79.

Merkle, R. C. (1989). A certified digital signature. In Gilles Brassard (Ed.), *Advances in Cryptology - Crypto '89, Lecture Notes in Computer Science, vol 435*, 218-238., Berlin: Springer-Verlag.

Minguillón J., Herrera-Joancomartí, J., & Megías, D. (2003, January). Empirical evaluation of a JPEG 2000 standard-based robust watermarking scheme. *Proceedings of SPIE: Security and Watermarking of Multimedia Contents V, 5020*, 717-727V (January 2003, Santa Clara, CA), vol. 5020, 717-727.

Nicchiotti, G., & Ottaviano, E. (1998, September). Non-invertible statistical wavelet watermarking. *Proceedings of the 9th European Signal Processing Conference EUPISCO '98*, 2289-2292. (September 1998, Island of Rhodes, Greece), 2289-2292.

Ohnishi, J., & Matsui, K. (1998). A method of watermarking with multiresolution analysis and pseudo noise sequences. *Systems and Computers in Japan, 29*(5), 11-19.

Peng, C., Deng, H. J. R., Wu, Y. D., & Shao, W. (2003). A flexible and scalable authentication scheme for JPEG 2000 codestreams. *Proceedings of the eleventh ACM international conference on Multimedia MULTIMEDIA '03*, 433-441.

Perreira, S., Voloshynovskiy, S., & Pun, T. (2000, April) Optimized wavelet domain watermark embedding strategy using linear programming. *SPIE AeroSence 2000: Wavelet Applications VII*, H. H. Szu, (Ed.)., (April 2000, Orlando, FL).

"Robustness: JPEG 2000 compression". (2007). Retrieved August 22, 2007, from http://www.cosy.sbg.ac.at/~pmeerw/Watermarking/attack_jpeg2000.html

Schneier, B. (1995). *Applied cryptography: Protocols, algorithms, and source code in C*, Second 2nd Edition. New York: John Wiley & Sons.

Seo, Y., Kim, M., Park, H., Jung, H., Chung, H., Huh, Y., & Lee, J. (2001, October). A secure watermarking for JPEG 2000. *Proceedings of the IEEE International Conference on Image Processing ICIP 2001*, 530-533. (October 2001, Thessaloniki, Greece), 530-533.

Su, P., & Kuo, C. (2003, May 25-28). Information embedding in JPEG-2000 compressed images. *ISCAS 2003*, (May 25-28, 2003, . Bangkok, Thailand).

Taubman, D. (2000). High performance scalable image compression with EBCOT. *IEEE Transactions on Image Processing, 9*(6), 1158-1170.

Taubman, D., & Zalkor, A. (1994). Multirate 3-D subband coding of Video. *IEEE Transactions on Image Processing, 3*(5), 572-578.

Taubman, D., Ordentlich, E., Weinberger, M., Seroussi, G., Ueno, I., & Ono, F. (2000, September). Embedded block coding in JPEG 2000. *Proceedings of IEEE International Conference on Image Processing ICIP 2000, 2*, 33-36. (September 2000, Vancouver, Canada), vol. II, 33-36..

Tzovaras, D., Karagiannis, N., & Strintzis, M. G. (1998, September). Robust image watermarking in the subband or discrete cosine transform. *Proceedings of the 9th European Signal Processing Conference EUPISCO '98*, 2285-2288. (September 1998, Island of Rhodes, Greece.), 2285-2288.

Usevitch, B. (2001). A tutorial on modern lossy wavelet image compression: Foundations of JPEG2000. *IEEE Signal Processing Magazine, 18*(5), 22-35.

Vetterli, M. (2001). Wavelets, approximation and compression. *IEEE Signal Processing Magazine, 18*(5), 59-73.

Walton, S. (1995). Image authentication for a slippery new age. *Dr. Dobb's Journal of Software Tools for Professional Programmers, 20*(4), 18-26.

Watson, A. B., Yang, G. Y., Solomon, J. A. & Villasenor, J. (1997). Visibility of wavelet quantization noise. *IEEE Transactions on Image Processing, 6*(8), 1164-1175.

"Welcome to JPEG". (2007). Retrieved August 07, 2007, from http://www.jpeg.org/jpeg2000/CDs15444.html

Wong, P. H. W., Yeung, G. Y. M., & Au, O.C. (2003, Baltimore). Capacity for JPEG2000-to-JPEG 2000 images watermarking. *Proceedings of 2003 IEEE International Conference on Multimedia & Expo ICME'03, 2, 485-488.* (2003, Baltimore), Vol. 2, 485-488.

Wu, M., & Liu, B. (1998). Watermarking for image authentication. *IEEE International Conference on Image Processing ICIP'98, vol.2,* 437-441.

Wu, Y., Deng, R., Di M., Peng, C., & Yang, Y. (2003). Authentication of JPEG 2000 Code-Streams and Files. ISO/IEC JTC1/SC29/WG1 N2809

Xia, X.-G., Boncelet, C. G., & Arce, G. R. (1998). Wavelet transform based watermark for digital images. *Optics Express 3*(12), 497-511.

Xie, L. & Arce, G.R. (1998). Joint wavelet compression and authentication watermarking. *Proceedings of the IEEE International Conference on Image Processing, ICIP '98,* (1998,. Chicago, IL).

Zhishou, Z., Gang, Q., Qibin, S., Xiao, L., Zhicheng, N., & Shi, Y.Q. (2004, June). A unified authentication framework for JPEG 2000. *Proceedings of 2004 IEEE International Conference on Multimedia & Expo ICME'04, 2,* 915-918. (June 2004, Taipei, Taiwan), vol. 2, 915-918.

ADDITIONAL READING

"JPEG 2000 DataCompression.info". (2007). Retrieved August 30, 2007, from http://datacompression.info/JPEG2000.shtml

Acharya, T., & Tsai, P. S. (2004). JPEG2000 Standard for image compression: Concepts, algorithms and VLSI architectures. Wiley-Interscience.

Arnold, M., Schmucker, M., & Wolthusen, S. D. (2003). Techniques and applications of digital watermarking and content protection. Boston, MA : Artech House.

Digital Watermarking and Steganography, Second Edition (The Morgan Kaufmann Series in Multimedia Information and Systems) Amsterdam Boston : Morgan Kaufmann.

Hanjalic, A. (2000). *Image and video databases: Restoration, watermarking, and retrieval.* Amsterdam Lausanne: Elsevier.

Johnson, N. F., Duric, Z. & Jajodia, S. (2001). *Information hiding: Ssteganography and Wwatermarking-- attacks and countermeasures.* Boston : Kluwer Academic Publishers.

Katzenbeisser, S., and & Petitcolas, F. (2000). *Information hiding techniques for steganography and digital watermarking.* Boston: Artech House.

Lu, C-S. (Ed.) (2004). *Multimedia security: Steganography and digital watermarking techniques for protection of intellectual property.* Hershey, PA; London: Idea Group.

Pan, J. S., Huang, H. C., Jain, L., and & Fang, W. C. (2007). Intelligent multimedia data hiding: New Directions (Studies in Computational Intelligence) Berlin / Heidelberg : Springer.

Rabbani, M. & Joshi, R. (2002). An Overview of the JPEG2000 Still Image Compression Standard, *Signal Processing Image Communication, 17*(1).

Seitz, J. (Ed.) (2005). *Digital watermarking for digital media.* Information Science Publishing.

Taubman, D. S. & Marcellin, M. W. (2002). *JPEG 2000: Image compression fundamentals, standards and practice.* Boston; Dordrecht : Kluwer Academic Publishers.

Wayner, P. (2002). *Disappearing cryptography: Information hiding: Steganography and watermarking* (2nd Edition). Amsterdam; Boston: Morgan Kaufmann.

Chapter VI
Securing and Protecting the Copyright of Digital Video Through Watermarking Technologies

Evanthia Tsilichristou
University of Patras, Greece

Spiridon Likothanasis
University of Patras, Greece

ABSTRACT

The basic principle of watermarking is the addition of the watermark signal to the host data that we wish to watermark. The addition is taking place in a way that the watermark signal is discreet and secure among the rest signals. Its retrieval, either partial or complete from the rest of signals, must be also possible only by using a secret key. In this chapter, we are going to deal with the digital video watermarking. First, we will name its applications, requirements, and the most important trends, then we will describe some of the most significant techniques of the specific process.

INTRODUCTION

Digital video watermarking techniques and algorithms offer a great support to real world digital video applications. These applications include the copy control, the broadcast monitoring, the fingerprinting, the video authentication, the copyright protection as well as the enhanced video coding.

Nowadays, the copying of a digital video is very simple by using a recorder. For this reason, a watermark is embedded to the digital video so that its copying through unauthorized recorders may not be possible. If the recorder is able to read the hidden information comprised into the watermark, then it is authorized to produce copies, otherwise it must not carry out the copying.

As to the broadcast monitoring, the aim of the watermarking is the determination of the identity of the video object transmitted. The owners having the right to create a video want to secure their privileges any time their property is broadcasted. The principal idea here embeds identification information (a unique watermark) into the data, which is identified by a computer. This identification information is obtained directly and with reliability after the decoding process.

In fingerprinting, the aim of the watermark is to show which user created the illegal copies. The problem arises when a 'traitor' spares the protected material without having any sort of permission on behalf of the holder of the right on intellectual property. In order to solve the problem, the basic idea is to be able to identify the identity of the traitor when detecting an illegal copy so that we can prosecute him in court. This can happen by embedding into data an indelible and invisible watermark which determines the client's identity.

The authentication techniques are useful for confirming that a video content is the original. Different methods for the verification of the video content authenticity as well as for the protection against falsification are proposed. Researchers have also studied the use of digital watermarking aiming at verifying the integrity of the digital video content. A basic technique is the typical embodiment of a timestamp into the video frames. The result of the aforementioned technique is that the detection of alterations may be possible.

REQUIREMENTS OF VIDEO WATERMARKING

A video watermarking technique must fulfil some requirements. We mention below the three most principal requirements for video watermarking. The first is that the technique above should be robust to non hostile video processing. The second is that it should be robust to collusions and the third one is that it should be performed in real-time.

The robustness of the digital watermarking is always estimated in regard to the survival of the watermark after the implementation of the attacks. In the environment of digital watermarking the future value of attacks that take place in the video is multiple. Many different, non hostile attacks in video are in fact likely to happen. The term non-hostile refers to those attacks where for example, the provider of the content processes a bit of information from his digital data for the most efficient handling of his sources. Afterwards, we name any procedures that can lead to non hostile attacks: the addition of noise during the transmission through a wireless network, the conversion of a digital to analog or analog to digital signal, the gamma correction in order to increase the contrast, the changes across display formats (4/3, 16/9, 2.11/1), the changes of spatial resolution (NTSC, PAL, SECAM), the attack by a handheld camera, the changes in frame rate, the video editing process (cut-and-splice or cut-insert-splice) and the overlay with a chart (logos and labels).

Another basic requirement is the robustness against collusions. The term collusion refers to all hostile users who unite their knowledge, for example the watermarked data they have in order to produce illegally the non-watermarked ones. There are two types of collusion: the type I collusion and the type II collusion. The same watermark is embedded into different copies of different data. The type I collusion estimates the watermark of every watermarked data. Then, it combines in a linear way the watermarks estimated and provides an exact estimation of it; for example, it measures the mean of various evaluations. Since the collusion obtained a good estimation of the watermark, it removes it from the rest and in this way we have the non-watermarked data. When different watermarks are embedded into different copies of the same data, type II collusion is applied. The only thing that this collusion can do is to apply a linear combination to different watermarked data so as to produce the non-watermarked ones. It can use the average as a linear combination. In general, the average of different watermarks points to zero.

The real-time constitutes the third requirement. It does not have any particular concern in the case of still images. When someone wishes to embed a watermark or to control its presence in an image, then few seconds of delay may be acceptable. However, such a delay is not realistic in a video environment. In fact, the frames are transmitted in a quite fair rate, usually 25 frames per second is a rate that can be achieved for a smooth video stream. The least the embedder or the detector of the watermark or in some cases even both of them can do is to be able to handle such a rate. While monitoring a broadcast, the detector should be capable of detecting an embedded watermark in real-time. In order to fulfil the real-time requirement, the complexity of the watermarking algorithm must be the lower possible.

THE MOST IMPORTANT TRENDS IN VIDEO WATERMARKING

Digital video watermarking is a relatively new area of research which uses the advantages resulting from the conclusions of the digital watermarking in still images. Many algorithms have been proposed and among them we have isolated the three most important trends existing. The simplest and most direct approach considers the video as a sequence consisting of still images and it applies to them one of the existing watermarking shapes for still images. The second approach makes use of the further dimension of time aiming at designing new robust algorithms for video watermarking. Finally, the last trend considers the video stream as compressed data that have been compressed following a specific method of video compression and its characteristics are used in the production of an efficient watermarking shape.

During the very first years, digital watermarking studied to a large extent the case of still images. Many interesting results and algorithms were developed and when new areas, such as the video watermarking, started to become a research issue, the basic idea was to test the reuse of former known results. As a consequence, the community of watermarking considered in the first place the video as a sequence of still images and adopted the existing watermarking shapes for images during video watermarking. A simple way to extend the shape above is to embed the same watermark into the video frames following a typical rate. From the detector's point of view, its presence is controlled for each frame. If the video is watermarked, then a typical vibration can be observed as a response to him. However, such a shape does not have any profitable load. The only thing the detector can do is to say if the watermark given appears or not but he does not extract any secret message. On the other side, host data are much bigger in size than a simple still image. Since it is possible to embed more bits into a larger host signal, we expect that video watermarks have a much more profitable load. This can be easily realized by embedding independent watermarks of many bits into each video frame. However, the benefit as to the profitable load is balanced with the loss of robustness.

The main disadvantage of concerning the video as a sequence of independent still images is that we do not take into great consideration the dimension of time. A number of researchers have studied how it is possible to reduce the visual impact that the watermark has on still images, taking into account the properties of the human visual system as well as the procedures of the frequency mask, the luminance mask and the contrast mask. These studies can be easily extended also in video through a direct frame after frame adaptation. However, the watermark resulting is not the ideal one in terms of visibility since it is not possible to study the sensitivity of the human eye in time. The motion is in fact a very particular characteristic of the video and the new video-based measurements of perceptibility need to be designed so that we will be able to make use of them during digital video watermarking. This simple example shows that the dimension of time is a crucial point in video and that it should be seriously considered for the creation of effective algorithms.

The last trend considers the video data as compressed ones that have been compressed based on a specific type of compression. In fact, the most of the time, a video is stored in a compressed version to save some space. The watermarking methods have been designed in such a way that the watermark is embedded directly into the compressed video stream. Therefore, we make use of a very specific part of this video compression (run length coding) aiming at hiding information. Alternative watermarking strategies can be used according to the type of frame under watermarking. If we embed the watermark directly into the stream of the compressed video, the real-time video processing is possible. However, the watermark is by nature connected to this compression and it may not survive after a standard video conversion.

The simplest way of watermarking a video is the straight change of pixel values of the video in spatial domain. Another way which has more advantages is embedding the watermark into the frequency domain, by using one of the much known transforms: Discrete Fourier Transform (DFT), Discrete Cosine Transform (DCT) and Discrete Wavelet Transform (DWT). Below we describe three important and interesting video watermarking techniques which have satisfying effects during experiments.

AN ADAPTIVE VIDEO WATERMARKING ALGORITHM

Robustness is the major issue arising in digital watermarking algorithms. An effective method applied for improving the watermark's robustness is that its embodiment is done adaptively to the perceptual property and the characteristics of the signal. Hong-mei Liu, Ji-wu Huang and Zi-mei Xiao suggest an adaptive video watermarking algorithm to the wavelet domain. According to the properties of the 2-D wavelet coefficients, the watermark is inserted into the coefficients of the low frequency sub-band in order to achieve better robustness. If we want to improve the strength of the watermark's components, we perform a classification of the coefficients of the low frequency sub-band based on the motion of the object and the texture complexity of the content in the video sequence. Following the results of this classification, the strength of the components of the watermark is adjusted adaptively. Results from experiments have shown that the watermark generated is robust to video degradation and distortions, while its transparency is guaranteed.

The Watermarking Algorithm

The algorithm of inserting the watermark consists of five steps: (1)DWT (Discrete Wavelet Transform), (2)motion detection and texture classification, (3)production of the watermark, (4)watermark coding, (5)IDWT (inverse DWT). In Figure 1 the diagram of this specific algorithm is illustrated.

Discrete wavelet transform
So that the watermark is more robust we apply a DWT of three levels. The DWT is applied to the Y component of each frame in video sequence and ten sub-bands result (LH_i, HL_i, HHi, LL_3, i=1-3), where LL_3 is the low-pass approximation of the original image.

Figure 1. Block diagram of the watermark inserting algorithm

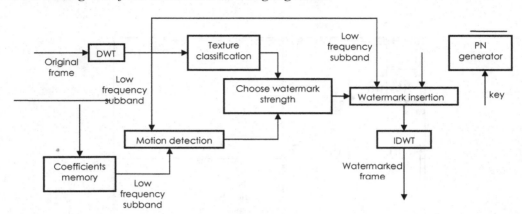

Motion Detection

Motion detection is applied to the part of the LL_3 sub-band in still or moving areas. The basic steps of this process are the following:

- We estimate the difference between the LL_3 sub-band coefficients of the current frame and of the last frame: FD $(i, j) = S_k (i, j) - S_{k-1} (i, j)$.
- We define the T_1 and T_2 thresholds and we decide upon the situation of each coefficient:

$$p(i, j) = \begin{cases} 0 & \text{still} & |FD(i,j)| < T_1 \\ X & \text{ambiguous} & T_1 \leq |FD(i,j)| \leq T_2 \\ 1 & \text{motion} & |FD(i,j)| > T_2 \end{cases}$$

- We abolish the ambiguous situation.
- We incorporate the areas of slow motion and abolish the still area which is surrounded by motion areas.

Due to the fact that the handling of the steps above is simple, the calculating power of the motion detection process is insignificant.

Texture Classification

Taking for granted that the watermark is inserted into the LL_3 band, the texture's characteristics (it is simple or complex) of the original frame need to be illustrated in this band. But from the simple coefficient of the LL_3 band, which represent an 8x8 block of the original frame, we cannot obtain the texture's characteristics. Therefore, if we use a 2x2 block of the LL_3 band, the corresponding block in the original frame should be 16x16 and then the transparency or the robustness of the watermark are influenced. For this reason the progressive prediction of the texture's characteristics of other bands than the LL_3 one is proposed.

Figure 2. Predict texture characteristics from LL$_3$ band

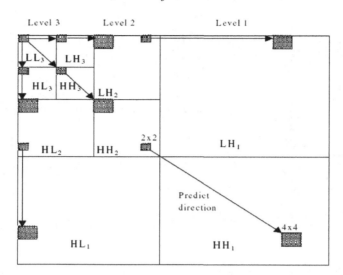

It is well-known that texture in different levels of the pyramid is highly correlated. Therefore, the texture's characteristics of the LH$_3$, HL$_3$ and HH$_3$ bands in level 3 are predicted by the LL$_3$ band. Then those characteristics are used for the prediction of the texture's characteristics of the bands in level 2 and so on.

The algorithm above is based on the progressive characteristics of the texture predicted by the LL$_3$ band. The process of predicting the texture's characteristics by this specific band is illustrated in Figure 2. After that, we describe how the texture's characteristics of the HH$_1$ band result from the LL$_3$ band. The procedure for the other bands remains the same. The steps performed are the following:

1. We set the threshold for each sub-band.
2. For each 2x2 block of the LL$_3$ band, we compare the standard deviation S with the threshold Th$_3$ of the HH$_3$. If S> Th$_3$, then we perform step 4, else
3. We mark the corresponding (in the same location in spatial domain) 2x2 block of the HH$_3$, the 4x4 block of the HH$_2$ and the 8x8 block of the HHi in '0' which represent the area of simple texture and then we perform step 12
4. We mark the corresponding 2x2 block of the HH$_3$ in '1' which represent the area of complex texture
5. We compare the standard deviation S of the 2x2 block of the HH$_3$ which has been marked in '1' with the Th$_2$ threshold of the HH$_2$. If S> Th$_2$ then we perform step 7, else
6. We mark the corresponding (in the same location in spatial domain) 4x4 block of the HH$_2$ and the 8x8 block of the HHi in '0' and afterwards we perform step 12
7. We mark the corresponding 4x4 block of the HH$_2$ in '1'
8. For each 2x2 block of the 4x4 block in step 6, we compare the standard deviation S with the Th$_1$ threshold of the HH$_1$, if S> Th$_1$ then we perform step 10, else
9. We mark the corresponding 4x4 block of the HHi in '0' and then we perform step 11
10. We mark the corresponding 4x4 block of the HH$_1$ in '1'

11. We repeat steps 8-11 until all 2x2 blocks of the 4x4 block in step 6 are used
12. We repeat steps 2-12 until all 2x2 blocks of the LL_3 are used
13. We map the characteristics of the texture of each 4x4 block of the HH_i band in the coefficient of the LL_3 band.

Watermark Insertion

The hidden bit of information is embedded into the components which present high perceptibility based on the robustness of the hidden information. The LL_3 sub-band consists of those components in the DWT domain and the value of the LL_3 coefficients is much greater than the value of the high frequency coefficients in general. That means that if the LL_3 coefficients have bigger perceptibility, then it is possible that the information shall be embedded without any perceptual distortions arising. On the other hand, the high-pass sub-band coefficients obey to Laplace distribution and most of them are small or tend to zero and that is why their alteration influences the invisibility of the watermarked image.

Based on all these reasons and on their experiments, the authors propose the use of the LL_3 sub-band for the watermark's embodiment. Experimental results support this procedure. If compared with a still image, the video sequence consists of moving components. It is well-known that the eye sensitivity is lowered when the object is moving. Thus, a watermark of great width is embedded in the area where there is motion. So that it is adapted to the video motion, we apply a detection of the motion among the LL_3 sub-bands of the current frame and the last one and then the LL_3 sub-band of the current frame is distributed in moving or still areas.

The texture masking constitutes a property of the human visual system and indicates that the more complex the texture is, the bigger the contrast sensitivity threshold is and the greater the width is concerning the embedded watermark. Following that, we apply the algorithm which rates based on the LL_3 texture (that is, the algorithm described above) and classifies the LL_3 coefficients in areas of simple texture and areas of complex texture and in the end a watermark arises which is adapted to the video content.

According to the results coming from the motion detection and the texture classification, the LL_3 coefficients are grouped into three sets:

- Still area with simple texture. The watermark's strength is the a_1.
- Still area with complex texture or area with motion and simple texture. The watermark's strength is the a_2.
- Area with motion and complex texture. The watermark's strength is the a_3.

Following the property of perception, we have $a_3 > a_2 > a_1$.

A special Gaussian ordinary sequence is generated as a watermark for each frame of the video sequence. Let N define the number of the coefficients of the low frequency sub-band, consequently the watermark of the kth frame is the $W^{(k)} = \{x_i^{(k)}, 0 \leq i < N\}$ and afterwards we insert it as follows: $\tilde{u}_i^{(k)} = u_i^{(k)} + ax_i^{(k)}$, where a defines the strength of the watermark and it has been selected so that it is adapted to the results of the classification. The $u_i^{(k)}$ and $\tilde{u}_i^{(k)}$ define the DWT coefficient of the LL_3 band before and after the insertion of the watermark.

Finally, we apply the IDWT and the watermarked frame turns up.

Watermark Detection

The detection algorithm is based on the control assumptions. Firstly, the similarity is measured:

$$\rho^{(k)}(\hat{\mathbf{W}}^{(k)}, \mathbf{W}^{(k)}) = \sum_{j=0}^{N-1} \hat{x}_j^{(k)} \cdot x_j^{(k)} \Big/ \sqrt{\sum_{j=0}^{N-1} (\hat{x}_j^{(k)})^2}$$

where $\hat{\mathbf{W}}^{(k)}$ defines the components of the watermark in the kth frame of the test sequence and we have $\hat{\mathbf{W}}^{(k)} = \{.\hat{x}_i^{(k)}, 0 \le i < N\}$ If there are L frames in the sequence, then the mean similarity is the following:

$$\rho = \frac{\sum_{i=0}^{L-1} {}^{(i)}(\hat{W}^{(i)}, W^{(i)})}{L}.$$

Moreover, we compare the mean similarity r with the threshold T (=5), so as to decide whether the watermarks match.

When certain frames are dropped or the sequence is chopped, we are able to measure the mean similarity of the auxiliary frames and in this way the watermark becomes robust to the frame dropping and to temporal down-sampling.

Let us note that during detection process, the original video process is useful, but it is not required that we know into which DWT sub-band the watermark's coefficient is inserted and which is its strength.

Experimental Results

The watermarking shape above was put into practice in the 32 frames of the Football sequence, of length 704x576 as well as in the 32 frames of the Flower garden sequence, of length 720x480. Part of the original frame and part of the watermarked frame of the Football sequence are illustrated in Figure 3.

We test the robustness of the adaptive watermarking algorithm suggested to video degradation and it is compared with the robustness of the non adaptive algorithm. Further Gaussian noise with different strength is added to video sequences with or without the watermark. Part of the watermarked frame which is corrupted by noise is illustrated in Figure 4(a). Even if the noise is quite loud (PSNR=14.78dB), the watermark can be detected. It is noticed that the robustness of the adaptive algorithm is generally better than that of the non adaptive one.

Figure 3. Demonstration of invisibility (a)Part of a original frame from Football and (b)Watermarked frame (PSNR=43.17dB)

(a)   *(b)*

Figure 4, The noised frame and MPEG coded frame from Football (a)Noised watermarked frame (PSNR=14.78dB) (b)MPEG-2 coded frame at 0.18bpp (PSNR=26.80)

(a)　　　　　　　　　　　　　　　*(b)*

Table 1. Results of frame dropping

Number of dropped frames	Similarity
1	64.8697
8	64.3288
16	65.4938
24	64.4752

We also test the robustness of the algorithm in the MPEG-2 coding with different rates of compression. Part of a MPEG codified and watermarked frame (with CR=66:1, Bit Rate=1.8M, PSNR=26.80dB) is illustrated in Figure 4(b). Even though the distortion of the reconstructed frame is obvious, the similarity obtained is greater than the threshold. It is remarked that the robustness to the MPEG coding of the adaptive watermark is much better than the one of the non adaptive watermark.

Finally, we test the ability to detect the watermark when frames of the video sequence are dropped and down-sampled in space. According to the results of Table 1, the watermark is nearly influenced by the dropping of the frame. When the video sequence is 2:1 down-sampled in space, then the detector's response is 21.4709 (watermark) which is much better than the T(=5) threshold.

MULTIRESOLUTION SCENE-BASED VIDEO WATERMARKING USING PERCEPTUAL MODELS

The authors Mitchell Swanson, Bin Zhu and Ahmed Tewfik have proposed a watermarking procedure to embed copyright protection into digital video. This procedure makes direct use of spatial masking, frequency masking as well as temporal properties in order to embed an invisible and robust watermark. The last one is composed of static and dynamic temporal components. These components are generated from a temporal wavelet transform which is applied to video scenes. The resulting frames with a wavelet coefficient are modified by a pseudorandom sequence. This one was shaped based on perception and represents the author of the watermark. The noise-like watermark is statistically undetectable and therefore its unauthorized removal is discouraged. Furthermore, the author's representation resolves the deadlock problem. The multiresolution watermark may be detected on single frames, without knowledge of the location of these frames in the video scene. The authors after some experiments have demonstrated that this watermarking procedure is robust to several video degradations and distortions.

Watermark Insertion

The first step of the watermarking algorithm presented in this paper consists of the splitting of the video sequence into scenes. This action allows the watermarking procedure to take into consideration the temporal excess. To visibly similar areas of the video sequence, such as the frames of the same scene, a consistent watermark must be embedded. So that pirate attacks will not affect it, the temporal wavelet transform is applied to video scenes. The multiresolution nature of the wavelet transform allows the watermark to exist across multiple temporal scales and in this way, we can overcome the aforementioned attacks. For example, the embedded watermark exists in all frames in the scene, in the lowest frequency (DC) of each wavelet frame.

The indexed temporal variables are denoted by capital letters, for example the ith frame of a video scene is the F_i. The frames are settled in progression along time. The circumflex is used for the definition of a wavelet representation, for example by $\tilde{F}_i$ we define the ith frame of the wavelet coefficient. Without loss of generality, wavelet frames are settled from the lowest to the highest frequency, e.g. $\tilde{F}_0$ is a DC frame. Finally, the grave capital letters, such as F_i' define the DCT representation of an indexed variable.

Figure 5 illustrates the video watermarking process. A scene of k frames in a video sequence is studied. Let each scene frame be of size nxm. The video can be of grey level (8 bit/pixel) or colored (24 bit/pixel). Let the term F_i define the frames in the scene, where i=0,…, k-1. Initially, the wavelet transform of k F_i frame is measured, so that the k frames of the $\tilde{F}_i$ wavelet coefficient, with i=0,…,k-1. The watermark is generated and added to the video based on the following steps:

1.   We group each $\tilde{F}_i$ wavelet frame into 8x8 block $\tilde{B}_{ij}, i = 0,1,...,\lfloor n/8 \rfloor$ and $j = 0,1,...,\lfloor m/8 \rfloor$
2.   For each block $\tilde{B}_{ij}$:
     a.   We measure the DCT, $\tilde{B}_{ij}'$, of the $\tilde{B}_{ij}$ block in the frame,
     b.   We measure the frequency masking, M_{ij}', for the DCT $\tilde{B}_{ij}'$ block,
     c.   We use the M_{ij}' masking to weigh the noise-like author Y_{ij}' for this frame block and the author's signature is generated in the frequency: $P_{ij}' = M_{ij}' Y_{ij}'$,
     d.   We generate the watermarked block of the $\tilde{W}_{ij}$ wavelet coefficient, by measuring the opposite DCT of the P_{ij}' and the watermark increases in the specific area in the level of the greatest error occurred through the $\tilde{S}_{ij}$ spatial mask (that is, the $\tilde{W}_{ij}$ watermark is multiplied by the $\tilde{S}_{ij}$ spatial mask),
     e.   we add the $\tilde{W}_{ij}$ watermark to the $\tilde{B}_{ij}$ block and the watermarked block is generated.
3.   This procedure is repeated for all frames of the wavelet coefficient, $\tilde{F}_i$ The watermark for each frame of the wavelet coefficient is the sequence of all 8x8 block of the $\tilde{W}_{ij}$ watermark for this frame. Finally, the watermarks generated according to this procedure are added to the video frame. The watermarked frames of the wavelet coefficient are transformed back in the spatial domain by using the opposite wavelet transform. Since the watermark has been designed and embedded into the wavelet domain, the single watermarks for each frame in the wavelet coefficient are spread out in

many levels so as to gain support by the temporal domain. For example, the watermarks embedded into the high-pass wavelet frames are temporally restricted. In reverse, the watermarks embedded into the low-pass wavelet frames in general are situated along the scene in the temporal domain.

Watermark Detection

The watermark has been designed in such a way that the owner shall be able to easily extract it even if signal processing operations are applied to the host video. When the embedded watermark is noise-like, the attacker does not have adequate knowledge of the watermark's direct removal. Consequently, efforts for the destruction of the watermark are made blindly. As opposed to other users, the owner has a copy of the original video as well as the author's signature which is noise-like and has been embedded into the video. Usually, the owner appears to maintain one or more video frames through which he wishes to prove that he is holding the right on intellectual property. In order to extract the potential watermark from a test video or test video frame, two methods were developed. Both hypotheses are experimentally tested. The first method requires index knowledge during detection process, as for example we shall know the placement of the test video frames relative to the original video. The second detection method does not require knowledge of the location of the test frames. This process is extremely useful while setting a video where thousands of frames may be similar and we do not know where each test frame resides.

Detection I-Watermark Detection with Index Knowledge

When the location of the test frame is known, a straightforward hypothesis test is applied. For each frame in the test video R_k, we perform the following hypothesis test:

$$H_0 : X_k = R_k - F_k = N_k \quad \text{(no watermark)}$$
$$H_1 : X_k = R_k - F_k = W_k^* + N_k \quad \text{(watermark)} \tag{1}$$

Figure 5. Diagram of video watermarking procedure

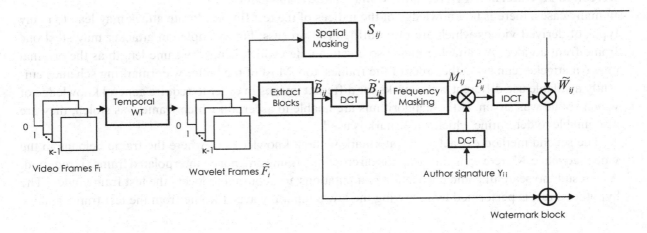

where F_k is the original frame, W_k^* is the (potentially modified) watermark recovered from the frame and N_k is noise. The decision on which hypothesis is valid is obtained by computing the scalar similarity between the extracted signal X_k and the original watermark W_k:

$$S_k = sim_k(X_k, W_k) = \frac{X_k \cdot W_k}{W_k \cdot W_k}.$$

(2)

The overall similarity between the extracted and the original watermark is measured as the mean of S_k for all k: S=mean (S_k). The overall similarity is compared with a threshold to define whether the test video is watermarked. The experimental threshold is chosen around 0.1. If the similarity value is bigger than 0.1, then the video is watermarked. In this case, the video is considered as the author's property and the copyright claim is valid. If the similarity value is smaller than 0.1, then the video is not watermarked.

When the length (in terms of frames) of the test video is equal to the length of the original video, the hypothesis test is performed in the wavelet domain. The temporal wavelet transform of the test video is estimated so as to obtain the wavelet coefficient frames $\tilde{R}_k$. In (1) we replace the values by the corresponding wavelet transformed ones and thus we have:

$$H_0 : \tilde{X}_k = \tilde{R}_k - \tilde{F}_k = N_k \qquad \text{(no watermark)}$$
$$H_1 : \tilde{X}_k = \tilde{R}_k - \tilde{F}_k = \tilde{W}_k^* + N_k \qquad \text{(watermark)}$$

(3)

where $\tilde{F}_k$ is the wavelet coefficient frame from the original video, $\tilde{W}_k^*$ is the potentially modified watermark from each frame and N_k is noise. The hypothesis is tested for each wavelet frame and $\tilde{X}_k$ results for all k. Similarity values are estimated as before, that is: $S_k = sim_k(\tilde{X}_k, \tilde{W}_k)$.

Using the original video signal to detect the presence of the watermark, the virtual handling of all types of distortions is possible. This specific action is taken by employing the generalized likelihood which is similar to test. The authors have also developed a second detection scheme which is capable of recovering a watermark from a video that has gone through several distortions without using the generalized likelihood which is similar to test. This procedure is fast and simple, especially when confronted with the large amount of data associated with video.

Detection II-Watermark Detection without Index Knowledge

In many cases, there is no knowledge of the indices of the test frames. Pirate attack may lead to many types of derived videos which are often difficult to process. For example, an attacker may steal one frame from a video. An attacker may also create a video which is not the same length as the original one. An attacker can swap the order of the frames, too. Most of the better watermarking schemes currently available use different watermarks for different images in order to require general knowledge of which frame was stolen. If these algorithms are unable to ascertain which frame was stolen, they are also unable to determine which watermark is used.

The second method extracts the watermark without knowledge of where the frame belongs in the video sequence. Moreover, no information on cropping, frame order or on interpolated frames is required. As a result, no searching and correlation computations are required to locate the test frame index. The hypothesis test is performed by removing the low temporal wavelet frame from the test frame and we estimate the similarity with the watermark for the low temporal wavelet frame. The hypothesis test lies below:

$$H_0 : X_k = R_k - \tilde{F}_0 = N_k \qquad \text{(no watermark)}$$
$$H_1 : X_k = R_k - \tilde{F}_0 = \tilde{W}_k^* + N_k \qquad \text{(watermark)} \qquad (4)$$

where R_k is the test frame in the spatial domain and $\tilde{F}_0$ is the low temporal wavelet frame. The decision is made by computing the scalar similarity between the extracted signal X_k and the original watermark for the low temporal wavelet frame $\tilde{W}_0 : sim_k(X_k, \tilde{W}_0)$. This approach is powerful and exploits the wavelet property of varying temporal support.

Experimental Results

Visual Results

The invisibility and robustness of the watermarking scheme is tested for two videos on grey level (8mpp): the Pingpong video and the Football video. Each frame is of length 240x352. An original frame from each video is illustrated in Figures 6(a) and 7(a). The corresponding watermarked frame for each video is illustrated in Figures 6(b) and 7(b). In both cases, the watermarked frame is visually identical to the original. In Figures 6(c) and 7(c) the watermark for each frame is illustrated. This one has changed scale on grey levels for the presentation. Even though the watermarks are measured in wavelet frames, they are

Figure 6. Frame from Pingpong video (a)original, (b)watermarked, and (c)watermark

(a) *(b)* *(c)*

Figure 7. Frame from Football video (a)original, (b)watermarked, and (c)watermark

(a) *(b)* *(c)*

exposed to the spatial domain for visual convenience. The watermark of each frame is the same in size as the host frame, that is, it is of size 240x352. For each frame, the watermark's values corresponding to areas of smooth block are in general smaller than those in locations near to areas of motion and edges. This is expected because areas of motion and edges have more favourable masking characteristics.

Certain statistical properties for each watermark are presented in Table 2. These values have been computed for frames illustrated in Figures 6 and 7, values that also represent other watermarks in other frames of each video. The maximum and minimum value is in terms of watermark values and is beyond the 240x352 watermark. The peak signal- to- noise ratio (PSNR) is a typical metric for image quality and is defined as $20\log_{10}(255/\sqrt{SNR})$. The signal-to-noise ratio (SNR) is computed for the original and watermarked frame.

So as to define the quality of the watermarked frame, a series of unofficial visual tests are performed. First of all, the original test video is presented to the observer. After that, two videos, A and B, are displayed which were selected by chance. These two videos are progressively displayed. The pair of the coordinates is accidentally chosen by the pair (original-watermarked) or by the pair (watermarked-original). The observer is asked to choose one of the A or B videos, that is, the one that is more visually pleasant to him. This test is performed ten times for each different video. A group of ten observers (the authors are not included) take part into this blind test. Its results are cited in Table 3. As predicted by the models of visual masking, the original and watermarked frames show visual similarity and each of them is preferred for around half of the time. Conclusively, the watermark does not cause visible degradation to host video.

Robustness Results

So that the watermark is effective, it must be robust to intentional and accidental distortions that the host video suffers. Apparently, each operation to loose signal which is applied to host video also affects the embedded watermark.

The robustness of the watermarking procedure is measured through the ability to detect the watermark when it appears in a video. The robustness depends also on the algorithm's ability to reject the video when the watermark does not appear. For a given distortion, the overall efficiency is ascertained by the relative difference between the similarity when a watermark appears (hypothesis H_1) and the similarity

Table 2. Statistical properties of the video watermark

Video	Maximum	Minimum	Variance	PSNR(dB)
Pingpong	42	-44	11.20	37.64
Football	43	-47	14.44	36.54

Table 3. Blind testing of watermarked videos

Video	Preferred original to watermarked
Pingpong	48.5%
Football	50.5%

when a watermark is absent (hypothesis H_0). In every experiment concerning the test of robustness, same results arise for both hypotheses. Particularly, the degradation is applied to the video when a watermark appears. It is also applied in the case where a watermark does not appear. The similarity is computed for the original watermark and the recovered signal (which may have or not a watermark). A great similarity indicates the presence of a watermark (H_1), whereas a small one indicates the absence of the watermark (H_0). According to tests, there is no covering among the hypotheses appeared during degradations and distortions. This connotes a great detection possibility and a small false alarm possibility.

During tests we use the first 32 frames of each video. Both detection approaches are applied during each experiment. Particularly, detection (3) is performed when the overall test sequence is available and the indices are known. Furthermore, detection (4) is performed when it takes place frame after frame and without frame index knowledge. In that case, we assume that the frame index is unknown and therefore there is no knowledge of the frame's placement in the video.

Colored Noise

In order to give a model to the techniques of perceptual coding, the watermark is corrupted with the worst colored noise, a process that is obtained by using visual masks. Colored noise is produced after modulating (as for example the multiplication) the white noise with the frequency and spatial masks for the video. Due to the fact that colored noise is produced in the same way as the watermark, it acts as another inconvenient watermark. Colored noise is produced and is added to the video with or without the watermark. Noise variance for each test sequence is chosen to be nine times greater than the watermark embedded into the video. For example, mean variance of the watermark on all frames of the Football video sequence is 14.0. The sequence of the colored noise is generated with variance around 126.0 (PSNR=27.1dB). A frame with noise for every watermarked video is illustrated in Figures 8(a) and 8(b). These frames correspond to frames in Figures 6 and 7.

For each video, this test process is repeated 100 times and a new noise sequence is applied to each repetition. During the first test, all video frames are used to detect (Detection I). Similarity values for each video sequence with or without the watermark are presented in Table 4. The maximum, mean and minimum similarity value is measured for all 100 repetitions with noise. It is important to notice that maximum similarity values with a watermark are much bigger than those without it. A covering between both of them indicates probable error during detection. In this case, for example, the minimum similarity value of the Pingpong sequence with a watermark is 0.91, which is much bigger than the

Figure 8. Frame from videos with colored noise (PSNR=25.1 dB) (a)pingpong and (b)football

(a)   *(b)*

Table 4. Similarity results for pingpong and football with colored noise

Video	PSNR(dB)	With watermark			No watermark		
		Max	Mean	Min	Max	Mean	Min
Pingpong	27.8	1.00	0.96	0.91	0.03	0.00	-0.02
Football	27.1	1.00	0.97	0.93	0.04	0.00	-0.03

maximum value 0.03 without it. As a result, it is easy for someone to decide when a watermark exists in a video. The selection of a decision threshold T around $0.1 \leq T \leq 0.9$ ensures the right decision-making concerning test videos that have colored noise.

Moreover, tests frame after frame are performed without frame index knowledge (Detection II). The detection is performed by removing the low-pass temporal frame $\tilde{F}_0$ from the test frame and afterwards we correlate the result of the removal to watermark $\tilde{W}_0$ which corresponds to $\tilde{F}_0$ During all distortion experiments, colored noise is added to each video before the distortion (for example the coding or printing etc.). Colored noise is used for the simulation of further attacks against the watermark. Its strength is almost the same as that of the watermark, which is invisible.

Coding

In most applications involving storage and transmission of digital video, lossy coding operations are performed on it to reduce bit rates and increase efficiency. We test whether the watermark is able to survive after the MPEG coding in the very low quality. After some experiments, MPEG tables were set on the most typical and probable levels of quantization so that compression is maximized.

A watermarked frame on the Pingpong video is coded by 0.08 bpp, as illustrated in Figure 9(a). The corresponding compression ratio (CR) is 100:1. The original (non-coded frame) is shown in Figure 9(b). Note that a large amount of distortion is present in the frame. Using the same quantization tables, a frame on the Football video is coded by 0.18 bpp (CR 44:1) as illustrated in Figure 9(b). Note that both videos make use of the same quantization tables. However, the Football sequence presents greater motion than the Pingpong sequence. As a result, further bits/pixel are required to code the Football video.

In order to simulate more attacks into the watermark, we add colored noise to each video before the MPEG coding. Each video is tested 100 times with a different sequence of colored noise being used in each repetition. During the first test, all video frames are used for the detection (Detection I). The maximum, mean and minimum similarity value for each video sequence with or without the watermark is presented in Table 5. Again, we see that the values of the minimum similarity with a watermark are much greater than the values of the maximum similarity without it. Even during coding in low quality, similarity values are much despread and thus, it is easy to ascertain the presence of the watermark. Detection is also performed in separate video frames (Detection II) without index knowledge.

Multiple Watermarks

We also test the ability of detecting watermarks when others turn up. Corruption may appear as a watermark which is progressively embedded by using the paths of legitimate multimedia distribution. Moreover, an attacker can use further watermarks to attack a valid watermark. Three consecutive wa-

Figure 9. MPEG coded frame from (a)pingpong (0.08 b/pixel, CR 100:1) and (b)football (0.18 b/pixel, CR 44:1)

(a)				*(b)*	

Table 5. Similarity results for pingpong and football after MPEG coding

Video	CR	PSNR(dB)	With watermark			No watermark		
			Max	Mean	Min	Max	Mean	Min
Pingpong	100:1	26.8	0.41	0.35	0.28	0.06	0.00	-0.08
Football	44:1	24.4	0.37	0.32	0.27	0.07	0.01	-0.05

termarks are embedded into each test video in a row during the experiment. All three of them use the original (non-watermarked) video as their original during detection. Afterwards, we add colored noise to videos and a MPEG coding is implemented to the result arising. The Pingpong sequence is coded by 0.28 bpp (CR 29:1, PSNR 27.45 Db). Using the same MPEG parameters, the Football sequence is coded by 0.51 bpp (CR 16:1, PSNR 25.43dB). Tests are performed 100 times and a new sequence of colored noise is applied to each repetition. The presence of the three watermarks is easily detected under these circumstances.

Frame Averaging

Some of the distortions which are particularly interesting as to video watermarking are those referring to temporal processing, for example the temporal cropping, the frame dropping and the frame interpolation. It is proved that temporal cropping is counterbalanced by the approach of Detection II which does not require frame indices knowledge. In order to test the case of frame dropping as well as the case of interpolation, we drop the frames of the video sequence that have an unnecessary index. The frames missing are replaced by the average of their adjacent frames, that is, by the frame $F_{2n+1}=(F_{2n}+F_{2n+2})/2$.

Printing and Scanning

A significant issue concerning the intellectual property is the protection of separate video frames against copyright during printing, as it happens for example in magazines. For this case, we create powerful copies of the original and watermarked frames as illustrated in Figures 6 and 7 and a flatbed scanner is used to re-digitize them. The similarity results arising from printing and scanning are presented in

Table 6. Similarity results after printing and scanning

Video Frame	Similarity	
	With watermark	Without watermark
Pingpong	0.734	0.011
Football	0.611	0.052

Table 6. The detection is performed without knowledge of the frame's location (Detection II). Similarity values imply an easy distinction between watermarked and non-watermarked printed frames even without knowledge of the frame's location in the video sequence.

A DWT-BASED DIGITAL VIDEO WATERMARKING SCHEME WITH ERROR CORRECTING CODE

The authors Pik-Wah Chan and Michael Lyu propose a digital video watermarking algorithm. The scheme performs a DWT-based blind digital watermarking with scrambled watermark and error correcting code. This scheme embeds different parts of a single watermark into different video scenes under the wavelet domain. To increase its robustness, the watermark is refined by applying the error correcting code. This last one is embedded as a watermark in audio channel. The video watermarking algorithm is robust against the attacks of frame dropping, averaging and statistical analysis. These attacks were not solved effectively in the past. Furthermore, it allows blind retrieval of the embedded watermark, that is, we do not need the original video for the watermark's retrieval. Finally, the watermark is perceptually invisible.

The Video Watermarking Scheme

The watermarking scheme described below is based on DWT and Figure 1 shows its description. In this scheme, the input video is split into two streams, the video and audio streams, which undergo watermarking. The overall watermark is decomposed into different parts which are embedded into the corresponding frames of different scenes in the original video.

Due to the fact that an image watermark is applied to each video frame, problems arise concerning the maintenance of the statistical and perceptual invisibility, whereas the scheme employs independent watermarks for successive but different scenes. Embedding independent watermarks to frames also presents a problem: there are areas in each video with little or no motion which remain the same frame after frame. These motionless areas are statistically compared and averaged to remove independent watermarks, so we embed an identical watermark into motionless scenes. With this mechanism, the proposed method is robust to frame dropping, averaging, swapping and statistical analysis. At the same time, error correcting codes are extracted from the video watermark and embedded as an audio watermark into the audio channel, which makes it possible to correct and detect the changes from the extracted watermarks. This addition protection mechanism enables the scheme to overcome the watermark's corruption and in this way its robustness is increased under common attacks.

Figure 10. Overview of the watermarking process

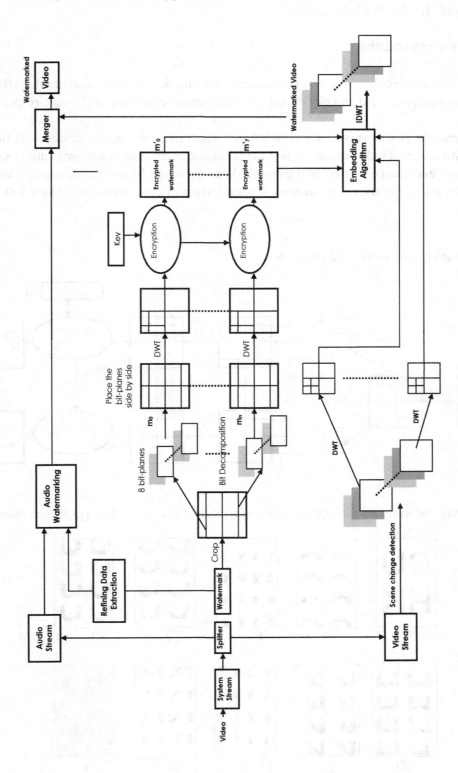

This scheme consists of four steps: (1) watermark preprocess, (2) video preprocess, (3) watermark embedding and (4) watermark detection.

Watermark Preprocess

The specific procedure consists of two parts, video watermark and audio watermark. After that, both watermarks are preprocessed and embedded into video channel and audio channel, respectively.

Video watermark: A watermark is scrambled into small parts during preprocess and then they are embedded into different video scenes so that the scheme can resist to a number of attacks.

A 256 grey level image is used as a watermark, as shown in Figure 12(a), whereas every pixel is represented by 8 bits. Firstly, the watermark is scaled to a particular size based on the following equa-

Figure 11. Overview of watermark preprocess

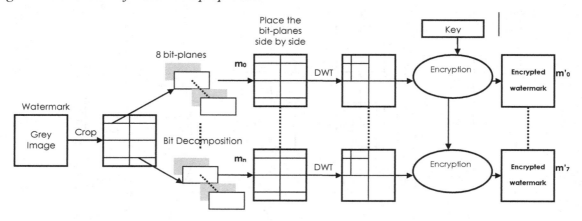

Figure 12. Original watermark (b-i)Preprocessed watermark m_0-m_7 (j)Encrypted watermark m'_0.

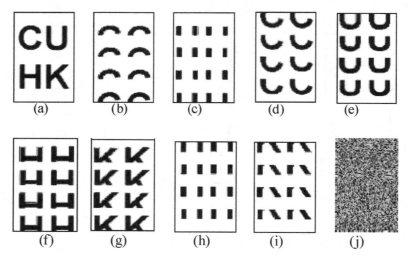

tion: p+q=n (1) where p and q > 0 is the number of scene changes and n, p, q is positive integers. The size of the watermark is: $64 \cdot 2^p x 64 \cdot 2^q$ (2).

Then the watermark is divided into 2^n small images with size 64x64. Figures 11 and 12 show the procedure and the result of the watermark preprocess with m=10, n=3, p=1 and q=2.

In the next step, each small image is decomposed into 8 bit-planes and a large image m_n is obtained by placing the 8 bit-planes side by side. The final image of the watermark consists only of '0' and '1'. These processed images are used as watermarks, and totally 2^n independent watermarks are obtained. To make the scheme more robust, the processed watermarks m are transformed to the wavelet domain and then they are encrypted. Samples of the preprocessed watermarks are shown in Figure 12, where (a) is the original watermark, (b)-(i) represent the scrambled watermarks in the spatial domain and (j) shows the watermark (b), as it should be if embedded into data, i.e. m'_0.

Audio watermark: Error correcting code is extracted from the watermark image and embedded into the audio channel as an audio watermark. This watermark provides the error correcting and detection capability for the video watermark. During detection phase, it is extracted and used for refining the video watermark. Different error correcting coding techniques can be applied.

Error correcting code plays an important role to the watermark, especially when the last one is corrupted, e.g. when it is significantly damaged. Error correcting code overcomes the corruption of the watermark and in this way it survives even after serious attacks. Moreover, the scheme has the advantages of watermarking in the audio channel because an independent channel is provided for embedding the error correcting code, which gives extra information for watermark extraction. Therefore, this scheme is more robust than others using only the video channel.

The key to error correcting is redundancy. Indeed, the simplest error correcting code simply repeats everything several times. However, in order to keep the audio watermark inaudible, we must not embed too much information into the audio channel. In this scheme, averaging is applied to achieve the error correcting code. Within a small area of an image, pixels are similar. Therefore, the average value of a small area can be used to estimate the pixels within that particular area. The average value of pixels in each area is calculated as follows:

$$Avg_k = \sum_{i=0}^{x} \sum_{j=0}^{y} W_{j*w+q*x+p*y*w+i} \qquad (3)$$

Figure 13. (a)Original video watermark (b)Visualization of averaging (c)Audio watermark (average of a)

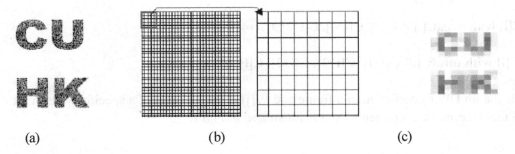

(a)　　　　　　　　　(b)　　　　　　　　　(c)

Figure 14. After scene change detection, watermark m₁ is used for the first scene. When there is a scene change, another watermark m₃ is used for the next scene

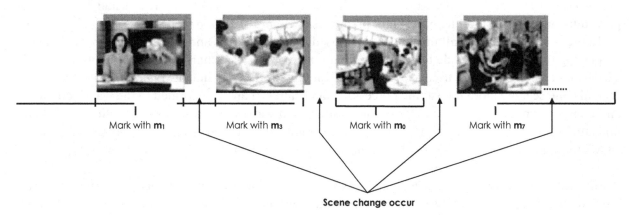

where k is the kth block of the average image, the pair (p, q) is the coordinates of area k, the pair (x, y) is the coordinates of the pixel in area k and xxy is the size of the block. An example of this procedure is illustrated in Figure 13.

Video Preprocess

This watermark scheme is based on 4 levels DWT. All video frames are transformed to the wavelet domain. Furthermore, scene changes are detected from the video by applying the histogram difference method on the video stream.

After scene change detection, as shown in Figure 14, independent watermarks are embedded into video frames of different scenes. Within a motionless scene, an identical watermark is used for each frame. The watermark for each frame is chosen with a pseudorandom permutation so that only one legitimate watermark detector can reassemble the original watermark.

Watermark Embedding

The watermark is then embedded into video frames by changing the position of a certain DWT coefficient and by applying the following condition:

if $W[j] = 1$,
exchange $C[i]$ with $\max(C[i], C[i+1], C[i+2], C[i+3], C[i+4])$
    else
exchange $C[i]$ with $\min(C[i], C[i+1], C[i+2], C[i+3], C[i+4])$ (4)

where $C[i]$ is the ith DWT coefficient of a frame and $W[j]$ is the jth pixel of a specific watermark. The sequence of the watermark coefficients used is illustrated in Figure 15.

Figure 15. Embedding watermarks in a frame. Higher frequency coefficients are embedded to higher frequency part of the video frame. Also, only the middle frequency wavelet coefficient of the frame (middle frequency sub-band) is watermarked.

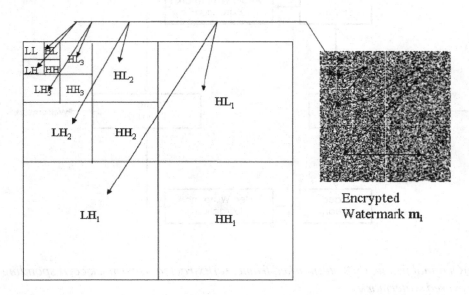

Encrypted
Watermark $\mathbf{m}_i$

In this scheme emphasis is put on the video watermark. The audio watermark is used to help the first one become more robust. Namely, the audio watermark is used for refining the video watermark in the detection phase, so the error correcting code is stored in the audio channel. Here, we have applied a simple audio watermarking technique, the spread spectrum.

Watermark Detection

The watermark is detected according to the process described below. Its overview is shown in Figure 16. A test video is split into video stream and audio stream and watermarks are extracted separately, that is, we perform the audio watermark extraction and video watermark extraction. Finally, the extracted watermark undergoes a refining process.

Video watermark detection: We process the video stream to get the video watermark. In this step, the changing scene is detected from the test video. Also, each video frame is transformed to the wavelet domain with 4 levels. Then the watermark is extracted under the following condition:

if WC[i] > median(WC[i], WC[i+1], WC[i+2], WC[i+3], WC[i+4])

        W[j] = 1

   else

        W[j] = 0   (5)

where WC[i] is the ith DWT coefficient of the watermarked video frame and W[j] is the jth pixel of the extracted watermark.

Figure 16. Overview of detection of the watermark

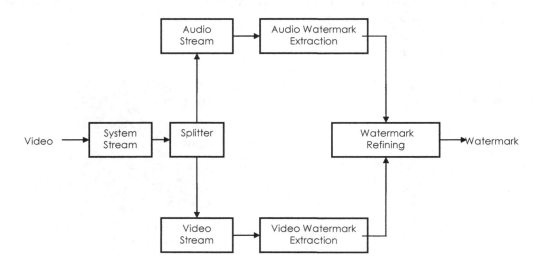

Figure 17. (a)Original frame, (b)Watermarked frame, (c)Extracted watermark corresponding to Figure 12(g), (d)Recovered watermark

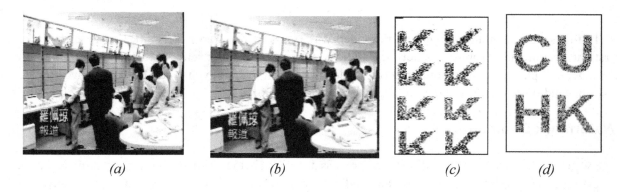

Since an identical watermark is used for all frames within a scene, multiple copies of each part of the watermark may be obtained. The watermark is recovered by averaging the watermarks extracted from different frames of a scene. This procedure reduces the effect of the attacks if carried out at certain frames. Then, we combine the 8 bit-planes and in this way we recover the 64x64 size image, i.e. the $1/2^n$ part of the original watermark.

If enough scenes are found and all parts of the watermark are collected, then the original watermark can be reconstructed. This can be shown in Figure 17, where the original frame, the watermarked frame and the extracted watermark are depicted. Moreover, the watermark can survive even if some of its parts are lost.

Audio watermark detection and refining: At the same time, error correcting codes are extracted from the audio stream and the video watermark recovered is refined by this information according to the following equation:

$$\hat{W}_{ij} = (\hat{W}_{ij} * P + Avg_k * Q) / (P + Q) \tag{6}$$

where k is the kth block of the average image of the watermark, the pair (i, j) are the coordinates of the video watermark and P:Q is the ratio of importance of the extracted video watermark to the audio watermark.

After extracting and refining the watermark, we measure the similarity between the extracted and the original watermarks which is used for objective judgement of the extracted fidelity defined as:

$$NC = \frac{\sum_i \sum_j w(i,j,)\hat{w}(i,j,)}{\sum_i \sum_j [W(i,j)]^2}$$

Normalized correlation: Which is the normalized cross-correlation of the referred watermark energy so that there is unity at the peak of the correlation. This measurement is used in experiments performed for this scheme.

Hybrid Approach Using Different Watermarking Schemes

In current bibliography, we have not found any watermarking scheme capable of resisting to all attacks applied to a watermark. Hybrid approach can be a probable solution to this problem. Independent watermarking schemes include either different watermarking schemes for different video scenes or different watermarking schemes for different parts of the same frame. Dependent watermarking schemes embed a watermark into each frame with different watermarking scheme.

The authors propose two different approaches of hybrid watermarking schemes. Initially, they combine strange watermarking schemes in dissimilar ways. Four watermarking schemes have been chosen and each one of them fights against a different set of attacks. These four schemes are: 1) watermarking that uses DWT, 2) watermarking that uses DCT, 3) watermarking that uses DFT and 4) watermarking that uses the Radon transform. All four of them embed the watermark into different domains, thus presenting the properties of their robustness. When we systematically combine the advantages of these watermarking schemes, the simultaneous confrontation of several attacks may be possible. Afterwards, we describe two approaches concerning how we can combine different watermarking schemes. In the first approach, we apply different watermarking schemes for different video scenes, whereas in the second we apply different watermarking schemes for different parts of each frame.

Different Schemes for Different Scenes

In this approach, the watermark is decomposed into different parts which are embedded into the corresponding frames of different scenes within the original video. However, each part of the watermark is embedded with a different watermarking scheme. The frames of a video scene are watermarked using the same part of the watermark and by applying the same watermarking scheme.

When an attack is taking place to a watermarked video, different watermarking schemes become robust against it. As a conclusion, certain parts of the watermark shall survive even after being attacked. Therefore, the specific approach gives video the opportunity to survive after applying various attacks and in this way the watermark's robustness is increased. The important thing is that only one part of the watermark is destroyed, if the watermarked video undergoes an attack. This is so because

Figure 18. Hybrid approach with different scheme for different scene

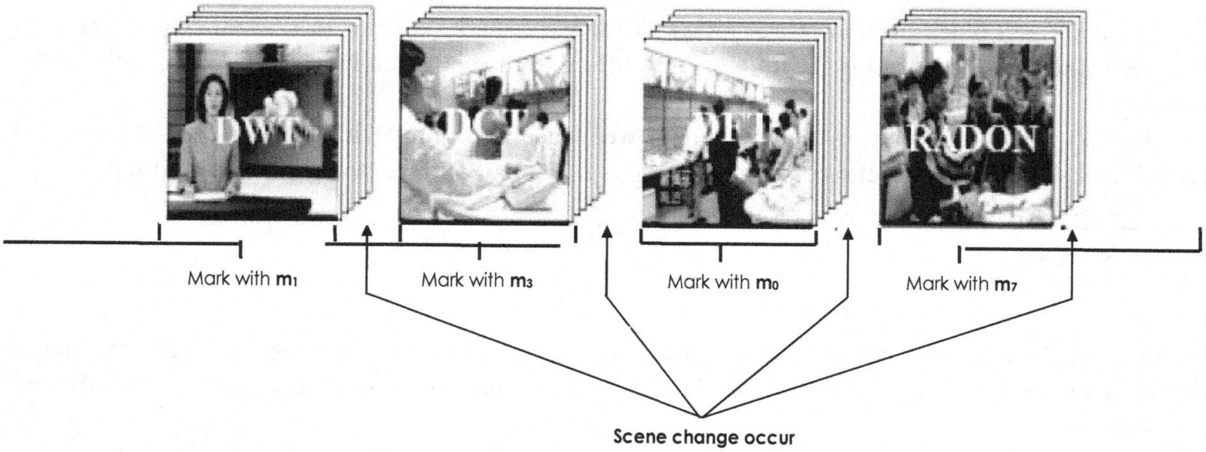

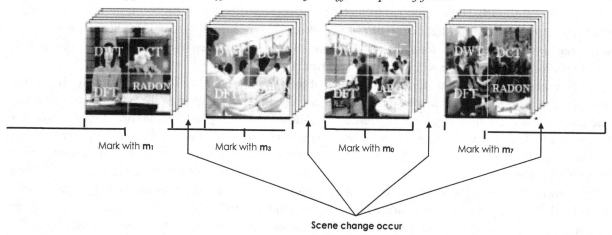

Figure 19. Hybrid approach with different scheme for different part of frame

there is at least one watermarking scheme that is robust to it. The disadvantage of this approach is the low fidelity of the extracted watermark, if compared to other watermarking schemes which specialize only in a specific attack.

Different Schemes for Different Parts of Each Frame

This approach is similar to the former one. But, the four different watermarking schemes are applied to each frame instead of being applied to different video scenes. Each video frame is divided into four parts and the watermark for this specific frame is also divided into four parts. Then, each part of the watermark is embedded into the video frame to a different domain.

If a watermarked video undergoes an attack, part of the watermark on each frame may survive. Consequently, it is possible to recover information on each part of the watermark and therefore it can be measured approximately. Even though fidelity of the extracted watermark is reduced, the watermark is more robust against various attacks.

Experimental Results

To evaluate the performance of the specific watermarking scheme, several experiments have been done such as: the experiment with various dropping ratio, the experiment with various numbers (of frames colluded), the experiment with various quality factors of MPEG and the experiment with various cropping ratio. Another watermarking scheme is used as compared the proposed one. It uses the DWT transform for embedding an identical watermark into all video frames. During experiments, we use a video clip with 1526 frames of size 352x288. The video consists of 10 different scenes. The NC values are computed for the watermarked video which has undergone several attacks.

Experiments with Frame Dropping

As a video contains a large amount of redundancy among its frames, it may suffer attacks by frame dropping. In this experiment, we examine the robustness of the scheme against frame dropping. During other experiments, different percentages of frames are dropped and the results obtained are shown in Figure 20.

Based on the above, it becomes evident that this scheme achieves better performance than the DWT-based scheme. This is so because in each scene, all frames have been watermarked by the same

Figure 20. NC values under frame dropping. From the experiment, we found that our scheme achieves better performance than the DWT-based scheme without scene-based watermarks

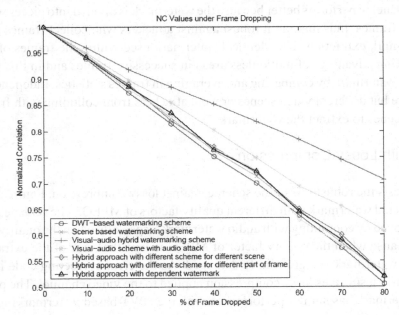

watermark. Therefore, attackers are not able to remove it by applying frame dropping. If they try to remove part of it, then they need to remove the whole scene and this leads to a significant damage to the video. In addition, when frames are dropped, an error is introduced only to the corresponding small part of the watermark. For the DWT-based watermarking scheme, the error is introduced to the whole watermark and thus, its performance is worse.

The scheme's performance is significantly improved by combining with the audio watermark, especially when the dropping rate of video frames is high. The improvement increases by increasing the frame dropping rate. This is so because when the dropping rates increases, the error in the extracted watermark increases too and it significantly damages the watermark. The error correcting code from the audio watermark provides information to correct the error and overcomes the part of the corruption of the video watermark, thus the NC values of the watermark are higher than the one without the error correcting code. Moreover, the error correcting code is embedded into the audio channel. Frame dropping does not affect the audio channel much. The scheme takes this advantage in so that it avoids destroying the information and the error correcting code is used to refine the watermark and improve the NC value.

When the audio channel also undergoes an attack, the NC values of the extracted watermark are reduced. Therefore, the error correcting codes located within the audio channel may alter after this attack. Even though the possibility of recovering the error from the video watermark is getting low, the result is even better than the result obtained from the scheme without the audio watermark because the last one that has been attacked still contains certain information on recovering the watermark from the video channel.

Experiments with Frame Averaging and Statistical Analysis

Frame averaging and statistical analysis is another common attack applied to a video watermark. When attackers collect a number of watermarked frames, they estimate the watermark by statistical averaging and then they remove it from the watermarked video.

The proposed scheme performs better because the watermark is divided into pieces which are embedded into different frames, thus making it robust against attackers who collect frames and estimate the average for watermark extraction. The identical watermark used within the frames of a scene prevent attackers from taking advantage of motionless areas in successive frames and in this way they are not able to remove the watermark by comparing and averaging in frames statistics. Independent watermarks used for successive but different video scenes prevent attackers from colluding with frames from completely different scenes to extract the watermark.

Experiments with Lossy Compression

This experiment tests the robustness of the scheme against lossy compression. Figure 22 shows the NC values of the extracted watermark with different quality factors of MPEG. The scheme's performance is significantly improved by combining with audio watermark, especially when the quality factor of MPEG is low. This is because when the quality factor of MPEG is low, the error of the extracted watermark increases and the watermark is significantly damaged. As the error correcting code is provided from the audio watermark, it survives lossy compression applied to the video channel. The proposed scheme without audio watermark has similar performance with the DWT-based watermarking scheme.

Figure 21. NC values under statistical averaging. After this attack is applied to the watermarked video with different numbers of video frame colluded, watermarks are extracted and NC values are obtained. It is found that the proposed scheme can resist to statistical averaging quite well.

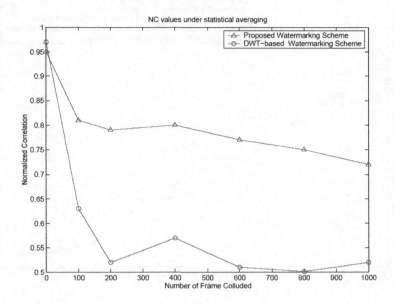

Figure 22. NC values under lossy compression. From the experiment, we found that the proposed scheme improves the robustness for watermark protection.

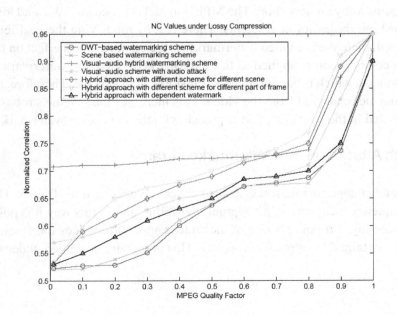

Figure 23. NC values under cropping

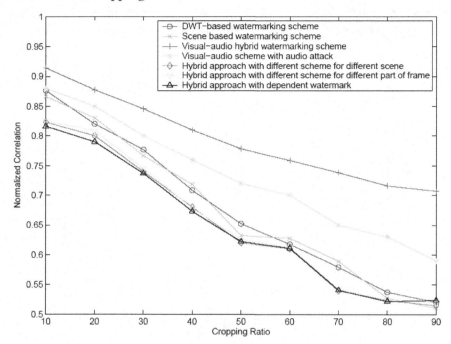

The scheme's performance is improved also in the case of hybrid approach using different watermarking schemes. NC values of the hybrid approach in the case of applying lossy compression are bigger than NC values of the scheme that apply only a simple watermarking scheme for video watermarking. According to the results evaluation, it becomes clear that the watermarking scheme based on DWT transform is the more robust one against lossy compression. The MPEG model is based on DWT and lossy compression mainly modifies the high frequency coefficients. Therefore, by modifying the coefficients of the middle sub-band on this domain during video watermarking, the compression's effect on the watermark is reduced. When the compression is applied to the watermarked video, the watermark embedded with the watermarking scheme which is based on DWT transform shall survive. Therefore, at least a quarter of the watermark may be recovered from the video. This increases the scheme's robustness. However, this one is not improved in the case of hybrid approach with the dependent watermark.

Experiments with Attacks on the Watermarked Frame

DWT inherits many advantages in robustness against attacks on watermarked frames. This fact achieves both spatial and frequency localization, perceptual invisibility and in this way it is possible to face attacks by image processing. Cropping is one of the attacks applied to videos too frequently. Figure 23 illustrates the results obtained by applying cropping. This procedure is applied under various ratios.

FUTURE RESEARCH DIRECTIONS

The copyright protection constitutes the principal aim of the digital watermarking applications for digital video in history. The main strategy embeds a watermark into the data of the digital video which indicates the identity of the person holding the right on intellectual property. If an illegal copy is found, this person can prove its authorship due to the embedded watermark and in this way he can sue the illegitimate user.

The video coding process is usually a sequence of two steps. During the source coding, all surplus information is removed so that the compressed representation of data arises, while the authenticity of visual quality is maintained. After that, the compressed representation of the video is subjected to channel coding where further surplus information is added in order to correct all errors. The channel coding is considered obligatory since errors may turn up during transmission. The digital watermarking is initiated as an alternative tactics for the introduction of information concerning the correction of an error after the source coding.

Experiments have shown the feasibility of this approach and following the conclusions it is clear that digital watermarking has more effective performances than the traditional mechanisms and future research direction will focus on this area.

REFERENCES

Chan, P-W., & Lyu, M. R. *A DWT-based digital video watermarking scheme with error correcting code.*

Chan, P-W., Lyu, M. R., Chin, R. T. *A novel scheme for hybrid digital video watermarking: Approach, evaluation and experimentation.*

Doerr, G., & Dugelay, J. L. (2003). A guide tour of video watermarking. *Signal Processing: Image Communication 18,* 263-282.

Liu, H-m., Huang, J-w., & Xiao, Z-m. (2001). An adaptive video watermarking algorithm. *IEEE International Conference on Multimedia and Expo,* 257-260.

Swanson, M. D., Zhu, B., & Tewfik, A. H. (1998, May). Multiresolution scene-based video watermarking using perceptual models. *IEEE Journal on Selected Areas In Communications, 16*(4), 540-549.

ADDITIONAL READING

Chan, P-W. (2004, July). *Digital video watermarking techniques for secure multimedia creation and delivery.*

Filipe, J., Coelhas, H., & Saramago, M. (2005, October 3-7). E-business and telecommunication networks. *Second International Conference, ICETE 2005.* Reading, UK, October 3-7, 2005. Selected Papers (Communications in Computer and Information Science), by (Paperback - Dec 14, 2007).

Hanjalic, A., Langelaar, G. C., van Roosmalen, P. M. B., & Biemond, J. *Image and video databases: Restoration, watermarking and retrieval.*

Section III
Distributing, Managing, and Transacting Digital Rights in E-Commerce Sytems

This section deals with the issues of distribution, management, and exploitation of copyrighted material and its digital rights through e-commerce systems. The issues are very important as they set the landscape and its restrictions regarding the transaction of digital rights via networks, Web services, and the Internet.

Chapter VII
Digital Rights Management of Images and Videos Using Robust Replica Detection Techniques

Nikos Nikolaidis
Aristotle University of Thessaloniki, Greece

Ioannis Pitas
Aristotle University of Thessaloniki, Greece

ABSTRACT

Intellectual property rights protection and management of multimedia data is essential for the deployment of e-commerce systems involving transactions on such data. Lately, replica detection or fingerprinting has emerged as a promising approach for the rights management of multimedia data. In this chapter, a review of 2 replica detection techniques is presented. The first technique utilizes color-based descriptors, an R-tree indexing structure, and Linear Discriminant Analysis (LDA) to achieve image replica detection. The second technique is a video fingerprinting method that utilizes information about the appearances of individuals in videos along with an efficient search and matching strategy.

INTRODUCTION

E-commerce systems have become an almost integral part of everyday life, introducing new distribution channels and bringing up a radical change to the way transactions are being conducted. This change is, without doubt, more evident in multimedia content, whose distribution is constantly shifting towards electronic means (online music stores and commercial image databases, video on demand services, etc). However, the successful deployment of e-commerce systems for multimedia data requires the resolution of the critical issues of intellectual property rights protection and management since their digital nature allows for arbitrary reproduction and distribution, without any control by the copyright holders. Replica detection or fingerprinting is an emerging technology that can be used as an alternative to watermarking for the efficient Digital Rights Management (DRM) of multimedia data. Two replica detection approaches are reviewed in this chapter. The first is an image fingerprinting technique that makes use of color-based descriptors, R-trees and Linear Discriminant Analysis (LDA). The second is a video fingerprinting method that utilizes information about the appearances of actors in videos along with an efficient search strategy. Experimental performance evaluation is provided for both methods.

BACKGROUND

Numerous systems addressing the issue of copyright protection and DRM in general can be found in the literature, the vast majority of them being based on watermarking. Watermarking is the technique of imperceptibly embedding information within a medium (Tefas et al. 2005). Although watermarking has been the subject of intensive research in both the industry and the academia, it has certain disadvantages. Embedding information inside a multimedia item before it becomes available to the public, implies that the data will be distorted up to a certain extent and that watermarking methods are not applicable to data that are already in the public domain and need to be protected. Moreover, watermarking is unable to cope with leakage of unprotected content, i.e., cases where a copy of the original item that bears no watermark is stolen and distributed.

Recently, the scientific community started to investigate digital rights management in multimedia data from an alternative point of view i.e. as a problem of similarity of such data, the similarity being defined in a robust way. These approaches, which come under different names, such as multimedia fingerprinting (Oostveen et al. 2002), robust or perceptual hashing (Michak & Venkatesan 2001), replica or near-replica recognition/detection (Ke et al. 2004) and copy detection (Kim & Vasudev 2005) aim at extracting from the data a feature vector, called perceptual hash, fingerprint or signature, that characterizes them in a unique, robust and discriminative way. This feature vector can be combined with a database of multimedia documents that need to be managed with respect to their digital rights, an appropriate similarity metric and an efficient database search strategy in order to devise a DRM system. More specifically, such a system can decide if a query digital item resembles a reference item in the database. If this is indeed the case, the query item is identified as being a copy (replica) of the corresponding item in the database and legal action can be pursued against its owner/distributor if he is not legally possessing/distributing it. In order to be of practical use, the feature vectors and the matching procedure involved in a fingerprinting system should be robust to manipulations that multimedia data might undergo, either due to their distribution and use or due to an intentional attempt to make them unrecognizable by the fingerprinting system. Unlike watermarking, no information needs to be embedded within the multimedia content in a fingerprinting system, thus ensuring perfect quality for the data to be protected and furthermore making the system applicable to data that are already in the public domain. It should be mentioned here that the term fingerprinting as used in this chapter and in other papers, should not be confused with the fingerprinting watermarking which is essentially a variant of watermarking.

The underlying hypothesis behind fingerprinting is that every multimedia document shares enough information with its modified copies to allow their identification as such, and yet this information is discriminative enough to allow identification of other documents as irrelevant. Furthermore, it is assumed that the modified data sufficiently resemble the original i.e., that they are of sufficient quality. In other words, a fingerprinting system is not expected to detect severely distorted copies since their commercial value is highly reduced. The problem of multimedia fingerprinting bears certain similarities with that of content-based indexing and retrieval but has also important differences. The major difference between fingerprinting and retrieval is that the similarity criterion is usually looser in retrieval, since the user is often interested not only in finding copies of the multimedia item used as a query, but also in retrieving different items that are perceptually similar to it. Moreover, retrieval applications do not require robustness to manipulations. Finally, in retrieval the search result is usually a set of multimedia items that resemble the query item whereas in a fingerprinting method the result is either a single item or an empty set.

In this chapter two fingerprinting systems are described. The first is an image fingerprinting system that utilizes a database of original images that can be queried with an image and decide whether this image is a possibly modified copy of a stored original. Images are represented by a feature vector comprising of color-based descriptors. The system utilizes a multidimensional indexing structure based on R-trees. Although substantially reduced, the probability that the R-tree returns more than one image as candidates for being the originals of the query is non-zero and prevents the system to decide unambiguously. Linear Discriminant Analysis, preceded by Principal Component Analysis (PCA) is applied in order to transform the solution space and yield more discriminant image representations. A more detailed description of this system can be found in Nikolopoulos et al. (2006). The second system makes use of information about the appearance of faces of distinct individuals (e.g. actors), in order to characterize a video segment in a robust way and use this information for video fingerprinting. Pulse-series-like signals that provide information on whether a certain actor appears or not in each frame of the video are used as feature vectors in this case. Additional details for this system (when used in a video indexing framework) can be found in Cotsaces et al. (2006).

RELATED WORK

A number of attempts towards devising efficient fingerprinting/ replica detection systems for images, video and other types of content have been published during the last years. In the following, a brief description for some typical state-of-the-art image replica detection techniques, followed by techniques targeting video, will be provided. Qamra et al (2005) propose an image replica detection system that is based on the so-called Dynamic Partial Functions (DPF) for measuring the similarity between images. DPF choose adaptively a different set of features for each image pair i.e. they use only the similar aspects of the images in order to measure their similarity. Features are selected from a large pool of global color and texture features as well as local features. DPFs are combined with thresholding, sampling and weighting schemes that help in evaluating the appropriate number of features for each image pair. In order to cope with large datasets and the high dimensionality of the feature space, the authors utilize the Locality-Sensitive Hashing (LSH) indexing scheme (Gionis et al., 1999). Maret, Dufaux, & Ebrahmi (2006) utilize weighted and statistically normalized 162-dimensional feature vectors representing texture, color and gray-level information for assessing image similarity. The method constructs a different decision/classification function for every original image in a database. This function is based on Support Vector Machines and is used to decide if a query image is a replica of the corresponding original. Local image descriptors extracted by PCA-SIFT (Ke & Sukthankar, 2003) are used by Ke et al. (2004) as elements of the feature vector. These descriptors are extracted from the intensity channel of an image and exhibit very interesting properties, i.e., they are scale and rotation invariant and robust to manipulations like Gaussian blurring, median filtering, additive noise, affine warping and changes in brightness and contrast. Since a single image can generate thousands of such features, Locality-Sensitive Hashing (Gionis et al., 1999), combined with offline indices that are optimized for disk access is used. Kim (2003) proposes an image fingerprinting method that uses the ordinal measure of DCT coefficients for representing images. The magnitudes of AC coefficients of 8x8 image blocks are ordered and a matrix (rank matrix) containing the ranks of these magnitudes is constructed. The distance of two images is subsequently defined as the $L1$ norm of the Minkowski metric of the respective rank matrices. A classifier whose thresholds are selected based on the maximum a posteriori-criterion, is used to determine whether a query image is a replica of an original image. In order to cope with large databases, k-means clustering of the feature vectors is employed. A framework that combines watermarking with fingerprinting was proposed by Roy et al. (2005). The authors focus on finding a feature space and a metric, such that the representations of any two database images are sufficiently separated from each other in this space. The original images are slightly modified so that their mutual separation within the selected feature space exceeds a certain threshold. At the same time, this modification is selected so as to ensure that the perceptual difference between the original and the modified image is kept to a minimum. The framework consists of a pre-processing and a detection stage. The feature space chosen by the authors is that of Analytical Fourier-Mellin Transform invariants (Ghorbel, 1994), that are robust to rotation, scaling and translation.

In what concerns video replica detection, Law-To et al (2006) propose a video characterization approach that is based on local descriptors of interest points and a robust voting system. In more detail, 20-dimensional local differential image descriptors are extracted for the regions around interest points detected by the Harris detector. This procedure is applied to all frames of the video sequences that are to be stored in the database and the trajectories of the interest points over time are evaluated using a simple tracking algorithm. These trajectories are subsequently described by the mean value of the corresponding local descriptors as well as the variation of the spatial position of the interest points and the length of the trajectories. A high level description in terms of two labels (background and moving) is also assigned to the interest points. The technique is asymmetric in the sense that the frames of the query videos are characterized only by the values of the local descriptors in selected frames. Matching between the query and the database videos is performed through a voting function that is robust to signal transformations. In Hampapur & Bolle (2002), the authors describe and compare three different fingerprint vectors for video replica detection. In the first method, the frames are split into blocks, a motion vector is associated with each block and a 4-bin histogram of vector directions is evaluated. Thus, the fingerprint consists of a series of motion vector direction histograms, one per frame. Searching and matching a query video in the video database is performed by evaluating the normalized correlation of the two fingerprints while the one is moved over the other. According to the second method, each frame is split into blocks. The average intensity of each block is evaluated and the corresponding values are sorted. The feature vector of each frame consists of the ranks of the frame blocks (ordinal measure) and the series of these vectors comprise the feature vector of the whole video segment. Finally, according to the third method, the feature vector of a video segment consists of a series of 64-bin concatenated

YUV color histograms (one per frame). Normalized histogram intersection is used for fingerprint vector matching. The experimental evaluation results provided by the authors for the three techniques prove that the method based on the ordinal measures achieves the best performance. The local image descriptors derived for the key frames of a video sequence in Joly, Buisson, & Frélicot (2007) are very similar to those used in Law-To et. al (2006), i.e. they consist of local differential descriptors extracted in regions around Harris interest points. The local features extracted from a query video, are individually searched in the database using a new approximate similarity search approach called distortion-based probabilistic query. This search provides, for each local feature in the query, a set of similar local features. The partial results obtained for all the local features are then merged by a post-processing step which consists of a registration and voting strategy that counts the number of geometrically consistent local matches between the candidate sequence and the database sequences contained in the partial results. The novelty of this work lies mainly on the distortion-based probabilistic queries. These queries rely on the distribution of the relevant similar features for searching only a subset of the database data, thus reducing the search time required to find a transformed document. In more detail, this approach (that requires the existence of a probabilistic model of the distortions induced to the features due to a transformation of the video) reduces the number of fingerprints to scan during the search by selecting only the regions of the feature space for which the probability of finding a distorted fingerprint is high. Spatio-temporal transform-based fingerprint vectors are utilized in Coskun, Sankur, & Memon (2006). More specifically, video clips (which are considered to be relatively small in length, i.e. up to several minutes) are first normalized i.e., converted to a standard video signal in terms of frame dimensions and number of frames via appropriate smoothing and sub-sampling. Subsequently the 3D DCT, or a variant that uses a randomized basis set (generated through a key in order to increase security) is evaluated and 64 transform coefficients from the low-pass band are selected. Next the median value of these coefficients is used as a threshold in order to quantize them into either zero or one. Thus the hash/fingerprint sequence for the video consists of a binary string of 64-bits. The Hamming distance is used in order to calculate the similarity of hash sequences corresponding to different videos. Finally, a comparative study of a number of video replica detection methods is provided in Law-To et. al (2007).

IMAGE REPLICA DETECTION USING COLOR DESCRIPTORS R-TREES AND LINEAR DISCRIMINANT ANALYSIS

System Overview

The construction of the proposed fingerprinting - image replica detection system can be split into two independent stages. The first stage deals with the database organization and creation. Whenever a new original, copyright protected image is to be added into the database, a series of predefined attacks (image manipulations) are applied to it. These attacks are selected according to the system's design specifications, i.e. they correspond to the attacks that the system should be able to cope with. Feature vectors are extracted from each attacked version and a feature table which contains samples from the feature space neighborhood of the original image is constructed. The latter is utilized for the calculation of an extent vector that specifies the extent of the neighborhood around each original image. Finally, the extent vector is used to index the original image within an R-tree structure. The above procedure is illustrated in Figure 1.

Figure 1. Database organization of the image fingerprinting system

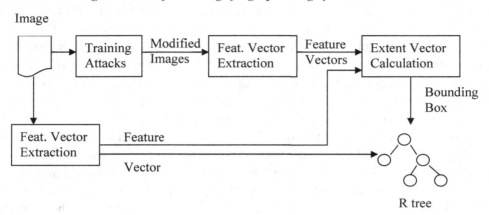

Figure 2. Querying the database

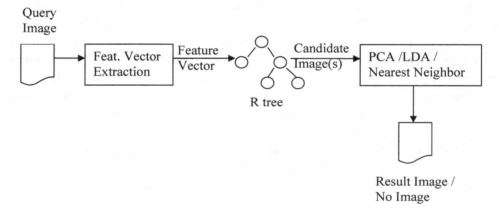

The second stage implements the querying and search procedure within the database constructed in the first stage. The feature vector of an arbitrary image is calculated and submitted as a query to the indexing structure. The R-tree prunes the redundant branches according to this feature vector and provides either a set of images that are candidates for being the originals of the query image or an empty set if none of the database images is related to the query. The next step attempts to enhance the system performance through a PCA dimensionality reduction step followed by LDA. Finally, the system returns the image that is closer to the query based on some similarity metric. Alternatively, the query image may be found to reside outside the neighborhoods formulated around each original image. In this case, the result is an empty set. Thus, the decision that the query image is not a (possibly modified) copy of the images in the database may be reached either while traversing the R-tree or after the application of the LDA step. Handling of the queries is exemplified in Figure 2.

Derivation of Feature Vectors

The proposed system is based on the results presented in Gavrielides et al. (2005) for image feature extraction. In this work, a comparative evaluation of various feature extraction methods has been performed. All methods are based on color histograms and try to benefit from its inherent resilience to a number of common manipulations, especially geometrical transforms. Dimensionality reduction is performed by quantizing the color histogram distribution with respect to a specific color palette. The comparative evaluation indicates that the best trade-off between data compaction and retained information is achieved when the quantization scheme utilizes the Macbeth color checker chart for constructing a feature vector containing 24 scalar values. It must be noted however, that the scheme described here can be combined with other feature vectors.

Indexing Structure

The R-tree (Gaede & Gunther, 1998) utilized by this method aims at reducing the computational cost of the database search. Originally, R-trees were created to index spatial objects using their bounding boxes (BBs). In our case, for a given image query, the R-tree returns all the records whose BBs include the query. This is because the proposed system is based on the assumption that the feature vectors of modified copies of an original image are concentrated around the feature vector of the original image. Therefore, the R-tree is constructed by associating a bounding box, defined using an extent vector, to every original image. In order to determine the extent vector for each image in the database, we simulate all image attacks that the system should be able to cope with. Thus, before inserting an image into the database, a series of predefined attacks are performed and the resulting images are used for determining the extent vector.

In more detail, a feature vector is extracted from every modified (attacked) version of an image and the distances in each dimension of the feature space between the original image and each modified version are calculated. For each dimension, the maximum distance is selected as the extent in this dimension. Through this procedure, an extent vector consisting of 24 scalar values that determines the extent of the neighborhood in each dimension of the feature space is evaluated for each original image.

It is obvious that the extent vector selection significantly affects the system behaviour. In order to fine-tune the system performance, a constant a that is multiplied with the values of all elements in the extent vector was introduced. By modifying a one can enlarge or shrink the bounding boxes and thus control the system's behaviour.

Linear Discriminant Analysis

The fact that the R-tree can return more than one database images as candidates for being the originals related to the query image is an issue that should be resolved, since a fingerprinting system should either return a single image or an empty set. In order to obtain a single result and, at the same time, reduce the number of decision errors discriminant feature selection through LDA (Duda et al., 2000), combined with a decision function were used. Prior to the application of the LDA, PCA is used to achieve dimensionality reduction. Elimination of the dimensions that correspond to the smaller eigenvalues results in an implicit denoising of the data. The set of classes that are involved in the LDA coincides with the set of images (classes) returned by the R-tree. Each of these classes consists of the original image feature vector along with the feature vectors of its attacked versions. These observations are employed in the calculation of the class statistics. The LDA space is trained every time a query is submitted. The result of LDA is a linear transformation $\mathbf{W}_o$ that transforms and/or reduces the dimensionality of the image feature vectors $\mathbf{x}_k$:

$$\mathbf{x}'_k = \mathbf{W}_o^T \mathbf{x}_k. \tag{1}$$

The goal of this linear transformation is to maximize the between class scatter while minimizing the within class scatter. Projection of the observations to the newly created solution space results in better separation of classes. A similarity metric is then used in this space to find the class (image) that is closest to the query image. If the query image is within a neighborhood defined around its closest original image, then the query image is declared to be a copy of the original image. Otherwise, the query image is considered as a non-replica. The neighbourhood involved in this decision-making procedure is defined by an extent vector whose selection is done through a procedure analogous to the one described in the Section titled Indexing Structure.

Experimental Performance Evaluation

A set of 2.232 images were used to populate the database of copyright protected images. The images were selected so as to form 12 content categories, each corresponding to a world famous architectural monument (Parthenon in Athens, Pyramids in Egypt, etc). Evaluation of the system performance on a database containing groups of similar images was done in an effort to assess its behaviour under the least favourable situation.

As already mentioned, a training image set that contains attacked versions of the originals is involved in three different stages of the system. More specifically, this set is involved in the evaluation of the extent vectors which define the bounding boxes that accompany each original image in the R-tree. Moreover, it is used for providing the observations utilized in the LDA for the evaluation of the linear transform $\mathbf{W}_o$ and for deriving the extent vectors involved in the final decision step in the LDA space. Essentially, the goal of the training set is to model effectively all possible distortions that can affect an original image.

A total of 77 attacks were applied on each original image for the construction of the training set, which consisted of 171.864 images. These attacks, which are applied each time a new original image is being inserted into the image database are: JPEG compression, resizing, cropping and rotation. Each attack is applied multiple times, with different parameter values, as explained in Table 1.

Two sets of experiments were conducted in order to evaluate the performance of the proposed fingerprinting system. The first set aimed at evaluating the performance of the system when being queried with images that are replicas of the images in the database. The percentage of the query images that are falsely identified as not being copies (false rejection rate) as well as the percentage of the query images that are identified as copies but are assigned to an erroneous original image in the database (misclassification rate) were evaluated. An image set containing more attacks than the training set was utilized as query image set in this experiment. This query set contained attacked versions derived from the same attack categories (compression, rotation, resizing, cropping) and parameters from the same range as those used in training. However in this case more parameter values were selected from within each range (Table 2). 240 images that reside in the database were randomly selected for this experiment. The

Table 1. Attacks on original images, utilized for constructing the training image set

Attack Category	Parameter Range	Step	Number of Generated Images
JPEG Compression	Quality Factor: 10-90	5	17
Rotation	1° - 359°	10°	36
Resizing	Scale Factor: 0.3 - 2.0	0.1	16
Cropping	Remaining Portion: 50%- 99%	5%	8
Total			77

Table 2. Attacks on original images utilized for the construction of the query image set used in testing

Attack Category	Parameter Range	Step	Number of Generated Images
JPEG Compression	Quality Factor: 10-90	1	80
Rotation	1°-359°	1°	360
Resizing	Scale Factor: 0.3 - 2.0	0.05	35
Cropping	Remaining Portion: 50%- 99%	1%	50
Total			525

attacks detailed in Table 2 were applied on these images and 525 modified versions were generated for each image. The resulting 126000 images were used as query images. It is obvious that, in this case, images that are not included in the training set are incorporated in the query set in order to devise a fair experiment. For the queries on this set, the false rejection and misclassification rates were 0.57% and 1.28% respectively.

The second set of experiments aimed to evaluate the performance of the system when being queried with images that are not copies of the images in the database. The percentage of such query images that are falsely identified as copies (false acceptance rate) was used as a performance measure in this case. 450 images that were not included in the image database formulated the content of this query set. The false acceptance rate in this case was equal to 7.33%.

VIDEO REPLICA DETECTION USING FACE-RELATED FINGERPRINT VECTORS

The video fingerprinting method presented in this section utilizes information regarding the existence of faces of individuals (e.g. actors in a movie) to robustly characterize a video. Some attempts to use information related to faces for video indexing or fingerprinting have already been reported in the literature. However the majority of these approaches (Eickeler et al., 2001; Satoh, 2005) are essentially face recognition approaches that briefly describe ways to explore the derived information for indexing. In this section, we do not propose a face detection and recognition method, since both subjects have attracted considerable attention in the last years (Zhao et. al, 2003). Instead, we examine the effect of the face detection and recognition modules on the performance of the proposed replica detection method. Since face-related information is of semantic nature, the proposed algorithm is robust to video noise and other types of video processing (e.g. color-related manipulations). Moreover, since the algorithm is convolution-based it is also robust to changes of query segment boundaries and to face detection and recognition errors. Finally, the algorithm can operate efficiently on databases containing a large amount of video data. The details of the proposed system will be described in the next sections.

Fingerprint Structure

Let $\mathbf{V} = \{f_1\ f_2\dots f_N\}$ denote a video segment consisting of N frames f_n. Let also $\mathbf{S} = \{s_1\ s_2\dots s_M\}$ be the set of all individuals $s_m, m = 1\dots M$ depicted in $\mathbf{V}$. Alternatively, $\mathbf{S}$ can be assumed to contain only the individuals of interest, e.g., the main actors in a movie.

Let us subsequently assume the availability of a face detection and recognition algorithm whose output is the certainty that a specific individual is depicted in a certain frame:

$$G(n,m) = Prob\{s_m \text{ is depicted in } f_n\} \tag{2}$$

The face recognizer can either generate a "hard" decision, which implies that $G(n,m) \in \{0,1\}$ or a soft one, in which case $G(n,m) \in [0,1]$. Using this information, it is possible to find, for each individual s_m, all non-overlapping frame intervals $I_i^m = [a_i^m, b_i^m]$ where s_m is present, i.e. intervals where $G(n,m) > 0, n \in [a_i^m, b_i^m]$ and $I_i^m \not\subset I_j^m, \forall i \neq j$. We can then define for each such interval I_i^m the average certainty within the in-

Figure 3. Fingerprint of a video segment. Different fill patterns correspond to distinct individuals. Fingerprint 4-tuples are represented by rectangles.

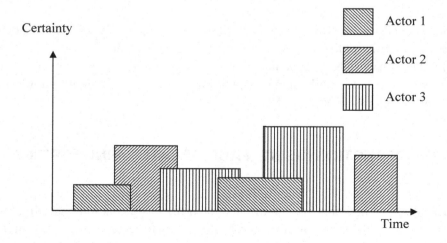

terval, that a person s_m is depicted in it and call it a *face occurrence* $F_i^m = \overline{F(n,m)}\big|_{n=a_i^m}^{b_i^m}$. Thus, we can approximate $G(n,m)$ by:

$$F(n,m) = \sum_i F_i^m \left[u(n-a_i^m) - u(n-b_i^m) \right]$$

(3)

where $u(n)$ denotes the unit step function.

For each person s_m, the triplets (F_i^m, a_i^m, b_i^m), $i = 1, \ldots, N$ can be considered as a pulse series, the independent variable being the video time. As a consequence, a certain video **V** can be characterized by a *fingerprint* that is made up of 4-tuples of the form $(s_m, F_i^m, a_i^m, b_i^m)$, $m = 1, \ldots, M$, $i = 1, \ldots, N$ (see Figure 3 for an example of such a fingerprint signal). Each 4-tuple conveys the information that individual s_m has been detected from frame a_i^m to frame b_i^m with an average certainty of F_i^m, i.e., it corresponds to a unique face appearance.

Measuring the Fingerprint Similarity

Let $F_1(n,m)$ and $F_2(n,m)$ be two fingerprints of the form presented in Equation , which refer to a common set **S** of M individuals and have been derived from (and thus characterize) two video segments. Let us also assume that we slide F_2 with respect to F_1 by a certain displacement d. We will define as *co-occurrence C* the evidence that the two fingerprints are the same. If the face recognizer provides a hard decision (i.e. its output is either 0 or 1), such evidence exists for a specific person s_m at a certain frame n, if the person exists in both fingerprints, i.e. $C_{hard}(d,n,m) = F_1(n,m) \cdot F_2(n+d,m)$. If the detector provides a soft decision, i.e., if it can provide the certainty that the person is imaged in a frame, the evidence that a specific person is present in both fingerprints depends on this certainty. In this case, co-occurrence can be defined as $C_{soft}(d,n,m) = \min(F_1(n,m), F_2(n+d,m))$. The overall evidence, for a specific displacement d, that $F_1(n,m)$ and $F_2(n,m)$ are similar can be evaluated by summing $C(d,n,m)$ over all frames and persons. If the lengths of the two video segments are N_1 and N_2, and assuming (without loss of generality) that $N_1 \leq N_2$, the normalized value of C for a hard detector can be expressed as:

$$C_{hard}(d) = \sum_{n=1}^{N_1} \sum_{m=1}^{M} \frac{F_1(n,m) \cdot F_2(n+d,m)}{N_1 M}$$

(4)

whereas in the case of a soft detector:

$$C_{soft}(d) = \sum_{n=1}^{N_1} \sum_{m=1}^{M} \frac{\min(F_1(n,m), F_2(n+d,m))}{N_1 M}$$

(5)

One can consider C as the overlap between the pulses that correspond to the 4-tuples which refer to the same individual in the two fingerprints. The similarity of $F_1(n,m)$, $F_2(n,m)$ can be defined as the maximum co-occurrence value $C_{max} = \max_d C(d)$, obtained when sliding F_2 over F_1. From the above description it is obvious that the procedure used to evaluate C_{max} is similar to a convolution. As a consequence, C_{max} is expected to be insensitive to small changes in the fingerprint. Such changes include splits, shifts and changes in width of the 4-tuple pulses as a result of face detection errors or changes in height of the pulses due to the face recognizer.

Having established a fingerprint similarity evaluation method, the search for a certain video in a database can be performed by evaluating the similarity of the fingerprint of this video with the fingerprints stored in the database and declaring a match when this similarity is above a pre-specified threshold. Obviously, performing this search using a brute-force approach is prohibitive in terms of computational time. For this reason an algorithm that utilizes indexing structures along with the properties and structure of the fingerprints in order to achieve almost logarithmic search time has been developed. More details on this procedure can be found in Cotsaces et al. (2006).

Experimental Performance Evaluation

Since a video fingerprinting method is expected to operate on video databases consisting of thousands of videos, the performance of the proposed method should be evaluated on experimental setups having similar characteristics. However, applying different types of existing face detectors and recognizers on such a database in order to use their results for the experimental performance evaluation of the method is a cumbersome procedure. For this reason, we selected to test the algorithm on artificial data. In order to do so, two probabilistic models have been devised. The first one models the ground truth of face appearances in videos, whereas the second one models errors of the face detection and recognition algorithms when applied on the query video in order to derive the corresponding fingerprint. The model of the face detector and recognizer errors was used to modify the face appearance ground truth sequences (fingerprints). Both statistical testing and analysis of the physical meaning of the random variables that appear in these models (number of persons in each shot, duration of appearances, etc) were used to select the distribution models used for these variables. The parameters of these distributions (mean, variance etc) were derived by annotating a moderately large video corpus and analyzing the results. The output of these models is a set of video fingerprints.

The following types of face detection and recognition errors (noise) have been taken into account in the corresponding model:

- Changes in the start and end frames of the 4-tuple, which is the most frequent error committed by face detectors and trackers and will be called face detector error. To model these errors, exponentially distributed noise has been added to the start time of a 4-tuple, whereas zero mean Gaussian noise was applied on the end time of the 4-tuple. Standard deviation values of 1 and 2 seconds, were used for both the start and end frame noise. The noise mean value was zero in the case of the 4-tuple's end frame. Since exponential noise was applied on the start frame, a mean value equal to the standard deviation was used.
- Change of the person's identity in a 4-tuple, a typical error committed by face recognizers. A probability of 5% or 10% that the true identity of a person would be randomly changed to another one was used in the experiments.

Phenomena such as compression, cropping, video noise etc were not modelled explicitly. This was due to the fact that such manipulations affect the output of the face detection and recognition modules. Thus, their effect can be included in the noise model of the face detection and recognition modules.

A number of experiments involving query videos that existed in the database as well as videos that did not exist in the database were performed in order to measure the algorithm's performance.

As already mentioned in this chapter, two sorts of errors can occur in the first case: false rejection and misclassification. The set of experiments in this case involved an artificially constructed fingerprint database consisting of 1000 videos, each being 65 minutes long. From this database we randomly extracted 3 sets, each consisting of 100 video segments. The segments in the three sets were respectively 5, 7.5 and 10 minutes long and contained 32, 48 and 64 4-tuples. Noise representing face detector and recognizer errors was added on each set, using the procedure described above, and the videos were used as queries to the system.

In the second case, we used the model described above to create 1000 videos (more specifically, fingerprints corresponding to videos) that differed from the videos in the database. Since the content of the new videos was not related to those in the database, these videos were not modified in order to model errors in face detection and recognition. Three sets, each containing 1000 videos and 32, 48 and 64 4-tuples per video (or equivalently 5, 7.5 and 10 minutes of video), were derived and used for querying the artificially created database described above. False acceptance is the only type of error in this case.

The results are presented in Table 3, where the strength of the face detector noise is presented as the mean deviation of the change in the start and end frames of the 4-tuples (in seconds), and the strength of the face recognizer noise is given as the probability of false recognition. The results show that the method performs very satisfactorily, especially when lengthy query videos are used. For example, for a query segment of 64 4-tuples (10 minutes), and with moderate noise (2 seconds detector noise and 5% recognizer noise) the false acceptance rate is 2.1%, the false rejection rate is 4% and the misclassification rate only 1%.

The computational complexity of the algorithm was also evaluated using an artificial video database. The experiments proved that the length of the query segments did not influence the search time and that

Table 3. Performance results of the video replica detection algorithm

Query Length (4-tuples)		32	48	64
Query Length (minutes)		5	7.5	10
False Acceptance (%)		6.6	3	2.1
Face Recognizer Noise	Face Detector Noise	False Rejection (%)		
5%	1sec	2	4	3
10%	1 sec	7	4	4
5%	2 sec	4	3	4
10%	2 sec	11	7	12
Face Recognizer Noise	Face Detector Noise	Misclassification (%)		
5%	1 sec	0	0	0
10%	1 sec	0	0	0
5%	2 sec	4	1	1
10%	2 sec	2	0	0

the performance of the algorithm is near-logarithmic with respect to the size of the database, requiring just 40 seconds for a search in a database consisting of 10,000 videos of duration 60 minutes each.

CONCLUSION

Fingerprinting or replica detection is an efficient alternative to watermarking for the digital rights management of multimedia data, having the additional advantage of leaving the data unaffected. Two fingerprinting approaches have been presented in this chapter. The first approach utilizes color-based descriptors along with R-trees and LDA in order to achieve identification of (possibly modified) copies of images from a database of originals. The second method deals with video data and combines semantic information about the appearances of actors in videos with a convolution-like search strategy to achieve the same goals in a fast and robust way. Experimental results show that the proposed techniques can be used for the efficient DRM of images and video.

FUTURE RESEARCH DIRECTIONS

A number of enhancements and variants of the methods outlined in this chapter can be envisioned. For the image replica detection algorithm, feature vectors different than the color-based one currently in use are being tested. Such feature vectors involve structural or spatial information like texture or edge characteristics or spatial distribution of colors within the image. Moreover, a variant of this algorithm that reduces the false acceptance rate by introducing, after the R-tree step, a module that performs image similarity computation using SIFT features (Lowe, 2004) is under investigation. One can also think of utilizing other indexing structures instead of the R-trees used in this study. The video replica detection algorithm is also tested on real video data with the use of existing face detection and recognition algorithms. Variants of this algorithm that operate on other types of semantic fingerprints with similar structure, such as fingerprints related to speaker identities derived through a speaker recognition algorithm, might be considered.

ACKNOWLEDGMENT

This work has been supported in part by the European Commission through the IST Programme under Contract IST-2002-507932 ECRYPT.

REFERENCES

Coskun, B., Sankur, B., & Memon, N. (2006). Spatio-temporal transform-based video hashing. *IEEE Transactions on Multimedia, 8*(6), 1190–1208.

Cotsaces, C., Nikolaidis, N., & Pitas, I. (2006). Video indexing by face occurrence-based signatures. *In IEEE International Conference on Acoustics Speech and Signal Processing (ICASSP 06)* (pp. II-137-II-140).

Duda, R., Hart, P., &. Stork, D. (2000). Pattern classification, 2nd edition. Wiley Interscience.

Eickeler, S., Wallhoff, F., Iurgel, U., & Rigoll, G. (2001). Content-based indexing of images and video using face detection and recognition methods. *In IEEE International Conference on Acoustics, Speech, and Signal Processing (ICASSP 2001)* (pp.III-1505-III-1508).

Gaede, V., & Gunther, A. (1998). Multidimensional access methods. *ACM Computing Surveys, 30*(2), 170-231.

Gavrielides, M., & Sikudova, E., & Pitas, I. (2005). Color-based descriptors for image fingerprinting. *IEEE Transactions on Multimedia, 8*(4), 740-748.

Ghorbel, F. (1994). A complete invariant description for gray-level images by the harmonic analysis approach. *Pattern Recognition Letters, 15*(10), 1043-1051.

Gionis, A., Indyk, P., & Motwani, R. (1999). Similarity search in high dimensions via hashing. *In 25th International Conference on Very Large Data Bases (VLDB '99)* (pp. 518–529).

Hampapur, A., & Bolle, R. (2002). Comparison of sequence matching techniques for video copy detection. *In Conference on Storage and Retrieval for Media Databases*, 194-201.

Joly, A., Buisson, O., & Frélicot, C. (2007). Content-based copy detection using distortion-based probabilistic similarity search. *IEEE Transactions on Multimedia, 9*(2), 293-306.

Ke, Y., & Sukthankar, R. (2003). PCA-SIFT: A more distinctive representation for local image descriptors. *In IEEE Computer Vision and Pattern Recognition*, (pp. II-506-II-513).

Ke, Y., Sukthankar, R., & Huston, L. (2004). An efficient parts-based near-duplicate and sub-image retrieval system. *In 12th annual ACM international conference on Multimedia* (pp. 869-876).

Kim, C. (2003). Content-based image copy detection. *Signal Processing: Image Communication, 18*(3), 169-184.

Kim, C., & Vasudev, B. (2005). Spatiotemporal sequence matching techniques for video copy detection. *IEEE Transactions on Circuits and Systems for Video Technology, 15*(1), 127-132.

Law-To, J., Buisson, O., Gouet-Brunet, V., & Boujemaa, N. (2006). Robust voting algorithm based on labels of behaviour for video copy detection. *In ACM Multimedia, (MM'06)* (pp. 835-844).

Law-To, J., Chen, L., Joly, A., Laptev, Y., Buisson, O., Gouet, V., Boujemaa, N., & Stentiford, F. (2007). Video copy detection: A comparative study. *In ACM International Conference on Image and Video Retrieval*, (pp. 371-378).

Lowe, D (2004). Distinctive image features from scale-invariant keypoints. *International Journal of Computer Vision, 60*(2), 91-110.

Maret, Y., Dufaux, F., & Ebrahmi, T. (2006). Adaptive image replica detection based on support vector classifiers. *Signal Processing: Image Communication, 21*(8), 688-703.

Mihcak, M. K., &. Venkatesan, R. (2001). New iterative geometric methods for robust perceptual image hashing. *In ACM Workshop on Security and Privacy in Digital Rights Management, LNCS 2320*, 13-21.

Nikolopoulos, S., Zafeiriou, S., Sidiropoulos, P., Nikolaidis, N., & Pitas, I. (2006). Image replica detection using R-trees and linear discriminant analysis. *In IEEE International Conference on Multimedia and Expo (ICME 06)* (pp. 1797-1800).

Oostveen, J., Kalker, T., & Haitsma, J. (2002), Feature extraction and a database strategy for video fingerprinting. *In 5th International Conference on Recent Advances in Visual I*

Qamra, A., Meng, Y., & Chang, E. (2005). Enhanced perceptual distance functions and indexing for image replica recognition. *IEEE Transaction on Pattern Analysis and Machine Intelligence, 27*(3), 379-391.

Roy, S., Chang, E.-C., & Natarajan, K. (2005). A unified framework for resolving ambiguity in copy detection. *In 13th annual ACM international conference on Multimedia* (pp. 648-655).

Satoh, S. (2000). Comparative evaluation of face sequence matching for content-based video access. *In 4th International Conference on Automatic Face and Gesture Recognition(FG2000)* (pp. 163 – 168).

Tefas, A., Nikolaidis, N., &. Pitas, I. (2005). Watermarking techniques for image authentication and copyright protection. In Bovik A. (Ed.) *The Handbook of Image and Video Processing*, 2nd edition (pp. 1083-1109). Elsevier.

Zhao, W., Chellappa, R., Phillips, P.-J., & Rosenfeld, A. (2003). Face recognition: A literature survey. *ACM Computing Surveys, 35*(4), 399--458.

ADDITIONAL READING

Berrani, S.-A., Amsaleg, L., & Gros, P. (2003). Robust content-based image searches for copyright protection. *In ACM International Workshop on Multimedia Databases*, (pp. 70–77).

Boujemaa, N., Fauqueur, J., & Gouet, V. (2003). What's beyond query by example?. In IAPR International Conference on Image and Signal Processing (ICISP'2003).

Chang, E., Wang, J., Li, C., & Wilderhold, G. (1998). Rime—A replicated image detector for the World Wide Web. *In SPIE Symosium on Voice, Video, and Data Communications*, (pp. 58–67).

Fridrich, J., & Goljan, M. (2000). Robust hash functions for digital watermarking. *In International Conference on Information Technology: Coding and Computing (ITCC'00)* (pp. 178-183).

Haitsma, J., & Kalker, T. (2002). A highly robust audio fingerprinting system. *In International Conference on Music Information Retrieval (ISMIR 02)*.

Hsu, C. Y., & Lu, C. (2004). Geometric distortion-resilient image hashing system and its application scalability. *In ACM International Conference on Multimedia: Proceedings of the 2004 workshop on Multimedia and security* (pp. 81-92).

Hua, X.-S., Chen, X., & Zhang, H.-J. (2004). Robust video signature based on ordinal measure. *In IEEE International Conference on Image Processing (ICIP 04)* (pp. 685-688).

Indyk, P., Iyengar, G., & Shivakumar, N. (1999). *Finding pirated video sequences on the Internet.* Technical report, Stanford University.

Iwamoto, K., Kasutani, E., & Yamada, A. (2006). Image signature robust to caption superimposition for video sequence identification. *In IEEE International Conference on Image Processing (ICIP 06)* (pp. 3185-3188).

Jaimes, A., Chang, S.-F., & Loui, A. C. (2002). Duplicate detection in consumer photography and news video. *In ACM International Conference on Multimedia*, (pp. 423–424).

Johnson, M., & Ramchandran, K. (2003). Dither-based secure image hashing using distributed coding. *In IEEE International Conference on Image Processing (ICIP 03)* (pp. 751-754).

Laptev, I., & Lindeberg, T. (2003). Space-time interest points. *In IEEE International Conference on Computer Vision (ICCV 03)*, (pp. 432–439).

Lefebvre, F., Macq, B., & Czyz, J. (2003). A robust soft hash algorithm for digital image signature. *In IEEE International Conference on Image Processing (ICIP 03)*, (pp. 495-498).

Li, Y., Jin, L., & Zhou, X. (2005). Video matching using binary signature. *In International Symposium on Intelligent Signal Processing and Communication Systems*, (pp. 317–320).

Maret, Y., Nikolopoulos, S., Dufaux, F., Ebrahimi, T., & Nikolaidis, N. (2006). A novel replica detection system using binary classifiers, R-trees and PCA. *In IEEE International Conference on Image Processing (ICIP 06)* (pp. 925-928).

Massoudi, A., Lefebvre, F., Demarty, C.-H., Oisel, L., & Chupeau, B. (2006). A video fingerprint based on visual digest and local fingerprints. *In IEEE Workshop on Signal Processing Systems (SiPS 2000)*, (pp. 2297–2300).

Meng, Y., Chang, E. Y., & Li, B. (2003). Enhancing DPF for near-replica image recognition. *In International Conference on Pattern Recognition*, (pp. 416–423).

Monga, V., & Mihcak, M. K. (2005). Robust image hashing via non-negative matrix factorizations. *In IEEE International Conference on Acoustics Speech and Signal Processing (ICASSP 06)*, (pp. II-225—II-228).

Radhakrishnan, R., Xiong, Z., & Memon, N. D. (2005). *On the security of visual hash.*

Roy, S., & Chang, E.-C. (2004). Watermarking with retrieval systems. ACM Multimedia Systems, 9(5), 433-440.

Seo, J., Haitsma, J., Kalker, T., & Yoo, C. D. (2003). Affine transform resilient image fingerprinting. *In IEEE International Conference on Acoustics Speech and Signal Processing (ICASSP 03)*,(pp. III-61-III-64).

Seo, J. S., Haitsma, J., Kalker, T., & Yoo C. D. (2004). A robust image fingerprinting system using the radon transform. *Signal Processing: Image Communication, 19*, 325-339.

Smeulders, A. W. M., Worring, M., Santini, S., Gupta, A., & Jain, R. (2000). Content-based image retrieval at the end of the early years. *IEEE Transactions on Pattern Analysis and Machine Inteligence, 22*(12), 1349-1380.

Swaminathan, A., Mao, Y., & Wu, M. (2004). Image hashing resilient to geometric and filtering operations. *In IEEE Workshop on Multimedia Signal Processing (MMSP'04)* (pp. 355-358).

Venkatesan, R., Kaon, S., Jakubowski, M. H., & Moulin, P. (2000). Robust image hashing. *In IEEE International Conference on Image Processing (ICIP 00)* (pp. 664-666).

Yang, S., & Chen, C. (2005). Robust image hashing based on SPIHT. *In International Conference on Information Technology: Research and Education (ITRE 05)* (pp. 110-114).

Yang, Z., Oop, W., & Sun, Q. (2004). Hierarchical non-uniform locally sensitive hashing and its application to video identification. *In IEEE International Conference on Image Processing (ICIP 04).*

Chapter VIII
Digital Fingerprinting Based Multimedia Content Distribution

Shiguo Lian
France Telecom R&D, Beijing, China

ABSTRACT

In this chapter, the digital fingerprinting technology that is used to trace illegal distributors in multimedia content distribution is investigated. Firstly, the background and basic knowledge of digital fingerprinting-based multimedia distribution are reviewed. Then, some existing fingerprinting algorithms are introduced and compared. Additionally, the methods to embed the fingerprint securely are overviewed and analyzed. As an example, the secure audio distribution scheme is presented, and its performances are evaluated. Finally, some open issues and the future trends in digital fingerprinting are proposed. It is expected to provide valuable information to the students, engineers or researchers interested in this research topic.

INTRODUCTION

With the development of network technology and multimedia technology, multimedia content transmission becomes more and more popular in e-commerce systems, such as video-on-demand, video conferencing, multimedia message sending, mobile TV, and so on. In these services, multimedia content protection is important and urgent, which protects the rights of content producer, service provider and customer.

Till now, various protection techniques have been reported, such as multimedia encryption (Furht & Kirovski, 2006), digital watermarking (Cox, et al., 2002), multimedia authentication ((Furht & Kirovski, 2006; Fridrich, 2002), etc. Multimedia encryption technique transforms multimedia content into an unintelligent form in order to forbid unauthorized customers from reading the content. In this technique, a key is required to encrypt or decrypt multimedia content, which determines the system's security. Differently, digital watermarking technique embeds such information as ownership, customer ID or label into multimedia content by modifying multimedia data slightly. The embedded information can be extracted from multimedia content and used to tell the ownership information. Another technique, multimedia authentication, can detect the malicious tampering in multimedia content. In this technique, the unique code is computed from multimedia content and then stored in a secret way (securely transmitted to receivers, or embedded into multimedia content with watermarking technique) before transmission. Then, at the customer side, a unique code is computed from the received multimedia content with the same method and compared with the received one (received from the sender, or extracted from the multimedia content) to tell the tampering results. Generally, these techniques are used together to realize secure multimedia transmission in e-commerce systems (Abijit & Kuilboer, 2002).

In some applications, such as IPTV (ITU IPTV) or Mobile TV (DVB), multimedia content distribution often faces such a problem: a customer may redistribute the received multimedia content to other unauthorized customers. This typical problem often causes great profit-losses of content producer or service provider. As a potential solution, new technique, named digital fingerprinting (Wu, et al., 2004), is reported. It embeds different information, such as Customer ID, into media content, produces different copy, and sends different copy to different customer. If a copy is spread to unauthorized customers, the unique information in the copy determines the illegal re-distributor. It seems a good solution. However, another question arises, i.e., different customer combines different copy through averaging or some other operations to produce a new copy. For there is often few differences between these copies, the collusion operation may make the embedded information lost. This kind of attack is named collusion attack (Wu, et al., 2004). Finding new solutions resisting collusion attacks attracts more and more researchers.

In this chapter, digital fingerprinting technique is investigated, including its basic knowledge, key difficulties, various solutions and practical applications. As an example, the secure audio distribution scheme based on digital fingerprinting is constructed and evaluated. Additionally, some open issues and future work in this topic are presented. The rest of the chapter is arranged as follows. In Section 2, the fundamental wok of secure multimedia distribution is introduced. Then, digital fingerprinting technique is investigated in detail in Section 3, including the biggest threat - collusion attack, robust fingerprinting algorithms, and secure fingerprint embedding schemes. In Section 4, an audio distribution scheme based on digital fingerprinting is proposed and evaluated. Some open issues and future trends are presented in Section 5. Finally, in Section 6, some conclusions are drawn.

BACKGROUND

In secure multimedia distribution, multimedia content is transmitted from the sender to the receivers in a secure manner. Generally, two techniques are used to protect multimedia content's ownership and confidentiality respectively, i.e., digital watermarking and multimedia encryption.

Digital watermarking technique (Cox, et al., 2002; Barni & Bartolini, 2004; Petitcolas, et al., 1999) embeds some information into multimedia content by modifying it slightly. The embedded information can be detected or extracted from multimedia content and used for some applications. For example, if the information of content owner is embedded as a watermark, then the watermark can be used to tell the ownership and protect the copyright. Generally, digital watermarking technique has some requirements (Barni & Bartolini, 2004), among which, imperceptibility and robustness are two typical ones. The imperceptibility means that the difference between the watermarked multimedia content and the original one can not be detected by human's eyes. The robustness means that the watermark can survive some operations on the multimedia content, such as recompression, A/D or D/A conversion, adding noise, filtering, etc. Till now watermarking techniques can be classified with different methods. According to the multimedia content, watermarking technique can be classified into image watermarking (Mohanty, et al., 2000; Cox, et al., 1997), video watermarking (Thiemert, et al., 2004; Simitopoulos, et al., 2002), audio watermarking (Dittmann, et al., 2006; Lang, et al., 2005), text watermarking (Huang, et al., 2001), software watermarking (Zhu, et al., 2002), etc. According to the embedding method, it can be classified into additive watermarking (Cox, et al., 1996), multiplicative watermarking (Barni, et al., 2001), quantitative watermarking (Chen & Wornell, 1998), etc.

Multimedia encryption technique (Furht & Kirovski, 2006) transforms multimedia content into an unintelligible form under the control of a key. It is used in multimedia distribution to confirm that only the authorized receivers can recover the multimedia content correctly. Generally, traditional ciphers can be used to encrypt all or part of multimedia data. The straightforward method (Mao, et al., 2004; Lian, et al., 2005) is to encrypt the raw data or compressed data completely. However, considering that multimedia content (e.g., video, image, etc.) is often of large volumes and multimedia related applications often needs real-time interaction, encrypting all the data is time cost. If the cipher needs complicated computing, it is not suitable for real-time applications. As an alterative, partial encryption method (Lian, et al., 2007a; Lian, et al., 2004a) encrypts only a part of multimedia data, such as the significant region in an image, or the objects in a video sequence. Because of reducing the encrypted data volumes, the time cost can be greatly reduced. Till now, many multimedia encryption algorithms have been reported, such as the speech or audio encryption algorithms (Servetti, et al., 2003; Cheng & Li, 2000), image encryption algorithms (Lian, et al., 2004b; Lian, et al., 2006a) or video encryption algorithms (Lian, et al., 2006b; Lian, et al., 2007b).

Figure 1. Typical application based on digital fingerprinting

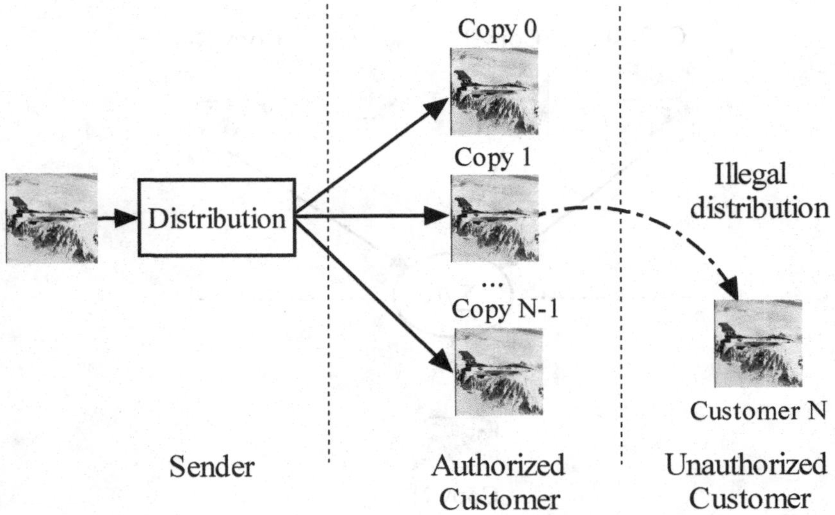

DIGITAL FINGERPRINTING

Digital fingerprinting (Wu, et al., 2004) is the technique that embeds unique information into multimedia content and traces the usage of the corresponding multimedia content. The typical application is shown in Figure 1. Here, the unique information is embedded into the image, which produces different copy for different customer. If one customer redistributes its copy to other unauthorized customers, the unique information can be extracted and used to tell the illegal redistributor. Digital fingerprinting is similar to digital watermarking, while it faces more challenges. And the challenges attract more researchers.

Collusion Attack

The biggest threat to digital fingerprinting is collusion attack. That is, several attackers fabricate a new copy through combining their unique copies in order to avoid the tracing. The colluders intend to remove the fingerprinting by use of the differences between different copies. This kind of attack is often classified into two categories (Wu, et al., 2004; Wu, 2005), i.e., linear collusion and nonlinear collusion. Among them, linear collusion means to average, filter or cut-and-paste the copies, while nonlinear collusion means to take the minimal, maximal or median pixels in the copies. Generally, four kinds of collusion attacks are often considered, i.e., averaging attack, min-max attack, negative-correlation attack and zero-correlation attack.

Figure 2 shows the example of averaging attack, in which, N number of copies are averaged to generate a new copy.

Fingerprinting Algorithms

To detect collusion attacks and detect the colluders, some fingerprinting algorithms have been studied, among which, three types are more attractive. They are orthogonal fingerprinting, coded fingerprinting and warping-based fingerprinting.

Figure 2. Example of averaging attack

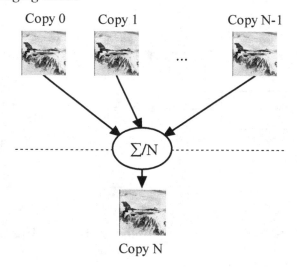

Orthogonal fingerprinting. Each fingerprinting is orthogonal to another (Trappe, et al., 2003; Herrigel, et al., 1998; Wang, et al., 2005), which keeps the colluded copy still detectable. According to the property of orthogonal sequence, such detection method as correlation detection is still practical although there is some degradation caused by collusion attacks. For example, the algorithm (Herrigel, et al., 1998) produces orthogonal fingerprinting for each customer, the fingerprinting is then modulated by the cover video, and correlation detection is used to determine the ownership or colluders. For example, orthogonal fingerprinting is generated from pseudorandom sequence generator and then embedded into the video to be transmitted, which produces different video copies. For each copy, correlation detection obtains a big correlation value that determines the customer who receives the copy. For the colluded copy (averaging two copies), correlation detection obtains a relative small correlation value that is still bigger than the threshold. Thus, the colluders can still be traced.

Coded fingerprinting. Fingerprinting can be carefully designed in codeword that can detect the colluders partially or completely. Till now, two kinds of encoding methods are often referenced. They are the Boneh-Shaw scheme (Boneh & Shaw, 1998) and the combinatorial design based code (Wu, et al., 2004; Kim & Suh, 2004). Boneh-Shaw scheme is based on the Marking assumption: only the different bits are changed by colluders, while the same bits can not be changed. By designing the primitive binary code, at least one colluder can be captured out of up to c colluders. And it can support more customers if it is extended to outer code. Differently, in combinatorial design based anti-collusion scheme, the fingerprinting acts as a combinatorial codeword. The combinatorial codes have the following property: each group of colluders' fingerprinting produces unique codeword that determines all the colluders in the group. The codeword is constructed based on combinatorial theory, such as AND-ACC (anti-collusion codes) or BIBD (Dinitz & Stinson, 1992).

Warping-based fingerprinting. This kind of fingerprinting aims to make collusion impractical under the condition of imperceptibility (Celik, et al., 2005; Mao & Mihcak, 2005). That is, to de-synchronize the carrier. Thus, the colluded copy is perceptible (generates perceptual artifacts). These de-synchronization operations include random temporal sampling (video frame interpolation, temporal re-sampling, etc.), random spatial sampling (RST operations, random bending, luminance filtering or parameter smoothing) or random warping. For example, the original video copy is warped under the control of customer ID, which produces different copies with slight degradation. In collusion attacks, the colluded copy is degraded so greatly that it can not be used in high definitional applications. According to this case, warping-based fingerprinting makes collusion attacks unpractical, and thus is secure against collusion attacks. However, this scheme has its own disadvantages. For example, the compression ratio is often changed because of the pre-warping operations. And the transmission cost is increased especially in multicast channels because multi-copies should be produced for multi-customers.

Secure and Efficient Fingerprint Embedding

In digital fingerprinting, the distribution efficiency (Simitopoulos, et al., 2003) is a problem. That is, each customer should be assigned a unique copy, which costs much in broadcast or multicast channel. Generally, the cost depends on the embedding point. For example, if the fingerprinting is embedded at the server end, then the server must deal with many copies before transmission, and much time or storage space will be cost. As a substitution, embedding at customer end (Bloom, 2003) is proposed, which

Figure 3. The scheme of Joint Fingerprint embedding and Decryption

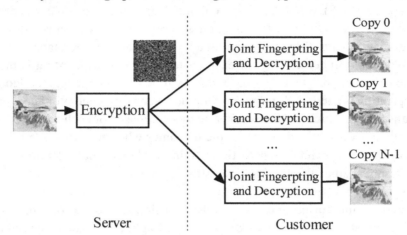

deals with only one copy at each end. However, this kind of embedding is not secure for some one may feign the server to sending copies. As a tradeoff, an algorithm embeds fingerprinting at the middle of the server end and customer end (Brown, et al., 1999), which strengthens the system while increasing its complexity. Thus, the suitable distribution system needs to be studied.

Recently, joint fingerprinting and decryption (JFD) scheme (Parnes & Parviainen, 2001; Anderson & Manifavas, 1997) is reported and attracts more and more researchers. As shown in Figure 3, in this scheme, the multimedia content is fingerprinted and decrypted simultaneously at the receiver end. For the fingerprinting operation and decryption operation are jointed together, there is no gap between them, and the multimedia content will not be leaked out. For example, the scheme (Parnes & Parviainen, 2001) is constructed on broadcasting encryption, the Chamleon method (Anderson & Manifavas, 1997) is based on stream cipher and Least Significant Bit (LSB) watermarking, the method (Kundur & Karthik, 2004) is based on partial encryption, the method (Lian, et al., 2006c) is based on codeword substitution, and another method (Lemma, et al., 2006) is based on partial encryption and stream cipher.

SECURE AUDIO CONTENT DISTRIBUTION

The Proposed JFD Scheme for Audio Data

The scheme, shown in Figure 4, gives the encryption process and decryption process that are implemented at the sender side and the receiver side, respectively. In encryption process, audio data P is modulated by n random sequences generated from random sequence generators. In decryption process, audio data C is decrypted into a unique copy P_k (k=0,1,...,M-1, M is the number of customers) by demodulation under the control of the k-th customer's fingerprint code F_k. The fingerprint code can be detected from the media copy P_k, which can determine the owner of the copy.

Audio Encryption

The encryption process, shown in Figure 4, is composed of two steps, i.e., random sequence generation and modulation.

Random sequences generation. Generate n random sequences $S_0, S_1, \ldots, S_{n-1}$ ($S_i = s_{i,0}s_{i,1}\ldots s_{i,d-1}$, $-L \leq s_{i,j} < L$, $i=0,1,\ldots,n-1$, $j=0,1,\ldots,d-1$, L is the range of the random data) with random number generator under the control of $R = r_0 r_1 r_2 \ldots r_{n-1}$ (r_i is a 32-bit integer, $i=0,1,\ldots,n-1$), as shown in Figure 4. Some existing random number generator can be used, such as the one proposed in (Viega, 2003). Here, R acts as the encryption key.

Modulation. The plain audio $P = p_0 p_1 \ldots p_{d-1}$ is modulated by the n sequences according to the following method.

$$c_i = p_i + \sum_{j=0}^{n-1} s_{j,i} \ (i = 0,1,\ldots,d-1) \tag{1}$$

Audio Decryption

The decryption process, shown in Figure 4, is composed of three steps, i.e., random sequence generation, fingerprint code generation and demodulation.

Random sequences generation. Generate n random sequences $S_0, S_1, \ldots, S_{n-1}$ ($S_i = s_{i,0}s_{i,1}\ldots s_{i,d-1}$, $-L \leq s_{i,j} < L$, $i=0,1,\ldots,n-1$, $j=0,1,\ldots,d-1$, L is the range of the random data) with random number generator under the

Figure 4. The JFD scheme for audio data

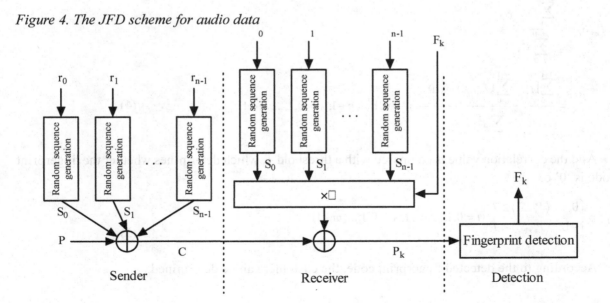

control of $R=r_0r_1r_2...r_{n-1}$ (r_i is a 32-bit integer, i=0,1,...,n-1), as shown in Figure 4. Some existing random number generator can be used, such as the one proposed in (Viega, 2003).

Fingerprint code generation. This step generates the fingerprint code $f_{k,0},f_{k,1},...,f_{k,n-1}$ ($f_{k,j}$=0 or -1, k=0,1,...,m-1, j=0,1,...,n-1, m is the number of customers) from the k-th customer information F_k. Generally, for k-th customer, the following conditions are satisfied: $f_{k,j}$=-1(j≠k) and $f_{k,k}$=0.

Demodulation. The cipher audio $C=c_0c_1...c_{d-1}$ is demodulated by the n sequences according to the following method.

$$p_{k,i} = c_i + \sum_{j=0}^{n-1} f_{k,j}s_{j,i} \ (i = 0,1,...,d-1, k = 0,1,...,m-1) \qquad (2)$$

And it is deduced as below.

$$p_{k,i} = p_i + \sum_{j=0}^{n-1} s_{j,i} + \sum_{j=0}^{n-1} f_{k,j}s_{j,i}$$

$$= p_i + \sum_{j=0}^{n-1} (f_{k,j}+1)s_{j,i} \ (i = 0,1,...,d-1, k = 0,1,...,m-1) \qquad (3)$$

As can be seen, whether a random sequence is added to the plaintext or not depends on the corresponding fingerprint code. When $f_{k,j}$=-1, the random sequence is not added, other wise, the random sequence is added.

Traitor Tracing

In detection process, the correlation between P_k and S_i (i=0,1,...,n-1) is computed, as defined below.

$$<P_k,S_i> = \frac{\sum_{j=0}^{d-1} p_{k,j}s_{j,i}}{\sum_{j=0}^{d-1} s^2_{j,i}}$$

$$= \frac{\sum_{j=0}^{d-1} [p_i + \sum_{t=0}^{n-1} (f_{k,t}+1)s_{t,i}]s_{j,i}}{\sum_{j=0}^{d-1} s^2_{j,i}} \ (i = 0,1,...,n-1, k = 0,1,...,m-1). \qquad (4)$$

And the correlation value is compared with a threshold T, which determines whether the fingerprint code is '0' or '-1'.

$$f_{k,i} = \begin{cases} 0, & \langle P_k,S_i \rangle \geq T \\ -1, & \langle P_k,S_i \rangle < T \end{cases} \ (i = 0,1,...,n-1, k = 0,1,...,m-1) \qquad (5)$$

According to the detected fingerprint code, the customer can be determined.

Collusion Resistance

Assume N customers $(t, t+1, ..., t+N-1)$ attend the collusion attack. In the average collusion, the N copies $P_t', P_{t+1}', \cdots, P_{t+N-1}'$ are averaged, which produces the colluded copy P''. In this case, the k-th fingerprint bit will be detected as follows.

$$< P''^k - P^k, S_1^j > = < \frac{P_t'^k + P_{t+1}'^k + \cdots + P_{t+N-1}'^k}{N} - P^k, S_1^j >$$

$$= \frac{\sum_{i=0}^{n/r-1} (\frac{p_{t,i}'^k + p_{t+1,i}'^k + \cdots + p_{t+N-1}'^k}{N} - p_i^k) s_{1,i}^j}{\sum_{i=0}^{n/r-1} s_{1,i}^j s_{1,i}^j}$$

$$= \frac{\frac{1}{N} \left[\sum_{i=0}^{n/r-1} s_{t,1,i}^{f_k} s_{1,i}^j + \sum_{i=0}^{n/r-1} s_{t+1,1,i}^{f_k} s_{1,i}^j + \cdots + \sum_{i=0}^{n/r-1} s_{t+N-1,1,i}^{f_k} s_{1,i}^j \right]}{\sum_{i=0}^{n/r-1} s_{1,i}^j s_{1,i}^j}$$

$$= \frac{1}{N} < S_{t,1}^{f_k}, S_1^j > + \frac{1}{N} < S_{t+1,1}^{f_k}, S_1^j > + \cdots + \frac{1}{N} < S_{t+N-1,1}^{f_k}, S_1^j >. \tag{6}$$

The correlation value is in close relation with the fingerprint encoding method. Taking the simplest fingerprint code for example, the 7-length code is defined as below.

$Customer\,0:$ 0   −1   −1   −1   −1   −1   −1
$Customer\,1:$ −1   0   −1   −1   −1   −1   −1
$Customer\,2:$ −1   −1   0   −1   −1   −1   −1
$Customer\,3:$ −1   −1   −1   0   −1   −1   −1
$Customer\,4:$ −1   −1   −1   −1   0   −1   −1
$Customer\,5:$ −1   −1   −1   −1   −1   0   −1
$Customer\,6:$ −1   −1   −1   −1   −1   −1   0

Seen from the fingerprint codes, there is only one '0' in each row or column. Taking the first column for example, to detect the first code '0' (j=1), the correlation value in Eq. (6) becomes

$$< P''^k - P^k, S_1^j > = \frac{1}{N} < S_{0,1}^{f_0}, S_1^1 > + \frac{1}{N} < S_{1,1}^{f_1}, S_1^1 > + \cdots + \frac{1}{N} < S_{6,1}^{f_6}, S_1^1 >$$

$$= \frac{1}{N} < S_{0,1}^{f_0}, S_1^1 > \tag{7}$$

As can be seen, with the rise of N, the correlation value decreases, and the fingerprint bit is difficult to detect.

Experimental Results

Perceptual Security

For multimedia content encryption, both cryptographic security and perceptual security (Lian, et al., 2006b; Lian, et al., 2007b) should be investigated. The former one refers to the security against such cryptographic attacks as brute-force attack, statistical attack, etc., while the latter one denotes the intel-

Figure 5. Relation between the perceptual security and n

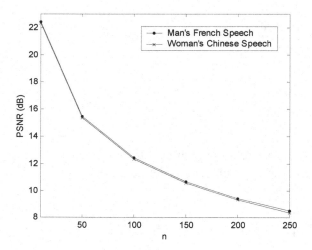

Figure 6. Results of audio encryption, decryption and fingerprinting ((a) original audio, (b) encrypted audio, (c) decrypted audio, and (d) fingerprinted audio)

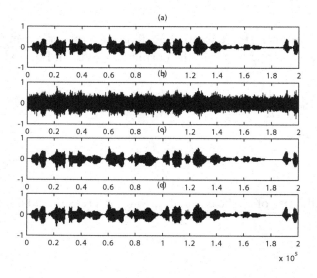

ligibility of the encrypted multimedia content. In the proposed scheme, the pseudorandom sequence is used to modulate multimedia content, which belongs to the stream cipher whose cryptographic security can be confirmed. However, the perceptual security is in close relation with the parameters, L and n. Taking the audio data of Man's French speech (16-bit, 44.1MHz, Stereo) and Woman's Chinese speech (16-bit, 44.1MHz, Single) for example, the relation between the peak signal-to-noise ratio (PSNR) of the encrypted audio data and the parameters is tested and shown in Figure 5. Here, L=250, and n ranges from 10 to 250. As can be seen, the bigger n is, the smaller the PSNR is. Generally, when n is no smaller than 200, the encrypted audio is greatly degraded and can not be used for commercial applications. The encrypted audio, decrypted audio and fingerprinted audio are shown in Figure 6. Here, the audio is Man's French speech (16-bit, 44.1MHz, Stereo), L=250, and n=200. As can be seen, the encrypted audio is degraded greatly by the random sequences, while the decrypted audio and fingerprinted audio are still of high quality. Thus, the proposed encryption scheme is of high perceptual security.

Collusion Resistance

As has been analyzed in Section 4.5, the proposed scheme is robust against collusion attacks in some extent. Taking averaging attack for example, one copy is generated by averaging two different copies, as shown in Figure 7. From the first copy (b), the first pseudorandom sequence can be detected with the correlation value of 0.97. For the second copy (c), the second pseudorandom sequence can be detected with the correlation value of 0.96. For the averaged copy (d), the first pseudorandom sequence can be detected with the correlation value of 0.51, and the second pseudorandom sequence can be detected with the correlation value of 0.46. That is, the correlation value decreases with the rise of colluders, as shown in Figure 8. Generally, when the number of colluders is no bigger than 9, the correlation value is no smaller than 0.1, which can still be detected.

Figure 7. Robustness against averaging attack ((a) original audio, (b) fingerprinted copy 1, PSNR=40.64dB, (c) fingerprinted copy 2, PSNR=40.65dB, and (d) averaged copy, PSNR=42.39)

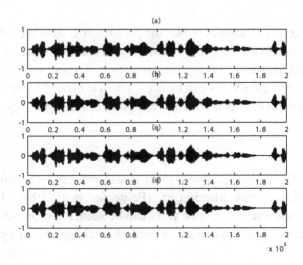

Figure 8. Relation between the correlation value and the number of colluders

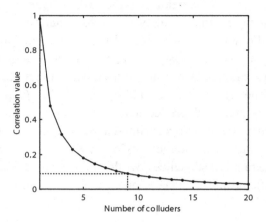

Figure 9. Relation between the imperceptibility and L

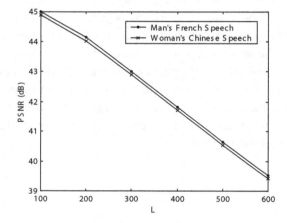

Imperceptibility

To keep the embedded fingerprint imperceptible, the parameter L should be chosen from a suitable collection. In the proposed scheme, the bigger L is, the smaller the PSNR is, and the worse the imperceptibility is. Otherwise, on the contrary. Taking the samples in Section 4.6.1, the relation between PSNR and L is tested and shown in Figure 9. As can be seen, when L is not bigger than 500, the fingerprinted audio's PSNR is not smaller than 40 dB, which keeps good imperceptibility.

Robustness

Besides collusion attacks, the embedded fingerprint is also robustness against some other operations, such as mp3 encoding, additive noise, filtering, etc (Petitcolas, et al., 1998). The correlation value after some operations are tested and shown in Table 1. As can be seen, the proposed fingerprinting algorithm is more robust against additive noise than against median filtering and mp3 encoding.

Table 1. Robustness against operations

L	MP3 encoding		Additive noise		Median filtering
	128kbps	64kbps	Factor =1	Factor =3	
100	0.06	0.04	0.25	0.11	0.02
200	0.08	0.08	0.37	0.28	0.13
300	0.16	0.12	0.42	0.36	0.21
400	0.27	0.19	0.56	0.49	0.33

CONCLUSION

In this chapter, the digital fingerprinting technique that is used to trace illegal distributor in multimedia services is investigated. Firstly, the basic techniques of digital watermarking and multimedia encryption are introduced. Then, the existing fingerprint techniques are reviewed and analyzed. Taking audio content for example, an audio distribution scheme based on digital fingerprinting is constructed and evaluated. Finally, some open issues and future trends in digital fingerprinting are presented. It is expected to provide valuable information to students, engineers, researchers interested in DRM for E-commerce.

FUTURE RESEARCH DIRECTIONS

Digital fingerprinting based multimedia distribution is now still in development. There are some hot topics in this research field.

Firstly, the fingerprint embedding method that makes the fingerprint survive such operations as camera-capture, filtering, adding noise, recompression and so on is expected. Till now, few embedding methods can survive most of the operations. Thus, better methods are expected.

Secondly, the fingerprint encoding method resisting collusion attacks is expected. Till now, the reported methods all have some disadvantages. For example, orthogonal fingerprint can not keep the detection rate when the colluders increase, coded fingerprint is fragile to linear combinatorial collusion attack, and desynchronized fingerprint affects the multimedia content's quality and is difficult to resist resynchronization attack.

Thirdly, secure and efficient distribution scheme suitable for different networks is to be studied. In unicasting, the fingerprint is embedded at the sender side, while in multicasting or broadcasting, the fingerprint should be embedded at the receiver side. When embedding at the receiver side, the security should be confirmed in order to resist the attackers who break the system by investigating the components at receiver side.

Fourthly, the performances of the joint fingerprint embedding and decryption schemes need to be improved. Generally, in the existing schemes, the fingerprint's robustness and the encryption algorithm's security contradict with each other. To keep the performances of both fingerprint embedding algorithm and encryption algorithm is the future work.

Fifthly, how to use the fingerprint in DRM systems is an open issue. Digital fingerprinting is based on watermarking technology that embeds the fingerprint into multimedia content and extracts the fingerprint from multimedia content. Additionally, fingerprint embedding should comply with the architecture of the practical application, such as p2p content sharing, IPTV, Mobile TV, etc. Using digital fingerprint in existing DRM systems is urgent, and much more work is expected in this topic.

REFERENCES

Abijit, C., & Kuilboer, J.-P. (2002). E-Business and E-Commerce infrastructure. McGraw-Hill. ISBN 0-07-247875-6.

Anderson, R., & Manifavas, C. (1997). Chameleon – A new kind of stream cipher. *In Lecture Notes in Computer Science, Fast Software Encryption*, (pp. 107-113), Springer-Verlag. .

Barni, M., & Bartolini, F. (2004). *Watermark systems engineering.* Marcel Dekker.

Barni, M., Bartolini, F., De Rose, A., & Piva, M. (2001). A new decoder for the optimum recovery of non-additive watermarks. *IEEE Trans. on Image Processing, 10*(5), 755-765.

Bloom, J. (2003). Security and rights management in digital cinema. *In Proc. IEEE Int. Conf. Acoustic, Speech and Signal Processing, 4*, 712-715.

Boneh, D., & Shaw, J. (1998). Collusion-secure fingerprinting for digital data. *IEEE Trans. Inform. Theory, 44*, 1897-1905.

Brown, I., Perkins, C., & Crowcroft, J. (1999). Watercasting: Distributed watermarking of multicast media. *In Proceedings of International Workshop on Networked Group Communication, 1736.* Springer-Verlag LNCS.

Celik, M. U., Sharma, G., & Tekalp, A. M. (2005). Collusion-resilient fingerprinting by random pre-warping. *IEEE Signal Processing Letters, Preprint.*

Chen, B., & Wornell, G. W. (1998). Digital watermarking and information embedding using dither modulation. *In Proceedings of the 1998 IEEE 2nd Workshop on Multimedia Signal Processing. Redondo Beach*, 273-278.

Cheng, H., & Li, X. (2000, August). Partial encryption of compressed images and videos. *IEEE Transactions on Signal Processing, 48*(8), 2439-2451.

Cox, I. J., Kilian, J., Leighton, T., & Shamoon, T. (1996). A secure, robust watermark for multimedia. *In Proceedings of the Inform. Hiding Workshop*, 147-158. Cambridge.

Cox, I. J., Kilian, J., Leighton, T., & Shamoon, T. G. (1997). Secure spread spectrum watermarking for multimedia. *In Proceedings of the IEEE International Conference on Image Processing, ICIP '97, 6*, 1673 – 1687. Santa Barbara, CA.

Cox, I. J., Miller, M. L., & Bloom, J. A. (2002). *Digital watermarking.* San Francisco: Morgan-Kaufmann.

Dinitz, J. H., & Stinson, D. R. (1992). Contemporary design theory: A collection of surveys. New York: Wiley.

Dittmann, J., Megias, D., Lang, A., & Herrera, J. (2006). Theoretical framework for a practical evaluation and comparison of audio watermarking schemes in the triangle of pobustness, transparency and capacity. *LNCS Transactions on Data Hiding and Multimedia Security*, 1-40.

DVB-Digital Video Broadcasting. http://www.dvb-h.org/

Fridrich, J. (2002). Security of fragile authentication watermarks with localization. *In Proceedings of SPIE Photonic West, 467). Electronic Imaging 2002: Security and Watermarking of Multimedia Contents IV*, 691-700. San Jose.

Furht, B., & Kirovski, D. (Ed.). (2006). Multimedia encryption and authentication techniques and applications. Boca Raton, FL: Auerbach Publications,.

Herrigel, A., Oruanaidh, J., Petersen, H., Pereira, S., & Pun, T. (1998). Secure copyright protection techniques for digital images. *In second Information Hiding Workshop (IHW), LNCS 1525*. Springer-Verlag.

Huang, D., & Yan, H. (2001). Inter-word distance changes represented by Sine Waves for watermarking text images. *IEEE Trans. on Circuits and Systems for Video Technology, 11*(12), 1237-1245.

ITU IPTV Focus Group. http://www.itu.int/ITU-T/IPTV/

Kim, W., & Suh, Y. (2004). Short N-secure fingerprinting code for image. *2004 International Conference on Image Processing*, 2167-2170.

Kundur, D., & Karthik, K. (2004). Video fingerprinting and encryption principles for digital rights management. *Proceedings of the IEEE, 92*(6), 918-932.

Lang, A., Dittmann, J., Lin, E. T., & Delp, E. J. (2005). Application-oriented audio watermark benchmark service. *Security, Steganography, and Watermarking of Multimedia Contents*, 275-286.

Lemma, A. N., Katzenbeisser, S., Celik, M. U., & Veen, M. V. (2006). Secure watermark embedding through partial encryption. *Proceedings of International Workshop on Digital Watermarking (IWDW 2006), 4283*, 433-445. Springer LNCS

Lian, S., Liu, Z., Ren, Z., & Wang, H. (2006a). Secure image communication for network applications. *2006 SPIE Symposium on Defense and Security, 6250*, 62500L0-8.

Lian, S., Liu, Z., Ren, Z., & Wang, H. (2006b). Secure advanced video coding based on selective encryption algorithms. *IEEE Transactions on Consumer Electronics, 52*(2), 621-629.

Lian, S., Liu, Z., Ren, Z., & Wang, H. (2006c). Secure distribution scheme for compressed data streams. *2006 IEEE Conference on Image Processing (ICIP 2006)*.

Lian, S., Liu, Z., Ren, Z., & Wang, Z. (2007a). Multimedia data encryption in block-based codecs. *International Journal of Computers and Applications, 29*(1).

Lian, S., Liu, Z., Ren, Z., & Wang, H. (2007b). Commutative encryption and watermarking in compressed video data. *IEEE Circuits and Systems for Video Technology, 17*(6), 774-778.

Lian, S., Sun, J., & Wang, Z. (2004a). Perceptual cryptography on JPEG 2000 compressed images or videos. *International conference on Computer and Information Technology (CIT)*, 78-83.

Lian, S., Sun, J., & Wang, Z. (2004b). A novel image encryption scheme based-on JPEG encoding. *In Proceedings of the Eighth International Conference on Information Visualization (IV)*, 217-220. London, UK.

Lian, S., Sun, J., & Wang, Z. (2005). A block cipher based on a suitable use of the chaotic standard map. *Chaos, Solitons and Fractals, 26*, 117-129.

Mao, Y., Chen, G., & Lian, S. (2004). A novel fast image encryption scheme based on 3-D chaotic baker maps. *International Journal of Bifurcation and Chaos, 14*(10), 3613-3624.

Mao, Y., & Mihcak, M. (2005). Collusion-resistant international de-synchronization for digital video fingerprinting. *IEEE Conference on Image Processing.*

Mohanty, S. P., Ramakrishnan, K. R., & Kanakanhalli, M. S. (2000) A DCT Domain Visible Watermarking Technique for Images. *In Proceedings of the IEEE International Conference on Multimedia and Expo (ICME) 2*, 1029-1032.

Parnes, R., & Parviainen, R. (2001). Large scale distributed watermarking of multicast media through encryption. *In Proc. IFIP Int. Conf. Communications and Multimedia Security Issues of the New Century*, 17.

Petitcolas, F., Anderson, R., & Kuhn, M. (1998, April). Attacks on copyright marking systems. In David Aucsmith (Ed), Information Hiding, *Second International Workshop, IH'98, Portland, USA, LNCS, 1525*, 219-239.

Petitcolas, F., Anderson, R., & Kuhn, M. (1999, July). Information Hiding – A Survey. *Proc. IEEE*, 1062-1078.

Servetti, A., Testa, C., Carlos, J., & Martin, D. (2003). Frequency-selective partial encryption of compressed audio. *Paper presented at the International Conference on Audio, Speech and Signal Processing.* Hong Kong.

Simitopoulos, D., Tsaftaris, S. A., & Boulgouris, N. V., et al. (2002). Compressed-domain video watermarking of MPEG streams. *2002 IEEE International Conference on Multimedia and Expo.*, 569-572. Lausanne, Switzerland.

Simitopoulos, D., Zissis, N., Georgiadis, P., Emmanouilidis, V., & G.Strintzis, M. (2003, September). Encryption and watermarking for the secure distribution of copyrighted MPEG video on DVD. *ACM Multimedia Systems Journal, Special Issue on Multimedia Security, 9(3)*, 217-227.

Thiemert, S., Vogel, T., Dittmann, J., & Steinebach, M. (2004). A high-capacity block based video watermark. *EUROMICRO 2004*, 457-460.

Trappe, W., Wu, M., Wang, Z. J., & Liu, K. (2003). Anti-collusion fingerprinting for multimedia. IEEE *Trans. Signal Processing, 51*, 1069-1087.

Viega, J. (2003, December). Practical random number generation in software. *In Proc. 19th Annual Computer Security Applications Conference.*

Wang, Z., Wu, M., Trappe, W., & Liu, K. (2005). Group-oriented fingerprinting for multimedia forensics. *Preprint.*

Wu, M., Trappe, W., Wang, Z., & Liu, R. (2004, March). Collusion-resistant fingerprinting for multimedia. *IEEE Signal Processing Magazine, , 21*(2), 15-27.

Wu, Y. (2005, March). Linear combination collusion attack and its application on an anti-collusion fingerprinting. *IEEE International Conference on Acoustics, Speech, and Signal Processing* (ICASSP '05), *2,* 13-16.

Zhu, W., Thomborson, C., & Wang, F. Y. (2002). A survey of software watermarking. *Lecture Notes in Computer Science-Volume, 3495*, 454-458.

ADDITIONAL READING

Aggelos, K., & Moti, Y. (2003). Breaking and repairing asymmetric public-key traitor tracing. *ACM Digital Rights,* 32-50. Berlin: Springer-Verlag.

Boneh, D., & Franklin, M. (1999). An efficient public key traitor tracing scheme. *Proc CRYPTO'99,* 338-353. Berlin: Springer-Verlag.

Chabanne, H., Phan, D. H., & Pointcheva, D. (2005). Public traceability in traitor tracing schemes. *Advances in Cryptology: EUROCRYPT 2005,* 542-558. Berlin: Springer.

Craver, S., Memom, N., & Yeo, B. (1998). Resolving rightful ownerships with invisible watermarking techniques: Limitations, attacks, and implications. *IEEE Journal on Selected Areas in Communications, 16*(4), 573-586.

Deguillarme, F., Csurka, G., & Ruanaidh, J. O. (1999). Robust 3D DFT video watermarking. *Proceedings of SPIE Security and Watermarking of Multimedia Contents,* 113-124. San Jose.

Hartung, F., & Girod, B. (1997). Digital watermarking of MPEG2 coded video in the bitstream domain. *IEEE International Conference on Acoustic, Speech, and Signal Processing,* 2621-2624. Munich, Germany.

Hartung, F., Girod, B. (1998). Watermarking of uncompressed and compressed video. *Signal Processing, Special Issue on Copyright Protection and Access Control for Multimedia Services, 66*(3), 283-301.

Hartung, F. H., Su, J. K., & Girod, B. (1999). Spread spectrum watermarking: Malicious attacks and counterattacks. *Proceedings of SPIE Security and Watermarking of Multimedia Contents,* 147-158. San Jose,.

He, S., & Wu, M. (2005). A joint coding and embedding approach to multimedia fingerprinting. *IEEE Trans. on Information Forensics and Security.*

Kurosaua, K., & Desmedt, Y. (1998). Optimum traitor tracing and asymmetric scheme. *Proc EURO-CRYPTO'98, 145-157.* Berlin: Springer-Verlag.

Lian, S., Sun, J., Zhang, D., & Wang, Z. (2004). A selective image encryption scheme based on JPEG2000 codec. *In Proceeding of 2004 Pacific-Rim Conference on Multimedia (PCM2004), LNCS, 3332,* 65-72. Springer

Lian, S., Wang, Z., & Sun, J. (2004). A fast video encryption scheme suitable for network applications. *In Proceeding of International Conference on Communications, Circuits and Systems, 1,* 566-570.

Linnartz, J., & Dijk, M. (1998, April). Analysis of the sensitivity attack against electronic watermarks in images. *In Workshop on Information Hiding,* Portland, 15-17.

Liu, Q., & Jiang X. (2005). Applications of mobile agent and digital watermarking technologies in mobile communication network. *2005 International Conference on Wireless Communications, Networking and Mobile Computing,* 1168-1170.

Servetti, A., & Martin, J. (2002a). Perception-based selective encryption of G. 729 speech. *Proceedings of IEEE ICASSP, 1,* 621-624. Orlando, FL.

Servetti, A., & Martin, J. (2002b). Perception-based selective encryption of compressed speech. *IEEE Transactions on Speech and Audio Processing, 10*(8), 637-643.

Shi, C., & Bhargava, B. (1998a). A Fast MPEG Video Encryption Algorithm. *In Proceeding of the 6th ACM International Multimedia Conference,* 81-88. Bristol, UK.

Shi, J., & Bhargava, B. (1998b). An efficient MPEG video encryption algorithm. *In Proceedings of the 6th ACM International Multimedia Conference,* 381-386. Bristol, United Kingdom.

Song, G., Kim, S., Lee, W., & Kim, J. (2002). Meta-fragile watermarking for wireless networks. *Proc. of Int'l Conf. of Communications, Circuits, and Systems.*

Swanson, M. D., & Zhu, B. (1998). Multiresolution scene based video watermarking using perceptual models. *IEEE Journal on Selected Areas in Communications, 16*(4), 540-550.

Teang, W. G., & Tzeng, Z. J. (2001). A public-key traitor tracing scheme with revocation using dynamical shares. *PKC'2001.*

Vogel, T., & Dittmann, J. (2005). Illustration watermarking: An object-based approach for digital images. *Security, Steganography, and Watermarking of Multimedia Contents,* 578-589.

Voloshynovskiy, S., Pereira, S., & Thierry, P. (2001). Attacks on digital watermarks: Classification, estimation based attacks, and benchmarks. *IEEE Communications Magazine, 39*(8), 118-126.

Wu, C., & Kuo, C. (2000). Fast encryption methods for audiovisual data confidentiality. In SPIE International Symposia on Information Technologies 2000, Boston, MA, USA. *Proceedings of SPIE, 4209, 284-295.*

Wu, C., & Kuo, C. (2001). Efficient multimedia encryption via entropy codec design. In SPIE International Symposium on Electronic Imaging 2001, San Jose, CA, USA. *Proceedings of SPIE, 4314,* 128-138.

Yu J. W., Goichiro, H., & Hidek, I. (2001). Efficient asymmetric public-key traitor tracing without trusted agents. *Proc CT-RSA, 392-407*. Berlin: Springer-Verlag,.

Zeng, W., & Lei, S. (2003). Efficient frequency domain selective scrambling of digital video. *IEEE Trans, Multimedia, 5*(1), 118-129.

Zhao, H. V., & Ray Liu, K. J. (2006). Fingerprint Multicast in Secure Video Streaming. *IEEE Transactions on Image Processing, 15*(1), 12-29.

Chapter IX
A Digital Rights Management System for Educational Content Distribution

Tom S. Chan
Southern New Hampshire University, USA

Shahriar Movafaghi
Southern New Hampshire University, USA

J. Stephanie Collins
Southern New Hampshire University, USA

ABSTRACT

While delivering content via the Internet can be efficient and economical, content owners risk losing control of their intellectual property. Any business that wishes to control access to, and use of its intellectual property, is a potential user of Digital Rights Management (DRM) technologies. Traditional DRM has a passive one-way downstream consumption of content from producer to consumer focus primarily concerns digital rights enforcement. This model does not translate well to the education environment where openness, informal decision making, sharing of ideas, and decentralization are valued. Collaboration and multiple authorships are common in the educational environment, as is the repurposing and modification of digital content used for teaching and learning. A DRM system for educational content distribution must be substantially more sophisticated and flexible than what is available right now to gain support in the educational community.

INTRODUCTION

A copyright is the legal right granted to an author, composer, playwright, publisher, or distributor to exclusive publication, production, sale, or distribution of a literary, musical, dramatic, or artistic work (American Heritage, 2006). It provides creators with the legal right to be paid for, and to control the use of their creations. As the unimpeded flow of information is fundamental to the mission and activities of teaching and learning, copyright law makes exceptions, such as the Fair Use Doctrine for educational institutions who access material protected under the copyright laws (LII, 2007a).

The Internet has made an unprecedented impact on the educational landscape. Today, 83% of US Higher Education institutions regularly use course management system (Green 2004). Broadband subscriber enrollment in the US is projected to jump from 24 million in 2003 to nearly 50 million in 2008 (Cravens, 2004). The penetration of digital technologies in homes, workplaces and public places means a rapidly growing number of people who can have access to digital information and knowledge. Contents for e-learning today are much more complex and dynamic than web pages; there are e-books, courseware, simulations, animation, and even access to live data and web casting. While these capabilities significantly enhance learning experiences, their complexity add many challenges to the management of digital rights as modern technology allows perfect and unlimited copying and distribution of content in very convenient and inexpensive ways.

A NEW ROLE FOR EDUCATIONAL CONTENT PROVIDERS

The Internet enables digital content to offer many more options to its users than print form can. Globally, the print media are under tremendous pressure. Circulation declines lead to staff reduction as print media are unable to compete with e-media for an audience that is younger, with a busier life style, and increasingly seeking information online (Ahrens, 2005). Similarly, e-learning technology is rapidly changing the landscape for education products and services. Publishers, the traditional undisputed leaders in the educational content market who based their business process on the production of textbooks, must now seriously rethink their role and business model. The digital educational content market has arrived. The focus is now shifted from the distribution and sale of tangible products to the distribution and licensing of intangible products, from products to the services, and perhaps phasing out the paper product all together.

While e-books have not experienced mass-market success, digital technology does provide ample opportunity for content marketers with the right strategy (Hasebrook, 2002). Today's educational market is truly global. Digital content can be packaged and customized for different market segments and electronically distributed to different geographic areas. Print materials are expensive to produce and store, while digital content lowers manufacturing and distribution cost. New technology now enables an entire reference library to be carried in a small lightweight portable device, making it convenient for field workers who need access to reference materials or consumers who want to take their personal libraries with them. Intranets and wireless networks extend on-line courses to non-traditional learners who are highly motivated, reducing the cost of corporate training. The use of virtual private networks and wireless LANs empowers an entire new educational paradigm: mobile, or m-learning.

Over the past few years, the world of textbook and educational material publishing has been shaken by the advent of technology. The ongoing process of innovation and media integration has led to a complete change in the book publishing industry. Several new business models have been suggested (Mazzucchi, 2005). First, a publisher can deliver its own content through its own web portal. Second, a public or private aggregator can gather and deliver third party content. Third, a public or non-profit institution can sponsor a gateway for metadata repository of digital content. Finally, publishers, aggregators, or courseware vendors can bundle educational content for schools. The winning formula is far from certain. Multiple and incompatible digital rights management (DRM) standards as they exist right now are impeding the development of the digital content market. Broad adoption of media sharing devices will be delayed as long as content owners disagree between themselves on how they wish to benefit from DRM technologies. Technology providers, in turn, cannot develop a horizontal market for connected devices until major content providers have agreed on a common framework of DRM interoperability. While the writing for print material is on the wall, it is not clear what will replace it. Most players in the educational content market have adopted an experimental and multi-pronged approach; everyone is waiting for a resolution of the technology standards and compatibility issues.

DIGITAL RIGHTS MANAGEMENT TECHNOLOGIES

The e-commerce paradigm is both an opportunity and challenge to business. While delivering content via the Internet can be efficient and economical, content owners risk losing control of their intellectual property. Digital content providers, such as the music industry are looking upon "copy-protection technologies" to enclose and protect their copyrighted digital content. Digital rights management (DRM) refers to protecting the copyright of digital content by restricting what actions an authorized recipient may take with regard to that content. DRM gives owners the ability to securely distribute their valued content and to control the use of this content, preventing it from unauthorized distribution (Russ, 2001). Whether the content is periodicals, books, photographs, music or video, DRM can be used to manage access and identify content. Furthermore, DRM can also be used to repackage content in different ways for specific market segments. The same content packaging can be adapted to create targeted versions at different prices for various customer groups.

The earliest forms of DRM in the Internet age can be traced back to the click-wrap license. The Uniform Computer Information Transactions Act (UCITA, 2002) was passed in 2001 to facilitate e-commerce. Basically, it is traditional commercial law with a digital twist. Software distributors can use click-wrap licenses as a convenient way to license software to end users on the Internet. The statements can be in unformatted text or in metadata with the rights holder's name and claims over the work provided to users. When a user agrees to the end user license agreement (EULA), that user is legally bound by its terms. There is no easy way for enforcement of the EULA except by counting on the user's good faith. The success of the DRM relies upon a high volume and low cost principle. By making contents affordable, users can easily acquire the product legally, making illicit activities less appealing. Furthermore, egregious infringements can be brought under control using the legal system; and measures such as registration make illegal copying more inconvenient and burdensome.

Whether the content is periodicals, books, photographs, music or video, DRM can be used to identify content and manage access. Steganography and cryptography are two essential ingredients in DRM techniques. While encryption allows only authorized users to access the message content, cryptographic algorithms generate messages that are easily recognizable as encrypted. Although the content remains illegible and protected, encrypted messages attract attention; thus their use is undesirable in some circumstances. Steganography, on the other hand, embeds a secret message into another message that serves as a carrier. The goal is to modify the carrier in an imperceptible way that reveals neither the embedding of a message, nor the embedded message itself.

Digital Watermark and Fingerprinting

Steganography is the science of hiding a message in a medium in a way that can defy detection. The rise of peer-to-peer (P2P) networks has been an inevitable outgrowth with the rise of the Internet. Unfortunately, P2P networks have grown from helpful tools in information sharing to havens for unauthorized distribution of copyrighted materials. Digital content identification or steganography is crucial in setting up a controlled distribution environment by providing an efficient mean for the tagging of copyright materials. Steganographic techniques can be divided into two broad categories: watermarking and fingerprinting.

A watermark is an image that appears on valuable documents to prove their authenticity and prevent counterfeiting. Digital watermarks are so named because they serve the same purpose as watermarks on paper. Since all software files have predefined formats that are deterministic, they can be modeled mathematically and used as a basis for comparison. Steganography programs alter the subtle characteristics, such as color, frequency, tone, noise and distortion, of a file to generate small variances in the digital content. Because "regular" software that creates the files would never produce these variances, the watermark can be detected and recovered. A fingerprint is a unique pattern characterizes the content, and that can be used for identification purposes. Fingerprinting cannot resist illegal copying, but it enables copyright owners to track recipients who leak or redistribute the fingerprinted content. Fingerprinting identification works by matching a small sample of suspected digital content to the original content against a database of fingerprints. Since digital fingerprinting does not add data to the content, it can be applied to contents that are already published.

Steganography is indispensable in the pursuit and location of illegal copyrighted material online. For example, a piece digital music can be watermarked. This allows the owner to create a search engine that can find the marked clip on the Internet. The owner can then determine its legality and seek remedy. Under US copyright law, to have an allegedly infringing material removed from a service provider's network, or to disable access to the material, the owner must provide notice to the provider. Once the notice is given, the provider is required to expeditiously remove, or disable access to, the material from its network. A more proactive approach is the fingerprint filtering technique. The technology examines a file and determines its identity by checking the content against digital fingerprints in a database. A service provider can either forbid the use of a file, or allow it only under specified conditions, should a match be detected. Several P2P sites have already adopted the technology to verify contents uploaded by their users so as to reduce the problem of copyright infringement. If the content is in the fingerprint database, upload is automatically blocked. Apart from the accurate monitoring of file transfer, the technology is also vital for payment accounting in determining the appropriate royalties to artists, publishers and record companies (Kellan, 2001).

Cryptography and Key Management

Encryption is the process of taking a message in plain text and scrambling it so it cannot be understood except by someone possessing the decryption key. Modern DRM technologies use cryptography to ensure that the permissions made available by the content owner are not breached. A media file is encrypted using a key specific to a user. A key for viewing or listening to the content is provided to the user with the purchase. But, the usage right can prohibit copying, printing, and redistribution of the content. When the user opens a content file, the DRM software checks the user's identity and contacts the owner's website. If permission is granted, the file is decrypted and access is granted. These types of systems can vary with a wide range of sophistication. In the simplest form, contents are encrypted using a single master key. But, such an approach is fragile, as compromising one key can compromise the entire system. The system can be strengthened using a "multiple keys multiple encryptions" approach similar to the Public Key Infrastructure (PKI) system. The loss of a single key only means the compromising of a single piece of content, and not the entire system.

In more complex systems, keys are unique not only for the content but also for function, lifetime, and device as well. Different keys denote different privileges, and are used for setting and automatically enforcing limits on user behavior. The content owner can configure access in many ways. For example, a document might be viewable but not printable. The owner may specify that the content only be used on a single device, for limited functions, and for a limited time. Under this approach, the user would be required to submit the serial numbers of the devices where content will be used. The encryption keys can be generated using the submitted numbers as a factor. This is a more complicated and persistent approach, and it requires ongoing and periodic contact between user and distributor. Users would want to be able to continue using the content when they are replacing an old device with new one. While information collected under this scenario will be minimal and not very sensitive, it does build up a device ownership database where information can be mined.

While most modern DRM technologies use encryption system such as PKI to control user access to digital content, some distributors opt for a strategy of distributing digital content with embedded DRM software. In this way, copyright protection would not rely solely upon a user's good faith. Once the content is downloaded onto a user's computer, there is no further contact with the distributor. Users access the digital content under restrictions. If one attempts a function not authorized under the EULA, the embedded DRM software downloaded and installed with the content will stop the computer's operating system from executing the requested task. On a positive note, this approach does not affect user privacy in terms of personal information gathering and the actual use of digital content can take place in total privacy, even offline, free of obstructions. However, apart from the obvious security risks, such an approach constitutes a more serious invasion of privacy by installing software onto a user's computer, which is personal property, without their full knowledge.

TRADITIONAL DRM SYSTEM FOR E-COMMERCE

E-commerce of digital content is a rapidly expanding market due to an abundant supply of digital content and the growing practicality of conducting transactions over the Internet. Delivering content directly to consumers online not only eliminates physical costs such as paper, printing and storage, it allows for highly customizable products and opens up numerous business opportunities. However, current

Figure 1. An example of digital content transaction

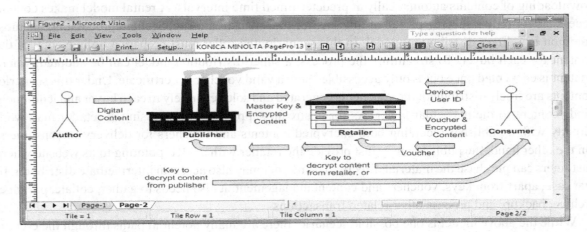

DRM technologies can support only a simple straightforward business model. It is a passive one-way downstream consumption of content from producer to consumer. These systems focus primarily on digital rights enforcement, managing content distribution functions such as repository, representation, control and monitoring. The keystone technology is the embedding of an encrypted file together with the downloaded content. The file contains identification information and the usage agreement, which is digitally signed to protect its integrity. The downloaded content is also fingerprinted and watermarked digitally to protect its authenticity. Together, the combination ensures the downloaded content is used only within the terms under which the material is acquired. Furthermore, it also monitors and tracks usage so that payment can be debited and credited properly. An example of business transaction under such scenario may be as the following (see Figure 1).

A customer visits the website of a content retailer and peruses merchandise on the online catalogue. Once the customer locates the desired material, the customer clicks on a button to make a purchase. A dialog box will pop up with the EULA. It then requests certain unique identifying information from the customer. It could be a CPU ID, user ID, and some other sort of device ID. The consumer can decide what information they are willing to disclose. If the retailer deems the information insufficient, they may decline to sell the product since it might not be able to uniquely tie the content to a specific environment. Upon confirmation, the retailer's website automatically verifies the information and asks permission to store a profile on the customer's computer to streamline future transactions. The customer then enters a credit card number or some other e-payment information to complete the purchase. The content is optimized for online use, encrypted and downloaded into the customer's computer. With the content, a small software voucher is attached which uniquely binds the customer to the content. Apart from terms of usage, the voucher is keyed to certain identifiers. Whenever the consumer opens the downloaded content, the accompanying voucher will be automatically recognized and checked. Upon validation, the content is decrypted and rendered. On the other hand, if someone attempts to access the content without a valid voucher, that person will be redirected to a URL to learn about purchasing the digital content.

Under this scenario, a retailer may establish different prices for different locking options. For example, the price may be differentiated between site licensing for all users in an organization or just for an individual user. The retailer may also use a variety of business models. A subscription model allows downloading of contents automatically at predetermined time intervals. A rental model makes content accessible for only a specific period of time. As for the downstream supply chain processing, the most common is a direct distribution model. In this scenario, the seller must prepare a unique copy of the content for each buyer. To streamline the process, a super distribution model can be adopted, where content is encrypted once but is only accessible using a valid voucher or certificate. Under this scenario, contents are freely distributed; the voucher is generated and sold separately to each buyer and it uniquely binds content to the particular buyer. As for upstream supply chain processing, a retailer may work directly with a publisher receiving both encrypted contents and vouchers for delivery to consumers. On the other hand, the publisher may just provide the retailer with a URL pointing to its website where customers can purchase the material directly. The retailer may also act as an intermediate distributor. In that case, apart from keys, vouchers and content management, it also needs to gather, collate, package, archive, backup, and process other related transactions.

While the above model is one possible scenario, there are many potential paths through the e-commerce supply chain, each with different implications for the individuals or organizations involved. An author has many alternatives in creating contents, establishing agreements with, and delivering contents to publishers. For the publisher, the main concern is in content distribution, i.e., the implementation of a secure and efficient transaction environment. Security and distribution issues aside, a retailer's focus is on content and voucher management, customer service, and of course, cost reduction as well. As for consumers, they too have a variety of options in receiving and using the digital contents. However, ingrained in most consumers' attitudes, there is a strong feeling that people should be allowed to do what they wish with the property they pay for and own, without restriction and fear of being controlled or monitored. The analogy is the purchased book that may be read in any location the buyer chooses, given away, or loaned without obtaining permission from the book seller. Thus, it is important that DRM technologies can meet such usage expectations. At a minimum, consumers should be able to use the digital content in any format on any device he or she owns; and it should also include fair use rights such as copying for research or personal non-commercial purposes. The technology must also be lightweight, seamless and user friendly. The system should be deployable on mass market legacy platforms such as PCs, preferably without adding new hardware or tedious software installation on the consumer's part. It should provide unbreakable security and without adverse effects to the consumer's platform. Finally, the system should support multiple content types such as audio, video, text, and software; multiple platforms and DRM vendors, and allow content migration between them. Furthermore, all operations should be as transparent and non-intrusive as possible.

The aforementioned scenario is one that most recognizable by the public. It is where a majority of consumers are exposed to the DRM technologies. As such, the "enforcement" approach to DRM has left many with serious doubts about the long term usability, interoperability, and acceptability of online digital content market place. Additionally, such systems are constantly under attack from the hacker community who are keen on breaking the new unbreakable encryption techniques. Nevertheless, by tying access rights directly to unique devices or users, content owners can and do control access to their copyrighted contents. Furthermore, the technology does also protect the content against illegal copying or sharing. When content is bound to a device, the user can sell, loan or give the device away, but when the content is copied, it would not be playable. This source management approach allows for only a simple consumption from owners to users. But, what if the relationship has to be bidirectional? The system can easily become useless if contents are to be edited, or multiple sources combined to form a new value added product (Godwin, 2006).

A NEW APPROACH TO DRM FOR TEACHERS AND LEARNERS

Early digital contents in the Internet were merely repurposed forms of the analog products in new digital format. As content distributors needed to find ways to overcome the liabilities of screen reading and to improve on consumer experiences, they slowly added interactive capabilities for user control features and user-centric contenting. The Internet is a powerful medium for communication. It possesses potential far greater than just merely a new distribution channel. Content owners look beyond their own websites and start sending contents to places where they may have more uses or audiences. Syndication refers to the process by which a website shares content with other websites to ensure the widest possible audience and more overall traffic. For example, a restaurant reviewer can syndicate its content to travel websites, a mutually beneficial arrangement for both the website and reviewer. The approach is similar to syndicated television shows that are produced by studios and sold to independent stations in order to reach a broader audience. Several vendors have tools for automating syndication relationships, and there is an open standard protocol for site interoperability. Taking one step further, and looking beyond content syndication, the syndication model can be expanded for content distribution to multiple and arbitrary parties. Under this model, the control and monitor over usage based on contractual agreements are mandatory as the trustworthiness of the other parties is unknown.

Educational content creation is more aligned with the syndication model. The content supply chain exhibits a complex circular two-way relationship between content producers and consumers. Collaboration and multiple authorships are common in the educational environment, as is the repurposing and modification of digital content used for teaching and learning. Educators produce and distribute their works with the goal of reaching the widest possible audience, often intended to be shared with current and future students. Educational contents are often stored on institutional repositories accessible globally, but other materials may exist solely within an instructor's personal computing environment. Still, other contents may be donated to, shared with, or purchased by institutions. Finally, dissemination occurs over distributed network environments through the use of course management systems, academic libraries, and websites. Individuals consume the content terminated in one's personal computing environments, after which modification might occur and be reintroduced back into the content supply chain. Often, the process crosses jurisdictional and domain boundaries. While a minute portion of educational content exist in a simple linear distribution chain, most contents are produced and consumed in a more circular fashion (Collier et al., 2004).

The Internet has forever changed the nature of content distribution from a passive one-way flow to an interactive two-way dialogue where contents are re-used, combined and extended ad infinitum. This trend can only continue in the future. Thus, for education purposes, digital content availability and usefulness may at first seem to be incompatible with DRM, as its restrictions undermine the educational mission of promoting access, scholarship and learning. Academics, teachers, and learners will expect to be able to reuse and repurpose digital content directly, to be able to edit digital content, and to be able to easily combine digital content. Given the collaborative and distributed nature of educational content and the multitude of possible authors involved, DRM is indeed a complex and challenging undertaking. As a starting point, the system must be able to function in a highly collaborative and distributed environment allowing the discovery and location of desired digital content. After that, content rights need to be negotiated, managed and honored. The system must also support granular and differential access to contents; support fair use; and be interoperable with existing and emerging standards. Finally, the resulting infrastructure must be able to manage the acquisition, distribution, and enforcement of digital rights and contents from end to end in order to ensure appropriate access, intellectual fidelity, and lawfulness. These requirements far exceed the capabilities of DRM systems and technologies that are currently available.

A TWO-WAYS CIRCULAR DRM FRAMEWORK

Duncan et al. (2004) divide rights management into policy creation and policy projection processes. Policy creation involves recognizing, asserting and expressing rights; and policy projection involves dissemination, exposure, and enforcement of rights. Recognition entails the identification of rights holders as well as any explicit permission to the content. Assertion is accomplished by means of a legally binding agreement. Expression takes the form of a copyright notice, either in human or machine readable form. Dissemination declares the use of rights data which accompanies a digital object wherever it goes. Exposure occurs when a user sees the title of rights associated with the content. Finally, enforcement involves the use of technological protection measures to ensure that rights are not infringed. For proper DRM in an educational environment, the above functionalities must be implemented for both the upstream and downstream business supply chain framework (see Figure 2).

Digital Content Management (DCM) is a system that manages the entire content lifecycle, from the content's creation to destruction without breaking its integrity. Content follows a standard lifecycle. It is created by authors, edited by editors, approved by managers, and published by the publisher. Content may have different life spans; a piece of news may become irrelevant quickly, while a historical archive may be relevant for centuries. Most content created will eventually become obsolete, expire, and need to be archived or deleted. Apart from managing the content's lifecycle, DCM should also support the categorizing, structuring, and storing of the content so that it can be searched and retrieved. Furthermore, DCM should allow users to navigate between stored contents and may even edit the content to create new contents (Boiko, 2002). In general, a DCM system automates the following processes in the management of content lifecycle:

Figure 2. DRM framework for educational content distribution

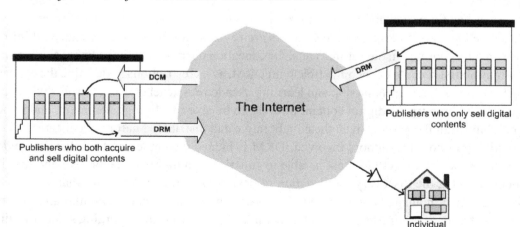

- Import acquired documents and multimedia material
- Identify key users and assign their roles
- Define workflow with messaging alerts to manager to changes in content
- Track and manage multiple versions of a single instance of content
- Publish the content to a repository
- Support the search and retrieval of content
- Manage content publishing, expiration, disablement and archiving

Content management is not an innovative idea, but it is essential in today's enterprises overburdened with content on their corporate networks. Different publications often share or reuse the same content. While the same basic content exists in several places, it is often edited by different people at various times. Often, there is no clear idea which content is correct and current. Maintaining multiple versions of the supposedly identical content only wastes resources and creates confusion. Even more troubling, incorrect information may be published. Not all content stored or used by an organization is authored by the organization. Some contents are acquired externally, i.e., provided by suppliers or business partners, or purchased from other companies or content aggregators. To facilitate the integration of internally authored and externally acquired contents, rights management functions must be added into the DCM infrastructure, establishing rules and standards for content integration, as well as processes for converting, using and tracking the use of these contents.

As content creation typically involves multiple personnel each playing a different role, DCM must define and designate user roles. Each person is assigned certain rights to support their assignments in the content lifecycle. For example, some persons are allowed to change the content while others can approve the content for publication and distribution. Since content can be originated internally or externally, similar to defining roles, ownership and terms of usage should also be designated for each piece of content used within the organization. The rights to use a piece of content can range in ways from very specific to totally unrestricted. Reusing and integrating a piece of content without knowing its associated rights could result in copyright or contractual violation. The publisher must have clear terms of use and evidence of the "title of rights" before incorporating any content into their works. In this way, they can in turn issue a good title to others acquiring and using the content down the business value chain. Downloaded with the digital content, there should always be the associated rights information. This title information should include at a minimum, a content description, rights holders information, the terms of usage, plus any prior existing terms of agreements. Of course, the title will also determine who should get paid and the amount of royalties for the future sale. It also affects all future terms of usage for the content down the value chain.

In the future, as the demand and supply of digital contents grow, a digital content registry may be established similar to the Universal Description, Discovery, and Integration (UDDI) registry to facilitate the discovery and trading of digital intellectual property. Based on existing standards, such as Extensible Markup Language (XML) and Simple Object Access Protocol (SOAP), UDDI provides one-stop shopping for information on businesses and electronic web services available on the Internet (UDDI, 2007). A digital content registry can be built upon data provided by copyright owners who wish to advertise and make their contents available. Companies register in the registry by providing content descriptions, rights holders information, the terms and conditions of the offers, and existing terms of agreements. The registry keeps track of all these entities by assigning each one a programmatically unique identifier. This key is guaranteed to be unique and never changes within the registry, and it is used to reference the entity with which they are associated. Clients, such as e-marketplaces, search engines, and other businesses can use the registry to locate contents of interest, and their terms of usage.

It is easy to confuse DCM with DRM as both share common techniques and requirements. DCM manages production of digital content in the upstream supply chain, but DRM handles content distribution in the publisher's downstream supply chain. As content is created, it is traded online and delivered to the consumer via a DRM system. However, a publisher may in turn act as a consumer and acquire content via e-commerce exchanges, and use this content to create new value added products. The terms and conditions agreed on during the exchanges must be forwarded to the DCM system, where the system must ensure contents are only used for the purpose acquired, in accordance with agreements. Naturally, systems that manage the supply and creation of content must interface and closely couple with systems that manage content distribution and exchange. In any event, DCM and DRM are highly dependent upon each other. Together, they ensure that the appropriate, correct, and accurate rights information is captured, followed and managed in both the content's acquisition and distribution processes.

PRIVACY COMPLIANCES

The term "privacy" is used frequently in ordinary language as well as in philosophical, political and legal discussions, yet there is no single definition of the term. Unauthorized breaches of privacy, such as surveillance, eavesdropping and appropriation of one's communication are a form of illegal search and seizure. It threatens rights of personal integrity and self-definition in subtle but powerful ways. In 1986, privacy protection was extended to cover electronic communications of the modern era with the Electronic Communications Privacy Act (LII, 2007b). In general, it is illegal to acquire and process personal data unless the persons involved have agreed with the acquisition and processing of their personal data and the personal data is required for the execution of whatever process it is used in. It is also illegal to keep personal data longer than necessary. But, personal privacy is now threatened even more in the digital information age. There are massive databases about individual financial and credit histories, medical records, daily purchases and contacts, all accessible via the Internet. There exists the capability for others to mine and link the databases, but there are few controls over how the information can be used and distributed. The predicament makes individual control over one's privacy next to impossible.

Historically, DRM has been focused on security and enforcement. A DRM system for an educational institute must also satisfy regulatory requirements, most prominently, the Family Educational Rights and Privacy Act (FERPA), the Health Insurance Portability and Accountability Act (HIPAA), and the Gramm Leach Bliley (GLB) Act. FERPA protects the privacy of student records. The act provides a student the right to inspect and review their education records; the right to seek to amend those records; and the right to control over the disclosure of information from those records. FERPA applies to all educational institutions receiving federal funding (LII, 2007c). HIPAA affects how health information will be used and released by the health center and physicians. Through HIPAA, US Congress charged the department of Health and Human Services with addressing the information concerns facing the healthcare industry. Some HIPAA rules are already in effect. They include standard requirements on various aspects of transaction, privacy and identification (HHS, 2007). The Financial Modernization, or GLB, Act, protects consumers' personal financial information held by financial institutions. GLB defines privacy requirements including both financial privacy and safeguards rules. It applies to companies, whether or not they are financial institutions, as long as they receive such information (FTC, 2007).

DRM with encryption is less intrusive as it does not involve installing software on a user's computer. Encryption keys are used to set and automatically enforce limits on user behavior. Different keys can have different privileges, and the keys can even be tied to a particular device or set of devices. While DRM encryption does not raise privacy issues in itself, the functional restrictions in place intrude upon the private space and autonomy to determine the circumstances of use for individual private property. Furthermore, requiring user authentication from a server each time digital content is accessed can constitute the worst sort of privacy invasion. No much different from the problem with spyware, information garnered by DRM systems in our highly networked society can be used to build a dossier of a user's preferences and usage patterns. Such information can in turn be sold to online marketers or even obtained by the government to keep a tight watch on its citizens (Cohen, 2003). For an educational institution, such information can constitute serious leakages of financial, health, or educational records as they leave a trail of documents that students have accessed.

Many people have become cautious online and are skeptical of e-commerce because of privacy and security concerns. One solution is to allow consumers to use software that generates an anonymous digital certificate or voucher from a trusted third party, such as schools in our case. The school would provide a credential containing a pseudo student number and expiration date that would be digitally sealed. The credential is presented to the content owner's server when an access to copyrighted content is made. As a result, student identity will never be revealed. To provide better security and anonymity, a new encrypted credential could be issued each time an access is made. This approach not only protects privacy, it also effectively reduces the risk of identity theft and personal data leakage by businesses (Prince, 2007).

Privacy control in DRM is a complicated matter because there are legitimate reasons for distributors to collect data about users and their activities. For example, the collected data can be used for traffic modeling, infrastructure planning, Quality of Service (QoS), and risk management. Data mining of aggregated, depersonalized data can be used for trend spotting, untargeted marketing and advertising. If the company is not able to gather information about its customers, the company will not be able to serve its market efficiently, potentially leading to higher prices. If data collection is inevitable, but the company has an established privacy policy and actually adheres to the policy, customers will also be more comfortable doing business with the company. However, data collected for legitimate reasons can also be used illegitimately, and by parties who are unknown when the data is gathered. These parties may be any of the following: future business partners that the data gatherer acquires, buyers of aggregated data, and any number of data brokers. While consumers may consent for data to be gathered by company X, the same data may end up being used by others of whom the consumer will never be aware (Estes, 2007). In today's dynamic business environment, the mergers, acquisitions, bankruptcies, and other changes over the life cycle of a corporation can radically change who has access to what information and how that information may be used and cross referenced.

THE INTEGRITY CHALLENGE

The biggest challenge for any digital content distribution system is the safeguard of information integrity. In the course of using and providing information, society has a shared understanding about the ways in which information will be allowed to flow, and who will get access to it. This understanding underlies our social and legal system, governing the production and dissemination of all information. Integrity is preserved, which means depending on situations, that nobody has seen that particular piece of information except for those who are supposed to have access to it, or that copies have been made only under certain circumstances and that all copies are in some way accounted for. In other words, information integrity is about the protection of privacy and confidentiality for customers, and the protection of copyright and licensing for intellectual properties.

One of the hallmarks of digital information is that it is extremely easy to disseminate and copy, this is because the basic distribution and copying costs are almost zero. This fact has had a greatly beneficial effect on our society and our civilization. However, it also makes the maintenance of information integrity, both the enforcement of privacy and copyright very difficult. Furthermore, once integrity is violated, it is difficult or impossible to restore the information's integrity completely. Large scale violations, such as multi-person identity theft or the republication of an entire database, can be detected with relative ease. Smaller scale violations, such as the exposure of a single reference transaction or a casual download, can be difficult to detect. However, they can potentially have severe repercussions on the lives of the people affected.

Since most digital contents are stored in networked electronic repositories, the provider must ensure that only authorized persons can access the information. Whenever a request was is over a network, typically to a database server, the server must then decide, based on the message's contents and context, whether or not to return the requested information. Since machines lack human intelligence, the system must rely on a strict and unvarying set of rules to make these decisions. The simplest approach is the username and password scheme. In general, an access control scheme restricts access to a certain set of information to a certain set of people. Under the above schema, access to information is denied unless the user enters a valid username and password pair. These are issued to customers, who agreed to rules and procedures that are mandated under copyrighted material licensing agreements.

With DRM's reliance on encryption, one of the challenges for publishers and retailers is to manage key distribution properly. A customer who is supposed to have access to copyrighted material needs to obtain the key. Thus, if many people are allowed to have access to the information, then the key must be widely distributed. The key cannot itself be encrypted and is thus vulnerable to being copied and used without authorization. If the key is encrypted, again, the user will still need to obtain another key so as to decrypt and use the key. In other words, as a key is distributed to more people, its integrity is more at risk. Consequently, the integrity of all of the information encrypted with that key is more at risk. Many secure information systems in theory turn out to be quite vulnerable in practice because the keys are handled carelessly, and are disclosed either accidentally or deliberately to people who should not have them.

With customers' information stored in a database to manage access control, the content provider must also ensure the integrity of its own server. As long as only authorized users are able to access the system, the integrity of its information is well preserved; and the primary responsibility for maintaining a secure server will rest with the technology staffs. Yet, human, rather than technical factors can be more significant in creating vulnerabilities. For example, someone who has been given access to information, and is not afraid to violate the terms of the contracts they agreed to, cannot be prevented from copying the information if they choose. Thus, it is impossible to have a system that cannot be broken into. The content repository administrator must ultimately decide how much of their resources to put into maintaining computer security, based on the level of risk they are willing to accept, which, unfortunately, is a difficult and uncertain decision.

CONCLUSION

It is understandable that academia would be skeptical of DRM technologies in general. Current DRM technologies can be cumbersome for conducting normal scholastic work allowed under the Fair Use Doctrine. As a case in point, DRM technologies often prevent cutting and pasting of text, forcing students and scholars to retype a passage that they are quoting. The practical outcome of such restrictions is perhaps what leads to the unpopularity of some e-books. Technologies that constrain user behavior narrow the zone of freedom traditionally enjoyed for activities in private. In so doing, they decrease the level of autonomy that users enjoy with respect to the terms of use and enjoyment of intellectual goods. It restricts the freedom of expression. DRM technologies restrict legitimate fair use and intrude into everyday life in innumerable and intolerable ways (Lohmann, 2002). Under fair use, a creative person can make some use of another's work that one believes to be fair. If the rights holder agrees, use continues. Otherwise, the case can be resolved in the courts. If, however, such a fair use attempt is prevented from the outset by DRM technologies, there will be no experimentation, no product innovations, and no evolution of new consumer markets. For DRM technologies to gain support in the educational community, the system must be substantially more sophisticated and flexible than what is available right now.

Education in the digital age means that teachers can use new technologies to teach and learners can use new technologies to learn. But, education in the digital age is a much more complex issue than it would at first appear: digitizing a book or document, and treating it the same way as a paper book or document is not enough. Digital content is different in that it allows for the interaction of the reader with the writer in a much more direct fashion than previously possible. Until recently, DRM research and development has been driven mainly by commercial content providers, protecting their commercial interests, and particularly as a reaction to violation of copyright law by consumers using peer-to-peer networks to share digital content such as music and movies. This approach heavily favored owners' rights over users' rights and has led to a much more restrictive copyright atmosphere. Clearly, this model does not translate well to the education environment where openness, informal decision making, sharing of ideas and decentralization are valued. Stronger privacy protection is not necessarily incompatible with stronger copyright enforcement. Educators should get involved with DRM development, in order that the emerging standards will not compromise user privacy or impede the free flow of information which is vital to the fundamental mission of education.

FUTURE RESEARCH DIRECTIONS

E-commerce of digital content is a rapidly expanding market due to an abundant supply of digital content and the growing practicality of conducting transactions over the Internet. Delivering content directly to consumers online not only eliminates physical costs such as paper, printing and storage, it allows for highly customizable products and opens up numerous business opportunities. There are many types of DRM system, and each supports a different business model. Some interesting topics for exploration include:

1. What are the benefits and challenges of different systems and business models?
2. What are the current trends in the digital content distribution and delivery market?

E-learning technology is rapidly changing the landscape for education products and services. Publishers, the traditional undisputed leaders in the educational content market who based their business process on the production of textbooks, must now seriously rethink their role and business model. The digital educational content market has arrived. The focus is now shifted from the distribution and sale of tangible products to the distribution and licensing of intangible products, from products to the services, and perhaps phasing out the paper product all together. While e-books have not experienced mass-market success, digital technology does provide ample opportunity for content marketers if one can find the right strategy and develop an effective business model.

For education purposes, digital content availability and usefulness may seem to be incompatible with DRM, as its restrictions undermine the educational mission of promoting access, scholarship and learning. Academics, teachers, and learners will expect to be able to reuse and repurpose digital content directly, to be able to edit digital content, and to be able to easily combine digital content. Historically, DRM has been focused on security and enforcement. A DRM system for an educational institute must also satisfy regulatory requirements, most prominently, the Family Educational Rights and Privacy Act (FERPA), the Health Insurance Portability and Accountability Act (HIPAA), and the Gramm Leach Bliley (GLB) Act. Furthermore, apart from Fair-Use, copyright laws governing an educational institute also include library exceptions and the TEACH Act. Given all these, a useful DRM system for educational content will indeed be a complex and challenging undertaking.

REFERENCES

Ahrens, F. (2005, February 20). Hard news, Daily papers face unprecedented competition. Washington Post Sunday, F01.

American Heritage® Dictionary of the English Language, 4th Edition. Retrieved 6/22/07 from http://dictionary.reference.com/browse/copyright

Boiko, B. (2002). Content management bible. New York, NY: Wiley Publishing Inc.

Cohen, J. (2003). DRM and privacy. *Communications of the ACM, 46*(4), 47-49.

Collier, G., Piccariello, H., & Robson, R. (2004). *Digital rights ,anagement: An ecosystem model and scenarios for higher education.* Educause Center.

Cravens, A. (2004, September). Speeding ticket: The U.S. residential broadband market by segment and technology. *In Stat/MDR.*

Duncan, C., Barker, E., Douglas, P., Morrey, M., & Waelde, C. (2004, August 25). JISC DRM Study Intrallect Ltd. Retrieved 6/22/07 from http://www.intrallect.com/drm-study/DRMFinalReport.pdf

Estes, A. (2007, May 6). Bill would ban lenders' alerts to homebuyers. *Boston Globe*, B3.

Federal Trade Commission (2007). Public Law 106-102, GLB..Retrieved 6/22/07 from http://www.ftc.gov/bcp/conline/pubs/buspubs/glbshort.htm

Godwin, M. (2006). *Digital rights management: A guide for librarians*. Office for Information Technology Policy, American Library Association.

Green, K. (2004). The 2004 National Survey of Information Technology in U.S. Higher Education. *The Campus Computing Project*. Retrieved 6/22/07 from http://www.campuscomputing.net/

HHS (2007). Public Law 104-191, HIPAA. Department of Health & Human Services. Retrieved 6/22/07 from http://aspe.hhs.gov/admnsimp/pl104191.htm

Hasebrook, J. (2002). International E-Learning business: Strategies & opportunities. *World Conference on E-Learning in Corp., Govt., Health & Higher Ed, 2002*(1), 404-411.

Kellan, A. (2001, July 5). Whiz kid has 'fingerprints' all over new Napster. *CNN Technology News*. Retrieved 6/22/07

LII (2007a). U.S. Code Collection 107, Limitations on Exclusive Rights: Fair Use, Legal Information Institute, Cornell Law School.

LII (2007b). U.S. Code Collection, Title 18, S 2510, The Electronic Communications Privacy Act of 1986, Legal Information Institute, Cornell Law School.

LII (2007c). U.S. Code 20.31.3.4.1232g, FERPA. Legal Information Institute, Cornell Law School.

Lohmann, F. (2002). *Fair use and digital rights management, computers, freedom & privacy*. Electronic Frontier Foundation.

Mazzucchi, P. (2005). Business models and rights management for eLearning in Europe. *INDICARE Monitor, 2*(7), 25-29.

Prince, B. (2007). *IBM shields online personal data, eWeek news & analysis*. Retrieved 6/22/07 from http://www.eweek.com/article2/0,1759,2095275,00.asp

Russ, A. (2001, July). *Digital rights management overview*. SANS Information Security Reading Room. Retrieved 6/22/07 from http://www.sans.org/reading_room/whitepapers/basics/434.php

UCITA (2002). Uniform Computer Information Transactions Act. *National Conference of Commissioners on Uniform State Laws*.

UDDI (2007). FAQs for UDDI Initiative and Standard. *OASIS Standards Consortium*. Retrieved 6/22/07 from http://www.uddi.org/faqs.html

ADDITIONAL READING

BEUC (2007). Consumers Digital Rights Initiative, European Consumers' Organization. Retrieved 6/22/07 from http://www.consumersdigitalrights.org

Brands, S. (2000). *Rethinking public key infrastructures and digital certificates; building in privacy.* Cambridge, MA: The MIT Press

ClickZ (2003, April 11). Users still resistant to paid content. Jupitermedia. Retrieved 4/16/07 from http://www.ecommerce-guide.com/news/news/print.php/2189551

Cohen, J. (2003). DRM and privacy. *Communications of the ACM, 46*(4), 47-49.

Cox, I., Miller, M., & Bloom, J. (2002). *Digital watermarking: Principles & practice.* San Diego, CA: Academic Press.

Cravens, A. (2004, September). Speeding ticket: The U.S. residential broadband market by segment and technology. *In Stat/MDR.*

EFF (2005). *Dangerous terms, a user's guide to EULA.* Electronic Frontier Foundation. Retrieved 6/22/07 from http://www.eff.org/wp/eula.php

EFF (2007). *A user's guide to DRM in online music.* Electronic Frontier Foundation. Retrieved 6/22/07 from http://www.eff.org/IP/DRM/guide/

EPIC (2000). *Pretty poor privacy: An assessment of P3P and Internet privacy.* Electronic Privacy Information Center. Retrieved 6/22/07 from http://www.epic.org/reports/prettypoorprivacy.html.

Godwin, M. (2006). *Digital rights management: A guide for librarians.* Office for Information Technology Policy, American Library Association.

Guibault, L., & Helberger, N. (2005). Copyright law and consumer protection European consumer law group. ECLG/035/05

Gunter, C., Weeks, S., & Wright, A. (2001). Models and languages for digital rights. *Technical Report STAR-TR-01-04.* InterTrust STAR Lab.

Kellan, A. (2001, July 5). Whiz kid has 'fingerprints' all over new Napster. *CNN Technology News.* Retrieved 4/16/07 from http://edition.cnn.com/2001/TECH/internet/07/05/napster.fingerprint/index.html

LII (2007a). U.S. Constitution Article I Section 8, Legal Information Institute, Cornell Law School.

LII (2007b). U.S. Code Collection, Title 17, Copyrights, Legal Information Institute, Cornell Law School.

LII (2007c). The Bill Of Rights: U.S. Constitution, Amendment IV, Legal Information Institute, Cornell Law School.

Morris, R., & Thompson, K. (1979). Password security: A case history. *Communication of the ACM, 22*(11).

Mulligan, D., & Schwartz, A. (2000). *P3P and privacy: An update for the privacy community.* Center for Democracy & Technology. Retrieved 4/16/07 from http://www.cdt.org/privacy/pet/p3pprivacy.shtml

National Research Council Panel on Intellectual Property (2000). *The digital dilemma: Intellectual property in the information age.* Washington, D.C.: National Academy Press.

Rosenblatt, B., Trippe, B., & Mooney, S. (2002). Digital rights management: Business and technology. New York, NY: M&T Books.

Schaub, M. (2006). A breakdown of consumer protection law in the light of digital products. *Indicare Monitor, 2*(5).

Schwartz, J. (2004). In survey, fewer are sharing files (or admitting it). *The New York Times, C*, 1.

Shapiro, C., & Varian, H. (1999). *Information rules: A strategic guide to the network economy.* Boston, MA: Harvard Business School Press.

USG (1998). The Digital Millennium Copyright Act of 1998. U.S. Copyright Office, Pub. 05-304, 112 Stat. 2860.

W3C (2002a). *How to create and publish your company's P3P policy in 6 easy steps.* W3C P3P Working Group. Retrieved 4/16/07 from http://www.w3.org/P3P/details.html

W3C (2002b). *The platform for privacy preferences 1.0 (P3P1.0) specification.* W3C P3P Working Group. Retrieved 4/16/07 from http://www.w3.org/TR/P3P/

Chapter X
Digital Rights Management and E-Commerce Transactions:
Online Rights Clearance

Dimitrios P. Meidanis
SilkTech S.A., Greece

Spiros N. Nikolopoulos
SilkTech S.A., Greece

Emmanouil G. Karatzas
SilkTech S.A., Greece

Athanasia V. Kazantzi
SilkTech S.A., Greece

ABSTRACT

This chapter investigates intellectual property rights clearance of as part of e-commerce. Rights clearance is viewed as another online transaction that introduces certain technological and organizational challenges. An overview of the current intellectual property rights legislation is used to describe the setting in which business models and digital rights management systems are called to perform safe and fair electronic trade of goods. The chapter focuses on the technological aspects of the arising issues and investigates the potentials of using advanced information technology solutions for facilitating online rights clearance. A case study that presents a working online rights clearance and protection system is used to validate the applicability of the proposed approaches.

INTRODUCTION

Rights clearance has always been an important issue in every transaction that involves copyrighted objects but even in other transactions such as land property acquisition. Typically the owner (seller) has to prove that he possesses the right to make the transaction and the buyer has to be sure of the legitimacy of the transaction that he is going to be part of. The general perspective of this chapter is to address every aspect of rights clearance in e-commerce transactions mainly from the technical point of view. The major topics that will be addressed in the remaining of this chapter are the investigation of on-line rights clearance background in terms of broad definitions, discussions and contradicting views, the inquire of intellectual property rights as part of a Digital Rights Management system and with respect to a plausible business model, the analysis of the technical components involved in on-line rights clearance, along with the arising flow control and engineering issues as well as the presentation of an operative DRM system integrating on-line rights clearance practices.

BACKGROUND

"Rights clearance" is a term often used indiscriminately to describe a set of processes that are followed both in the physical and digital world. As a consequence, the "bad" use of this term and in general the terminology related to rights clearance is usually a source of many ambiguities and misconceptions that prevent readers from acquiring a common understanding on the issue. The goal of this section is to outline the related topics, address controversial issues and eventually formulate a clear basis that will help the reader gain an insightful view of the subject.

Intellectual Property Rights (IPR) and Current Legislation

Current legislation concerning intellectual property primarily aims at protecting artworks that exhibit a considerable level of creativeness and novelty, such as works originating from literature, theatre, music, art etc. Among the large corpora of law proceedings that concern intellectual properties, there is a considerable portion that attempt to address intellectual properties as formulated by digitizing and distributing content through computer networks. There is a very strong tradition that seeks to harmonize the activities of all European countries under a common, international action line, with the aim to tackle the problems generating from the misuse of intellectual properties. The need for common treatment of such issues is considered essential in the context of a European market, mainly due to differences in conception of intellectual property and the obstacles arising by the enforcement of domestic copyright restrictions. If we consider the pace by which digital information is being generated and the practices that are often used for its distribution and sharing, it is evident that individual national legislations are inadequate to guarantee the interests of intellectual property owners, in the light of an emerging and without boundaries digital trade.

The purpose of national legislation is to determine the amount of actions that are considered legitimate within the nation boundaries. However, the study of a national legislation should not be carried out independently from the international status quo. The international state of affairs is constituted by international conventions and directives that act normatively in the establishment of national laws. The most important international conventions are:

- Berne convention (supervised by World Intellectual Property Organization) [WIPO]
- The international convention regarding copyright (UCC)
- TRIP's agreement (Trade Related Intellectual Property Rights) under the auspices of World Trade Organization

The purpose of the aforementioned conventions is to introduce a set of minimum requirements to be adopted by all member states. In this context, the European Commission (EC) envisages the establishment of a European legislation that will be founded on the international conventions and will be adopted by all European countries, in order to facilitate a global, liberal European market where the trade of goods will be conducted in a smooth and unrestricted manner.

Originality is the essential characteristic that an artwork should exhibit in order to allow for its rights to be granted under intellectual property laws. Berne convention does not provide an explicit definition describing which artworks should be considered copyright protected and which not. However, an artwork should be more than a simple digital representation of a physical object in order to be considered original. Berne convention does not treat the digitized version of an original artwork as a "new original artwork" with completely independent intellectual properties, despite the fact that under certain circumstance such rights can be granted. The copyright holder of an artwork is by default the person who has created it. In the case where the artwork has been generated by more than one creator, intellectual properties are assigned to all participants. Concluding, we can claim that the intellectual properties legislation framework in each European country derives from the combination of Berne convention, European directives and national laws.

Rights Clearance

The term "Rights Clearance" refers to the overall process of determining the terms and conditions that constrain the use of an artwork, identifying the person or organization that holds the right to grant its usage permissions and eventually trasnfering these permissions on the ground of a license agreement.

Although different types of intellectual properties exist such as a) copyright b) database right c) moral rights d) rights bound to patents e) execution right etc, the process of rights clearance can be considered roughly uniform.

The outcome of rights clearance is a set of rules that constrain the use of an artwork, always with respect to a certain agreement. This outcome is described by a license that serves as a contract between the rights owner and the final user. The license is a document that details the terms and conditions under which the content is allowed to be exploited by the end user without committing copyright violation. Hence, as long as the license counterparts obey to the conditions of the agreement, rights violation is not an issue. Nevertheless, this process can either be performed in the digital or the physical world raising important differentiations to its interpretation.

Rights Clearance in the Physical world is a process quite straightforward since it has been exercised for many decades and its long established practice has set a frame of rules that must be followed. It is usually transacted by attorneys or other professions or organizations with adequate knowledge and access to records describing the rights applied on an object.

Rights clearance in the Digital world has become an absolute necessity, since e-commerce plays a vital role in modern transactions. After the transition to the Digital world, rights clearance became a more complex procedure and a number of arising issues has to be studied. A key element of this study must be the dissimilarities between the original digital resources and the digitized ones which are bound by different kinds of intellectual property rights. Another important issue introduced by the digital world is the rights on purely digital objects. Such a study will set the foundations on which some standards for on-line rights clearance will be defined.

Digital Rights Management (DRM)

Rights management involves the registration, maintenance, monitoring and administration of the protected content property rights in an efficient and profitable way. Services like tracking the usage of content engaged to a certain license, as well as identifying new rights that bring added value to the content at hand, are considered essential functionalities of a rights management framework. Since rights, as indicated previously, can either refer to physical (i.e., statues, paintings etc) or digital objects (i.e., computer graphics, multimedia content etc), rights management should facilitate both cases. As the number of artworks, digitized or digitally generated, that are being distributed over computer networks rapidly increases, the need for developing advanced digital rights management systems becomes apparent.

Enabling rights management on highly heterogeneous and complex environments as in the case of WWW, requires the extraction and representation of a sufficiently large amount of information in a manner that can be shared among computer systems of the same purpose. Metadata is data about data that aim at describing an object or a resource independently of its nature, physical or digital. Particularly, metadata try to describe sources in a systematic and structured way in order to facilitate their easy sharing and re-use. In this context, intellectual property rights are also information that has to be retained and organized in an interoperable way.

Numerous initiatives, each one with its own advantages and disadvantages, have attempted to establish a set of metadata able to sufficiently capture the information required for managing property rights. Among them, Dublin Core Metadata Initiative [DCMI] has emerged as an international standard that receives considerable support from both industry and academia.

Protecting Digital Rights

Despite the fact that rights clearance, and digital rights management in general, is still in its infancy, numerous technological solutions deriving either from industry or academia have been recorded. The engineering of a holistic rights management system that could meet the requirements of all existing business models seems particurarly difficult. However, certain aspects of the problem have been tackled successfully by custom solutions. The aim of this paragraph is to provide an overview of the current state in the field of digital rights protection and identify the areas open to further improvements.

As mentioned previously registration, maintenance, monitoring and administration of intellectual properties are among the most important requirements that a digital rights management system should fulfill. The design and development of technological means that will facilitate the aforementioned operations are considered essential, especially for tracking distributed content. The mechanisms that incorporate technological protection means, work complementary to the digital rights management systems in order to defend the financial interests of content creators.

There are several ways by which technology can be employed to serve the purposes of digital rights protection. The dominant trends can be categorized as follows:

- **Distribute digital content of low quality:** Constitutes a simple, economical and widely adopted technique for preventing unauthorized actions of content misuse (e.g., printing, replicating etc).

For instance, an image resolution of 72 dpi (dots per inch) is high enough to retain the image visual quality for preview purposes but very low to allow exploitation actions such as publishing printed copies.

- **Distribute encrypted content:** A popular method for protecting digital content, adopted by famous DRM systems is the distribution of multimedia content in an encrypted format. In this case only the user having payed a certain fee, obtains a use license which serves as the decryption key.
- **Steganography:** Protecting digital content using steganographic techniques involves the use of specialized mechanisms that hide encoded messages within the actual content. In this way tracking of content through computer networks is possible, via the transmission of data concerning the content users.
- **Digital watermarking:** Digital watermarking constitutes one of the most modern technological solutions for protecting digital content and has been adopted by a number of content providers. Digital watermarking introduces an additional level of protection and has been particularly popular in the field of digital images. Digital watermarks can be either visible or invisible and their purpose is to provide evidence for supporting the copyright holder ownership over the watermarked content.

RIGHTS CLEARANCE AND DRM

The process of rights clearance involves many different players interacting in various modes. The purpose of this section is to describe a case of electronic trade with special focus on rights clearance. The key-entities will be identified and their interrelations will be outlined. This process is motivated by the necessity to trace the slots in the electronic transaction sequence where advanced technologies can be attached and bridge the gap between physical and electronic commerce. Rights clearance can be regarded as part of the general digital rights management objective that has emerged as one of the greatest challenges for content distribution. First-generation DRM systems, used to rely on encryption techniques, limiting content distribution to a very restricted amount of legitimate users. Second-generation DRM systems facilitate the description, identification, trading, protection, monitoring and tracking of all forms of rights usage over both tangible and intangible assets.

Motivating Example

A typical example of a Digital Rights Management system that incorporates rights clearance functionality can be taken from the E-book sector. OzAuthors (OZAUTHORS) is a service provided by the Australian society of authors in a joint venture with IPR Systems, (Renato 2001). Their goal is to provide an easy way for society members (including Authors and Publishers) to deliver their content to the market place at low cost and with fair royalties for content owners.

Figure 1 shows the OzAuthors' interface for collecting rights related information. In this example, the "Usage Rights and Pricing" frame, allows the content provider to specify "Read" and/or "Print" permissions, pricing, and security options for the ebook. Additionally, a number of pages can be specified for free preview. The second frame of the interface allows the content provider to specify all involved rights holders, their roles, and their percentage on the royalty split. Each time the ebook is sold, the rights holders will automatically receive the indicated amount. By inspecting the front end of a DRM

Figure 1. DRM: Front end example application

system it is evident that there are two critical architectures to consider. The first is the Functional Architecture, which covers the high-level architectural components of a DRM system. The second critical architecture is the Information Architecture, which covers the modelling of the key-players within a DRM system as well as their relationships. In the following, indicative diagrams will be used to illustrate an electronic transaction, in terms of the aforementioned architectures, with special focus on the process of removing the constraints on the use of a digital asset by clearing the rights and obtaining on-line licenses for its use.

Functional Architecture

The core functionality of a DRM framework can be separated in the following three main areas:

- **Intellectual property (IP) asset creation and capture:** Refers to the circumstances under which content is created in order to favor its trade. Asserting rights when content is initially created is one such example, since it reduces the complexity of subsequent rights clearance.
- **IP asset management:** Asset management and trade, follows its creation and is carried out by a system that addresses trading requirements, such as descriptive and rights metadata management.
- **IP asset usage:** Monitoring of content usage once it has been traded is the primary goal of this component, which involves applying usage rules over traded content.

While the above core components comprise the broad trucks for DRM, these models need to be further extended in order to fully describe the functionality required by a DRM system (see Figure 2).

The Functional Architecture stipulates the roles and behavior of a number of cooperating and interoperating modules under the three areas of Intellectual Property (IP): Asset Creation, Management, and Usage. Each of these modes is attached with a model hierarchy that provides more detailed description

Figure 2. DRM functional architecture

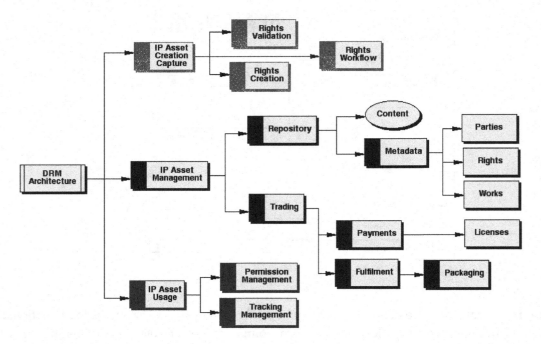

of DRM functionalities. A thorough analysis of the functional architecture can be found in (Renato 2001). However, Functional Architecture is only part of the answer to the challenges of DRM, since rights management can become complex remarkably quickly. As a result, DRM systems must follow the, more flexible, information model that addresses these complex and layered relationships.

Information Architecture

Entities and relations are two widely established notions that are used to model certain aspects of the real world. In this context, information architecture is primarily concerned with the entities and relations governing DRM functionality. Modeling all different aspects of DRM functionality requires the following actions:

- Model the entities
- Identify and describe the entities, and
- Express the rights statements

Modeling the Entities

A clear and complete model that incorporates all existing entities and relations is useful for identifying the underlying technologies of a DRM framework. The <indecs> project (INDECS) introduces a model where the three core entities: Users, Content, and Rights, are clearly separated as shown in Figure 3. The Users entity encompasses any type of user, from a rights holder to an end-consumer. Content can

Figure 3. DRM information architecture: Core entities Model

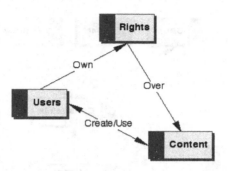

Figure 4. DRM information architecture: Content Model

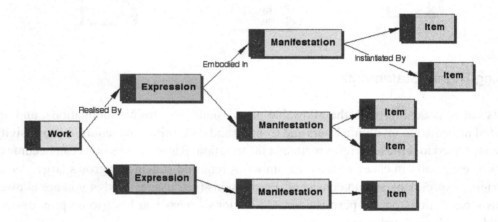

be any type of content that is subject to electronic trade and the Rights entity is an expression of the permissions, constraints, and obligations between the Users and the Content. The main advantage of this model is that it provides the greatest flexibility when assigning rights to any combination or layering of Users and Content. The core entities model is highly adjustable and can be used to model the needs of new and evolving business models.

The core entities diagram depicted above, constitutes a rather abstract modeling of DRM functionality and indicates that all three entities need to incorporate a mechanism for communicating metadata between them. Attempting a more thorough analysis of the model would require the Content and Rights entities to be further extended by more fine grained entities and relations. International Federation of Library Associations (IFLA) has proposed an extended model for Content entity that is based on many "layers" from various intellectual stages or evolution of its development. The goal behind this extended model is to enable clearer (i.e., more explicit and/or appropriate) attribution of rights information. According to this model, Content can be identified at the Work, Expression, Manifestation, and Item layers, as shown in Figure 4. At each of these layers, different rights and rights holders may need to be supported. Further explanations of the extended model for Content entity can be found in (Renato 2001).

Figure 5. DRM information architecture: Rights Expression Model

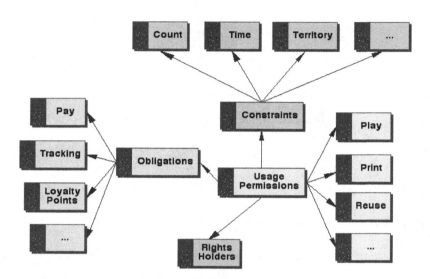

Expressing Rights Statements

The Rights entity is dealing with the allowable permissions, constraints, obligations, and any other rights-related information involving Users and Content and determines the required expressivity power of the language used to represent rights metadata information. Rights expressions can become complex quite quickly, especially in cases where the number of required statements grows large. As shown in Figure 5, rights expressions should consist of: Permissions (i.e., usages) - what you are allowed to do, Constraints - restrictions on the permissions, Obligations - what you have to do/provide/accept and Rights Holders - who is entitled to what.

For example, as demonstrated by the motivating example, a rights expression may state that a particular ebook can be read and printed (i.e., a usage permission), for a $10 fee (i.e., an obligation to pay) and a maximum of 5 pages can be used for preview purposes (i.e., a count constraint). Additionally, each time the ebook is used, Libby, Renato, and Dale (the rights holders) receive a percentage of the fee.

RIGHTS CLEARANCE & BUSINESS MODEL

After identifying and describing the key-entities and relations of DRM functionality, it is interesting to consider the aforementioned observations in the context of a more general business model. The aim is to investigate inherent weaknesses of on-line rights clearance activities and trace pitfalls that are likely to arise. Eventually, technology potentials will be investigated for tackling these weaknesses.

General Architectural Model

For the purposes of our investigation we will use the business model developed as part of the IMPRI-MATUR Project (ESPRIT 20676) (IMPRIMATUR). The validity of this model was further certified

Exhibit 1.

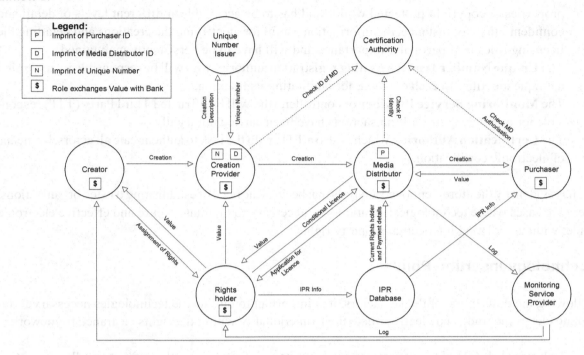

via its subsequent adoption by the TRADEX (TRial Action for Digital object EXchange) Project (IST 21031) (TRADEX). For an extensive description of this model in the context of a cultural information system, the interested reader is referred to (Tsolis 2005).

The actors (stakeholders) identified in this model are:

- The **Creator** is the author of the copyrighted work.

- The **rights-holder** (or copyright owner), acts of behalf of the **Creator** and is responsible for licensing the use of the creation. Specifically, he defines the conditions of use, records the IPR information at a registry and collects the royalties deriving from trading of the works which he is in charge to administer.

- The **content provider** (or service producer), is in charge to prepare content for being traded electronically, and thus, for example, to embed into creations those mechanisms that will allow the tracking of copyright (watermarks). This player has to employ the necessary technological means so as to ensure that copyright can always be protected.

- The **media distributor** (or service provider), who has the responsibility to distribute to purchasers the creations, and thus to satisfy the request of his clients. This involves re-assuring that the IPR on the distributed material is protected and the related fees paid. This actor requires accessing the databases where IPR information is stored and using all the technological means needed to protect the copyright of the creations he trades (watermarking, cryptography, secure protocols). Moreover, he will have to offer the purchasers electronic licenses that determine the permissions, constraints and obligations of content use, as well as provide the authors, right-holders and other authorized actors a set of services to monitor and control the trading of their works.

- The **IPR Database** or register, is the repository of all information related to the intellectual properties of copyright protected works, and has to be accessible at different levels of detail and confidentiality. For instance, the information useful for identifying the creations and detailing the licensing rules is of particular importance and will have to be persistently maintained.

- The **Unique Number Issuer**, a naming registration authority who will be responsible for assigning a unique identifier to each creation, for facilitating its tracking.

- The **Monitoring Service Provider** or controller, who will be a Trusted Third Party (TTP) responsible for monitoring that all transactions have been carried out legally.

- The **Certification Authority**, which is also a TTP, with the task to authenticate all actors, by means of electronic certification.

It is evident by the aforementioned analysis that besides the need of establishing trusted organizations, there are cases where technological solutions are necessary to facilitate secure and effective electronic trade, without violating intellectual property rights.

Technology Insertion Points

Following the description of the key actors, it is important to outline the technologies necessary to facilitate electronic trade and clearly situate their functionality within the rights clearance framework.

- **Relational databases,** can serve as the repository infrastructure that will store all information required by the framework.

- **Communication protocol,** will allow different components to seamlessly communicate. As suggested by the diagram depicting the IMPRIMATUR business model, engineering an information system for performing electronic trade, would require the existence of many distributed functional components. Employing a standardized communication protocol would make binding between components more loosely-coupled and greatly benefit the reusability of components and extensibility of the framework.

- **IPR Metadata standards,** are essential for representing intellectual property information in an interoperable manner. These standards are particularly important for the **IPR Database** and **Rights holder** actors and its proper use and adjustment will favor the openness of the developed framework.

- **Rights Expression Language**, will try to cope with the increased level of complexity stemming from the number of conditions, restrictions and obligations included in the license documents. The **Rights holder** along with the **Media Distributor** will be the main consumers of this technology and is particular important for implementing a valid rights clearance service.

- **Technological Protection Means** such as watermarking, encryption etc, are the key functional component used for the protection and management of intellectual property rights. The DRM framework requires for a means to prevent unauthorized users from violating the intellectual property rights of traded content. In the case of watermarking (Tsolis 2001), copyright information is invisibly embedded inside the image digital content and technological evidence of the image ownership can be obtained by extracting this information. The embedded information typically corresponds to the **Rights holder** copyright notice and according to the aforementioned business model, the player that benefits more from utilizing this technology is the **Content Provider**.

- **Uniform resource identifiers**, are the cornerstone of services involving transaction tracking, since all entities need to be both identified and described uniformly. Identification should be accomplished via open and standard mechanisms that will facilitate the association of metadata records with creations. Open standards such as Uniform Resource Identifiers (URI) and Digital Object Identifiers (DOI), as well as the emerging ISO International Standard Textual Work Code (ISTC) are typical schemes for producing uniform resource identifiers.

RIGHTS CLEARANCE TECHNOLOGIES

The purpose of this section is to elaborate on the technologies that are more tightly related to on-line rights clearance and not DRM in general.

Communication Standards

Traditionally, information systems are architected using a component-based approach. Typically, the distinct components of the information system are closely interrelated, in such a way that modifications in any one of them subsequently causes extensive changes to other parts. This fact restricts their maintainability and limits their future expansion. Web Services are a set of open standards and protocols that were introduced to increase the reusability and interoperability of the components, by making the binding between them more loosely-coupled. Further elaboration on the topic of web services is out of the scope of this chapter, but the interested reader can refer to (Tsolis 2005).

IPR Metadata Standards

Independently of the adopted rights protection and management strategy, information is considered of vital importance. It is the information that allows the rights administrator to check the validity of content use, to trace potential usage violations, to grant the copyright of an artwork, etc. Information is also the mean that allows the end user to communicate with the copyright holder in order to file a request for using the copyright protected content or acquire the pricing policy of an artwork available on-line. The data comprising this type of information concerns various aspects of object property status such as, a) the intellectual property rights owner b) the intellectual property rights holder in case he is different from the owner c) communication details of the rights holder d) technological means used to protect and manage property rights, etc.

This type of information should accompany the digital artwork and be easily and directly accessible. The amounts of information that is related with a digital object and describe their technical and semantic characteristics are addressed by the term metadata. The set of metadata is intended to capture the information that the content creator chooses to preserve. With regards to the protection and management of intellectual property rights, it is very important that the set of metadata chosen to document the digital artwork, also incorporates data related to intellectual property. These data will formulate the means on which digital rights management systems will base their functionalities. The need for including rights related metadata has been recognized by dominant standardization bodies and is reflected to some of the most widely accepted metadata standards.

Open standards were established to facilitate the description of digital resources. The introduction of XML (Extensible Markup Language) (XML) by W3C has launched numerous resultant languages, protocols and technologies, which are commonly used today by both research projects and commercial applications. XSD (XML Schema Definition) [XSD] and RDF (Resource Description Framework) (RDF) have standardized the processes of defining metadata sets and characterizing resources. In order to accommodate the requirements of vertical applications, specialized metadata sets were also introduced, such as Dublin Core (DC) (DCMI), DIG35 (DIG35), MPEG-7 (MPEG7) to name only a few.

Amongst the various metadata standardization initiatives, Dublin Core (DC) (DCMI) has gained significant visibility and appeal. Dublin Core is a metadata standard that supports the diversity, convergence and interoperability of digital cultural objects and aims at supporting a wide range of business models. The basic schema proposed by Dublin Core is a simple content description model, defined by its 15 elements, out of which four are related with intellectual property rights namely, creator, publisher, contributor, rights.

The Digital Image Group (DIG) [DIG35] is a non-profit cooperation between the industrial players of digital image such as software companies, consumers of digital images, etc. The primary goal of DIG35 is to establish an open framework for the exchange of ideas concerning the investigation, implementation and exploitation of methods and technologies that will boost the market related to digital imaging. This metadata standard is already being widely used in simple end-user devices and even to worldwide networks. DIG35 constitutes a rather extensive metadata set and includes information for a large set of digital image technical and semantic characteristics. Despite the fact that DIG35 is mainly oriented to digital images, the intellectual property related metadata are valid for all different types of multimedia content. The total amount of DIG35 metadata that are directly or indirectly related to intellectual property rights can be divided in 7 categories namely, names, description, dates, exploitation, digital rights management system, identification info and communication info.

Rights Expression Languages

MPEG-REL

MPEG - Rights Expression Language is a machine translatable description language, suitable for defining intellectual property rights, grants and licenses. Its role, in the context of rights clearance, is to provide a flexible and interoperable scheme for large scale consumption of digital objects and facilitate the distribution of digital content while protecting its intellectual properties. The Rights Expression Language defines the linguistics for expressing rules through rights statements. License rules can be rather simple such as, "this content is allowed to be replicated or reproduced" or more complicated such as, "this content is allowed to be reproduced on Tuesday on 7 of March and at 6:00 am, under the condition that the reproducing device satisfies a number of criteria". Such expressions are likely to be created for every person that has the authority to transfer the copyright of protected content. Rights Expression Language is considered a fundamental part of MPEG-21 (MPEG21) mainly due to the intention of MPEG group in establishing a protocol that will allow heterogeneous systems to seamlessly communicate. Thus, the existence of a standardized language for incorporating digital content rights into machine understandable licenses is considered very important. The aim of this section is to investigate the REL data model, analyze its structure identify the key-components and summarize the relevant technological platforms.

Figure 6. REL Data Model

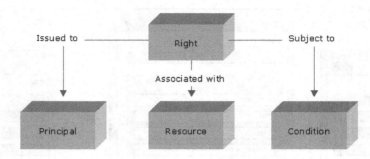

The REL data model (REL), as realized by MPEG-21, incorporates a simple and extensible data model for representing the basic concepts and components. Specifically, it is consisted of four basic entities and the relations among them. The following diagram depicts the fundamental entities and their interrelations.

- **Principle:** The principle entity models the potential users involved in the process of distribution, usage, and content consumption.
- **Right:** Right is the "action" the practice of which is being transferred to the Principle.
- **Resource:** Resource is considered the "object" the rights of which are being transferred to the principle.
- **Condition:** The condition entity determines the terms, restrictions and obligations under which the right is allowed to be exercised.

The four aforementioned entities, comprise a grant. By itself, a grant is not a complete rights expression that can be transferred unambiguously from one party to another. A full rights expression is called a license. A typical license consists of one or more grants and an issuer, which identifies the party who issued the license. In case the licence publisher wants to grant distribution rights to an e-shop or DRM, he signs a distribution license. The grant of a distribution license, instead of the right to be tranfered, contains a new grant as seen in Figure 7 .

The procedure of implementing the MPEG-21 REL initiated with the establishment of a set consisting of 48 requirements. Experts from heterogeneous sectors agreed that the fulfilment of the aforementioned requirements would suffice to guarantee the success of the initiative. The set of requirements extends to various fields ranging from the language expressivity to security. Eventually, the XrML (eXtensible Rights Markup Language) (XrML) technological platform was selected to serve as the groundwork of MPEG-21 REL. To promote interoperability, MPEG has developed the Rights Data Dictionary (RDD) to ensure that the semantic interpretation of new verbs is unambiguously understood. The RDD comprises a set of clear, consistent, structured, integrated and uniquely identified Terms to support the MPEG-21 REL. As well as providing definitions of Terms for use in the REL, the RDD specification is designed to support the mapping and transformation of metadata from the terminology of one namespace (or Authority) into that of another namespace (or Authority) in an automated or partially-automated way, with the minimum ambiguity or loss of semantic integrity.

Figure 7. MPEG 21 - REL data model

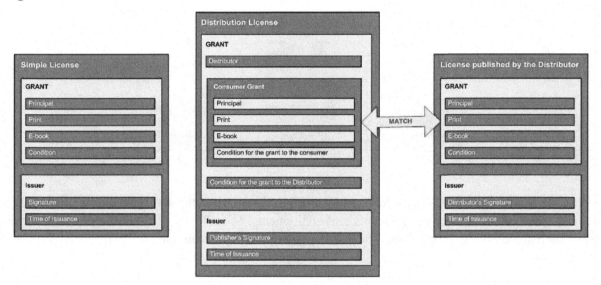

Figure 8. The ODRL foundation model

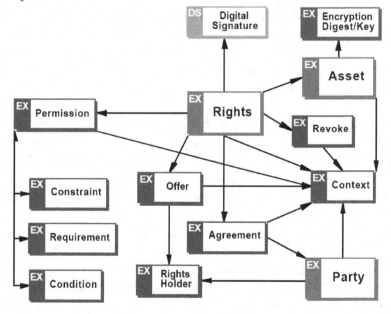

Open Digital Rights Language (ODRL)

ODRL complements existing analogue rights management standards by providing digital equivalents, and supports an expandible range of new services that can be afforded by the digital nature of the assets in the Web environment.

ODRL is a standard language and vocabulary for the expression of terms and conditions over assets. It covers a core set of semantics for these purposes including the rights holders and the expression of permissible usages for asset manifestations. Rights can be specified for a specific asset manifestation or could be applied to a range of manifestations of the asset. *ODRL* is focused on the semantics of expressing rights languages and definitions of elements in the data dictionary.

ODRL does not enforce or mandate any policies for DRM, but provides the mechanisms to express such policies. Communities or organisations, that establish such policies based on *ODRL*, do so based on their specific business or public access requirements. *ODRL* depends on the use of unique identification of assets and parties The *ODRL* model is based on an analysis and survey of sector specific requirements (including models and semantics), and as such, aims to be compatible with a broad community base.

ODRL is based on an extensible model for rights expressions which involves a number of core entities and their relationships. This *ODRL* Foundation Model is shown in Figure 8.

The model, as shown in Figure 8, consists of the following three core entities: Assets, Rights, Parties. The Assets include any physical or digital content. The Assets must be uniquely identified and may consist of many subparts and be in many different formats. The Rights include Permissions which can then contain Constraints, Requirements, and Conditions. Permissions are the actual usages or activities allowed over the Assets (e.g., Play a video Asset). Constraints are limits to these Permissions (e.g., Play the video for a maximum of 5 times). Requirements are the obligations needed to exercise the Permission (e.g., Pay $5 each time you Play the video). Conditions specify exceptions that, if become true, expire the Permissions and renegotiation may be required (e.g., If Credit Card expires then all Permissions are withdrawn to Play the video). The Parties include end users and Rights Holders. Parties can be humans, organisations, and defined roles. End users are usually the asset consumers. Rights Holders are usually parties that have played some role in the creation, production, distribution of the Asset and can assert some form of ownership over the Asset and/or its Permissions. Rights Holders may also receive royalties.

Most entities in the model can support a specific Context. A Context, which is relative to the entity, can describe further information about that entity or the relationship between entities. For example, the Context of an Agreement may specify the date of the transaction, the Context of a Party may specify their role.

The Asset entity (sometimes referred to as a Work, Content, Creation, or Intellectual Property), is viewed as a whole entity. If the Rights are assigned at the Asset's subpart level, then such parts would require to also be uniquely identifiable. However, *ODRL* can specify constraints on subparts of the asset. Additionally, Assets can be identified as to their layer of intellectual property as defined by the IFLA model. These include Work, Expression, Manifestation, and Item. These features also allow rights to be expressed over non-tangible assets and individual instances.

These core Entities together allow for a wide and flexible range of *ODRL* expressions to be declared. Additionally, the expressions can be digitally signed.

Watermarking

Watermarking can be considered as an integrated service, providing protection and assisting management of intellectual property rights. Watermark technology incorporates encryption methods to ensure unambiguous and categorical proof of ownership, as well as image processing techniques for conveying useful information inside the digital content, (Cox 2002). The level of functionality that can be achieved by the proposed scheme depends upon the usage policy of the conveyed information. A typical scenario involves an organization that owns a great collection of digital images and is willing to sale high quality copies of collection objects for a standard price. Prior to delivery, the organization embeds a digital watermark inside the image content. The watermark serves three different purposes, a) give proof of ownership, b) identify the transaction that took place and c) correlate the transaction description with the specific image copy. All details necessary for describing a transaction are included within the image metadata information maintained within the content provider's database infrastructure.

In this case, the input arguments of watermark embedding mechanism consist of two integer numbers. The first number corresponds to the encryption key while the second to the transaction identification number. The encryption key is used for invoking the core cryptographic module that guarantees for watermark's security. It's a unique private number that constitutes the key of the system's cryptographic attributes and is used by the right's holder for proving his ownership.

Thus, there is a need for universal administration of such numbers in order to avoid conflicts and irresolvable disputes. This role is appointed to uniform resource identifier systems that will be described at a later section. If we consider that a uniform resource identifier is consisted of two distinct numbers, a prefix and a suffix, the watermarking scheme performs the following actions. By using the prefix number as seed for cryptographically encoding the watermark information within the image digital content, the proposed scheme exploit's the handle system administration facilities for resolving ownership disputes. The suffix is an independent number selected by the institution protocol service; it is administered locally and can be regarded as the transaction identification number. This number is encoded inside the digital image content and can be retrieved by the decryption mechanism.

Unique Resource Identifier

Open object identification systems are deemed very important for distributed environments like the ones encountered in electronic commerce. Global identifiers should allow for unique identification of digital objects in order to facilitate the operations of rights clearance.

Handle System

The Handle System, (Kahn 2006), is a distributed information system designed to provide an efficient, extensible and confederated name service that allows any existing local namespace to join the global handle namespace by obtaining a unique Handle System naming authority. Local names and their value-binding(s) remain intact after joining the Handle System. Any handle request to the local namespace may be processed by a service interface speaking the Handle System protocol. Combined with the unique naming authority, any local name is guaranteed unique under the global handle namespace.

It is probably best to view the Handle System as a name-attribute binding service with a specific protocol for securely creating, updating, maintaining, and accessing a distributed database. It is designed to be an enabling service for secured information and resource sharing over networks such as the public Internet. Applications of the Handle System could include metadata services for digital publications, identity management services for virtual identities, or any other applications that require resolution and/or administration of globally unique identifiers.

Handle Namespace

Every handle consists of two parts: its naming authority, otherwise known as its prefix, and a unique local name under the naming authority, otherwise known as its suffix:

<Handle> ::= <Handle Naming Authority> "/" <Handle Local Name>

The naming authority and local name are separated by the ASCII character "/". The collection of local names under a naming authority defines the local handle namespace for that naming authority. Any local name must be unique under its local namespace. The uniqueness of a naming authority and a local name under that authority ensures that any handle is globally unique within the context of the Handle System.

For example, "1082.5000/image1" is a handle for a digital image published on a cultural website. Its naming authority is "1082.5000" and its local name is "image1". The handle namespace can be considered a superset of many local namespaces, with each local namespace having a unique naming authority under the Handle System. The naming authority identifies the administrative unit of creation, although not necessarily continuing administration, of the associated handles. Each naming authority is guaranteed to be globally unique within the Handle System. Any existing local namespace can join the global handle namespace by obtaining a unique naming authority so that any local name under the namespace can be globally referenced as a combination of the naming authority and the local name as shown above.

Naming authorities under the Handle System are defined in a hierarchical fashion resembling a tree structure. Each node and leaf of the tree is given a label that corresponds to a naming authority segment. The parent node notifies the parent naming authority of its child nodes. Unlike DNS, handle naming authorities are constructed left to right, concatenating the labels from the root of the tree to the node that represents the naming authority. Each label is separated by the octet used for ASCII character ".". Each naming authority may have many child naming authorities registered underneath. Any child naming authority can only be registered by its parent after its parent naming authority has been registered. However, there is no intrinsic administrative relationship between the namespaces represented by the parent and child naming authorities. The parent namespace and its child namespaces may be served by different handle services, and they may or may not share any administration privileges.

Handle System Architecture

The Handle System defines a hierarchical service model. The top level consists of a single handle service, known as the Global Handle Registry (GHR). The lower level consists of all other handle services, generically known as Local Handle Services (LHS).

The Global Handle Registry can be used to manage any handle namespace. It is unique among handle services only in that it provides the service used to manage naming authorities, all of which are managed as handles. The naming authority handle provides information that clients can use to access and utilize the local handle service for handles under the naming authority.

Local Handle Services are intended to be hosted by organizations with administrative responsibility for handles under certain naming authorities. A Local Handle Service may be responsible for any number of local handle namespaces, each identified by a unique naming authority. The Local Handle Service and its responsible set of local handle namespaces must be registered with the Global Handle Registry.

Figure 9. Example of handle resolution process

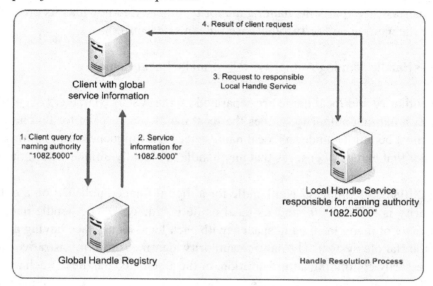

The Global Handle Registry maintains naming authority handles. Each naming authority handle maintains the service information that describes the "home" service of the naming authority. The service information lists the service sites of the given handle service, as well as the interface to each handle server within each site. To find the "home" service for any handle, a client can query the Global Handle Registry for the service information associated with the corresponding naming authority handle. The service information provides the necessary information for clients to communicate with the "home" service.

Figure 9 shows an example of a typical handle resolution process. In this case, the "home" service is a Local Handle Service. The client is trying to resolve the handle "1082.5000/1" and has to find its "home" service from the Global Handle Registry. The "home" service can be found by sending a query to the Global Handle Registry for the naming authority handle for "1082.5000". The Global Handle Registry returns the service information of the Local Handle Service that is responsible for handles under the naming authority "1082.5000". The service information allows the client to communicate with the Local Handle Service to resolve the handle "1082.5000/1".

To improve resolution performance, any client may choose to cache the service information returned from the Global Handle Registry and use it for subsequent queries. A separate handle caching server, either stand-alone or as a piece of a general caching mechanism, may also be used to provide shared caching within a local community. Given a cached resolution result, subsequent queries of the same handle may be answered locally without contacting any handle service. Given cached service information, clients can send their requests directly to the correct Local Handle Service without contacting the Global Handle Registry.

CASE STUDY: SilkDRM

SilkDRM is a new Digital Rights Management System that provides on-line Rights Clearance for digital images (or other digital assets). Individuals and/or institutions who own the Intellectual Property Rights of digital images can use SilkDRM in order to ensure the authenticity of their content. Additionally, the system can be authorized by the right holder to issue distribution licenses for the digital resources. This is done by signing a special license which describes the set of rights that can be assigned for a specific resource, as well as the equivalent necessary conditions under which the assignment can be made.

System Functionality

SilkDRM is accessible to internet users through its easy to use web interface. A number of Cultural Institutions who created websites for their digitized content, used the system in order to document their rights on the content and as a mechanism for the production of digital licenses on its use. In practice, the Cultural Institutions registered their content in the system and in parallel, in the webpages presenting the digital assets they provide a hyperlink to SilkDRM. By following that hyperlink, the visitor is directed to the corresponding page from where he can retrieve information about the intellectual propery rights binding the digital resource, as well as the conditions for obtaining a use license. If the rights holder decides to use digital watermarking for protecting his content, he is able to embody the unique code created by SilkDRM in the watermark. In this case, the detection of the watermark can lead one to the corresponding page of the DRM (through the code retrieved).

System Users

The two basic system user types involved in SilkDRM are Content Providers and Content Consumers. Content Providers include single users or members of a Cultural Organization aiming in registering

Figure 10. SilkDRM system functionality

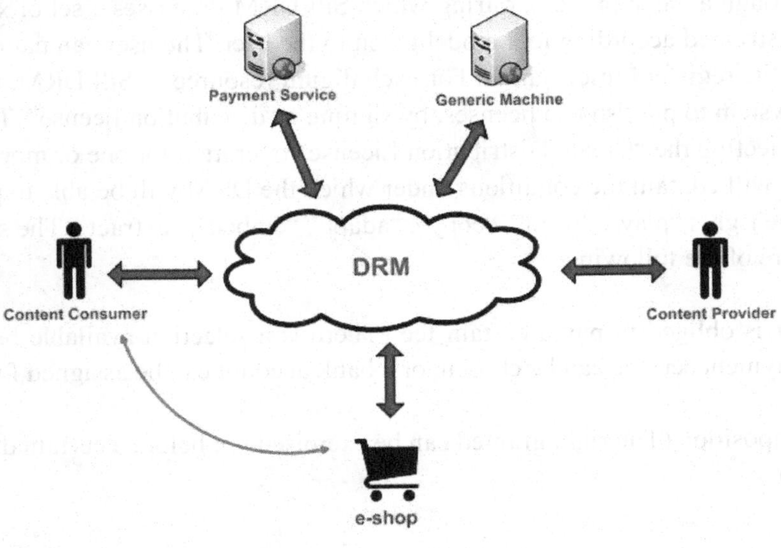

their digital content in order to authenticate their ownership over the content and pursue its commercial exploitation. A Content Consumer is browsing the DRM webpages, receiving intellectual property information on specific digital resources and potentially apply for a use license. A Content Consumer can be not only an individual but also an e-shop. In this scenario, the rights holder has assigned the distribution of his content to an e-shop. The e-shop contacts the DRM in order to retrieve information concerning the terms and conditions set by the owner for the selling of the digital resource and present them to the potential buyers. In case the item is sold, the DRM is responsible for publishing the corresponding use license and forward it to the e-shop. SilkDRM is able to communicate with various payment services over the web, achiving this way transaction monitoring as well as the validation of published licenses. Beside the aforementioned users, any generic machine, implementing a specific communication protocol based on standard web technologies, is able to connect and transact with the system.

Content Providers

When a content provider browses our web pages for the first time, he is prompted to fill in an application form for the creation of an account. This form includes personal and corporate information in case the user acts on behalf of an organization/institution. SilkDRM administrator processes the application and contacts the applicant in order to retrieve information about the resourses that he intends to register in the DRM. The next step includes the preparation of a legal contract, in which the applicant declares that he or the institution that he represents is the intellectual property rights holder of the content that will be registered in SilkDRM. When the contract is signed, a new account is created and the applicant becomes a registered user of the system. The first account created, is an account of the organization administrator having full rights to all system functionalities. The administrator can create new accounts and assign user rights to the people he chooses. The "register procedure" for a new digital resource in the DRM, is implemented by filling in some forms containing descriptive information about the resource and its intellectual propery. In parallel, a preview picture (eg. thumbnail) can be uploaded. In case the rights holder has decided to watermark the resource, he can ask the DRM to produce a unique identification number, in order to be embedded in the watermark. SilkDRM can also produce a handle for the resource, in order to facilitate a unique addressing method. The registration of digital assets to the DRM can also be acomplished through a batch process, during which SilkDRM processes a set of xml files (one for each resource), constructed according to a model given to the user. The user can navigate through his collection and edit the registerd information. For each digital resource in SilkDRM, the rights holder can authorize the system to publish use licenses, by signing a "distribution license". This procedure is accomplished by selecting the "Create Distribution License" operation for one or more resources. The licese to be created will contain the conditions under which the DRM will be able to publish licenses, granting some of the rights "play", "print", "copy", "adapt", "embed", "extract". The set of conditions, could be one or more of the following:

- The consumer is obliged to pay a certain fee (There is a selection available between payment methods. A payment service can be chosen, or a bank account can be assigned for a deposit to be made)
- Time Limit Imposition (The right granted can be exercised not before a certain date and not after a certain date)

- Exercise Limit (There is a specific number of executions allowed for the right(s) granted)
- Geographical Restrictions (The right granted can be exercised only in a specified country)

When the conditions are selected, the license is published and the DRM acquires the authorization to create and publish use licenses for specific digital resources, due to the conditions of the distribution license signed. The last service offered to the content provider, is a license management service. The user can browse a list of all the licenses published by SilkDRM for his digital resources. For each license, the system provides information about the principal to whom the rights are granted as well as the potential use of the Validator. The Validator is a subsystem of the SilkDRM which is able to read a license and respond whether it is valid or not. This is accomplished by checking the fullfilment of the conditions set (e.g., fee payment, time limitations). The Validator is not a single "valid" or "not valid". It can indicate the specific terms that are not satisfied.

Content Consumers

The two main services offered to a content consumer, are browsing the collections of registered resources and managing obtained licenses. The resources collections are sorted by rights holder but there is also a search engine available. For each digital resource exists a page demonstrating all available information (e.g., for a digital image elements such as title, legent, description, rightsholder, creator, digitizer etc. are presented). In case the appropriate distribution license is issued, the choice of obtaining a use license is provided. If the user selects to obtain a license, he will be directed to the license creation page. In this page, the user can see all the rights the DRM is empowered to distribute and select those he wants to receive a license. For each right, the consumer must agree with the conditions set by the rights holder and finally affirm that he wants to obtain the license. Finally the license is published and sent to the user via e-mail. The e-mal, except from the license attached, contains a hyperlink to the Validator, where the obtained licese can be validated. The licence management service, provides a list of all the licenses granted to the user. The licenses are sorted by date and are accompanied by information about the resource and a link to the Validator.

Figure 11. SilkDRM system architecture

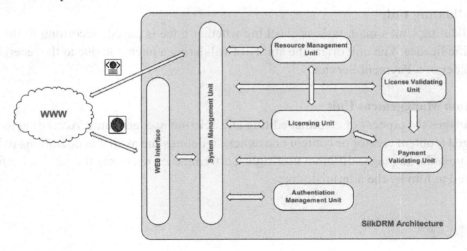

System Architecture

The system comprises of six distinct units, the functionality of which is described in the following paragraphs. These units are designed and constructed independenly, as the main goal was the production of a system with the highest possible maintenability and scalability.

System Management Unit

This is the unit that executes the system operation protocol. It receives requests from the web interface or another input (eg. Web service) and orchestrates system units by triggering the appropriate ones at a time, passing messages to them.

Resource Management Unit

This particular unit is responsible for the process of registering and documenting a digital resource. It also undertakes the task of retrieving the documentation and potentially editing and deleting it. Additionally, the Resource Management Unit embraces two distinct sub-units. The Unique Indentifier Generator and the Handle Creation Unit which create and register handles for the unequivocal addressing of the digital items.

Licensing Unit

This is the unit responsible for creating and processing licenses for digital resources. For each item, the unit can check whether a distribution licese has been published. If such a license is present, the unit is able to read it and dynamically create the terms and conditions a content consumer must agree with, in order to obtain a use license. When a license is published, the unit sends it via e-mail to the holder.

License Validating Unit

This unit receives a license as an input, and checks whether the conditions set in order the grant to be valid, are satisfied. For checking the validity of the payments, the unit is able to communicate with the Payment Validating Unit. Special response messages are produced, according to the results of the validity test. In case a license is not valid, the unit provides detailed information on which of the conditions are not met.

Payment Validating Unit

Payment Validating Unit's main task, is checking whether a fee is payed, according to the conditions set in a specific license. The unit offers the ability of validating a payment, due to the received input by the rights holder or a Payment Service.

Authentication Management Unit

This unit manages the process of creating, editing and deleting user accounts. According to the type of the user logged (content creator or content consumer), it defines the available operations to him on the system. The unit also manages different user rights, offering each user only the services defined by the rights assigned to him by the administrators.

Implementation Details

Registering a Digital Object

The process followed for registering a digital object in SilkDRM, is described in this paragraph.

1. An application is received by System Management Unit, from a system user wanting to register a digital resource.
2. System Management Unit contacts Authentication Management Unit, to certify that the user is permitted to perform the action.
3. Authentication Management Unit responds whether the user has the right to register the content or not.
4. If the response received is positive, Resource Management Unit is initiated in order to start the registering process.
5. Resource Management Unit provides all necessary data, for the creation of the registering interface. In case of digital images, SilkDRM uses the DIG-35 Intellectual Property Rights Metadata set and when handling other digital resources the Dublin Core Metadata set is used for the registration process.
6. Content Provider fills in the forms with the appropriate data
7. Resource Management Unit receives and stores the data, using a selected format. Relational Database schemes are used for the data storage. The unit is able to export inserted data in xml files. According to the user's demands, the Unique Indentifier Generator and the Handle Creating Unit will be triggered. The Handle Creating Unit includes a Handle Server playing the role of the Local Handle Service responsible for the naming authority "1082.xxxx" Finally the output (the results of the registration process, the unique identification number, the handle etc.) is passed to the content provider (through the System Management Unit).
8. The user wants to create a distribution license for the resource.

Figure 12. SilkDRM flow-chart

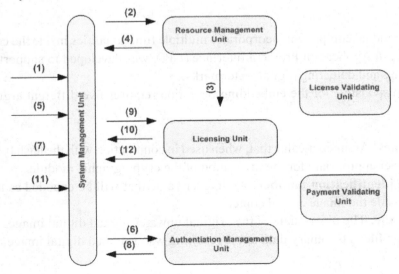

9. Licensing Unit is called, for the creation of the license.
10. License Unit provides the necessary data for the production of the license creation interface. For the creation of a license, MPEG – Rights Expression Language is used.
11. The user fills in the form selecting rights and conditions and submits it, thus giving the order for the creation o a license.
12. Licensing Unit receives the data, creates the license, and e-mails it to the content provider. The licenses are created and stored in the xml format specified by the MPEG-REL specifications.

The Licensing Process

The next bullets describe the process followed for the creation of a digital license.

1. A system user (content consumer) wants to browse the collections of registered digital items
2. Resource Management Unit is triggred for the presentation of the collection items.
3. Resource Management Unit contacts Licensing Unit to retrieve information about whether a distribution license is published, for each digital resource it will present.
4. Resource Management Unit presents the documentation for the registered items. In case a distribution license is published, the content consumer has the ability to request a lisence for the resource.
5. The user makes a license request for a specific digital resource.
6. System Management unit calls Authentication Management Unit to authenticate the user.
7. The user logs on the system if he has an account, or is taken through the steps to create one
8. Authentication Management Unit authenticates the user
9. The request is passed to the Licensing Unit
10. Licensing Unit retrieves and reads the distribution license, in order to produce the forms for the creation of the license.
11. The User accepts the licensing conditions and requests the finalization of the process.
12. Licensing Unit receives the final data, creates and stores the license and finally sends it to the user via e-mail.

Watermarking

Watermarking functional component incorporates multiple functionalities inside the content provider's operational chain. An Application Protocol Interface (API), was developed to support two basic interfaces for embedding and detecting digital watermarks.

The interface responsible for the embedding operation requires five different arguments from the service user:

- **Encryption key:** An integer value that, when used in conjunction with the hash function, produces a secret number appropriate for the invocation of the cryptographic module.
- **Transaction identification number:** An integer value that will be encoded as an imperceptible watermark inside the image digital content.
- **Input image file:** The binary data of the original unwatermarked digital image.
- **Output image file:** The binary data of the resulting watermarked digital image.

- **Strength modifier:** An integer between 1 and 4 indicating the embedding strength of the water-mark procedure. A value of 4 produces more robust watermarks, but introduces more distortion to image quality.The interface response returns a zero value on success of the watermarking process and a negative value in case of failure.Respectively, the interface responsible for detecting digital watermarks requires the following input arguments.
- **Decryption key:** The integer used during the embedding procedure. With regards to the specific watermarking system, the encryption and decryption keys must be identical in order for the detection to be successful.
- **Input image file:** The binary data of the image under detection. The detector's response, as already mentioned, is consisted of two parts.
- **Detection intensity:** Indicating the existence possibility of the watermark inside the image content. If this value is well above a predefined threshold the watermark is considered detected.
- **Decrypted information:** An integer value representing the number encoded during the embedding procedure. Normally, this number corresponds to the transaction identification number.

CONCLUSION

Rights Clearance has always been an important issue in human transactions. The Internet revolution made the issue a lot more complicated since we passed from the material to the digital substance of an asset. Multiple copies of a digital resource exist over the internet, thus making the monitoring of its use and the identification of its origin an extremely difficult task. Throughout this chapter, we described the rights clearance process in the physical and digital world and the ways it can be accomplished on-line through a Digital Rights Management system. Important issues concering a DRM system are the definition of key-entities and relations of its functionality, the way a digital resource is represented, protected bound with metadata sets, uniquely identified and the way rights are digitally expressed and assigned. Finally we present an application of all discussed attributes of a DRM system, in an existing system (SilkDRM) that provides on-line Rights Clearance for digital images (or other digital assets).

FUTURE RESEARCH DIRECTIONS

Future research involves integrating Rights Clearance as a fully functional component of second-generation DRM systems. More specifically, as opposed to first-generation DRM systems where the enforccment of encryption techniques allowed very limited access to content, second generation DRMs introduce more flexible content delivery schemes at the expense of balancing between a set of diverse features such as:

- Uniformly describe and identify an asset (both tangible or intangible).
- Adhere to a globally estrablished protocol for registering rights-holders as well as the set of rights they are allowed to grant.
- Support rights expression languages that are able to describe different types of property rights and facilitate their transfer to a person or an organization.

- Seamlessly co-operate with technological protecting means both for the tasks of copyright protection and transanction tracking
- Finally, to make all the above work in a unified e-commerce business model.

Each bullet can be considered as a different research field. Although several DRM systems have been developed none of them manages to successfully address all aforementioned aspects. A unified DRM system that operates over the internet is envisaged as the only plausible solution for providing consistent and bulletproof protection of Intellectual Property Rights.

REFERENCES

ContentGuard, http://www.contentguard.com

Cox, I., Miller, M. L. & J. A. Bloom. (2002) *Digital watermarking*. San Francisco, CA, USA: Morgan Kaufmann Publishers Inc.

DCMI, Dublin Core Metadata Initiative, Last checked: October 11 2007, <http://www.dublincore.org/>

DIG35, Digital Image Group - DIG35 Specification – Metadata for Digital Images. Last checked: 11 October 2007, http://www.i3a.org/i_dig35.html

DOI, Digital Object Identifier. Last checked: 11 October 2007, http://www.doi.org

IFLA, Functional Requirements for Bibliographic Records, IFLA Study Group on the Functional Requirements for Bibliographic Records, (Approved September 1997) K . G. Saur München, 1998. Not available, http://www.ifla.org/VII/s13/frbr/frbr.htm

IMPRIMATUR, Intellectual Multimedia Property RIghts Model and Terminology for Universal Reference, Not available, http://www.imprimatur.alcs.co.uk/index.htm

INDECS, Interoperability of data in e-commerce systems, Last checked: October 11 2007, <http://www.indecs.org>

ISTC, ISO International Standard Textual Work Code. Last checked: 11 October 2007, http://www.nlc-bnc.ca/iso/tc46sc9/istc.htm

Kahn, R. & Wilensky, R. (2006). A Framework for Distributed Digital Object Services. *International Journal on Digital Libraries*, 6(2). Springer.

MPEG21, MPEG-21 Overview v5, Last checked: 11 October 2007, http://www.chiariglione.org/mpeg/standards/mpeg-21/mpeg-21.htm

MPEG7, ISO/IEC Moving Picture Experts Group. Last checked: 11 October 2007, < http://www.chiariglione.org/mpeg/standards/mpeg-7/mpeg-7.htm >

Open Digital Rights Language (ODRL), version 1.1 (2002) from http://odrl.net

OZAUTHORS, OzAuthors Online Ebook Store, Last checked: October 11 2007, http://www.ozauthors. com

RDF, Resource Description Framework. Last checked: 11 October 2007, http://www.w3.org/RDF/

REL (2003). The MPEG-21 Rights Expression Language, A White Paper, Rightscom Ltd,

Renato, I. (2001). Digital rights manegement (DRM) architectures. *D-Lib Magezine Article*, 7(6).

Sun, S., Lannom, L., & Boesch, B. Handle system overview. *Internet Engineering Task Force (IETF) Request for Comments (RFC), RFC 3650*, November 2003 from http://www.handle.net

TRADEX, TRial Action for Digital object EXchange, Not available, http://www.iccd.beniculturali. it/download/tradex.pdf

Tsolis, G. K., Nikolopoulos, S. N., Kazantzi, N.V., Tsolis, D. K. & Papatheodorou, T. S. (2005, August 15-17). Re-Engineering digital watermarking of copyright protected images by using xml web services. *In Proc. of the Ninth IASTED International Conference on INTERNET & MULTIMEDIA SYSTEMS & APPLICATIONS (IMSA 2005)*, 264-270. Honolulu, Hawaii, USA.

Tsolis, G. K., Tsolis, D. K. & Papatheodorou, T. S. (2001). A watermarking environment and a metadata digital image repository for the protection and management of digital images of the hellenic cultural heritage. *Proc. IEEE International Conference on Image Processing 2001*, 566-569. Thessaloniki, Greece

URI, Uniform Resource Identifiers (URI): Generic Syntax, IETF RFC2396. Last checked: 11 October 2007, http://www.ietf.org/rfc/rfc2396.txt

WIPO, World Intellectual Property Organization, Last checked: October 11 2007, <http://www.wipo. int>

XML, eXtensive Markup Language. Last checked: 11 October 2007, http://www.w3.org/XML/

XrML, eXtensive rights Markup Language. Last checked: 11 October 2007, http://www.xrml.org

XSD, eXtensible Markup Language Schema, Last checked: 11 October 2007, <http://www.w3.org/ XML/Schema>

ADITTIONAL READING

DCMI, Dublin Core Metadata Initiative, Last checked: October 11 2007, <http://www.dublincore. org/>

DIG35, Digital Image Group - DIG35 Specification – Metadata for Digital Images. Last checked: 11 October 2007, http://www.i3a.org/i_dig35.html

DOI, Digital Object Identifier. Last checked: 11 October 2007, http://www.doi.org

MPEG21, MPEG-21 Overview v5, Last checked: 11 October 2007, http://www.chiariglione.org/mpeg/ standards/mpeg-21/mpeg-21.htm

MPEG7, ISO/IEC Moving Picture Experts Group. Last checked: 11 October 2007,   < http://www. chiariglione.org/mpeg/standards/mpeg-7/mpeg-7.htm >

URI, Uniform Resource Identifiers (URI): Generic Syntax, IETF RFC2396. Last checked: 11 October 2007, http://www.ietf.org/rfc/rfc2396.txt

WIPO, World Intellectual Property Organization, Last checked: October 11 2007, <http://www.wipo. int>

XML, eXtensive Markup Language. Last checked: 11 October 2007, http://www.w3.org/XML/

XrML, eXtensive rights Markup Language. Last checked: 11 October 2007, http://www.xrml.org

XSD, eXtensible Markup Language Schema, Last checked: 11 October 2007, <http://www.w3.org/ XML/Schema>

Section IV
Strategies and Case Studies

This section is presenting strategies and case studies of the use of digital rights management in organizations and sectors like cultural heritage.

Chapter XI
Digital Rights Management in Organisations:
A Critical Consideration with a Socio–Technical Approach

Dimitra Pappa
National Centre for Scientific Research "Demokritos", Greece

Lefteris G. Gortzis
Telemedicine Unit Department of Medical Physics, University of Patras, Greece

ABSTRACT

With emerging technologies constantly creating new possibilities for organisations to manage their information resources, this chapter proposes a model for designing systems to control access to, and usage of, digital resources in organisations. The authors argue that Digital Rights Management (DRM) is a socio-technical challenge that requires a holistic approach. The resulting socio-technical forces model, titled SYNAPSIS, includes the following interdependent dimensions: Technology, Task, Structure, People, and Organisation External Forces, which act as interrelated forces. The application of the SYNAPSIS model can help identify complex interdependencies among the involved dimensions, as well as their evolution with time. Models, like the one proposed, may provide significant support on the underlying field.

INTRODUCTION

Mapping the Organisational Landscape

With the pace of change and the complexity constantly increasing and compromising productivity and performance, new organisational structures are emerging and new approaches are adopted by modern enterprises, with regards to the way they plan, structure and manage their activities, in order to gain or maintain the competitive advantage. Information technology infrastructures play a significant role in this direction. Computer networking is changing the way people work and the way organisations function, by facilitating the geographic distribution of work, including remote access to and exchange of resources and tele-collaboration (Kiesler & Hinds, 2002). Joint international ventures among companies and global expansion into new markets have become common practice.

Modern companies are drifting away from the conventional model of independent, "all-in-one", business units and more towards dynamically interconnected organisational environments, where companies have one or multiple network identities and complex relationships and dependencies among companies exist. Networking and digital distribution enable the establishment of new business models. Around each company a larger network of partner organisations can thus be formed (Figure 1), including customers, suppliers of raw materials and/or components, providers of low-skill services (outsourced tasks) etc. Often instead of simple contractual relations, organisations are bound together by long-term strategic collaboration agreements. For example, such is the case of automobile manufacturing. While originally car manufacturers relied almost exclusively upon their in-house parts manufacturing for their production, since the late 1970s they began buying complete subassemblies from outside suppliers instead of individual components, to subsequently build around them the auto body (US Department of Commerce, 2006). As a result, today, more than ever, car manufacturers and their suppliers are closely cooperating in the design and manufacture of new cars.

Enterprises in all branches of industry are becoming increasingly customer centric. Robert H. Anderson's vision of the "creative consumer" (Toffler, 1980) implies placing the demands and wishes

Figure 1. Business environment of organisations

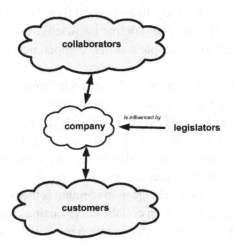

of each single customer at the centre of value creation. According to the mass customisation and personalisation concept, organisation systems, processes and business models should adapt, so that goods and services are produced to meet individual customers' needs "with near mass production efficiency" (Tseng & Jiao, 2001). This involves addressing different issues that evolve around developing, producing, and selling individualised products and services for rather large customer segments. Customers are allowed to define, configure, match or modify their individual solution from of a list of options and/or pre-defined components. Therefore, consumers can become an integral part of the value creation process with strong ties to company operations (Figure 1).

In today's dynamic business environment, an organisation has to adapt to change, constantly re-aligning organisational systems and processes, in order to gain or maintain its competitive advantage. New approaches are needed for companies to effectively plan, structure and manage their activities to increase productivity and organisational performance. Holstius and Malaska (2004) view business as "a continuous flow of opportunistic, strategic and visionary decisions and their modifications according to situational opportunities and challenges". Companies undergo transition in order to manage change.

Modern organisations are increasingly **knowledge-driven**. Knowledge is a valuable asset and its effective management emerges as a critical prerequisite for the long-term success and survivability of modern companies (Stewart, 1998). Long term excellence calls for new and effective ways for handling knowledge assets. Sveiby et al. (1997) argue that the information and knowledge assets of an organisation are strictly linked with its "capacity to act". The effective management of knowledge can offer significant competitive advantages to organisations. Knowledge Management (KM) is defined as the "systematic, explicit, and deliberate building, renewal, and application of knowledge to maximise an enterprise's knowledge-related effectiveness and returns from its knowledge assets" (Liebowitz and Beckman, 1998).

Information Technologies (IT) facilitate knowledge creation and transfer. Nowadays, large efforts are made for capturing and documenting organisational knowledge. The term "knowledge" is widely used, yet there is little agreement with regards to its precise definition (Biggam, 2001). Additionally, the terms "information" and "knowledge" are often mistakenly used interchangeably, as also the terms "data" and "information" are often considered synonyms.

Davenport & Prusak (1998) describe data as "a set of discrete, objective facts existing in symbolic form that have not been interpreted". Data is usually organised into structured records, but only when it is shaped and formed with the addition of context, it can become information. Information is "data that have been shaped by humans into a meaningful and useful form" (Laudon & Laudon 1998). Knowledge is deterministic. Gupta, Sharma & Hsu (2004) define knowledge as "the full utilisation of information and data coupled with the potential of people's skills, competencies, ideas, intuitions, commitments and motivations".

The ways an institution is using to organise and store its information are changing rapidly, as emerging technologies constantly create new options (e.g. data warehouses, relational databases). Elaborate **Enterprise Content Management (ECM)** systems provide the means to capture, manage, store, preserve, and deliver content and documents related to organisational processes. ECM systems facilitate the management of corporate documents and other types of information for use internally as well as externally with a company's business partners, customers, regulators, and the general public.

A particularly important aspect of knowledge management is the protection of **organisational information** and **knowledge assets**. In the modern collaborative business landscape, knowledge flows often transcend organisational boundaries. Knowledge creation is a collaborative process that is embedded in all business activities of an organisation. New knowledge is produced through the interactions amongst people or between people and their environment, rather than by an individual operating alone (Nonaka & Takeuchi, 1995; Nonaka et al., 2000) Value is created by knowledge generated and exchanged not only within the company, but also between the company and its business associates and customers. As a result, knowledge management and rights protection approaches are conditioned by and need be adapted to both organisation-internal restrictions and inter-organisational relationships.

A large percentage of the data global organisations collect, use and exchange, often in real-time, is considered to be confidential information. This includes operational data related to business-critical activities (such as customer behaviour analysis, business process performance measurements etc), employee data (e.g. competency profiles, healthcare records etc) and customer information, as well as information related to the organisation's core competency (intellectual property, such as state-of-the-art, patented know-how etc).

Organisations, as **rights holders** to the intellectual property they own, have a legitimate expectation that they can authorise the exploitation of this asset, but also need to have the means to define, manage, and track rights to digital content. An accidental or malicious disclosure of regulated data can interrupt business operations, cost time, effort and money to amend, affect the organisation's profitability and even threaten its market viability. Similarly, content misuse can cause grave implications.

Therefore, mechanisms, policies and procedures are necessary so as to protect data confidentiality and integrity and to ensure its "proper" use in every phase of the information management process. Access privileges to Knowledge Management Systems (KMS) need to be carefully examined, defined and implemented, otherwise the competitive advantage or even the existence of a company may be jeopardised. Increasingly sophisticated technologies are emerging in the field of **Digital Rights Management** (DRM) and are used to control access to and usage of digital resources and to enforce applying restrictions. DRM includes "all technologies and/or processes that are applied to digital content to describe and identify it and/or to define, apply and enforce usage rules in a secure manner" (WIPO, 2003). DRM deals with the persistent protection of content, tracking access and operations on content, the definition and implementation of contract rights to content (rights licensing). The term "Digital", as included in the DRM, denotes the medium of the material over which the rights exist.

A DRM framework essentially comprises four different entities: the **digital content** to be protected, the **holder of rights** to this content, the **end-user**, to whom a right to "consume" this content is granted, and the **usage rights** that determine what the end-user can do with the content. Aim of DRM is to concretely identify these entities and determine and implement the relationships among them.

In the quest for performance improvement, business processes in modern organisations are constantly under scrutiny and often subject to modifications or reengineering. DRM systems, put in place to protect information and manage **Intellectual Property Rights** (IPR), throughout the life-cycle of business knowledge creation, need to keep up with organisational development efforts and respond to the frequent changes and the complexity of the corporate environment. Typically the life-cycle of knowledge involves the following stages: Acquisition, Identification, Retention, Utilisation, Development, Sharing/distribution **(Probst et al. 1999). Technologies associated with the life-cycle of digital content include: Database management systems, content storage systems, indexing and search technologies, metadata technologies, workflow engines etc.**

The effects of digital content misuse can be severe. Therefore, instead of identifying and fixing DRM problems as they arise, a proactive approach is needed during the system and service design phase, including a thorough planning of DRM measures based on an in depth investigation of potential risks to content. In addition, since organisations go through constant changes, which often largely affect their knowledge-assets (more specifically the physical artefacts, in which the information is embedded, as well as the acquisition, management, processing and distribution of critical knowledge across the community of stakeholders), it is imperative for DRM solutions to be flexible and allow for continuous improvement. In order to be effective, DRM measures should be able to support organisational change and adjust to a changing operations scenario, recognising and adapting to opportunities and/or potential threats as they emerge. Therefore, in order to guarantee quality of service, the performance of DRM systems should be under constant monitoring and revision.

In the following sections we look into the implications of effective DRM systems design and propose a holistic socio-technical model for implementing DRM in organisations.

BACKGROUND

In principle, DRM is about "**management**", i.e. about defining and managing the policies under which protected content will be made available and about ensuring that these policies are respected. Policies should reflect all **rights** linked to the material.

According to the socio-technical perspective on organisational change and development, organisations are complex **socio-technical entities,** influenced by both social and technological determinants. Knowledge management is recognised as the continued interaction between technologies, techniques and people (Bhatt, 2001). The **socio-technical systems (STS) theory** (Trist and Bamforth, 1951; Mumford 1995), recognising the existence of a two-way relationship between people and machines, argues that the effective design of technology-based work processes can only be achieved through the simultaneous optimisation of both technical and social elements. Similarly, Information Systems (IS) employed by organisations involve both technical and social elements (e.g., Hirschheim 1985; Eason, 1988). Their implementation presents technical challenges, yet is closely linked to and driven by business priorities and legal concerns. Technology, as well as social forces and the organisational context play a role in shaping the produced outcomes. Data protection and rights management, being related to knowledge, cannot be regarded as a mere technical issue, because this entails the risk of other important dimensions being neglected. Instead, a thorough investigation of the entire socio-technical system is required while developing a corporate IS. This is imperative also in the case of turnkey systems, which need to be adapted to better serve organisational needs, in accordance to applying legal requirements.

In the past, various approaches have been proposed for the management of digital rights. Dhamija and Wallenberg (2003) suggest that the following questions are important to ask with respect to the evaluation of DRM systems: (i) Is the proposal technically feasible? (ii) What are the incentives to circumvent legal and technical protections for all parties in the transaction? (iii) What is the burden of monitoring for compliance in the system, and on which parties does this burden fall? (iv) What is the efficiency of the collection and distribution of funds from consumers to rights holders? (v) What are the impacts on user privacy and fair use? vi) What is the feasibility of legal enforcement, both domestically and internationally? Dhamija and Wallenberg compare and contrast the proposals for DRM along the following dimensions: technical feasibility, incentives to cheat, burden of monitoring, efficiency of collection and distribution of funds, privacy, fair use, feasibility of legal enforcement and flexibility. These dimensions are usually interrelated, making comprehensive evaluations difficult.

In the context of eGovernment Abie et al. (2004) propose an integrated DRM research framework for policy, privacy, security, trust and risk management for DRM, though the establishment of a virtual competence centre that will provide a flexible context of technologies and concepts. Their framework builds on the collaboration of experts from four different areas: Technology, Business, Social science & Ethics and Legal & Regulatory.

In a study of the different aspects of DRM in the field of eLearning (i.e. issues related to sharing teaching and learning resources, publication and digital library management, providing access to research data, and using resources from third party sources etc) the UK Joint Information Services Committee (JISC) adopts the **Six Stage Model** of rights expressions and licence requirements (JISC, 2004). This model proposes a framework for action for DRM that views rights management as a step-by-step process, featuring tasks for policy creation and projection. The steps include:

- Recognition of rights (recognising the rights that need to be expressed)
- Assertion of rights (asserting rights in relation to the shared content)
- Expression of rights   (digital rights expression languages (DRELs))
- Dissemination of rights (describing the applying rights for every resource, e.g. legal framework, licensing schemes)
- Exposure of rights (disseminating license information for every resource, i.e. making potential users of content aware of the rights information associated with this resource)
- Enforcement of rights (taking protective measures and monitoring use, e.g. through authentication /authorisation)

In principle, all scholars acknowledge that technology is the common denominator in tackling DRM issues. Nonetheless, it is evident that it is not sufficient for DRM measures to be based on selected individual dimensions (e.g. technical, or social, etc.), and usually it is necessary to pursue the complex processes that contribute to outcomes (to ask why those outcomes come about) and consider relationships between dimensions, individual characteristics, organisational characteristics, and effects among them.

SYNAPSIS: A NEW SOCIO-TECHNICAL FORCES MODEL

A **holistic framework** is needed in order to recognise data flows, including hidden data patterns, embedded in workflows and business processes (Russell et al, 2004), to then be able to develop appropriate DRM policies and measures and to successfully address the changing operating conditions. Ultimate objective of this effort is the semi-automation of this process.

We argue that effective DRM systems need to take into account both technical and social aspects. In order to draw an accurate picture of the situation to be addressed and define a suitable solution, technological options need to be examined in context. Technology needs to be positioned in relationship to the tasks to be carried out, the people involved and the organisational structure. Overlooking a set of indicators or failing to balance the four dimensions may jeopardise the success of the DRM system.

In this chapter we discuss and investigate a holistic framework for the development of value added DRM solutions using as basis Leavitt's diamond. In his effort to analyse organisational change, Leavitt

Figure 2. The Leavitt diamond, 1965

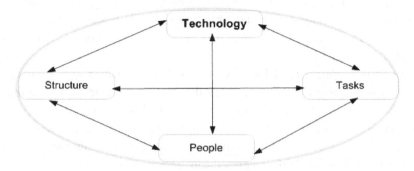

Figure 3. The SYNAPIS model

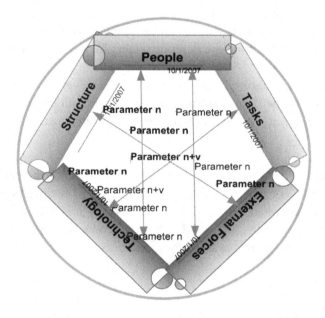

(1965) proposed the classification of organisations as a four-dimensional diamond (Figure 2), in which Task, Technology, People, and Structure are interrelated and mutually adjusting.

Leavitt argued that when one dimension is changed, the impact of the innovation is often balanced by the other components (compensatory or retaliatory change). Consequently, while planning a change, a holistic examination of all aspects is required.

Similarly, when designing a DRM system, an integrated view over a number of parameters is required, so as to understand their interdependencies. The external business environment, as determined by market conditions and related decisions of regulatory and normative authorities can play a significant role. For example, DRM measures have to comply with intellectual property laws that provide a framework for protecting different forms of subject matter (copyright, patent, trademark, industrial design rights, trade secret etc).

In light of the above, we believe that the Leavitt model provides a good starting point for the development of an effective DRM design framework. Yet, Leavitt's methodology builds on a more introvert view of the organisation. External influences are considered indirectly and only after they have been assimilated to the organisation's structure, tasks, people and/or technology. Instead, effective planning calls for a more proactive approach that will guarantee timely feedback. For this reason one additional dimension needs to be introduced, in order to better capture the influence of the business environment and the effect of the interactions with other organisations, regulatory authorities etc and the market in general. The resulting **socio-technical forces model,** titled **SYNAPSIS** (Figure 3) includes the following interdependent dimensions: **Technology**, **Task**, **Structure** (including partnerships**), People** (actors), and organisation **External Forces,** which act as interrelated forces.

External "collaborators" and "customers" (Figure 1) fall under the People dimension, together with the personnel of the organisation. The influence of regulatory and normative authorities ("legislators" in Figure 1) is taken into consideration under External Forces. This dimension also includes market forces etc.

In the following sections we investigate DRM from each of the aforementioned dimensions and highlight crucial parameters and/or requirements that shape the solution.

Technology Dimension

Information represents a vital asset for organisations, which nowadays is usually captured in digital form and managed using digital means. Digital content should be protected during the entire life-cycle from its creation to the time it becomes obsolete and is destroyed. Nowadays, the security policy of a large organisation comprises many elements (mail, WAN and remote-access systems, and intranet) and many points of enforcement, often controlled by different administrative entities. DRM activities may comprise policies in servers set to block the forwarding of sensitive email by its employees, the copying and distributing of electronic material by its customers (e.g. audiovisual content) etc.

DRM-conscious system and service design implies having a clear understanding of the technology requirements, solutions, and obstacles for any given application scenario.

Central to DRM measures and solutions are the topics of privacy, policy, security, trust management, risk management, protection mechanisms, and information representation semantics. These solutions should guarantee security, privacy, safety, and quality of data and processes throughout the entire life-cycle of content, including both the communication and the application phase.

DRM stand-alone and/or add-on software modules should allow for the unambiguous identification and description of intellectual property, including the rights and permissions associated with it.

Data protection mechanisms used for the identification of original content include **watermarking** and **fingerprinting. Encryption** techniques (e.g. PKI infrastructure, security tokens etc) can protect the confidentiality of exchanged information, making it "unreadable" to anyone except its intended recipient. **Digital signatures** allow users to verify the integrity and authenticity of content or software and identify third party modifications.

Depending on the application domain and specific constraints that may apply, Enterprise IS can range from providing the maximum possible privilege for accessing data and services to enforcing the strongest restrictions. With regards to "off–the-shelf" products, this translates into highly permissive applications in which security rights can be determined by configuration.

On the application level, XML technologies can play a significant role in rights management and overall data protection (content description and rights expression languages).

The Security Assertion Markup Language (SAML) is an XML standard for exchanging authentication and authorisation information. SAML defines XML-based assertions and protocols, bindings, and profiles, allowing business entities to make assertions regarding the identity, attributes, and entitlements of a subject (an entity that is often a human user) to other entities, such as a partner company or another enterprise application. SAML is a product of the OASIS Security Services Technical Committee.

OASIS has developed the eXtensible Access Control Markup Language (**XACML**) for the expression of authorisation policies against objects. It is a declarative access control policy language implemented in XML and a processing model, describing how to interpret the policies.

Other initiatives in the area include the **EPAL** (Enterprise Privacy Authorization Language), a formal language for writing enterprise privacy policies to govern data handling practices in IT systems according to fine-grained positive and negative authorization rights. EPAL was submitted to the World Wide Web Consortium (W3C) by IBM. It is used for exchanging privacy policy in a structured format between applications or enterprises, supporting the ability to encode an enterprise's privacy-related data-handling policies and practices and providing a language that can be imported and enforced by a privacy-enforcement system.

The **Digital Signature Service Core Protocols, Elements, and Bindings** specification was published by the OASIS Digital Signature Services (DSS) Technical Committee in October 2005. The document defines XML request/response protocols for signing and verifying XML documents and other data. Through these protocols a client can send documents to a server and receive back a signature on the documents; or send documents and a signature to a server, and receive back an answer on whether the signature verifies the documents. The DSS Core specifications provide the basic protocols and elements which are adapted to support specific use cases in the DSS profiles.

Information and Content Exchange (ICE) is an XML-based protocol used for content syndication via the Internet. By using XML both sender and receiver have an agreed-upon language in which to communicate.

XrML (eXtensible Rights Markup Language) is a rights specification language developed by Content-Guard and standardised as the Rights Expression Language (REL) for MPEG-21 (defined in ISO/IEC 21000-5). The MPEG-21 standard (ISO 21000.) developed by the Moving Picture Experts Group defines an open framework for multimedia applications. In this context a REL is used for the implementation of Intellectual Property Management & Protection (IPMP), i.e. the MPEG equivalent of DRM).

New industry initiative such as the Trusted Computing Group (TCG), which is supported by several hardware developers, is proposing a new model where security becomes an essential service built into the IT infrastructure. The Trusted Computing Group (TCG) develops and promotes open, vendor-neutral, industry standard specifications for **Trusted Computing** (TC) building blocks and software interfaces across multiple platforms. Trusted Computing technologies use a combination of hardware and software on specific microprocessor-based devices (e.g. PCs, PDAs, mobile phones, etc) to help enforce the protection of content. The word "trust" denotes the access and permissions that one entity (i.e. application, system, or user) has with another. All information exchanged between trusted entities can be encrypted and integrity-checked in order to make it tamperproof and protect if from network sniffing or man-in-the-middle attacks (Oltsik, 2007).

Modern information and communication technologies have enabled the emergence of distributed and extended organisations, with staff residing at multiple locations and with business applications being made available across corporate wide area networks and where remote access to key systems and data is possible. DRM is affected by the resulting ubiquity of digital content. In developing a DRM framework for a geographically distributed organisation, it is thus of paramount importance to take into consideration the limitations and inherent risks of the information and communication infrastructures. Openness and interoperability are mandatory also on a security services design level, in order to achieve seamless interconnection and cooperation.

The emergence of Web services technologies has allowed for the loose-coupling of applications within organizations, across enterprises, and across the Internet in a language-neutral, platform-independent way. In this context, OASIS is elaborating a WS-SecurityPolicy specification. The Web Services Security Policy Language (**WS-SecurityPolicy**) specification indicates the policy assertions which apply to Web Services Security: SOAP Message Security, WS-Trust, and WS-SecureConversation. Web Services Trust Language (**WS-Trust**) uses the secure messaging mechanisms of WS-Security to define additional primitives and extensions for security token exchange to enable the issuance and dissemination of credentials within different trust domains.

Grid technologies are also expected to play an important role in the corporate sector, as they provide the means for a flexible, secure, coordinated resource sharing among dynamic collections of individuals, institutions, and resources (Foster et al., 2001). The underlying principles of the Grid are virtualisation and dynamic provisioning of resources across organisational boundaries, forming temporary Virtual Organisations to solve specific problems. Although initially viewed as an enabler of e-Science (computational Grid), the Grid is beginning to exploit technologies developed for Web Services and the Semantic Web (Goble and De Roure, 2002). The Grid Security Infrastructure (**GSI**) specification allows for secret, tamper-proof communication between software in a grid computing environment, using digital signature technology for authentication.

Task Dimension

DRM is closely linked to business processes and as such should conform to and support the implementation of overarching business imperatives.

Cross-organisational border content exchanges often come across a patchwork of IS and database implementations, which makes access to services and retrieval of data from repositories a challenging area. IS integration, calls for the adoption of common standards and the development of communication interfaces. All operations need to be secure and transparent and guided by well defined policies.

Furthermore, in the extended business environment, **cross-organisational workflows** can emerge. Hence, workflow concepts are applicable for both intra-organisational applications, as also for inter-organisational collaboration and commercial exchanges in the B2B domain. Organisation-internal processes need to be aligned inter-organisationally for the duration of the enactment of a business transaction.

Web Services technologies allow for the loose-coupling of IS and the implementation of application-level collaboration procedures on top of interacting Web Services. Composite services that may span multiple organisational domains, can be produced from the joining together of basic Web Services. Service-oriented Business Process Integration can thus support both external Business-to-Business (B2B) and internal Enterprise Application Integration (EAI) efforts.

A number of XML-based standards have been developed for creating business processes from multiple Web services, formalising the specification of Web services, their flow composition and execution. Three main viewpoints can be distinguished, namely the orchestration, the behavioural interface and choreography. Orchestration languages like OASIS' Business Process Execution Language (**BPEL4WS** or **BPEL**) are used to specify business processes and business interaction protocols, by defining flows of control and data between Web Service operations (end-point approach). The choreography model adopts a more global approach, looking into the interactions of all involved users, applications and services. W3C's Web Services Choreography Definition Language (**WS-CDL**) provides a set of rules about how different components should act together and in what sequence for a flexible, systemic view of the process.

The Electronic Business using eXtensible Markup Language (**ebXML**) is a global electronic business standard, sponsored by OASIS and UN/CEFACT, whose mission is to define an open, XML-based framework that will enable the global use of electronic business information in an interoperable, secure, and consistent manner by all trading partners. The **ebXML Business Process Specification Schema** is a standard for representing models for collaborating e-business public processes to allow businesses to find each other and conduct business using well-defined messages and standard business processes.

Similarly, the XML-based **RosettaNet** standard defines message guidelines, business processes interface and implementation frameworks for interactions between companies. Mostly addressed is the supply chain area, but also manufacturing, product and material data and service processes are in scope.

While typically the focus of workflow management is put on the process aspect of business processes, particular attention should be placed on the management and handling of the different kinds of business data involved in the process.

Van der Aalst and van Hee (2002) define a workflow on three dimensions: the case dimension, the process dimension, and the resource dimension. **Workflow Management systems** (WfMSs) rely strongly on business information in order to make valid control flow decisions. A uniform and transparent access method to all related business data stored in any data source is hence required (e.g. XML-based data wrappers).

Russell et al. (2004) have studied the use of data patterns for the modelling of the data aspect of workflow management systems. They concluded that the data representation in different workflow tools and business process modelling paradigms has a number of common characteristics and identified 39 different recurring **data patterns**, which can be divided into four distinct groups.

Data employed in workflows should be described, represented and processed uniformly across the involved IS. Seamless integration with external systems can be achieved by exchange of process and application data in XML format.

The Electronic Data Interchange (**EDI**) standards for structuring information is used to formally guide the electronic exchange of information between "trading partners", i.e. between and within businesses, organisations, government entities and other groups. EDI covers the transmission, message flow, document format, and software used to interpret the documents.

The use of standardised languages to describe privacy and security policies can facilitate seamless interoperability on a DRM level.

People Dimension

In order to be effective, organisational content and services should be made available to the right people, at the right place, at the right time and in the correct form. Communities may form around tasks requiring collaboration (e.g. communities for collaborative co-design). These may span functional boundaries (traditional approach) and/or extend beyond organisational structures, in order to create common knowledge and value as part of an interactive learning process (Gibbert, Leibold, & Probst, 2002). Community members interact intensively on problem solving in the framework of a shared work environment with similar tools and joint sources of information.

Content is intended for consumption by specific individuals, groups or organisations. Only authorised users are allowed to create, store, access, manipulate and communicate information objects within or across organisational boundaries, depending on their business role and authorisation rights. Rights are defined through corporate regulations, existing law and contracts. Rights can be acquired automatically (e.g. authorisation rights pertaining to a specific business role are automatically passed to the individual holding this position) or distributed (e.g. by contract).

Among the aims of DRM is to manage rights holder's relationships, ensure the **privacy of personal information** (what personal information can be shared with whom and under which conditions), enforce **accountability** or allow for user **anonymity** (depending on the application setting) etc.

Different combinations of access and usage rights are possible, ranging from unrestricted access and unrestricted modification rights (GNU-licensed public content), to restricted access and limited usage rights (e.g. confidential content, access granted to authorised individuals only).

Security infrastructures need to be put in place in order to control the movement of digital information within and outside the user domain (**access control**) and protect content from unauthorised distribution and usage (**usage control**).

Therefore the information management plan of an organisation needs to include an **authentication and authorisation framework** to assure that content is solely used by the intended users within the extended organisation and in the accordance to the applying usage rules. DRM solutions linked together as part of a specific organisational environment need to be interoperable and provide a guaranteed end-to-end quality-of-service. Establishing standards-based infrastructures emerges as an imperative requirement. Ideally, a DRM system should be flexible with regards to the definition of content protection rules and entirely transparent to the users of this content.

Structure Dimension

The day-to-day business praxis and longer-term strategic planning activities of an organisation increasingly rely on the collection, sharing and distribution of information within its extended business environment (Figure 1). Sensitive information that relates to the organisation's internal operations, its transactions with business partners, customers, and regulators and the market conditions is regularly exchanged among involved stakeholders.

The establishment of trust and confidence between consumers and providers of services and content implies the setting up of appropriate **trust management processes** to ensure user privacy. Furthermore, a common policy language is required, in order to allow the organisation to manage the enforcement of a "corporate" security policy, across all organisational units and their respective IS.

The exchange of digital content within the organisation is conditioned by its **organisational structure** and the **administrative procedures** that are in place.

On the other hand, cross-border content exchange between the organisation and third-party collaborators and/or customers is defined on a **contractual** basis. This gives rise to business models involving the sale of physical artefacts, whose only value is the embedded information. Consumer rights should be clearly defined and implemented in the DRM framework, so as to avoid tensions between the two parties.

A DRM scheme serves a threefold purpose, namely to:

- Define rights for any given piece of protected content (i.e. establish a copyright),
- Manage the distribution of the copyrighted content and,
- Monitor and control what the end-user can do with that content once it has been distributed.

In practice, DRM systems seek to control viewing, copying, printing, altering etc of digital content.

Rights specifications languages (e.g. XrML) can facilitate the definition of rules and the exchange of user-rights related information. This is of particular importance when digital content is transferred across different IS between partner-organisations.

A common policy language is required in order to allow the organisation to manage the enforcement of its security policy across organisational entities and ISs.

The organisational structure and other circumstances that may affect human interaction may be the source of risk for sensitive digital content, and as such should be taken into consideration is typically influenced (situational trust), beliefs and inclinations (human centric trust), during the design of the DRM framework.

Technological advances in the area of information and communication technologies (ICT) create new distribution channels and lead to new Business Models for networked delivery. For example, the advent of peer-to-peer networking has made the process of making content available on the Internet even more straightforward for the individual user, and facilitated the unauthorised distribution of material. DRM frameworks had to adjust to this new reality.

External Forces Dimension

Market conditions influence business decisions and shape corporate strategies and partnerships with third parties, including both customers and external collaborators. New **business models** have emerged following the advent of novel media, such as the Internet, which have impacted the methods of doing business and generating revenue of modern companies (e.g. Internet broadcasting services as part of Internet commerce). Other tried-and-true models are placed under scrutiny and are being reinvented under the light of the new technologies (e.g. online auctions). Internet business models continue to evolve, constantly producing new and interesting variations. The mutability of the business environment results in a dynamic set of partnerships, rich in **rights transactions**. To a large extent, the rights to be transferred by the rights holders (i.e. the organisation) to the end-user of some digital content are negotiated and determined in the context of this dynamic business environment.

Rights holders have a legitimate expectation that they can authorise the exploitation of the asset they own, which needs to be weighted against the expectations of the intended user, in the context of the actual market and societal conditions. All involved stakeholders, (staff, employers, suppliers etc) need to be aware of who the rights holders are, which rights are concerned (e.g. copyright and moral rights), as well as the extent to which some rights might be relaxed to permit certain uses.

The World Intellectual Property Organisation (WIPO) describes intellectual property as the legal rights which result from intellectual activity in the industrial, scientific, literary and artistic fields. Intellectual property can be divided into two main branches: **Industrial property**, which includes inventions (patents), trademarks, industrial designs, and geographic indications of source; and **Copyright**, which relates to artistic creations, i.e. literary and artistic works such as novels, poems and plays, films, musical works, artistic works such as drawings, paintings, photographs and sculptures, and architectural designs (WIPO, 2004). Governmental actions (i.e. laws and regulations) set strict rules with regards to content protection, so as to safeguarding creators and other producers of intellectual goods and services.

Copyright is a set of exclusive rights regulating the use of a particular expression of an idea or information and not the content itself. Unlike copyright, protection of inventions covers any case of use of an invention without the authorisation of the owner. Inventions represent new solutions to technical problems and as such are considered to be "ideas".

Innovations in the area of ICT have added new challenges to the traditional regime of IPRs. In particular, the complexity and jurisdictional issues relating to the utilisation of the Internet are drastically challenging the IPR regime. Emerging cases of conflict of law call for the international harmonisation of IPR legislation. The 1995 World Trade Organisation (WTO) TRIPS Agreement is an international treaty for rights holders who are distributing their content through the means of e-Commerce, including via DRM schemes. It provides protection and enforcement for various types of intellectual property rights, including copyrights, patents, trademarks and trade secrets etc.

Legislation defines the context in which rights holders can assert their rights in a form that is defendable under law (copyright, moral rights, permitted uses and exclusions). Copyright and other applicable laws form the **legal context** in which DRM systems are established. For example, copyright laws allow copyright owners to prohibit others from making some uses of the work in question, such as copying, distributing or making a derivative work.

DRM systems should facilitate the implementation of these restrictions and permit end-users to make only what is defined as "**fair use**" of a given work. Consequently, all provisions referring to the protection of digital content owned by the organisation and are included in **contractual agreements** with external collaborators and/or customers, should be also in line with the **existing legal framework and trade policies**. The legal requirements for DRM result from an interaction between legal norms and private sector contractual agreements. Different laws may apply depending on the country in which an action takes place and, putting the emphasis on either side, i.e. strict legal framework or privately defined rules.

In the context of DRM, digital information should be handled in accordance with the applying rules and policies that specify the rights of both the rights holders and the end-users of content. For any given DRM implementation:

- All possible cases of "fair use" should be well-described and encoded as automatic defaults into the DRM system (e.g. using Rights Expression Languages), i.e. license terms, fair use exceptions etc;
- The rights of all involved actors (both organisation internal and external) should be identified and catered for by the DRM system (e.g. protection of personally identifying information)

The implementation of the later requirement is not always straightforward For example, there are certain situations that negate copyright protection in favour of the content user, e.g. copying protected material for personal use, that practically would call for the DRM systems to make difficult "per-case" decisions.

CONCLUSION

The effective management of knowledge can provide significant competitive advantages to organisations, while its misuse can cause severe implications. Aim of DRM is to provide technical means to assure that the rights holders can maintain control of their content. DRM measures are thus embedded in corporate IS and processes.

During the early years of DRM, scholars often failed to address the topic in its entirety, some considering business or legal abstractions without a proper grounding in technology and others focusing too deeply on narrow technologies without providing necessary and useful context. Nowadays it is widely recognised that DRM design is a challenging task, full of constrains that can vary depending on the application environment. Furthermore, it is acknowledged that in each case a framework for policy, privacy, security, trust and risk management for DRM needs to be in place.

DRM is increasingly regarded as a **socio-technical** challenge that requires a holistic examination of several determinants, without overemphasising either the technical capabilities of systems, tools and infrastructures supporting information exchange or the limitations posed by the application framework

DRM solutions design should comprise a detailed investigation of the application environment for the identification of requirements and risks, to allow for the subsequent application of appropriate provisions to fulfil the requirements and controls to eliminate of mitigate the risks. Furthermore, since the external and internal environment of an organisation is in a state of constant change, DRM solutions should be adaptable.

At any time, the application of the hereby discussed **socio-technical forces model** can:

- Provide a holistic view of the complexities that affect IS design, and/or operation by positioning each dimension in a strong relationship with the others (e.g. tasks carried out to the actors participating in these tasks etc).
- Can help monitor the evolution of these variables and their interdependencies over time.
- Support the adaptation and continuous improvement of rights protection schemes.

To ensure its effective application, the dimensions of the socio-technical forces model and their corresponding parameters should be identified, reviewed, and classified simultaneously, to obtain efficiently distributed resources (inputs), to transform them by interactions (services), to eventually produce high quality services (outputs) improving the overall organisational operation (outcomes).

In this sense it is critical for IS designers to overcome the vagueness that characterises specific dimensions interconnections, to identify exactly the relationship between the dimensions and appropriate ways to analyse them.

The wide application of this framework in organisations is expected to demonstrate its value and also provide valuable empirical knowledge and insight to support the future automation of the DRM design process.

FUTURE RESEARCH DIRECTIONS

The need for a functional integration of diverse business environments calls for a holistic approach, in order to identify knowledge objects, recognise data flows and develop appropriate DRM policies and measures.

An integrated vision on information management, including intensive standardisation efforts are required for data collections to become the shared commodity among involved stakeholders. The standardisation of content representation schemes and business workflows can provides a solid base for supporting data integration and facilitate the harmonisation of rights protection solutions. Furthermore, the use of standardised languages to describe privacy and security policies can facilitate seamless interoperability on a DRM level.

A holistic socio-technical approach is required in order to address DRM within the dynamic landscape of modern organisations. It is not sufficient for DRM measures to be based on selected individual criteria. DRM system design needs to pursue the complex processes that contribute to outcomes and consider relationships between dimensions, individual characteristics, organisational characteristics, and effects among them.

The application of the SYNAPSIS socio-technical forces model can help identify complex interdependencies among important variables, as well as their evolution with time. It can thus help provide a timely response to parameters that may influence the effectiveness of the solution (e.g. external factors) by identifying issues as they emerge, assessing their impact and guiding the design or re-design process accordingly.

The systematic application of this framework in enterprises in all branches of industry will provide valuable knowledge to develop **benchmarks** to improve the effectiveness of DRM solutions and lead to a future automatisation of the DRM design process.

REFERENCES

Aalst, W. M. P. van der & Hee, K. van (2002). *Workflow management: Models, methods, and systems.* Cambridge, MA: MIT press.

Abie, H., Bing, J., Blobel, B., Delgado, J., Foyn, B., Karnouskos, S., Pharow, P., Pitkänen, O., & Tzovaras, D. (2004). The need for a digital rights management framework for the next generation of E-Government services. *International Journal of Electronic Government, 1*(1), 8-28.

Avgerou, C. (1993). Information systems for development planning. *International Journal of Information Management, 13,* 260-73.

Bainbridge, D. I. (2006). *Intellectual Property.* 6th edition. Pearson Education

Bhatt, G. D. (2001). Knowledge management in organisations: Examining the interaction between technologies, techniques, and people. *Journal of Knowledge Management, 5*(1), 68-75.

Biggam, J. (2001). Defining knowledge: An epistemological foundation for knowledge management. *Paper presented to 34th Hawaii International Conference on System Sciences.* Hawaii.

Dhamija, R., & Wallenberg, F. (2003). A framework for evaluating digital rights management proposals. *In Proceedings of the First International Mobile IPR Workshop: Rights Management of Information Products on the Mobile Internet.* Helsinki, Finland.

Dana, L. P., Korot, L., & Tovstiga, G. (2005). A cross-national comparison of knowledge management practices. *International Journal of Manpower, 26*(1), 10-22.

Davenport, T. H., & Prusak, L. (1998). Working knowledge: How organisations manage what they know. Boston, MA: Harvard Business School Press.

Eason, K. (1988). *Information technology and organisational change*. London UK: Taylor and Francis.

El Sawy, O. A. (2001). Redesigning enterprise processes for E-Business. Boston MA: McGraw-Hill Irwin.

Figallo, C., & Rhine, N. (2002). *Building the knowledge management network: Best practices, tools, and techniques for putting conversation to work*. New York, NY: John Wiley & Sons, Inc.

Foster, I., Kesselman, C., & Tuecke, S. (2001). The anatomy of the grid: Enabling scalable virtual organizations. *International Journal of High Performance Computing Applications, 15*, 200-222.

Goble, C., & De Roure, D. (2002). The grid: An application of the Semantic Web. *SIGMOD Record, 31*(4).

Goh, A. (2004). Enhancing organisational performance through knowledge innovation: A proposed strategic management framework. *Journal of Knowledge Management Practice*, (5)

Gupta, J. N. D., Sharma, K. S., & Hsu, J. (2003): An overview of knowledge management. In Gupta, J. N. D. (Ed.): *Creating knowledge-based organizations*. Hershey, PA, USA: Idea Group Publishing.

Hirschheim, R. A. (1985). *Office automation: A social and organizational perspective*. New York: John Wiley and sons.

Holstius, K., & Malaska, P. (2004). Advanced strategic thinking. *Visionary management*. Publications of the Turku School of Economics & Business Administration, ISBN: 95-564-187-x

Kiesler, S. & Hinds, P. (Ed.) (2002). *Distributed work*. Cambridge, MA: The MIT Press

Laudon, K. & Laudon, J. (1998). *Information systems and the Internet*, 4th ed., Orlando, FL: Dryden Press.

Leavitt, H. J. (1965). Applied organizational change in industry: Structural, technical, and humanistic approaches. In March, J. (Ed.). *Handbook of Organizations* (pp. 1144-70). Chicago IL: Rand McNally & Co.

Leibold, M., Probst, J. B. & Gibbert, M. (2002). *Strategic management in the knowledge economy*. Wiley, Chichester.

Liebowitz, J., & Beckman, T. (Eds) (1998) *Knowledge organizations: What every manager should know*. Boca Raton, FL: St. Lucie Press.

Mumford, E. (1995). Effective systems design and requirements analysis. London, UK: Macmillan.

Nonaka, I., & Takeuchi, H. (1995). *The knowledge-creating company: How Japanese companies create the dynamics of innovation*. New York, NY: Oxford University Press.

Nonaka, I., Toyama, R., & Konno, N. (2000). SECI, Ba and Leadership: A Unified Model of Dynamic Knowledge Creation. *Long Range Planning, 33*, 5-34.

Oltsik, J. (2007). *The trusted computing group (TCG) storage specification: Securing storage and information lifecycle management.* Enterprise Strategy Group White Paper

Polanyi, M. (1966). *The tacit dimension.* London,UK: Routledge & Kegan Paul.

Probst, G., Raub, S., & Romhardt, K. (1999). Managing knowledge: Building blocks for success. Chicester: Wiley.

Rao, M. (Ed.). (2004). Knowledge management tools and techniques: Practitioners and experts evaluate KM solutions. Burlington, MA: Elservier Butterworth-Heinemann.

Russell, N., Hofstede, A. H. M. ter, Edmond, D., Aalst, & W.M.P. van der (2005). Workflow data patterns: Identification, representation and tool support. In L. Delcambre, C. Kop, H.C. Mayr, J. Mylopoulos, O. Pastor, (Ed.) *24nd International Conference on Conceptual Modeling (ER 2005)* (pp. 353-368) Berlin: Springer-Verlag.

Sproull, L., & Kiesler, S. (1992). *Connections: New ways of working in the networked organization.* Cambridge, MA: The MIT Press.

Sveiby, K. (1997). *The new organizational wealth: Managing and measuring knowledge-based assets.* San Francisco, CA: Berrett Koehler.

Stewart, T. (1999). Intellectual capital: The new wealth of organizations. New York, NY: Bantam Press.

Toffler, A. (1980). The third wave. New York: Bantam Books.

Trist, E. L. & Bamforth, K. W. (1951). Some social and psychological consequences of the longwall method of coal getting. *Human Relations, 4*(1), 3-38.

Tseng, M. M. & Jiao, J. (2001) Mass customization. In G. Salvendy (Ed.) *Handbook of Industrial Engineering* (pp. 684-709), 3rd edition, New York: John Wiley & Sons, Inc.

UK Joint Information Services Committee (JISC)/Intrallect (2004), Digital Rights Management Study and appendices, from www.intrallect.com/drm-study/

UK Joint Information Systems Committee (JISC) Legal Information Service, Web site: http://www.jisclegal.ac.uk/

U.S. Department of Commerce, The International Trade Administration, The American Automotive Industry Supply Chain – In the Throes of a Rattling Revolution, from www.ita.doc.gov/td/auto/domestic/SupplyChain.pdf

Weisburd, S.I. (2004). Handling Intellectual Property Issues in Business Transactions. New |York, NY: Practising Law Institute

World Intellectual Property Organization (WIPO) (2004). WIPO Intellectual Property Handbook: Policy, Law and Use, Geneva CH: WIPO Publications (NO. 489)

World Trade Organisation (WTO). Trade-related aspects of intellectual property rights (TRIPS) agreement, from http://www.wto.org/english/tratop_e/trips_e/trips_e.htm

ADDITIONAL READING

UK Joint Information Services Committee (JISC)/Intrallect (2004), Digital Rights Management Study and appendices, from www.intrallect.com/drm-study/

World Trade Organisation (WTO). Trade-related aspects of intellectual property rights (TRIPS) agreement, from http://www.wto.org/english/tratop_e/trips_e/trips_e.htm

U.S. Department of Commerce, The International Trade Administration, The American Automotive Industry Supply Chain – In the Throes of a Rattling Revolution, from www.ita.doc.gov/td/auto/domestic/SupplyChain.pdf

Kiesler, S. & Hinds, P. (Ed.) (2002). *Distributed work*. Cambridge, MA: The MIT Press

Avgerou, C. (1993). Information systems for development planning. *International Journal of Information Management, 13*, 260-73.

Chapter XII
An Advanced Watermarking Application for the Copyright Protection and Management of Digital Images of Cultural Heritage Case Study:
"Ulysses"

Georgios Stilios
TEI of Ionian Islands, Greece

Dimitrios K. Tsolis
University of Patras, Greece

ABSTRACT

The issue addressed in this chapter is the design, implementation, and evaluation of a watermarking application, especially focused on the protection of cultural heritage. The application described here is focusing on protecting digital surrogates of high-quality photographs of artifacts, monuments and sites, and on countering copyright infringement of online digital images. This is achieved by the integration of an innovative watermarking method to a specialized and usable user–interface. The system is specifically applied to "Ulysses," the Official Cultural Portal of the Hellenic Ministry of Culture (HMC). The chapter is structured in 7 main sections where an overview of the issue is presented, the watermarking method is analyzed, and the user-interface is described in detail. Finally, an evaluation of the overall watermarking application is presented and specific on-site implementation issues are analyzed.

INTRODUCTION

The Origins of the Problem

The great value of cultural content is by now well recognized as it relates directly not only to culture in general but to important and vast markets, mainly Education, Tourism, Entertainment and Research. Wide access and delivery of valuable content raise several critical issues, pertaining to management, protection and exploitation of digitized cultural content. These include the critical problem of IPR (Intellectual Property Rights), protection and the unauthorized use and exploitation of digital data ("electronic theft"). Besides economical and other implications, such problems create considerable skepticism to cultural organizations and individual content owners. As a result content of great educational and economical value is often held secret and private.

The issue is gradually becoming critical mostly due to the following reasons:

1. Advances in technology have improved the ability to reproduce, distribute, manage and publish information (CSTB, 99). Reproduction costs are much lower for both right holders (content owners) and infringers, and digital copies are perfect replicas. The average computer owner today can easily do the kind and the extent of copying that would have required a significant investment a few years ago. The computer networks have changed the economics of distribution. Networks enable sending multimedia content worldwide, cheaply and at a high speed. As a consequence, it is easier and less expensive both for a rights holder to distribute a work and for an individual to make and distribute unauthorized copies. Finally, the World Wide Web has altered at a fundamental way the publication of information, allowing everyone to be a publisher with worldwide reach. The variety of documents and multimedia content of all sorts on the Web demonstrate that many people worldwide are making use of that capability. This is affecting the Cultural Sector too.

2. The information structure has been integrated into everyday life, affecting directly the intellectual property legislation (House, 98). Today, actions that can be taken casually by the average citizen – downloading files, forwarding information found on the Web – can at times be violations of intellectual property laws. Others as such as making copies of information for private use may require difficult interpretation of the law simply to determine their legality. Consequently, individuals in their daily lives have the capability and the opportunity to access and copy vast amounts of digital information, yet lack a clear picture of what is acceptable or legal. On the other hand, the necessary amendments of the copyright legislation in several cases do not cope with the entirety of the problem, resulting in certain legislative weaknesses.

The issue of copyright infringement in the Cultural Heritage sector is mainly observed to the commercial exploitation of digital images. Some prevailing examples of copyright infringement especially for digital images of Cultural Heritage could be viewed in many corporate web sites, where the unauthorized commercial exploitation of digital images is conducted in an every day basis. This improper exploitation of digital images is proving the lack of awareness of both content holders and content users.

Legislation and Key Documents: Summary

The protection of intellectual property rights or copyright have both economic, social and cultural aspects and this is proved through a World Wide political will for resolution expressed by Laws, Directives and Provisions. Most of them are aiming at protecting the artistic creation in general, in which Cultural Heritage is included.

In the United States the most important initiative is the "Digital Millennium Copyright Act". The legislation implements two 1996 World Intellectual Property Organization (WIPO) treaties: the WIPO Copyright Treaty and the WIPO Performances and Phonograms Treaty. The Act includes:

- The "Online Copyright Infringement Liability Limitation Act," which creates limitations on the liability of online service providers for copyright infringement when engaging in certain types of activities.
- The "Computer Maintenance Competition Assurance Act," creates an exemption for making a copy of a computer program or object by activating a computer for purposes of maintenance or repair.

In addition it contains several miscellaneous provisions, relating to distance education, the exceptions in the Copyright Act for libraries and for making ephemeral recordings, "webcasting" of sound recordings on the Internet, and the applicability of collective bargaining agreement obligations in the case of transfers of rights in motion pictures (Cox, 02).

European initiatives formulate a political will for protecting copyright in the Cultural Sector. The significance of the issue has been justified in European Commissions Directives and laws. The creation of the European single market and the fast development of new technologies made it necessary for the Community to create legal protection for copyright. Accordingly, since 1991 a number of directives aimed at protecting intellectual and artistic creativity have been adopted. In December 1997 the Commission presented a proposal for a Directive on copyright and selected rights in the Information Society (COM(97)628) aiming to extend copyright protection to new forms of technology in the digital area such as Internet, CD-Roms, CDs and Digital Video Discs. The European Parliament in the first reading on 10 February 1999 adopted many amendments to the proposal many of which the Commission included in its amended proposal. Based on this proposal the Member States have been invited to harmonize their national laws towards a common legislative framework across Europe. Recently in Greece the Intellectual Property Rights legislation has been harmonized both with the Digital Millennium Copyright Act and the Directives of the European Parliament.

The most important recent amendments of the legislation are focusing on the next issues:

- In the digital world, even the most routine access to information invariably involves making a copy, as well as copies of copies, and this can be done easily without proper authorization. Consequently the electronic distribution and sale of digitized material presents considerable risks for the Cultural Sector. The amendments are aiming at creating legal exceptions for the inevitable copying of a digital work only for distribution over computer networks.
- The technical means for copyright protection and management are being recently identified and protected within the legislative framework. Watermarking, encryption and other technologies are legally protected and every action against them (e.g. attack to the watermark of a digital image) is

legally prosecuted. This is enabling the content and copyright owners to legally demand financial measures if their protection systems (e.g. watermarks) are proved to be attacked by individuals.

Technological Solutions for Copyright Protection: Overview

The technical part of the copyright protection of digital objects problem is focusing on how to provide access without giving up control. Many solutions have been proposed relying on a combination of encryption, watermarking and rights management software. Encryption encodes information so it can be accessed only with the appropriate key. Watermarking is usually embedding an imperceptible key within the digital data itself. The rights – management software enables fine-grain control of access, specifying such thing as the number of accesses permitted and whether the material may be printed (Katzenbeisser, 00). A complete technological schema which incorporates all possible means for copyright protection includes:

- Security and integrity of operating systems and computer networks.
- Rights – management programming languages and software.
- Encryption of transferred data.
- Watermarking of multimedia content (digital images, sound, video and computer graphics).

The above generic schema is applying, amongst other, to the Cultural sector too and provides the basis of an efficient copyright protection and management of digital objects.

"ULYSSES": THE OFFICIAL WEB PORTAL OF THE HELLENIC CULTURE

Technical Specifications

"Ulysses" is one of the largest and most highly acclaimed cultural web sites worldwide. As the primary WWW site of the Hellenic Ministry of Culture (HMC), "Ulysses" provides bilingual information on almost every aspect of Greek culture through 15,000 web pages with rich multimedia content. Sections on Greek cultural heritage and contemporary cultural creation are available, including hundreds of archaeological sites, museums and monuments, cultural organizations, exhibitions, special issues. Numerous international awards from established organizations have been received, as well as broad public acceptance. The number of "Ulysses" visitors exceeds a monthly average of 100,000 guests, 85% of whom live abroad. "Ulysses" has been used in education by schools from various countries, including Greece, the US and Germany. On-line since 1995, "Ulysses" has been established as the most effective ambassador of Greek Culture on the Internet. "Ulysses" is constantly expanding in content as well as in services, including:

- An interactive cultural map of Greece
- Multilingual full text search system
- On-line access to database-supported volatile information, such as cultural activities, press releases, etc.
- A subject catalogue on cultural sites from all over the world

- Detailed coverage and special reviews of cultural events

Especially focusing on the digital images management infrastructure it should be noted that:

- The images are being selected by the archaeologists, scanned at a high quality (tiff compression).
- The digital images are stored simply in a logically structured file system and managed at a simple way.
- Metadata for the digital images are not being used and preserved.
- The digital images are being hard coded into HTML.
- The published on-line digital images are being compressed to JPEG format (medium quality of compression).
- The copyright of the digital images is not being protected. Access control, watermarking and encryption are being applied neither to the high quality digital images nor to their compressed surrogates.
- A copyright management framework does not exist.

The requirements above prove that the architecture used for the "Ulysses" portal especially for the digital images management and copyright protection surely does not reflect to an efficient and adequate infrastructure. The main weaknesses could be summarized to the next important points:

- The images should be digitized using custom made scanning tools and interfaces which should utilize the existing network infrastructure.
- The digital images should be stored in a relational and distributed database system.
- International metadata standards should be used for the description of the digital images.
- The copyright of the digital images should be protected using imperceptible and robust watermarking.
- The watermarking method should be robust mainly at Jpeg compression and the usual geometrical attacks (rotation, cropping, etc.).
- The copyright management should be based on international metadata standards for IPR.

Based on the above important points a Watermarking Application dealing with the above issues should be designed and implemented.

WATERMARKING METHOD

Watermarking principles are used whenever the cover-data is available to parties who know the existence of the hidden data and may have an interest removing it. In this framework the most popular and demanding application of watermarking is to give proof of ownership of digital data by embedding copyright statements. For this kind of application the embedded information should be robust against manipulations that may attempt to remove it. Many watermarking schemes show weaknesses in a number of attacks and specifically desynchronization is a very efficient tools against most marking techniques. This is leading to the suggestion that detection, rather than embedding, is the core problem of digital watermarking (Fotopoulos 02), (Skodras, 02).

According to the above the first most important step towards the implementation of the Watermarking Application is the selection and evaluation of the watermarking method. The method chosen is mainly based on the further elaboration of the MCWG watermarking tool, focusing on constructing a more efficient detection mechanism, which is resulting to a more robust watermarking technique. The core of the MCWG tool is a transform domain technique that is based on the use of the Subband DCT transform (Fotopoulos, 00). The marking formula is the same well known multiplicative rule used in the large majority of the existing literature. The tool has performed positively in the past in a large variety of attacks, including those that an application like Ulysses would require. It did not though provide support for geometrical attacks. Thus some improvements were considered necessary.

There were two main directions for improvement. The first one was to maximize the detector's performance. As known from the literature, in the case of such systems, the detector's output is a function of two parameters that have to do with the selection of the marked coefficients vector: size and length. An adaptive algorithm has been designed and included into the system that fine-tunes the selection of these parameters (Barni, 98). The results of this improvement are clearly beneficial to the system. The other improvement direction has to do with the geometric attacks problem. A supplement to the system was created based on the notion of the center of mass. This familiar term from the classical mechanics theory has been introduced in the image domain by carefully selecting two different logical representations of the image array (Barni, 98). Extensive tests performed on images that were rotated, scaled and changed by means of aspect ratio, has proved that those changes can be satisfactory restored, thus providing a positive response from the re-synchronized system. This extension was also included into the original watermarking method.

The MCWG watermarking method was tested particularly with digital images provided by the Hellenic Ministry of Culture and fine-tuned in accordance with the produced results. In addition, certain actions were taken for the further development of the method so as to incorporate multi-file support, monochrome and colour images and multidimensional digital images.

WATERMARKING APPLICATION

Introduction

The main objective of the Watermarking Application is to deal with the weaknesses stated above. This is achieved firstly by the implementation of a basic infrastructure which is consisted of a Digital Image Repository and based on international metadata sets for the digital image management. The next step is to transform the MCWG watermarking method into a usable format and integrate it to the Watermarking Application. Finally, a user – interface is created which is based on the basic infrastructure and integrates the watermarking method. The result is a modular application which can serve as a platform for the efficient copyright management and protection of digital images.

Basic Infrastructure

The design and implementation of the basic infrastructure is required for further development of the watermarking application. The basic infrastructure is consisting of the Digital Image Repository and the Metadata sets which are described in detail.

Digital Image Repository

The efficient management of the digital images is based on an advanced database system. The design and implementation of the digital image repository for this platform is a very important task.

The Digital Image Repository is designed and developed in accordance with metadata sets described in the paragraph (par. 5.2.2). The metadata sets are incorporated through tables, fields, triggers and views in the Database. The specific tables and fields, which are used for the repository, were selected on the basis of the next requirements:

- Custom metadata of the Hellenic Ministry of Culture.
- International metadata for the dissemination of culture (e.g. Dublin Core).
- The international standards for describing, characterizing and identifying digital images.
- The international standards for managing and protecting the Intellectual Property Rights.

The database repository is implemented using the IBM DB2 Universal Database, with the assistance of the IBM DB2 XML and AIV Extenders. The specific system provides advanced services for searching and retrieving digital images. For example it supports digital image retrieval using similarity criteria (color, histogram, shape, etc.). In this case the user can use a color specification or even a digital image as a query to the repository.

Metadata

The need for adopting international metadata standards is profound, especially for applications aiming at cultural content exchange. The DIG 35 Specification "Metadata for Digital Images", Version 1.1 (DIG35, 00) has a very important role in the selection of fields and tables, as far as the metadata for the digital images are concerned. This metadata standard is already being widely used in simple end-user devices and even to worldwide networks. The database structure has also a special focus on metadata for the Intellectual Property Rights management. In particular, these sets were divided in five major sectors:

- **Technical metadata.** Technical metadata are related to the image parameters, such as the image format, the image size, the compression method, and the color information.
- **Image creation metadata.** The image creation metadata include general information concerning the creation of the digital image. This information involves the time and date of the creation, the name of the creator, and information about the capturing device.
- **History metadata.** The history metadata are necessary so as to identify and record the processing steps that might have been applied to a digital surrogate. This may help to avoid any further processing steps, and to identify independent objects in a composition of digital pictures. This set of metadata contains information on whether or not a digital image is cropped, rotated, retouched, or suffered a color adjustment.
- **Content description metadata.** The content description metadata contain descriptive information about the location, the capture time and date, etc.
- **IPR related metadata.** This important metadata set is related with the intellectual property rights and involves information about the copyright, the image creator and rights holder, the restriction of use and contact points.

Table 1.

DIG-35 Mapping (Ref. No. DIG35 Specification)	HMC Metadata
BasicImageParameter.Title (A.3.1.2)	Image Id
ContentDescription.Caption (C.3.2)	Monument
ContentDescription.Thing (C.3.6.)	Content Type
ConentDescription.Caption (C.3.2)	Description
IPR.OriginalWorkCreation (E.3.3)	Coverage
ContentDescription.CaptureTime (C.3.3)	Capture Time
IPR.ImageCreator (E.3.1)	Photographer

Amongst the various metadata standardization initiatives, Dublin Core (DC) (Dublin Core, 00) has gained significant visibility and respect. Dublin Core is a metadata standard fully applied to cultural heritage and supports the diversity, convergence and interoperability of digital cultural objects. The basic Dublin Core data model is a simple content description model, defined by its 15 elements. The need for incorporating the DC elements in the digital repository is significant mainly because many cultural organizations are already using the DC model and this will support the wider interoperability of the system.

The most common practice of efficiently combining two or more metadata standards is mapping. Mapping between metadata formats requires the creation of a mapping table. The advantage is that this mapping makes it possible for both simple DC-based as well as more detailed DIG 35 (Digital Imaging Group) content-based search to be done. The main difficulty of mapping DIG 35 to DC is the difference of granularity. The DC element set has only 15 elements and on the other hand DIG 35 is a highly structured and detailed metadata set. The mapping table of the two standards was developed. In addition a mapping table was developed between the custom made metadata set of the Hellenic Ministry of Culture and the Dig 35 correspondent set. This table is shown bellow (Table 1).

Watermarking

Integration Strategy

The integration strategy is referring to the methodology and process of incorporating the watermark embedment and detection to the Watermarking Application. The strategy selected is considering the watermarking method, described above, as a "black box". The technical requirement of this strategy is the watermarking method to be available at a re-usable format (Software Development Kit and Dynamic Link Libraries). The watermarking is seen as a generic class, with specific attributes, functions, arguments, parameters and return values. The advantage of this strategy is that the watermarking method is independent from the development of the basic infrastructure (databases) and the user interfaces. The drawback is that the watermarking method cannot be further elaborated and fine-tuned in accordance with the specific needs of the final user.

Implementation

As long as the watermarking method is considered as a black box it is important to analyze its actual integration to the entire watermarking application. The watermarking method should be incorporated into the user-interface (client) part of the watermarking application. As a result the user – interface, apart from the storage and management of the digital images, is responsible for the watermarking of the digital images. The user – interface part of the watermarking application is constructed in a Visual Basic environment. The watermarking method is utilized by constructing a DLL (the Watermarking Type Library 1.0.) and referencing it as a class in the main watermarking application.

The DLL of the watermarking application includes two useful methods, Embed and Detect. These methods implement the watermarking embedding and detection mechanisms. The Embed and Detect methods require a number of parameters as an input and they in response are returning specific values (outputs).

The Embed method: The input parameters of this method are more or less the usual parameters that every watermarking scheme requires in order to incorporate the watermark into a digital image. The most significant parameter is the ImageID. The definition of the class method is:

Embed (long ImageID , long Key, string InputFile, string OutputFile, int Strength)

- The ImageID parameter is representing the id that corresponds to the image stored in the Digital Image Repository.
- The Key parameter is a long integer which is referring to the watermark id. The Key is common for all the digital images. As a result the key is uniquely related to the Ministry of Culture, which is identified as a copyright owner of the digital image.
- The InputFile parameter refers to the path of the file of the digital image, which will be watermarked.
- The OutputFile parameter is the file path where the watermarking tool will store the watermarked image. As mentioned previously all watermarked images are being stored directly to the repository. During this storage procedure temporary files in the user's hard disk are created. After insertion the temporary images files are deleted.
- Finally the Strength parameter is determining the robustness of the watermark. It is strongly related with the magnitude of the parameter "α" used in the DCT based watermarking schemes.

One of the most important aspects of the system is its ability to preprocess the image and preserve some valuable side information in the Digital Image Repository. The ImageID parameter is associating the digital images with this side information. The watermarking application depending on the ImageID manages to connect to the repository and store the side information that has acquired from the preprocessing. In this way the ImageID associates uniquely the actual image and its related side information. The best way to demonstrate how the embedding method works is to present the next scheme (Figure 1).

The Detect Method: Along with the embedding method the watermarking application has the capability of detecting the watermark. The detection can be activated by the application's end-user. The class method that performs this task is the detect method.

Figure 1.

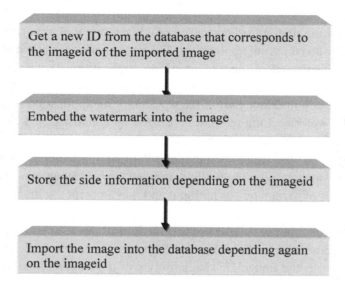

Detect (long ImageID, long Key, string InputFile)

- The ImageID parameter in the detect method is being used by the watermarking application, in order to retrieve the side information from the Digital Image Repository. The detection method is impossible to work if the side information is unavailable. It includes values of vital importance for the detection method and the inability of finding these values will end up in false results. The ImageID selection is achieved with an image content - based query supported by the DB2 AIV Extenders.
- The Key parameter must be the same with the value used during the embedding process. The reason that this value is used again as an input parameter, even if it is common for all the digital images, is for future development of the application.
- The InputFile is the path to the image file, to which the detection method will be applied.

The detection scheme is presented in the next figure (Figure 2).

The watermarking method is depending on the L, M values (common for the watermarking research area) that are vital for the detection process, which are also stored in the repository. It's obvious that in case that the selected ImageID doesn't correspond to the correct digital image the detect process will fail. Although the DB2 AIV Extenders work quite well it is essential to have a safety net in case of a misleading ImageID selection. For this reason a selection threshold has been specified. If the similarity score returned from the image content query is above the threshold then the detection method selects the L, M values from scratch. Even though this process is time consuming it is necessary for the robustness of the watermark application. In this framework, there is no point in using the image registration method as long as the proper side information is unavailable.

Figure 2.

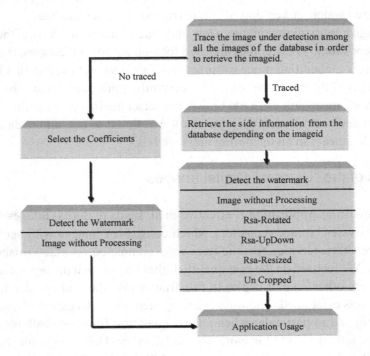

Box 1.

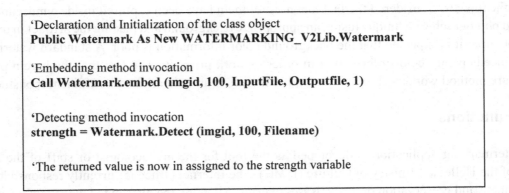

```
'Declaration and Initialization of the class object
Public Watermark As New WATERMARKING_V2Lib.Watermark

'Embedding method invocation
Call Watermark.embed (imgid, 100, InputFile, Outputfile, 1)

'Detecting method invocation
strength = Watermark.Detect (imgid, 100, Filename)


'The returned value is now in assigned to the strength variable
```

The integration of the watermarking method to the application is achieved by referencing the correspondent Type Library. A pseudocode example is shown in Box 1.

Watermarking Utilities

Whenever a new digital image is being inserted into the Digital Image Repository the Embed method is activated by default. The user does not have the permission to override this activation. As a result, it is impossible for a digital image to be stored in the repository without having been watermarked first. An image is considered watermarked only if it is extracted from the database.

Apart from the high quality digital image, a low and a medium quality copy of the image is produced and stored into the repository. These copies are used for web based applications, thumbnail representation etc. The watermark embedding process cannot be overridden not even in this low quality copies.

The implementation of the detection scheme is certainly more interactive. The user must navigate to the appropriate choice menu and use a file browser to select the image file path. The system response is a message box that declares whether the watermark was found or not, and in case the answer is yes, the detection strength appears in an upcoming message box.

Special Features of the "Ulysses" Digital Images

Although the Watermarking Application is effective in all kinds of digital images, the specific system is focusing on the "Ulysses" image repository which consists of images with special characteristics. In order to find these characteristics specific tests were completed on a 220 image sample set of the "Ulysses" repository. We focused on the best quality digital images that the repository holds since these are the source for every other kind of copies.In this framework, the average size for every dimension of the digital images was calculated. The watermarking method works extremely well when the size of the images is quite big and in particular when a large quadratic frame is available at the center of the image. A frame of the size of 512x512 is more than satisfactory. The average for the Height and Width dimension was calculated automatically to the values of [945.2954 , 708.5636] proportionally. Conclusively, the "Ulysses" image repository fits perfectly to the requirements.

Another special feature of the "Ulysses" digital image repository is the amount of information carried by the images. Considered the fact that most of them have been captured inside a museum, with a standard photographic technique (using an appropriate background and placing the artifact in the center of the picture), it is expected that the background color information is poor. A standard watermarking scheme needs plenty color information in order to work properly. The fact that the herein proposed watermark method works well with this kind of images is an indication of its efficient robustness.

User Functions

The watermarking application is developed as the tool for the archaeologist or staff of the Internet Office of the Hellenic Ministry of Culture (HMC). The Internet Office is currently responsible for the management and preservation of the "Ulysses" Portal. Allowing the distributed management of digital images, the application serves specific functions and transparently embeds watermarks into the pictorial representation of objects of the Hellenic Cultural Heritage. This client has already been installed and is under pilot testing. The user functions have been selected and implemented by taking into account:

- The needs of the organization to automate certain procedures (digital image management, content and metadata management, etc.).
- The user requirements and the organizational structure, equipment and the personnel skill status.
- The end user profile (age, technical experience, etc.)

The main functions of the user – interface (client) part of the watermarking application are presented bellow.

Watermarking: As described previously, the watermark is embedded transparently into the digital image. An insertion of a digital surrogate into the central database causes the inevitable embedding of the appropriate digital watermark. This function is incorporated into the client, not the server, and is implemented on Microsoft Windows Operating Systems. This was chosen mainly for the following reasons:

- The installment of the central Digital Image Repository is independent from the operating system and platform. The client is remotely connected to the central Digital Image Repository.
- The Microsoft Windows operating system provides for efficient communication with scanners and digitization tools and is the standard operating system for the Internet Office of the HMC.

During the embedding a standard copyright ID number that actually declares Hellenic Ministry of Culture as the copyright owner of the digital image is incorporated into the digital image. The user has the capability of initiating the detection of a watermark.

Database Connection: Whenever a user is using the watermarking application, a permanent connection exists, between the client and the central Digital Image Repository. This connection is established during the user authentication and is preserved until the user exits from the client.

Disconnect: When the user exits, certain steps are applied for the appropriate disconnection of the client from the database. The connection and disconnection procedures are part of a custom library (DLL) that serves for special functions such as user authentication, data logging, etc.

Image and Metadata Management Functions: The functions that are already implemented include basic image management procedures. A part of the basic image management functions are implemented by dynamic link libraries in Microsoft Visual C++ and the other part using Microsoft Visual Basic. The dynamic link libraries submit SQL instructions to the central Digital Image Repository and consist of the following basic functions:

- Connect and Disconnect (previously described)
- Retrieve and Import
- Search by using a unique identifier and similarity criteria (color, histogram, shape, etc.)

The rest of the functions, mainly consisting of image scanning, caching and printing, are implemented using the Microsoft Visual Basic Form Controls, the Microsoft Web Browser Control, the Kodak Imaging Controls and the ADO Data Binding Control. In addition, image insertion can be done directly from a TWAIN source (such as a scanner or a digital camera) or from external files. All the above technologies are provided by the Microsoft Visual Basic programming environment.

Importing, retrieving and searching of metadata are implemented using HTML forms, which are integrated into the client of the watermarking application. The HTML forms are based on an XML Schema. Their implementation is completed with the transformation of the XML Schema, throughout XSL, with

Figure 3.

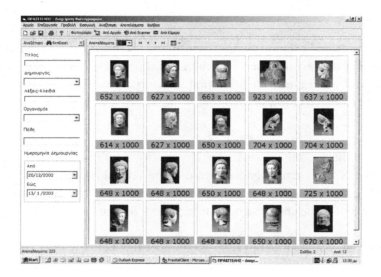

the use of MSXML 3.0. In addition, the XML Schema is used as a solution for the permanent storage of the search queries for future use. As a result the end – user has a "save as query" capability.

The presentation of the results (especially metadata information) retrieved by the repository is supported by the creation of XML documents. The XML documents are produced by user-defined SQL queries. The XML documents are based on an XML schema, which is derived from the XML schema of the DIG35 Metadata Standard and is modified in accordance with the specifications of the Hellenic Ministry of Culture. The output files are automatically populated with XML Template Files. These template files interconnect the database and the XML schemas. The presentation of the results is accomplished through the transformation of XML files to HTML, using Microsoft XSLT Processor or the IBM XML Lightweight Extractor (XLE). This feature enables the end – user to store the results of a query as an XML of an HTML file. A screenshot of the client is presented in the next figure (Figure 3).

For this project the usage of XML is recommended as the standard metadata interchange format. The primary reasons are the following. XML is widely adopted as an Internet-based language. XML is highly extensible and device independent. In addition, XML is an application independent language.

Finally, automated batch insert and export of digital images from and to the database is supported. This function aims at the mass processing of digital images stored in a CD-ROM.

Evaluation

The image repository of the Official Web Portal is open to public via the Internet. As a result, the watermarking robustness evaluation against jpeg compression, rescaling, cropping and analog to digital attacks is the most appropriate.

In order to make our tests we used a 220 – image sample from the Ulysses repository. In order to test the robustness of the system to jpeg compression all digital images were compressed after they had been watermarked. The evaluation was based on six different kinds of compression. The results are shown in the following table (Table 2).

Table 2.

Compression Name	Down sampling	Miss-Rate
High compression, Low quality	1:96	18%
High compression, Medium quality	1:56	11%
High compression, High quality	1:20	1%
Medium compression, Low quality	1:85	12%
Medium compression, Medium quality	1:57	5%
Medium compression, High quality	1:18	0%

Table 3.

Tiff Image format	
Down Sampling	Miss Rate
1:2	3%
1:3	5%

It is important to mention that except for the third and the sixth compression type in all other cases (1:96, 1:56, 1:85 and 1:57) the images were severely damaged and their commercial exploitation is impossible.

Another very usual attack is the rescaling of the images. It is a very common procedure for someone to download the image from the web, rescale it and put it in his web page or another electronic edition. It is though very important for the proposed watermarking application to be able to counter this kind of attacks. In the above sample of images a downscaling of 2 and 3 times was performed and the results were quite encouraging.

Along with the rescaling attack the watermarking application was tested against the cropping attack. Most of the digital images in the "Ulysses" repository depict a statue or an artifact centrally placed in the picture. A cropped version of the image including only the interesting part is undoubtedly valuable in a commercial way. The watermark application showed satisfactory robustness mainly because of the use of the side information. On the contrary when the cropped version of the image was too small and without content information, the detection failed.

The last of the attacks is the digital to analog one. It is a very powerful feature for a watermarking application to be able to detect the watermark, even if the image is printed, using a scanner. For this kind of attack the 220 – image sample was not used since it would be a very time consuming and expensive procedure; instead a small random sample was selected. In order to have a more realistic attack except for the digital to analog attack the jpeg compression was performed additionally. Some results are shown in the following table (Table 4).

FUTURE RESEARCH DIRECTIONS

Designing and implementing a watermarking application for "Ulysses" the official portal of the Hellenic Culture is a demanding and important task. Most of effort was dedicated to meet the watermarking

Table 4.

Image Type	Image Compression	Print Quality	Result
Tiff	None	Best	Detected
Tiff	None	Normal	Detected
Jpeg	Medium Compression High Quality	Best	Detected
Jpeg	Medium Compression High Quality	Normal	Detected
Jpeg	Medium Compression Medium Quality	Best	Detected
Jpeg	Medium Compression Medium Quality	Normal	Missed

functional and technical requirements and to deal with the lack of basic infrastructure. The result is a modular watermarking application which serves as an integrated platform for digital image management, metadata management and copyright protection via digital watermarking.

The MCWG watermarking method was further elaborated mainly towards a more powerful detection method and transformed to a reusable Dynamic Link Library. The watermarking application was structured upon this method, benefiting by its robustness, and proposed a detection scheme based on side information stored into a repository and related to the digital images. The side information retrieval is supported by an image content similarity query (Query By Image Content). The main advantages of this scheme is the improvement of robustness against geometrical attacks and the ability of proving that a random watermarked image, probably downloaded through the Internet, corresponds to a specific image stored in the "Ulysses" repository. Consequently, a) it is proved that the HMC is the copyright owner of the specific image and b) the necessary key for retrieving from the repository all the copyright related information (copyright plate, important dates, contact points, etc.) is available.

Based on the above, in order to optimize the robustness of the watermarking application a more thorough research on the image content query should be initiated. In addition, the user – interface (client) should be developed focusing on the copyright information retrieval and management towards a more complete digital rights management system.

REFERENCES

Barni., M., Bartolini., F., Cappellini., V., Piva., A. (1998). A DCT-domain system for robust image watermarking. *Signal Processing. Special Issue on Watermarking, 3*(66), 357-372.

Cox., I. J., Miller., M., & Bloom., J. (2002). *Digital watermarking.* Morgan Kaufann Publishers.

Computer Science and Telecommunications Board, National Research Council. (1999). *The digital dilemma: Intellectual property in the information age*, 2-3. Washington: National Academy Press.

DIG35 Specification - Metadata for Digital Images. Version 1.0. (2000). Digital Imaging Group.

Dublin Core Metadata Standard. (2000). Dublin Core.

Fotopoulos.,V., & Skodras., A. N. (2000). A subband DCT approach to image watermarking. *X European Signal Processing Conference (EUSIPCO-2000).* Tampere, Finland.

Fotopoulos.,V., & Skodras., A. N. (2002). *Adaptive coefficients selection for transform domain watermarking.* Technical Report TR2002/10/02. Patras, Greece: Computer Technology Institute.

Fotopoulos.,V., &Skodras., A. N. (2002, September). *Geometric deformations and watermarking.* Technical Report TR2002/09/02. Patras, Greece: Computer Technology Institute.

House of Representatives. (1998). Digital Millennium Copyright Act.

Katzenbeisser. S., & Petitcolas., F. A. P. (2000). *Information hiding - Techniques for steganography and digital watermarking,* 95-172. Artech House, Computer Series.

ADDITIONAL READING

Wayner. (2002). *Disappearing cryptography - Information hiding: Steganography and watermarking* (Second, pp. 291-318). Morgan Kaufmann.

Computer Science and Telecommunications Board, National Research Council. (1999). *The digital dilemma: Intellectual property in the information age,* 2-3. Washington: National Academy Press.

House of Representatives, Digital Millennium Copyright Act, October 28, 1998.

The Hellenic Cultural Heritage Portal, http://www.culture.gr.

Randall Davis (2001, February). The digital dilemma. *Communications of the ACM, 44,* 80.

IBM, IBM DB2 Digital Library, http://www.ibm.com.

Tsolis, G. K., Tsolis, D. K., & Papatheodorou, T. S. (2001). A watermarking environment and a metadata digital image repository for the protection and management of digital images of the Hellenic Cultural Heritage. *In 2001 International Conference on Image Processing.* Greece.

World Wide Web Consortium. Extensible Markup Language (XML). http://www.w3.org/XML.

The IBM AlphaWorks. (2001). XML Access Service Lightweight Extractor (XLE).

Chapter XIII
Digital Rights Management in the Cultural Heritage Arena:
A Truth or a Myth

Andrea de Polo
Alinari 24 ORE SpA, Italy

ABSTRACT

Digital Rights Management (DRM) describes a set of functionalities which control access to, and the use of, copyright material. In particular, they focus on the acquisition of revenue from copyright material, and the prevention of its re-use and misuse in the online environment. This document describes the DRM system in the cultural heritage sector; the value of the DRMS to the content repositories and also to the end users is described. Managing digital rights is a focal point for any content provider.

INTRODUCTION

DRM is the necessary building block on which to build online content-trading processes. Every day a vast amount of material is distributed online, through the Internet and private networks. Owners of digital material need to protect their digitized goods without inhibiting their trade. In economic terms, the contribution made by (digital and non-digital) copyright-based goods and services to the Community's GDP is significant and rising (around 6% of GDP).

The aim of a reliable and trusted DRM system should be as follows:

1. A trusted photographic licensing and IPR solution
2. Third party content providers
3. A "trusted" network of providers and users. Trusted because the access will be through a subscription fee and because the end user will have to agree to certain IPR and image usage regulations before entering into the site. A specific IPR image licensing model will be available for download, through the content provider site

4. The "standard" DRMS solution described here is related to the "Standard" IPR image licensing form
5. The images are watermarked (statically and-or dynamically, on the fly) and by carry on a small visible copyright logo
6. The system is monitored remotely by the content provider personnel in order to assure the most reliable usage of the system
7. A Web crawler monitor the download of the images and their possible (not legal) usage, after words, on the Web.

The future of internet based solutions for content delivery are further enhanced, beside still jpeg images also by MPEG audio and video through greater choice in the content with which the user can choose to interact. In structured audio books, for example, a specific chapter from a text book can be provided in a specific form.

Business solutions can also be incorporated through the use of DRM, allowing several user types or profiles to co-exist in one revenue stream. At a consumption level, the common user can then specify how that content is delivered and save these preferences for their particular user scenario.

The aim of this document is to define the rule that governs the usage of the images and video shared by content providers. This IPR guideline document is meant to encourage also to use text and other content.

Definition of "DRM"

A system, comprising technological tools and a usage policy, that is designed to securely manage access to and use of digital information. By "technological tools," we refer to both hardware-based and software-based measures. In the copyright context, these tools are often called "technological protection measures" ("TPMs") or, simply, "technical measures." In this report, we distinguish between DRM systems and TPMs: DRM systems often utilize TPMs – the "technological tools" of our definition – as component parts.

The term "TPM" typically refers to technologies that control access to or use of information, or both. A TPM that controls access to information might be as simple as a password protection. More complex access-control TPMs use encryption to regulate access to information by encrypting it and permitting decryption and access only by authorized individuals or devices.

Use-control TPMs control the uses that can be made of a work after an individual accesses it. The most common type of use-control TPM is a copy-control mechanism which regulates or prevents duplication of all or part of a work. Macrovision technology, for example, is a copy-control technology which prevents or distorts copying of Macrovision-protected DVDs.

THE DRMS AND THE CONTENT REPOSITORIES

The digital rights management system embedded in cultural heritage online sites (mainly stock agencies, galleries, photo archives and content providers) is an important element of the value proposition to content repositories. By protecting the rights of the content owners, it provides the platform whereby revenue can be derived from online virtual access to their important material. Without such a system, the value of having online material is greatly decreased, and is reduced to merely advertising for 'real' visits to the institutions which host the source material, or to sell physical prints and copies of images.

Having a strong DRMS makes cultural sites attractive as a business partner to those institutions which host the content. By utilizing the DRMS, the memory institution or image repository gains the benefits of a DRMS, without having to implement its own.

The DRMS and Large Repositories

Large content providers should adopt a DRMS policy in order to be sure to place their valuable content into a trusted repository, even through a shared network. This means increased Web traffic, more visibility and better chances for selling content.

The unity and standardization of the tools used within the DRMS system are some of the main reasons why large archives should license their content to large online repositories.

The DRMS and Small Repositories

The objective of the DRMS is to provide the small content provider with a quality set of legal and technical solutions which securely protect their content. Often, small archives do not have the budget for marketing, promotion or technical security; they can achieve this through financially inexpensive solution.

The DRMS and the End User

While protecting the Content Repositories is an essential part of the DRMS, the end users must have a simple and effective method for accessing content – otherwise the commercial offerings of the Repositories will not be attractive.

Essentially, a DRMS is a system which restricts the activities of end users, in terms of re-use of copyright material. However, if the DRMS is seen to be excessively restrictive, or to hamper the activities of the user, this makes the whole solution unattractive. The aim of the DRMS, with regard to end users, is to control their activity in an **unobtrusive** manner.

Four aspects of the DRMS are considered here, with discussion explaining how they serve the end user, and not just the online system and the content repositories:

1. Access control
2. Use restrictions
3. Visible watermarking
4. Invisible watermarking

DRM Requirements for Research and Education

DRM is recognized as a complex and critical aspect of the lifecycle of a digital object. In Research and Education (R&E), we are currently witnessing a surge of interest in DRM for several reasons. An obvious reason is the need for DRM to support digital library collections, code and software development, distance education, and networked collaboration, among other applications. Many institutions, for example, have completed the first step in the development of digital collections — the digitization and storage of content, and the development of descriptive metadata schemes for discovery and retrieval of that content. Progressing to the next step of enabling global access to that content will require DRM.

There is also evidence of a growing interest in academia for open publishing models, such as the Budapest Open Access Initiative. These new models are emerging in response to escalating commercial journal costs and restrictive publishing practices, which are perceived as disenfranchising the journal authors from their own intellectual property. Open publishing models require new DRM strategies that emphasize fair use, protection of intellectual property from misuse, and multiple subscription models, which include both fee-based and non-fee based access.

Finally, many in R&E consider that commercial DRM solutions tip the balance between the rights owner and the user too much in favor of the rights owner, undermining fair use and the first sale doctrine in the process — two critical and cherished principles in R&E. There is also concern that some DRM implementations compromise the privacy of the user.

In response to this growing need to support expanding digital collections and new scholarly publishing models, as well as networked collaboration, there is a movement underway to develop DRM solutions to specifically meet R&E requirements. These requirements include: accommodating the highly collaborative and distributed aspect of many R&E activities; supporting fair use of copyrighted materials for educational purposes; supporting granular and differential access to resources; preventing misuse of resources; insuring the integrity of resources; and interoperating with existing and emerging infrastructure.

Two points are worth noting here. The first is that R&E requirements reveal a distinction between conventional definitions of DRM (the e-commercial model, which functions solely to protect the rights of the owner) and the broader definition emerging in the R&E community. The latter includes access management as well as intellectual property rights management, and is as concerned with the rights of the user as with those of the rights owner. Indeed, given this difference in interpretation, it has been suggested that the term "DRM" has been appropriated by the publishing industry and that the goals of the R&E community in this space would be better served using a different term. The second point is that, whether fair use is interpreted as a declarative right or a defense, methods have been proposed to accommodate fair use either in trusted systems or by means of third-party escrow. The notion, therefore, that an accommodation of fair use is beyond the province of DRM technologies is being challenged.

The VidMid Video-on-Demand Working Group is exploring how far middleware (identity management, authentication, authorization, security and metadata) and the establishment of communities of trust might go towards implementing customized, open and interoperable DRM systems. This focus is the theme of an invitational workshop planned for September 2002; the "NSF Middleware Initiative and DRM Workshop is being funded by the NSF NMI program to bring together content management, copyright law, and middleware experts to explore cooperative DRM development to meet R&E needs. The workshop will be facilitated by the authors, and is supported by the Coalition for Networked Information, EDUCAUSE, Internet2, the Southeastern Universities Research Association, and the Video Development Initiative.

An additional and very significant focus for the "NMI and DRM Workshop" is the presentation of a proposal to cooperatively develop a rights metadata core. Equivalent to the Dublin Core for descriptive metadata, the rights core will be cooperatively developed to meet R&E requirements, and will map to existing and future rights languages, as well as interoperating with descriptive metadata schemas. There is a proliferation of rights languages currently, but, for the most part, these support one-to-one e-commercial transactions. A sufficient user base is not yet established to determine whether these languages are flexible and extensible enough for R&E purposes, or whether their use is going to be encumbered by patent claims. The rights core data element set and application schema will be developed by identifying the core DRM needs for R&E, and mapping the data elements required to document and support those needs against existing rights schemas. One of the significant benefits of this process will be the identification of R&E needs that are not currently addressed by existing schemas. The authors expect to propose changes and additions to existing schemas to provide more relevance and utility for R&E among commercial and open source DRM implementations.

A DRM implementation, obviously, entails more than technology. There are complex legal and policy issues implicit in any DRM implementation, as well as a need to support gradations of risk. The FDRM project is a first step for VidMid in testing the hypothesis that it is possible to develop a DRM solution to meet R&E requirements — it does not attempt to address all of these complexities. Our approach to the DRM problem is focused on flexible access management rather than enforcement of rights after the user has legitimately accessed the resource. Our primary goal in this article is to present a reference architecture for FDRM to demonstrate how emerging middleware infrastructure might be leveraged as a foundation and framework for an effective DRM implementation.

Access Control

Access to the online repository is available only to the holders of valid passwords. This ensures that all use of the system has been paid for, and thus that the content providers receive revenue from the use of their material.

At the same time, such access control ensures the **highest level of performance** for the end user. With restricted user numbers, system response time are rapid and the use of the system involves the minimum delay and waiting. This is of particular importance when dealing with large image files, which have their own inherent delays.

Use Restrictions and User Scenario

The DRMS controls the end user by restricting the amount of material which he can view, manipulate or download via the online portal. A counter tracks how many images each subscriber has downloaded or can access, view or download and print. Typically, a user can download a certain number of images per annual subscription. Once no more credits are left, the user can acquire further credits.

The portal makes it clear to the user at all times how many credits he has remaining in his account, and how many credits each operation will cost him. This allows the user to budget his use of the system appropriately, and ensures that he has no unpleasant surprises when he wishes to use the system for research, education, training, etc.

Visible Watermarking

The use of a visible watermark on the content can be viewed by the end user as a 'necessary evil'. While the visible watermark does not enhance the value of the image from the user's point of view, it is an integral part of the system, which is itself of great value to the user. In order to minimize the intrusion and impact on the end user, the visible watermark is translucent and subtle, and is placed non-centrally on the image.

Invisible Watermarking

The invisible watermark on the images has no impact whatsoever on the legitimate user of the content. This powerful and important element of the DRMS thus serves the user particularly well – it has no impact whatsoever on the user, while being an important enabler of the useful and valuable IPR system.

TECHNICAL INVESTIGATION RESULTS

Introduction

In presenting the results of our technical investigations in this Report, it is helpful to draw a distinction between what we have coined as "autonomous DRM" and "netdependent DRM." Although useful for presenting the results here, this distinction did not factor into our technical investigations or our *PIPEDA* assessments substantively in any way.

Autonomous DRM refers to DRM that needs no outside interaction to fulfill its purpose. Software that requires a CD-Key before becoming usable, DVDs that will only work with DVD players in certain regions and software that deactivates after a given number of uses are all examples of autonomous DRM.

Net-dependent DRM refers to a growing trend in DRM schemes that involves either internet authentication, internet surveillance of uses and/or the tying of content to an online platform. Online music subscription services that deploy digital licenses to allow the use of locked content, Web-enabled software validation and the tying of content to an online platform are all examples of net-dependent DRM.

In our technical investigations, we found that many, but not all, autonomous DRMs connect to and communicate with external computers during the course of the operation of the DRM. Conversely, *all* of the net-dependent DRM systems that we investigated communicated with external computers.

We also found that a number of the DRM products we investigated communicated with the same third parties: Akamai Technologies, Omniture and DoubleClick.

Autonomous DRM

Six of the products that we investigated used *Autonomous DRM*. Four of these showed no communications. Since autonomous DRM does not appear to need to communicate to fulfill rights management purposes, it is natural to ask questions regarding those that do engage in external communications. Our assessment revealed that these communications appeared in most cases to be linked to advertising and Web metrics.

Consider our investigation of Disney's *Pirates of the Caribbean* DVD (disc 2). When we inserted the DVD, a pop-up window appeared asking us to install the Interactual Player, software that plays DVDs on computers. Once we installed the software, a configuration window appeared with a tab marked

"Privacy." We deselected all agreements to information transfers. Nonetheless, we captured communications to InterActual servers. Indeed, the software placed a cookie onto our test computer.

The cookie itself can only be read by an InterActual Web site, but this does mean that InterActual may have collected our IP address, Web browser and operating system information through the cookie request from our computer. As the InterActual interface window does not go through a Web browser, it is likely that an unsophisticated user would not know that he or she is downloading advertising from the internet or delivering information to InterActual.

Net-Dependent DRM

Products Purchased in Physical Form

Net-dependent DRM systems rely on internet communications to fulfill their rights management purposes.. Whereas *autonomous DRM* authentication usually requires a user to enter a valid identification key as pre-determined by the software, *net-dependant DRM* goes one step further and, for example, cross-references this key with a database to ensure that the key is not already being used by another user.

Our investigation revealed that many store-bought net-dependent DRM-protected products allow users a limited number of uses or limited functionality; others simply will not work until authenticated *via* the internet or sometimes by telephone.

Online Products and Services

Online content subscription services such as the Ottawa Public Library (OPL) and Napster deploy digital licenses to allow the use of locked content. The downloaded content. For example, our investigations revealed that if a user pays for a one-month subscription with Napster and tries to play Napster acquired songs through Windows Media Player while Napster is uninstalled, then the digital license attached to the song will require the reinstallation of Napster. This is not a format issue; songs can be played outside of Napster. If Napster is installed on a user's computer, the user can play Napster-acquired songs through other platforms such as Windows Media Player.

All of our investigations involving online services revealed communications to third party sites belonging to companies such as Akamai Technologies, Omniture and DoubleClick. Although we know something about the general nature of these businesses, we do not know what information was sent to them.

Case Descriptions

- **Fratelli Alinari Photo Archive (now called Alinari 24 ORE SpA),** founded in Florence in 1852, is the oldest firm in the world in the field of photography and more in general in that of the image and communication. The birth of photography and the history of the firm go hand in hand in their development and growth, as witnessed by the immense fund of *over 4,500,000* photographs Alinari owns today. The Internet related business can be roughly illustrated by the following descriptive criteria.
  - o **Number of images online:** More than 330.000 images . **Format:** jpeg, tiff, and soon with the newest compression encoding as Jpge-xr

- o **Resolution:**
  - ➤ **Thumbnails:** 128x128 pixels
  - ➤ **Low resolution:** 256x256 pixels
  - ➤ **Low-medium resolution:** 480x480 pixels
  - ➤ **Medium resolution:** 800x800 pixels (internal use only)
  - ➤ **High resolution:** 4000x6000 pixels (on demand)
- o **Watermarking:** Watermark on the fly
- o **Digitised:** More than 350,000 images
- o **Catalogued:** More than 350,000 images

Key words for the search engine: About 8,000 (chosen with the collaboration of the University of Florence). The images are digitised from originals (films, slides, vintage prints, daguerreotypes, collotype, stereotypes…).

- • **Total Alinari's archive amount of images (owned):** Over 4,500,000
- • **Total images (owned plus managed):** About 20,500,000

  - o **Areas of interest:** Art, Architecture, Traveling, Agriculture, Industry, History, Movie, Fashion, Theatre, Science, Technology,…
  - o **Number of photographers:** 2,500 (from 1852 till nowadays)
  - o **Number of artists represented:** 5,000 artists (whose works are preserved in more than 200 museums: Gallery of Uffizi, Museum of Louvre, British Museum, National Gallery, Musée D'Orsay, Pinacoteca of Brera, Palatino Gallery of Florence, Vatican Museums, Museum of Egypt in Cairo, Ermitage of Pietroburgo, etc..)
  - o **Archives managed or represented by Alinari:** Italian Touring Club (about 500,000 images); Ansaldo Industry (about 200,000 images); TEAM Archive (about 50,000); RMN, ONB, Interfoto, Bridgeman, Corbis, and some more.
  - o **Customers:** Graphic designers, editors, reporters; advertisement; restorers; police; medical; Web designers; architects; art buyers; writers; Web advertisement; designers; researchers; students; professors
  - o **Transactions via Internet:** More than 400 transactions/ year
  - o **Number of online-clients:** More than 8,000 online business clients, more than 7,000 online education clients
  - o **Payments:** By credit card, off-line by post or wire transfer.

The knowledge presentation in the cultural heritage domain and the basis for an approach towards interoperability must take into account the actual status of the art in the professional context and the on going researches projects that have been set up.

Business

    http://business.alinari.it

Educational and multilingual

    http://edu.alinari.it

    http://www.orpheus-edu.org

    http://www.euridice-edu.org

Exhibit 1.

Name:	**ALINARI BUSINESS.COM**
Address:	Http://www.business.alinari.com
	ALINARI
Description:	It's a business to business site, developed since 1999, featuring 330.000 images, bilingual.
	Images can be downloaded at high resolution once the user has registered to the Alinari picture library
Target:	B2B market
Key points:	• This site is used only by professional users (jurnalists, newsagents, editors, etc.)

Exhibit 2.

Name:	**ALINARI EDU.COM**
Address:	Http://www.edu.alinari.com
	ALINARI
Description:	It's a multilingual e-learning photographic site featuring 85.000 images, powered by XLImage zooming technology.
	It can be accessed through a flat fee subscription business model (30 euros for 1 year for the single student, 10.000 euros for flat fee for a whole university)
Target:	B2B and B2C market in educational area
Key points:	• Difficulties in finding in Europe a proper market to sell easily this kind of services, probably for two main reasons: a *financial reason*, i.e. universities are often short in money; a *pragmatic reason*, i.e. universities have often their own e-learning system or methodology and joining an independent service can create some problems

New research projects, including metadata, multilingual access, geo-tagging, visual retrieval, immersive navigation solutions can be viewed through the R&D portal at http://www.alinari.it/it/progetti-europei.asp

Meaning, Digital Policy Enforcement and Governance Issues

There is a need for digital rights management infrastructure, as a tool for content management (both commercial and noncommercial).

But digital rights management, even in the limited context of the management of "content" on the network, has at least four different components:

- A "policy metadata" layer, which allows for the structured description of policies – what permissions relate to this item of content, under what conditions of use (for example, attribution, period of use, payment), and what is not permitted (for example, adaptation);

- An "authentication, authorization and access" layer – which allows for the structured identification and authorization of different users (or classes of users) and the matching of their privileges with the permissions relating to content;
- An "enforcement" layer, which is the technology most commonly associated with the acronym "DRM"
  - The technology which allows policies relating to content to be enforced even after content has been released from a controlled local network into the (uncontrolled) global network;
- An "audit" layer, which allows activities to be recorded and compliance with policies to be monitored.

In essence, a perfect software for the delivery of high quality images should have the following features:

- Allow quick and easy view of even huge (up to gigabytes) image files.
- Not require plug-ins or special client software.
- Not require proprietary image formats and instead support the most popular ones.
- Allow interactivity with the end user, offering advanced functionalities such as zooming, panning, dragging, comparing of more images, editing of remote images, one-on-one editing sessions.
- Guarantee colour accuracy, enabling the server to deliver image ICC colour profiles and by having the profiles interpreted on the client side, therefore ensuring colour accuracy on user's display.
- Ensure implicit protection of image by not allowing copy of the whole image file.
- Allow the image to be protected by dynamic digital watermark.
- Enable tracking of the watermarked image and its users.
- Allow easy integration within existing Web site architecture
- Allow integration with databases.
- Allow full customization for specific functionalities and user interfaces.
- Be browser independent.

Figure 1.

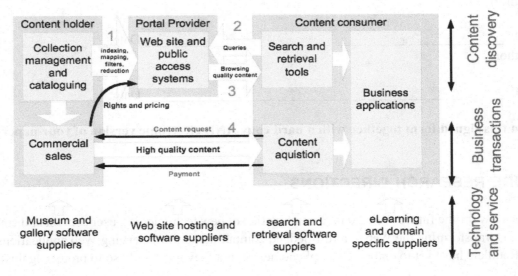

- Require minimal hardware power on user's side (low computing power, low RAM, average speed Internet connection)

EXAMPLE OF DRM STANDARD SIGN FORM

Copyright Release Form

I / we agree that the abstract/paper entitled:

_____

_____

is original work and has not been published in any other publication

I/We give my/our permission for the written paper to be published in the Journal 'Forum' by … if and when the manuscript is accepted for publication.

The author(s) reserve(s) all proprietary rights such as patent rights.

The author(s) retain the right to use all or part of this manuscript in future works of their own, such as lectures, press releases, reviews or text books.

The presenting author is responsible for providing evidence of copyright clearance or authority on any items subject to copyright which are included in the manuscript.

Signed: _____ Date:_____
(presenting author)

Signed: _____ Date:_____
(co-author)

Signed: _____ Date:_____
(co-author)

Signed: _____ Date:_____

Return this signed form together with a hard copy AND electronic version of your paper to:…

FUTURE RESEARCH DIRECTIONS

Gartner view for the future Web 2.0 is "a combination of new technologies, user content and communities that is transforming the Web to a full-fledged computing platform serving Web applications to end users. Retailers have yet to embrace this phenomenon, but they need to do so to protect against threats

Table 1. New approach to the Web services

Web 1.0		Web 2.0
Personal Web sites	→	Blogging
Domains speculation	→	Optimisation of positioning in Web crawlers
Business on page views	→	Cost per click
Content publication	→	Content creation in networked partnerships
Content management systems	→	Wikis (editing the contents)
Taxonomy (top-down and rigid classification of contents)	→	Folksonomy: the users classify autonomously the contents
Stikiness (try to keep the visiting users as long as possible on the site)	→	Syndication (portion of the site is made available to other sites that share users and contents)

to their brands." Consequently the majority of the big enterprises is expected to have the technology to use the new Web 2.0 possibilities but they will be late to apply the most promising aspects of this advance which should respect the social aspect of the new services. The social aspects is evidenced by the following Table 1 where it is clear the user participation to the empowering of the new Web contents and services.

Based on the above table DRMSs will be made available through numerous e-commerce sites and their services will support users to transact and share contents. The DRMS will be a part of the Syndication characteristic of the Web 2.0.

REFERENCES

Cappellini, V., Piva, A., Dawson, D., & Tsolis, D. (2003, June). Technological solutions for copyright protection and management of cultural heritage: Best practices and guidelines. Workshop on Digitization of Cultural Content, 27-28 June 2003, Corfu, Greece.

DIG35 Specification - Metadata for Digital Images. Version 1.0. (2000). Digital Imaging Group.

Digital Object Identifier. http://www.doi.org

Digital watermarking. (2002). Morgan Kaufann Publishers.

Rosenblatt, B., Trippe, B., & Mooney, S. (2002). Digital rights management – Business and technology. *Professional Mindware.* , New York: M & T Books.

Tsolis, G. K., Tsolis, D. K., & Papatheodorou, T. S. (2001). A watermarking environment and a metadata digital image repository for the protection and management of digital images of the Hellenic Cultural Heritage. *International Conference on Image Processing, Thessalonica.* Greece, 2001.

ADDITIONAL READING

Federated Digital Rights Management (D-Lib Magazine, July/August 2002)

Digital Rights Management and Copy Protection Schemes (EFF org)

ηττπ://εν.ωικιπεδια.οργ/ωικι/ΔPM

ηττπ://ωωω.δρμωατχη.χομ/

http://drm.info/

Section V
Legislative Issues

The legal issues are being analyzed, aiming at pointing out the most crucial legislative parameters that affect digital rights management and the distribution of copyrighted material online through e-commerce systems.

Chapter XIV
Digital Rights Management:
A European Law Perspective

Christos Golfinopoulos
Attorney at Law, Golfinopoulos Law Office, Patra, Greece

ABSTRACT

The purpose of this chapter is to provide a brief overview of the legal framework that applies to Digital Rights Management (DRM) information and Technological Protection Measures at the EU level. For this reason, the relevant legal instruments are identified and briefly described, while at the same time, an effort has been made to identify the most important points of concern that arise from the interpretation and application of the law. The review concludes by reference to the ongoing discussion over DRM designs to best incorporate the requirements of the law into technological solutions.

EU COPYRIGHT LAW AND DRM

Copyright Law is based on the right of the author or producer of a protected work to forbid unauthorized reproduction. In order to apply this principle in practice, one would have to formulate rules to define (a) what is a protected work, (b) who is the holder of the rights to this work; (c) what are, if any, the exceptions or limitations to those rights and (d) how to enforce those rights and/or exceptions. These rules are defined in law, creating a framework for rightholders to exploit their rights when making their works available to third parties and the public in general.

The larger the number or protected works; the wider their distribution and exploitation, the more vital becomes the need for an effective way for authors to manage their rights. In the world of internet, e-commerce, network effects and fast emerging new technologies, legislation often seems inadequate to deal with situations that arise faster than traditional law-making can cope with. This is most evident when considering Intellectual Property rights in the digital world.

Digital Rights Management (DRM) systems are currently the technical means used to facilitate management of rights.[1] "The term DRM refers to the use of technology to describe and identify digital content protected by intellectual property rights, and which enforces usage rules set by rightholders or prescribed by law for digital content".[2] Digital rights refer to copyright and related rights in the digital environment, whereas digital content is works created, distributed and/or exploited digitally.

The above definition indicates the two main elements of DRM: (a) identification of protected digital content and (b) enforcement of usage rules. Identification is achieved by digitally marking the protected work so that anyone accessing or using it should be at any time aware of the proprietor of rights and the level of protection of that particular work. Enforcement is achieved technically by limiting the actual uses of a protected work by the rightful user, for example via encryption or watermarking.

The main legal instrument on the functioning and application of DRM technologies at EU level is the Copyright Directive[3,] which contains the legal provisions regarding protection of copyright and related rights in the information society and defines the European Commission's policy in the area of Digital Rights Management. The Directive sets the principle goals and the level of protection that Member States must provide for in their national legal systems, yet it leaves Member States to decide on the exact implementing measures in order to achieve the result envisaged in the Directive.[4]

DRM technology, therefore, in Europe must apply and police the provisions of the Directive, safeguarding the rights of IP owners. Rightholders identified and protected in the Directive (authors, producers and/or broadcasting organizations) shall be uniquely identified when incorporating DRM technology into protected content; the ownership rights shall also be manifested via marking/registration. Further, the Copyright Directive spells out a number of exceptions to the rights of content owners. DRM technology should allow for certain uses, which the copyright owner must allow on the basis of the rights conferred to him by the Directive. As a result, legislation and its intended effect must be translated into the technological process that will safeguard the proper implementation of the rules. Assuming that this process has been completed in a fair and proportionate way, violation of the provisions of the law should not be possible without tampering with the DRM instrument.

In the digital world, legislation on rights and exceptions is not adequate to safeguard the interests of IP owners against damage incurred by unauthorized acts. Legislation must also allow for the protection of DRM instruments against circumvention and against the production and marketing of circumvention devices. The latter is an indispensable condition for the functioning of electronic commerce and for its acceptance among rightholders and commercial users or even for consumers alike.[5] Using those technological measures to achieve control over the uses allowed by law, allows for direct and "real" compensation to content owners for every protected use. In other words, safeguarding business and financial rights of IP owners depends on achieving the technological challenge of enforcement.

The Directive contains an exhaustive list of the rights and exceptions or limitations to those rights. "Fair compensation" is due to copyright owners in specific cases where exceptions or limitations to the exclusive rights of content-owners are imposed in favour of users (articles 2-5 of the Directive). The Directive also contains provisions regarding the legal protection against circumvention of any effective technological measures (chapter III, articles 6-8). In terms of policy orientation, the Directive expressly encourages compatibility and interoperability of the different technical systems of identification of works and protected subject matter in digital format, voting for global standardization.

As stated in the recital of the Directive, at paragraph 13, "A common search for, and consistent application at European level of, technical measures to protect works and other subject-matter and to provide the necessary information on rights are essential insofar as the ultimate aim of these measures is to give effect to the principles and guarantees laid down in law." Digital Rights Management technologies aim at giving effect to the principles and provisions of the Directive and the implementing legislative measures of the Member States.

THE PROVISIONS OF THE COPYRIGHT DIRECTIVE 2001/29

The EU Copyright Directive attempted the harmonization of the laws of the Member States on copyright and related rights, under Articles 47(2), 55 and 95 of the EC Treaty establishing an internal market and safeguarding competition in the internal market,[6] also implementing in the European legal system the WIPO Copyright Treaty and the WIPO Performances and Phonograms Treaty. The main policy decision behind the harmonization of copyright law in the EU is to provide for a high level of protection of Intellectual Property, having as ultimate goal to boost investment, innovation and competitiveness of European industry.

The justification behind the introduction of the Directive is that differing Member States' legislations on the level of protection of intellectual property could result in restrictions on the free movement of services and products incorporating, or based on, intellectual property, especially due to the continuous and fast development of technologies and the information society. Furthermore, one of the main benefits of ensuring high level copyright protection, is that the appropriate compensation for creators and authors can be guaranteed, which by itself is a major incentive for copyright owners to continue their creative work. The management of rights in the digital environment helps ensure that all commercial and transactional aspects of distribution, licensing and use of digital content are administered in such a way that content owners' rights are safeguarded and the agreed remuneration for the licensed act or use of the content is returned to the content owner.

The Directive ensures that maximum protection is offered to copyright owners, save for a number of exhaustively listed exceptions. Once the basic policy line was decisively in place, discretion was left to Member States to decide on certain important aspects on implementation, in order to achieve the Community goal.

The Directive grants content owners three main rights: (a) the right of *reproduction* (article 2), (b) the right of *communication* to the public including the right of making available (article 3) and (c) the right of *distribution* (article 4). Exceptions or limitations to these rights are listed exhaustively in Article 5 of the Directive. It requires Member States to limit the –otherwise absolute- rights granted to authors and producers, on the basis of *inter alia* public policy, social and cultural considerations as well as use for purposes other than commercial exploitation under circumstances that are explicitly described.

The exceptions and limitations provided for in the Directive are grouped in different categories depending on their purpose and the discretion Member States enjoy in adopting such measures, offering an explicit interface between the protection and exceptions to the rights. In particular:

a. Member States *have* to provide for exceptions to temporary acts of *reproduction* which are transient or incidental and an integral and essential part of a technological process use to enable transmission in a network or any lawful use of a work or other subject matter, provided they have no independent economic significance.

b.   Member States *may* provide for exceptions or limitations to the *reproduction* right in cases of:
- o   Reproductions on paper or any similar medium, provided that the right-holders receive fair compensation;
- o   Reproductions for *private use* and, in general, non-commercial purposes, on condition that fair compensation to rightholders takes into account the implementation of technological measures, as described below;
- o   Specific acts of reproduction for educational purposes e.g. by libraries, educational institutions and museums, which are not for economic or commercial advantage;
- o   Ephemeral recordings of works by broadcasting organisations by means of their own facilities and for their own broadcasts;
- o   Reproductions of broadcasts made by social institutions pursuing non-commercial purposes, such hospitals and prisons, on condition that the rightholders receive fair compensation.

c.   Member States *may*, under specific circumstances, provide for a number of exceptions or limitations to the *reproduction* right and the right of *communication* to the public. From the rather detailed list of article 5 paragraph 3 of the Directive, we distinguish here the following *public* or *social* policy exceptions i.e.:
- o   Teaching or scientific research for non-commercial purposes;
- o   Uses that are necessary for the benefit of people with a disability;
- o   Use for the purposes of public security or to ensure the proper performance or reporting of administrative, parliamentary or judicial proceedings;

In addition to the above, article 5 paragraph 3 of the Directive allows Member States to decide whether to provide for a number of exceptions, which mainly relate to everyday commercial uses of protected subject matter for specific uses, where no direct or indirect commercial advantage derives from 'exploitation' of the protected work itself.

All the above exceptions and limitations may be similarly provided with regards to the right of *distribution*. In any case, however, exceptions and limitations must be applied, according to the Directive, only in "certain special cases which do not conflict with a normal exploitation of the work or other subject-matter and do not unreasonably prejudice the legitimate interests of the right holder".

A detailed list of potentially allowed uses avoids at first sight the vagueness in the interpretation of the law, a situation that is most evident in the US where the focus is on courts and their interpretation of the notion of *fair use*.[7] On the other hand, Member States are not obliged to incorporate into their national legislation all of the above exceptions and limitations. In fact, they *may* only provide for any one of those listed, or even *none*, save for those of an obligatory nature. In that respect, especially in jurisdictions where the legislator may have transposed into national law only the minimum level of protection required by the Directive, a policy choice of using 'fair use' notions rather than exhaustive criteria for exempting certain uses would have been much more generous towards protecting user rights.

The specific provisions of the Directive that are of particular relevance regarding DRM technologies are:

- •   Article 5.2.(b) allows for an exception or limitation to the general *reproduction* right of authors and producers, "in respect of reproductions on any medium made by a natural person for private use and for ends that are neither directly nor indirectly commercial, on condition that the right-holders receive fair compensation, which takes account of the application or non-application of technological measures referred to in Article 6 to the work or subject-matter concerned". It is left to Member States to determine the form, detailed arrangements and possible level of such fair compensation, taking into account the particular circumstances of each case.[8]

- Chapter III of the Directive entitled "Protection of Technological Measures and Rights-Management Information" lists the obligations on Member States to provide for the legal protection of technological measures (Article 6) and rights-management information (Article 7).

The area of law regarding the actual application of DRM technology remains unharmonised and most of these issues are left to Member States. However, the Directive emphasizes on (a) the protection of technological measures and (b) taking into account the application of technological measures when providing for fair compensation for the specific uses of content allowed.

The justification behind excluding from harmonization those areas of law that deal with the development and application of DRM technology, as the Commission recognizes, is that legislation depends largely on the development of technological measures: *"such technology needs to be agreed upon, developed and deployed by the private sector... these criteria should be determined by the market with the risk that possibly divergent or even incompatible standards will emerge"*. Digitization is also transforming the ways content in its different forms is developed, distributed and exploited, with emerging new models such as open source, peer-to-peer, flat rate subscriptions etc.[9]. It seems, therefore, that the move for harmonization reflects the industry's need to safeguard its proprietary rights over content, by ensuring that the main policy objective of the EU is to remain faithful to traditional copyright protection. The political choice to adopt the principle of protection of technological measures as such was necessary for the industry to invest in resources and effort to develop and implement effective DRM solutions. Thus, the market has been left free to develop its own models of content distribution, licensing and remuneration systems, in a legal environment, however, where the balance leans in favor of rightholders and safeguarding IP rights against almost any use, save for a limited number of exceptions that the users, in any event, would have to claim against rightholders. In order to encourage uniform technological systems for the management of digital rights, the EU Commission places its entire focus of the Working Paper in listing and describing the available –at the time of the report- DRM Systems and introducing a number of initiatives aiming at promoting such technology and standardization, through consensus of stakeholders and relevant bodies and organizations.

Protection of Technological Measures under the Copyright Directive[10]

The Directive defines, at article 6 paragraph 3, 'technological measures' as "any technology, device or component that, in the normal course of its operation, is designed to prevent or restrict acts, in respect of works or other subject matter, which are not authorised by the rightholder of any copyright or any right related to copyright as provided for by law or the sui generis right provided for in Chapter III of Directive 96/9/EC."

By means of such technological measures, rightholders should be in a position to control and enforce digitally their rights, *"as provided for by law"*. The latter refers to any legal provision regarding copyright, any right related to copyright as well as the *sui generis* right on the legal protection of databases.

The wording of the law obliges rightholders to build their protective mechanisms in such a way so as to prevent acts or uses that would violate their rights but also *to allow* for the statutory exceptions and limitations specifically provided by law.

The Directive considers those technological measures to be 'effective' where "the use of a protected work or other subject-matter is controlled by the rightholders through application of an access control or protection process, such as encryption, scrambling or other transformation of the work or other subject-matter or a copy control mechanism, which achieves the protection objective." The level of protection is, as already seen, *provided by law*, i.e. it comprises implementation of the rights as well as their exceptions and limitations.

Protection is twofold and is achieved through the general prohibition (a) against circumvention of technological measures, where the offender acts either in knowledge or with reasonable grounds to know that he is pursuing that objective and (b) against the manufacture, import, distribution, sale, rental, advertisement for sale or rental, or possession for commercial purposes of devices, products or components or the provision of services that promote, advertise, enable or facilitate the circumvention of technological measures.[11] In both situations, it is left to Member States' discretion to decide on what legislation to enact in order to provide for adequate legal enforcement of said prohibitions. Such legal protection must be proportionate, allowing research, development and commercial exploitation of devices implementing such technology (e.g. cryptography) for uses other than to circumvent the technical protection.[12]

Adopting the criterion of *effectiveness* in the Directive meets the necessary requirement of proportionality. It is meant to exclude protection of technological measures that do not achieve the protection objective or offer only very limited protection of copyright and related rights on the subject-matter, in such a way that circumvention would be too easy. It is questionable, however, whether protection should actually extend to those technological measures that prevent *access* to a protected work.[13] It should be accepted that, as the Directive stipulates, control of use of a protected work or other subject-matter *must achieve the protection objective*. If an access control technological measure is implemented by the rightholders within the boundaries of protection of subject-matter *as provided by law*, then it should also receive legal protection under article 6 paragraph 3 of the Directive.

Voluntary Measures vs. Legislation

As it is evident from the objective pursued by the technological measures envisaged in the Directive, incorporating into technological measures the exceptions and limitations provided by law could prove to be a rather daunting task. Due to the complexity of the technology and the fact that translating complicated legal notions into technological functions is far from guaranteed, most aspects of the implementation of the provisions of the Directive were left unharmonized.

Therefore, it is not entirely surprising that the Directive encourages *voluntary measures* by rightholders, including agreements between them and other parties concerned, allowing legitimate users (beneficiaries) the benefit of an applicable (to electronic communications such as e-commerce) exception or limitation, as provided for by the Directive (at article 6 paragraph 4). Where such voluntary measures or private agreements apply technological measures according to the provisions of the law, they shall enjoy the equivalent legal protection afforded to technological measures by article 6 paragraph 1 of the Directive.

This, in turn, means that either technological measures must be built in such a way so as to identify in each case the use that falls within an exception (on rightholder's initiative), or beneficiaries should have recourse, for example on the basis of a separate *voluntary* agreement with the rightholder or through national legislation, to some means of claiming their right to a use exempted by law, to the extent necessary to fulfil the purpose of the exception.

Where national legislation incorporates one or more of the specific exceptions or limitations of the Directive (listed above, bulleted items under (b) and (c)), in the absence of voluntary measures, Member States are obliged to take appropriate measures to ensure that rightholders make that exception, or the means to benefit from that exception, available to its intended beneficiary and lawful user.

The *private use* exception to the *reproduction* right was not vested with a similar level of protection. In the absence of voluntary agreements, it is left to Member States to decide whether to enforce the private use exception on rightholders. Even then, the right of rightholders to limit the number of copies to the extent they deem justified and proportionate in order to protect their legitimate interests, cannot be withdrawn or prevented. Moreover, *private use* justifies the imposition of *fair* compensation, for example in the form of royalty payments, which should take into account the application or non-application of technological measures to the work concerned.

This more lenient approach towards the private use exception signifies the expected reduction or phasing out of copyright levies applied in most Member States and their substitution with levies on the basis of the actual use of a protected work, via DRM control measures. This switch will only be possible once technological measures are effectively in operation and are accepted by all stakeholders. Therefore, imposing *ab initio* an obligation on rightholders to allow for the *private use* exception without having established that *fair* compensation would be due by legitimate users only once, would create unnecessary excess costs for beneficiaries. As noted by Reinbothe (2002), the issue of private copying may easily be the catalyst for the successful introduction of technological measures.[14]

It follows from the above, that the Directive initially transfers the authority on rightholders to safeguard the exceptions and limitations to their rights through technological or other voluntary measures.[15] The requirement is optional on rightholders, since failure to provide said voluntary measures shall cause national legislation to intervene in favour of the beneficiary and lawful user. In the absence of voluntary measures or private agreements, Member States are obliged to ensure that beneficiaries enjoy the minimum rights granted to them by the Directive and national implementing legislation against the rightholders.

It is not indicated what measures Member States may impose by legislation in order for legitimate users (that is users who already have lawful access) to benefit from the exceptions to the controlled through technological measures use of a copyrighted work. Furthermore, it is not clear how long a Member State must wait, in the absence of voluntary agreements or other voluntary measures before taking action. According to recital 51 of the Directive, this should happen within a "reasonable period of time". As correctly pointed out, "it is unclear under which conditions the mere authority to impose obligations changes to a duty to impose obligations. It is questionable, for example, whether this duty only emerges once an abusive behaviour by a rightholder has become apparent."[16]

Since either voluntary or State measures should make possible for the users to exercise an exception to the rights of the content owners, it is widely supported that acts of circumvention needed to exercise a lawful exception are not permitted. The wording of the final text of Article 6 paragraph 1 of the Directive, when compared to the original text of the proposal, has lead to ambiguity as to whether the prohibition of circumvention of technological measures should only be linked to acts of infringement of copyright and related rights over a protected work. Commentaries conclude that the protection afforded under the Information Society Directive can, in principle, be invoked even for acts of circumvention accomplished for purposes that would be lawful under the copyright act.[17]

As it has been generally accepted in literature, "even if article 6(4) creates an obligation to provide the means to exercise a limitation, this obligation is imposed on rights owners and does not give users any authority to perform acts of circumvention themselves. In other words, this provision "does not introduce exceptions to the liability of the circumvention of technological measures in a traditional sense, but rather introduces a unique legislative mechanism which foresees an ultimate responsibility on the rightholders to accommodate certain exceptions to copyright or related rights".[18]

This approach is justified, assuming that voluntary or State measures actually grant users the right to an exempted use to the effect fully permitted by law and under circumstances that allow the legitimate user to take advantage to the fullest extent possible of his rights. In cases, however, where no voluntary measures or an agreement between the rightholder and a legitimate user exist and national legislation measures are either inadequate or too burdensome and time consuming for the legitimate user to invoke, would the legitimate user be held liable for circumventing those technological measures in order to pursue his legitimate right to an exception or limitation?

The general principle behind the provisions of the Directive is that a *fair balance* of rights and interests between rightholders and users of protected subject-matter must be safeguarded.[19] The definition of 'technological measures' in the Directive refers to measures designed to prevent or restrict acts "which are not authorised by the rightholder of any copyright *as provided for by law*".[20] In effect, rightholders do not have *ab initio* the absolute right to prohibit any act with regards to a copyrighted work; rather, their very right is limited in scope at its birth, in a sense that the exceptions and limitations provided by law do not fall within the realm of the exclusive rights of the content owner. In the wording of the Directive, "*they [exceptions] are exempted from the right.*"

The way one interprets the Law on this point is of particular importance. Circumvention is not allowed for technological measures built to protect the rightholder's right. It is certainly not for the rightholder to prevent legitimate uses which have been explicitly identified in law as exempted from the protected right, but rather his duty to allow them. While the wording of the Directive, as already noted above, indicates that one would have committed an unlawful act, in case of circumvention in order to benefit from an exception or limitation,[21] a teleological interpretation of this very provision of the Directive could reach the opposite conclusion. Holding a user liable for claiming his right to an exempted use, where voluntary measures or national legislation in effect preempt his right, as provided for by the Directive, runs against the very principles of fairness and proportionality. An equitable rule-of-reason analysis on a case-by-case basis would probably support the same view. Excluding *a priori* an interpretation of the anti-circumvention rules of the Directive in favor of the rightful user, could lead to situations where although all measures and legislation are in place, the actual benefit of an exception to any legitimate user is limited for merely practical reasons, due to the complexities of the technology involved and the inadequacy of those entrusted to deal with disputes to promptly react to a request for an exempted use by the rightful user.[22]

Legislation grants authors and producers the right to control the use of their works. To challenge that right, one must refuge to litigation, mediation or other procedures provided by law. Likewise, legislation also grants users the right to use lawfully acquired works for a number or exempted uses, which in turn means that technological protection mechanisms used to restrict access may not be circumvented and should remain unaffected. Nevertheless, it is the rightful user once again who would have to pursue litigation or mediation, as provided for in law, if his right to an exempted use is violated by the rightholder. This formulation places unreasonable burden on the user -especially the single not easily identified user[23]- despite the fact that most of the exempted uses have been placed in order to safeguard 'public policy' objectives, which should take precedent over authors' rights. It is the very right of the user to an exempted use that should allow for circumvention of DRM technologies without any sanctions in order for the user to exercise the right to that use.[24]

Adopting that approach is necessary in order to safeguard users' rights and protect the lawful consumer. Relying solely on DRM solutions to ensure that the intended user of the content is not subject to any unlawful constraint,[25] makes lawful use conditional on explicit permission from rightholders. If circumvention is in every situation unlawful, then enforcement of users' rights is compromised in favor of absolute —even abusive- enforcement of IP rights. In this respect, the proposal put forward to expressly recognize by law the imperative character of some or all limitations on copyright and related rights is to be welcomed.[26]

On-Demand Services: A Troublesome Provision

Article 6 paragraph 4 of the Directive, fourth subparagraph reads as follows:

The provisions of the first and second subparagraphs [obligation on MSs to provide necessary means for users to benefit from exceptions] shall not apply to works or other subject-matter made available to the public on agreed contractual terms in such a way that members of the public may access them from a place and at a time individually chosen by them.

As indicated at the recital of the Directive at paragraph 53, the above exclusion refers to the provision of interactive on-demand services, as opposed to non-interactive forms of online use, where such services are governed by contractual arrangements. With regards to those services, the obligation to safeguard the exceptions through voluntary or State measures, to ensure that users enjoy the benefits of limitations to the content owners' rights, as described above, does not apply.

At first reading, the wording of this provision is rather alarming, as it seems to remove any obligation or limitation to the basic rights of the Directive in almost every e-commerce activity or relationship. The purpose of the provision is to cover situations were the provision of certain services are tailor-made to individual requests for the provision at a specific place and for a limited duration of time, as per the contractual agreement between the right's owner and the user. In a situation like that, the agreement includes licensing and fee arrangements appropriate and analogous to the use and duration of that use of the transmitted copyrighted content. Furthermore, the provision of the service covers the specific need of a member of the public as requested for a particular point in time, event or situation. Under those circumstances, it is, therefore, reasonable to assume that the contracting parties have specifically taken into consideration the very specific use of the sought on-demand service, adjusting accordingly the royalties, in a sense that no exceptions to the sought on-demand use should be allowed.

Nevertheless, the concerns expressed against the actual application of this provision in the future, where online on-demand interactive services might become the norm in e-commerce, remain valid.[27]

Protection of Rights Management Information under the Copyright Directive

Article 7 of the Directive imposes obligations regarding protection of electronic Rights Management Information analogous to those for protection of technological measures. The Directive defines this term as "any information provided by rightholders which identifies the work or other subject-matter referred to in this Directive or covered by the sui generis right provided for in Chapter III of Directive 96/9/EC, the author or any other rightholder, or information about the terms and conditions of use of the work or other subject-matter, and any numbers or codes that represent such information." With regards to such information, removal or alteration is strictly forbidden. Accordingly, circulation to the public in any way of works or other subject-matter products without the rights management information initially attached to them, where the offender knows or has reasonable grounds to know that such an act may ultimately lead to infringement of copyright or any related rights (including the *sui generis* right for the protection of databases) is also forbidden. The Directive requires Member States to provide for adequate legal protection against any of those acts.

As opposed to Technological Protection Measures, whose purpose is to control access and/or copying of a protected work, it is clear from the definition in the Directive that DRM is used to identify the protected work and the terms and conditions of use of the protected work or subject matter. Enforcement comes as a necessary step and may be effectuated through the implementation of various technological measures, depending on the rules set by rightholders or imposed by law, regarding the allowed uses of protected content. The distinction between technological measures and electronic rights management information in the Directive, therefore, is more of a technical nature rather than of substance. The Commission, in effect, recognises that protection of rights in the digital world does not necessary lie on measures that ultimately render a certain use or reproduction of copyrighted material impossible but also the intended protection may be achieved through less restrictive and more flexible approaches, whereby information on the IP rights over a work remain inextricably linked to that particular work and compliance is monitored when accessed by any user.

Sanctions and Remedies under the Copyright Directive

The Directive, at article 8, calls for "effective, proportionate and dissuasive" sanctions and remedies in respect of infringements of the rights and obligations set out in its provisions, as well as all the measures necessary to ensure that these sanctions and remedies are applied.

The minimum level of protection shall include damages actions as well as injunctions by rightholders against infringers and infringing activities and, where appropriate "for the seizure of infringing material as well as of devices, products or components" that facilitate circumvention of technological measures. Intermediary service providers used by a third party to commit an infringement may also face injunction orders.[28]

It is apparent that Member States enjoy wide discretion in deciding what sanctions or measures to introduce against infringers. Hence, implementation has resulted in various approaches in different Member States, most notably with the imposition of criminal sanctions (especially imprisonment) as opposed to civil sanctions, which seem to be the most common.[29]

OTHER EU LEGISLATION RELEVANT TO TECHNOLOGICAL MEASURES AND DRM INFORMATION

Directive 2000/31 on E-Commerce

As already seen, the principle legal basis for the protection of IP rights, technological measures and DRM information in Europe is the Copyright Directive. Protection of copyright liability in the network environment further requires a number of measures to regulate electronic commerce, dealing with issues such as defamation, misleading advertising, infringement of trademarks. These concerns are addressed horizontally in Directive 2000/31/EC of the European Parliament and of the Council of 8 June 2000 on certain legal aspects of information society services, in particular electronic commerce, in the internal market (E-Commerce Directive).[30] The timescale for implementation by Member States of both the Copyright Directive and the E-Commerce Directive has been similar and the need for coordinated introduction of both measures, as complementary to each other and based on similar principles, has been clearly spelled out in both legal texts.

The objective of the E-Commerce Directive has been to create a legal framework to ensure the free movement of information society services between Member States. The definition of information society services already exists in Community law in Directive 98/34/EC of the European Parliament and of the Council of 22 June 1998 laying down a procedure for the provision of information in the field of technical standards and regulations and of rules on information society services[31] and in Directive 98/84/EC of the European Parliament and of the Council of 20 November 1998 on the legal protection of services based on, or consisting of, conditional access[32]; this definition covers any service normally provided for remuneration, at a distance, by means of electronic equipment for the processing (including digital compression) and storage of data, and at the individual request of a recipient of a service.[33]

The Directive requires Member States to lay down in their legal systems requirements applicable to information society services according to the distinctions provided for by the Directive (coordinated field), which cover on-line activities such as on-line information, on-line advertising, on-line shopping and on-line contracting. Information society services explicitly include on-demand services which are transmitted point to point, such as video-on-demand.[34] Such requirements also concern, under Article 3 of the Directive, the content of the service and the liability of the service provider.

In that respect, service providers have a duty to act, under certain circumstances, with a view to preventing or stopping illegal activities. The Directive encourages the development of rapid and reliable procedures for removing and disabling access to illegal information, primarily by developing such mechanisms on the basis of voluntary agreements between all parties concerned that should be encouraged by Member States. Furthermore, the provisions of the Directive relating to liability in no way precludes the development and effective operation, by the different interested parties, of technical systems of protection and identification and of technical surveillance instruments made possible by digital technology within the limits laid down by Directives 95/46/EC and 97/66/EC on data protection and privacy. To this effect, interoperability and compatibility of electronic means, not only within the EU but also on a global scale, is necessary in order to make laws and procedures compatible.[35] The reference to the technological measures, DRM information and voluntary agreements envisaged in the Copyright Directive is direct and unequivocal.

Liability of service providers is only excluded, under certain circumstances, in cases of 'mere conduit', 'cashing' and 'hosting', as those terms are specifically described in the Directive. A service provider, however, who deliberately collaborates with one of the recipients of his service in order to undertake illegal acts, cannot benefit from the liability exemptions established for these activities. The Directive's provisions on liability exceptions of service providers in cases of 'mere conduit', 'caching' and hosting, pinpoint to the major problem posed, for example, by peer-to-peer technology which has to a great extend facilitated copyright violations of massive scale. Effective DRM systems may offer solutions to this problem since protection of content transmitted lies on mechanisms incorporated in the content itself rather than solely at the level of the service provider through which content is disseminated.

Similarly to the Copyright Directive, necessary sanctions against violators must be in place, and especially injunctions of different kind should be available, consisting in particular of orders by courts or administrative authorities requiring the termination or prevention of any infringement, including the removal of illegal information or the disabling of access to it.[36]

Under Article 3 of the Directive, Member States may not restrict the freedom to provide information society services from another Member States (for reasons falling within the coordinated field), save for reasons –inter alia- relating to public policy and the protection of consumers. Under the public policy umbrella, the Directive places most emphasis on serious criminal offences, such as those against minors, against human dignity and those of grounds or race, sex, religion or nationality discrimination. Nevertheless, public policy is a wide area and could cover a number of infringements set for the protection of various public policy objectives, when criminal sanctions have been chosen my Member States as means of ensuring compliance.

It is apparent from the provisions of the Directive, when read in conjunction with those of the Copyright Directive, that reliance on private sector initiatives to develop interoperable state-of-the-art technological measures and DRM systems as well as on interested stakeholders (including consumers) to enter into *voluntary agreements* for the exploitation of rights and dissemination of copyrighted material through e-commerce systems, allowing for full application of the law to the benefit of all interested parties, is a policy objective of EU legislation in the area of IP protection and e-commerce systems. The question once again turns to the vital issue of translating legal restrictions into electronic measures, further allowing for negotiation and private contractual solutions, whereas state intervention remains the last resort. The balance of rights in favor of IP owners and service providers indicates that State intervention must in any case be available, offering swift and workable solutions to situations where the rights of lawful content users are at stake. State mechanisms to safeguard the legality and proportionality of any *voluntary* measures must also exist, since the balance of powers against the consumer – final user is bound to undermine the creation of a level playing field for all stakeholders.

Data Protection and Privacy

Data about how the protected works are used is of additional economic value. The discussion around application of various DRM designs entails a thorough consideration of issues that could arise in terms of data protection and privacy. It is not within the scope of this chapter to deal with those aspects of law; hence this brief reference is made for informational purposes only.

The protection of individuals with regard to the processing of personal data is governed by Directive 95/46/EC of the European Parliament and of the Council of 24 October 1995 on the protection of individuals with regard to the processing of personal data and on the free movement of such data (OJ L 281, 23.11.1995, p. 31.) and Directive 97/66 EC of the European Parliament and of the Council of 15 December 1997 concerning the processing of personal data and the protection of privacy in the telecommunications sector (OJ L 24, 30.1.1998, p. 1.). These two legal instruments establish a Community legal framework in the field of personal data that is fully applicable to information society services.

Legal Protection of Computer Programs. The legal protection of technological measures under the Copyright Directive does not affect the specific provisions on protection provided for by the Directive on the legal protection of Computer Programs[37]. In particular, it does not apply to the protection of technological measures used in connection with computer programs, which is exclusively addressed in that Directive. As stipulated at paragraph 50 of the recital of the Copyright Directive, its provisions should neither inhibit nor prevent the development or use of any means of circumventing a technological measure that is necessary to enable acts to be undertaken in accordance with the terms of Article 5(3) or Article 6 of the Computer Programs Directive.

In particular, article 5(3) of the Computer Programs Directive allows a lawful user of a computer program to observe, study or test the functioning of the program in order to determine the ideas and principles of the program, if he does so while performing any lawful use of the program. Article 6 of same Directive describes the terms and conditions under which a rightful user may perform acts of decompiling of a computer program without the authorization of the rightholder.

On the other hand, article 7 of the Directive contains itself a provision on protection of technological measures, requiring Member States to provide for adequate remedies against a person committing any act of circulating or possessing for commercial purposes of any means intended to facilitate the unauthorised removal or circumvention of any technical device which may have been applied to protect a computer program.

It is apparent that Community law comprises two legal regimes applicable to technological protection measures: on the one hand, a regime that prohibits the business of trafficking in illicit devices, pursuant to the Computer Programs Directive; and, on the other hand, a regime that prohibits both the act of circumvention of TPMs, as well as the business of trafficking in illicit devices or circumventing services.[38]

ONGOING DISCUSSION OVER DRM SYSTEMS

The discussion over the impact of DRM systems and effective protection of technological measures has for some years now hoped for a shift in online practices and markets. A wide variety of views have been expressed, all stressing the importance of interoperability and flexibility in allowing technology markets to develop the necessary standards for administering IP rights through technological measures.

Interoperability is in almost every case presented as indispensable to user acceptance of technological measures and DRM designs. Unavoidably, this principle leads the discussion to Open DRM standards, which may guarantee content distribution over a multitude of platforms and user devices.[39] The concern that in a horizontal market, access to services by consumers and access to consumers by providers had to remain technology neutral still existed in mid-2005, despite the hopes expressed a couple of years earlier that markets would find their way towards standardization and interoperability.[40]

The European Commission, in its 2002 Staff Working Paper, expressed the hope that "DRM systems would enable rightholders [...] to adopt new business models, which would open up new and alternative revenue streams for their content. Ultimately, one solution could be to create an environment where content creators are able to choose whether they wish to protect their rights and receive remuneration or not on a voluntary basis."[41] It goes on to specify an example, drawn from industry interviews, where a single dedicated environment, in the form of a distribution channel, could be used as a platform to ensure compliance with copyright exemptions in favour of beneficiaries.[42] In that case, all content falling within a certain exemption (for example reproduction for educational and public institutions such as libraries, where users could be identified as members of the same group, such as library patrons) would be administered and distributed through a single content platform. This proposal, while it seems viable for a specific content use, it would still require protection of content by DRM systems, in order to prohibit unauthorised copying and redistribution of content from lawful users, for purposes other than their strict intended use. Unauthorised circulation of protected content e.g. in University networks, even were such content is in no way serving an educational cause, is far from limited.

A further passing ascertainment in the Commission Staff Working Paper, is that technological protection measures, in sectors with numerous unidentifiable users such as the music industry, could be applied not by rights holders but rather by an intermediary, like the content or service provider. Lionel S.Sobel elaborated on a similar model in 2003.[43] Based on a comparative presentation of the available at that time business models for distributing copyrighted content, Sobel proposed that Internet Service Providers (ISPs) could act as Digital Retailers, controlling content distribution through their servers. Content would be identified through watermarking, fingerprinting or other technologies, while technology used to identify protected content would reside on ISP's servers. "ISPs would detect and record those watermarks as files flow through their servers [...] and that data would be used to allocate collections proportionately among copyright owners." In that way, Sobel supports, "ISPs would monitor the flow of copyrighted works through their servers, looking for watermarks and recording the recipients of watermarked files. A database would identify the owner of the copyright to each watermarked file, as well as the wholesale price the copyright owner decided to charge for its use." A similar database could be created for fingerprinted files.[44] This model appears to be a realistic proposal that takes advantage of the currently available distribution channels over the internet and exploits the access rights enjoyed by current industry players, such as the ISPs, in order to create a control mechanism of online use of protected content. It certainly requires resolving a number of licensing and royalty issues. Also, an immediate reaction would come from advocates of personal data protection and privacy, since ISPs would gain control over all uses of copyright material over the internet. Nevertheless, in most network industries, network administrators and service providers already have access to user data and it is a matter of legislation and proper controls to ensure that privacy rights will be respected.

When elaborating the way DRM mechanisms should be built, the way users may invoke their rights is of critical importance. A proposal that has been put forward involves DRM designs where users would be allowed "to Challenge the Code".[45] Users would be provided with the ability to request authorisation for controlled actions that should be allowed, as stipulated by law, thus challenging the code of a given DRM mechanism. It is not clear, as Armstrong (2006) points out, whether denial of a requested use could be subjected to a further review either outside or inside the DRM system, nevertheless "the proposal hints at a possible opening-up of DRM mechanisms". This notion of giving users the ability to "assert their rights" through the DRM mechanism seems to gain wider consensus in different model proposals to date.[46] The discussion seems to flirt –now stronger that ever- with the long-established and increasingly accepted principles of Open Source technology and Open Source Licensing practices and models. A strong indication of this trend can be found in most relevant literature with presentations of Open Source Licensing examples, most notably by reference to the Creative Commons initiative, which strives to balance the two ends between full copyright control and free public works. [47]

FUTURE RESEARCH DIRECTIONS

The discussion over DRM systems as means of enforcing IP rights and controlling user rights seems to be dependent on the degree of technological development in this area. The requirements as well as the application of the law shall remain blurred for as long as no standardised solutions or generally accepted principles are adopted by the industry. Since the possibility of achieving such a consensus has been on the table for quite a few years now, Open Source principles and technology would inevitably prevail as the most suitable candidate: interoperability and standardisation can be guaranteed from the outset, without however holding back technological progress and development. It is a matter of turning the discussion from the question of how to protect content and enforce proprietary rights effectively to the point of achieving wide dissemination of content to lawful users, to the benefit of both creative producers and consumers.

REFERENCES

Armstrong, T. K. (2006). Digital rights management and process of fair use. *Harvard Journal of Law & Technology, 20*(1).From http://papers.ssrn.com/sol3/papers.cfm?abstract_id=885371#PaperDownload.

Commission of the European Communities Staff. (2002, February 14). *Digital Rights, Background, Systems, SEC(2002) 197* Working Paper *Assessment*, Brussels.

Curran, T. (2002). Chief Technology Officer, Bertelsmann at the Digital Rights Management Workshop, February 28, 2002, Brussels (from http://ec.europa.eu/information_society/eeurope/2005/all_about/digital_rights_man/index_en.htm).

Dusollier S. (2001, April). Fair use by design in the european copyright directive of 2001. *Communications of the ACM, 46*(4), 51.

Fox L. B., & LaMacchia, B. A. (2003, April). Encouraging recognition of fair uses in DRM systems. *Communications of the ACM, 46*(4), 61-63.

Evain, J-P. (2005, April 6). *Open standards: The path to interoperability. EBU, Towards Reaching Consensus on Digital Rights Management.* Brussels.

Gasser, U., & Girsberger, M. (2004, November 10). *Transposing the copyright directive: Legal protection of technological measures in EU-member states.* Berkman Publication Series. From http://cyber.law.harvard.edu/publications.

Government of France. (2004). *Charter of agreement for the development of a legal supply of on-line music, respect for intellectual property and the fight against digital piracy*, Paris, 28 July 2004, from http://ec.europa.eu/information_society/eeurope/2005/all_about/digital_rights_man/doc/drm_workshop_2005/charte_en.pdf).

Institute for Information of Law (2001, February). *Study on the Implementation and Effect in Member States' Laws of Directive 2001/29 on the Harmonisation of Certain Aspects of Copyright and Related Rights in the Information Society.* University of Amsterdam.

Reinbothe, J. (2002, February 28). *The legal framework for digital rights management. European Commission, submission at the Digital Rights Management Workshop*, Brussels.

Samuelson, P. (2003, April). *DRM (and or vs.) the law. Communications of the ACM, .46*(4).

Sobel, S. L. (2003). *DRM as an enabler of business models: ISPs as digital retailers.* Entertainment Law Reporter, Distinguished Scholar, Berkeley Center for Law & Technology; Lecturer, Boalt Hall (Spring 2003), from https://www.law.berkeley.edu/institutes/bclt/drm/papers/sobel-drm-btlj2003.html

Von, F. L. (2002, April 16). *Fair use and digital rights management: Preliminary thoughts on the (Irreconcilable?) tension between them.* Electronic Frontier Foundation, Computers, Freedom & Privacy 2002. From http://w2.eff.org/IP/DRM/fair_use_and_drm.html.

ADDITIONAL READING

Braun, N. (2003). *The Interface between the Protection of Technological Measures and the Exercise of Exceptions to Copyright and Related Rights: Comparing the Situation in the United States and the European Community, 25*(EIRP 11), 49(.

Byers, S., Cranor, L., Korman, D., McDaniel, P., & Cronin, E. (2003, October 27). *Analysis of Security Vulnerabilities in the Movie Production and Distribution Process, DRM'03.* Washington, DC, USA.

Cheun Ngen, C., Yee Wei, L., Sandro, E., & Pieter, H. H. *Approximating fair use in licenseScript.* The Netherlands: Faculty of EEMCS, University of Twente.

de Rosnay, M. D. (2002). *Digital rights management systems and European law: Between copyright protection and access control.* Web Delivering of Music, 2002. WEDELMUSIC 2002. *Proceedings Second International Conference on,* 117–124.

Dreier, T. P., & Hugenholtz, B. (ed.) (2006). *Concise on European copyright law,* 393. Alphen aan den Rijn, Kluwer Law Intermational.

European Commission (2003). *First Report on the application of Directive 2000/31/EC of the European Parliament and of the Council of 8 June 2000 on certain legal aspects of information society services, in particular electronic commerce, in the Internal Market (Directive on electronic commerce),* Brussels, 21.11.2003, COM(2003) 702 final

European Commission, Digital Rights Management, High Level Group Documents, at http://ec.europa.eu/information_society/eeurope/2005/all_about/digital_rights_man/documents/index_en.htm

GartnerG2, *Copyright and Digital Media in a Post-Napster World,* Version 2 (Updated January 2005), by GartnerG2 and The Berkman Center for Internet & Society at Harvard Law School.

Internet Resource For Digital Rights Management: http://www.drmwatch.com/legal/

Picot, A., & Fielder, M. (2006). *Property rights and openness as factors of innovation.* In Bindseil, U., Haucap, J., & Wey, C. *Institutions in Perspective.* Tübingen, Germany:Mohr Siebeck.

Schneider, M., & Henten, A. (2003, June 27-28). DRMS and TCP: Technology and law. *CTI Working Papers,76, Center for Tele-Information, COST A20 Conference*

Towards New Media Paradigms (2003, June 27-28). Pamplona.

ENDNOTES

[1]   See Commission of the European Communities Staff Working Paper, *Digital Rights, Background, Systems, Assessment*, Brussels, 14-2-2002, SEC(2002) 197. See also Pamela Samuelson, *DRM {AND, OR, VS.} THE LAW*, Communications of the ACM, April 2003/Vol.46, No.4, at p. 45: "DRM has more than one potential relationship with the law: it can enforce, displace, and override legal rights, while the law can constrain the design of DRM."

[2]   Commission Staff Working Paper, supra note 1 at p.6

[3]   Directive 2001/29 of the European Parliament and of the Council of 22 May 2001 on the harmonisation of certain aspects of copyright and related rights in the information society, OJ L167/10, 22.6.2001

[4]   This chapter focuses only on legislation at EU level. For an analysis of Member States' implementing legislation see *Study on the Implementation and Effect in Member States' Laws of Directive 2001/29 on the Harmonisation of Certain Aspects of Copyright and Related Rights in the Information Society*, Institute for Information of Law, University of Amsterdam, February 2001, at Part II (Study commissioned by the European Commission's Internal Market Directorate-General), from http://ec.europa.eu/internal_market/copyright/studies/studies_en.htm. See also Urs Gasser and Michael Girsberger, *Transposing the Copyright Directive: Legal Protection of Technological Measures in EU-Member States*, Berkman Publication Series No.2004 -10 November 2004, from http://cyber.law.harvard.edu/publications.

[5]   Jörg Reinbothe, European Commission, submission at the Digital Rights Management Workshop, Brussels, 28 February 2002, "The Legal Framework for Digital Rights Management".

[6]   For an assessment of the impact of the implementation of the Directive's provisions regarding rights and limitations see Study on Directive 2001/29, supra note 4, under 2.4 at p. 73.

[7]   For a detailed analysis of the fair use doctrine see Fred Von Lohmann, *Fair Use and Digital Rights Management: Preliminary Thoughts on the (Irreconcilable?) Tension between Them*, Electronic Frontier Foundation, Computers, Freedom & Privacy 2002, 16 April 2002, from http://w2.eff.org/IP/DRM/fair_use_and_drm.html. See also Timothy K. Armstrong, *Digital Rigths Management and Process of Fair Use,* Harvard Journal of Law & Technology, Volume 20, Number 1 Fall 2006, from http://papers.ssrn.com/sol3/papers.cfm?abstract_id=885371#PaperDownload.

[8]   recital of the Directive, paragraph 35.

[9]   See Commission Staff Working Paper, supra note 1 p. 9

[10]   For an overview of the Legal Protection of Technological Measures outside Europe and a comparative remark see Study on Directive 2001/29, supra note 4, under 3.3. at p.81

[11]   At article 6 paragraphs 1 and 2 of the Directive. Member States are allowed to go further and prohibit also the private possession of devices, products or components for the circumvention of technological measures (recital of the Directive, paragraph 49).

[12]   recital of the Directive, paragraph 48

13 See Study on Directive 2001/29, supra note 4, pp. 75-76.

14 See Jörg Reinbothe, supra note 5, p.2

15 For an analysis of the intricacies of Article 6(4) of the Directive see Séverine Dusollier, *Fair Use By Design in the European Copyright Directive of 2001*, Communications of the ACM, April 2003/Vol.46, No.4, p.51

16 See Study on Directive 2001/29, supra note 4, at p.109 and reference therein to S. Bechtold, "Comment on Directive 2001/29/EC", in T. Dreier P.B. Hugenholtz (ed.), *Concise on European Copyright Law*, Alphen aan den Rijn, Kluwer Law Intermational, 2006, p.393

17 See Study on Directive 2001/29, supra note 4, pp.78-79 and references therein, see also Séverine Dusollier, supra note 14

18 See Study on Directive 2001/29, supra note 4, p.106 and reference therein to Nora Braun, *The Interface between the Protection of Technological Measures and the Exercise of Exceptions to Copyright and Related Rights: Comparing the Situation in the United States and the European Community*, 25 EIRP 11, 499 (2003).

19 recital of the Directive, paragraph 31

20 See Study on Directive 2001/29, supra note 4, at p.48 and references there in: "According to recital 33 of the Directive, a use should be considered lawful "where it is authorised by the rightholder or not restricted by law". [...] The qualification "not restricted by law" primarily refers to copyright limitations. This expression covers temporary copies that are created to enable uses authorised under existing copyright limitations. The provision ensures that the right of reproduction "cannot be used by rights holders to undermine the copyright limitations listed in Article 5(2) and (3) of the Directive"[...] In principle any limitation of the copyright monopoly may be relevant".

21 This view is further supported by paragraph 5, Article 5 of the Directive according to which "the exceptions and limitations provided for in paragraphs 1, 2, 3 and 4 shall only be applied in certain special cases which do not conflict with a normal exploitation of the work or other subject-matter and do not unreasonably prejudice the legitimate interests of the rightholder". Priority is given to the rightholder and its legitimate interests which take precedent over legitimate users rights for fair use. See also Gasser and Girsberger, supra note 4, p.17 and reference therein to Nora Braun, 2003,pp. 496, 498 (2003).

22 See in this respect the proposal by Barbara L.Fox and Brian A. LaMacchia, *Encouraging Recognition of Fair Uses in DRM Systems,* Communications of the ACM, April 2003/Vol.46, No.4, pp. 61-63 for the creation of safe harbors for modelling fair use rights in DRM systems, starting from approximating in machine-interpretable form fair use features that are a priori declared non-infringing.

23 See Study on Directive 2001/29, supra note 4, p.108, "In other sectors of the copyright industry, where users do not belong to easily identifiable groups and where the negotiation of acceptable agreements is more difficult, rights holders appear to ignore the obligation."

24 See P.Samuelson supra note 1, p.45, on the proposition to reform the US Digital Millenium Copyright Act (DMCA) in order to "allow lawful acquirers of copyrighted material to circumvent technical measures if necessary to make noninfringing uses of the work if the copyright owner has not made publicly available the necessary means to permit the noninfringing uses without additional cost or burden to users."

25 See Commission Working Paper, supra note 1, p.13

26 See Study on Directive 2001/29, supra note 4, p. 160-164

27   Séverine Dusollier, supra note 14, p.54

28   Protection of IP rights in terms of enforcement has been significantly enhanced following the introduction of Directive 2004/48/EC of the European Parliament and the Council of 29 April 2004 on the enforcement of intellectual property rights (OJ L157, 30 April 2004, p.45-86)

29   See Gasser and Girsberger, supra note 4, p.28 for a comparative analysis of the applicable regimes in some Member States.

30   OJ L 178, 17.7.2000, p. 1

31   OJ L 204, 21.7.1998, p. 37. Directive as amended by Directive 98/48/EC (OJ L 217, 5.8.1998, p. 18).

32   OJ L 320, 28.11.1998, p. 54.

33   recital of the E-Commerce Directive, paragraph 17. Those services referred to in the indicative list in Annex V to Directive 98/34/EC that do not imply data processing and storage, are not covered by this definition.

34   Ibid. at paragraphs 18 and 21

35   Ibid. at paragraph 61

36   Ibid. at paragraph 41

37   Council Directive 91/250/EEC of 14 May 1991 on the legal protection of computer programs, *OJ L 122, 17.5.1991, p. 42–46*

38   See Study on Directive 2001/29, supra note 4, p. 86 and references therein.

39   Remarks by Thomas Curran, Chief Technology Officer, Bertelsmann at the Digital Rights Management Workshop, February 28, 2002, Brussels (from http://ec.europa.eu/information_society/eeurope/2005/all_about/digital_rights_man/index_en.htm). Curran noted, however, that if by year 2003, the industry were not closer to an open DRM standard, it would be time for the EC and its counterparts in other regions of the world, to switch from a facilitating role to a more activist role. Note in this respect the "Charter of agreement for the development of a legal supply of on-line music, respect for intellectual property and the fight against digital piracy", signed in Paris on 28 July 2004, between the Government of France, access providers, rightholders, producers and platforms of on-line distribution, aiming at coordinating efforts, *inter alia*, to develop the availability for all platforms under transparent and non-discriminatory conditions of digitised content, to study filtering solutions in the area of peer-to-peer at the level of access providers and to take the necessary measures to develop compatibility between the formats for encoding and downloading music on the one hand, and the software and equipment for reading music files on the other, while ensuring a secure environment for the contents (from http://ec.europa.eu/information_society/eeurope/2005/all_about/digital_rights_man/doc/drm_workshop_2005/charte_en.pdf).

40   Presentation by Jean-Pierre Evain, EBU, Towards Reaching Consensus on Digital Rights Management, Brussels 6 April 2005, Open Standards: The path to interoperability: "the answer to the question what can be standardised and how, remains blurred".

41   See Commission Working Paper, supra note 1, p.16

42   Ibid. p.108

43   Lionel S.Sobel, Editor, Entertainment Law Reporter; Distinguished Scholar, Berkeley Center for Law & Technology; Lecturer, Boalt Hall (Spring 2003), paper entitled *DRM as an Enabler of Business Models: ISPs as Digital Retailers*, from https://www.law.berkeley.edu/institutes/bclt/drm/papers/sobel-drm-btlj2003.html

44   Ibid. pp.5, 13-14

45   See Timothy K. Armstrong, supra note 7, p.89-90 with reference to Erickson and Mulligan.

46   An aspect of this proposal, i.e. the right of users to have recourse to a third party to assert their rights, has to a certain extent been formulated in some Member States' legislation, where mediators (most commonly in a form or government or other administrative body or authority) are entrusted with the task of resolving disputed and intervening by regulating markets where necessary. The introduction of such mechanisms by some Member States was the result of the implementation of their obligation under the Copyright Directive to provide for appropriate measures in the absence of voluntary agreements between rightholders and users, see Study p. 124-132. See also summary of Armstrong's proposal, supra note 7, at p. 108, where users would be empowered to assert fair use rights over purchased content, a record of the asserted fair uses in the form of an audit trail would be preserved by the system and user-identifying information would be escrowed with a third party.

47   See http://creativecommons.org/

Chapter XV
Legal Issues for DRM:
The Future

Vagelis Papakonstantinou
University of Patras, Greece & PKpartners Law Firm, Greece

ABSTRACT

DRM systems have been implemented in the past few years by the Content Industry as the panacea against all copyright (and Intellectual Property Rights in general) infringements over the Internet. The validity of this statement shall be assessed in this analysis, identifying its strengths and record to-date and highlighting its shortcomings in an increasingly complex e-commerce (Web 2.0) environment. While doing this, particular attention shall be given to (mostly EU) Intellectual Property Law, Consumer Law, Data Protection Law, and Competition Law.

THE (LEGAL) BACKGROUND

Before embarking upon the legal analysis of contemporary DRM e-commerce systems, as elaborated in other chapters of this book, a short presentation of the background that led to their development is deemed essential. DRM systems, as it will immediately be seen, have been the Content Industry's technical, but not necessarily legal, response to a relatively recent and otherwise unprecedented volume of attacks against the copyright scheme, that could have ultimately brought its demise. Nevertheless, DRM e-commerce systems, essentially reflecting business rather than technical models, it remains to be seen whether they will indeed fare well under the legislative environment that regulates a number of their aspects.

The Digitization of Information

The digitization of information signaled the first difficulties for the copyright scheme[1]. Until that time the copyright system for protecting intellectual property had worked relatively successfully for around

200 years. It was first developed in the United Kingdom back in 1709[2], when the development of printing and the sale of legislative (and Shakespearean) texts begun evolving into an industry[3]. Law-makers of the time identified thus a new type of property, "intellectual" property. This had not been as evident then, as it perhaps appears to us today: for thousands of years before that time, property was divided into only two categories, fixed assets (land) and mobile assets (furniture, equipment, garments etc.). Only at that time did mankind realize that works of the intellect could be of an economic value, and therefore constituted "property" of their author (or right-holder). In this sense, the system that was then developed, and is still in use today, focused upon protection of the "work" of the intellect against unauthorized reproductions (copyright = right to copy). The author of such a protected work deserved compensation for each and every use (reproduction, copying) of his work by others.

The digitization of information challenged the practical, not theoretical, parts of this scheme. Until then reproductions (copies) of any "work" were relatively easy to control (and thus, ask for a fee): books had to be printed and sold on bookshelves, music had to be copied into vinyl and sold on record stores, paintings could only be seen at the premises of the person who owned them. All these actions of reproduction included cost (and thus could not be undertaken by anyone), and were controllable because of the relatively small distribution channels (shops) and the fragmented market (international commerce meant totally different things at the time). The digitization of information managed the first blow to this scheme: once texts and music and pictures became digital, anyone could reproduce them at minimum cost. No more were printing and binding machines or vinyl-cutting industries needed; once "works" became digital, anyone, even home users, could easily copy and store them in their computer systems for (unlimited) future use. Evidently, the 17th century scheme, whereby any act of copying would confer money to the author of the work automatically became obsolete: copying became so vast that the Content Industry could no longer control it as effectively as it did in the past. Even when new "works" emerged (for instance, movies) it was only a matter of time before digitization affected them in the same way too.

The Internet (Mostly P2P) Factor

The Internet managed the second, and crucial, blow to the copyright scheme: it increased exponentially the distribution channels. Until its emergence the digitization of information, regardless whether annoying in itself for the content industry, remained inevitably "computer-isolated": any user could store tons of protected material in his computer, but use essentially was confined to his computer alone. Because networks did not exist (at least outside the academic or work environment) any exchange of protected works with other users had to be performed physically, by means of copying onto a disk and carrying the disk to another computer in person. Consequently, even at that time the Content Industry was not particularly discomforted[4]: although its property was digitized and copied massively, user-isolation meant that purchases of originals were not substantially affected.

Once the Internet emerged this was no longer the case: connected users were suddenly able to exchange "files" (incorporating unauthorized copies of copyrighted material) without moving from their homes, at a single press of a button and at a marginal cost. Traditional distribution channels (i.e., shops) were shattered. No longer was it necessary at least for some users to purchase the original in order to digitize the work in it – the, vast, Internet community made sure that once a single user in the whole wide world purchased the original and digitized it everybody could then have it for free through a simple download[5].

To make things worse, e-commerce systems emerged that enthusiastically (probably too enthusiastically if they knew what was good for them) facilitated the exchange of files among users, namely Peer-to-Peer (P2P) networks. This development was probably inevitable, given the user interest in it. E-commerce systems are inevitably innovative ways of transforming user interest into money[6]. They may not be predicted beforehand, because they are inherently innovative, transforming new technology into user trends. This has been as much valid ten years ago, when P2P networks were state-of-the-art as it is today, when IPTV, VOD and Web 2.0 systems (for instance, YouTube) are the talk of the day.

At any event, the Content Industry now had to face new e-commerce systems that demonstrated a new way of exploitation of its works. The first to have been affected was the music industry, obviously because songs took up less storing space (with the help of the .mp3 format) and were thus easier to be exchanged through the bandwidth then available. At the peak of an era that such P2P networks as Napster[7] initiated, millions of users rather than buying whole CDs, they broke them apart separating songs and exchanged them for free among them, while income was realized by the facilitator (P2P network, essentially an e-commerce company) through other ways (mainly advertisement).

The battle between the Content Industry (as represented by its music branch) and new e-commerce players (P2P networks) was fierce and lasted a decade. Although a number of cases were initiated by music labels against P2P networks, the one that finally did make it to the US Supreme Court was the one by Metro-Goldwyn-Mayer against Grokster. The question at hand was whether a P2P networks facilitator could be held indirectly ("secondary") liable for the uses of its software by its users (that is, for the unauthorized exchange of copyrighted material among its users). At first[8] the P2P operators seemed like they could get away with it: courts were confused with the, relatively recent VCR cases where VCR manufacturer Sony was not held responsible for copying of TV shows performed by users using its sets[9], and drew the analogy between this case and P2P networks facilitators. Nevertheless, the US Supreme Court held otherwise[10]: based on quantitative and qualitative criteria (for instance, 90% of content stored on P2P networks is copyrighted material, 100 million users exchanged more than 1 billion files on a monthly basis, plus the fact that P2P operators actually advertised this aspect of their systems) it decided, in short, that P2P networks operators are ultimately liable for the actions of their users, and thus made the continuation of their operation in their then form no more viable.

The, American, verdict on Grokster unavoidably affected the way all countries around the world viewed P2P networks. This happened not only because P2P networks could no longer operate lawfully in the USA, but also because copyright legislation constitutes in practice international law. Indeed, the WIPO and the international legal instruments in effect (TRIPS, Berne Convention etc.) have established more or less the same legal scheme internationally. Therefore, although the case on Grokster in not typically enforceable in any other country other than the USA whose Supreme Court issued it, any judge in any other country of the world that will be confronted with it (a task diligently undertaken by lawyers of the music industry[11]) would evidently have to explain extremely well any derogation from its findings. This, in practice, has expectedly put an international lid on all P2P network providers, at least as they were known until then[12].

Emergence of the First DRM Systems for E-Commerce: The iTunes Case

Once the Content Industry had won its battle against the first generation of e-commerce newcomers (namely, P2P networks providers) and it became clear that its content (songs, texts, pictures, and, given bandwidth, films[13]) could not be distributed over the Internet for free, the second generation of e-commerce contestants assessed the situation. After Grokster what was known to everyone in the on-line market was that, first, a tremendous users' interest and know-how existed in the on-line provision of content, and that, second, the Content Industry would not be deprived of its lawful interest to compensation for every use of its content, regardless whether on-line or off-line.

DRM technologies for e-commerce applications emerged as the natural response to the above gap: having a strong market of millions of users on the one hand (who, after the P2P demise, where left "homeless"), and, on the other, an industry that was unwilling to provide its merchandise unless assured that its rights would not be compromised, inevitably led to a technology that would gap this gap[14]. DRM e-commerce systems promised to do exactly that: to secure lawful provision (or, to be exact, provision that is according to the preferences of the Content Industry) of content to users.

The legal considerations behind such DRM e-commerce systems will be discussed in the following chapter. Here it is enough to be noted that DRM e-commerce systems ultimately appeal not only to the Content Industry, for self-evident reasons, but to users as well[15]. Users ought not be perceived as systematic law-breakers. Despite of any doubts anyone may cast upon the copyright (and patent) scheme today, the fact remains that users are aware of law-breaking when downloading content online without paying anything for it. On the other hand, the on-line provision of content undoubtedly has its merits: content is available to take with everywhere, to save in various means for reproduction, to process in play lists, and, ultimately, it constitutes, allegedly, a far more enjoyable option that typical CD or DVD purchasing or cinema viewing. DRM e-commerce systems address concerns of those law-abiding users who see no reason why they should be deprived of the merits of the on-line provision of content. By providing a lawful alternative, DRM systems helped the on-line market mature.

An economic model thus had to be devised. DRM e-commerce systems constitute essentially technical solutions – they do not guarantee in themselves any financial success (any more than they guarantee their own lawfulness, as it will later be seen). At any event, the first comprehensive solution that, combined with the appropriate hardware, had tremendous success in the market and today constitutes the "standard" is undoubtedly Apple's iTunes[16].

The iTunes on-line store is a case study in itself that will be revisited many times during this analysis[17]; being the leader in the market, it has attracted international attention not only on its approach (using DRM technologies for the on-line provision of content) but also on some of its finer features (almost exclusive connection to Apple's hardware -iPod, uniform charges for songs regardless of their age or popularity, fragmented, country-specific provision of content etc.)[18].

An analysis of the iTunes model is here only performed for consistency's purposes; readers are indeed encouraged to visit and purchase at least some content, and also try to store it into Apple-connected (iPod) and non-Apple (other mp3 players) means, in order to acquire a first-hand experience of the standard-setting model in the market. At any event, here it is enough to be noted that Apple has setup on-line music stores in several countries of the world; users from each country connect to their respective on-line store, having installed the appropriate software in their computer, and purchase content (mostly music, but also films, TV shows and other items). Content is priced in a uniform way (for instance, each song costs 99p, regardless whether a song of the 60's or the latest hit) and users cannot shop but only in the shop of their country of residence. Once users have purchased a song, it is downloaded in their account. Use of purchased content is far from unlimited: (through use of appropriate DRM technologies) users can, most notably: (a) use their content on "up to five iTunes-authorised devices" (i.e., computers) at any time, (b) store their content "from up to five different accounts on certain devices, such as iPod, at a time", (c) burn an audio play list up to seven times, (d) are not allowed to burn video content, (e) not allowed to use their content (songs) "as a musical ringer in connection with phone calls"[19].

In the iTunes model we therefore see a DRM e-commerce system in full operation. Its owner (Apple) is using it to restrict use of purchased content. Users buy content (songs, shows, films, audiobooks etc.) at competitive prices, but their rights are effectively limited: they can only use a song they bought in five computers or they can burn it onto a CD only up to seven times. Users are also manipulated into purchasing only from their country's store (thus allowing Apple to gain from exchange rate differences). Appropriate DRM e-commerce systems make sure that these rules are obeyed.

Apple's iTunes is by no means the only DRM model used in the on-line market for the provision of content. Since its first appearance (and success) all possible alternatives have appeared in the market[20]: by now users may pay monthly fees and indeed acquire content without DRM, only streamline content, or pay for any other combination in-between; even Apple (after public criticism, as it will later be seen) has made available, for an additional fee, DRM-free content in its iTunes store. In all these cases DRM systems are the e-commerce providers' such as Apple only weapon, first, to convince the Content Industry to make its products available through their on-line services, and, second, to ensure that rules are observed and their business thus flourishes.

DRM SYSTEMS FOR E-COMMERCE: A LEGAL APPROACH

As already seen, DRM systems for the on-line provision of content have been the e-commerce industry's technical, but not necessarily legal, response to conditions in the market after the Grokster decision. Once it was established that content could no longer be made available on-line without adequate compensation mechanisms for the Content Industry, e-commerce players (most notably, Apple) devised business and technical systems whereby the use of content made available on-line would be controlled according to the standards of the Content Industry who owned it. DRM systems were thus put to this cause.

Of course, DRM systems are by no means newcomers in the field of protecting the interests of the Content Industry. As seen above, off-line DRM systems impeded (and continue to do so) unlimited copying from, for instance, VCRs or DVDs or even CDs[21]. Nevertheless, it was the emergence of e-commerce and the advent of the factors mentioned above (digitization of information, P2P networks) that intensified their use; by now all users over the Internet are familiar with the term and its effect in practice.

It shall therefore be the on-line, e-commerce implementations of DRM systems that shall form the basis of their legal analysis in this chapter. Readers, for practical purposes, may keep in mind while going over this chapter Apple's iTunes; being a leader in the market, its technical implementation and legal approach shall inevitably be repeatedly used as an example.

As regards the particular fields of law that appear to be affected by DRM e-commerce systems, despite of the obvious connection with Intellectual Property (copyright) law, their implementation in contemporary e-commerce practice seems to make several other fields relevant. Most notably, contemporary DRM e-commerce systems find themselves entangled with, at least, Consumer Law, Competition Law and Data Protection Law (Privacy Law) issues. All these fields of law will be elaborated upon in the following paragraphs.

Before embarking upon their examination under a legal point of view a few technical clarifications are deemed essential. Trying to keep the level of analysis as non-technical as possible (technical implementations are elaborated in other parts of this book), within a typical e-commerce DRM system as perceived in this chapter content is expected to follow the so-called *superdistribution* model, whereby *"rules governing its usage are cryptographically attached to the content either directly and or can be dynamically acquired on-line"*[22]. What we therefore have in effect is a system that at its one end attaches cryptographic information onto content, while, at its other end, it sets rules for use of the same content. Evidently, all these actions are undertaken or authorized by the lawful owners (rightholders of the respective economic intellectual property rights) of such content.

DRM e-commerce systems consequently perform two basic tasks: first, they affect "works", in the intellectual property protection sense, by attaching additional information onto them in view of their future use in DRM systems; and, second, they set and implement rules for the further use of such works. It is essentially these two tasks that shall be examined under the said different fields of law in the following analysis.

DRM E-Commerce Systems and Intellectual Property Law

DRM e-commerce systems, as already noted, are the technical, but not necessarily legal, response of the Content Industry to challenges to the intellectual property protection (copyright) scheme. The digitization of information and the emergence of Information and Communication Technologies challenged the viability of a legal framework aimed only at protecting works of the intellect from unauthorized copying. The framework devised in the 17th century withstood all technological and market changes (and the invention of new "works"), based on its strong, factual hold upon acts of copying. When information and communication technologies made copying (private or other) uncontrollable, the whole system crumbled. DRM e-commerce systems aim at re-awarding to rightful owners of "works" control over the use of their property by third parties.

From this point of view DRM e-commerce systems are essentially intellectual property tools. Exactly as with their off-line predecessors (the most recent example pertaining to DVDs), they were created out of a need of the Content Industry, and they purport to properly implement Intellectual Property (copyright) law. It is therefore within this field that the core of the legal analysis pertaining to these systems lies, regardless of the fact that contemporary e-commerce implementations also step into other fields of law such as Consumer Law, Competition Law or Data Protection Law. Such stepping into other fields of law is a by-product of business strategies (for instance, when requesting that content be reproduced only on certain hardware, or that prices are uniform around the world, or that consumers' preferences be recorded) that have ultimately nothing to do with the true nature of DRM e-commerce systems: the protection of intellectual property, within intellectual property law limits, online.

Because Intellectual Property Law constitutes by now more or less international law (thanks to a series of international regulatory instruments, for instance, the WIPO Treaty, the Berne Convention etc.[23]), the approach in this analysis shall essentially focus on the common notions of Intellectual Property Law and not to any, if at all, national particularities. This is deemed necessary, not only because of the, international, nature of Intellectual Property Law itself, but also because DRM e-commerce systems are ultimately e-commerce business models that are addressed to the whole wide world. Being made available over the Internet, their end-users may reside in various parts of the world but, in this context, are subjected to the same, uniform (DRM) rules. For instance, iTunes users acquire the same rights over content purchased regardless whether they reside within the EU or in America[24]. It is with this in mind that we shall resort to the Intellectual Property Law fundamentals, rather than to, local, particularities.

In the same context, it is evident that when we speak of DRM e-commerce systems and Intellectual Property Law, we speak of copyright. Patents have very little to do with implementing DRM e-commerce systems, at least from an end-user perspective; if any one of those systems infringes existing patents, then this is a totally different issue whose analysis largely exceeds the purposes of this chapter. It is therefore basic copyright legislation that shall form the basis of analysis here.

Intellectual Property Law: A "Safe Harbor" for DRM (E-Commerce) Systems?

Intellectual Property Law is an, ultimately, DRM-friendly field of law; this, however, is done in an indirect way. As far as Intellectual Property Law is concerned, only *"technological measures that restrict acts unauthorized by authors"*, the so-called Technical Protection Measures (TPMs), are explicitly acknowledged and protected. In this context, according to the WIPO Copyright Treaty[25], *"contracting parties shall provide adequate legal protection and effective legal remedies against the circumvention of effective technological measures that are used by authors in connection with the exercise of their rights under this Treaty or the Berne Convention and that restrict acts, in respect of their works, which are not authorized by the authors concerned or permitted by law"*[26]. TPMs are thus passively protected in the wording above, by means of explicit recognition of their existence in the Treaty. This is, nevertheless, not the only layer of protection afforded to TPMs: in addition to their passive protection, they are also actively protected against (in the case of e-commerce, at least) "hackers": *"contracting parties shall provide adequate and effective legal remedies against any person knowingly performing any of the following acts knowing [...] that it will induce, enable, facilitate or conceal an infringement of any right covered by this Treaty or the Berne Convention: (i) to remove or alter any electronic rights management information without authority; (ii) to distribute, import for distribution, broadcast or communicate to the public, without authority, works or copies of works knowing that electronic rights management information has been removed or altered without authority"*. Technical Protection Measures (regardless whether in the e-commerce context or other) are thus protected twofold: first, their existence is explicitly acknowledged in the text of law; second, anybody who tempers with them or anybody who passes along content whose TPM have been tempered with, shall be persecuted.

The obvious question now relates to the relationship between TPM and DRM. Despite of the fact that certain views have highlighted their differences (in most of cases with an ultimate aim of justifying attempted circumventions of DRM systems[27]), judging even from their wording their actual relationship becomes clear: TPM are the measures upon which DRM is based. In other words, TPM corresponds to the first of the two basic tasks of DRM systems described above (under 2): the attachment of additional information onto content in view of its later use in DRM systems. And, in the same context, if the act of attaching TPM onto content is recognized and protected by law, most certainly the introduction of (DRM) rules for the use of such (TPM enriched) content is also, indirectly, equally recognized and protected. The use of DRM systems, regardless whether off- or online, is therefore, technically, lawful under Intellectual Property (copyright) Law[28].

Indeed, the e-commerce environment does not seem to affect in any way this statement. In e-commerce models, at least according to the *superdistribution* model seen above, digitised content is affixed with data that shall later be used as instructed by the DRM (e-commerce) system. Evidently, the analysis above is still valid: TPM is data affixed on works regardless whether they shall be used in the off- or on-line environment. And, DRM e-commerce systems, regardless of technology implemented, essentially use such TPM data in order to regulate users' use of content according to their rules. From this point of view the WIPO Copyright Treaty may be used to accommodate DRM e-commerce systems in exactly the same way it has been used so far to accommodate their, off-line, predecessors.

The same is more or less the situation by now in both sides of the Atlantic. In Europe, the Copyright Directive devotes a whole Chapter (Chapter III) to the *"Protection of Technological Information and Rights-Management Information"*. In this context the Directive's Articles 6 and 7 repeat, in effect, the WIPO Treaty's provisions seen above. In the USA, Section 103 of the Digital Millennium Copyright Act (the so-called *"anti-circumvention provisions"*) effectively implemented the same WIPO Treaty provisions. It is therefore safe to say that by now the lawfulness of DRM systems according to Intellectual Property (copyright) Law and as far as its scope is concerned should be taken for granted, both in the off-line and in the online environment.

The DRM E-Commerce Systems Core: The License Agreement

Having established that the first task of DRM e-commerce systems, that is, affixing DRM-related data (in other words, TPM) onto content, is a lawful act performed by rightholders as far as Intellectual Property Law is concerned (and, indeed, Intellectual Property Law is the only field of law that tells us how to deal with "works" or "content"), we now have to establish whether the second DRM e-commerce task is also lawful under the same point of view. In order to do this within an intellectual property context we will inevitably have to look at the terms and conditions of the DRM e-commerce system License Agreement.

It is by now common knowledge that the license to use (but not own) is one of the two ways an author (or, a rightsholder) can make money out of his work. The other way being the transfer of ownership, the license to use shall, for obvious reasons, be the rule in contemporary market conditions. Such "license to use" granted by the rightholder to a user is incorporated into a License Agreement (the all-too-known at least in the Information Technology environment, End-User License Agreement – EULA). However, the particular terms and conditions in a License Agreement are only broadly sketched by (intellectual property) law: apart from a couple of restrictions for the benefit of users (for instance, reverse engineering is allowed regardless what the license says but only for interoperability purposes[29]), an author (or rightsholder) may draw the License Agreement for use of his work by users as he sees fit. It is, after all, under this *laissez-faire* approach that such diverse types of licenses as the standard (commercial) proprietary license (for instance, the MS Windows EULA) and the GPL have been hosted under essentially the same legislative provisions, regardless of their profound differences.

And, it is exactly this possibility for practically endless licensing schemes that makes the task of assessing DRM e-commerce systems' licenses impossible. E-commerce DRM systems do what their owners want them to do. Once it is established, as seen above, that they are allowed to exist, their internal policies and use-specific rules may be as their owners please, provided of course that no mandatory legal provision (and there is only a handful of those in copyright legislation) is infringed. From this point of view, it is simplistic to call DRM (e-commerce or other) systems "good" or "bad"; in themselves, they only constitute tools that (lawfully) regulate use of (copyrighted) works. The use such systems are being put by those who implement them for profit is a totally different issue (and, in most cases, their lawfulness is not for copyright legislation alone to decide).

This is why the License Agreements, the agreements, that is, under which users acquire content, in DRM e-commerce systems should be judged on a case-by-case basis according to Intellectual Property (or other, as seen in the following chapters) legislation. While doing this attention should at first be given to the mandatory provisions of copyright law. Irrevocable rights awarded to users by Intellectual Property legislation cannot be infringed by any contractual terms included in DRM systems' License Agreements. In this context, the European Copyright Directive expressly sets that "*notwithstanding the legal protection provided for [...], in the absence of voluntary measures taken by rightholders, including agreements between rightholders and other parties concerned, Member States shall take appropriate measures to ensure that rightholders make available to the beneficiary of an exception or limitation provided for in national law the means of benefiting from that exception or limitation, to the extent necessary to benefit from that exception or limitation and where that beneficiary has legal access to the protected work or subject-matter concerned*"[30]. What the Directive says, in a perhaps not so straightforward way, is that whenever users benefit from any rights under copyright legislation such rights should continue to be applicable under DRM e-commerce systems as well.

The above been said, it is in fact very few irrevocable rights that are awarded to users by intellectual property legislation that pertain to use of content. Apart from certain categories where special rules may apply (for instance, libraries, education), the rule is that usual, typical users are very much left helpless by copyright law when it comes to DRM systems' policies imposed upon them. Rightholders (the Content Industry) is more or less free to draft the terms and conditions of its (DRM) license agreements as it pleases, at least from a copyright law perspective (other fields of law may not be as accommodating, as it will later be seen).

The only two issues the content industry has to tackle while drafting its DRM license agreements relate to "fair use" in the USA and "private copying" in Europe. According to well-known copyright provisions respectively, in America users are entitled to reproduce works for "fair use" purposes[31]; in Europe, users are entitled to one copy of each work, used for their private purposes[32]. DRM e-commerce systems sometimes (and, it is again reminded that their License Agreements reflect the business models of their owners) get in the way of the above two rights. DRM adversaries have most of the times barricaded themselves behind these two issues. The (legal) analysis of these two cases would largely exceed the limits of this chapter, but would most probably also prove unfruitful[33]. As already seen, it is not in the nature of DRM systems to infringe, for instance, the right to fair use of copyrighted material. DRM e-commerce systems, in their contemporary form (see, for instance, iTunes) only reflect business models, not technological limitations; evidently, if a new law or a court decision set what exactly constitutes "fair use" with regard to current DRM systems implementation, then DRM systems could do nothing but comply; it is therefore to this end that any adversary-DRM resources should be spent. From a *prima facie* approach on typical license agreements of e-commerce DRM systems, it would appear that most of the times they do reflect the existing (regardless how limiting, from the user's perspective) standard copyright provisions.

DRM E-Commerce Systems from the User Perspective

DRM e-commerce systems affect the user perspective, from an Intellectual Property (copyright) Law point of view, in two ways: first, they affect the product he buys. And second, they regulate this, already purchased, product's use in his own hardware. Nevertheless, as it will immediately be seen, the user had better looked elsewhere for effective protection of his rights, than into copyright law.

In the first instance, as already seen, the user, from his own point of view, is interested in purchasing a license to use a specific work, but he ends us with a work that is "DRM-enriched". Whether the user has an option to purchase DRM-without content, or DRM-enriched works is his only way of acquiring them does not constitute an Intellectual Property Law consideration (but rather a Consumer Law or Competition Law question that shall be elaborated in the respective chapters). For the time being it is enough to note that, according to copyright law seen above (under 2.1.1) it is lawful for rightholders to make available media files that do not contain only the work but also other (DRM related) data. From a user point of view therefore, the fact that, rather than buying for instance a license to use a song, he buys a media file containing the song and DRM data, is perfectly fine according to copyright law.

The second task of DRM e-commerce systems is more subtle; they control reproduction of the work, implementing the terms of the respective License Agreement. For instance, a specific song purchased in .mp3 format by a user may not play on all mp3 players, but only on the seller's marketed ones. Again from Intellectual Property (copyright) Law perspective, the user's right to reproduce the work, whose license to use he just acquired, is limited as per the same License's terms. These limitations of reproduction are technically implemented through a DRM system (in the above example, the song just won't load in another mp3 player). Nevertheless, no matter how frustrating this situation may be for the user, the rightholder has in effect all the economic (intellectual property) rights over a work (content), and part of these rights is to grant licenses to use with as many limitations as he wishes (and the market can handle). As long as the rightholder (or, the Content Industry) keeps away from the few (very few indeed, in the case of content) mandatory legal provisions of Intellectual Property Law, the user's right to reproduce the work acquired under a License Agreement may be as limited as (feasibly) possible. DRM e-commerce systems merely reflect this generosity of copyright law to rightholders, but under no means can they be blamed for it by users[34].

DRM E-Commerce Systems from the Author Perspective

Author's rights are probably more relevant when it comes to implementing DRM e-commerce systems under Intellectual Property (copyright) Law. Of course, "authors" in this case do not coincide with rightholders; authors in this chapter shall mean the actual artists who have created the content. As known, when a work is created in the copyright sense, its author automatically acquires economic and moral rights over it; in today's market conditions authors usually transfer their economic rights over their works to the Content Industry (obviously, in return of a fee) and they keep their moral rights (mostly, the right to be recognized as author of the work).

In view of all the above, authors are faced today with some basic questions: first, whether to allow the Content Industry to apply DRM (TPM, actually) data onto their works. Second, whether they do want their works to be made available to users under a DRM e-commerce scheme.

The replies to these answers may not always be straightforward. Although one would expect that the Content Industry, in its contract with the author for transfer of his economic rights, will have provided expressly that the author leaves it at its discretion whether and how to make available the work through DRM e-commerce systems, sometimes this will conflict with the author's inalienable moral rights – and the latter shall prevail. According to the Berne Convention, "*Independently of the author's economic rights, [...]the author shall have the right to [...]object to any distortion, mutilation or other modification of, or other derogatory action in relation to, the said work, which would be prejudicial to his honour or reputation*"[35]. These rights may not be forfeited under contract.

Authors' therefore do appear to have a choice. The insertion of DRM data onto their works by the Content Industry may be claimed that it worsens the quality of reproduction[36], constituting thus a, forbidden, "*distortion*" or even "*mutilation*" of their work. In the same context, perhaps distribution of a certain work through a DRM e-commerce system that is particularly restrictive and has grown a bad reputation among Internet users may be construed as "*a derogatory action, prejudicial to his honour or reputation*". In all those instances authors do have a right to object against the Content Industry and the DRM systems it implements for distribution of their works. Although here again the lawfulness of distributing works under a DRM e-commerce scheme *per se* may not be challenged by authors (as much as by users), authors have an extra set of rights, their moral rights, from which they could draw if they wished to limit or amend the distribution of their works under DRM e-commerce schemes.

DRM E-Commerce Systems and Consumer Law

As already noted, DRM e-commerce systems essentially constitute "systems" for the on-line use of content: these systems are composed of technical data (TPM, affixed on each "work" in the intellectual property sense) and rules for the use of such (TPM-enriched) content. Once it is established that their existence is basically justified by Intellectual Property (copyright) law, that, as seen above, allows the insertion of DRM-related data onto content, only the rules of these "systems" may be scrutinized under other fields of law. Nevertheless, not all DRM e-commerce systems are run by the same rules; because they ultimately reflect business models of those who implement them, their rules may vary from strict, hardware-limited control over the reproduction of content, to laid back simple cataloguing of users' preferences. This, inevitable, lack of uniformity makes the task of drawing general conclusions on DRM e-commerce systems examined from other fields of law perspective quite impossible. Rather than that, a case by case legal analysis of the rules of each DRM e-commerce systems should be performed each time, in order to assess conformity with other fields of law (that may, after all, be many more than those referred to in this analysis)[37].

This being said, Consumer Law is a field of law that has proven particularly relevant in contemporary DRM e-commerce implementations[38]. Because the Content Industry has often chosen to bind users with strict rules that affect not only the content itself but also the hardware used to reproduce it, more than once Consumer Law, at least in Europe, has come to users' assistance. The analysis in this Chapter shall therefore focus upon these cases, that have formed a first background upon which to judge future DRM e-commerce implementations.

The (Re)quest for Interoperability

Interoperability is seen by many as the "Holy Grail" in the contemporary digital economy. Indeed, after some forty years since the Information and Communications Technologies emergence, the widespread use of computing systems that not always understand each other threatens the foundations of society itself. Our digital economy has come to be based so much in the seamless operation of Information and Communications Technologies that it is unthinkable that any contemporary system will not undertake its best efforts to work in harmony with other (even competitive) systems (evidently, much to the resentment of such systems' owners, who would very much prefer to bind users for ever)[39]. It is after all with this in mind that reverse engineering is allowed by law notwithstanding anything to the contrary in any End User License Agreement:

The authorization of the rightholder shall not be required where reproduction of the code and translation of its form [...] are indispensable to obtain the information necessary to achieve the interoperability of an independently created computer program with other programs [...][40].

DRM e-commerce systems ever since their first appearance in the on-line environment flirted with the idea of binding users to specific hardware[41]. Because their owners sometimes also sold their own hardware, the idea of using on-line purchased content to push users towards specific (their own) hardware was understandably tempting; so tempting indeed, that it was put to the test.

It is in this context that iTunes' given preference for the iPod mp3 player should be examined. Apple has implemented in its iTunes Store a DRM system (called FairPlay) that binds together content purchased in it and its iPod reproduction hardware. This has raised considerable criticism on the basis of Consumer Law, at least in Europe. Not only has the EU Commissioner for Consumer Protection asked Apple to change its policy (in her own words, *"Do you find it reasonable that a CD will play in all CD players, but an iTunes song will only play on an iPod? It doesn't to me. Something must change"*[42]), but some Member-States also took action. Most notably in Norway, the Consumer Council filed a complaint with the country's Consumer Ombudsman, accusing Apple of violating the country's Marketing Control Act, and eventually won its case[43]. By early 2007 almost all Member-States (including Germany and France) joined the action against Apple and its iTunes DRM system; by the time this analysis was prepared, however, the negotiations were not concluded.

Sony, nevertheless, has not been as lucky as Apple. Early in 2007 Sony UK and Sony France lost a case against the French Consumer Protection Association UFC Que Choisir, because they did not inform consumers about the lack of interoperability of their mp3 music player with any other content than that purchased from a specific on-line store (Connect). The lack of interoperability worked, in effect, in two ways: Sony's mp3 player did not play any other content than that purchased from the Connect Internet site, and music purchased at the Connect Internet site could be read only by Sony's mp3 players. This tight grip on consumers was too much for French courts, who forced Sony to change it[44].

At the other side of the Atlantic it appears that e-commerce DRM systems have not attracted as much attention as their off-line relatives. Therefore, although Apple's iTunes is prevalent in the American on-line market too, no Norwegian-like claims have been raised so far. On the other hand, Sony BMG's DRM system on its music CDs has attracted so much criticism that it eventually had to settle with the US Government[45].

The above developments clearly set the scene from the Consumer Law perspective. DRM e-commerce systems constitute systems of rules, and it is ultimately these rules that shall be assessed against Consumer Law provisions. The existence of DRM e-commerce systems *per se*, as established by Intellectual property (copyright) Law, may not be challenged by Consumer Law; it is only the rules of these systems that have to be weighted against consumer concerns. In this context, the first years of DRM e-commerce implementation appear to be the probing stage of the Content Industry. Once the on-line model was established (setting-up shops that sell TMP-enriched content aimed at downloading onto computers and/or hardware players) it was worth a try attempting to bind consumers who purchase content on-line to their own hardware, increasing thus their sources of income exponentially. This model, bluntly implemented by Sony and more reservedly by Apple's iTunes, does present the tendency to becoming obsolete. Not only are strict consumer-binding rules clearly not tolerated by, at least EU, Consumer Law, but also the Content Industry itself is trying to detach itself from such image-ruing practices (see, for instance, Apple's sale of DRM-free content, admittedly for an increased price, next to its other DRM-enriched content). From this point of view consumers seem to have avoided the worst for now; Consumer Law has proven in practice that it is in possession of the filters that will keep the e-commerce DRM model as open (and interoperating) as possible.

DRM E-Commerce Systems and the Protection of Privacy

Contemporary DRM e-commerce systems are expected to gather personal information[46]. Such data may pertain to users' financial information (for instance, credit card details) that will facilitate on-line transactions for the purchase of DRM-enhanced content, users' preferences (simply recorded or actively used to create profiles and suggest further "compatible" sales), users' hardware (if applicable, for interoperability or non-interoperability purposes), users' address (in country-fragmented systems such as iTunes, see below under 2.4.1), etc. This on-line collection and processing of personal information, however, shall invariably fall within the limits of data protection (in Europe) or privacy protection (in the USA) legislation.

Once again it must be made clear before embarking upon any privacy-related analysis that DRM e-commerce systems are perceived as lawfully operating e-commerce systems for the on-line sale of content according to basic Intellectual Property (copyright) legislation. As already established (see above, under 2.1), copyright law justifies all steps necessary for the introduction and operation of a typical DRM e-commerce system. Once this is confirmed, one can only judge this system's rules according to other fields of law: because DRM e-commerce systems essentially reflect the business rules of the business plan of those implementing them, it is only those business rules that shall be assessed against other legislative provisions. And, as far as this Chapter is concerned, typical contemporary DRM e-commerce systems do tend to step into Data Protection (or Privacy Protection, respectively) legislation, through the almost invariable collection and processing of personal information[47].

One further clarification needs to be made before going any further: perceptions of privacy protections vary deeply between both sides of the Atlantic. In Europe (in the EU) a data protection approach has been adopted, whereby formalised rules protect individuals' personal information and state agencies make sure that these rules are observed. In the USA a more *laissez-faire* approach has been adopted, whereby it is individual privacy that is broadly protected (that is, not particularly the processing of personal information) mostly by means of sector-specific legislation; in addition, no federal or state agency is established to centrally monitor the protection of individual privacy. At any event, for the purposes of this analysis, first, "data protection" and "privacy" shall be used as synonyms, and, second, a typical contemporary DRM e-commerce system (along the lines of iTunes) shall form the reference standard.

Collection and Processing of Personal Information

Typical DRM e-commerce systems place personal information at the basis of their operation. Personal data gathered through a fairly typical user-login process may involve names and e-mail addresses, home addresses, credit card information etc. These data enable the operators of DRM e-commerce systems (the Content Industry or others) to establish a possibly "personal" relationship with users, creating their on-line "accounts" and completing payment processes through simplified steps. Unavoidably, these data also assist in imposing restrictions according to the DRM system's rules to the use of acquired content: for instance, iTunes connects users to home computers and allows for reproduction of purchased content only on five computers per user. All these operations would have been impossible without the creation of user "accounts", whereby content purchased, hardware identification and other details are interconnected.

Nevertheless, collection of personal data will normally not go unchallenged in Europe (or, at least, in EU Member-States). According to the Data Protection Directive, "*processing of personal data' ('processing') shall mean any operation or set of operations which is performed upon personal data, whether or not by automatic means, such as collection, recording, organization, storage [...]*"[48]; and, accordingly, "*this Directive shall apply to the processing of personal data wholly or partly by automatic means, and to the processing otherwise than by automatic means of personal data which form part of a filing system or are intended to form part of a filing system*"[49]. It becomes therefore clear that the collection of personal information within DRM e-commerce systems does constitute an activity falling within the scope of the EU Data Protection Directive; the Directive has by now been implemented in all Member-States, constituting thus national law, and therefore each and every one EU Member-State, to which DRM e-commerce systems such as iTunes are addressed, now has to assess their rules according to its Data Protection legislation.

Collection and processing of personal information has to be performed "*fairly and lawfully*", collected information may be used only for "*specified, explicit and legitimate purposes and not [be] further processed in a way incompatible with those purposes*", it must be "*adequate, relevant and not excessive in relation to the purposes for which it is collected, accurate and, where necessary, kept up to date*"; in other words, in Europe DRM e-commerce systems will have to conform to all fundamental data protection principles[50]. Furthermore, the operators of such systems will most probably have to register with the Data Protection Authorities their creation of a filing system and processing of personal information. And, all these will have to be observed in each and every one EU Member-State locally (for instance, if iTunes sells to Greece, it has to register with the Greek Data Protection Authority and observe the Greek Data Protection Act – notwithstanding the fact that the Act is more or less the same as the Data Protection Directive).

Perhaps of more relevance to DRM e-commerce systems is the matter of international transfers of personal data. Although it is to be expected that all international DRM e-commerce operators are aware of and shall probably have allocated enough resources to comply with data protection requirements in all European states they aim to sell, where their infrastructure (servers) is located may be a totally different (and interesting) issue. Exports of EU personal information are only allowed under very strict rules: "*the Member States shall provide that the transfer to a third country of personal data which are undergoing processing or are intended for processing after transfer may take place only if, without prejudice to compliance with the national provisions adopted pursuant to the other provisions of this Directive, the third country in question ensures an adequate level of protection*"[51]. There is no need to go into the details of the negotiations between American and EU authorities, assessing whether the American level of protection can be deemed "*adequate*" in order for data exports to be permitted[52]; instead, it is sufficient to be noted that, if the servers of a DRM e-commerce operator are located outside the EU and personal information of EU residents is collected there, then all requirements of the EU Data Protection Directive must be met, in order for such processing to be lawful.

Profiling, Data Matching and Other Marketing Processing Methods

Because DRM e-commerce systems are essentially business systems, maximizing profit constitutes evidently one of their major concerns. To this end they might be tempted to use personal information stored in them in marketing campaigns or processes to offer "personalized" services to their customers, with a view to increasing sales[53]. Or, they might be tempted to use customer personal information to combat piracy or even fraud or other lawful and worthy purposes[54]. Nevertheless, in all those cases to the extent that personal information of EU residents is being processed, the EU Data Protection Directive provisions shall have to apply (making the lawfulness of such processing questionable).

With regard to profiling (the creation of customer-specific profiles that record preferences based on purchases or Web browsing and the subsequent use of such profiles in order to promote services or goods deemed compatible), it ought to be noted that the (EU Data Protection Directive) finality principle requires that personal information be processed for *"specified, explicit and legitimate purposes and not [be] further processed in a way incompatible with those purposes"*[55]. In this context, personal information transmitted to a DRM e-commerce system operator by one of its clients in order to execute an on-line purchase is not clear that it may be used in order to create a profile for the same individual and forward to its inbox material particular to its perceived preferences. On the contrary, each client has to be informed, at the time he fills-in the form necessary for the purchase process, of the (legal) person that is collecting his data and the purposes for which such data shall be used. The most common way-out for DRM e-commerce operators shall be acquiring the individuals' consent (through, for instance, opt-in and opt-out boxes placed at the bottom of the relevant form), but it should nevertheless be noted that the lawfulness of such *opt-in* techniques is questioned in several EU Member-States.

The finality principle becomes even more relevant when DRM e-commerce operators use personal information of their clients for other, undoubtedly worthy, purposes: the combating of piracy or even the operation of their own DRM systems (by limiting uses per user). Again in these cases the finality data protection principle, at least in Europe, prohibits that stored personal data be put to any other purposes that the ones they were collected for in the first place. With regard to DRM e-commerce systems, obviously personal data will have been collected with a purpose of executing a purchase; whether these data may be used in order, for instance, to "tag" users and prohibit unauthorized use through DRM techniques of their purchased content (for instance, reproduction on other mp3 players) remains questionable. It is equally questionable whether personal information collected under DRM e-commerce systems may be used for the fulfillment of other lawful purposes, as is the combating of piracy: for instance, if a user has given his personal information to the Content Industry in order to purchase music within a DRM e-commerce system, the Content Industry is not unequivocally allowed to keep a file on this user (IP, personal details) in order to tag use over the Internet and identify potential acts of (content) piracy – here again, the principles of data protection on the fair and lawful use of personal information ought to be observed.

In view of the above, DRM e-commerce operators might find it useful to observe closely (European) data protection legislation while drafting and implementing their DRM techniques on EU residents.

Other Legal Concerns

As repeatedly discussed in this Chapter, DRM e-commerce systems constitute essentially business systems that, once the lawfulness of their existence has been confirmed by Intellectual Property (copyright)

Law, will have to be judged on an *ad hoc* basis. In this subchapter a brief analysis shall be undertaken on certain legal issues that were raised through the implementation in the market of contemporary DRM e-commerce systems, particularly with regard to EU law.

DRM E-Commerce Systems and Competition Law

Because DRM e-commerce systems may be equipped with the functionality to identify the location of users (customers), obviously based on their IP address, some operators (for instance, Apple) have used it in order to setup a country-specific sales system. For instance, users in the UK are guided to the UK-online shop and are allowed to purchase content only from it (evidently, at UK-specific prices). In this way the DRM e-commerce system operator benefits from currency exchange rates in a world that is artificially divided by its e-commerce system.

Such DRM e-commerce systems implementations *per se* hurt competition and international trade. Probably because they are based on single-user purchases, no formal claims have been raised so far against this "functionality". Nevertheless, this implementation does infringe EU law as well: because EU law aims at the creation of a common market, an e-commerce system that, based on DRM technologies, sells at different rates between Member-States of the EU unavoidably violates substantial EU Competition Law[56].

EU Law Requirements for E-Commerce Systems

Again within the EU, DRM e-commerce systems should be setup in order to conform with basic EU e-commerce legislation. Although these do not pertain to the core technologies of DRM e-commerce systems, they do affect the way they do business: a series of legal requirements, for instance, on information that should be readily provided to customers in on-line shops, on the execution of contracts on-line, or on the protection of consumers once a purchase has been completed indirectly affect DRM e-commerce systems – their implementation is mandatory, in order for their operators to lawfully use them in Europe.

THE FUTURE(?): WEB 2.0, IPTV, VOD AND OTHER MARKET (& RESEARCH) DIRECTIONS

DRM systems for the on-line or off-line world are evidently here to stay. Once basic Intellectual Property Law has secured their existence, they are still considered an invaluable (if not the only) tool for the Content Industry to make its products available in contemporary market conditions. The dissemination of broadband networks among users and the digitisation, by now, of every conceivable "work" in the intellectual property sense (music, movies, pictures) has made unavoidable a future whereby users in an international market exchange files of any size at an uncontrollable pace. More substantially, this situation is affecting the market itself: no more are CDs considered the prime source of revenue for the Content Industry or even artists: by the time these lines are being written practically all major labels have announced on-line systems of content sales[57], while, at the same time, popular groups and artists discover that money is to be made from now on mostly from concerts and other channels of distribution (and are quitting music labels in the process[58]).

DRM e-commerce technologies are essentially found in the middle of all this: the Content Industry advocates their widest possible use now more than ever, as a matter of life and death. Users are shopping around on-line providers for the one who offers the least DRM-infected content. And, e-commerce entrepreneurs keep pushing the technology further, through innovative business methods.

A number of fields may be identified where DRM technologies could play or are already playing a central role. Web 2.0 implementations is an obvious candidate: the Content Industry is increasingly annoyed at user-created content that uses extracts of copyrighted material (TV shows, films, music) without permission – DRM systems could present a solution, either blocking this altogether or creating an adequate way of compensation for the Content Industry (because today infringements cannot be counted, the Content Industry is usually settling with blanket, arbitrary agreements with e-commerce operators such as YouTube for all and any of their content used in their Web pages). IPTV implementations is another potential field for DRM systems exploitation: because the Content Industry has learned its lesson from the online provision of music, by now it only makes available its content in IPTV applications when strong DRM systems are in place – as long as broadband access increases, these systems shall also gain in significance. Evidently, the same applies to Video-on-Demand (VoD) implementations: a number of, mostly telecommunications, service providers, in their attempt to increase revenue after the demise of their voice earnings, have introduced VoD systems, whereby users, through a set-top box installed at their TV set, are able to download films: here again the Content Industry (namely, studios) is only making its content available whenever strong DRM systems are in place to protect it from unauthorised reproduction.

DRM e-commerce systems, regardless whether users like them or not, are here to stay: their existence is secured by law (copyright) and strong proponents (the Content Industry) and their future well-being is warranted by always-increasing e-commerce innovative business methods. Being essentially technology-neutral systems that, at their most basic functionality, only protect content from unauthorised reproductions, it remains to be seen whether the business models they are put to serve shall alienate them from the public (that misguidedly identifies them as the problem) or shall integrate them effortlessly into an environment aiming towards ubiquitous computing, where, however, authors too have to make a decent living.

REFERENCES

Maillard, T., & Furon, T. (2004). Towards digital rights and exemptions management systems. *Computer Law & Security Report, 20*(4), 281-287.

Morin, J-H. & Pawlak, M. (2007, July 1-5). A model for credential based exception management in digital rights management systems, Internet monitoring, and protection. *ICIMP 2007. Second International Conference,* 41. Digital Object Identifier   10.1109/ICIMP.2007.3

Park, Y., & Scotchmer, S. (2005, August). Digital rights management and the pricing of digital products. *NBER Working Paper, W11532.* Available at SSRN: http://ssrn.com/abstract=778105

Tehranian, J. (2002, November). All rights reserved? Reassessing copyright and patent enforcement in the digital age. Available at SSRN: http://ssrn.com/abstract=351480 or DOI: 10.2139/ssrn.351480

WIRED (2006, April 3). Reasons to love open-source DRM. Available at http://www.wired.com/entertainment/music/commentary/listeningpost/2006/04/70548)

ADDITIONAL READING

Fairfield, J. (2005). Virtual property. *Boston University Law Review, 85,* 1047. Available at SSRN: http://ssrn.com/abstract=807966

Lessig, L. (2006). *Code version 2.0.* Basic Books

Zittrain, J. (2006, May). The generative Internet. *Harvard Law Review, 119,* 1974. Available at SSRN: http://ssrn.com/abstract=847124

ENDNOTES

1   See also Petrick, Paul, Why DRM Should be Cause for Concern: An Economic and Legal Analysis of the Effect of Digital Technology on the Music Industry (November 2004), *Berkman Center for Internet & Society at Harvard Law School Research Publication No. 2004-09.* Available at SSRN: http://ssrn.com/abstract=618065

2   The Statute of Anne.

3   For a concise analysis, see Lloyd, I. *Information Technology Law,* Oxford University Press, Fourth Edition, pp.363ff.

4   While not being particularly discomforted at that time by what essentially was computer-copying the Content Industry suffered a serious blow in another field and thus learned a lesson that proved invaluable in the very near future: VCRs. During the 80ies the VCR technology became immensely popular: for the first time in human history non-expert home-users at a minimum effort and cost could copy and reproduce at the ease of their home valuable copyrighted material (films and other TV material). The Content Industry reacted to such technology and sued those who profited from it, namely SONY Corp. After bitter and long court struggle, in the milestone SONY/BETAMAX case video copying was ruled lawful (see below, footnote 10). The flaws of the Content Industry in that case proved of invaluable importance a few years later, when P2P networks came into play. The Content Industry ultimately won this battle, not least because it did not step into the traps of the BETAMAX case (while the P2P industry seemed poised to do so).

5   See also Petrick, P, *ibid.*

6   See Zittrain, J, The Generative Internet, *Harvard Law Review,* Vol. 119, p. 1974, May 2006, available at SSRN: http://ssrn.com/abstract=847124

7   Now transformed into fee-based service, at www.napster.com.

8   Court of Appeals (Ninth Circuit) 380 F 3d 1154.

9   *Sony Corp. of America v. Universal City Studios Inc.* 464 US 417 (1984, *BETAMAX case*).

10   *Metro-Goldwin-Mayer Studios Inc. et al. v. Grokster Ltd., et al.,* 27 June 2005.

11   See IFAA press articles.

12   P2P technology was nevertheless under no circumstances abandoned. A similar implementation may be met today in networks such as Skype. This evidently does not include any content exchange; when P2P networks did become again involved in content exchange, this time it was done with strict observation of copyright rules (and with full implementation of DRM systems, see, for instance, Joost at www.joost.com).

13   On "content" see also WIPO, Standing Committee on Copyright and Related Rights, *Automated Rights Management Systems And Copyright Limitations and Exceptions*, April 27, 2006 (SCCR/14/5), p.13.

14   Probably confirming Lessig's assertion that "code is law" (Lessig L, *Code version 2.0*, Basic Books 2006).

15   Also see, however, David Weinberger, *Copy Protection is a Crime against Humanity: Society is based on bending the rules*, at WIRED, http://www.wired.com/wired/archive/11.06/view.html

16   For a broader analysis of typical (at least contemporary) DRM e-commerce applications see *Center for Democracy and Technology*, September 2006 (version 1), pp.8ff., available at www.cdt.org/copyright/20060907drm.pdf, pp.8ff.

17   See also Gasser, Urs, iTunes: How Copyright, Contract, and Technology Shape the Business of Digital Media - A Case Study (June 2004), *Berkman Center for Internet & Society at Harvard Law School Research Publication No. 2004-07.* Available at SSRN: http://ssrn.com/abstract=556802

18   See, The Economist, Music wants to be free, February 8, 2007 (available at http://www.economist.com/opinion/displaystory.cfm?story_id=8668981).

19   Terms found at http://www.apple.com/legal/itunes/uk/service.html/

20   See WIRED, *The year of living DRMishly*, January 24, 2006 (available at http://www.wired.com/science/discoveries/news/2006/01/70049)

21   See *Evaluating DRM: Building a Marketplace for the convergent world*, pp.5ff.

22   Felten, E *DRM and Public Policy* in Communications of the ACM, V. 48, No. 7, July 2005, p. 112, but also see WIPO, Standing Committee on Copyright and Related Rights, *Automated Rights Management Systems And Copyright Limitations and Exceptions*, April 27, 2006 (SCCR/14/5), pp.17ff.

23   See WIPO's official site at www.wipo.org.

24   See the, essentially identical, texts under http:// www.apple.com/legal/itunes/ww/.

25   Its provisions, with regard to DRM at least, have been implemented in the USA through the Digital Millennium Copyright Act (DMCA), and in Europe through the Directive 2001/29/EC of the European Parliament and of the Council of 22 May 2001 on the harmonization of certain aspects of copyright and related rights in the information society (EU Copyright Directive).

26   Art. 11 WCT.

27   See, for instance, the, largely legalistic, argumentation whether TPM that can be circumvented can be "effective" or not, in order to infer whether they are protected by the WCT (see, however, Art. 6 par. 3 of the EU Copyright Directive, and, recently, *Helsinki District Court Decides That CSS Used in DVDs Is "Ineffective*, International Law Office Information Technology Update, available at http://www.internationallawoffice.com/Newsletters/Detail.aspx?g=c720e545-425b-4f73-93de-cf2ed7638764).

28   After all, the regulation of TPM is as far as Intellectual Property Law is allowed to go. DRM systems constitute "systems" that regulate the use of content. As such, only their case-specific rules for such use may be assessed (on an ad hoc basis) according to Intellectual Property Law

provisions (see, for instance, the *fair use* principle, wherever applicable). This assessment of their rules does not refuse DRM systems their right to exist (perhaps, using other rules). Intellectual Property Law deals with works, and the act of attaching TPM onto them, thus amending them, is an act that may or may not be accepted as such under its provisions. Once it is established that attaching TPM onto works is lawful, self-evidently some (DRM) rules for the use of this TPM content are to be expected.

[29] See Art. 6 of the European Directive on the legal protection of computer programs (91/250/EEC)

[30] Article 6.4.

[31] See US Copyright Office under http://www.copyright.gov/fls/fl102.html, and the respective entry in Wikipedia under http://en.wikipedia.org/wiki/Fair_use .

[32] In the DRM context see Reinbothe J, *Private Copying, Levies and DRMs against the Background of the EU Copyright Framework*, available at http://ec.europa.eu/internal_market/copyright/documents/2003-speech-reinbothe_en.htm .

[33] See, however, The Economist, *Criminalising the Consumer*, April 27, 2007 (available at http://www.economist.com/science/displaystory.cfm?story_id=9096421).

[34] Naturally, it is a totally different issue if, for instance, implementation of a DRM system eventually harms hardware or software owned by the user. Although this has nothing to do with copyright law examined here, evidently the owner of the DRM system shall be fully liable to indemnify the user for any damage suffered while using lawfully acquired content (see also Evaluating DRM: Building a Marketplace for the convergent world, p.20).

[35] Berne Convetnion, Art. 6bis par. 1.

[36] See, for instance, the iTunes Terms of Sale: "iTunes Plus content does not contain security technology that restricts your usage of such content, and is encoded at a higher audio bit rate than the DRM-protected songs or music videos available on the iTunes Store" (under http://www.apple.com/legal/itunes/uk/sales.html).

[37] See WIPO, Standing Committee on Copyright and Related Rights, *Automated Rights Management Systems And Copyright Limitations and Exceptions*, April 27, 2006 (SCCR/14/5), p.13.

[38] See Evaluating DRM: Building a Marketplace for the convergent world, p.21.

[39] See, however, WIRED, *Reasons to love open-source DRM*, April 3, 2006 (available at http://www.wired.com/entertainment/music/commentary/listeningpost/2006/04/70548)

[40] Art. 6.1, European Council Directive 91/250/EEC of 14 May 1991 on the legal protection of computer programs

[41] See also Center for Technology and Democracy, *Evaluating DRM: Building a Marketplace for the convergent world*, pp.15ff.

[42] http://www.focus.de/digital/multimedia/ipod/apple_aid_50327.html

[43] The Ombudsman ruled that that the terms of the iTunes License Agreement (in its then version of 2006) were "unreasonable" with respect to the Norwegian Marketing Control Act, that it was unlawful to submit the License Agreement to English law, as well as, that the same Agreement's disclaimer on Apple's liability for possible damage its software may cause was equally unlawful (see http://forbrukerportalen.no/Artikler/2006/1149587055.44 , and also http://www.out-law.com/page-7691).

[44] See, among others, the EDRI relevant entry at http://www.edri.org/edrigram/number5.1/drm_sonyfr. It should also be noted that France has provided for an "Authority for DRM" to be established under its DADVSI Act

[45] As per Electronic Frontier Foundation (EFF)'s description, "at issue are two software technologies - SunnComm's MediaMax and First4Internet's Extended Copy Protection (also known as XCP) - which Sony BMG claims to have placed on the music CDs to restrict consumer use of the music on the CDs but which in truth do much more, including reporting customer listening of the CDs and installing undisclosed and in some cases hidden files on users' computers that can expose users to malicious attacks by third parties, all without appropriate notice and consent from purchasers. The CDs also condition use of the music on unconscionable licensing terms in the End User Licensing Agreement (EULA)" (http://www.eff.org/cases/sony-bmg-litigation-info).

[46] See Evaluating DRM: Building a Marketplace for the convergent world, pp.19ff.

[47] See Coher J, DRM and Privacy, *Berkeley Technology Law Journal*, available at https://www.law.berkeley.edu/institutes/bclt/drm/papers/cohen-drmandprivacy-btlj2003.html

[48] Art. 2b, EU Data Protection Directive (95/46/EC).

[49] Art. 3.1, EU Data Protection Directive (95/46/EC).

[50] Art. 6.1, EU Data Protection Directive (95/46/EC).

[51] Art. 25.1, EU Data Protection Directive (95/46/EC).

[52] On this issue see the official EU site at http://ec.europa.eu/justice_home/fsj/privacy/thridcountries/index_en.htm

[53] See Kerr, Ian R. and Bailey, Jane, The Implications of Digital Rights Management for Privacy and Freedom of Expression, *Journal of Information, Communication & Ethics in Society*, Vol. 2, 2004, Troubador Publishing Ltd. Available at SSRN: http://ssrn.com/abstract=705041

[54] In this context it should be noted that, at least in Europe, the notion of "personal information" largely exceeds the routine use of the term in everyday life, in order to include any piece of information that may have even a remote connection to an individual – for instance, IP addresses, even if not connected to users, do constitute "personal information" for the purposes of data protection legislation in Europe (see Working Party Opinion 4/2007).

[55] Art. 6.1, EU Data Protection Directive (95/46/EC).

[56] See COMPUTERWORLD, *Apple drops iTunes prices, EU drops antitrust action*, January 9, 2008 (available at http://www.computerworld.com/action/article.do?command=viewArticleBasic&articleId=9056458)

[57] See WIRED, *Death of DRM could weaken iTunes, boost iPod*, January 4, 2008 (available at http://www.wired.com/entertainment/music/news/2008/01/rip_drm)

[58] See The Economist, *Online Music: The slow death of digital rights*, available at http://www.economist.com/business/displaystory.cfm?story_id=9963252

Additional Reading

Section I
Overview

Chapter I
Intellectual Property Rights

Berne Convention: http://www.wipo.int/treaties/en/ip/berne/trtdocs_wo001.html

The Digital Millennium Copyright Act (DMCA) Software Copyright: http://www.copyright.gov/legislation/dmca.pdf

TRIPS - Agreement on Trade-Related Aspects of Intellectual Property Rights: http://www.wto.org/english/tratop_e/trips_e/t_agm0_e.htm

The Community Directive on software copyright Directive 91/250/EEC: http://europa.eu.int/ISPO/legal/en/ipr/software/software.html

Creative Commons web site http://creativecommons.org

Ronchi, Alfredo M., eCulture: cultural content in the digital age, Springer, ISBN: 978-3-540-75273-8

OASIS, Policy on Intellectual Property Rights: http://www.oasis-open.org/who/intellectualproperty.php

Intellectual Property aspects of World Wide Web authoring : www. http://www.ipr-helpdesk.org

ISO, "MPEG Strides Forward with ISO/IEC 14496-2" in ISO Bulletin May 2002. http://www.iso.ch/iso/en/commcentre/isobulletin/articles/2002/pdf/mpeg02-05.pdf

ANSI, Guidelines for Implementation of the ANSI Patent Policy: http://public.ansi.org/ansionline/Documents/Standards%20Activities/American%20National%20Standards/Procedures,%20Guides,%20and%20Forms/PATPOL.DOC

Microsoft's Standards Licensing Program: http://www.microsoft.com/mscorp/ip/standards/

IEEE, Understanding Patent Issues During IEEE Standards Development: http://standards.ieee.org/board/pat/guide.html

Caplan, P., Patents and Open Standards (2003): http://www.niso.org/press/whitepapers/Patents_Caplan.pdf

Chapter II
Digital Rights Management: A New Trend or a Necessity?

Gantz, J., & Rochester, J. (2004). Pirates of the Digital Millennium: How the Intellectual Property Wars Damage Our Personal Freedoms, Our Jobs, and the World Economy. FT Prentice Hall.

Harte, L. (2006). Introduction to Digital Rights Management (DRM); Identifying, Tracking, Authorizing and Restricting Access to Digital Media. Althos Publishing.

Rosenblatt, B., Trippe, B., & Mooney, S. (2001). Digital Rights Management: Business and Technology. Wiley Publications.

Safavi-Naini, R., & Yung, M. (2005). Digital Rights Management: Technologies, Issues, Challenges and Systems. Lecture Notes in Computer Science.

Tassel, J. (2006). Digital Rights Management: Protecting and Monetizing Content. Focal Press.

Zeng, W., Yu, H., & Lin, C. (2006). Multimedia Security Technologies for Digital Rights Management. Academic Press.

Section II
Protecting Digital Rights in E-Commerce Systems

Chapter III
Image Watermarking

Certimark. Available at http://vision.unige.ch/certimark/.

Checkmark. Available at http://watermarking.unige.ch/checkmark/.

Openwatermark. Available at http://www.openwatermark.org/.

Optimark. Available at http://poseidon.csd.auth.gr/optimark/.

Stirmark audio. https://amsl-smb.cs.uni-magdeburg.de/smfa//main.php

Stirmark. Available at http://www.petitcolas.net/fabien/watermarking/stirmark/.

Watermark Evaluation Testbed. Available at http://www.datahiding.com/.

Juergen Seitz, Ed. Digital Watermarking for Digital Media. ISBN 1-59140-518-1 Idea Group, Inc. 2005.

Mauro Barni and Franco Bartolini. Watermarking Systems Engineering. ISBN: 0-8247-4806-9 Marcel Dekker, Inc. 2004.

Ingemar Cox, Jeffrey Bloom, and Matthew Miller. Digital Watermarking, Principles & Practice. Morgan Kaufmann, first edition, 2001.

Wei Lu, Hongtao Lu, Fu-Lai Chung. Feature based watermarking using watermark template match. ISSN:0096-3003 Applied Mathematics and Computation, Volume 177, Issue 1, June 2006.

Benoit Macq, Jana Dittmann, and Edward J. Delp. Benchmarking of image watermarking algorithms for digital rights management. Proceedings of the IEEE, 92(6):971–984, June 2004.

J. F. Delaigle, C. Devleeschouwer, B. Macq, and I. Langendijk. Human Visual System Features Enabling Watermarking. Proc. IEEE Int. Conf. Multimedia Expo, vol. 2, 2002, pp. 489—492.

J. Dittmann, P. Wholmacher, and K. Nahrstedt. Using cryptographic and watermarking algorithms. IEEE Multimedia, 8(Oct-Dec):54–65, 2001.

V. Solachidis, A. Tefas, N. Nikolaidis, S. Tsekeridou, A. Nikolaidis, and I. Pitas. A benchmarking protocol for watermarking methods. In IEEE Int. Conf. on Image Processing (ICIP'01), Thessaloniki, Greece, pages 1023–1026, 2001.

S. Voloshynovskiy, S. Peirera, V. Inquise, and T. Pun. Attack-modeling: towards a second generation watermarking benchmark. Signal Processing, 81:1177–1214, 2001.

S. P. Mohanty, K. R. Ramakrishnan, and M. S. Kanakanhalli, "A DCT Domain Visible Watermarking Technique for Images", in Proceedings of the IEEE International Conference on Multimedia and Expo (ICME) (Vol. 2), pp.1029-1032, 2000.

G.Voyatzis and I.Pitas, "Protecting Digital Image Copyrights: A Framework", IEEE Computer Graphics & Applications, Jan/Feb 1999, pp.18-24.

M.Ramkumar and A.N.Akansu, "Image Watermarks and Counterfeit Attacks: Some Problems and Solutions", Proc. of Content Security and Data Hiding in Digital Media, Newark, NJ, USA, May 14 1999.

Liehua Xie and Gonzalo R. Arce. Joint wavelet compression and authentication watermarking. In Proceedings of the IEEE International Conference on Image Processing, ICIP '98, Chicago, IL, USA, 1998.

J.J.K. O'Ruanaidh and T.Pun, "Rotation, Scale and Translation Invariant Spread Spectrum Digital Image Watermarking", Signal Processing, Vol.66, No.3, May 1998, pp.303-317.

Wenwu Zhu, Zixiang Xiong, and Ya-Qin Zhang. Multiresolution watermarking for images and video: a unified approach. In Proceedings of the IEEE International Conference on Image Processing, ICIP '98, Chicago, IL, USA, October 1998.

J.P.M.G. Linnartz, A.C.C. Kalker, G.F. Depovere and R. Beuker, "A reliability model for detection of electronic watermarks in digital images", Benelux Symposium on Communication Theory, Enschede, October 1997, pp. 202-209.

M.D.Swanson, et al., "Transparent Robust Image Watermarking", Proc IEEE International Conf. on Image Processing, ICIP-96, Vol.3, pp 211-214.

Chapter IV
Watermarking Techniques for DRM Applications

Adelsbach, A. & Sadeghi, A.-R., (2001). Zero-knowledge watermark detection and proof of ownership. In 4th International Workshop on Information Hiding, IH'01, Springer Lecture Notes in Computer Science, Vol. 2137 (pp. 273-288). Pittsburgh, PA, USA.

Adelsbach, A., Rohe, M., & Sadeghi, A.-R., (2005). Non-interactive watermark detection for a correlation-based watermarking scheme. In Communications and Multimedia Security, Springer Lecture Notes in Computer Science, Vol. 3677 (pp. 129-139). Salzburg, Austria.

Adelsbach, A., Huber, U., & Sadeghi, A.-R., (2006). Fingercasting – joint fingerprinting and decryption of broadcast messages. In 11th Australasian Conference on Information Security and Privacy, Springer Lecture Notes in Computer Science, Vol. 4058 (pp 136-147). Melbourne, Australia.

Ahmed, F., Sattar, F., Siyal, M. Y., & Yu, D., (2006). A secure watermarking scheme for buyer-seller identification and copyright protection. EURASIP Journal on Applied Signal Processing.

Anderson, R. J., & Manifavas, C., (1997). Chameleon - a new kind of stream cipher. In 4th International Workshop on Fast Software Encryption, FSE '97, Springer-Verlag, (pp. 107-113). London, UK.

Celik, M., Lemma, A., Katzenbeisser, S., & van der Veen, M., (2007). Secure embedding of spread-spectrum watermarks using look-up tables. In International Conference on Acoustics, Speech and Signal Processing, ICASSP'07, IEEE Press, Vol. 2 (pp. 153-156). Honolulu, Hawaii, USA.

Craver, S., (1999). Zero knowledge watermark detection. In 3rd International Workshop on Information Hiding, IH'99, Springer Lecture Notes in Computer Science, Vol. 1768 (pp. 101-116). Dresden, Germany.

Craver, S., & Katzenbeisser, S., (2001). Security analysis of public-key watermarking schemes. In M. S. Schmalz (Ed.) SPIE, Mathematics of Data/Image Coding, Compression and Encryption IV, with Applications, Vol. 4475, (pp 172-182). San Diego, CA.

Crowcroft, J., Perkins, C., & Brown, I., (2000). A method and apparatus for generating multiple watermarked copies of an information signal. WO Patent No. 00/56059.

Emmanuel, S., & Kankanhalli, M., (2001). Copyright protection for MPEG-2 compressed broadcast video. In IEEE Int. Conf. on Multimedia and Expo, ICME 2001 (pp. 206-209). Tokio, Japan.

Kundur, D., (2004). Video fingerprinting and encryption principles for digital rights management. Proceedings of the IEEE, 92(6), 918-932.

Kuribayashi, M., & Tanaka, H., (2005). Fingerprinting protocol for images based on additive homomorphic property. IEEE Transactions on Image Processing, 14(12), 2129-2139.

Lei, C.-L., Yu, P.-L., Tsai, P.-L., & Chan, M.-H., (2004). An efficient and anonymous buyer-seller watermarking protocol. IEEE Transactions on Image Processing, 13(12), 1618-1626.

Lemma, A., Katzenbeisser, S., Celik, M., & van der Veen, M., (2006). Secure watermark embedding through partial encryption. In International Workshop on Digital Watermarking (IWDW 2006), Springer Lecture Notes in Computer Science, Vol. 4283 (pp. 433-445), Jeju Island, Korea.

Malkin, M. & Kalker, T., (2006). A cryptographic method for secure watermark detection. In 8th International Workshop on Information Hiding, IH'06, Springer Lecture Notes in Computer Science, Vol. 4437 (pp.26-41). Old Town Alexandria, Virginia, USA.

Memon, N., & Wong, P., (2001). A buyer-seller watermarking protocol. IEEE Transactions on Image Processing, 10(4), 643-649.

Parviainen, R., & Parnes, P., (2001). Large scale distributed watermarking of multicast media through encryption. In International Federation for Information Processing, Communications and Multimedia Security Joint working conference IFIP TC6/TC11, Vol.192 (pp 149-158). Darmstadt, Germany.

Piva, A., Cappellini, V., Corazzi, D., De Rosa, A., Orlandi, C., and Barni, M., (2006). Zero-knowledge ST-DM watermarking. In P. W. Wong and E. J. Delp (Ed.), Security, Steganography, and Watermarking of Multimedia Contents VIII, Proc. SPIE, Vol. 6072 (pp. 291-301). San Jose, CA, USA.

Troncoso, J. R., & Perez-Gonzalez, F., (2007). Efficient non-interactive zero-knowledge watermark detector robust to sensitivity attacks. In P. W. Wong and E. J. Delp (Ed.), Security, Steganography, and Watermarking of Multimedia Contents IX, Proc. SPIE Vol. 6505. San Jose, CA, USA.

Zhang, J., Kou, W., & Fan, K., (2006). Secure buyer-seller watermarking protocol. IEE Proceedings on Information Security, 153(1), 15-18.

Chapter V
Watermarking and Authentication in JPEG2000

Taubman, D.S. & Marcellin, M.W. (2002). JPEG2000: Image Compression Fundamentals, Standards and Practice. Boston Dordrecht : Kluwer Academic Publishers.

Rabbani, M. & Joshi, R. (2002). An Overview of the JPEG2000 Still Image Compression Standard, Signal Processing Image Communication, 17(1).

Acharya, T. & Tsai, P.S. (2004). JPEG2000 Standard for Image Compression: Concepts, Algorithms and VLSI Architectures. Wiley-Interscience

"JPEG2000 DataCompression.info". (2007). Retrieved August 30, 2007, from http://datacompression. info/JPEG2000.shtml

Watermarking, Data hiding & Authentication:

Cox, I., Miller, M., Bloom, J., and Fridrich J., (2007)

Digital Watermarking and Steganography, Second Edition (The Morgan Kaufmann Series in Multimedia Information and Systems) Amsterdam Boston : Morgan Kaufmann.

Hanjalic, A. (2000). Image and video databases: restoration, watermarking and retrieval. Amsterdam Lausanne : Elsevier.

Katzenbeisser, S. and Petitcolas, F. (2000). Information Hiding Techniques for Steganography and Digital Watermarking. Boston, MA : Artech House.

Wayner P. (2002). Disappearing cryptography: information hiding: steganography and watermarking (2nd Edition). Amsterdam Boston : Morgan Kaufmann.

Arnold, M., Schmucker, M. & Wolthusen, S.D. (2003). Techniques and applications of digital watermarking and content protection. Boston, MA : Artech House.

Lu, C-S. (Ed.) (2004). Multimedia security: steganography and digital watermarking techniques for protection of intellectual property. Hershey, Pa. ; London : Idea Group.

Johnson, N.F., Duric, Z. & Jajodia, S. (2001). Information hiding: steganography and watermarking-attacks and countermeasures. Boston : Kluwer Academic Publishers.

Seitz J. (Ed.) (2005). Digital Watermarking for Digital Media. Information Science Publishing.

Pan, J.S., Huang, H.C., Jain, L., and Fang, W.C. (2007). Intelligent Multimedia Data Hiding: New Directions (Studies in Computational Intelligence) Berlin / Heidelberg : Springer

Chapter VI
Securing and Protecting the Copyright of Digital Video Through Watermarking Technologies

A. Hanjalic, G.C. Langelaar, P.M.B. van Roosmalen, and J. Biemond, "Image and Video Databases: Restoration, Watermarking and Retrieval".

Joaquim Filipe, Helder Coelhas, and Monica Saramago, "E-business and Telecommunication Networks: Second International Conference, ICETE 2005", Reading, UK, October 3-7, 2005. Selected Papers (Communications in Computer and Information Science), by (Paperback - Dec 14, 2007).

Pik-Wah Chan, "Digital Video Watermarking Techniques for Secure Multimedia Creation and Delivery", July 2004.

Section III
Distributing, Managing, and Transacting Digital Rights in E-Commerce Systems

Chapter VII
Digital Rights Management of Images and Videos Using Robust Replica Detection Techniques

Berrani, S.-A., Amsaleg, L., & Gros, P. (2003). Robust content-based image searches for copyright protection. In ACM International Workshop on Multimedia Databases, (pp. 70–77).

Boujemaa, N., Fauqueur, J., & Gouet, V. (2003). What's beyond query by example?. In IAPR International Conference on Image and Signal Processing (ICISP'2003).

Chang, E., Wang, J., Li, C., & Wilderhold, G. (1998). Rime—a replicated image detector for the worldwide web. In SPIE Symosium on Voice, Video, and Data Communications, (pp. 58–67).

Fridrich, J., & Goljan, M. (2000). Robust hash functions for digital watermarking. In International Conference on Information Technology: Coding and Computing (ITCC'00) (pp. 178-183).

Haitsma, J., & Kalker, T. (2002). A highly robust audio fingerprinting system. In International Conference on Music Information Retrieval (ISMIR 02).

Hsu, C. Y., & Lu, C. (2004). Geometric distortion-resilient image hashing system and its application scalability. In ACM International Conference on Multimedia: Proceedings of the 2004 workshop on Multimedia and security (pp. 81-92).

Hua, X.-S., Chen, X., & Zhang, H.-J. (2004). Robust video signature based on ordinal measure. In IEEE International Conference on Image Processing (ICIP 04)(pp. 685-688).

Indyk, P., Iyengar, G., & Shivakumar, N. (1999). Finding pirated video sequences on the internet. Technical report, Stanford University.

Iwamoto, K., Kasutani, E., & Yamada, A. (2006). Image signature robust to caption superimposition for video sequence identification. In IEEE International Conference on Image Processing (ICIP 06) (pp. 3185-3188).

Jaimes, A., Chang, S.-F., & Loui, A. C. (2002). Duplicate detection in consumer photography and news video. In ACM International Conference on Multimedia, (pp. 423–424).

Johnson, M., & Ramchandran, K. (2003). Dither-based secure image hashing using distributed coding. In IEEE International Conference on Image Processing (ICIP 03),(pp. 751-754).

Laptev, I., & Lindeberg, T. (2003). Space-time interest points. In IEEE International Conference on Computer Vision (ICCV 03), (pp. 432–439).

Lefebvre, F., Macq, B., & Czyz, J. (2003). A robust soft hash algorithm for digital image signature. In IEEE International Conference on Image Processing (ICIP 03), (pp. 495-498).

Li, Y., Jin, L., & Zhou, X. (2005). Video matching using binary signature. In International Symposium on Intelligent Signal Processing and Communication Systems, (pp. 317–320).

Maret, Y., Nikolopoulos, S., Dufaux, F., Ebrahimi, T., & Nikolaidis, N. (2006). A novel replica detection system using binary classifiers, R-trees and PCA. In IEEE International Conference on Image Processing (ICIP 06) (pp. 925-928).

Massoudi, A., Lefebvre, F., Demarty, C.-H., Oisel, L., & Chupeau, B. (2006). A video fingerprint based on visual digest and local fingerprints. In IEEE Workshop on Signal Processing Systems (SiPS 2000), (pp. 2297–2300).

Meng, Y., Chang, E. Y., & Li, B. (2003). Enhancing DPF for near-replica image recognition. In International Conference on Pattern Recognition, (pp. 416–423).

Monga, V., & Mihcak, M. K. (2005). Robust image hashing via non-negative matrix factorizations. In IEEE International Conference on Acoustics Speech and Signal Processing (ICASSP 06), (pp. II-225—II-228).

Radhakrishnan, R., Xiong, Z., & Memon, N. D. (2005). On the security of visual hash

Roy, S., & Chang, E.-C. (2004). Watermarking with retrieval systems. ACM Multimedia Systems, 9(5), 433-440.

Seo, J., Haitsma, J., Kalker, T., & Yoo, C. D. (2003). Affine transform resilient image fingerprinting. In IEEE International Conference on Acoustics Speech and Signal Processing (ICASSP 03),(pp. III-61—III-64).

Seo, J. S., Haitsma, J., Kalker, T., & Yoo C. D. (2004). A robust image fingerprinting system using the radon transform. Signal Processing: Image Communication, 19, 325-339.

Smeulders, A. W. M., Worring, M., Santini, S., Gupta, A., Jain, R. (2000). Content-based image retrieval at the end of the early years. IEEE Transactions on Pattern Analysis and Machine Inteligence., 22(12), 1349–1380.

Swaminathan, A., Mao, Y., & Wu, M. (2004). Image hashing resilient to geometric and filtering operations. In IEEE Workshop on Multimedia Signal Processing (MMSP'04) (pp. 355-358).

Venkatesan, R., Kaon, S., Jakubowski, M. H., & Moulin, P. (2000). Robust image hashing. In IEEE International Conference on Image Processing (ICIP 00) (pp. 664-666).

Yang, S., & Chen, C. (2005). Robust image hashing based on SPIHT. In International Conference on Information Technology: Research and Education (ITRE 05) (pp. 110-114).

Yang, Z., Oop, W., & Sun, Q. (2004). Hierarchical non-uniform locally sensitive hashing and its application to video identification. In IEEE International Conference on Image Processing (ICIP 04).

Chapter VIII
Digital Fingerprinting Based Multimedia Content Distribution

Aggelos, K., & Moti, Y. (2003). Breaking and repairing asymmetric public-key traitor tracing. ACM Digital Rights Management. Berlin: Springer-Verlag, 32-50.

Boneh, D., & Franklin, M. (1999). An efficient public key traitor tracing scheme. Proc CRYPTO'99, Berlin: Springer-Verlag, 338-353.

Chabanne, H., Phan, D. H., & Pointcheva, D. (2005). Public traceability in traitor tracing schemes. Advances in Cryptology: EUROCRYPT 2005. Berlin: Springer, 542-558.

Craver, S., Memom, N., & Yeo, B. (1998). Resolving rightful ownerships with invisible watermarking techniques: Limitations, attacks, and implications. IEEE Journal on Selected Areas in Communications, 1998, 16(4), 573-586.

Deguillarme, F., Csurka, G., & Ruanaidh, J. O. (1999). Robust 3D DFT video watermarking. Proceedings of SPIE Security and Watermarking of Multimedia Contents, San Jose, 113-124.

Hartung, F., & Girod, B. (1997). Digital watermarking of MPEG2 coded video in the bitstream domain. IEEE International Conference on Acoustic, Speech, and Signal Processing, Munich, Germany, 2621-2624.

Hartung, F., Girod, B. (1998). Watermarking of uncompressed and compressed video. Signal Processing, Special Issue on Copyright Protection and Access Control for Multimedia Services, 66(3), 283-301.

Hartung, F. H., Su, J. K., & Girod, B. (1999). Spread spectrum watermarking: Malicious attacks and counterattacks. Proceedings of SPIE Security and Watermarking of Multimedia Contents, San Jose, 147-158.

He, S., & Wu, M. (2005). A Joint Coding and Embedding Approach to Multimedia Fingerprinting. IEEE Trans. on Information Forensics and Security.

Kurosaua, K., & Desmedt, Y. (1998). Optimum traitor tracing and asymmetric scheme. Proc EURO-CRYPTO'98, Berlin: Springer-Verlag, 145-157.

Lian, S., Sun, J., Zhang, D., & Wang, Z. (2004). A Selective Image Encryption Scheme Based on JPEG2000 Codec. In Proceeding of 2004 Pacific-Rim Conference on Multimedia (PCM2004), Springer LNCS, 3332, 65-72.

Lian, S., Wang, Z., & Sun, J. (2004). A fast video encryption scheme suitable for network applications. In Proceeding of International Conference on Communications, Circuits and Systems, 1, 566-570.

Linnartz, J., & Dijk, M. (1998). Analysis of the sensitivity attack against electronic watermarks in images. In Workshop on Information Hiding, Portland, 15-17 April.

Liu, Q., & Jiang X. (2005). Applications of mobile agent and digital watermarking technologies in mobile communication network. 2005 International Conference on Wireless Communications, Networking and Mobile Computing, 1168-1170.

Servetti, A., & Martin, J. (2002a). Perception-based selective encryption of G. 729 speech. Proceedings of IEEE ICASSP, Orlando, Florida, 1, 621-624.

Servetti, A., & Martin, J. (2002b). Perception-based selective encryption of compressed speech. IEEE Transactions on Speech and Audio Processing, 10(8), 637-643.

Shi, C., & Bhargava, B. (1998a). A Fast MPEG Video Encryption Algorithm. In Proceeding of the 6th ACM International Multimedia Conference, Bristol, UK, 81-88.

Shi, J., & Bhargava, B. (1998b). An efficient MPEG video encryption algorithm. In Proceedings of the 6th ACM International Multimedia Conference, Bristol, United Kingdom, 381-386.

Song, G., Kim, S., Lee, W., & Kim, J. (2002). Meta-fragile Watermarking for Wireless Networks. Proc. of Int'l Conf. of Communications, Circuits, and Systems.

Swanson, M. D., & Zhu, B. (1998). Multiresolution scene based video watermarking using perceptual models. IEEE Journal on Selected Areas in Communications, 16(4), 540-550.

Teang, W. G., & Tzeng, Z. J. (2001). A Public-Key Traitor Tracing Scheme with Revocation Using Dynamical Shares. PKC'2001Vogel, T., & Dittmann, J. (2005). Illustration watermarking: an object-based approach for digital images. Security, Steganography, and Watermarking of Multimedia Contents 2005, 578-589.

Voloshynovskiy, S., Pereira, S., & Thierry, P. (2001). Attacks on digital watermarks: Classification, estimation based attacks, and benchmarks. IEEE Communications Magazine, 39(8), 118-126.

Wu, C., & Kuo, C. (2000). Fast encryption methods for audiovisual data confidentiality. In SPIE International Symposia on Information Technologies 2000, Boston, MA, USA. Proceedings of SPIE, 4209, 284-295.

Wu, C., & Kuo, C. (2001). Efficient multimedia encryption via entropy codec design. In SPIE International Symposium on Electronic Imaging 2001, San Jose, CA, USA. Proceedings of SPIE, 4314, 128-138.

Yu J. W., Goichiro, H., & Hidek, I. (2001). Efficient asymmetric public-key traitor tracing without trusted agents. Proc CT-RSA 2001, Berlin: Springer-Verlag, 392-407.

Zeng, W., & Lei, S. (2003). Efficient frequency domain selective scrambling of digital video. IEEE Trans, Multimedia, 5(1), 118-129.

Zhao, H. V., Ray Liu, K. J. (2006). Fingerprint Multicast in Secure Video Streaming. IEEE Transactions on Image Processing, 15(1), 12-29.

Chapter IX
A Digital Rights Management System for Educational Content Distribution

BEUC (2007). Consumers Digital Rights Initiative, European Consumers' Organization. Retrieved 6/22/07 from http://www.consumersdigitalrights.org

Brands, Stefan (2000). Rethinking Public Key Infrastructures and Digital Certificates; Building in Privacy. The MIT Press, Cambridge, MA.

ClickZ (2003). Users Still Resistant to Paid Content, Jupitermedia, April 11, 2003. Retrieved 4/16/07 from http://www.ecommerce-guide.com/news/news/print.php/2189551

Cohen, Julie (2003). DRM and Privacy, Communications of the ACM, 46(4), 47-49.

Cox, I., Miller, M. & Bloom, J. (2002). Digital Watermarking: Principles & Practice. San Diego, CA: Academic Press.

Cravens, Amy (2004), Speeding Ticket: The US Residential Broadband Market by Segment and Technology, September 2004, In-Stat/MDR.

EFF (2005). Dangerous Terms, a User's Guide to EULA, Electronic Frontier Foundation. Retrieved 6/22/07 from http://www.eff.org/wp/eula.php

EFF (2007). A User's Guide to DRM in Online Music, Electronic Frontier Foundation. Retrieved 6/22/07 from http://www.eff.org/IP/DRM/guide/

EPIC (2000). Pretty Poor Privacy: An Assessment of P3P and Internet Privacy, Electronic Privacy Information Center. Retrieved 6/22/07 from http://www.epic.org/reports/prettypoorprivacy.html.

Godwin, Michael (2006). Digital Rights Management: A Guide for Librarians, Office for Information Technology Policy, American Library Association.

Guibault, Lucie & Helberger, Natali (2005). Copyright law and Consumer Protection European Consumer Law Group. ECLG/035/05

Gunter, Carl, Weeks, Stephen & Wright, Andrew (2001). Models and languages for digital rights. Technical Report STAR-TR-01-04, InterTrust STAR Lab.

Kellan, Ann (2001). Whiz Kid has 'Fingerprints' all over New Napster, CNN Technology News, July 5, 2001. Retrieved 4/16/07 from http://edition.cnn.com/2001/TECH/internet/07/05/napster.fingerprint/index.html

LII (2007a). United States Constitution Article I Section 8, Legal Information Institute, Cornell Law School.

LII (2007b). US Code Collection, Title 17, Copyrights, Legal Information Institute, Cornell Law School.

LII (2007c). The Bill Of Rights: US Constitution, Amendment IV, Legal Information Institute, Cornell Law School.

Morris, R. & Thompson, K. (1979). Password Security: A Case History. Communication of the ACM, 22(11).

Mulligan, D. & Schwartz, A. (2000). P3P and Privacy: An Update for the Privacy Community. Center for Democracy & Technology. Retrieved 4/16/07 from http://www.cdt.org/privacy/pet/p3pprivacy.shtml

National Research Council Panel on Intellectual Property (2000). The Digital Dilemma: Intellectual Property in the Information Age. National Academy Press, Washington, D.C., 2000.

Rosenblatt, B., Trippe, B. & Mooney, S. (2002). Digital Rights Management: Business and Technology. New York, NY:: M&T Books.

Schaub, M. (2006). A Breakdown of Consumer Protection Law in the Light of Digital Products, Indicare Monitor, 2(5).

Schwartz, John (2004). In Survey,Fewer Are Sharing Files (Or Admitting It),. The New York Times, Jan. 5, 2004. Section C, Page 1.

Shapiro, Carl & Varian, Hal (1999). Information Rules: A Strategic Guide to the Network Economy. Harvard Business School Press, Boston, MA.

USG (1998). The Digital Millennium Copyright Act of 1998, U.S. Copyright Office, Pub. 05-304, 112 Stat. 2860.

W3C (2002a). How to Create and Publish Your Company's P3P Policy in 6 Easy Steps. W3C P3P Working Group. Retrieved 4/16/07 from http://www.w3.org/P3P/details.html

W3C (2002b). The Platform for Privacy Preferences 1.0 (P3P1.0) Specification. W3C P3P Working Group. Retrieved 4/16/07 from http://www.w3.org/TR/P3P/

Chapter X
Digital Rights Management and E-Commerce Transactions: Online Rights Clearnance

DCMI, Dublin Core Metadata Initiative, Last checked: October 11 2007, <http://www.dublincore.org/>

DIG35, Digital Image Group - DIG35 Specification – Metadata for Digital Images. Last checked: 11 October 2007, http://www.i3a.org/i_dig35.html

DOI, Digital Object Identifier. Last checked: 11 October 2007, http://www.doi.org

MPEG21, MPEG-21 Overview v5, Last checked: 11 October 2007, http://www.chiariglione.org/mpeg/standards/mpeg-21/mpeg-21.htm

MPEG7, ISO/IEC Moving Picture Experts Group. Last checked: 11 October 2007,   < http://www.chiariglione.org/mpeg/standards/mpeg-7/mpeg-7.htm >

URI, Uniform Resource Identifiers (URI): Generic Syntax, IETF RFC2396. Last checked: 11 October 2007, http://www.ietf.org/rfc/rfc2396.txt

WIPO, World Intellectual Property Organization, Last checked: October 11 2007, <http://www.wipo.int>

XML, eXtensive Markup Language. Last checked: 11 October 2007, http://www.w3.org/XML/

XrML, eXtensive rights Markup Language. Last checked: 11 October 2007, http://www.xrml.org

XSD, eXtensible Markup Language Schema, Last checked: 11 October 2007, <http://www.w3.org/XML/Schema>

Section IV
Strategies and Case Studies

Chapter XI
Digital Rights Management in Organisations: A Critical Consideration with a Socio-Technical Approach

U.K. Joint Information Services Committee (JISC)/Intrallect (2004), Digital Rights Management Study and appendices, from www.intrallect.com/drm-study/

World Trade Organisation (WTO). Trade-related aspects of intellectual property rights (TRIPS) agreement, from http://www.wto.org/english/tratop_e/trips_e/trips_e.htm

U.S. Department of Commerce, The International Trade Administration, The American Automotive Industry Supply Chain – In the Throes of a Rattling Revolution, from www.ita.doc.gov/td/auto/domestic/SupplyChain.pdf

Kiesler, S. & Hinds, P. (Ed.) (2002). Distributed Work. Cambridge, MA: The MIT Press

Avgerou, C. (1993). Information systems for development planning. International Journal of Information Management,13, 260-73.

Chapter XII
An Advanced Watermarking Application for the Copyright Protection and Management of Digital Images of Cultural Heritage Case Study: "Ulysses"

Wayner, Disappearing Cryptography - Information Hiding: Steganography and Watermarking (Second, pp. 291-318). (2002). Morgan Kaufmann.

Computer Science and Telecommunications Board, National Research Council, The Digital Dilemma: Intellectual Property in the Information Age, National Academy Press, Washington, 1999, pp. ES 2-3.

House of Representatives, Digital Millennium Copyright Act, October 28, 1998.

The Hellenic Cultural Heritage Portal, http://www.culture.gr.

Randall Davis, "The Digital Dilemma", Communications of the ACM, Volume 44, February 2001, pp. 80.

IBM, "IBM DB2 Digital Library", http://www.ibm.com.

G. K. Tsolis, D. K. Tsolis and T. S. Papatheodorou, "A watermarking environment and a metadata digital image repository for the protection and management of digital images of the Hellenic Cultural Heritage", in 2001 International Conference on Image Processing, Greece.

World Wide Web Consortium. Extensible Markup Language (XML). http://www.w3.org/XML.

The IBM AlphaWorks. (2001). XML Access Service Lightweight Extractor (XLE).

Chapter XIII
Digital Rights Management in the Cultural Heritage Arena: A Truth or a Myth?

Federated Digital Rights Management (D-Lib Magazine, July/August 2002)

Digital Rights Management and Copy Protection Schemes (EFF org)

http://en.wikipedia.org/wiki/DRM

http://www.drmwatch.com/

http://drm.info/

Section V
Legislative Issues

Chapter XIV
Digital Rights Management: A European Law Perspective

Braun Nora, The Interface between the Protection of Technological Measures and the Exercise of Exceptions to Copyright and Related Rights: Comparing the Situation in the United States and the European Community, 25 EIRP 11, 499 (2003).

Byers Simon, Cranor Lorrie, Korman Dave, McDaniel Patrick and Cronin Eric,

Analysis of Security Vulnerabilities in the Movie Production and Distribution Process, DRM'03, October 27, 2003, Washington, DC, USA.

Cheun Ngen Chong, Yee Wei Law, Sandro Etalle, and Pieter H Hartel, Approximating Fair Use in LicenseScript, Faculty of EEMCS, University of Twente, The Netherlands

de Rosnay, M.D., Digital rights management systems and European law: between copyright protection and access control, Web Delivering of Music, 2002. WEDELMUSIC 2002. Proceedings. Second International Conference on Volume , Issue , 2002 Page(s): 117 - 124

Dreier T. P.B. Hugenholtz (ed.), Concise on European Copyright Law, Alphen aan den Rijn, Kluwer Law Intermational, 2006, p.393

European Commission, First Report on the application of Directive 2000/31/EC of the European Parliament and of the Council of 8 June 2000 on certain legal aspects of information society services, in particular electronic commerce, in the Internal Market (Directive on electronic commerce), Brussels, 21.11.2003, COM(2003) 702 final

European Commission, Digital Rights Management, High Level Group Documents, at http://ec.europa.eu/information_society/eeurope/2005/all_about/digital_rights_man/documents/index_en.htm

GartnerG2, Copyright and Digital Media in a Post-Napster World, Version 2 (Updated January 2005), by GartnerG2 and The Berkman Center for Internet & Society at Harvard Law School.

Internet Resource For Digital Rights Management: http://www.drmwatch.com/legal/

Picot Arnold and Fielder Marina, Property Rights and Openness as Factors of Innovation, in Bindseil U., Haucap J. and Wey C. Institutions in Perspective, 2006 Mohr Siebeck, Tübingen, Germany

Schneider Markus and Henten Anders, DRMS and TCP: Technology and Law, CTI Working Papers, no. 76, Center for Tele-Information, COST A20 Conference

Towards New Media Paradigms, Pamplona 27-28 June 2003

Chapter XV
Legal Issues for DRM: The Future

A Model for Credential Based Exception Management in Digital Rights Management Systems, Jean-Henry Morin, Michel Pawlak, Internet Monitoring and Protection, 2007. ICIMP 2007. Second International Conference on Volume , Issue , 1-5 July 2007 Page(s):41 – 41 Digital Object Identifier 10.1109/ICIMP.2007.3

WIRED, Reasons to love open-source DRM, April 3, 2006 (available at http://www.wired.com/entertainment/music/commentary/listeningpost/2006/04/70548)

Towards Digital Rights and Exemptions Management Systems, Computer Law & Security Report, Vol. 20, No.4, pp. 281-287, 2004 Thierry Maillard and Teddy Furon

Compilation of References

Aalst, W. M. P. van der & Hee, K. van (2002). *Workflow management: Models, methods, and systems.* Cambridge, MA: MIT press.

AAP (2000). *Association of American Publishers - AAP, numbering standards for E-Books*, Version 1.0. Retrieved February 1, 2008 from http://www.publishers.org/digital/numbering.pdf.

AAP (2007). Association of American Publishers - AAP. Retrieved February 1, 2008 from http://www.publishers.org.

Abie, H., Bing, J., Blobel, B., Delgado, J., Foyn, B., Karnouskos, S., Pharow, P., Pitkänen, O., & Tzovaras, D. (2004). The need for a digital rights management framework for the next generation of E-Government services. *International Journal of Electronic Government, 1*(1), 8-28.

Abijit, C., & Kuilboer, J.-P. (2002). E-Business and E-Commerce infrastructure. McGraw-Hill. ISBN 0-07-247875-6.

ACM, pp. 15-20. http://doi.acm.org/10.1145/285070.285073

Adams, M., & Kossentini, F. (2000). Reversible Integer-To-Integer Wavelet Transforms for Image Compression: Performance Evaluation and Analysis. *IEEE Transactions on Image Processing, 9*(6), 1010-1024.

Adelsbach, A., Katzenbeisser, S., & Sadeghi, A.-R. (2002). Crytpography meets watermarking: Detecting watermarks with minimal or zero knowledge disclosure. *In XI European Signal Processing Conference, EUSIPCO' 02, 1,* 446-449. Toulouse, France.

Ahrens, F. (2005, February 20). Hard news, Daily papers face unprecedented competition. *Washington Post Sunday*, F01.

American Heritage® Dictionary of the English Language, 4th Edition. Retrieved 6/22/07 from http://dictionary.reference.com/browse/copyright

Anderson, R., & Manifavas, C. (1997). Chameleon - A new kind of stream cipher. *In Lecture Notes in Computer Science, Fast Software Encryption*, (pp. 107-113), Springer-Verlag. .

Antonini, M., Barlaud, M., Mathieu, P., & Daubechies, I. (1992). Image Coding Using The Wavelet Transform. *IEEE Transactions on Image Processing, 1*(2), 205-220.

Armeni, S., Christodoulakis, D., Kostopoulos, I., Stamatiou, Y., & Xenos, M. (2000, June). A transparent watermarking method for color images. *First IEEE Balcan Conference on Signal Processing, Communications, Circuits, and Systems.* Istanbul, Turkey.

Armstrong, T. K. (2006). Digital rights management and process of fair use. *Harvard Journal of Law & Technology, 20*(1). From http://papers.ssrn.com/sol3/papers.cfm?abstract_id=885371#PaperDownload.

Arnold, M., & Schmucker, M., & Wolthusen, S. D. (2003). Techniques and applications of digital watermarking and content protection. Artech House.

Avgerou, C. (1993). Information systems for development planning. *International Journal of Information Management, 13*, 260-73.

Ayars, J. (2002). *XMCL - eXtensible media commerce language.* RealNetworks, Inc., W3C. Retrieved February 1, 2008 from http://www.w3.org/TR/xmcl.

Bainbridge, D. I. (2006). *Intellectual Property.* 6th edition. Pearson Education

Barni, M., & Bartolini, F. (2004). Watermarking systems engineering: Enabling digital assets security and other applications. *Signal Processing & Communication.* Marcel Dekker.

Barni, M., Bartolini F., & Fridrich, J. (2000, September). Digital Watermarking for the Authentication of the AVS Data. *Eusipco2000.* (Sep. 4-8, 2000, Tampere, Finland).

Barni, M., Bartolini, F., & Furon, T. (2003). A general framework for robust watermarking security. *Signal Processing, 83*(10), 2069-2084.

Barni, M., Bartolini, F., Cappellini, V., Lippi, A., & Piva, A. (1999). A DWT-based technique for spatio-frequency masking of digital signatures. *Proceedings of the 11th SPIE Annual Symposium, Electronic Imaging '99, Security and watermarking of Multimedia Contents,* P. W. Wong (ed.), *3657,* 31-39.(January 1999, San Jose, CA), P. W. Wong (Ed.), vol. 3657, 31-39.

Barni, M., Bartolini, F., De Rosa, A., & Piva, A. (2001). A new decoder for the optimum recovery of non-additive watermarks. *IEEE Transactions on Image Processing, 10*(5), 755-766.

Barni, M., Bartolini, F., De Rosa, A., & Piva, A. (2003). Optimum decoding and detection of multiplicative watermarks. *IEEE Transactions on Signal Processing, 51*(4), 1118-1123.

Barni., M., Bartolini., F., Cappellini., V., Piva., A. (1998). A DCT-domain system for robust image watermarking. *Signal Processing. Special Issue on Watermarking, 3*(66), 357-372.

Bartolini, F., Barni, M., Cappellini, V., & Piva, A. (1998). Mask building for perceptually hiding frequency embedded watermarks. *In 5th IEEE International Conference on Image Processing ICIP'98, 1,* 450-454. Chicago, Illinois, USA.

Berne Convention (1886). *Summary of Berne Convention for the protection of literary and artistic works.* Retrieved February 1, 2008 from http://www.wipo.int/treaties/en/ip/berne/summary_berne.html.

Berne Convention (1979). *Berne Convention for the protection of literary and artistic works.* Retrieved February 1, 2008 from http://www.wipo.int/export/sites/www/treaties/en/ip/berne/pdf/trtdocs_wo001.pdf.

Bhatt, G. D. (2001). Knowledge management in organisations: Examining the interaction between technologies, techniques, and people. *Journal of Knowledge Management, 5*(1), 68-75.

Bhattacharjee S., & Kutter, M. (1998, October 4-7). Compression Tolerant Image Authentication. *International Conference on Image Processing ICIP'98.* (October 4-7, 1998, Chicago, IL).

Biggam, J. (2001). Defining knowledge: An epistemological foundation for knowledge management. *Paper presented to 34th Hawaii International Conference on System Sciences.* Hawaii.

Bloom, J. (2003). Security and rights management in digital cinema. *In Proc. IEEE Int. Conf. Acoustic, Speech and Signal Processing, 4,* 712-715.

Boiko, B. (2002). Content management bible. New York, NY: Wiley Publishing Inc.

Boliek, M., Houchin J. S., & Wu, G. (2000, September). JPEG 2000 Next Generation Image Compression System Features And Syntax. *Proceedings of the Intl Conf. on Image Processing ICIP 2000 2,* 45-48. , (September 2000, Vancouver, Canada), vol. II, 45-48.

Boneh, D., & Shaw, J. (1998). Collusion-secure fingerprinting for digital data. *IEEE Trans. Inform. Theory, 44,* 1897-1905.

BOWS (2006). *Break our watermarking system.* From http://lci.det.unifi.it/BOWS.

BOWS-2 (2007). *Break our watermarking system*, 2nd Ed., From http://bows2.gipsa-lab.inpg.fr.

Bricks Project, (2007). From http://www.brickscommunity.org/

Brown, I., Perkins, C., & Crowcroft, J. (1999). Watercasting: Distributed watermarking of multicast media. *In Proceedings of International Workshop on Networked Group Communication, 1736.* Springer-Verlag LNCS.

Caldelli, R., Piva, A., Barni, M., & Carboni, A. (2005). Effectiveness of ST-DM watermarking against intra-video collusion. *In 4th International Workshop on Digital Watermarking, IWDW 2005, LNCS, 3710,* 158-170. Siena, Italy.

Cappellini, V., Piva, A., Dawson, D., & Tsolis, D. (2003, June). Technological solutions for copyright protection and management of cultural heritage: Best practices and guidelines. Workshop on Digitization of Cultural Content, 27-28 June 2003, Corfu, Greece.

Celik, M. U., Sharma, G., & Tekalp, A. M. (2005). Collusion-resilient fingerprinting by random pre-warping. *IEEE Signal Processing Letters, Preprint.*

Chan, P.-W., & Lyu, M. R. (2003). A DWT-Based Digital Video Watermarking Scheme with Error Correcting Code. *Lecture Notes in Computer Science.* (2836), 202-213.

Chan, P. W., Lyu, M. R., & Chin, R. T. (2005). A Novel Scheme for Hybrid Digital Video Watermarking: Approach, Evaluation and Experimentation. *IEEE TRANSACTIONS ON CIRCUITS AND SYSTEMS FOR VIDEO TECHNOLOGY. 15*(12), 1638-1649.

Chen, B., & Wornell, G. (2000). Preprocessed and post-processed quantization index modulation methods for digital watermarking. *Proceedings of SPIE: Security and Watermarking of Multimedia Contents II, Electronic Imaging 2000,* (January 2000, . San Jose, CA).

Chen, B., & Wornell, G. (2001). Quantization index modulation: A class of provably good methods for digital watermarking and information embedding. *IEEE Transaction on Information Theory, 47,* 1423-1443.

Chen, B., & Wornell, G. W. (1998). Digital watermarking and information embedding using dither modulation. *In Proceedings of the 1998 IEEE 2nd Workshop on Multimedia Signal Processing. Redondo Beach,* 273-278.

Chen, T. P.-C., Chen, Y.-S., & Hsu, W.-H. (1999, July). Adaptive-rate image watermarking based on spread spectrum communication technique. *3rd World Multiconference on Circuits, Systems, Communications and Computers (CSCC'99).* Athens, Greece.

Cheng, H., & Li, X. (2000, August). Partial encryption of compressed images and videos. *IEEE Transactions on Signal Processing, 48*(8), 2439-2451.

CIAGP (Conseil International des Auteurs des Arts Graphiques et Plastiques et des Photographes): cisac.org

CISAC (Conféderation Internationale des Sociétés d'Auteurs et Compositeurs): cisac.org

Clarendon Press. (1933). *The Oxford English dictionary: Being a corrected re-issue.* Oxford.

Cohen, J. (2003). DRM and privacy. *Communications of the ACM, 46*(4), 47-49.

Cohen, J. E. (2001). *DRM and privacy.* ACM, pp. 46-49. http://doi.acm.org/10.1145/641205.641230.

Collier, G., Piccariello, H., & Robson, R. (2004). *Digital rights management: An ecosystem model and scenarios for higher education.* Educause Center.

Commission of the European Communities Staff. (2002, February 14)., *Digital Rights, Background, Systems, SEC(2002) 197* Working Paper *Assessment,* Brussels.

Computer Science and Telecommunications Board, National Research Council. (1999). *The digital dilemma: Intellectual property in the information age,* 2-3. Washington: National Academy Press.

Corvi, M., & Nicchiotti, G. (1997, June). Wavelet-based image watermarking for copyright protection. *Scandinavian Conference on Image Analysis SCIA '97.,* (June 1997, Lappeenranta, Finland).

Coskun, B., Sankur, B., & Memon, N. (2006). Spatio-temporal transform-based video hashing. *IEEE Transactions on Multimedia, 8*(6), 1190-1208.

Costa, M. (1983). Writing on dirty paper. *IEEE Transaction on Information Theory, 29*, 439-441.

Cotsaces, C., Nikolaidis, N., & Pitas, I. (2006). Video indexing by face occurrence-based signatures. *In IEEE International Conference on Acoustics Speech and Signal Processing (ICASSP 06)* (pp. II-137-II-140).

Cox, I. J., Kilian, J., Leighton, F. T., & Shamoon, T. (1995). Secure spread spectrum watermarking for multimedia. *Technical Report 95-10*. NEC Research Institute.

Cox, I. J., Kilian, J., Leighton, T., & Shamoon, T. (1996). A secure, robust watermark for multimedia. *In Proceedings of the Inform. Hiding Workshop*, 147-158. Cambridge.

Cox, I. J., Kilian, J., Leighton, T., & Shamoon, T. (1997). Secure spread spectrum watermarking for multimedia. *IEEE Transaction on Image Processing, 6*, 1673-1687.

Cox, I. J., Miller, M. L., & Bloom, J. A. (2002). *Digital watermarking*. San Francisco: Morgan-Kaufmann.

Cox, I., & Miller, M. L. (1997, February). A review of watermarking and the importance of perceptual modeling. *Proceedings of SPIE, 3016. Human Vision and Electronic Imaging II*, 92-99. Bellingham, WA.

Cravens, A. (2004, September). Speeding ticket: The U.S. residential broadband market by segment and technology. *In Stat/MDR*.

Craver, S., Yeo, B., & Yeung, M. (1998). Technical trials and legal tribulations. *Communications of the ACM, 41*(7), 44-54.

Crawford, D. (1999). *Intellectual property in the age of universal access*. ACM Publications.

CSTB (1999). *The digital dilemma: Intellectual property in the information age*. Prepublication Copy, Computer Science and Telecommunications Board, US National Research Council: National Academy Press.

Curran, T. (2002). Chief Technology Officer, Bertelsmann at the Digital Rights Management Workshop, February 28, 2002, Brussels (from http://ec.europa.eu/information_society/eeurope/2005/all_about/digital_rights_man/index_en.htm).

Dana, L. P., Korot, L., & Tovstiga, G. (2005). A cross-national comparison of knowledge management practices. *International Journal of Manpower, 26*(1), 10-22.

Davenport, T. H., & Prusak, L. (1998). Working knowledge: How organisations manage what they know. Boston, MA: Harvard Business School Press.

Davis, R. (2001). *The digital dilemma*. ACM, pp. 77-83. http://doi.acm.org/10.1145/359205.359234.

Davoine, F. (2000). Comparison of two wavelet based image watermarking schemes. *Proceedings of the IEEE International Conference on Image Processing ICIP 2000*, (September 2000,. Vancouver, Canada).

DCITA (2003). *A guide to digital rights management*. Department of Communications Information Technology and the Arts. Retrieved February 1, 2008 from http://www.dcita.gov.au/drm.

DCMI, Dublin Core Metadata Initiative, Last checked: October 11 2007, <http://www.dublincore.org/>

Delannay, D. (2004, April). Digital watermarking algorithms robust against loss of synchronization. *PhD thesis*. Laboratoire de Telecommunications et Teledetection : Universite Catholique de Louvain.

Dhamija, R., & Wallenberg, F. (2003). A framework for evaluating digital rights management proposals. *In Proceedings of the First International Mobile IPR Workshop: Rights Management of Information Products on the Mobile Internet*. Helsinki, Finland.

DIG35 Specification - Metadata for Digital Images. Version 1.0. (2000). Digital Imaging Group.

DIG35, Digital Image Group - DIG35 Specification - Metadata for Digital Images. Last checked: 11 October 2007, http://www.i3a.org/i_dig35.html

Digital Object Identifier. http://www.doi.org

Dinitz, J. H., & Stinson, D. R. (1992). Contemporary design theory: A collection of surveys. New York:

Wiley.

Dittmann, J., Megias, D., Lang, A., & Herrera, J. (2006). Theoretical framework for a practical evaluation and comparison of audio watermarking schemes in the triangle of robustness, transparency and capacity. *LNCS Transactions on Data Hiding and Multimedia Security*, 1-40.

DMCA (1998). *Digital millennium copyright act*. Retrieved February 1, 2008 from http://www.gseis.ucla.edu/iclp/dmca1.htm.

Doerr, G., & Dugelay, J. L. (2003). A guide tour of video watermarking. *Signal Processing: Image Communication 18*, 263-282.

Doerr, G., & Dugelay, J. L. (2003). New intra-video collusion attack using mosaicing. *In IEEE International Conference Multimedia Expo., 2,*505-508. Baltimore, USA.

DRM (2000). *Digital rights management workshop*. Retrieved February 1, 2008 from http://www.w3.org/2000/12/drm-ws/.

DRRL (1998). *Digital property rights language - DPRL, manual and tutorial - XML edition, Version 2.00*. Retrieved February 1, 2008 from http://xml.coverpages.org/DPRLmanual-XML2.html.

Dublin Core Metadata Standard. (2000). Dublin Core.

Duda, R., Hart, P., &. Stork, D. (2000). Pattern classification, 2nd edition. Wiley Interscience.

Duhl, J., & Kevorkian, S. (2001). *Understanding DRM systems*. IDC White Paper.

Duncan, C., Barker, E., Douglas, P., Morrey, M., & Waelde, C. (2004, August 25). JISC DRM Study Intrallect Ltd. Retrieved 6/22/07 from http://www.intrallect.com/drm-study/DRMFinalReport.pdf

Dusollier S. (2001, April). Fair use by design in the European copyright directive of 2001. *Communications of the ACM, 46*(4), 51.

DVB-Digital Video Broadcasting. http://www.dvb-h.org/

Eason, K. (1988). *Information technology and organisational change*. London UK: Taylor and Francis.

EDItEUR ONIX (n.d.). *EDItEUR ONIX international standard*. Retrieved February 1, 2008 from http://www.editeur.org/onix.html.

Eggers, J., & Girod, B. (2000). Quantization Watermarking. *Proceedings of SPIE: Security and Watermarking of Multimedia Contents II, Electronic Imaging 2000*, (January 2000,. San Jose, CA).

Eickeler, S., Wallhoff, F., Iurgel, U., & Rigoll, G. (2001). Content-based indexing of images and video using face detection and recognition methods. *In IEEE International Conference on Acoustics, Speech, and Signal Processing (ICASSP 2001)* (pp.III-1505-III-1508).

El Sawy, O. A. (2001). Redesigning enterprise processes for E-Business. Boston MA: McGraw-Hill Irwin.

Electronic Frontier Foundation (EFF): www.eff.org

Erickson, J. (2001). Information objects and rights management. *D-Lib Magazine, 7*(4). Retrieved February 1, 2008 from http://www.dlib.org/dlib/april01/erickson/04erickson.html.

Erickson, J. S. (2001). *Fair use, DRM, and trusted computing*. ACM, pp. 34-39, http://doi.acm.org/10.1145/641205.641228.

ESA (2001). *Electronic signature act*. Retrieved February 1, 2008 from http://unpan1.un.org/intradoc/groups/public/documents/APCITY/UNPAN025695.pdf.

Eskicioglu, A. M. (2003). Protecting Intellectual Property in Digital Multimedia Networks (Invited Paper). *IEEE Computer, Special Issue on Piracy and Privacy, 36*(7), 39-45.

Estes, A. (2007, May 6). Bill would ban lenders' alerts to homebuyers. *Boston Globe*, B3,.

Evain, J-P. (2005, April 6). *Open standards: The path to interoperability. EBU, Towards Reaching Consensus on*

Digital Rights Management. Brussels.

Fabien A. P., Petitcolas, R. Anderson, J., .& Kuhn, M. G. (1999). Information hiding - A survey. *Proc. IEEE 87,* 1062-1078.

Federal Trade Commission (2007). Public Law 106-102, GLB..Retrieved 6/22/07 from http://www.ftc.gov/bcp/conline/pubs/buspubs/glbshort.htm

Figallo, C., & Rhine, N. (2002). *Building the knowledge management network: Best practices, tools, and techniques for putting conversation to work.* New York, NY: John Wiley & Sons, Inc.

Foster, I., Kesselman, C., & Tuecke, S. (2001). The anatomy of the grid: Enabling scalable virtual organizations. *International Journal of High Performance Computing Applications, 15,* 200-222.

Fotopoulos, V., & Skodras, A. N. (2002, July 1-3). JPEG2000 Parameters against Watermarking. *Proceedings of the 14th Int. Conf. on Digital Signal Processing DSP 2002* (July 1-3, 2002, , Santorini, Greece), vol. 2, 713-716. Santorini, Greece

Fotopoulos.,V., & Skodras., A. N. (2000). A subband DCT approach to image watermarking. *X European Signal Processing Conference (EUSIPCO-2000).*Tampere, Finland.

Fotopoulos.,V., & Skodras., A. N. (2002). *Adaptive coefficients selection for transform domain watermarking.* Technical Report TR2002/10/02. Patras, Greece: Computer Technology Institute.

Fotopoulos.,V., &Skodras., A. N. (2002, September). *Geometric deformations and watermarking.* Technical Report TR2002/09/02. Patras, Greece: Computer Technology Institute.

Fox L. B., & LaMacchia, B. A. (2003, April). Encouraging recognition of fair uses in DRM systems. *Communications of the ACM, 46*(4), 61-63.

Frank, S. (2005, September). RFID is x-ray vision. Communication *of the ACM, 48*(9).

Fridrich, J. (2002). Security of fragile authentication watermarks with localization. *In Proceedings of SPIE Photonic West, 467). Electronic Imaging 2002: Security and Watermarking of Multimedia Contents IV,* 691-700. San Jose.

Furht, B., & Kirovski, D. (Ed.). (2006). Multimedia encryption and authentication techniques and applications. Boca Raton, FL: Auerbach Publications,.

Furon, T., Venturini, I., & Duhamel, P. (2001). An unified approach of asymmetric watermarking schemes. In E.J. Delp and P.W. Wong (Ed.), *Security and Watermarking of Multimedia Contents III, Proc. SPIE, 4314 ,* 269-279). San Jose, CA.

Gaede, V., & Gunther, A. (1998). Multidimensional access methods. *ACM Computing Surveys, 30*(2), 170-231.

Gasser, U., & Girsberger, M. (2004, November 10). *Transposing the copyright directive: Legal protection of technological measures in EU-member states.* Berkman Publication Series. From http://cyber.law.harvard.edu/publications.

Gavrielides, M., & Sikudova, E., & Pitas, I. (2005). Color-based descriptors for image fingerprinting. *IEEE Transactions on Multimedia, 8*(4), 740-748.

Ghorbel, F. (1994). A complete invariant description for gray-level images by the harmonic analysis approach. *Pattern Recognition Letters, 15*(10), 1043-1051.

Gilani, S., Kostopoulos, I., & Skodras, A. (2002, July 1-3). Adaptive color image watermarking. *14th IEEE International Conference on Digital Signal Processing.* Santorini, Greece.

Gionis, A., Indyk, P., & Motwani, R. (1999). Similarity search in high dimensions via hashing. *In 25th International Conference on Very Large Data Bases (VLDB '99)* (pp. 518-529).

Goble, C., & De Roure, D. (2002). The grid: An application of the Semantic Web. *SIGMOD Record, 31*(4).

Godwin, M. (2006). *Digital rights management: A guide for librarians.* Office for Information Technology Policy, American Library Association.

Goh, A. (2004). Enhancing organisational performance through knowledge innovation: A proposed strategic management framework. *Journal of Knowledge Management Practice*, (5)

Government of France. (2004). *Charter of agreement for the development of a legal supply of on-line music, respect for intellectual property and the fight against digital piracy*, Paris, 28 July 2004, from http://ec.europa.eu/information_society/eeurope/2005/all_about/digital_rights_man/doc/drm_workshop_2005/charte_en.pdf).

Green, K. (2004). The 2004 National Survey of Information Technology in U.S. Higher Education. *The Campus Computing Project*. Retrieved 6/22/07 from http://www.campuscomputing.net/

Grosbois, R., Gerbelot, P., & Ebrahimi, T. (2001, July 29th-August 3rd). Authentication and access control in the JPEG 2000 compressed domain. *Proceedings of the SPIE 46th Annual Meeting, Applications of Digital Image Processing XXIV* (July 29th- August 3rd, 2001,. San Diego, CA).

Gunter, C., Weeks, S., & Wright, A. (2001). *Models and languages for digital rights*. InterTrust Star Lab Technical Report STAR-TR-01-04. Retrieved February 1, 2008 from http://www.star-lab.com/tr/star-tr-01-04.pdf.

Gupta, J. N. D., Sharma, K. S., & Hsu, J. (2003): An overview of knowledge management. In Gupta, J. N. D. (Ed.): *Creating knowledge-based organizations*. Hershey, PA, USA: Idea Group Publishing.

Hampapur, A., & Bolle, R. (2002). Comparison of sequence matching techniques for video copy detection. I*n Conference on Storage and Retrieval for Media Databases*, 194-201.

Hasebrook, J. (2002). International E-Learning business: Strategies & opportunities. *World Conference on E-Learning in Corp., Govt., Health & Higher Ed, 2002*(1), 404-411.

Heng, G. (2001). Digital rights management (DRM) using XrML. *T-110.501 Seminar on Network Security*.

Herrigel, A., Oruanaidh, J., Petersen, H., Pereira, S., & Pun, T. (1998). Secure copyright protection techniques for digital images. *In second Information Hiding Workshop (IHW), LNCS 1525*. Springer-Verlag.

HHS (2007). Public Law 104-191, HIPAA. Department of Health & Human Services. Retrieved 6/22/07 from http://aspe.hhs.gov/admnsimp/pl104191.htm

Hirschheim, R. A. (1985). *Office automation: A social and organizational perspective*. New York: John Wiley and sons.

Hofmeister, C., Nord, R., & Soni, D. (2000). *Applied software architectures*. Addison-Wesley.

Holstius, K., & Malaska, P. (2004). Advanced strategic thinking. *Visionary management*. Publications of the Turku School of Economics & Business Administration, ISBN: 95-564-187-x

House of Representatives. (1998). Digital Millennium Copyright Act.

Huang, D., & Yan, H. (2001). Inter-word distance changes represented by Sine Waves for watermarking text images. *IEEE Trans. on Circuits and Systems for Video Technology, 11*(12), 1237-1245.

Hunt, B. (2000). *Information and content exchange (ICE) reference version*. Retrieved February 1, 2008 from http://www.infoloom.com/gcaconfs/WEB/paris2000/S21-04.HTM.

ICE (1998). *Information and content exchange protocol - ICE*. W3C. Retrieved February 1, 2008 from http://www.w3.org/TR/NOTE-ice.

IFLA, Functional Requirements for Bibliographic Records, IFLA Study Group on the Functional Requirements for Bibliographic Records, (Approved September 1997) K . G. Saur München, 1998. Not available, http://www.ifla.org/VII/s13/frbr/frbr.htm

IMPRIMATUR, Intellectual Multimedia Property RIghts Model and Terminology for Universal Reference, Not available, http://www.imprimatur.alcs.co.uk/index.

htm

IMS (n.d.). *IMS learning resource meta-data information model (Version 1.1).* Retrieved February 1, 2008 from http://www.imsproject.org/metadata/mdinfov1p1.pdf.

INDECS (2002). *Interoperability of data in E-Commerce systems.* Retrieved February 1, 2008 from http://www.indecs.org.

Ingemar, C., Miller, M., & Bloom, J. (2002). *Digital watermarking.* Morgan Kaufmann Publishers.

Institute for Information of Law (2001, February). *Study on the Implementation and Effect in Member States' Laws of Directive 2001/29 on the Harmonisation of Certain Aspects of Copyright and Related Rights in the Information Society.* University of Amsterdam.

Intellectual property related organisations (Web sites tested on Aug 2007)

IPR Helpdesk organization: http://www.ipr-helpdesk.org

ISO (n.d.). *ISO international standard textual work code.* Retrieved February 1, 2008 from http://www.nlc-bnc.ca/iso/tc46sc9/istc.htm.

ISO/IEC JTC1/SC29 15444-1. (2007). Information technology -- JPEG 2000 image coding system: Core coding system.

ITU IPTV Focus Group. http://www.itu.int/ITU-T/IPTV/

JPEG 2000. (2007). Retrieved August 07, 2007, from http://www.jpeg.org/jpeg2000.html

Joly, A., Buisson, O., & Frélicot, C. (2007). Content-based copy detection using distortion-based probabilistic similarity search. *IEEE Transactions on Multimedia, 9*(2), 293-306.

Kahn, D. (1996). The history of steganography. *Proceedings of the First International Workshop on Information Hiding.*

Kahn, R. & Wilensky, R. (2006). A Framework for Distributed Digital Object Services. *International Journal on Digital Libraries, 6*(2). Springer.

Kailasanathan, C., Safavi-Naini, R., & Ogunbona, P. (2001, June 3-6). Image Authentication Surviving Acceptable Modifications. *IEEE-EURASIP Workshop on Nonlinear Signal and Image Processing NSIP '01.1* (June 3-6, 2001).

Kalker, T. (2001). Considerations on watermarking security. *In IEEE Multimedia Signal Processing, MMSP '01 Workshop*, 201-206. Cannes, France.

Kalker, T., Depovere, G., Haitsma, J., & Maes, M. (1999). A video watermarking system for broadcast monitoring. In E.J. Delp and P.W. Wong (Ed.), *Security and Watermarking of Multimedia Contents, Proc. SPIE, 3657*, 103-112. San Jose, CA.

Katzenbeisser, S., & Petitcolas, F. (2002). *Information hiding - Techniques for steganography and digital watermarking.* Atrech House Inc.

Katzenbeisser. S., & Petitcolas., F. A. P. (2000). *Information hiding - Techniques for steganography and digital watermarking,* 95-172. Artech House, Computer Series.

Ke, Y., & Sukthankar, R. (2003). PCA-SIFT: A more distinctive representation for local image descriptors. *In IEEE Computer Vision and Pattern Recognition,* (pp. II-506-II-513).

Ke, Y., Sukthankar, R., & Huston, L. (2004). An efficient parts-based near-duplicate and sub-image retrieval system. *In 12th annual ACM international conference on Multimedia* (pp. 869-876).

Kellan, A. (2001, July 5). Whiz kid has 'fingerprints' all over new Napster. *CNN Technology News.* Retrieved 6/22/07

Kerckhoffs, A. (1883). La cryptographie militaire. *Journal des sciences militaires, 9,* 5-83.

Kiesler, S. & Hinds, P. (Ed.) (2002). *Distributed work.* Cambridge, MA: The MIT Press

Kim, C. (2003). Content-based image copy detection. *Signal Processing: Image Communication, 18*(3), 169-

184.

Kim, C., & Vasudev, B. (2005). Spatiotemporal sequence matching techniques for video copy detection. *IEEE Transactions on Circuits and Systems for Video Technology, 15*(1), 127-132.

Kim, J. R., & Moon, Y. S. (1999, October). A robust wavelet-based digital watermark using level-adaptive thresholding. *Proceedings of the 6th IEEE International Conference on Image Processing ICIP '99, (October 1999, Kobe, Japan), vol.II2*, 226-230. Kobe, Japan

Kim, W., & Suh, Y. (2004). Short N-secure fingerprinting code for image. *2004 International Conference on Image Processing*, 2167-2170.

Kim, Y.-S., Kwon, O.-H., & Park, R.-H. (1999). Wavelet- based watermarking method for digital images using the human visual system. *Electronic Letters 35*(6), 466-467.

Koch, E., & Zhao, J. (1995, June). Towards robust and hidden image copyright labeling. In I. Pitas, (ed.), *Proceedings of 1995 IEEE Workshop on Nonlinear Signal and Image Processing*. Neos Marmaras, Greece, (pp. 452-455).

Kostopoulos, I., Gilani, S. A. M., & Skodras, A. N. (2002, July 1-3). Color Image Authentication Using a Self-embedding Technique. *Proceedings of the 14th Int. Conf. on Digital Signal Processing DSP 2002* (July 1-3, 2002, . Santorini, Greece).

Kundur, D. (1999, October). Improved digital watermarking through diversity and attack characterization. *Proceedings of the ACM Workshop on Multimedia Security '99*, 53-58, (October 1999,. Orlando, FL), .53-58.

Kundur, D., & Hatzinakos, D. (1999, July). Digital watermarking for telltale tamper proofing and authentication. *Proceedings of the IEEE, 87*(7), 1167-1180.

Kundur, D., & Karthik, K. (2004). Video fingerprinting and encryption principles for digital rights management. *Proceedings of the IEEE, 92*(6), 918-932.

Kundur, D., Lin, C.-Y., Macq, B., & Yu, H. (2004).

Special issue on enabling security technologies for digital rights management. *Proceedings of the IEEE, 92*(6), 879-882.

Kutter, M., Jordan, F., & Bossen, F. (1997). Digital signature of color images using amplitude modulation. *Proceedings of the SPIE, Storage and Retrieval for Image and Video Databases V*, 518-526.

Lang, A., Dittmann, J., Lin, E. T., & Delp, E. J. (2005). Application-oriented audio watermark benchmark service. *Security, Steganography, and Watermarking of Multimedia Contents*, 275-286.

Laudon, K. & Laudon, J. (1998). *Information systems and the Internet*, 4th ed., Orlando, FL: Dryden Press.

Law-To, J., Buisson, O., Gouet-Brunet, V., & Boujemaa, N. (2006). Robust voting algorithm based on labels of behaviour for video copy detection. *In ACM Multimedia, (MM'06)* (pp. 835-844).

Law-To, J., Chen, L., Joly, A., Laptev, Y., Buisson, O., Gouet, V., Boujemaa, N., & Stentiford, F. (2007). Video copy detection: A comparative study. *In ACM International Conference on Image and Video Retrieval*, (pp. 371-378).

Leavitt, H. J. (1965). Applied organizational change in industry: Structural, technical, and humanistic approaches. In March, J. (Ed.). *Handbook of Organizations* (pp. 1144-70). Chicago IL: Rand McNally & Co.

Legal Advisory Board (LAB) of the European Commission: http://europa.eu.int/ISPO/legal/en/lab/labdef. html

Leibold, M., Probst, J. B. & Gibbert, M. (2002). *Strategic management in the knowledge economy.* Wiley, Chichester.

Lemma, A. N., Katzenbeisser, S., Celik, M. U., & Veen, M. V. (2006). Secure watermark embedding through partial encryption. *Proceedings of International Workshop on Digital Watermarking (IWDW 2006), 4283*, 433-445. Springer LNCS

Lian, S., Liu, Z., Ren, Z., & Wang, H. (2006). Secure

image communication for network applications. *2006 SPIE Symposium on Defense and Security, 6250,* 62500L0-8.

Lian, S., Liu, Z., Ren, Z., & Wang, H. (2006). Secure advanced video coding based on selective encryption algorithms. *IEEE Transactions on Consumer Electronics, 52*(2), 621-629.

Lian, S., Liu, Z., Ren, Z., & Wang, H. (2006). Secure distribution scheme for compressed data streams. *2006 IEEE Conference on Image Processing (ICIP 2006).*

Lian, S., Liu, Z., Ren, Z., & Wang, H. (2007). Commutative encryption and watermarking in compressed video data. *IEEE Circuits and Systems for Video Technology, 17*(6), 774-778.

Lian, S., Liu, Z., Ren, Z., & Wang, Z. (2007). Multimedia data encryption in block-based codecs. International Journal of Computers and Applications, *29*(1).

Lian, S., Sun, J., & Wang, Z. (2004). Perceptual cryptography on JPEG 2000 compressed images or videos. *International conference on Computer and Information Technology (CIT),* 78-83.

Lian, S., Sun, J., & Wang, Z. (2004). A novel image encryption scheme based-on JPEG encoding. *In Proceedings of the Eighth International Conference on Information Visualization (IV),* 217-220. London, UK.

Lian, S., Sun, J., & Wang, Z. (2005). A block cipher based on a suitable use of the chaotic standard map. *Chaos, Solitons and Fractals, 26,* 117-129.

Liang, J., Xu, P., & Tran, T. D. (2000, March). A robust DCT-based low frequency watermarking scheme. *34th Annual Conference on Information Sciences and Systems, 1,* TA5 1-6. (March 2000, Princeton, NJ), vol. *1,* TA5 1-6.

Liebowitz, J., & Beckman, T. (Eds) (1998) *Knowledge organizations: What every manager should know.* Boca Raton, FL: St. Lucie Press.

LII (2007). U.S. Code Collection 107, Limitations on Exclusive Rights: Fair Use, Legal Information Institute, Cornell Law School.

LII (2007). U.S. Code Collection, Title 18, S 2510, The Electronic Communications Privacy Act of 1986, Legal Information Institute, Cornell Law School.

LII (2007). U.S. Code 20.31.3.4.1232g, FERPA. Legal Information Institute, Cornell Law School.

Lin, C.-Y., & Chang, S.-F. (2000, January). Semi-Fragile Watermarking for Authenticating JPEG Visual Content. *Proceedings of the SPIE International Conference on Security and Watermarking of Multimedia Content II, 3971,* 140-151. (Jan 2000, San Jose, CA), vol. 3971, 140-151.

Liu, H-m., Huang, J-w., & Xiao, Z-m. (2001). An adaptive video watermarking algorithm. *IEEE International Conference on Multimedia and Expo,* 257-260.

Lohmann, F. (2002). *Fair use and digital rights management, computers, freedom & privacy.* Electronic Frontier Foundation.

Lowe, D (2004). Distinctive image features from scale-invariant keypoints. *International Journal of Computer Vision, 60*(2), 91-110.

Lu, C. S., & Liao, H. Y. M. (2001). Multipurpose Watermarking for Image Authentication and Protection. *IEEE Transactions on Image Processing, 10*(10), 1579-1592.

Lyon, G. (2001). The Internet marketplace and digital rights management. *Report to the U.S. Department of Commerce,* USA.

Maillard, T., & Furon, T. (2004). Towards digital rights and exemptions management systems. *Computer Law & Security Report, 20*(4), 281-287.

Mao, Y., & Mihcak, M. (2005). Collusion-resistant international de-synchronization for digital video fingerprinting. *IEEE Conference on Image Processing.*

Mao, Y., Chen, G., & Lian, S. (2004). A novel fast image encryption scheme based on 3-D chaotic baker maps. *International Journal of Bifurcation and Chaos, 14*(10), 3613-3624.

MARC (n.d.). *MARC code list for relators*. Retrieved February 1, 2008 from http://lcweb.loc.gov/marc/relators/re0003r2.html.

Marcellin, M. W., Gormish, M., Bilgin, A., & Boliek, M. (2000, March). An Overview of JPEG 2000. *Proceedings of IEEE Data Compression Conference*, 523-541(March 2000, . Snowbird, UT), 523-541.

Maret, Y., Dufaux, F., & Ebrahmi, T. (2006). Adaptive image replica detection based on support vector classifiers. *Signal Processing: Image Communication, 21*(8), 688-703.

Mazzucchi, P. (2005). Business models and rights management for e-Learning in Europe. *INDICARE Monitor, 2*(7), 25-29.

Meerwald, P. (2001, May). Quantization Watermarking in the JPEG 2000 Coding Pipeline. Communications and Multimedia Security Issues of the New Century., *IFIP TC6/TC11, Fifth Joint Working Conference on Communications and Multimedia Security, CMS'01, 69-79.* (May 2001, Darmstadt, Germany), 69-79.

Merkle, R. C. (1989). A Certified Digital Signature. In Gilles Brassard (Ed.), *Advances in Cryptology - Crypto '89, Lecture Notes in Computer Science, vol 435*, 218-238., Berlin: Springer-Verlag.

Michiels B., & Benoit, M. (2006). Benchmarking image watermarking algorithms with open watermark. *14th European Signal Processing Conference - EUSIPCO06*, Florence, Italy.

Microsoft (n.d.). Retrieved February 1, 2008 from http://www.microsoft.com.

Mihcak, M. K., &. Venkatesan, R. (2001). New iterative geometric methods for robust perceptual image hashing. *In ACM Workshop on Security and Privacy in Digital Rights Management, LNCS 2320*, 13-21.

Minguillón J., Herrera-Joancomartí, J., & Megías, D. (2003, January). Empirical Evaluation of a JPEG 2000 Standard-based Robust Watermarking Scheme. *Proceedings of SPIE: Security and Watermarking of Multimedia Contents V, 5020*, 717-727V (January 2003, Santa Clara, CA), vol. 5020, 717-727.

Mintzer, F., Braudaway, G. W., & Yeung, M. M. (1992, October). Effective and ineffective digital watermarks. *Image Processing, 3*, 9-12.

Mohanty, S. (1999). *Digital watermarking: A tutorial review.*

Mohanty, S. P., Ramakrishnan, K. R., & Kanakanhalli, M. S. (1999). A dual watermarking technique for images. *In Proceedings of the 7th ACM International Multimedia Conference (ACMMM,) 2*, 49-51.

Mohanty, S. P., Ramakrishnan, K. R., & Kanakanhalli, M. S. (2000) A DCT Domain Visible Watermarking Technique for Images. *In Proceedings of the IEEE International Conference on Multimedia and Expo (ICME) 2*, 1029-1032.

Mohanty, S. P., Ranganathan, N., & Balakrishnan, K. (2006, May). A dual voltage-frequency VLSI chip for image watermarking in DCT domain. *IEEE Transactions on Circuits and Systems II (TCAS-II), 53*(5), 394-398.

Morimoto, N. (1999). Digital watermarking technology with practical applications. *Information Science Special Issue on Multimedia Information Technology, 1,2*(4).

Morin, J-H. & Pawlak, M. (2007, July 1-5). A model for credential based exception management in digital rights management systems, Internet monitoring, and protection. *ICIMP 2007. Second International Conference*, 41. Digital Object Identifier 10.1109/ICIMP.2007.3

MPEG REL, ISO/IEC FDIS 21000-5 (2003). *Information technology - Multimedia framework - Part 5: Rights expression language.*

MPEG21, MPEG-21 Overview v5, Last checked: 11 October 2007, http://www.chiariglione.org/mpeg/standards/mpeg-21/mpeg-21.htm

MPEG7, ISO/IEC Moving Picture Experts Group. Last checked: 11 October 2007, < http://www.chiariglione.org/mpeg/standards/mpeg-7/mpeg-7.htm >

Mumford, E. (1995). Effective systems design and requirements analysis. London, UK: Macmillan.

N5229 (2002). Requirements for the persistent association of identification and description of digital items, ISO/IEC JTC1/SC29/WG11, (MPEG-21—Requirements).

NetAssociate / MacAfee: www.nai.com

Nic, G., Digital rights management, copyright, and napster. *ACM Communications*. www.acm.org/sigs/sigecom/exchanges/volume_2/2.2-Garnett.pdf.

Nicchiotti, G., & Ottaviano, E. (1998, September). Non-invertible statistical wavelet watermarking. *Proceedings of the 9th European Signal Processing Conference EUPISCO '98*, 2289-2292. (September 1998, Island of Rhodes, Greece)., 2289-2292.

Nikolopoulos, S., Zafeiriou, S., Sidiropoulos, P., Nikolaidis, N., & Pitas, I. (2006). Image replica detection using R-trees and linear discriminant analysis. *In IEEE International Conference on Multimedia and Expo (ICME 06)* (pp. 1797-1800).

Nonaka, I., & Takeuchi, H. (1995). *The knowledge-creating company: How Japanese companies create the dynamics of innovation*. New York, NY: Oxford University Press.

Nonaka, I., Toyama, R., & Konno, N. (2000). SECI, Ba and Leadership: A Unified Model of Dynamic Knowledge Creation. *Long Range Planning, 33*, 5-34.

ODRL (n.d.). *Open digital rights language*. Retrieved February 1, 2008 from http://odrl.net/.

Ohnishi, J., & Matsui, K. (1998). A method of watermarking with multiresolution analysis and pseudo noise sequences. *Systems and Computers in Japan, 29*(5), 11-19.

Oltsik, J. (2007). *The trusted computing group (TCG) storage specification: Securing storage and information lifecycle management*. Enterprise Strategy Group White Paper

Oostveen, J., Kalker, T., & Haitsma, J. (2002), Feature extraction and a database strategy for video fingerprinting. *In 5th International Conference on Recent Advances in Visual I*

Owens, R., & Akalu, R. (2004). Legal policy and digital rights management. *Proceedings of the IEEE, 92*(6), 997-1003. Retrieved February 1, 2008 from http://ieeexplore.ieee.org/Xplore/login.jsp?url=/iel5/5/28864/01299173.pdf.

OZAUTHORS, OzAuthors Online Ebook Store, Last checked: October 11 2007, http://www.ozauthors.com

Paris Convention (1883). *Paris Convention for the Protection of Industrial Property*. Retrieved February 1, 2008 http://www.wipo.int/export/sites/www/treaties/en/ip/paris/pdf/trtdocs_wo020.pdf.

Park, Y., & Scotchmer, S. (2005, August). Digital rights management and the pricing of digital products. *NBER Working Paper, W11532*. Available at SSRN: http://ssrn.com/abstract=778105

Parnes, R., & Parviainen, R. (2001). Large scale distributed watermarking of multicast media through encryption. *In Proc. IFIP Int. Conf. Communications and Multimedia Security Issues of the New Century, 17*.

Peng, C., Deng, H. J. R., Wu, Y. D., & Shao, W. (2003). A Flexible and Scalable Authentication Scheme for JPEG 2000 codestreams. *Proceedings of the eleventh ACM international conference on Multimedia MULTIMEDIA '03*, 433-441.

Pereira, S., Voloshynovsiy, S., & Pun, T. (2001). Optimal transform domain watermark embedding via linear programming. *Signal Processing, 81*(6), 1251-1260.

Perreira, S., Voloshynovskiy, S., & Pun, T. (2000, April) Optimized wavelet domain watermark embedding strategy using linear programming. *SPIE AeroSence 2000: Wavelet Applications VII*, H. H. Szu, (Ed.)., (April 2000, Orlando, FL).

Petitcolas, F., Anderson, R., & Kuhn, M. (1998, April). Attacks on copyright marking systems. In David Aucsmith (Ed), Information Hiding, *Second International Workshop, IH'98, Portland, USA, LNCS, 1525*, 219-239.

Petitcolas, F., Anderson, R., & Kuhn, M. (1999, July). Information Hiding - A Survey. *Proc. IEEE*, 1062-1078.

Pfitzmann, B. (1996). Information hiding terminology - Results of an informal. ISBN 3-540-61996-8. *Results of an informal plenary meeting and additional proposals*, pp. 347-350.

Piva, A., Barni, M., & Bartolini, F. (1998). Copyright protection of digital images by means of frequency domain watermarking. In Schmalz (Ed.), *Mathematics of Data/Image Coding, Compression, and Encryption, Proc. of SPIE, 3456*, 25-35. San Diego, California.

Piva, A., Barni, M., Bartolini, F., Cappellini, V., De Rosa, A., & Orlandi, M. (1999). Improving DFT watermarking robustness through optimum detection and synchronisation. In *GMD Report 85, Multimedia and Security Workshop at ACM Multimedia '99*, 65-69. Orlando, Florida.

Podilchuk, C. I., & Delp, E. J. (2001, July). Digital watermarking: algorithms and applications. *IEEE Signal Processing Magazine, 18*(4), 33-46.

Polanyi, M. (1966). *The tacit dimension*. London, UK: Routledge & Kegan Paul.

Prince, B. (2007). *IBM shields online personal data, eWeek news & analysis*. Retrieved 6/22/07 from http://www.eweek.com/article2/0,1759,2095275,00.asp

Probst, G., Raub, S., & Romhardt, K. (1999). Managing knowledge: Building blocks for success. Chicester: Wiley.

Qamra, A., Meng, Y., & Chang, E. (2005). Enhanced perceptual distance functions and indexing for image replica recognition. *IEEE Transaction on Pattern Analysis and Machine Intelligence, 27*(3), 379-391.

Qiong, L., Safavi-Naini, R., & Sheppard, N. (2003). Digital rights management for content distribution. *Australian Information Security Workshop (AISW2003)*. Adelaide, Australia.

Rao, M. (Ed.). (2004). Knowledge management tools and techniques: Practitioners and experts evaluate KM

solutions. Burlington, MA: Elservier Butterworth-Heinemann.

RDF, Resource Description Framework. Last checked: 11 October 2007, http://www.w3.org/RDF/

Reinbothe, J. (2002, February 28). *The legal framework for digital rights management. European Commission, submission at the Digital Rights Management Workshop*, Brussels.

REL (2003). The MPEG-21 Rights Expression Language, A White Paper, Rightscom Ltd,

Renato, I. (2001). Digital rights management (DRM) architectures. *D-Lib Magazine, 7*(6).

Renato, I. (2001, January 22-23). Open digital rights management. *W3C Digital Rights Management Workshop*. Sophia Antipolis, France.

RFC (n.d.). *RFC 2426 vCard Profile*. Retrieved February 1, 2008 from http://www.ietf.org/rfc/rfc2426.txt.

Robustness: JPEG 2000 compression. (2007). Retrieved August 22, 2007, from http://www.cosy.sbg.ac.at/~pmeerw/Watermarking/attack_jpeg2000.html

Rosenblatt, B., Trippe, B., & Mooney, S. (2002). Digital rights management - Business and technology. *Professional Mindware.*, New York: M & T Books.

Rosenblatt, R. (1997). Solving the dilemma of copyright protection online. *The Journal of Electronic Publishing (JEP), 3*(2). Retrieved February 1, 2008 from http://www.press.umich.edu/jep/03-02/doi.html.

Roy, S., Chang, E.-C., & Natarajan, K. (2005). A unified framework for resolving ambiguity in copy detection. *In 13th annual ACM international conference on Multimedia* (pp. 648-655).

Russ, A. (2001). *Digital rights management overview*. SANS Institute.

Russ, A. (2001, July). *Digital rights management overview*. SANS Information Security Reading Room. Retrieved 6/22/07 from http://www.sans.org/reading_room/whitepapers/basics/434.php

Russell, N., Hofstede, A. H. M. ter, Edmond, D., Aalst, & W.M.P. van der (2005). Workflow data patterns: Identification, representation and tool support. In L. Delcambre, C. Kop, H.C. Mayr, J. Mylopoulos, O. Pastor, (Ed.) *24nd International Conference on Conceptual Modeling (ER 2005)* (pp. 353-368) Berlin: Springer-Verlag.

Sai Ho, K. (2002, August). Digital rights management for the online music business. *ACM SIGecom Exchanges, 3(3)*, 17-24.

Samuelson, P. (2001). Does information really have to be licensed.

Samuelson, P. (2001). Intellectual property for an information age: Introduction. ACM, pp. 66-68. http://doi.acm.org/10.1145/359205.359230.

Samuelson, P. (2003, April). *DRM (and or vs.) the law. Communications of the ACM, .46*(4).

Samuelson, P. (2006, June). Copyrighting standards: Should standards be eligible for copyright protection. *Communication of the ACM, 49*(6).

Satoh, S. (2000). Comparative evaluation of face sequence matching for content-based video access. *In 4th International Conference on Automatic Face and Gesture Recognition(FG2000)* (pp. 163-168).

Schmidt, A., Tafreschi, O., & Wolf, R. (2004). Interoperability challenges for DRM systems. *Reviewed Papers about Virtual Goods.* Technische Universitat Ilmenau, Germany.

Schneier, B. (1995). *Applied Cryptography: Protocols, Algorithms, and Source Code in C*, Second 2nd Edition. New York: John Wiley & Sons.

SDMI (2001). *Reading between the lines: Lessons from the SDMI challenge.* Princeton University. Retrieved February 1, 2008 from http://www.cs.princeton.edu/sip/sdmi.

SDMI (n.d.). *Secure digital music initiative - SDMI, protection through encryption.* Retrieved February 1, 2008 from http://www.benedict.com/Digital/Internet/SDMI.aspx.

Seo, Y., Kim, M., Park, H., Jung, H., Chung, H., Huh, Y., & Lee, J. (2001, October). A sSecure wWatermarking for JPEG 2000. *Proceedings of the IEEE International Conference on Image Processing ICIP 2001*, 530-533. (October 2001, Thessaloniki, Greece), 530-533.

Servetti, A., Testa, C., Carlos, J., & Martin, D. (2003). Frequency-selective partial encryption of compressed audio. *Paper presented at the International Conference on Audio, Speech and Signal Processing.* Hong Kong.

Shih, F., & Wu, S. (2003). Combinational image watermarking in the spatial and frequency domains. *Elsevier, Pattern Recognition, 36*, 957-968.

Simitopoulos, D., Tsaftaris, S. A., & Boulgouris, N. V., et al. (2002). Compressed-domain video watermarking of MPEG streams. *2002 IEEE International Conference on Multimedia and Expo.*, 569-572. Lausanne, Switzerland.

Simitopoulos, D., Zissis, N., Georgiadis, P., Emmanouilidis, V., & G.Strintzis, M. (2003, September). Encryption and watermarking for the secure distribution of copyrighted MPEG video on DVD. *ACM Multimedia Systems Journal, Special Issue on Multimedia Security, 9(3)*, 217-227.

Simmons, G. J. (1984). The prisoners' problem and the subliminal channel. *In Proc. CRYPTO'83*, 51-67. Plenum Press.

Sobel, S. L. (2003). *DRM as an enabler of business models: ISPs as digital retailers.* Entertainment Law Reporter, Distinguished Scholar, Berkeley Center for Law & Technology; Lecturer, Boalt Hall (Spring 2003), from https://www.law.berkeley.edu/institutes/bclt/drm/papers/sobel-drm-btlj2003.html

Società Italiana Autori ed Editori - www.siae.it

Sproull, L., & Kiesler, S. (1992). *Connections: New ways of working in the networked organization.* Cambridge, MA: The MIT Press.

Stewart, T. (1999). Intellectual capital: The new wealth of organizations. New York, NY: Bantam Press.

Stirmark [online]. Available at http://www.petitcolas. net/fabien/watermarking/stirmark/.

Su, P., & Kuo, C. (2003, May 25-28). Information eEmbedding in JPEG-2000 cCompressed iImages. *ISCAS 2003*, (May 25-28, 2003, . Bangkok, Thailand).

Sun, S., Lannom, L., & Boesch, B. Handle system overview. *Internet Engineering Task Force (IETF) Request for Comments (RFC), RFC 3650*, November 2003 from http://www.handle.net

Sveiby, K. (1997). *The new organizational wealth: Managing and measuring knowledge-based assets.* San Francisco, CA: Berrett Koehler.

Swanson, M. D., Zhu, B., & Tewfik, A. H. (1998, May). Multiresolution scene-based video watermarking using perceptual models. *IEEE Journal on Selected Areas In Communications, 16*(4), 540-549.

Swanson, M., Kobayashi, M., & Tewfik, A. (1998, June). Multimedia data embedding and watermarking technologies. *IEEE Proceedings, 86*(6), 1064-1087.

Taubman, D. (2000). High Performance Scalable Image Compression with EBCOT. *IEEE Transactions on Image Processing, 9*(6), 1158-1170.

Taubman, D., & Zalkor, A. (1994). Multirate 3-D subband coding of Video. *IEEE Transactions on Image Processing, 3*(5), 572-578.

Taubman, D., Ordentlich, E., Weinberger, M., Seroussi, G., Ueno, I., & Ono, F. (2000, September). Embedded Block Coding in JPEG 2000. *Proceedings of IEEE International Conference on Image Processing ICIP 2000, 2,* 33-36. (September 2000, Vancouver, Canada), vol. II, 33-36..

Tefas, A., Nikolaidis, N., &. Pitas, I. (2005). Watermarking techniques for image authentication and copyright protection. In Bovik A. (Ed.) *The Handbook of Image and Video Processing*, 2nd edition (pp. 1083-1109). Elsevier.

Tehranian, J. (2002, November). All rights reserved? Reassessing copyright and patent enforcement in the digital age. Available at SSRN: http://ssrn.com/abstract=351480 or DOI: 10.2139/ssrn.351480

Tewfik, A. H., & Swanson, M. (1997, July). Data hiding for multimedia personalization, interaction, and protection. *IEEE Signal Processing Magazine, 14*(4), 41-44.

The Content ID Forum, (2002). *cIDf Specification v. 1.1.* Tokyo, Japan.

Thiemert, S., Vogel, T., Dittmann, J., & Steinebach, M. (2004). A high-capacity block based video watermark. *EUROMICRO 2004*, 457-460.

Toffler, A. (1980). The third wave. New York: Bantam Books.

TRADEX, TRial Action for Digital object EXchange, Not available, http://www.iccd.beniculturali.it/download/tradex.pdf

Trappe, W., Wu, M., Wang, Z. J., & Liu, K. (2003). Anticollusion fingerprinting for multimedia. IEEE *Trans. Signal Processing, 51*, 1069-1087.

TRIPS (1994). *Agreement on trade-related aspects of intellectual property rights.* Retrieved February 1, 2008 from http://www.wto.org/english/tratop_e/trips_e/t_agm0_e.htm.

Trist, E. L. & Bamforth, K. W. (1951). Some social and psychological consequences of the longwall method of coal getting. *Human Relations, 4*(1), 3-38.

Tseng, M. M. & Jiao, J. (2001) Mass customization. In G. Salvendy (Ed.) *Handbook of Industrial Engineering* (pp. 684-709), 3rd edition, New York: John Wiley & Sons, Inc.

Tsolis, G. K., Nikolopoulos, S. N., Kazantzi, N.V., Tsolis, D. K. & Papatheodorou, T. S. (2005, August 15-17). Re-Engineering digital watermarking of copyright protected images by using xml web services. *In Proc. of the Ninth IASTED International Conference on INTERNET & MULTIMEDIA SYSTEMS & APPLICATIONS (IMSA 2005)*, 264-270. Honolulu, Hawaii, USA.

Tsolis, G. K., Tsolis, D. K., & Papatheodorou, T. S. (2001). A watermarking environment and a metadata digital image repository for the protection and management of digital images of the Hellenic Cultural Heritage. *International Conference on Image Processing, Thessalonica.* Greece, 2001.

Tzovaras, D., Karagiannis, N., & Strintzis, M. G. (1998, September). Robust image watermarking in the subband or discrete cosine transform. *Proceedings of the 9th European Signal Processing Conference EUPISCO '98, 2285-2288.* (September 1998, Island of Rhodes, Greece.), 2285-2288.

U.S. Department of Commerce, The International Trade Administration, The American Automotive Industry Supply Chain - In the Throes of a Rattling Revolution, from www.ita.doc.gov/td/auto/domestic/SupplyChain.pdf

UCITA (2002). Uniform Computer Information Transactions Act. *National Conference of Commissioners on Uniform State Laws.*

UDDI (2007). FAQs for UDDI Initiative and Standard. *OASIS Standards Consortium.* Retrieved 6/22/07 from http://www.uddi.org/faqs.html

UK Joint Information Services Committee (JISC)/Intrallect (2004), Digital Rights Management Study and appendices, from www.intrallect.com/drm-study/

UK Joint Information Systems Committee (JISC) Legal Information Service, Web site: http://www.jisclegal.ac.uk/

URI (n.d.). *Uniform resource identifiers (URI): Generic syntax.* IETF RFC2396. Retrieved February 1, 2008 from http://www.ietf.org/rfc/rfc2396.txt.

Usevitch, B. (2001). A Tutorial On Modern Lossy Wavelet Image Compression: Foundations of JPEG2000. *IEEE Signal Processing Magazine, 18*(5), 22-35.

Van Schyndel, R., Tirkel, A., & Osborne, C. (1994). A digital watermark. *Proceedings of IEEE International Conference on Image Processing (ICIP-94), 2,* 86-90.

Vetterli, M. (2001). Wavelets, Approximation and Compression. *IEEE Signal Processing Magazine, 18*(5), 59-73.

Viega, J. (2003, December). Practical random number generation in software. *In Proc. 19th Annual Computer Security Applications Conference.*

Von, F. L. (2002, April 16). *Fair use and digital rights management: Preliminary thoughts on the (Irreconcilable?) tension between them.* Electronic Frontier Foundation, Computers, Freedom & Privacy 2002. From http://w2.eff.org/IP/DRM/fair_use_and_drm.html.

Walton, S. (1995). Image Authentication for a Slippery New Age. *Dr. Dobb's Journal of Software Tools for Professional Programmers, 20*(4), 18-26.

Wang, X., Lao, G., DeMartini, T., Reddy, H., Nguyen, M., & Valenzuela, E. (2002). XrML - eXtensible rights markup language. *Proceedings of the ACM Workshop on XML Security.* New York: ACM Press. (pp. 71-79).

Wang, Z., Wu, M., Trappe, W., & Liu, K. (2005). Group-oriented fingerprinting for multimedia forensics. *Preprint.*

Watson, A. B., Yang, G. Y., Solomon, J. A. & Villasenor, J. (1997). Visibility of Wavelet Quantization Noise. *IEEE Transactions on Image Processing, 6*(8), 1164-1175.

Watson, A.B. (1993). DCT quantization matrices visually optimized for individual images. *In Human Vision, Visual Processing and Digital Display IV, Proc. SPIE, 1913* 202-216. Bellingham, WA.

WCT (1996). *WIPO copyright treaty.* Retrieved February 1, 2008 from http://www.wipo.int/treaties/en/ip/wct/trtdocs_wo033.html.

Weisburd, S.I. (2004). Handling Intellectual Property Issues in Business Transactions. New York, NY: Practising Law Institute

Welcome to JPEG. (2007). Retrieved August 07, 2007, from http://www.jpeg.org/jpeg2000/CDs15444.html

Wikipedia (n.d.). *Wikipedia.* Retrieved February 1, 2008 from http://www.wikipedia.com.

Willingmyre, G. T. Current topics in IPR protection in the context of global standard-Setting processes. http://www.wipo.int/sme/en/documents/ip_standards2.htm

WIPO (2007). *World intellectual property organization.* Retrieved February 1, 2008 from http://www.wipo.org.

WIPO Convention (1967). Convention establishing by the world intellectual property organization. *Preamble, Second Paragraph.* Retrieved February 1, 2008 http://www.wipo.int/treaties/en/convention/trtdocs_wo029.html.

WIPO, World Intellectual Property Organization, Last checked: October 11 2007, <http://www.wipo.int>

Wipro Technologies (2001). *Digital watermarking: A technology overview.* White Paper.

WIRED (2006, April 3). Reasons to love open-source DRM. Available at http://www.wired.com/entertainment/music/commentary/listeningpost/2006/04/70548)

Wolfgang, R. B., Podilchuk, C. I., & Delp, E. J. (1999, July). Perceptual watermarks for digital images and video. *Proceedings of IEEE, 87*(7), 1108-1126.

Wong, P. H. W., Yeung, G. Y. M., & Au, O.C. (2003, Baltimore). Capacity for JPEG2000-tTo-JPEG 2000 Images Watermarking. *Proceedings of 2003 IEEE International Conference on Multimedia & Expo ICME'03, 2, 485-488.* (2003, Baltimore), vol. 2, 485-488.

World Intellectual Property Organization (WIPO) (2004). WIPO Intellectual Property Handbook: Policy, Law and Use, Geneva CH: WIPO Publications (NO. 489)

World Trade Organisation (WTO). Trade-related aspects of intellectual property rights (TRIPS) agreement, from http://www.wto.org/english/tratop_e/trips_e/trips_e.htm

WPPT (1996). *WIPO performances and phonograms treaty.* Retrieved February 1, 2008 http://www.wipo.int/treaties/en/ip/wppt/trtdocs_wo034.html.

Wu, M., & Liu, B. (1998). Watermarking for Image Authentication. *IEEE International Conference on Image Processing ICIP'98, vol.2,* 437-441.

Wu, M., Trappe, W., Wang, Z., & Liu, R. (2004, March). Collusion-resistant fingerprinting for multimedia. *IEEE Signal Processing Magazine, , 21*(2), 15-27.

Wu, Y. (2005, March). Linear combination collusion attack and its application on an anti-collusion fingerprinting. *IEEE International Conference on Acoustics, Speech, and Signal Processing* (ICASSP '05), *2,* 13-16.

Wu, Y., Deng, R., Di M., Peng, C., & Yang, Y. (2003). Authentication of JPEG 2000 Code- Streams and Files. ISO/IEC JTC1/SC29/WG1 N2809

Xia, X.-G., Boncelet, C. G., & Arce, G. R. (1998). Wavelet transform based watermark for digital images. *Optics Express 3*(12), 497-511.

Xie, L. & Arce, G.R. (1998). Joint wavelet compression and authentication watermarking. *Proceedings of the IEEE International Conference on Image Processing, ICIP '98,* (1998,. Chicago, IL).

XMCL (2001). *XMCL - eXtensible media commerce language.* Retrieved February 1, 2008 from http://www.xmcl.org/index.html.

XML, eXtensive Markup Language. Last checked: 11 October 2007, http://www.w3.org/XML/

XrML (2007). Extensible rights markup language - XrML. *2.0 Specification.* Retrieved February 1, 2008 from http://www.xrml.org.

XrML, eXtensive rights Markup Language. Last checked: 11 October 2007, http://www.xrml.org

XSD, eXtensible Markup Language Schema, Last checked: 11 October 2007, <http://www.w3.org/XML/Schema>

Yeung, M. M., & Mintzer, F. C. (1998, July). Invisible watermarking for image verification. *Journal of Electronic Imaging, 7*(3), 578-591.

Yeung, M., & Mintzer, F. (1997). An invisible watermarking technique for image verification. *Proceedings of ICIP '97.* Santa Barbara, CA.

Yu, G., Lu, C., & Liao, H. (2003). A message-based cocktail watermarking system. *Elsevier, Pattern Recognition, 36,* 969-975.

Zhao, W., Chellappa, R., Phillips, P.-J., & Rosenfeld, A. (2003). Face recognition: A literature survey. *ACM Computing Surveys, 35*(4), 399--458.

Zhishou, Z., Gang, Q., Qibin, S., Xiao, L., Zhicheng, N., & Shi, Y.Q. (2004, June). A Unified Authentication Framework for JPEG 2000. *Proceedings of 2004*

IEEE International Conference on Multimedia & Expo ICME'04, 2, 915-918. (June 2004, Taipei, Taiwan), vol. 2, 915-918.

Zhu, W., Thomborson, C., & Wang, F. Y. (2002). A survey of software watermarking. *Lecture Notes in Computer Science-Volume, 3495,* 454-458.

About the Contributors

Lambros Drossos graduated from the Department of Mathematics of the University of Thessaloniki in Greece. He received his PhD from the Department of Mathematics of the University of Patras in 1993. His research area is focusing on dynamic systems and analytical arithmetic methods which apply to chaotic dynamics. He is a professor at the Department of Applied Informatics in management and Finance of the Technical Educational Institute of Messolonghi. He has published an important number of papers in international scientific journals and conferences.

Spyros Sioutas obtained his diploma and PhD from the Department of Computer Engineering and Informatics of the University of Patras. His current research interests include spatio-temporal databases, data structures, algorithms and I/O complexity, computational geometry, peer-to-peer networks, knowledge management and advanced information systems. He has published about 60 articles in international conferences, books, journals and technical reports. Main research interests include: spatio-temporal and multimedia databases; efficient I/O algorithms and data structures; computational geometry and computer graphics; P2P computing; information systems and Web services; and educational software.

Dimitrios Tsolis is an associate professor (with contract) of the Department of Computer Engineering and Informatics of the University of Patras. He is responsible for the courses "Legal and Social Aspects of New Technologies", "Quality in Software Engineering", "Internet Technologies" and "Introduction to Informatics". His PhD was focusing on digital rights management systems for e-commerce. He has over 30 publications in journals, conferences and technical reports about DRMS, copyright management and protection, e-commerce and DRMs, etc.

Theodore Papatheodorou has held several academic and consulting positions in Greece and the United States. Since 1984 he has been a professor at the Department of Computer Engineering and Informatics of the University of Patras, the first Computer Science/Engineering Department in Greece. He developed the HPCLab of the University of Patras, which now employs about fifty faculty members, graduate researchers and computer engineers. Currently he is the director of this laboratory. He also initiated the establishment of the Computer Technology Institute (CTI). As the first director of CTI (1985-1990) he led the Institute's development and R&D work. Prof. Papatheodorou has received wide recognition for his work and several international awards. Most recent distinctions include: The Best Paper Award in Supercomputing, Dallas, Texas, November 2000; first price in the Moebius Competition

(Hellenic Section) for the CD-ROM on the life of Melina Merkouri; the selection of this CD-ROM in the top 4 in Europe (Europrix Competition – Cultural Section). He has authored numerous publications in several areas of computer engineering and computer science.

* * *

Mauro Barni was born in Prato, Italy, in 1965. He received his BS in electronic engineering at the University of Florence in 1991. He received the PhD in informatics and telecommunications in October 1995. From 1991 through 1998 he was with the Department of Electronic Engineering, University of Florence, Italy, where he worked as a postdoctoral researcher. Since September 1998, he has been with the Department of Information Engineering at the University of Siena, Italy, where he works as assistant professor. His main interests are in the field of digital image processing and computer vision. His research activity is focused on the application of image processing techniques to copyright protection and authentication of multimedia data (digital watermarking), and to the transmission of image and video signals in error-prone, wireless, environments. He is author/co-author of more than 100 papers published in international journals and conference proceedings. Mauro Barni is member of the IEEE, where he serves as member of the Multimedia Signal Processing Technical Committee (MMSP-TC).

Roberto Caldelli was born in Figline Valdarno (Florence), Italy, in 1970. He graduated (cum laude) in electronic engineering from the University of Florence, in 1997, where he also received his PhD degree in computer science and telecommunications engineering in 2001. He works now as a postdoctoral researcher with the Department of Electronics and Telecommunications at the University of Florence. He holds one Italian patent in the field of digital watermarking. His main research activities, witnessed by several publications, include digital image sequence processing, digital filtering, image and video digital watermarking, image processing applications for the cultural heritage field, and multimedia applications.

Vito Cappellini was born in Pistoia, Italy, in 1938. In 1961 he obtained the degree in electronic engineering from the Politecnico di Torino. In 1975 he obtained the Full Professor Degree in electrical communications at Florence University, being later appointed director of the Istituto di Elettronica for the period 1977-79. In 1981-1989 he was director of the IROE Institute in Florence. In 1993-1995 he was Dean of the Engineering Faculty of Florence University. His main research interests are: digital signal-image processing, digital communications, remote sensing, biomedicine, robotics and art work analysis-restoration. He has published over 250 papers in the above fields and contributed to several books: co-author of *Digital Filters and Their Applications* (Academic Press, 1978), editor of *Data Compression and Error Control Techniques with Applications* (Academic Press, 1985), editor of *Time-Varying Image Processing and Moving Object Recognition* (North-Holland, 1987). He is in the editorial board of several international journals: *Signal Processing* (North Holland), *Circuits, Systems, and Signal Processing* (Birkhauser), *European Transactions onTelecommunications*. He was chairman of the IEEE Middle & South Italy Section. He has been the Italian representative in the Seven Nations Cooperation Program on "Remote Sensing from Space". He is the Italian representative in the EARSeL (European Association of Remote Sensing Laboratories). He is in the Committee of the Italian Telecommunications Group (TTI). He is president of the Scientific-Tecnhical commettee of ITINERA (Italian Info-structure for European Research in Advanced Communications). He is member of the Scientific Committee of

CSELT. He is vice president of the Foundation on Applied Meteorology. In 1981 he received the "Clerk Maxwell Premium" by IERE and in 1984 the "IEEE Centennial Medal". Professor Cappellini is fellow of the IEEE, member of EURASIP, AEI, ANIPLA and AIT.

Tom S. Chan is an associate professor at the Information Department, Southern New Hampshire University at Manchester, New Hampshire, U.S.A. He holds a EdD from Texas Tech University, and MSCS from the University of Southern California. Prior to SNHU, he was an assistant professor at Marist College, and a project manager and software designer specializing in data communication at Citibank. He has published works in the area of instructional design, distance learning, technology adaptation, information security and Web design.

J. Stephanie Collins earned a PhD in management information systems in 1990 from the University of Wisconsin. She has taught in the field since 1988, and has published papers in various journals, and presented at conferences. She has published papers on information technology outsourcing and technology applications for economic development, IT education, and on technical issues. She has also worked as an IT consultant, and has developed several systems. Her current research is focused on how the uses of internet technologies change the environment for business and for education.

Alessia De Rosa was born in Florence, Italy, in 1972. In 1998, she graduated in electronic engineering at the University of Florence, Italy. In February 2002, she received the PhD degree in informatics and telecommunications from the University of Florence. At present she is involved in the research activities of the Image Processing and Communications Laboratory of the Department of Electronic and Telecommunications of the University of Florence, where she works as a postdoc researcher. Her main research interests are in the field of digital watermarking, human perception models for digital image watermarking and quality assessment, image processing for cultural heritage applications. She holds an Italian patent in the field of digital watermarking. She is lecturer for the "Comunicazioni Elettriche 2" (Communication Systems) course of the Laurea Degree in Information Engineering (University of Florence, PRATO).

Andrea de Polo, Fratelli Alinari Photo Archives and Museums (Italy) Andrea de Polo manages and directs a staff of 12, including a multimedia development manager and 7 support personnel responsible for the online indexing. His main expertise is in the following applications: selected to become permanent beta tester for any future new software; and past or current collaboration and testing with HP, Splash Technology, Digital Corp., Xerox, Digimarc, Signum, Nikon, Apple, Telecom Italy. His main areas of interest and activities are: IPR-watermarking, data encryption-image security, compression, high speed broadband transmission, information technlogy, cultural heritage, colour correction-image enhancement, pattern recognition-image similarity retrieval, edge detection/wavelet compression, Jpeg 2000, I3A Consortium.

Vassilis Fotopoulos was born in Patras in 1972. He graduated from the University of Patras, Department of Physics in 1995 and received his MSc degree from the Electronics Laboratory of the same department in 1998. He received his PhD in 2003 from Patras University as well. He is lecturing digital design, computer architecture and microprocessors for the Hellenic Open University (HOU) Computer Science department and the Technological Educational Institute of Patras, department of Electrical

Engineering. His research interests include digital watermarking, digital image and video processing, image and video compression algorithms, for which he has published 25 works in various international conferences and journals. He is currently a member of the CAS, SP and Computer societies of the IEEE and a member of SPIE. He is also a reviewer for many journals and conferences.

Christos Golfinopoulos Education: University of Athens, Faculty of Law (LL.B. 1997); University of Essex, UK (LL.M. in EC Law, 2001); University of Athens, Faculty of Law, PHD Candidate (October 2004), doctoral dissertation on "Legal protection of software programs. Prior work experience includes an in-service traineeship (stage), European Commission, Directorate General for Competition, State Aids Unit (March 2001-July 2001); associate at Herbert Smith Law Firm, Brussels EU Competition law department, Belgium (September 2001-July 2004). Building on his academic background and extensive prior work experience, Christos has brought to the office significant capabilities in specialised areas such as EU and competition law, vertical agreements, IP and licensing, state aid and public procurement. He has also been practicing extensively commercial/company law, contracts and tax law. Selected publications: Greece chapter of *Getting the Deal Through - Vertical Agreements 2007*, March 2007; Hellenic Competition Commission's Leniency Programme and its weaknesses, Business and Company Law, 10/2006 (Vol.12), 994 (in Greek); state aid in the air transport sector: useful guidance following the Commission's decision on Ryanair, (2005) Public procurement and State Aid Law Review, 1/2005 p.51, CIEEL (in Greek); concept of selectivity criterion in State aid definition following the Adria-Wien judgment – measures justified by the 'nature or general scheme of a system', (2003) European Competition Law Review, vol.24, October issue, p.543, Sweet & Maxwel; the Permissibility of Post-Selection Modifications in a Tendering Procedure: Decision by the European Commission that the London Underground Public-Private Partnership does not involve State Aid, (2003) 12 Public Procurement Law Review, issue 3, NA47, Sweet & Maxwell (co-writer); "Access to content" – Challenges for developing third generation (3G) technology, [2003] Entertainment Law Review, issue 3, p.56, Sweet & Maxwell.; legality of national measures to promote the procurement of energy from renewable sources, European Court of Justice, Judgment of March 13, 2001, Case C-379/98, PreussenElektra AG v. Schleswag AG, (2002) 11 Public Procurement Law Review, issue 1, NA8, Sweet & Maxwell.

Lefteris Gortzis is a fellow at the Medical Physics Department of University of Patras. He studied physics. He received his MSc degree in medical physics and his PhD in medical informatics from the University of Patras. His PhD thesis is under the title *Design Methodologies for Supporting Telediagnostic and Telesurgical Services Over Web*. His research interests include the design and evaluation of telemedicine applications and specific collaborative clinical systems, and the use of information technology to increase patient's safety. He has designed many collaborative clinical systems, which are already in use at the University Hospital of Patras. He has published one monograph and several articles in peer-reviewed journals and proceedings of conferences in the field of medical informatics. Additionally, he has served as reviewer for a number of scientific journals -including IEEE Transactions on Biomedical Engineering and the British Medical Association.

Emmanouil G. Karatzas received his diploma degree in Electrical and Computer Engineering and the MSc degree in Computer Science & Technology from the University of Patras, Greece in 1999 and 2002, respectively. He is currently the CEO of SilkTech, a computer informatics company, and a researcher at the University of Patras. He has participated in a number of IST projects as well as European comities and his work has been published in many international conferences.

Athanasia V. Kazantzi received her diploma degree in computer engineering and informatics and the MSc degree in computer science & technology from University of Patras, Greece in 2002 and 2005 respectively. She is currently working as a developer and researcher at SilkTech O.E and High Performance Information Systems Laboratory, University of Patras. She has participated in a number of European and regional research projects, for some of which she was responsible for the design and technical implementation.

Ioannis Kostopoulos was born in Athens, Greece, in November 18, 1972. He received the bachelor degree in mathematics, from the University of Patras, in 1995. He holds a PhD in computer engineering and informatics from 2003 and he has 15 years of experience in the fields of information technology and medium and large scale project management. He was member of the Database Laboratory of Computer Engineering and Informatics Department and member of the Multimedia Coding and Watermarking Group. He was also an IEEE Student member (Circuits and Systems Society and Signal Processing Society) and his main research interests include digital watermarking of still images and Video, data hiding and cryptography and e-government. He is currently member of the Information Systems and Business Intelligence Lab of the Business Administration Department of University of Patras. He has 18 publications in International Journals and Conferences.

Shiguo Lian, member of IEEE, SPIE and EURASIP, got his PhD degree in multimedia security from Nanjing University of Science and Technology in July 2005. He was a research assistant at City University of Hong Kong from March to June of 2004, studying multimedia encryption. He has been with France Telecom R&D Beijing since July 2005, focusing on multimedia content protection, including digital rights management (DRM), image or video encryption, watermarking and authentication, etc. He is the author or co-author of more than 50 referred journal and conference articles. He has contributed 9 chapters to books and holds 6 filed patents.

Spiridon Likothanasis is a professor at the Department of Computer Engineering and Informatics of the University of Patras. His research activities focus on genetic algorithms and artificial intelligence. He has published numerous papers to international research journals and conferences.

Christos Makris entered the Department of Computer Engineering and Informatics, School of Engineering, University of Patras in September 1988 and received his diploma, as a computer engineer, in December 1993. In November 1997 he received his PhD in computer science. The title of his dissertation was *Elementary Data Structures and their application in Computational Geometry and Information Retrieval* and his advisor was Professor Athanasios Tsakalidis. From November 1997 to May 1999 he served in the military. From May 1999 till today he cooperates with the Research Academic Computer Technology Institute, from August 2003 to October 2004 he was assistant professor in the Department of Applied Informatics in Management & Finance, Technological Educational Institute of Mesolonghi, while from October 2004 till today he is assistant professor in the Department of Computer Engineering and Informatics, University of Patras.

Penelope Markellou is a computer engineer and researcher in the Department of Computer Engineering and Informatics at the University of Patras. She obtained her PhD in *Techniques and Systems for Knowledge Management in the Web* (2005) and her MSc in *Usability Models for e-Commerce Systems and Applications* (2000) from the above University. Her research interests focus on algorithms, techniques and approaches for the design and development of usable e-applications including e-commerce, e-learning, e-government and business intelligence. She has published several research papers in national and international journals and conferences and is co-author of two books and eight book chapters.

Dimitrios P. Meidanis received his diploma degree in computer engineering and informatics in 2004 and his MSc degree in computer science and technology in 2006 from University Of Patras, Greece. He is currently preparing his PhD thesis on *Protection of Intellectual Property Rights and Digital Rights Management*. He is working as researcher for High Performance Information Systems Laboratory since 2004 and as a computer engineer for SilkTech O.E. since 2005.

Shahriar Movafaghi received a PhD in computer science from Northwestern University, with over twenty years of hands on technical experience. Dr. Movafaghi has published numerous papers in area of digital rights, data warehousing, databases, system architecture, software engineering, object-oriented technology, application development, and teaching techniques for IT. He has architected and led many software system projects in the financial, apparel, publishing, and computer hardware/software industries as well as directed government-funded research and development projects. He has taught courses at various universities including SNHU, UNH, BU, and UMASS Lowell.

Nikos Nikolaidis received the Diploma of Electrical Engineering in 1991 and the PhD degree in electrical engineering in 1997, both from the Aristotle University of Thessaloniki, Greece. From 1998 to 2002 he was postdoctoral researcher and teaching assistant at the Department of Informatics, Aristotle University of Thessaloniki. He is currently an assistant professor in the same Department. Dr. Nikolaidis is the co-author of the book *3-D Image Processing Algorithms* (Wiley, 2000). He has co-authored 7 book chapters, 26 journal papers and 89 conference papers. His research interests include computer graphics, image and video processing and analysis, copyright protection of multimedia, computer vision and 3-D image processing. Dr. Nikolaidis is currently serving as associate editor for the *EURASIP Journal on Image and Video Processing*, the *International Journal of Innovative Computing, Information and Control* and the *Innovative Computing, Information and Control Express Letters*.

Spiros N. Nikolopoulos received his diploma degree in computer engineering and informatics and the MSc degree in computer science & technology from University of Patras, Greece in 2002 and 2004 respectively. He is currently working as a research associate with the Informatics and Telematics Institute (ITI) and he is a member of Multimedia Knowledge Group (MKG). He has participated in a number of IST projects and his work has been published in many international conferences.

Ioannis Panaretou was born in Leycosia, Cyprus, on April 20, 1974. He received the diploma and the MSc degree from the computer engineering and informatics department of University of Patras, in 1998 and 2001 respectively. He is now a PhD candidate in Business Management & Administration Department of Patras University. His research interests include information systems, decision support systems, e-democracy, data protection, e-government and digital rights management. He has a working experience of more than 8 years. Since October 2000 he was the IT Project Manager of Options and since 2003 the General Manager and Legal Representative. He managed successfully more than 30 IT Project's and participated as an expert in several committees. He also acts as an external IT expert for various public bodies and organizations.

Evaggelos Papakonstantinou is a lawyer with specialization in issues concerning protection of personal data, copyright protection and e-commerce. He is practicing law in Greece and has had a parallel academic career in the Department of Computer Engineering and Informatics of the University of Patras for the past 4 years. He is responsible for the undergraduate course "social and legislative views of new technologies". He has numerous publications in scientific journals and conferences.

Dimitra Pappa is currently working at the National Centre for Scientific Research "Demokritos", for the Division of Applied Technologies. The research activity is focusing on designing platforms for the delivery of e-government services to the public. On this research field she has many publications in international journals and conferences.

Ioannis Pitas received the Diploma of Electrical Engineering in 1980 and the PhD degree in electrical Engineering in 1985 both from the Aristotle University of Thessaloniki, Greece. Since 1994, he has been a professor at the Department of Informatics, Aristotle University of Thessaloniki. From 1980 to 1993 he served as scientific assistant, lecturer, assistant professor, and associate professor in the Department of Electrical and Computer Engineering at the same University. He has served as a visiting research associate or visiting assistant professor at several Universities. He has published 157 journal papers, 405 conference papers and contributed to 23 books in his areas of interest and edited or co-authored another seven. He has also been an invited speaker and/or member of the program committee of several scientific conferences and workshops. In the past he served as associate editor or co-editor of four international journals and general or technical chair of three international conferences. His current interests are in the areas of digital image and video processing and analysis, multidimensional signal processing, copyright protection of multimedia and computer vision.

Alessandro Piva was born in Florence, Italy, on 1968. He graduated cum laude in electronic engineering from University of Florence on February 1995. He obtained the PhD degree in *Computer Science and Telecommunications Engineering* from the University of Florence on February 1999. From July 2002 until July 2004 he was research scientist at the National Inter-university Consortium for Telecommunications (CNIT). He is at present assistant professor at the Faculty of Engineering of the University of Florence. His main research interests are: technologies for multimedia content security, image processing techniques for cultural heritage applications, video processing techniques and multimedia applications in the cultural heritage field. He is co-author of more than 90 papers published in international journals and conference proceedings. He holds three Italian patents and one International patent regarding watermarking techniques. He is lecturer for the "Terminali Multimediali" (Multimedia Terminals) and Sicurezza dei Contenuti Multimediali (Multimedia Contents Security) course of the Laurea Degree in Telecommunications Engineering.

Alfredo M. Ronchi teaches Assisted Building Design in the Department of Engineering of Building Systems in the Engineering Faculty of Milan Polytechnic. Born in Milan in 1956, he graduated in engineering in 1981 and was appointed as researcher in 1984. In 1975 Ronchi became interested in the use of information technology in the field of assisted design. Since 1983 he has worked on the possible applications of artificial intelligence and expert systems to building design. He has been actively working on virtual reality since 1989, bringing together his experience in computers, multimedia and lighting engineering. In 1994 he organised the *"First International Day of Virtual Reality and advanced Computer Aided Architectural Design"* in Bologna. He is an active member of the ECAADE (Education in Computer Aided Architectural Design in Europe), Eurographics, ACM Siggraph and IES (Illuminating Engineering Society).He is currently working on multimedia, virtual reality and computer-aided building design. Ronchi has put forward a series of projects for the promotion and study of cultural heritage through the use of IT, in particular adapting techniques from computer graphics and multimedia applications. Since 1993 he has presented a number of projects to the European Community within the framework of Telematics Application, Info2000 and TEN Telecom. After two successful results in TA, the project Mosaic Net Virtual Museums presented in the TEN Telecom 96 programme for cultural heritage was approved and financed by the European Community. The projects currently under development include among their partners the Lombardy region, the Province of Milan, the Chamber of Commerce and Telecom. Alfredo Ronchi has published numerous articles in scientific journals and contributed to several collective works, as well as a series of academic monographs. He has actively participated in many conferences an seminars. He is a contributor to *Modulo, Virtual*; the weekly magazine *Panorama*; the dailies *Corriere della Sera, la Repubblica, il Sole24Ore, il Bollettino d'Informazioni della Scuola Normale Superiore di Pisa e dell'Enea*; and to the television magazines *Albedo* and *Mediamente*.

Georgios Stylios was born in Arta in 1971. He has studied physics at the Aristotle University of Thessaloniki and Informatics in the City University of London. He has worked at the Technical Educational Institute of Epirus as a professor and manager of European research programmes. He is a professor in the Department of Applied Informatics in Management and Finance at the Technological Educational Institute of Ionian Islands and a PhD candidate of the Computer Engineering and Informatics Department of the University of Patras. Since June 2006 he is a lecturer at the Technological Educational Institute of Ionian Islands in Greece (www.teiion.gr) at the department "Applied Informatics in Management & Finance." His research interests is focused at the area of e-government, e-culture, e-citizen, data mining, log analysis, and algorithm related to web analysis.

Athanasios Tsakalidis obtained his Diploma in mathematics from the University of Thessaloniki, Greece (1973), his Diploma in computer science (1981) and his PhD (1983) from the University of Saarland, Saarbuecken, Germany. His is currently a full professor in the Department of Computer Engineering and Informatics, University of Patras and the R&D Coordinator of the Research Academic Computer Technology Institute (RACTI). His research interests include data structures, graph algorithms, computational geometry, expert systems, medical informatics, databases, multimedia, information retrieval, and bioinformatics. He has published several research papers in national and international journals and conferences and is co-author of the *Handbook of Theoretical Computer Science* and other book chapters.

Evanthia Tsilichristou is a graduate student of the Department of Computer Engineering and Informatics of the University of Patras. She is an MSc candidate and she is specialized in the research area of digital watermarking for video archives. She has numerous publications in scientific conferences.

Nikos Tsirakis is a PhD candidate in the Computer Engineering and Informatics Department in the University of Patras (Advisor Assis. Prof. Christos Makris). In September 1999 he entered the Department of Computer Engineering and Informatics, School of Engineering, University of Patras and he received his Diploma, as a computer engineer, in December 2004. In October 2006 he received his Master in Computer Science in the same Department. His research interests are the design and analysis of data mining algorithms and applications (especially for huge data manipulation ex. databases, data streams, XML data), hypertext, software quality assessment and finally Web technologies.

Index